Lecture Notes in Computer Science 8671

Commenced Publication in 1973
Founding and Former Series Editors:
Gerhard Goos, Juris Hartmanis, and Jan van Leeuwen

T0214879

Leszek J. Chmielewski   Ryszard Kozera
Bok-Suk Shin   Konrad Wojciechowski (Eds.)

Computer Vision and Graphics

International Conference, ICCVG 2014
Warsaw, Poland, September 15-17, 2014
Proceedings

 Springer

Volume Editors

Leszek J. Chmielewski
Warsaw University of Life Sciences (SGGW), Poland
E-mail: leszek_chmielewski@sggw.pl

Ryszard Kozera
Warsaw University of Life Sciences (SGGW), Poland
E-mail: ryszard_kozera@sggw.pl

Bok-Suk Shin
The University of Auckland, New Zealand
E-mail: b.shin@auckland.ac.nz

Konrad Wojciechowski
Silesian University of Technology, Gliwice, Poland
and Polish-Japanese Institute of Information Technology, Warsaw, Poland
E-mail: konrad.wojciechowski@polsl.pl

ISSN 0302-9743   e-ISSN 1611-3349
ISBN 978-3-319-11330-2   e-ISBN 978-3-319-11331-9
DOI 10.1007/978-3-319-11331-9
Springer Cham Heidelberg New York Dordrecht London

Library of Congress Control Number: 2014947891

LNCS Sublibrary: SL 6 – Image Processing, Computer Vision, Pattern Recognition,
and Graphics

Typesetting: Camera-ready by author, data conversion by Scientific Publishing Services, Chennai, India

Printed on acid-free paper

Springer is part of Springer Science+Business Media (www.springer.com)

Preface

The International Conference on Computer Vision and Graphics, organized since 2002, is the continuation of The International Conferences on Computer Graphics and Image Processing, GKPO, held in Poland every second year from 1990 to 2000. The founder and organizer of these conferences was Prof. Wojciech Mokrzycki. The main objective of ICCVG is to provide an environment for the exchange of ideas between researchers in the closely related domains of computer vision and computer graphics.

ICCVG 2014 brought together about 100 authors. The proceedings contain 81 papers, each accepted on the grounds of at least two independent reviews. During the conference special sessions on Medical Ultrasound Image Processing and on Human Motion Acquisition, Processing, Analysis and Synthesis, and a poster session, were organized.

ICCVG 2014 was organized by the Association for Image Processing, Poland (Towarzystwo Przetwarzania Obrazów – TPO), the Faculty of Applied Informatics and Mathematics, Warsaw University of Life Sciences (WZIM SGGW), and the Polish-Japanese Institute of Information Technology (PJWSTK), together with the supporting organizers: Faculty of Information Science, West Pomeranian University of Technology (WI ZUT), Szczecin, and The Vistula University, Warsaw.

The Association for Image Processing integrates the Polish community working on the theory and applications of computer vision and graphics. It was formed between 1989 and 1991.

The Faculty of Applied Informatics and Mathematics, established in 2008 at Warsaw University of Life Sciences, offers two programs of study: Informatics, and Informatics and Econometrics. Its main advantage stems from merging technical education with applied sciences, including the application of computer sciences to the management and analysis of the agricultural industry.

The Polish-Japanese Institute of Information Technology founded in 1994 by the Computer Techniques Development Foundation under the agreement of the Polish and Japanese governments is one of the leading, non-state (private) Polish universities. We are very grateful that the institute hosted and supported the conference.

We would like to thank all the members of the Scientific Committee, as well as the additional reviewers, for their help in ensuring the high quality of the papers. We would also like to thank Grażyna Domańska-Żurek for her excellent work on technically editing the proceedings, and Dariusz Frejlichowski, Henryk Palus, Marcin Bator, Mariola Rejmund, and Bernadeta Bonio for their engagement in the conference organization and administration.

September 2014   Leszek J. Chmielewski
                                                                      Ryszard Kozera
                                                                       Bok-Suk Shin
                                                              Konrad Wojciechowski

Organization

- Association for Image Processing (TPO)
- Faculty of Applied Informatics and Mathematics, Warsaw University of Life Sciences (WZIM SGGW)
- Polish-Japanese Institute of Information Technology (PJWSTK)
- Faculty of Information Science, West Pomeranian University of Technology (WI ZUT), Szczecin
- The Vistula University, Warsaw

Conference General Chairs:

L.J. Chmielewski, Poland
R. Kozera, Poland

B.-S. Shin, New Zealand
K. Wojciechowski, Poland

Scientific Committee:

Ivan Bajla, Slovakia
Prabir Bhattacharya, USA
Gunilla Borgefors, Sweden
M. Emre Celebi, USA
Leszek Chmielewski, Poland
Dmitry Chetverikov, Hungary
Piotr Czapiewski, Poland
László Czúni, Hungary
Silvana Dellepiane, Italy
Marek Domański, Poland
Mariusz Flasiński, Poland
Paweł Forczmański, Poland
Dariusz Frejlichowski, Poland
Maria Frucci, Italy
André Gagalowicz, France
Samuel Morillas Gómez, Spain
Marcin Iwanowski, Poland
Adam Jóźwik, Poland
Heikki Kälviäinen, Finland
Andrzej Kasiński, Poland
Włodzimierz Kasprzak, Poland
Bertrand Kerautret, France
Nahum Kiryati, Israel
Reinhard Klette, New Zealand

Witold Malina, Poland
Radosşaw Mantiuk, Poland
Tomasz Marciniak, Poland
Andrzej Materka, Poland
Nikolaos Mavridis, United Arab Emirates
Przemysşaw Mazurek, Poland
Tomasz Mąka, Poland
Wojciech Mokrzycki, Poland
Mariusz Nieniewski, Poland
Sławomir Nikiel, Poland
Lyle Noakes, Australia
Antoni Nowakowski, Poland
Adam Nowosielski, Poland
Krzysztof Okarma, France
Maciej Orkisz, France
Arkadiusz Orłowski, Poland
Henryk Palus, Poland
Wiesław Pamuła, Poland
Volodymyr Ponomaryov, Mexico
Piotr Porwik, Poland
Artur Przelaskowski, Poland
Ferran Reverter, Spain
Przemysław Rokita, Poland
Khalid Saeed, Poland

Table of Contents

Computer Graphics

Computer Vision

A Validation of Combined Metrics for Color Image Quality Assessment

Krzysztof Okarma

West Pomeranian University of Technology, Szczecin
Faculty of Electrical Engineering
Department of Signal Processing and Multimedia Engineering
26. Kwietnia 10, 71-126 Szczecin, Poland
okarma@zut.edu.pl

Abstract. Since most of even recently proposed image quality assessment metrics are typically applied for a single color channel in both compared images, a reliable color image quality assessment is still a challenging task for researchers. One of the major drawbacks limiting the progress in this field is the lack of image datasets containing the subjective scores for images contaminated by color specific distortions. After the publication of the TID2013 dataset, containing i.a. images with 6 types of color distortions, this situation has changed, however there is still a need of validation of some recently proposed grayscale metrics in view of their applicability for color specific distortions.

In this paper some results obtained using different approaches to color to grayscale conversion for some well-known metrics as well as for recently proposed combined ones, are presented and discussed, leading to meaningful increase of the prediction accuracy of image quality for color distortions.

Keywords: color image quality assessment, combined metrics, image analysis.

1 Introduction

A growing interest in automatic image quality assessment algorithms, which has taken place during last several years, is one of the main reasons of development of many new metrics which are better and better correlated with perception of various image distortions by the Human Visual System (HVS). Most of such universal metrics are full-reference ones which are based on the comparison of the reference image with the distorted one, usually assuming the presence of only a single color channel in both images. For the RGB images the conversion to grayscale is typically required before calculations of an image quality metric.

Considering the importance of the luminance information and the fact that many types of image distortions affect the local brightness of images, the simplified approach to image quality assessment based on the luminance is justified in many cases. Analyzing the available image quality databases, containing

L.J. Chmielewski et al. (Eds.): ICCVG 2014, LNCS 8671, pp. 1–8, 2014.

images subjected to various distortions, together with subjective quality scores, expressed as Mean Opinion Scores (MOS) or Differential MOS (DMOS) values, most of distortions are not color specific even though the reference files are usually full-color RGB images. In such case the subjective scores have been collected by presenting the distorted color images to the human observers so the possible color disturbances might have an impact on the perceived quality of images. Nevertheless, such influence is rather indirect, so the subjective evaluation of images with color specific distortions may be different and therefore some other objective metrics may perform better.

In order to propose a reliable color image quality assessment metric a dataset of numerous images with color specific distortions and their subjective scores is necessary. Currently, there is only one such publicly available dataset which could be efficiently applied for such experiments, namely the newest version of Tampere Image Database (TID2013) containing 3000 distorted images (24 types of distortions with 5 levels each applied for 25 reference images) assessed by 971 observers conducting over million evaluations of relative visual quality in image pairs [15,16].

2   Relationships between Subjective and Objective Image Quality Assessment

One of the crucial requirements of further development of image quality assessment methods is the availability of subjective scores gained from human observers for images contaminated by various types of distortions. Verification of each newly developed objective metric is conducted by calculation of the correlation coefficients of the proposed metric with MOS or DMOS values provided for the specified database.

The most relevant feature of an objective image quality metric is good prediction accuracy of the perceived image quality which can be determined by calculation of the Pearson's Linear Correlation Coefficient (PCC) between the subjective and objective scores. In an ideal case the high values of the PCC should be obtained for raw scores obtained for the objective metric without the necessity of any nonlinear mapping. Nevertheless, due to a nonlinear characteristics of the Human Visual System, many researchers apply the nonlinear regression using e.g. polynomial or logistic function according to the recommendation of the ITU [4]. In practical applications such solution is hard to accept since the parameters of the mapping functions, obtained as the result of optimization, are different for each dataset, similarly as the values of the correlation coefficients [18]. Therefore the direct usage of the objective scores does not lead to expected results, consistent with subjective evaluations.

The definition of a single metric characterized by high linear correlation with MOS or DMOS values for the most relevant image quality databases is still a challenging task as the results reported for the best metrics are still far from perfection, especially for large databases containing numerous images contaminated by many types of distortions, such as TID2013 or its predecessor - TID2008 [14].

The additional benchmarks used for verification of the consistency of the objective metrics with subjective scores are rank order correlation coefficients, related to prediction monotonicity. For this purpose two such factors may be used: Spearman Rank Order Correlation Coefficient (SROCC) and Kendall Rank Order Correlation Coefficient (KROCC). Both those measures assess how well the relationship between the subjective and objective metrics values can be described using a monotonic function, analyzing the sequence order in two image lists sorted according to subjective and objective scores. However, such measures of accordance with subjective evaluations should be treated rather supplementary to the PCC values.

3 Combined Full-Reference Image Quality Metrics

One of the methods leading to increase of the linear correlation between the subjective and objective quality scores, without the necessity of using any nonlinear mapping functions, is applying the nonlinearity inside the metric by using a nonlinear combination of different image quality assessment methods. The first such approach (further referred to as the Combined Quality Metric - CQM), presented in the paper [12], is the nonlinear combination of three metrics: Multi-Scale Structural Similarity (MS-SSIM) [19], Visual Information Fidelity (VIF) [17] and R-SVD metric [9] based on the Singular Value Decomposition, according to the formula:

$$CQM = (MS\text{-}SSIM)^{\alpha} \cdot (VIF)^{\beta} \cdot (R\text{-}SVD)^{\gamma} . \tag{1}$$

After the optimization of weights (values of the exponents α, β and γ) using the TID2008 database, PCC=0.86 has been achieved.

Probably the best results using a single metric can be obtained for the most relevant datasets by the application of the Feature Similarity (FSIM) metric proposed in 2011 [20], especially for its color version (denoted as FSIMc). The FSIM metric is based on the comparison of gradient magnitude, calculated using Scharr filter, and the phase congruency, leading to the local similarity index, further aggregated using the additional masking based on the maximum phase congruency values. A similar approach (known as RFSIM), based on the application of Riesz transform, has been earlier described by the same authors [21], and the weighted combination of these two metrics has been analyzed in the paper [13], leading to further increase of the correlation with subjective scores for the most relevant image quality databases.

Since the performance of the FSIM metric is much better than the results achieved using the R-SVD metric, a modified version of the combined metric, based on the VIF and two similarity based image quality assessment methods (MS-SSIM and FSIMc), has been proposed in the article [10]. Proposed Combined Image Similarity Metric (CISI) defined as

$$\text{CISI} = (\text{MS-SSIM})^a \cdot (\text{VIF})^b \cdot (\text{FSIMc})^c \tag{2}$$

allows to increase the Pearson's correlation for TID2008 database to 0.8752. Further extension of such metric (referred to as Extended Hybrid Image Similarity - EHIS) allows to increase this value to 0.9105 due to the application of the weighted combination of the FSIMc and RFSIM instead of FSIMc metric [11].

An additional verification of the advantages of the approach based on the nonlinear combination of various metrics has been provided in the recent paper [8] where good results have also been achieved using the multi-method fusion approach. However, it is worth noticing that the results presented in this article have been obtained after the additional nonlinear regression and therefore they cannot be compared directly with the other combined metrics.

Nevertheless, a common disadvantage of the state-of-the-art metrics, including the combined ones, is low use of color information, since only the FSIMc metric partially utilizes such data. Due to the availability of the TID2013 dataset, containing much more images with color specific distortions, the calculations of the correlation coefficients of known metrics with MOS values provided for this database has been the first step of conducted experiments. Nevertheless, the best performance has been achieved for the FSIMc metric.

Due to high correlation of the recently proposed combined metrics with subjective scores as well as their ability to optimize, they have been chosen as the most promising for experimental verifications, assuming the necessary conversion of assessed images to grayscale.

4   The Impact of the Grayscale Conversion

Since most of the well-known image quality assessment methods, as well as recently proposed approaches, are based mainly (or even exclusively) on the luminance comparison, an important issue is related to the verification of the impact of the color to grayscale conversion method on the results of image quality assessment obtained using various metrics. A similar problem occurs also in image recognition systems as illustrated in the paper [7] and is also relevant in view of subjective evaluations [1].

During the experiments some typical color to grayscale conversion methods have been used such as the luminance channels from the HSV and CIELAB color spaces as well as the luminance (Y) calculation according to ITU recommendations. The Y component has been calculated according to the Recommendation BT.601-7 [6] for SDTV as

$$Y_{601} = 0.299 \cdot R + 0.587 \cdot G + 0.114 \cdot B , \tag{3}$$

and also for the Recommendation BT.709-5 [5] for HDTV as

$$Y_{709} = 0.2126 \cdot R + 0.7152 \cdot G + 0.0722 \cdot B . \tag{4}$$

Additionally, one of the contrast enhancing color to grayscale conversion methods, namely Decolorize [3], working in real-time, has been applied for comparison. Some other algorithms, which are more computationally demanding, such as e.g. well-known Color2Gray proposed by Gooch et al. [2], have not been analyzed due to limited practical applicability for image quality assessment purposes, especially for combined metrics which require more computations in comparison to single image quality assessment metrics.

The experiments have been conducted for the whole TID2013 database as well as for the color subset containing 750 images out of 3000, being contaminated by six types of color specific distortions (noise in color components, quantization noise, JPEG compression, change of color saturation, image color quantization with dithering and chromatic aberrations). During the calculations three combined metrics (CQM, CISI and EHIS) have been used and the optimization of the exponent weights have been conducted independently for the whole dataset and for the color subset. Additionally, the CISI metric has been optimized in two versions: grayscale only (applying the specified color to grayscale conversion method also for the FSIM component) and using the original color FSIMc metric together with grayscale versions of MS-SSIM and VIF.

The obtained results of the Pearson's Linear Correlation Coefficient with the MOS values are presented in Tables 1 and 2 where the combined metrics with weights optimized for the TID2013 database are marked by asterix (*). The bold numbers indicate the best results obtained for the combined metrics with weights obtained earlier using the TID2008 database and their new versions optimized using the TID2013 database. The highest results achieved for the CISI* metric have been obtained using the following sub-optimal weights: $a = 0.34$, $b = -0.09$ and $c = 8.9$ for the whole dataset using the L component, and $a = 2$, $b = -0.75$, $c = 20$ for the color subset using the V component.

Table 1. Obtained results of the Pearson linear correlation coefficients of combined metrics with MOS values for the whole TID2013 database using various grayscale conversion methods

Conversion / Metric	Y_{601}	Y_{709}	Value (HSV)	L (CIELAB)	Decolorize
CQM	0.7737	0.7946	0.7654	0.0812	0.7435
CISI	0.8534	**0.8546**	0.8436	0.7353	0.8398
EHIS	0.7995	0.8079	0.7746	0.5163	0.7448
CQM*	0.8400	0.8363	0.8120	0.6132	0.7726
CISI* (with FSIM)	0.8558	0.8567	0.8377	0.6186	0.8112
EHIS*	0.8604	0.8657	0.8552	0.6284	0.8162
CISI* (with FSIMc)	0.8752	0.8747	0.8743	**0.8788**	0.8743

Table 2. Obtained results of the Pearson linear correlation coefficients of combined metrics with MOS values for the color subset of the TID2013 database using various grayscale conversion methods

Metric \ Conversion	Y_{601}	Y_{709}	Value (HSV)	L (CIELAB)	Decolorize
CQM	0.6149	0.6750	0.6222	0.6482	0.5703
CISI	0.8006	**0.8080**	0.7604	0.7926	0.7531
EHIS	0.7349	0.7652	0.7202	0.6994	0.6579
CQM*	0.8817	0.8467	0.7571	0.6738	0.6430
CISI* (with FSIM)	0.8127	0.8061	0.7853	0.6660	0.7362
EHIS*	0.8096	0.8176	0.8098	0.7093	0.7306
CISI* (with FSIMc)	0.8744	0.8639	**0.8937**	0.8558	0.8811

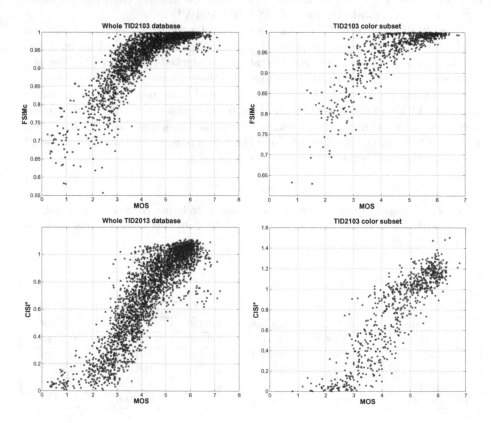

Fig. 1. Scatter plots of the FSIMc and CISI* metrics optimized for the whole TID2013 database (left) and its color subset (right) versus MOS values

As mentioned earlier, the best results obtained for the single metrics have been achieved for the FSIMc metric - the PCC value for the whole dataset equal to 0.8322 and the PCC=0.8046 for the color subset. Those values are lower than reported for some other datasets and can be considered as another proof of the high demands of the TID2013 dataset in terms of the metrics' performance defined as the correlation with subjective evaluations.

5 Analysis of Results and Conclusions

As can be observed during the analysis of achieved results a significant increase of the correlation with subjective scores can be obtained mainly by applying the Combined Image Similarity Index both for the whole TID2013 dataset and for the color subset. The best results for the application of the original CISI metric can be achieved for the Y_{709} component (4) calculated according to the ITU Recommendation BT.709-5 [5].

After the optimization of the weighting exponents using the MOS values derived in the TID2013 database, the most linear correlation with them can be observed for the CISI* index calculated for the luminance from CIELAB color space (for MS-SSIM and VIF) and FSIMc metric. Similar optimization conducted for the color subset leads to the best performance for the value component (V) from the HSV color space applied for MS-SSIM and VIF parts of the optimized CISI* metric (a significant increase of the PCC from 0.8046 form FSIMc and 0.8080 for CISI to 0.8937 can be observed). A highly linear relationship of the CISI* metric with MOS values is illustrated in Fig. 1.

Application of the combined metrics for different color spaces is an interesting direction of further research which can be focused on combining different metrics calculated for different color models and their possible further extensions toward color video quality assessment. Nevertheless, further optimization of such metrics is limited by the availability of subjective scores for images and video sequences containing color specific distortions.

References

1. Čadík, M.: Perceptual evaluation of color-to-grayscale image conversions. Comput. Graph. Forum 27(7), 1745–1754 (2008)
2. Gooch, A.A., Olsen, S.C., Tumblin, J., Gooch, B.B.: Color2gray: saliencepreserving color removal. ACM Transactions on Graphics 24(3), 634–639 (2005)
3. Grundland, M., Dodgson, N.A.: Decolorize: Fast, contrast enhancing, color to grayscale conversion. Pattern Recognition 40(11), 2891–2896 (2007)
4. International Telecommunication Union: Recommendation P.910 - Subjective video quality assessment methods for multimedia applications (1999)
5. International Telecommunication Union: Recommendation BT.709-5 - Parameter values for the HDTV standards for production and international programme exchange (2002)
6. International Telecommunication Union: Recommendation BT.601-7 - Studio encoding parameters of digital television for standard 4:3 and wide-screen 16:9 aspect ratios (2011)

7. Kanan, C., Cottrell, G.W.: Color-to-grayscale: Does the method matter in image recognition? PLOS One 7(1), e29740 (2012)
8. Liu, T.J., Lin, W., Kuo, C.C.J.: Image quality assessment using multi-method fusion. IEEE Trans. Image Processing 22(5), 1793–1807 (2013)
9. Mansouri, A., Mahmoudi-Aznaveh, A., Torkamani-Azar, F., Jahanshahi, J.: Image quality assessment using the Singular Value Decomposition theorem. Optical Review 16(2), 49–53 (2009)
10. Okarma, K.: Combined Image Similarity Index. Optical Review 19(5), 349–354 (2012)
11. Okarma, K.: Extended hybrid image similarity – combined full-reference image quality metric linearly correlated with subjective scores. Elektronika Ir Elektrotechnika 19(10), 129–132 (2013)
12. Okarma, K.: Combined full-reference image quality metric linearly correlated with subjective assessment. In: Rutkowski, L., Scherer, R., Tadeusiewicz, R., Zadeh, L.A., Zurada, J.M. (eds.) ICAISC 2010, Part I. LNCS, vol. 6113, pp. 539–546. Springer, Heidelberg (2010)
13. Okarma, K.: Hybrid feature similarity approach to full-reference image quality assessment. In: Bolc, L., Tadeusiewicz, R., Chmielewski, L.J., Wojciechowski, K. (eds.) ICCVG 2012. LNCS, vol. 7594, pp. 212–219. Springer, Heidelberg (2012)
14. Ponomarenko, N., Lukin, V., Zelensky, A., Egiazarian, K., Carli, M., Battisti, F.: TID2008 - a database for evaluation of full-reference visual quality assessment metrics. Advances of Modern Radioelectronics 10, 30–45 (2009)
15. Ponomarenko, N., Ieremeiev, O., Lukin, V., Jin, L., Egiazarian, K., Astola, J., Vozel, B., Chehdi, K., Carli, M., Battisti, F., Kuo, C.C.J.: Color image database TID2013: Peculiarities and preliminary results. In: Proc. 4th European Workshop on Visual Information Processing, EUVIP 2013, Paris, France, pp. 106–111 (2013)
16. Ponomarenko, N., et al.: A new color image database TID2013: Innovations and results. In: Blanc-Talon, J., Kasinski, A., Philips, W., Popescu, D., Scheunders, P. (eds.) ACIVS 2013. LNCS, vol. 8192, pp. 402–413. Springer, Heidelberg (2013)
17. Sheikh, H., Bovik, A.: Image information and visual quality. IEEE Transactions on Image Processing 15(2), 430–444 (2006)
18. Tourancheau, S., Autrusseau, F., Sazzad, Z., Horita, Y.: Impact of subjective dataset on the performance of image quality metrics. In: Proc. 15th IEEE Int. Conf. Image Processing, San Diego, California, pp. 365–368 (2008)
19. Wang, Z., Simoncelli, E., Bovik, A.: Multi-Scale Structural Similarity for image quality assessment. In: Proc. 37th IEEE Asilomar Conf. Signals, Systems and Computers, Pacific Grove, California (2003)
20. Zhang, L., Zhang, L., Mou, X., Zhang, D.: FSIM: A Feature Similarity index for image quality assessment. IEEE Trans. Image Processing 20(8), 2378–2386 (2011)
21. Zhang, L., Zhang, L., Mou, X.: RFSIM: A feature based image quality assessment metric using Riesz transforms. In: Proc. 17th IEEE Int. Conf. Image Processing, Hong Kong, China, pp. 321–324 (2010)

Quartic Orders and Sharpness
in Trajectory Estimation
for Smooth Cumulative Chord Cubics

Ryszard Kozera[1], Lyle Noakes[2], and Piotr Szmielew[1,3]

[1] Warsaw University of Life Sciences - SGGW
Faculty of Applied Informatics and Mathematics
Nowoursynowska str. 159, 02-776 Warsaw, Poland
[2] Department of Mathematics and Statistics, The University of Western Australia
35 Stirling Highway, Crawley W.A. 6009, Perth, Australia
[3] University of Warsaw, Institute of Philosophy
Krakowskie Przedmieście str. 3, 00-927 Warsaw, Poland
{ryszard_kozera,piotr_szmielew}@sggw.pl, lyle.noakes@maths.uwa.edu.au

Abstract. This paper discusses the issue of fitting reduced data $Q_m = \{q_i\}_{i=0}^m$ with smooth interpolant by piecewise-cubics to estimate an unknown curve γ in arbitrary Euclidean space. The interpolation knots $\{t_i\}_{i=0}^m$ satisfying $\gamma(t_i) = q_i$ are assumed to be unknown and guessed according to so-called cumulative chords. More specifically, first estimates of the derivatives at interpolation points Q_m are found by using piecewise-cubics combined with cumulative chords. Next Hermite interpolation is applied to construct C^1 piecewise-cubic yielding the interpolant with no cusps and corners. At least quartic orders of convergence for both trajectory and length estimations are analytically established in [1]. However their sharpness was exclusively tested for length estimation. This paper verifies experimentally the latter with respect to the trajectory approximation. Additionally, an excellent performance of the interpolant in question on sparse data is also confirmed experimentally. Fitting reduced data is used in computer vision and graphics, engineering, physics as well as in medical and biological sciences. A specific example of medical application is also presented in this paper.

1 Introduction

The sampled data points $Q_m = \{q_i\}_{i=0}^m$ with $\gamma(t_i) = q_i \in E^n$ define the pair $(\{t_i\}_{i=0}^m, Q_m)$ commonly coined as *non-reduced data*. We also require here that $t_i < t_{i+1}$ and $q_i \neq q_{i+1}$ hold. Moreover, assume that $\gamma : [0, T] \to E^n$ (with $0 < T < \infty$) is sufficiently smooth (to be specified later) and defines a regular curve $\gamma'(t) \neq \mathbf{0}$. In order to estimate the unknown curve γ with an arbitrary interpolant $\bar{\gamma} : [0, T] \to E^n$ it is necessary to assume that $\{t_i\}_{i=0}^m \in V_G^m$, i.e. that the following *admissibility condition* holds:

$$\lim_{m \to \infty} \delta_m = 0, \quad \text{where} \quad \delta_m = \max_{0 \leq i \leq m-1} (t_{i+1} - t_i).$$

L.J. Chmielewski et al. (Eds.): ICCVG 2014, LNCS 8671, pp. 9–16, 2014.
© Springer International Publishing Switzerland 2014

We omit here the subscript m in δ_m by setting $\delta = \delta_m$. In case when the interpolation knots $\{t_i\}_{i=0}^m$ are unknown a common approach is to choose the so-called cumulative chords. Namely, one sets:

$$\hat{t}_0 = 0 \quad \text{and} \quad \hat{t}_j = \hat{t}_{j-1} + \|q_j - q_{j-1}\|, \tag{1}$$

for $j = 1, 2, \ldots, m$. Let $\hat{\gamma}_3^i$ be *cumulative chord cubic* polynomial approximation to γ (see e.g. [2]) defined by quadruples $Q_m^i = (q_i, q_{i+1}, q_{i+2}, q_{i+3})$ and (1) over $[\hat{t}_i, \hat{t}_{i+3}]$ (see Newton's interpolation formula in [3]) according to:

$$\begin{aligned}\hat{\gamma}_3^i(\hat{t}) = \hat{\gamma}_3^i[\hat{t}_i] + \hat{\gamma}_3^i[\hat{t}_i, \hat{t}_{i+1}](\hat{t} - \hat{t}_i) + \hat{\gamma}_3^i[\hat{t}_i, \hat{t}_{i+1}, \hat{t}_{i+2}](\hat{t} - \hat{t}_i)(\hat{t} - \hat{t}_{i+1}) \\ + \hat{\gamma}_3^i[\hat{t}_i, \hat{t}_{i+1}, \hat{t}_{i+2}, \hat{t}_{i+3}](\hat{t} - \hat{t}_i)(\hat{t} - \hat{t}_{i+1})(\hat{t} - \hat{t}_{i+2}),\end{aligned} \tag{2}$$

where $f[x_0, x_1, \ldots, x_k]$ denote respective divided differences (see e.g. [3]).

Cumulative chord piecewise-cubics $\hat{\gamma}_3$ (a sum-track of $\hat{\gamma}_3^i$) approximate trajectory of γ at least to order four which matches the same orders as if $\{t_i\}_{i=0}^m$ are given (see [2]).

Unfortunately, cumulative chord piecewise-polynomials (including piecewise--cubics defined above) are usually not C^1 at junction points. The purpose of this paper is to rectify this deficiency by studying cumulative chord piecewise-cubics $\hat{\gamma}_H \in C^1$. In chapter 2 we discuss the construction of Hermite smooth interpolant $\hat{\gamma}_H$. Next in chapter 3 we confirm experimentally the sharpness of quartic convergence order in estimating the unknown curve γ by $\hat{\gamma}_H$. Some application for tumor's segmentation in medical images is also provided.

2 Problem Formulation and Motivation

We say that the family $F_\delta : [0, T] \to E^n$ satisfies $F_\delta = O(\delta^\alpha)$ if $\|F_\delta\| = O(\delta^\alpha)$, where $\|\cdot\|$ denotes the Euclidean norm. Another words there are constants $K > 0$ and $\bar{\delta} > 0$ such that $\|F_\delta\| \leq K\delta^\alpha$, for all $\delta \in (0, \bar{\delta})$ and $t \in [0, T]$ - see also [4]. Note that constant K depends here on each sampling $\{t_i\}_{i=0}^m$ and curve γ.

Recall the following smooth interpolation scheme based on reduced data and cumulative chords (see [1] and [5]):

1. First, for each $i = 0, 1, \ldots, m - 3$ let $\hat{\gamma}_3^i : [\hat{t}_i, \hat{t}_{i+3}] \to E^n$ be the cumulative chord cubic interpolating $(q_i, q_{i+1}, q_{i+2}, q_{i+3})$ at $(\hat{t}_i, \hat{t}_{i+1}, \hat{t}_{i+2}, \hat{t}_{i+3})$ (see (1) and (2)), respectively. Those cumulative chords cubics permit to approximate with high accuracy the derivatives of γ at $\{q_i\}_{i=0}^m$ (or more precisely at $\{t_i\}_{i=0}^m$ - see [1]). To be specific, for each consecutive overlapping subinterval $[\hat{t}_i, \hat{t}_{i+3}]$ we estimate the velocity $v(q_i) \in \mathbb{R}^n$ of γ at q_i as $v(q_i) = \hat{\gamma}_3^{i'}(\hat{t}_i)$. Note that for the last four points $(q_{m-3}, q_{m-2}, q_{m-1}, q_m) \subset Q_m$ the respective derivative estimation $(v(q_{m-3}), v(q_{m-2}), v(q_{m-1}), v(q_m))$ is obtained by calculating the velocities applying $\hat{\gamma}_3^{m-3}$ on $(q_{m-3}, q_{m-2}, q_{m-1}, q_m)$ at $(\hat{t}_{m-3}, \hat{t}_{m-2}, \hat{t}_{m-1}, \hat{t}_m)$ - see Fig. 1 illustrating the first part of the discussed fitting algorithm on sparse data.

2. Then let $\hat{\gamma}_H^i : [\hat{t}_i, \hat{t}_{i+1}] \to E^n$ be the Hermite cubic polynomial satisfying:

$$\hat{\gamma}_H^i(\hat{t}_{i+k}) = q_{i+k} \quad \text{and} \quad \hat{\gamma}_H^{i'}(\hat{t}_{i+k}) = \hat{\gamma}_3^{i+k'}(\hat{t}_{i+k}), \quad \text{for } k = 0, 1, \quad (3)$$

defined again by Newton's Interpolation Formula over $[\hat{t}_i, \hat{t}_{i+1}]$ as

$$\hat{\gamma}_H^i(\hat{t}) = \hat{\gamma}_H^i[\hat{t}_i] + \hat{\gamma}_H^i[\hat{t}_i, \hat{t}_i](\hat{t} - \hat{t}_i) + \hat{\gamma}_H^i[\hat{t}_i, \hat{t}_i, \hat{t}_{i+1}](\hat{t} - \hat{t}_i)^2 + \\ \hat{\gamma}_H^i[\hat{t}_i, \hat{t}_i, \hat{t}_{i+1}, \hat{t}_{i+1}](\hat{t} - \hat{t}_i)^2(\hat{t} - \hat{t}_{i+1}), \quad (4)$$

with $i = 0, 1, 2, \ldots, m - 1$. Define now $\hat{\gamma}_H : [0, \hat{T}] \to E^n$ (called *cumulative chord C^1 piecewise-cubic*) as a track-sum of the $\{\hat{\gamma}_H^i\}_{i=0}^{m-1}$.

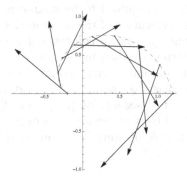

Fig. 1. γ_{sp} (see (6)) with derivative estimation at interpolation knots, for $m = 10$

The following result holds (see [1] and [5]):

Theorem 1. *Suppose γ is a regular C^4 curve in E^n. Let $\hat{\gamma}_H : [0, \hat{T}] \to E^n$ be the cumulative chord C^1 piecewise-cubic defined by Q_m as in (3) and (4). Then there is a piecewise-C^∞ reparameterization $\varphi : [0, T] \to [0, \hat{T}]$, such that*

$$\hat{\gamma}_H \circ \varphi = \gamma + O(\delta^4). \quad (5)$$

Recall (see [1] and [5]) that here φ is a piecewise-cubic Hermite reparameterization between each $[t_i, t_{i+1}]$ and $[\hat{t}_i, \hat{t}_{i+1}]$ defined as:

1. First, for each $i = 0, 1, \ldots, m - 3$ let $\psi^i : [t_i, t_{i+3}] \to [\hat{t}_i, \hat{t}_{i+3}]$ be the cumulative chord cubic interpolating $(\hat{t}_i, \hat{t}_{i+1}, \hat{t}_{i+2}, \hat{t}_{i+3})$ at $(t_i, t_{i+1}, t_{i+2}, t_{i+3})$, respectively. Those cumulative chords cubics permit to approximate the derivatives of reparameterization φ^i at $\{t_i\}_{i=0}^m$. More specifically, for each consecutive subinterval $[t_i, t_{i+3}]$ we estimate the velocity $\bar{v}(t_i) \in \mathbb{R}^1$ of φ^i at t_i as $\bar{v}(t_i) = \varphi'(t_i)$. Note that for the last four knots $(t_{m-3}, t_{m-2}, t_{m-1}, t_m)$ the respective derivative estimation is obtained by calculating the velocities $(\bar{v}(t_{m-3}), \bar{v}(t_{m-2}), \bar{v}(t_{m-1}), \bar{v}(t_m))$ using interpolant ψ^{m-3} applied to $(\hat{t}_{m-3}, \hat{t}_{m-2}, \hat{t}_{m-1}, \hat{t}_m)$ at $(t_{m-3}, t_{m-2}, t_{m-1}, t_m)$, respectively.

2. Let $\varphi^i : [t_i, t_{i+1}] \to [\hat{t}_i, \hat{t}_{i+1}]$ be the Hermite cubic polynomial satisfying:

$$\varphi^i(t_{i+k}) = \hat{t}_{i+k} \quad \text{and} \quad \varphi^{i'}(t_{i+k}) = \psi^{i'}(t_{i+k}), \quad \text{for } k = 0, 1,$$

defined by *Newton's Interpolation Formula* according to:

$$\varphi^i(t) = \varphi^i[t_i] + \varphi^i[t_i, t_i](t - t_i) + \varphi^i[t_i, t_i, t_{i+1}](t - t_i)^2$$
$$+ \varphi^i[t_i, t_i, t_{i+1}, t_{i+1}](t - t_i)^2(t - t_{i+1}).$$

Then define $\varphi : [0, T] \to [0, \hat{T}]$ (forming a reparameterization - see [1] or [5]) as a track-sum of the $\{\varphi^i\}_{i=0}^{m-1}$.

The construction of the above reparameterization φ is in fact not possible on real data since $\{t_i\}_{i=0}^m$ are assumed to be unknown. However, the latter is invoked here only for the verification of the asymptotics claimed in (5). On the other hand the interpolant $\hat{\gamma}_H$ can be constructed exclusively based on Q_m, guessed knots (1) and interpolation scheme (3) and (4).

In many applications in computer vision and graphics, engineering, physics as well as in medical and biological sciences it is required for the interpolant to be smooth i.e. at least of class C^1 (see e.g. [6], [7], [8], or [9]). The latter is met by $\hat{\gamma}_H$ defined by (3) and (4). The next section tests experimentally the sharpness of (5) and includes the example of using $\hat{\gamma}_H$ for medical image segmentation.

3 Experiments

All tests presented in this paper are performed in *Mathematica 9.0.1* [10] on a 2.4GHz Intel Core 2 Duo computer with 16GiB RAM (see [11]; pp. 29) and on PlGrid infrastructure [12]. Note that since $T = \sum_{i=1}^m (t_{i+1} - t_i) \le m\delta$ the following holds $m^{-\alpha} = O(\delta^\alpha)$, for $\alpha > 0$. Hence, the verification of any asymptotics expressed in terms of $O(\delta^\alpha)$ can be performed by examining the claims of Th. 1 in terms of $O(1/m^\alpha)$ asymptotics.

Recall that for a parametric regular curve $\gamma : [0, T] \to E^n$ and m varying between $m_{min} \le m \le m_{max}$ the i-th error for γ estimation over $[t_i, t_{i+1}]$ is defined as follows:

$$E_m^i = \sup_{t \in [t_i, t_{i+1}]} \|(\hat{\gamma}_H^i \circ \varphi^i)(t) - \gamma(t)\| = \max_{t \in [t_i, t_{i+1}]} \|(\hat{\gamma}_H^i \circ \varphi^i)(t) - \gamma(t)\|.$$

In the latter we exploit the continuity of $\tilde{E}_m^i(t) = \|(\hat{\gamma}_H^i \circ \varphi^i)(t) - \gamma(t)\| \ge 0$ over each compact subinterval $[t_i, t_{i+1}] \subset [0, T]$. The maximal value E_m of $\tilde{E}_m(t)$ (the track-sum of $\tilde{E}_m^i(t)$) for each m is found by using the Monte Carlo method (see e.g. [13]). From the set of *absolute errors* $\{E_m\}_{m=m_{min}}^{m_{max}}$ the numerical estimate $\bar{\alpha}$ of a genuine order α is subsequently computed by applying *a linear regression* to the pairs of points $(\log(m), -\log(E_m))$ - see also [5].

The *Mathematica* built-in functions *LinearModelFit* permits to estimate numerically the coefficient $\bar{\alpha}$ from the computed regression line $y(x) = \bar{\alpha}x + b$ based on pairs of points $\{(\log(m), -\log(E_m))\}_{m=m_{min}}^{m_{max}}$.

3.1   Curves and Samplings

In this subsection the testing curves and samplings are introduced.

a) Curves: We begin with the introduction of the curves used in our experimentation.

Example 1. (i) Define first a simple planar spiral γ_{sp} - see Fig. 2a:

$$\gamma_{sp}(t) = ((t + 0.2)\cos(\pi(1 - t)), (t + 0.2)\sin(\pi(1 - t))) \in E^2, \text{ for } t \in [0, 1], \quad (6)$$

and also another planar spiral γ_{spl} - see Fig. 2b:

$$\gamma_{spl}(t) = ((6\pi - t)\cos(t), (6\pi - t)\sin(t)) \in E^2, \text{ for } t \in [0, 5\pi].$$

(ii) Define next a spatial curve γ_{eh} in E^3, i.e. an elliptical helix - see Fig. 2c:

$$\gamma_{eh}(t) = (1.5cos(t), sin(t), t/4) \in E^3, \text{ for } t \in [0, 2\pi].$$

As easily verifiable all γ_{sp}, γ_{spl} and γ_{eh} are regular curves.

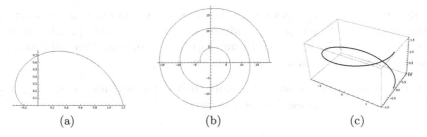

(a)   (b)   (c)

Fig. 2. Testing curves: a) γ_{sp}, b) γ_{spl}, c) γ_{eh} □

We recall now a definition of a special subfamily of admissible samplings (see [14], [15], [16] and [17]) i.e. *more-or-less uniform samplings* satisfying:

$$\kappa\delta \leq t_{i+1} - t_i \leq \delta, \quad (7)$$

where $\kappa \in (0, 1]$ (here κ depends on each sampling), for all $i \in [0, m]$.

b) Samplings

Example 2. Consider first the sampling:

$$t_i = \frac{i}{m}, \quad \text{for } i \text{ even}; \quad t_i = \frac{i}{m} + \frac{1}{m} - \frac{1}{m^2}, \quad \text{for } i \text{ odd}; \quad t_m = 1. \quad (8)$$

An easy verification shows that (8) is admissible but not more-or-less uniform as $t_2 - t_1 = 1/m^2$. On the other hand the following admissible sampling:

$$t_i = \begin{cases} \frac{i}{m}, & \text{if } i \text{ is even,} \\ \frac{i}{m} + \frac{1}{2m} & \text{if } i = 4k + 1, \\ \frac{i}{m} - \frac{1}{2m} & \text{if } i = 4k + 3, \end{cases} \quad (9)$$

satisfies more-or-less uniformity (see (7)), for $\kappa = \frac{1}{3}$.

The last admissible sampling used (with $\kappa = \frac{1}{5}$ in (7)) is defined as

$$t_i = \frac{i}{m} + \frac{(-1)^{i+1}}{3m}. \tag{10}$$

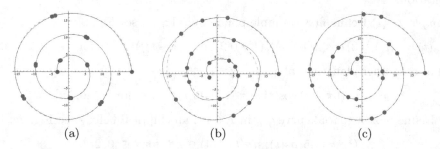

(a)   (b)   (c)

Fig. 3. $\hat{\gamma}_H$ (continuous) and γ_{spl} (dashed) for $m = 18$ sampled as in a) (8), b) (9), c) (10)

Visibly (see Fig. 3) interpolant $\hat{\gamma}_H$ is smooth with no cusps and corners at junction points i.e. at each $q_i \in Q_m$. Moreover, due to the high quartic orders in (5) for trajectory estimation (see [1] and [5]), the interpolant $\hat{\gamma}_H$ approximates accurately curve γ_{spl}, even on sparse data ($m = 18$). □

In the next subsection a medical example using Hermite interpolation $\hat{\gamma}_H$ (see (3) and (4)) based on sparse data is presented.

3.2   Example Based on Sparse Data

Example 3. One of the possible application of Hermite interpolation scheme $\hat{\gamma}_H$ ((3) and (4)) on sparse data is segmentation of tumor in images from CT scan or from ultrasonography (USG) (e.g. [18]). The physician in the first step marks the interpolation points - forming our reduced data Q_m. Next the interpolant

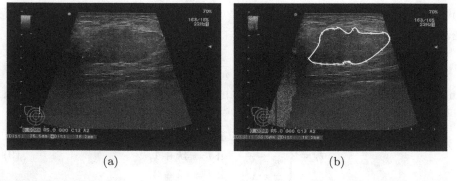

(a)   (b)

Fig. 4. *Hamartoma mammae* a) original USG image and b) encircled by Hermite interpolant ($m = 24$)

$\hat{\gamma}_H$ fitting Q_m is constructed. The example of such segmentation applied to USG image of *Hamartoma mammae* (a benign breast tumor), is shown in Fig. 4.

Again the interpolant $\hat{\gamma}_H$ is perfectly applicable on real life sparse data (as shown in Fig. 4 for $m = 24$). Note that in this particular application a C^1 piecewise-cubic interpolant $\hat{\gamma}_H$ forms a loop (i.e. $q_0 = q_m$). For such curves $\hat{\gamma}_H$ will generically produce a cusp or a corner only at a single junction point $q_0 = q_m$ as demonstrated in Fig. 4. This small deficiency in global smoothness of $\hat{\gamma}_H$ can be easily alleviated by e.g. adjusting $v_a(q_m) = v_a(q_0) = (v(q_m) + v(q_0))/2$. Evidently the average preserves the asymptotics in question.   □

3.3 Experimental Results

The numerical tests performed on curves and samplings introduced in subsection 3.1 are presented in Table 1. They all confirm the sharpness of the asymptotic estimate from (5) established in Th. 1.

Table 1. Estimated $\alpha \approx \bar{\alpha}$ with the aid of interpolant $\hat{\gamma}_H$

Curves	Samplings	m	$\alpha = 4$
γ_{spl}	uniform	$\{99, 100, \ldots, 120\}$	4.055
γ_{sp}	uniform	$\{99, 100, \ldots, 120\}$	4.044
γ_{eh}	uniform	$\{99, 100, \ldots, 199\}$	3.977
γ_{spl}	(8)	$\{99, 100, \ldots, 199\}$	3.955
γ_{sp}	(8)	$\{99, 100, \ldots, 120\}$	4.013
γ_{eh}	(8)	$\{99, 100, \ldots, 120\}$	4.003
γ_{spl}	(9)	$\{99, 100, \ldots, 120\}$	4.012
γ_{sp}	(9)	$\{99, 100, \ldots, 120\}$	3.950
γ_{eh}	(9)	$\{99, 100, \ldots, 200\}$	3.982
γ_{spl}	(10)	$\{99, 100, \ldots, 120\}$	4.014
γ_{sp}	(10)	$\{99, 100, \ldots, 120\}$	4.022
γ_{eh}	(10)	$\{99, 100, \ldots, 120\}$	3.985

The results from Table 1 indicate the sharpness of the asymptotics established in Th. 1.

4 Conclusion

In this paper we verified experimentally the sharpness of Th. 1 establishing quartic order in approximating regular curves $\gamma \in E^n$ by cumulative chord C^1 piecewise-cubics $\hat{\gamma}_H$. The experiments (conducted here for both planar and spatial curves) fully confirm the sharpness of (5) as demonstrated for to the length estimation in [1] and [5]. The fast quartic orders of convergence yield also a very good performance of our interpolant $\hat{\gamma}_H$ on sparse multidimensional data, which is presented in this paper on examples. A possible extension of this work includes first a theoretical proof of sharpness established in Th. 1. Secondly a comparison between two smooth interpolants, namely C^1 piecewise-cubic $\hat{\gamma}_H$ and C^2 spline based on cumulative chords [3], [19] and [20] could also be examined.

Acknowledgement. This research was supported in part by PL-Grid Infrastructure [12].

References

1. Kozera, R., Noakes, L.: C^1 interpolation with cumulative chord cubics. Fundamenta Informaticae 61(3-4), 285–301 (2004)
2. Noakes, L., Kozera, R.: Cumulative chords, piecewise-quadratics and piecewise-cubics. In: Klette, R., Kozera, R., Noakes, L., Weickert, J. (eds.) Geometric Properties for Incomplete Data, vol. 31, pp. 59–75 (2006)
3. De Boor, C.: A Practical Guide to Splines. Springer, Heidelberg (2001)
4. Ralston, A.: A First Course in Numerical Analysis. Mc-Graw Hill (1965)
5. Kozera, R.: Curve modeling via interpolation based on multidimensional reduced data. Studia Informatica 25(4B-61), 1–140 (2004)
6. Janik, M., Kozera, R., Kozioł, P.: Reduced data for curve modeling - applications in graphics, computer vision and physics. Advances in Science and Technology 7(18), 28–35 (2013)
7. Kocić, L.M., Simoncelli, A.C., Della Vecchia, B.: Blending parameterization of polynomial and spline interpolants. Facta Universitatis (NIŠ), Series Mathematics and Informatics 5, 95–107 (1990)
8. Kvasov, B.I.: Methods of Shape-Preserving Spline Approximation. World Scientific Publishing Company, Singapore (2000)
9. Piegl, L., Tiller, W.: The NURBS Book. Springer, Heidelberg (1997)
10. Wolfram Mathematica 9, Documentation Center, http://reference.wolfram.com/mathematica/guide/Mathematica.html
11. Taylor, B.N., Thompson, A. (eds.): The International System of Units (SI). National Institute of Standards and Technology Gaithersburg, MD 20899 (2008)
12. PL-Grid Infrastructure, http://www.plgrid.pl/en
13. Graham, C., Talay, D.: Stochastic Simulation and Monte Carlo Methods. Springer, Heidelberg (2013)
14. Kozera, R., Noakes, L., Szmielew, P.: Length estimation for exponential parameterization and ϵ-uniform samplings. In: Huang, F., Sugimoto, A. (eds.) PSIVT 2013. LNCS, vol. 8334, pp. 33–46. Springer, Heidelberg (2014)
15. Kozera, R., Noakes, L., Szmielew, P.: Trajectory estimation for exponential parameterization and different samplings. In: Saeed, K., Chaki, R., Cortesi, A., Wierzchoń, S. (eds.) CISIM 2013. LNCS, vol. 8104, pp. 430–441. Springer, Heidelberg (2013)
16. Kozera, R., Noakes, L.: Piecewise-quadratics and exponential parameterization for reduced data. Applied Mathematics and Computation 221, 620–638 (2013)
17. Noakes, L., Kozera, R.: More-or-less uniform sampling and lengths of curves. Quarterly of Applied Mathematics 61(3), 475–484 (2003)
18. Cho, Z.H., Jones, J.P., Singh, M.: Foundations of Medical Imaging. John Wiley & Sons (1993)
19. Morken, K., Scherer, K.: A general framework for high-accuracy parametric interpolation. Mathematics of Computation 66(217), 237–260 (1997)
20. Floater, M.S.: Chordal cubic spline interpolation is fourth order accurate. IMA Journal of Numerical Analysis 26, 25–33 (2006)

Parallel Simulation of Atmospheric Halo Phenomena

Marek Bejgier and Janusz Rzeszut

Warsaw University of Technology, Department of Electronics
and Information Technology, Warsaw, Poland
marek.bejgier@gmail.com, j.rzeszut@ii.pw.edu.pl

Abstract. The paper is an analysis of a parallelized simulation of solar halo phenomena based on an algorithm of inverse ray tracing with the use of Monte Carlo methods. In addition to the description of the basis for the phenomena the simulation algorithm is also discussed. In order to present it in an accessible way, a sequential algorithm is described at first and it is followed by its parallelization method. Both sequential and parallelized approaches are already implemented in author's solar halo effect simulators so that the practical use of these methods constitutes an excellent base to carry out useful comparisons of performance and quality in the context of obtaining very subtle details in varying types of solar halo phenomena.

1 Foundation of the Solar Halo Effect

The solar halo effect should be included in the family of optical phenomena. For its inception, the presence of ice crystals formed at a temperature oscillating around -30°C is indispensable. The ice crystals mainly occur in cirrostratus clouds high in the upper troposphere (up to 10 kilometers above the ground). In such conditions, they take a hexagonal prism shape with various ratios of height to radius of circle circumscribing their base. The crystals' sidewalls form 120° prisms between each other. In addition, if we number them consecutively from 0 to 5, we will further distinguish 60° prisms between the sidewalls with indices equal to $n+2 \mod 6$. Moreover, 90° prisms also occur in the crystals, appearing between the crystals' sidewalls and bases.

Another essential factor for the solar halo effect is the arrangement of the ice crystal during its free fall, which is firmly dependent upon the ratio of its height to radius of circle circumscribing its base. According to the classification presented by R. Greenler [1], columnar[1] and plate[2] crystals can be distinguished. As a consequence of aerodynamics, the plate crystals fall with their bases positioned almost parallel whereas the bases of the columnar crystals are arranged almost perpendicular to the surface of the Earth. We can also distinguish plate crystals in Lowitz orientation that rotate around an axis crossing opposite crystals' side

---

[1] Ice crystals with a large ratio of height to radius of circle circumscribing the base.
[2] Ice crystals with a small ratio of height to radius of circle circumscribing the base.

L.J. Chmielewski et al. (Eds.): ICCVG 2014, LNCS 8671, pp. 17–24, 2014.

Fig. 1. Photograph of solar halo phenomena taken on August 24, 2013 on the Solovetsky Islands. Several phenomena can be observed: 22° and 46° halos, sun dogs, parhelic circle, upper and lower tangent arcs, supralateral and infralateral arcs, Wegener arc [13].

walls. Thanks to the regular shapes of the ice crystals, a large diversity within the halo effect can be classified. The most common is a 22° ring which is formed when ice crystals of all kinds are present at the same time.

The halo arcs are a consequence of transitions and reflections of light rays which occur on the ice prisms. The path of a single ray that collides with the prism can be easily explained through four principles of optical physics: refraction, reflection, polarization and dispersion. The ice prisms simply send sunlight in particular directions. The angle of incidence of the light ray on the first wall of the prism only slightly affects its final deviation angle after exiting the prism (i.e. for 60° prisms the deviation angle equals around 22°, for 90° prisms the deviation angle equals around 46°), so we can observe that phenomena shapes are both regular and surprisingly complex at the same time.

2 The Inverse Ray Tracing Approach and Monte Carlo Methods

In the classical approach, the ray tracing method is the technique of generating images of three-dimensional scenes based on analyzing only those rays of light which get into the eye of the observer. As a consequence, the light rays are tracked at every destination from the observer's eye, through the surface that corresponds to the screen, and finally to the light source. For the purpose of

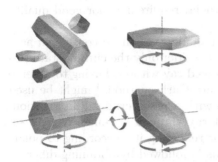 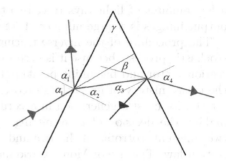

(a) Types of ice crystals and their free fall arrangements: random crystal (top left corner), plate crystal (top right corner), columnar crystal (bottom left corner), plate crystal in Lowitz orientation (bottom right corner).

(b) Light transition through a prism. Typical paths of sunrays through an ice crystal.

Fig. 2. Laws of optics and aerodynamics underlying the creation of halo effect

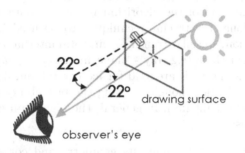

Fig. 3. Inverse ray tracing mechanism

the halo effect simulation, the approach to the ray tracing method is reversed so the light rays' paths are calculated from the light source to the drawing surface, taking into account the collision with a single ice crystal. Although such an approach violates the assumption that only the rays paths that go directly into the eye of the observer should be calculated, the inverse ray tracing approach is still highly more efficient than the classical solution, thanks to the fact that there is no need to create a whole three-dimensional scene containing millions of randomly generated virtual ice crystals which, from a technical point of view, cannot collide with light rays coming out from the drawing surface due to its limited resolution. The inverse method is widely used in halo simulation algorithms, because it simply guarantees a higher ratio of hit spots in the ice crystal to the number of traced light rays than the classical convention.

A relatively major disadvantage of the inverse ray tracing method is that the resulting simulation images do not have all their pixels filled (unfilled pixels take the background color). This is mainly visible when the images are generated with a low amount of light rays traced so the crucial requirement for good quality output images is a large number of traced rays.

The procedure of the inverse tracing of a single ray can be considered as a stochastic process, because it is necessary to consider only the current state (direction vector and beginning point) of the traced ray without having to observe the entire history of its path. Moreover, Monte Carlo methods[3] might be used for i.e., ice crystal generation in accordance with a predetermined distribution, making the decision of transmitting a light ray through a boundary between two different isotropic media (ice and air) or reflecting it - according to polarization law. The use of Monte Carlo methods is followed by obtaining different output images (a different set of pixels) each time the simulation is run, but the subjective impression remains almost identical to the observer.

2.1   Sequential Simulation Algorithm

The presented algorithm is a simplified set of steps that need to be followed in order to pursue a single ray of light through a single ice crystal. To achieve a complete halo output image, the algorithm has to be repeated multiple times. Moreover, implementation of the algorithm needs to contain several sophisticated three-dimensional ray tracing techniques to be used for surface physics (e.g. specular reflection, specular transmission, total internal reflection) and surface intersection algorithms (e.g. ray - plane intersection, ray - polygon intersection). Monte Carlo methods are used for ice crystal and light ray generation routines and for polarization modeling (using the probability of transmission or reflection of the traced light ray). In general, the algorithm can be categorized into three main steps:

1. Generate a single crystal (taking its geometry and corresponding free-fall orientation into account).
2. Cast a single ray from a light source through the ice crystal.
3. Calculate an intersection point of the ray and a drawing surface.

Light rays with different refractive indices should be traced separately to achieve colorful output images[4].

3   Parallelized Halo Effect Simulation Algorithm

Jackèl and Walter[8] have already proposed a parallel rendering method in order to achieve good quality halo output images by using a parallel computation for different wavelength calculations. The parallel method proposed in this article is emphatically different.

---

[3] A class of computational algorithms that benefits from repeated random sampling for resolving complicated numerical problems.

[4] For better performance the tracing procedure might be branched after calculating an intersection point with the first encountered ice crystal wall.

The halo phenomena simulation method is based on three main stages. The first is the ice crystal generation in terms of its population distribution. After identifying the height of the Sun above the horizon, the characteristics of the light ray need to be determined to make the light ray collide with the previously created ice crystal. The third simulation stage consists of modyfing the ray's path by a collision with the ice crystal together with marking an intersection point with the drawing surface.

In the case of the simulation carried out in a sequential manner, it seems to be obvious that the best idea is to perform the steps listed above individually for the ice crystal - light ray couples. So this method can be presented as a loop which performs all three simulation stages in its single iteration and each iteration is responsible for tracing a single light ray through a single ice crystal.

It should be mentioned that the above procedure has to performed sequentially (nevertheless its subalgorithms can be parallelized) so that the three simulation steps constitute a critical path of the halo effect simulation method. On the other hand, execution of several crital paths can parallelized. Thanks to that, the parallelization is perfectly scalable so that every processing unit is able to take care of the inverse tracing process for one ice crystal and light ray pair. The bottleneck of such an approach is the memory limit of the processing system in both efficiency and size aspects. On the other hand, the efficiency issue can by bypassed when using a separate memory bank for each processing unit in order to avoid a shared memory bus slowdown effect. Another doubt concerns an effect described in Amdahl's [10] law[5]. Fortunately, the sequential part of the parallelized algorithm is negligibly small and as mentioned before, the algorithm is scalable, so when enlarging the number of light rays to be traced, the influence of the sequential section is greatly reduced - according to Gustafson's [11] law.[6]

3.1   Parallel Nvidia CUDA Implementation

The sequential algorithm was parallelized using Nvidia CUDA SIMT (Single Instruction, Mulitple Thread) architecture. Three independent computational kernels were created and each of them separately implemented the corresponding simulation stage. The first two kernels, generating ice crystals and light rays respectively, were performed sequentially involving all CUDA cores. All objects representing crystals and rays were stored in the memory of the GPU and were accessed by the third computation kernel that implemented calculating the light rays' paths. Moreover, all the functions of the subalgorithms used in particular kernel implementations were parallelized thanks the use of CUDA threads. The interaction between the CPU and the GPU running the simulation consisted only of copying simulation input data (e.g. the Sun's elevation, number of rays

---

[5] This specifies the maximum parallelization benefit to a system when only part of the system is parallelized. It predicts the theoretical maximum speedup when using multiple processors.

[6] A counterpoint to Amdahl's law. It says that well scalable computations involving respectively large data sets can be efficiently parallelized.

to be traced, ice crystal population distribution) from RAM memory to the GPU device's memory and this was performed only once in a single simulation run.

4 Simulation Results

The approach presented in the article makes it possible to achieve output images of all known halo effect types, taking into account some subtle halo genres that can be simulated when the multiple scattering[9] technique is applied. Although the inverse ray tracing technique has already been presented by R. Greenler[1], the fully parallelized approach is innovative and provides a stunning simulation performance and good quality output images. Furthermore, all simulation results were compared to real halo effect photographs to verify their correctness. An output image that imitates the photograph from Solovetsky Islands (Fig. 1) is shown in Fig. 4.

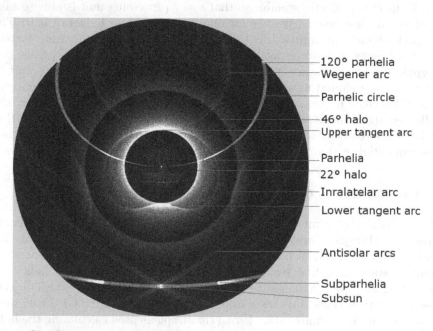

Fig. 4. Simulation output image that mirrors Fig. 1. Ice crystal population: random crystals - 63%, plate crystals - 5%, columnar crystals - 32%.

4.1 Performance Notes

A comparison of the time of parallel computation performed on the GPU to the time of computation carried out in a sequential manner on the CPU shows very favorable results for the first solution. For 1 million rays traced and exactly the same input simulation data the calculations lasted 0.6s and 26s respectively

for the GPU[7] and CPU[8]. The calculations were therefore speeded up about
43 times. Unfortunately, the comparison is not exactly certain as it depends
directly on the test kit (mainly a combination of the CPU and GPU). On the
other hand, comparing the performance makes sense, because it clearly shows
the profitability of the computiation transfer on the GPU.

Therefore, let's consider a different kind of test, conducted exclusively on
the GPU that relies on computation time analysis as a function of the number
of CUDA cores enabled. Such a comparison is reliable, because all CUDA cores
included in the system are symmetric. Despite the fact that all the subalgorithms
used to trace a single ray remain parallelized, the experiment shows an effect
of 'high-level' parallelization of the critical paths. The results of the experiment
are shown in Fig. 5.

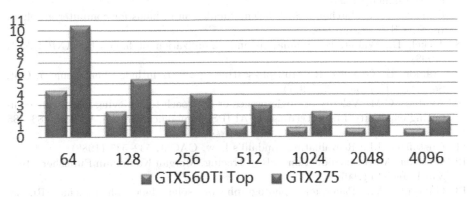

Fig. 5. Logarithmic chart of computation time in seconds as a function of the number
of enabled CUDA blocks in the range of 32 to 16384 (for 1 million rays traced). The
number of enabled CUDA blocks which is higher than 384 (the number of CUDA cores
in the test device) further reduces the computation time, because the CUDA kernels
need to be invoked fewer times (each kernel invocation causes some computational
overhead). The number of CUDA blocks that can be used at the same time is limited
by the memory size of the GPU.

5   Summary

The inverse ray tracing parallelization method presented in the article is an
effective way of shortening the computation time in halo effect simulations, taking into account the Nvidia CUDA architecture that provides parallelization of
calculations in many dimensions. Such an approach not only makes it possible
to speed up the execution time of particular algorithms of inverse ray tracing method, but it also makes the approach to the simulation greatly scalable.
Thanks to that, the parallelized inverse ray tracing approach can be reused to
illustrate other optical phenomena such as rainbows and glories, which are also
caused by a large number of relatively small objects.

---

[7] Nvidia GeForce GTX560 Ti Top.
[8] Intel Core i7 2600K. A single core of the CPU was used for the simulation.

References

1. Greenler, R.: Rainbows, halos, and glories. Cambridge University Press, Cambridge (1980)
2. Baranoski, G., Hong, S.: A Study on Atmospheric Halo Visualization, Technical Report CS-2003-26. School of Computer Science University of Waterloo, Ontario, Canada N2L 3G1 (2003)
3. Tränkle, E., Pattloch, F.: Monte Carlo Simulation and Analysis of Halo Phenomena. J. Opt. Soc. Am. A 1(5), 520–526 (1984)
4. Cowley, L.: HaloSim Homepage, http://www.atoptics.co.uk/halosim.htm
5. Glassner, A.: Computer-generated solar halos and sun dogs. IEEE Computer Graphics and Applications, 77–81 (1996)
6. Glassner, A.: Solar halos and sun dogs. IEEE Computer Graphics and Applications, 83–87 (January 1996)
7. Gonzato, J.C., Marchand, S.: Efficient simulation of halos for computer graphics. In: 8 ECS & IA, pp. 1–6.
8. Jackèl, D., Walter, B.: Simulation and visualization of halos. In: ANIGRAPH (1998)
9. Tränkle, E., Greenler, R.: Multiple-scattering effects in halo phenomena. J. Opt. Soc. Am. 4(3), 591–599 (1987)
10. Amdahl, G.M.: Validity of single-processor approach to achieving large-scale computing capability. In: Proceedings of AFIPS Conference, Reston, VA, pp. 483–485 (1967)
11. Gustafson, J.L.: Reevaluating Amdahl's Law. CACM, 532–533 (1988)
12. Glassner, A.: An Introduction to Ray Tracing. Morgan Kaufmann Publishers, Inc., San Francisco (2007)
13. Gnatyuk, Y.: Panoramic photograph of solar halo phenomena, Russia, Arkhangelsk, http://gnatyuk.ru/3d/galo/1.html

Mandelbrot- and Julia-Like Rendering of Polynomiographs

Krzysztof Gdawiec

Institute of Computer Science, University of Silesia
Będzińska 39, 41-200, Sosnowiec, Poland
kgdawiec@ux2.math.us.edu.pl

Abstract. Polynomiography is a method of visualization of complex polynomial root finding process. One of the applications of polynomiography is generation of aesthetic patterns. In this paper, we present two new algorithms for polynomiograph rendering that allow to obtain new diverse patterns. The algorithms are based on the ideas used to render the well known Mandelbrot and Julia sets. The results obtained with the proposed algorithms can enrich the functionality of the existing polynomiography software.

Keywords: polynomiography, rendering, Julia set, Mandelbrot set, computer art.

1 Introduction

One of the most elusive goals in computer aided design is artistic design and pattern generation. Pattern generation involves diverse aspects: analysis, creativity, development [11]. We must deal with all the three aspects in order to obtain an interesting pattern that could be later used in jewellery design, carpet design, as a texture etc.

Many methods of pattern generation exist in the literature, but we will mention only those which are needed in the paper. First such method is polynomiography. The method was introduced by Kalantari and it is based on the root-finding methods of complex polynomials [4]. Other known methods of pattern generation are Mandelbrot and Julia sets [3]. The methods are based on the iteration of a complex function, usually a quadratic function. In this paper, we combine concepts taken from the rendering methods of the Mandelbrot and Julia sets with the polynomiography, obtaining in this way new methods of artistic pattern generation. The patterns obtained with the help of our algorithms could find similar applications as the standard polynomiography, i.e., creating paintings, carpet design, tapestry design, animations etc. [5].

The paper is organized as follows. In Sec. 2 we introduce some basic informations about polynomiography and a standard algorithm for polynomiograph rendering. Then, in Sec. 3 we present two algorithms of polynomiograph rendering that are based on the ideas used in the rendering of Mandelbrot and Julia sets. We present some exemplary polynomiographs obtained with the proposed algorithms in Sec. 4. Finally, in Sec. 5 we give some concluding remarks.

L.J. Chmielewski et al. (Eds.): ICCVG 2014, LNCS 8671, pp. 25–32, 2014.

2 Polynomiography

Polynomiography is the art and science of visualization in approximation of the zeros of complex polynomials, via fractal and non-fractal images created using the mathematical convergence properties of iteration functions [4]. A single image created using the mentioned methods is called a polynomiograph.

In the polynomiography we can use different polynomial root finding methods, e.g., Newton method [9], Traub-Ostrowski method [9], Harmonic Mean Newton's method [1], Halley method [1], Whittaker method [9] etc. Because in the literature there is such multiplicity of root finding methods in the paper we will limit to the so-called parametric basic family [6].

Let us consider a polynomial $p \in \mathbb{C}[Z]$, $\deg p \geq 2$ of the form:

$$p(z) = a_n z^n + a_{n-1} z^{n-1} + \ldots + a_1 z + a_0.$$

To define the parametric basic family we need to introduce a sequence of functions $D_m : \mathbb{C} \to \mathbb{C}$. For $z \in \mathbb{C}$ the D_m function is defined as follows [6]:

$$D_0(z) = 1,$$

$$D_m(z) = \det \begin{pmatrix} p'(z) & \frac{p''(z)}{2!} & \cdots & \frac{p^{(m-1)}(z)}{(m-1)!} & \frac{p^{(m)}(z)}{m!} \\ p(z) & p'(z) & \ddots & \ddots & \frac{p^{(m-1)}(z)}{(m-1)!} \\ 0 & p(z) & \ddots & \ddots & \vdots \\ \vdots & \vdots & \ddots & \ddots & \frac{p''(z)}{2!} \\ 0 & 0 & \cdots & p(z) & p'(z) \end{pmatrix} \tag{1}$$

for $m \geq 1$.

Now, the parametric basic family is a sequence of functions $B_{m,\alpha} : \mathbb{C} \to \mathbb{C}$ for $m = 2, 3, \ldots$ and $\alpha \in \mathbb{C}$ of the following form [6]:

$$\forall_{z \in \mathbb{C}} \quad B_{m,\alpha}(z) = z - \alpha p(z) \frac{D_{m-2}(z)}{D_{m-1}(z)}. \tag{2}$$

When we take $m = 2$ and 3 it turns out that B_2 and B_3 are the parametric Newton method and the parametric Halley method (respectively):

$$B_2(z) = z - \alpha \frac{p(z)}{p'(z)}, \tag{3}$$

$$B_3(z) = z - \alpha \frac{2p'(z)p(z)}{2p'(z)^2 - p''(z)p(z)}. \tag{4}$$

To render a single polynomiograph we can use Algorithm 1. In the algorithm we use the so-called iteration colouring, i.e., colour is determined according to the number of iteration in which we have left the while loop. Other colouring methods exist in the literature, e.g., basins of attraction, mixed colouring [6].

Algorithm 1. Polynomiograph rendering

Input: $p \in \mathbb{C}[Z]$, $\deg p \geq 2$ – polynomial, $A \subset \mathbb{C}$ – area, k – number of
    iterations, ε – accuracy, $m \geq 2$ – number for $B_{m,\alpha}$, $\alpha \in \mathbb{C}$ – parameter
    for $B_{m,\alpha}$, $colours[0..k]$ – colourmap.
Output: Polynomiograph for the area A.

1 **for** $z_0 \in A$ **do**
2     $i = 0$
3   **while** $i \leq k$ **do**
4         $z_{i+1} = B_{m,\alpha}(z_i)$
5   **if** $|z_{i+1} - z_i| < \varepsilon$ **then**
6   break
7         $i = i + 1$
8   Print z_0 with $colours[i]$ colour

---

3   Algorithms of Mandelbrot- and Julia-Like Rendering of Polynomiographs

When we generate Julia and Mendelbrot sets, similar to the polynomiography, for each point in the area $A \subset \mathbb{C}$ we make some iterative process. For the Mandelbrot set this iterative process is following:

$$z_{i+1} = z_i^2 + c, \tag{5}$$

where constant c is equal to the considered point, and $z_0 = 0$. If z_{i+1} fulfils the escape criteria, i.e., $|z_{i+1}| > 2$, then the point do not belongs to the Mandelbrot set and we draw it with colour corresponding to the number of iteration.

We can transfer the concept with the constant c from the Mandelbrot algorithm to the polynomiography. In the original polynomiography algorithm we replace the standard iteration of $B_{m,\alpha}$ with:

$$z_{i+1} = B_{m,\alpha}(z_i) - c. \tag{6}$$

The constant c, unlike in the Mandelbrot algorithm, is taken as a value of a mapping $f : \mathbb{C} \to \mathbb{C}$ in the considered point. Moreover, at the end of each iteration constant c is transformed with an additional mapping $g : \mathbb{C} \to \mathbb{C}$. Algorithm 2 presents the complete pseudocode of the proposed algorithm.

The iterative process for the Julia sets is the same as for the Mandelbrot set, but this time c is constant for all the points in A, and the starting point is equal to the considered point. Moreover, in the escape criteria we have different threshold value: $\max\{2, |c|\}$.

In the Julia-like version of the rendering algorithm for polynomiography we change the standard iteration process with:

$$z_{i+1} = B_{m,\alpha}(z_i) + c, \tag{7}$$

Algorithm 2. Mandelbrot-like Polynomiograph rendering

Input: $p \in \mathbb{C}[Z]$, $\deg p \geq 2$ – polynomial, $A \subset \mathbb{C}$ – area, k – number of iterations, ε – accuracy, $m \geq 2$ – number for $B_{m,\alpha}$, $\alpha \in \mathbb{C}$ – parameter for $B_{m,\alpha}$, $f, g : \mathbb{C} \to \mathbb{C}$ – mappings, $colours[0..k]$ – colourmap.

Output: Polynomiograph for the area A.

1 **for** $z_0 \in A$ **do**
2 $\quad$ $c = f(z_0)$
3 $\quad$ $i = 0$
4 $\quad$ **while** $i \leq k$ **do**
5 $\quad\quad$ $z_{i+1} = B_{m,\alpha}(z_i) - c$
6 $\quad\quad$ **if** $|z_{i+1} - z_i| < \varepsilon$ **then**
7 $\quad\quad\quad$ break
8 $\quad\quad$ $c = g(c)$
9 $\quad\quad$ $i = i + 1$
10 $\quad$ Print z_0 with $colours[i]$ colour

Algorithm 3. Julia-like Polynomiograph rendering

Input: $c \in \mathbb{C}$ – parameter, $p \in \mathbb{C}[Z]$, $\deg p \geq 2$ – polynomial, $A \subset \mathbb{C}$ – area, k – number of iterations, ε – accuracy, $m \geq 2$ – number for $B_{m,\alpha}$, $\alpha \in \mathbb{C}$ – parameter for $B_{m,\alpha}$, $f : \mathbb{C} \to \mathbb{C}$ – mapping, $colours[0..k]$ – colourmap.

Output: Polynomiograph for the area A.

1 **for** $z_0 \in A$ **do**
2 $\quad$ $i = 0$
3 $\quad$ **while** $i \leq k$ **do**
4 $\quad\quad$ $z_{i+1} = B_{m,\alpha}(z_i) + c$
5 $\quad\quad$ **if** $|z_{i+1} - z_i| < \varepsilon$ **then**
6 $\quad\quad\quad$ break
7 $\quad\quad$ $c = f(c)$
8 $\quad\quad$ $i = i + 1$
9 $\quad$ Print z_0 with $colours[i]$ colour

---

and at the end of each iteration we use mapping $f : \mathbb{C} \to \mathbb{C}$ to transform the constant c. Algorithm 3 presents the complete pseudocode of the proposed algorithm.

In both the proposed algorithms we use a standard test for the convergence of the iteration process, i.e., $|z_{i+1} - z_i| < \varepsilon$, but we can use different convergence tests as was proposed in [2] for the standard polynomiography rendering algorithm.

4   Examples

In this section, we present some examples of polynomiographs obtained using algorithms proposed in Sect. 3.

We start with examples of polynomiographs obtained using the Mandelbrot-like rendering algorithm. The polynomiographs are presented in Fig. 1, and the parameters used were following:

(a) $p(z) = z^3 - 1$, $A = [-2, 2]^2$, $k = 40$, $\varepsilon = 0.001$, $m = 2$, $\alpha = 0.75$, $f(z) = 0.1 \sin z + 0.33 + \cos z$, $g(z) = \cos z$,

(b) $p(z) = z^3 - 1$, $A = [-2, 2]^2$, $k = 40$, $\varepsilon = 0.001$, $m = 3$, $\alpha = 0.75$, $f(z) = 0.1 \sin z + 0.33 + \cos z$, $g(z) = \cos z$,

(c) $p(z) = z^3 - 1$, $A = [-2, 2]^2$, $k = 40$, $\varepsilon = 0.001$, $m = 2$, $\alpha = 0.75$, $f(z) = z$, $g(z) = \log(\cos z)$,

(d) $p(z) = z^4 + 4$, $A = [-2, 2]^2$, $k = 40$, $\varepsilon = 0.001$, $m = 3$, $\alpha = 0.75 - 0.8\mathbf{i}$, $f(z) = 2z$, $g(z) = z$.

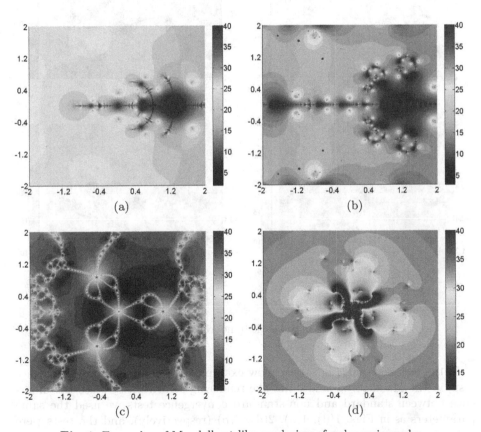

Fig. 1. Examples of Mandelbrot-like rendering of polynomiographs

Fig. 2 presents some examples of polynomiographs obtained with the Julia-like rendering algorithm. The parameters used to obtain the images were following:

(a) $c = 0.285$, $p(z) = z^3 - 1$, $A = [-3.2, 0.7] \times [-2, 2]$, $k = 25$, $\varepsilon = 0.001$, $m = 2$, $\alpha = 1.0$, $f(z) = \sin(\cos(z))$,

(b) $c = 0.285$, $p(z) = z^3 - 1$, $A = [-3.2, 0.7] \times [-2, 2]$, $k = 25$, $\varepsilon = 0.001$, $m = 3$, $\alpha = 1.0$, $f(z) = \sin(\cos(z))$,

(c) $c = -0.8$, $p(z) = z^4 + 4$, $A = [-2, 2]^2$, $k = 30$, $\varepsilon = 0.001$, $m = 2$, $\alpha = 0.85$, $f(z) = 0.2 \cos z$,

(d) $c = -5.8$, $p(z) = z^4 + 4$, $A = [-2, 2]^2$, $k = 30$, $\varepsilon = 0.001$, $m = 2$, $\alpha = 0.85$, $f(z) = 0.2 \cos z$.

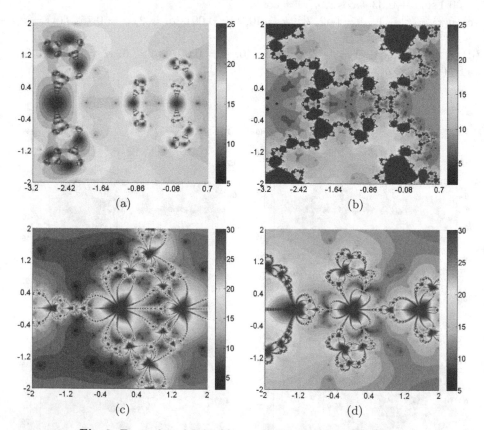

Fig. 2. Examples of Julia-like rendering of polynomiographs

In the last example (Fig. 3) we show examples of using different convergence tests in the Mandelbrot- and Julia-like rendering algorithms. To see the difference between standard and non-standard convergence tests we used the same parameters as in Figs. 1(d), 1(a), 2(d), 2(b) (respectively), and the tests were following:

(a) $||z_{i+1}|^2 - |z_i|^2| < \varepsilon$,
(b) $|0.01(z_{i+1} - z_i)| + |0.0285|z_{i+1}|^2 - 0.029|z_i|^2| < \varepsilon$,
(c) $|0.01(z_{i+1} - z_i)| + |0.029|z_{i+1}|^2 - 0.03|z_i|^2| < \varepsilon$,
(d) $|0.08\Re(z_{i+1} - z_i)| < \varepsilon \vee |0.08\Im(z_{i+1} - z_i)| < \varepsilon$,

where $\Re(z)$, $\Im(z)$ denote the real and imaginary part of z (respectively).

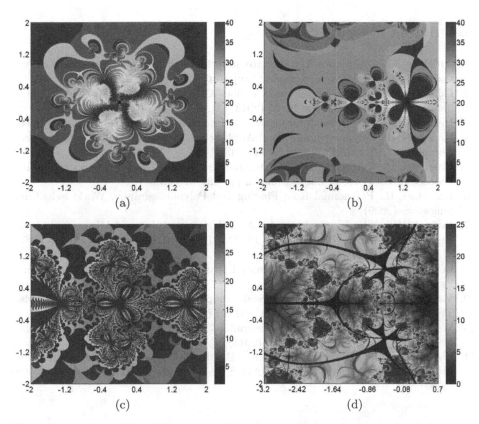

Fig. 3. Examples of Mandelbrot- and Julia-like rendering of polynomiographs with different convergence tests

5   Conclusions

In this paper, we presented two algorithms for the rendering of polynomiographs that are based on the ideas used in the rendering of the well known Mandelbrot and Julia sets. The presented examples show that using the proposed algorithms we are able to obtain very interesting and diverse patterns, and that these patterns are different from those obtained with the standard rendering method of the polynomiographs.

Polynomiography is based on the complex polynomials. In the literature we can find methods of obtaining interesting patterns using instead of the complex numbers the q-systems numbers [8] and bicomplex numbers [10]. Moreover, in the standard polynomiography we can use different iteration processes, e.g. Mann, Ishikawa [7]. The use of q-system and bicomplex numbers in the polynomiography together with the different iteration schemes can probably further enrich the obtained patterns, what would be examined in our future work.

References

1. Ardelean, G.: Comparison Between Iterative Methods by Using the Basins of Attraction. Applied Mathematics and Computation 218(1), 88–95 (2011)
2. Gdawiec, K.: Polynomiography and Various Convergence Tests. In: WSCG Communication Proceedings, pp. 15–20 (2013)
3. Herrmann, D.: Algorithmen für Chaos und Fraktale. Addison-Wesley, Bonn (1994)
4. Kalantari, B.: Polynomiography and Applications in Art, Education and Science. Computers & Graphics 28(3), 417–430 (2004)
5. Kalantari, B.: Two and Three-dimensional Art Inspired by Polynomiography. In: Proceedings of Bridges, Banff, Canada, pp. 321–328 (2005)
6. Kalantari, B.: Polynomial Root-Finding and Polynomiography. World Scientific, Singapore (2009)
7. Kotarski, W., Gdawiec, K., Lisowska, A.: Polynomiography via Ishikawa and Mann Iterations. In: Bebis, G., et al. (eds.) ISVC 2012, Part I. LNCS, vol. 7431, pp. 305–313. Springer, Heidelberg (2012)
8. Levin, M.: Discontinuous and Alternate Q-System Fractals. Computer & Graphics 18(6), 873–884 (1994)
9. Varona, J.L.: Graphics and Numerical Comparison Between Iterative Methods. The Mathematical Intelligencer 24(1), 37–46 (2002)
10. Wang, X.-Y., Song, W.-J.: The Generalized M-J Sets for Bicomplex Numbers. Nonlinear Dynamics 72(1-2), 17–26 (2013)
11. Wannarumon, S., Unnanon, K., Bohez, E.L.J.: Intelligent Computer System for Jewelry Design Support. Computer-Aided Design & Applications 1(1-4), 551–558 (2004)

Time Compensation in Perceptual Experiments

Anna Lewandowska (Tomaszewska)

West Pomeranian University of Technology, Szczecin
Faculty of Computer Science and Information Technology
Żołnierska 49, 71-210, Szczecin, Poland
atomaszewska@wi.zut.edu.pl

Abstract. Image quality plays important role in many image processing applications. To provide a convincing proof that a new method is better than the state-of-the-art, computer graphics projects are often accompanied by user studies, in which a group of observers rank or rate results of several algorithms. Such user studies, known as subjective image quality assessment experiments, are very time consuming. This paper is intended to help design time compensated quality assessment experiment.

1 Introduction

When developing a new imaging or algorithm, there is often a need to compare the results with the state-of-the-art methods. The vast majority of publications in computer graphics rely on rather informal validation, in which several examples included in the paper can be carefully inspected and compared with the results of competitive algorithms. This is an effective method, which often provides a sufficiently convincing proof of superiority of a new algorithm, but only if the visual difference is unquestionably large. If the differences are subtle, such informal comparison is often disputable. The most reliable way of assessing the quality of an image is by subjective evaluation. Indeed, the mean opinion score (MOS), a subjective quality measure requiring the services of a number of human observers, has been long regarded as the best method of image quality measurement. However, the MOS method is expensive, and time-consuming.

In this work we address the problem of reducing the time of subjective quality assessment experiments and analyzing the results. The paper complements our approach presented in [6]. The most prominent experimental methods, pair-wise, are analyzed and described in detail.

The paper is organized as follows. In section 2, previous works are discussed. In section 3, the pair-wise experiments are presented. Time compensation of the experiments in Section 4. Section 5 shows and discusses results achieved. The last section presents conclusions and suggestions for possible future work.

2 Previous Work

The subjective image quality assessment methods originate from a wider group of psychometric scaling methods, which were developed to measure psychological

L.J. Chmielewski et al. (Eds.): ICCVG 2014, LNCS 8671, pp. 33–40, 2014.

attributes [1]. Image quality is one such attribute that describes preference for a particular image rendering. The interest in image and video quality assessment has been predominantly focused on video compression and transmission applications, resulting in several recommendations for the design of quality assessment experiments [2–4]. The documents recommend experimental procedures (some of them evaluated in this study), viewing conditions, display calibration parameters and the methods for experimental data processing. The subjective quality assessment are used in different applications [5–10].

Quality assessment would be a much easier task if it could be performed by a computational algorithm without a need for a subjective experiment. A large number of such algorithms, known as objective quality metrics, have been proposed over the years [11, 12]. Their predictions can correlate well with the subjective experiments if trained for a restricted set of distortions [13], but their accuracy decreases with the growing variety of distortions [14].

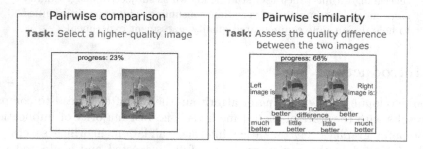

Fig. 1. Overview of the four subjective quality assessment methods we investigate in this work. The diagram shows the timeline of each method and the corresponding screens.

Relatively little work has been devoted to the user study optimization. As the experiments are time-consuming, in the paper we focus on the problem of time compensation.

3   Pair-Wise Assessment

For comparison the results we investigate two commonly used experimental methods of quality assessment, illustrated in Figure 1.

Ordering by Force-Choice Pairwise Comparison. The observers are shown a pair of images (of the same scene) corresponding to different conditions and asked to indicate an image of higher quality (see Figure 1a). Observers are always forced to choose one image, even if they see no difference between them (thus a forced-choice design). There is no time limit or minimum time to make the choice. The method is straightforward and thus expected to be more accurate than rating methods. But it also requires more trials to compare each possible pair of conditions: $0.5\,(n{\cdot}(n-1))$ for n conditions. The number of trials can be

lighthouse   saliling2   woman   womanhat

bikes   buildings   flowersonih35

parrots   plane   churchcapitol

Fig. 2. The reference images (scenes) from the public domain Kodak Photo CD used in the experiments

limited using balanced incomplete block designs [15] in which all possible paired comparisons are indirectly inferred. But even more effective reduction of trials can be achieved if a sorting algorithm is used to choose pairs to compare [16].

Efficient sorting algorithms, such as *quicksort*, can reduce the number of comparisons necessary to order a set of conditions to about $n \log n$, which could be significantly less than the full comparison, especially if the number of conditions n is large. When incorporated into an experiment, the sorting algorithm decides in an on-line fashion which pairs of images to compare based on the previous comparisons made in the same experimental session. Each comparison necessary to sort a set of conditions requires one trial with a two-alternative-forced-choice decision. Because such decisions are noisy and non-deterministic, such sorting rarely reflects the ranking of the true means. However, Monte-Carlo simulations have shown that gains in performance outweigh the loss of accuracy due to the incomplete design [16]. This is because sorting tends to concentrate comparisons around very similar images, which are the most sensitive to subjective variations. For our experiments we used the sorting algorithm based on the self balancing binary trees (Red-Black Trees), as it results in low and stable number of comparisons. Balance is preserved by painting each node of the tree with one of two colors (typically called 'red' and 'black') in a way that satisfies certain properties, which collectively constrain how unbalanced the tree can become in the

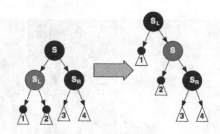

Fig. 3. Example of a Red-Black Tree balancing

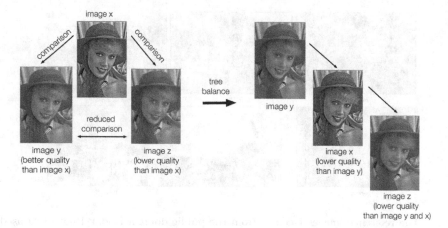

Fig. 4. Example of comparison reduction based on Red-Black Tree

worst case. When the tree is modified, the new tree is subsequently rearranged and repainted to restore the coloring properties. The properties are designed in such a way that this rearranging and recoloring can be performed efficiently (Figure 3). In our case, the left tree from Figure 4 denotes two pairs of images comparison *image x* → *image y* and *image x* → *image z*, where, *image y* has better quality than *image x* and *image z* is of inferior quality than *image x*. The tree balance hereby eliminate the pair *image y* → *image z* comparison.

The balancing of the tree is not perfect but it is good enough to allow it to guarantee searching in $O(logn)$ time, where n is the total number of elements in the tree. The insertion and deletion operations, along with the tree rearrangement and recoloring, are also performed in $O(logn)$ time.

Pairwise Similarity Judgements. While the forced-choice method orders images according to quality, it does not tell how different the images are. In pairwise similarity judgements observers are not only asked to mark their preference, but also to indicate on a continuous scale how large the difference in quality is between the two images (see Figure 1b). Observers can choose to leave the marker in the '0' position if they see no difference between the pair. The same sorting algorithm can be used for the similarity judgements as for the pairwise comparisons. The position of the marker (on the left or right side of '0') decides on the ranking of the image pair. If '0' is selected, the images are ranked randomly. The sorting algorithm used for the pairwise comparisons can also be used for the similarity judgements. The position of the marker (on the left or right side of 0) decides on the ranking of the image pair. If 0 is selected, the images are ranked randomly.

3.1 Experiment Design

Observers. The images were assessed by naïve observers who were confirmed to have normal or corrected to normal vision. The age varied between 22 and 43. 11 observers completed the two pairwise comparison experiments. For additional reliability, all observers repeated each experiment three times, but no two repetitions took place on the same day in order to reduce the learning effect.

Display Conditions. The experiments were run in two separate laboratories on two different displays: 26" NEC SpectraView 2690 and 24" HP LP2480zx. Both are high quality, 1920×1200 pixel resolution, LCD displays offering very good color reproduction. The display responses were measured with the Minolta CS-200 colorimeter and Specbos 1201 spectroradiometer. The measurements were used to calibrate the displays and ensure that all images were reproduced in the sRGB colour space.

Images and Distortions. Selected 10 images from the Kodak Photo CD photo sampler collection, shown in Figure 2. This is the subset of images used to collect data for the LIVE quality database [13]. They contain a broad range of content type, including faces, animals, man-made objects and nature.

We selected JPEG 2000 (JP2K) compression distortions and unsharp masking based on the bilateral filter ($\sigma_s = 8$, $\sigma_r = 50$) as the two evaluated algorithms, both at three levels of either distortion (JP2K) or enhancement (unsharp masking). The JP2K test images are the same as in the LIVE quality database [13] while unsharp masking is a new algorithm that we decided to include in our study.

Experimental Procedure. Following the ITU-R500 recommendation [4] we design experimental procedure. No session took longer than 30 minutes to avoid fatigue.

4   Experiment Optimisation

The measure of the experiment is computed as the number of votes (the number of times one algorithm is preferred to another) assuming that all pairs of algorithms are compared. The result is averaged across the observers and models for every algorithm. To stabilize results we compute the score by dividing the votes by standard deviation computed per observer.

Transitive Relation. Since a reduced pairwise comparison design was used for both the force-choice and the similarity judgement methods, several assumptions must be made to infer data for missing comparisons. The most obvious assumption is that the quality estimates are in the transitive relation: if image A is better than image B and B is better than C, then A is better than C. It must be noted that this does not need to be true for actual data collected in the full pairwise comparison experiment. Cyclic relations, in which the assumption is violated, are quite common in the full design, especially when images are similar.

Forced Choice. Assuming the transitive relation, it is not difficult to compute the number of votes for each condition — the number of times one condition is preferred to other assuming that all pairs of conditions are compared. The vote count is also equivalent to the position in the ranking.

Similarity Judgements data contains signed quality differences, where the sign indicates which image was judged as better. Because each observer could use a different range of values, the quality differences are divided by the overall standard deviation for a particular observer.

We need to make one more assumption to find unambiguous quality scores from the quality differences between pairs of images. The quality differences given by the observers rarely correspond to distances in one-dimensional space. That is, if $|| \cdot ||$ is the magnitude estimate between a pair of conditions, $||AB|| + ||BC||$ is rarely equal to $||AC||$. We could use 1D scaling to project the difference data to one dimensional space under the least-square criterion, but this would introduce further complications in the analysis of variance. Instead, to find the quality scores in the 1D space, we take into account only the quality difference values between the closest (in terms of ranking) pairs of images while ignoring all other magnitude estimates in the data. This is motivated by the fact that the magnitude estimates of the most similar images should be the most reliable. This simplification gives unique (up to a constant) projection to a 1D space for each set of conditions. An example of computing such a projection is shown in Figure 5.

	jp2k high	jp2k med	jp2k low	
jp2k_high	0	3	6	←ignored
jp2k_med	-3	0	2	
jp2k_low	-6	-2	0	
score	-3	1	2	

Fig. 5. Example of projecting pairwise similarity scores into 1-dimensional scale. The table contains the dissimilarity judgements (differences), where positive values mean that the condition in the column was selected as better than the condition in the row. The conditions are ordered from the lowest to the highest quality, so that the values just above the diagonal line are all positive. The final score is the sum of columns but computed only for the nearest (in terms of ranking) condition pairs, which lie just above and below the diagonal. All other difference values are ignored.

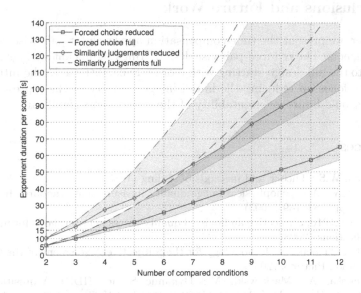

Fig. 6. The time required to compare the given number of conditions (x-axis) using each experimental method. The plot is based on the average time recorded in our experiments. Because the number of trials in reduced pairwise methods depends on the complexity of a sorting algorithm, the shaded regions represent the bounds between the best- and worst-case scenario. The continuous lines indicate the times based on the average complexity. The times include the assessment of a reference image for all methods, i.e. 2 conditions point corresponds to the assessment of two test images and one reference image.

5   Results and Analysis

When choosing an experimental method it is important to consider not only the sensitivity of a statistical test, but also the time that observers need to complete the experiment. After all, even a less accurate method may result in smaller confidence intervals if more measurements are collected. For each run of the main sessions of the experiment we recorded the total time as well as the number of trials. The data was averaged over all observers to compute the mean time required for a single trial. We used this data as well as the expected number of trials for each method to plot in Figure 6 the time required to compare a single scene at a given number of conditions. It is important to note that the experiment time for the reduced pairwise design can vary depending on the number of comparisons that is required to sort conditions. Therefore the timing for these methods is shown as the upper and lower bound of the sorting algorithm complexity (shaded region), together with the average complexity (the line with markers). The timing for the full design (all pairs compared with each other) is shown as the dashed lines.

6 Conclusions and Future Work

In the paper, we present the time-compensation approach for pair-wise, perceptual experiments. The reduced pairwise design brings significant savings in time compared to the full design starting with 6 or more conditions. In the future, we are going to focus on reducing the initial images dataset to the representative ones, that should improve executability of the experiments significant.

References

1. Torgerson, W.S.: Theory and methods of scaling (1985)
2. Keelan, B.W.: A psychophysical image quality measurement standard. In: SPIE, vol. 5294, pp. 181–189 (2003)
3. ITU-T.Rec.P.910, Subjective audiovisual quality assessment methods for multimedia applications (2008)
4. ITU-R.Rec.BT.500-11, Methodology for the Subjective Assessment of the Quality for Television Pictures (2002)
5. Tomaszewska, A., Markowski, M.: Dynamic Scenes HDRI Acquisition. In: Campilho, A., Kamel, M. (eds.) ICIAR 2010, Part II. LNCS, vol. 6112, pp. 345–354. Springer, Heidelberg (2010)
6. Mantiuk, R., Tomaszewska, A., Mantiuk, R.: Comparison of four subjective methods for image quality assessment. Computer Graphics Forum (2012)
7. Tomaszewska, A.: Blind Noise Level Detection. In: Campilho, A., Kamel, M. (eds.) ICIAR 2012, Part I. LNCS, vol. 7324, pp. 107–114. Springer, Heidelberg (2012)
8. Tomaszewska, A., Stefanowski, K.: Real-Time Spherical Harmonics Based Subsurface Scattering. In: Campilho, A., Kamel, M. (eds.) ICIAR 2012, Part I. LNCS, vol. 7324, pp. 402–409. Springer, Heidelberg (2012)
9. Tomaszewska, A.: User Study in Non-static HDR Scenes Acquisition. In: Bolc, L., Tadeusiewicz, R., Chmielewski, L.J., Wojciechowski, K. (eds.) ICCVG 2012. LNCS, vol. 7594, pp. 245–252. Springer, Heidelberg (2012)
10. Mantiuk, R., Mantiuk, R., Tomaszewska, A., Heidrich, W.: Color correction for tone mapping. Computer Graphics Forum 28, 193–202 (2009)
11. Wang, Z., Bovik, A.C.: Modern Image Quality Assessment. Morgan & Claypool Publishers (2006)
12. Pedersen, M., Hardeberg, J.Y.: Full-Reference Image Quality Metrics: Classification and Evaluation. Foundations and Trends in Computer Graphics and Vision 7(1), 1–80 (2011)
13. Sheikh, H.R., Sabir, M.F., Bovik, A.C.: A Statistical Evaluation of Recent Full Reference Image Quality Assessment Algorithms. IEEE Transactions on Image Processing 15(11), 3441–3452 (2006)
14. Ponomarenko, N., Lukin, V., Zelensky, A., Egiazarian, K., Carli, M., Battisti, F.: TID2008 - A database for evaluation of full-reference visual quality assessment metrics. Advances of Modern Radioelectronics 10, 30–45 (2009)
15. Gulliksen, H., Tucker, L.R.: A general procedure for obtaining paired comparisons from multiple rank orders. Psychometrika 26, 173–184 (1961)
16. Silverstein, D.A., Farrell, J.E.: Efficient method for paired comparison. Journal of Electronic Imaging 10, 394 (2001)

Fur Visualisation for Computer Game Engines and Real-Time Rendering

Dominik Szajerman and Adam Jurczyński

Institute of Information Technology
Lodz University of Technology, Łódź, Poland
dominik.szajerman@p.lodz.pl
http://it.p.lodz.pl/

Abstract. In this paper there is a method of real-time rendering of fur presented. Physical-based properties of a hair and fur strands are analysed. The work develops shell based method of rendering hair and fur, by new approach to strand modelling and rendering. Thanks to using efficient algorithms the presented method works in interactive, on-line mode and is less demanding in terms of an artist work. Thus it could be used in the production process of real-time rendering applications and computer games of various genres.

Keywords: real-time hair and fur rendering, physical simulation, computer game engines.

1 Introduction

Three-dimensional rendering is an area of computer graphics, that was naturally developing with technological advancement. Nowadays computers capabilities allows handling increasingly complex issues, inter alia, simulations of physical phenomena.

Hair or fur rendering are one of the most challenging and well known problems, albeit they are not always solved similarly. Some methods are designed and fit better to human hair while the others prove correct in animal fur rendering. However quite a few contemporary and advanced methods (e.g. [1]), including this work, can be applied to both hair and fur rendering. Usually it is done by tweaking of simulation parameters. For this reason, this paper uses "hair" and "fur" term interchangeably.

2 Evolution of Approach to Hair and fur Rendering

Methods developed throughout history of computer games and real time simulations to render hair and fur evolved with the development of computer graphics and the graphics hardware.

Textured static model is the first approach to character's hair representation in three-dimensional games, was based on static model. Obtained by deforming

L.J. Chmielewski et al. (Eds.): ICCVG 2014, LNCS 8671, pp. 41–48, 2014.

a)   b)   c)

Fig. 1. a) Static mesh hair; b) Hair planes with and without texture applied, presented in game The Last of Us, created by Naughty Dog; c) Hair based on control hair strands, created by nVidia

mesh to imitate hair structure, it was the simplest way to create and render hair, however very unnatural. Whole model of character, either human or animal, is joint as one mesh which is presented in the picture 1a.

Extension of this method allows diversifying main model by attaching separate models of hair mesh, however it requires skeletal based animation.

Animated Textured Planes. Reflecting on hair structure, it is concluded that hair need to be shown with a volume. First attempt to imitate this effect with static mesh, was focused around making layers of hair strips. Similarly to previous example of static mesh models, hair are simple textured objects. However, with the use of alpha blending, they are placed as a multiple planes stacked on each other. In the end resolving in volumetric effect, as hair gains depth with partially transparent objects, what describes picture 1b.

Texture-Based Hair - Shells. Previous solution introduced volumetric property of hair, whereas hair based on textures excels in this matter. This two methods are completely different even though both evolved around similar concept. Animated planes are representation of whole hair strip, it means that the textures are placed along the lines of strands. Whereas this technique bases on textures across hair[2,3], each shell is another layer of hair represented by strips.

Control Hair Strands. Up to this point methods of hair rendering are simplification of realistic physical objects by merging hair, control hair strands technique is an effort to imitate each hair as unique entity[4]. Control hair is very complex way to present structure of hair, as it is procedurally generating cylinders for each strand (fig. 1c). The process of rendering with control hair strands is started with creating two models, one is the mesh of a character and the other is hair in special file format, which contains hair with its shape. This poses one of the most important issues, as creating that kind of model requires special tools or necessity of dynamically modified width of strand in order to get proper rendering of it.

2.1   Comparison of Methods

Due to huge differences between presented methods it is no use to compare them to each other. Textured static model and textured planes are based on standard mesh rendering and always would be faster than the others because they are not as time or memory demanding as more contemporary methods. At the same time they give least plausible hair visualisations. On the other side there is control hair method which uses completely different rendering technique based on different data structures. It allows to introduce new simulation parameters such as wind and gravitation.

The method presented in this paper could be evaluated in comparison to the standard shells method because it is its improvement. Thus such comparison of time requirements and visual plausibility was presented in the Results section.

3   Development of Shells Method - Our Approach

During above review eveloved a question, which technique is best suited for the improvement and adaptation to game engine. Final solution was actually selected by the needs in games industry and lack of fur simulations working in real time. This choice directed further actions on shell based hair technique.

At the course of the work, it was noted that fur consisting of textured shells makes an impression of natural strands with inconsiderable amount of resources.

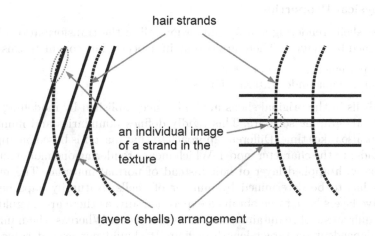

Fig. 2. Hair strands and their images in textures representing layers. Comparison between shells method (left) and improved method developed in this work (right).

In view of limitations that hardware imposed on developers, a game "Shadow of the Colossus" rendered up to 6 layers shells. The reason why this was sufficient number is the way how hair textures were generated. Strands were arranged aslant to shell instead of perpendicularly, this solution is presented in the picture 2.

Hardware limitations are now less an issue, what results in possibility of far greater number of layers. Hair strands can be drawn on texture as dots, perpendicularly to their line. Furthermore, that improvement solves multiple additional matters.

First appearing subject is distance between shells. To keep continuity of hair strands, this gaps have to be as small as possible. Increase in number of layers allows closing them to minimum, without loss of hair length. Another subject covered with that solution is density of hair. Aslant layout on texture occupies more space than perpendicular one, while strands thickness has to be sufficient for rendering on screen.

3.1   The Length of Strands

Following task requires some assumptions. Rendering one texture on every shell would cause in constant diameter of strands at its entire length. That is why there should be generated multiple different textures, however generating more than 6 textures which were used in "Shadow of the Colossus" would be unnecessary resource exploitation. Final number of textures can be different from number of shells, the effect of narrowing strand towards its end can be obtained stepwise. Hair strands have small diameter, so the difference on transition between different diameters would be unnoticeable. This effect can be imitated with simple increase in transparency with every layer.

3.2   Physical Properties

Regarding shells rendering and fur animation, all of the transformations has to be performed by shaders. There are two main aspects that concur to this area:

– shells placement,
– hair movement under external forces.

Placing shells in the original shells method is accomplished by modelling static objects in 3D graphic software. This rigidly defines boundaries and number of layers, but also takes time. Different approach to that matter is based on applying vertex shader to the character model. Which means rendering one model multiple times, but with applied layer of hair instead of normal material. The number of passes has to be determined by number of shells. Naturally gaps between consecutive layers have to be obtained experimentally, as there are no guidelines except requirement of maintaining continuous strands. Whereas, the number of shells is dependent on target length of hair. It should not exceed value of 50 layers, otherwise it would not be the optimal solution.

There are multiple forces that can change shape of hair by setting it into motion. The main three are: wind, gravity and character movement. As hair shells are separate objects treated in individual passes, each part of hair has to be transformed independently. External forces can be treated as vectors, which simplifies all of the computations into combining all of the vectors into one resultant vector.

4   Implementation

Rendering hair is a process in which hair is applied to the character, it follows that there are required two parts. The former one is character model, an underlay for hair. It is rendered using fur texture (fig. 3a) as a background for actual fur. The latter piece of work necessary in model preparations is a texture of hair length. Since hair are procedurally generated, there was a requisition for solution to constraint hair length. The first idea that arose was to set length values directly on the model, therefore it was created grayscale texture. Areas of the longest hair strands are represented by black colour and it is gradually shortened with brightness, white colour indicates regions without hair. This texture is presented in the picture 3b and what is important because of memory use optimization, it is stored in alpha channel of basic model texture.

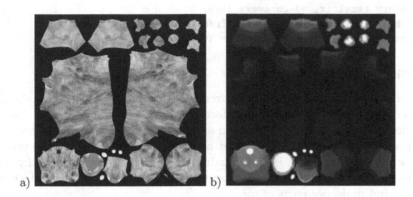

Fig. 3. Base colour fur texture (a) and hair length texture (b)

The main clue of the work is contained in generating cross-sections of hair strands throughout shells (texture layers) and in shaders applying effects to them. Next subsections describe the both.

4.1 Fur Texture Generation

The algorithm shown below creates the set of textures containing the shells. Generation of strands is actually a process of changing values in random pixels. The amount of changes is set by *density* (in the listing below) value. Noted previously, through course of experiments the best value oscillates at 35-40% of whole number of pixels in texture.

Next transformation performed on hair textures is decaying with length. Since hair are tapering towards end of a strands, this characteristic must be represented in created structure. The solution to this issue is changing alpha value with length of a strands. This means bottom layer is drawn as opaque object, while the uppermost one is nearly transparent. Blurriness advancing along hair imitates decaying visually without changing actual diameter of strands.

```
1. Fill every element of outputShellsTexture with zero vectors
2. Generate hair strands - "density" times fill in random texel of every
layer of outputShellsTexture with the value of corresponding texel from
```

```
inputHairLengthTexture
  for i = 1 to denstity:
    x = random(0, size)
    y = random(0, size)
    for every layer k:
      shellsTexture[k][x][y].xyz = inputHairLengthTexture[x][y]
      shellsTexture[k][x][y].alpha = 1
3. Decay hair with their length:
  for every texel (x, y) on every layer k:
    outputShellsTexture[k][x][y].alpha *= k/layers
4. Remove hair form bald spots
  for every texel (x, y) on every layer k:
    if hairLengthTexture[resize(x)][resize(y)] > 0.99
      outputShellsTexture[k][x][y] = (0,0,0,0)
```

4.2 Shaders in Rendering

The second part of implementing hair rendering method is included in shaders. It includes computation of external forces. The first is *gravity*. This force is simplified to a vector added to position of a vertex, its value is constant and set only in vertical axis. Next force is *wind*, added similarly to the previous vectors, which is generated on CPU. However, hair dampens wind force, that is why there was created variable to control this aspect - *dampen*. This attribute decreases force of wind in deeper parts of fur.

Layers of generated hair strands are placed along normal vector value (*Normal*) and fibers would be straight. However, a fur is in general tousled. Due to the usage of UV map (*randomTex()*), there are created slight deflections from normal vectors. Positions of consecutive shells are displaced slightly in random direction. Moreover, since differences in hair length between adjacent hair patches were not accounted in texture generation, this shader computes length for each vertex.

Finally, all of the computations are applied to the position of vertex (*vertexPosition*).

```
1. Generate wind and dampen
   windMovement = dot(Wind, Normal)
   dampen = abs(windMovement) / (length(Wind) * length(Normal)) + 1
2. Length and normal transformations modifying hair
   fLength = pow((hairLen+hairLen*randomTex()*0.5)/385.0, 1.7) * FurLength
   stiffness = pow(fLength , 3)
   transformedNormal = Normal + ((randomTex()-0.5 f) * pow((hairLen), 10))
3. Transform vertex to final position
   X = transformedNormal * fLength
   X += gravity * stiffness
   X += Wind * stiffness / dampen
   X -= Movement * stiffness * 50
   if (length(X) > fLength)
     vertexPosition += normalize(X) * fLength
   else
     vertexPosition += X
```

5   Results

Visual result of developed algorithm is shown in the picture 4. Rendered model with a fur consists of 19113 vertices. Lighting is calculated according to Kajiya-Kay model[6]. The number of layers used in simulation is 35. Such number of layers allows to simulate a relatively long hair. It combines plausible visual effect with acceptable processing time.

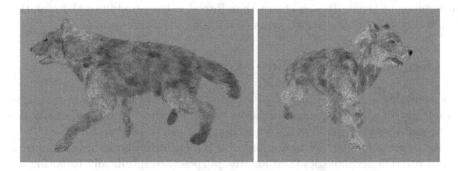

Fig. 4. Final result of rendering a wolf with fur

The improved method has been tested in two ways. The first test was the comparison of the visual effect with the standard shells method. In the picture 5 there is the comparison presented. The same input data was used and similar hair length was set. In the left picture it can be seen artifacts as gaps between individual shells (layers). Standard shell method requires compromise between visual quality and hair length. Our improved method lacks of this drawback.

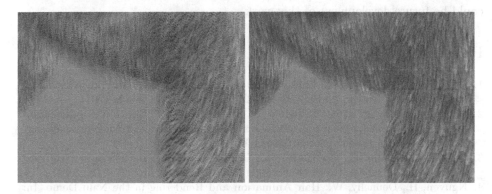

Fig. 5. Comparison between shells method (left) and developed method (right)

The second test was measuring the rendering time. A dependence of rendering time on number of layers was estimated for nVidia GPU GT 630M. The results are listed in Table 1. As expected, processing time is almost proportional to

Table 1. Computation times in [ms] required for rendering of 1024×768pix. images of a furry animal.

number of layers	6	12	18	24	30	35
no wind and no gravity	5.5	10.7	15.7	20.7	26.0	29.9
wind and gravity included	5.4	10.6	15.7	20.8	25.8	30.0

the number of layers. It also shows that introduction of additional simulation parameters (wind and gravitation) does not affect the execution time.

6   Conclusions and Future Work

Hair rendering is a crucial aspect of creating animated characters in real time. Complexity of this issue affects results, as in search of optimized method a compromise between quality and rendering time has to be found.

This paper is an attempt to compromise the optimization issues and natural look of fur. The technologies used for this purpose are specifically targeting application in computer game engines and real-time rendering. Easiness of creating different hair lengths and introduced parameters, such as gravity, strand stiffness and wind reduce the amount of work for graphic designers.

Regarding visual effects of fur rendering, this work proposes the method giving more plausible effects. Less artifacts - gaps between individual shells are visible. Whereas the processing times below 30ms (for large number of 35 layers) allows to apply the method in real-time rendering (at least 30 frames per second).

The only issue that appears in final visualisation is short hair rendering. This problem is not caused by method itself, but due to model preparation. However, this issue could be solved with properly worked out 3D modelling methods, which could be future development of this work.

References

1. Hedberg, V., Lagergren, M., Limsäter, F.: SpeedFur - A GPU based procedural hair & fur modeling system. In: SIGGRAPH 2011, Vancouver, Canada (2011)
2. Hair rendering in game "Shadow of the Colossus". Electronic publication (June 2013), http://teamico.wikia.com/wiki/Graphics_and_post-processing_effects_used_in_Shadow_of_the_Colossus
3. Lengyel, J., Praun, E., Finkelstein, A., Hoppe, H.: Real-Time Fur over Arbitrary Surfaces. In: I3D 2001, Research Triangle Park, NC USA, pp. 227–232 (2001)
4. Nguyen, H., Donnelly, W.: Hair Animation and Rendering in the Nalu Demo. In: GPU Gems 2, ch. 23. Addison-Wesley (July 2013)
5. Scott, G.V., Robbins, C.R.: Stiffness of human hair fibers. New Youk, J. Soc. Cosmet. Chem. 29, 469–485 (1978)
6. Kajiya, J.T., Kay, T.L.: Rendering fur with three dimensional textures. ACM, Computer Graphics 23(3), 271–280 (1989)

Multiple Scattering in Cumulus Clouds

Błażej Marcinkiewicz and Jacek Raczkowski

Warsaw University of Technology, Institute of Computer Science
Nowowiejska 15/19, 00-665 Warsaw, Poland
J.Raczkowski@ii.pw.edu.pl

Abstract. The paper presents an improved algorithm for realistic imaging of cumulus clouds. The technique is based on the lattice-Boltzmann method and takes into account multiple scattering of light in the participating medium of high albedo. Relevant estimation of a phase function for such environment is proposed. Acceleration technique with specific initialization of boundary conditions for light propagation is postulated. Obtained results are discussed and compared to existing techniques. Sample renderings are provided.

1 Introduction

Dense low-level clouds, especially cumulus and cumulonimbus, are a big challenge for realistic imaging in computer graphics. Modeling their shape and variability is troublesome as well as the propagation of light through the area occupied by the cloud. In this work the second issue is considered assuming that the cloud model is given and consists of a set of voxels with defined physical parameters. Light propagating through cumulus type clouds is strongly scattered on the molecules of water vapor. High albedo of cumulus clouds significantly impacts on the direction of light rays propagation and consequently on observer's visual impression.

Jim Kajiya and Brian Von Herzen [1] proposed the method of realistic rendering of clouds based on their physical parameters. The paper described two rendering algorithms. In the first one light was propagated through the volumetric cloud and the impact of each light source on the brightness of a point in space was calculated. The multiple scattering effects were ignored. The brightness was depended only on the light absorption. Finally brightness values for each ray from the camera were accumulated.

The other method used spherical harmonics to find the brightness of light at each point as a function of direction [2]. The obtained set of partial differential equations was attempted to be resolved analytically.

Lattice-Boltzmann method can be used to take into account multiple scattering effect [3]. A beam of discrete directions in which light is propagated is selected in order to obtain the optimal Gaussian quadrature. This method produces rays effect because it does not consider the area between the selected directions of propagation. Max [4] presented the method that allowed reducing the undesired effect.

L.J. Chmielewski et al. (Eds.): ICCVG 2014, LNCS 8671, pp. 49–56, 2014.

In this paper the extension of Max's algorithm [4] is presented. In particular the improved estimation of the phase function and the new idea of boundary conditions initialization for light propagation are postulated. It improves reality of final images and efficiency of the algorithm.

2   Transport of Light in Clouds

Both absorption and scattering provide the highest impact on the light transport in clouds. The emission of light does not occur and therefore is neglected:

$$\frac{dL(\boldsymbol{x}, \boldsymbol{\omega})}{ds} = -K(\boldsymbol{x})L(\boldsymbol{x}, \boldsymbol{\omega}) + aK(\boldsymbol{x}) \int_{4\pi} P(\boldsymbol{x}, \boldsymbol{\omega}, \boldsymbol{\omega}')L(\boldsymbol{x}, \boldsymbol{\omega}')d\boldsymbol{\omega}' \qquad (1)$$

where $\boldsymbol{\omega}'$ is the direction of incoming light, K is a total coefficient of absorption and scattering, and a is albedo.

The first component in the equation (1) is responsible for the extinction of light. It takes into account the light that has been absorbed by the medium as well as that which has been refracted in other direction than the direction of propagation. The integral in the equation is responsible for the rays which at a given point refract in the direction of propagation. P is a phase function which describes the angular distribution of scattered radiation for a given object.

Generally the light transport equation does not have an analytical solution. Therefore some simplifications are applied:

- assumption of isotropic medium (the value of the phase function depends only on the angle)
- assumption of homogeneous medium
- assumption of low albedo

Low albedo of a rendered object allows eliminating the factor responsible for multiple scattering. However such assumption does not work properly for cumulus clouds. Their high albedo forces using the multiple scattering in rendering. If that effect is omitted the resulted image suffers with unnatural darkened areas which in reality would be lit up by the refracted light.

Phase function describes the angular radiance distribution of scattered light. The shape of the function depends on the size of the object. The value of the phase function may also depend on the wavelength of refracted light. For particles much smaller than the wavelength of light the phase function is approximated using the Rayleigh model:

$$P(\Phi) = \frac{3}{4}(1 + \cos^2 \Phi) \qquad (2)$$

Such estimation is correct for the Earth's atmosphere. In clouds light is scattered on the water molecules whose diameter is close to the wavelength. This results in much stronger forward scattering than in the Rayleigh model. Therefore Henyey-Greenstein functions are commonly used:

$$P(\Phi) = \frac{1 - g^2}{(1 + g^2 - 2g \cos \Phi)^{\frac{3}{2}}} \qquad (3)$$

where g is the asymmetry coefficient in the range $-1 < g < 1$. Negative values correspond to backward scattering, the positive to forward scattering, and 0 is for isotropic scattering.

For cumulus clouds the Henyey-Greenstein model may be insufficient because it significantly underestimates the impact of backward scattering. That is why some researchers use Mie theory functions as an alternative solution. As a result of multiple refractions the shape of these functions changes. It may also lead to underestimating of backward scattering [5]. In this work the effect was taken into account. For cumulus clouds phase function values for the corresponding wavelengths are slightly different and related effects may be neglected.

3   Lattice-Boltzmann Method

Lattice-Boltzmann method simplifies the solution of the equation (1) assuming local interactions. Scattering in this method is considered in several (usually 18) selected directions. Each voxel stores the amount of energy that actually propagates in a given direction.

The algorithm starts with determining of illuminated walls and setting fixed values of light energy for the voxels located at the borders. Then in each iteration the light rays are propagated in selected directions. The directions indexed 1,...,6 are from the center of the voxel to the walls and 7,...,18 from the center of the voxel to its edges. In addition the direction of 0 is the direction from the voxel to itself to indicate the absorption of energy.

3.1   Edge Voxels Initialization

At the beginning of each iteration a portion of energy should be added to the boundary voxel. The subsequent propagation needs to select a minimum set of directions that have positive scalar product with the direction of light (due to the large distance from the light source it can be assumed that the rays are parallel). Directions should be sorted by the value of the scalar product. The initial value of the energy is normalized to 1. Then the following steps are performed starting from the direction of the largest scalar product:

For each edge voxel:
1. For the selected direction calculate the minimum value of the scalar product with the direction of the light and the remaining energy in voxel
2. Calculated minimum is the energy propagating in the given direction
3. From the remaining energy subtract the energy propagating in a given direction
4. If remaining energy is still greater then 0 choose another direction and repeat from step 1. Otherwise the procedure ends.

3.2 Light Ray Propagation Procedure

Each iteration of the propagation procedure consists of two phases. In the first phase light scattering in all directions is calculated in a way to obtain highly anisotropic forward scattering. To achieve it the entry point is an isotropic case with uniform energy distribution. Half of the energy is equally distributed to directions 1,...,6 and other half to directions 7,...,18. Next the coefficient defining what fraction of energy is distributed into specific direction i is modified by the phase function corresponding to the scattering of light from the incoming direction j to the direction i. Additionally all the coefficients are multiplied by the density at that point to achieve medium density dependence. Then in the second phase the light ray is propagated based on the guidelines set out in the previous phase. Both steps are executed synchronously.

3.3 Limitations of the Method

Lattice-Boltzmann method implementation is relatively simple and well suited for parallel computing. However high memory consumption (for each voxel the quantity of energy propagating in each direction should be stored) and a large number of iterations required to achieve a solution (proportional to the size of the simulation grid) are disadvantages of the method. In the next section the idea how to speed up the whole procedure is proposed.

Lattice-Boltzmann method involves a division of space into discrete elements. This method used to render real objects assumes a certain voxel size. In practice it may be more than one refraction between two adjacent voxels depending on the scale adopted. Multiple refraction affects the value of the phase function. In the next section the method of phase function estimation after n refractions is presented.

4 Estimation of Phase Function after Multiple Refraction

Multiple refraction of light rays engages an analytical model in order to estimate the value of the phase function. The model uses single refraction parameters (phase function and albedo) to determine the values after multiple refractions [5].

After two consecutive refractions with angles θ_1 and θ_2 the ray will propagate at an angle θ to the original direction:

$$\cos\theta = \cos\theta_1 \cos\theta_2 + \sin\theta_1 \sin\theta_2 \cos\psi \tag{4}$$

where ψ is the azimuthal angle between the second and first scattering events.

The probability that the ray will propagate in the direction θ_1 is $P(\theta_1)\sin\theta_1\Delta\theta_1$. The phase function after n refractions can be calculated using the equation:

$$P_n(\theta_n) = 4\pi \frac{\sum_{\theta_1,\theta_2,\psi} P_{n-1}(\theta_1)\sin\theta_1\Delta\theta_1 \cdot P_1(\theta_2)\sin\theta_2\Delta\theta_2}{\sum_{\theta_1,\theta_2,\psi} \sin\theta_1\Delta\theta_1 \cdot \sin\theta_2\Delta\theta_2} \tag{5}$$

The values of θ_n are determined by each combination of θ_1, θ_2, ψ in the equation 4.

5   Light Propagation Algorithm

In a real cumulus cloud an average straightforward path of light ray is approximately 20 meters. Assuming a voxel size of $100m \times 100m \times 100m$ there are about 5 refractions between two adjacent voxels. The method described in section 4 allows to determine the value of the phase function after the corresponding number of refractions. Mie phase function (data were generated by the program MiePlot [6]) was adopted as a base function for the calculation. The values of this function depend only on the angle of incidence so they can be stored in a lookup table to speed up the calculation.

The lattice-Boltzmann method is time costly due to significant number of iterations required for the propagation of energy until reaching the wall opposite to the light direction. However typically cloud does not occupy the whole area of simulation. Therefore one can apply a single scattering algorithm as a good approximation of light actual behavior inside the dispersive medium and adopt these values as initial values instead of zeros in the original algorithm. It significantly speeds up the transport of energy through the area of simulation.

In order to calculate the initial energy in voxels light intensity along the ray path $\Gamma_{x,y,z}$ needs to be calculated:

$$I_i(x, y, z) = e^{-\kappa \int_{\Gamma_{x,y,z}} \rho(\gamma) d\gamma} \tag{6}$$

where $I_i(x, y, z)$ is luminous intensity in voxel (x, y, z), κ is an absorption coefficient, and ρ is density of the medium.

The calculated values of intensity should be distributed to m scattering directions. For this purpose the procedure identical to that described in section 3.1 is applied with the initial value of the energy assigned according to the equation 6.

Next steps of the algorithm are the same as those described in section 3. The values inside the simulation area are propagated in the appropriate directions and values at the edges are initiated in accordance with 3.1.

6   Results

In the testing environment the rendering of an animation frame with single scattering takes about $0.2s$, for multiple scattering and lattice-Boltzmann method approximately $12s$ (with 64 iterations of the algorithm). The used cumulus cloud model was generated based on the fluid mechanics and thermodynamics. The mesh size was $128 \times 64 \times 128$. The light falling angle is $40°$ to the horizon.

The test object (Stanford bunny scaled to resolution of $128 \times 128 \times 128$) is additionally lighted by the source located at the angle of $20°$ to the zenith. Basic lattice-Boltzmann method needed 128 iterations to get a correctly rendered image. For algorithm with initial single scattering values the same result was achieved with 64 iterations. Both images are indistinguishable (figure 1).

Use single scattering to initiate values of energy speeds up the energy propagation through the whole area of the simulation (figure 2).

Fig. 1. Left: Rendering with basic lattice-Boltzmann algorithm, 128 iterations. **Right**: Rendering with lattice-Boltzmann algorithm initiated with single scattering, 64 iterations.

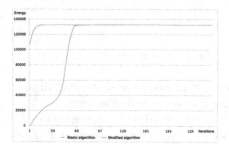

Fig. 2. (Left): Comparison of the amount of energy in each iteration for both algorithms. To reach the same level of energy the basic algorithm requires 128 iterations (the graph in blue), the modified algorithm needs only about 32 iterations. The data is collected only from the area where the cloud exists.

Fig. 3. (Right): Energy in the simulation as a function of the number of iterations. Energy is collected only from the area where the cloud exists. The use of modified phase function gives about 1.5% higher value of the total energy.

The modified phase function in the lattice-Boltzmann method results in higher total energy inside the area of simulation. All images were rendered with the light incidents at an angle of 40° to the horizon.

Pictures at figure 4 show the object observed from the direction of the light source. In figure 5 the object is between observer and the light source. Left pictures at both figures show the images rendered using the algorithm with single scattering. There are some unnaturally dark areas of the cloud. The edges of the

Fig. 4. Left: Single scattering. **Middle**: Lattice-Boltzmann method with non-modified phase function. **Right**: Lattice-Boltzmann method with modified phase function.

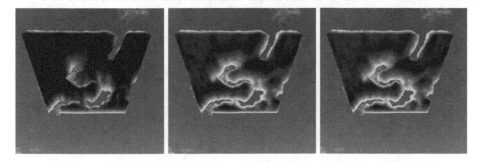

Fig. 5. Left: single scattering. **Middle**: lattice-Boltzmann method with non-modified phase function. **Right**: lattice-Boltzmann method with modified phase function.

cloud are clearly blacked out. Middle pictures present the images rendered by the lattice-Boltzmann method using the basic Mie phase function. In contrast to the single scattering algorithm these images are properly illuminated. The edges of the clouds are clear everywhere as in reality. Right pictures at figures 4 and 5 show the images rendered by the lattice-Boltzmann method using the modified Mie phase function after five refractions of ray. Again images look natural. The differences between the two methods are not significant. The total energy stored in the simulation differs by about 1.5% in favor of the modified phase function (figure 3).

7   Conclusion

The improved algorithm presented in this paper provides a significant performance increase compared to the basic lattice-Boltzmann method without losing the quality of the resulting image. Strictly comparable results are achieved using only half time. Modified phase function taking into account multiple ray refractions between two neighboring voxels supports higher brightness and thus the better realism of the rendered object.

References

1. Kajiya, J.T., Von Herzen, B.P.: Ray tracing volume densities. SIGGRAPH Computer Graphics 18(3), 165–174 (1984)
2. Chandrasekhar, S.: Radiative Transfer (1984)
3. Geist, R., et al.: Lattice-Boltzmann lighting. In: Proceedings of the 15th Eurographics Conference on Rendering Techniques, EGSR 2004, pp. 355–362 (2004)
4. Max, N.: Efficient Light Propagation for Multiple Anisotropic Volume Scattering. In: Proceedings of the 5th Eurographics Workshop on Rendering, pp. 87–104 (1994)
5. Piskozub, J., McKee, D.: Effective scattering phase functions for the multiple scattering regime. Optics Express 19(5), 4786–4794 (2011)
6. Philip Laven, P.: MiePlot (2013), http://www.philiplaven.com/mieplot.htm

Component Weight Tuning of SSIM Image Quality Assessment Measure

Przemysław Skurowski[1] and Mateusz Janiak[2]

[1] Institute of Informatics, Silesian University of Technology
Gliwice, Poland
przemyslaw.skurowski@polsl.pl
http://inf.polsl.pl
[2] Polish-Japanese Institute of Information Technology
Bytom, Poland
mjaniak@pjwstk.edu.pl
http://pjwstk.edu.pl

Abstract. The article describes a method for a parameter tuning for a family of image quality assessment methods based on the concept of SSIM. The method employs curve fitting to model SSIM-MOS relationship then uses inverse relationship to calculate intended measure values and finally the log-log regressive model to estimate parameters for components constituting the measure. The regression was implemented by minimizing of least squares (L2) and least absolute deviation (L1). The results were verified against well tested reference databases.

1 Introduction

The structural similarity index [13] (SSIM) was a seminal proposal- of an image quality assessment (IQA) method. By using complex correlations, which are relatively simple mathematical tools it offers reasonably high relevance of objective measure to the subjective human quality perception responses. It was used in numerous applications and it inspired creation of various further methods which improve precision of the original measure and share the general outline of the design. These are: information weighting (IWSSIM) [14], multiscale approach (MS-SSIM) [12], incorporating color information (CID) [5] and others. Moreover, SSIM is also a basis for quality measures of other types of signals like sound [3] or video [15]. The generalized measure formula (m) and basic $SSIM$ for a pair (x, y) of signals are product of a form:

$$m(x,y) = \prod_{i=1}^{N}[f_i(x,y)]^{\alpha_i}, \quad SSIM(x,y) = [l(x,y)]^{\alpha}[c(x,y)]^{\beta}[s(x,y)]^{\gamma} \quad (1a,b)$$

where: f_i are [0,1] valued components, describing similarity - in particular l, c, s are: luminance, contrast and structure measures respectively; α_is and in SSIM case α, β, γ are corresponding weights. The SSIM components are computed as correlation based statistical parameters:

L.J. Chmielewski et al. (Eds.): ICCVG 2014, LNCS 8671, pp. 57–65, 2014.

$$l(x,y) = \frac{2\mu_x\mu_y + C_1}{\mu_x^2 + \mu_y^2 + C_1}, \quad c(x,y) = \frac{2\sigma_x\sigma_y + C_2}{\sigma_x^2 + \sigma_y^2 + C_2}, \quad s(x,y) = \frac{\sigma_{xy} + C_3}{\sigma_x\sigma_y + C_3} \quad (2)$$

where: μ_x, μ_y are mean values of compared signals, $\sigma_x, \sigma_y, \sigma_x^2, \sigma_y^2, \sigma_{xy}$ are standard deviations, variances and covariance of respective signals, C_1, C_2, C_3 are small constant values to avoid division by zero problem. The default implementation mean SSIM (MSSIM) is computed as an average of a local SSIM values (see Eq. 10a), which are computed using local, Gaussian weighted statistical parameters.

In the original paper, for the sake of proposal clarity, the weights of SSIM components in Eq. (1b) were equally set up to 1, although, as it has been demonstrated by Rouse [9] these components are not of the equal relevance to the human quality perception (see also Fig. 1). Component weight tuning was considered in dedicated experiments [12,1] but for multiscale MS-SSIM only and to the authors knowledge that aspect of single scale SSIM have never been deliberated. Although, other tunable aspects of measure such as spatial pooling [11] and content weighting [14,6] were studied extensively. Therefore, component weighting still remains promising field for improvement for fine tuning of the measure both in terms of accuracy and precision.

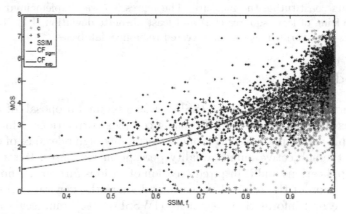

Fig. 1. SSIM components l, c, s vs TID2008 MOS judgements and their nonlinear regressive models (CF - sigmoidal and exponential)

In further parts of this paper, the proposal of regression based method for parameters computation is described. The proposal results in an improvement of both accuracy and precision of SSIM value. As a ground truth, there are used reference databases TID2008, LIVE and CSIQ.

2   The Idea

In order to verify the objective quality measure (m), its results are compared to the subjective judgments provided as MOS values (mean opinion score) which in a numerical scale represent mean values of human quality judgments of an image. The relationship between the IQAs and MOS judgments is modeled by a fitting curve (CF) - which have to be monotonic. Then the prediction (p) of an average human response for a pair of reference distorted images x, y is:

$$p_{x,y} = CF\left(m(x,y)\right) \tag{3}$$

Which has to be compared versus the $MOS(x, y)$ value. Since the MOS values should be treated as a ground truth, so any adjustments, should be done to the SSIM value. Therefore, let's define the intended measure value as:

$$\tilde{m}(x,y) = CF^{-1}\left(MOS(x,y)\right), \tag{4}$$

the value of measure (SSIM) which *should be* according to inverse fit curve (CF^{-1}) for the given x, y pair. This value can be used to formulate a regressive model on the basis of Eq. (1a) and logarithm:

$$\log(\tilde{m}(x,y)) = \sum_{i=1}^{N} \alpha_i \log(f_i(x,y)). \tag{5}$$

Taking the latter for a large enough set of (x, y) pairs, we get an overdetermined system of equations. In matrix notation, where $\tilde{M}_{\log}$ is a column vector of $\log(\tilde{m}(x, y))$s, A is a column vector of α_i-s and $F_{\log}$ contains log-component values $\log(f_i(x, y))$ as rows, the problem gets a form and least squares method solution (L2) as follows:

$$\tilde{M}_{\log} = F_{\log}\ A \tag{6}$$

$$A = (\tilde{M}'_{\log}\ \tilde{M}_{\log})^{-1} \tilde{M}'_{\log}\ F_{\log} \tag{7}$$

The vector A of results in Eq. (7) consists of weights to be used in Eqs. (1a,b). However, one should be slightly sceptical of the results returned by LSM, since it

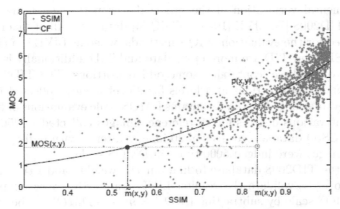

Fig. 2. Exemplary measure value m, prediction p, and intended value $\tilde{m}$

is sensitive to the outliers. In case of image quality reference databases the data is heavily dispersed, so it is also worth to consider alternative methods of solving the problem (Eq. (6)). Such a solution is least absolute error minimization - L1 regression that can be noted as an optimization problem:

$$A = \min_{A} |\tilde{M}_{\log} - F_{\log}\, A|, \tag{8}$$

which can be expressed as an augmented linear program (using slack variables [2]) to be calculated using an ordinary linear solver.

There is one more potential pitfall to discuss. Since the SSIM is usually (MSSIM) computed by averaging of local SSIM values, therefore l, c, s values are not to be used explicitly in the regression model, due to windowed averaging they are used indirectly. Luckily one can use the approximation - since expected value of product of two random variables X, Y is:

$$\mathbb{E}(XY) = \mathbb{E}(X)\mathbb{E}(Y) - \mathrm{cov}(X, Y) \tag{9}$$

assuming low spatial covariance of the image data, we can also suppose parameters to be of a low statistical spatial dependence. Therefore one can approximate:

$$MSSIM = \tfrac{1}{N}\sum_{i=1}^{N} SSIM(x_i, x_i) = \tfrac{1}{N}\sum_{i=1}^{N} [l_i c_i s_i] \tag{10a}$$

$$\approx \tfrac{1}{N}\sum_{i=1}^{N} l_i \tfrac{1}{N}\sum_{i=1}^{N} c_i \tfrac{1}{N}\sum_{i=1}^{N} s_i = \mu_l \mu_c \mu_s \tag{10b}$$

Please see Fig. 3 demonstrating the empirical verification of the above hypothesis. For the images from the TID2008 database the Pearson CC (PCC) btween MSSIM and approximation is 0.9984 and the maximal absolute difference (MAD) is about 0.0671 and mean absolute error (MAE) is 0.0045. These values for the LIVE database are PCC: 0.9993, MAD: 0.0538, MAE: 0.004.

3   Experiments

3.1   The Data and Evaluation Criteria

The experimental verification of the proposal was performed using reference databases: TID2008 [7], LIVE [10] and CSIQ [4] database. All of them are commonly applied for the evaluation of IQA methods, whereas LIVE is a classic one and both CSIQ and TID are more up-to-date and TID additionally is the most comprehensive of these, containing some odd distortions. The TID2008 database consists of 17 distortions at 4 levels for 25 ref images collected in 256428 MOS scale evaluations. The LIVE contains DMOS scale evaluations of five image distortions at various degrees for 29 reference images collected in 25000 evaluations. The CSIQ database consists of 30 images altered with 6 distoritons at 5 levels, the images were judged 5000 times in DMOS scale.

We used the TID2008 database to find out the weights and LIVE and CSIQ databases to cross-validate the results. LIVE And CSIQ were adopted from DMOS to MOS scale by subtracting ($MOS = max - DMOS$). The evaluation procedure, after [12], involved following criteria:

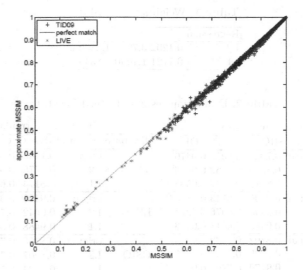

Fig. 3. Approximate MSSIM vs actual MSSIM for TID2008 and LIVE databases

- Relevance to the human perception - *monotonicity* - measured using Spearman rank order CC (SROCC) - it describes the precision of a measure.
- *Accuracy* of a prediction (dispersion of results) was measured using *Coefficient of Determination* (COD) [8] which is a fraction of variance explained by the model (CF): $COD = 1 - \sum_i(y_i - \hat{y}_i)^2 / \sum_i(y_i - \bar{y})^2$. It outperforms mean absolute error or root means square error (RMS) as it provides the error with respect to the proper prediction.
- Prediction *consistency* measured with *outlier ratio* (OR) as a fraction of MOS measures oustide ±2 standard deviations form the prediction.
- Scatter plots for visual qualitative examination.

In order to verify the results, the weights obtained for the TID database were cross-validated against LIVE database. Such a choice of the roles for the databases stems from the fact that the TID2008 is more comprehensive (17 classes of distortions) so the weights for this test set should be more general.

The key role of a CF both in the procedure and in evaluation requires careful choice of adequate curve to fit. The common choice in such cases is to use sigmoid, although fitting its parameters can be cumbersome, requiring numerous search evaluations due to start point sensitivity - to overcome that problem, for the assumed data sets, one can use the exponential function $y = ae^{bx}$ as in this case it conforms the sigmoid function very well, it achieves fine fit to the data very fast and gives robust results regardless on the starting point for the curve fitting.

3.2   The Results

Optimizing SSIM measure using L1 and L2 regressions gives weights (of Eq. (1b)) provided in Table 1. In the Table 2 there are provided quality evaluation

Table 1. Weights for MSSIM

Regression	α	β	γ
L2	0.1292	3.7979	1.2862
L1	0.1121	1.1640	0.8345

Table 2. Evaluation results of tuned MSSIM

A.) Approximate form						B.) Exact formula			
database	weights	SROCC	COD	OR		database	weights	SROCC	COD	OR
	original	0.7921	0.6019	0.0476			original	0.7749	0.5854	0.0541
TID2008	L2	0.8279	0.6462	0.0476		TID2008	L2	0.7775	0.5936	0.0606
	L1	0.8315	0.6447	0.0535			L1	0.8174	0.6314	0.0541
	original	0.9496	0.6743	0.0153			original	0.9496	0.6758	0.0153
LIVE	L2	0.9440	0.6976	0.0224		LIVE	L2	0.9442	0.7111	0.0193
	L1	0.9486	0.6611	0.0153			L1	0.9488	0.6634	0.0173
	original	0.8792	0.7239	0.0520			original	0.8755	0.7123	0.0554
CSIQ	L2	0.9025	0.7431	0.0647		CSIQ	L2	0.8907	0.7131	0.0658
	L1	0.9179	0.7795	0.0600			L1	0.9124	0.7675	0.0612

criteria for both exact and approximate values of MSSIM (Eq. 10b) for the tuned (TID) and cross validation (LIVE, CSIQ) datasets. Scatter plots of the results for these datasets are provided in Fig. 4.

3.3   Discussion of Results

The proposed method for fine tuning worked well for the original measure MSSIM and approximation as well. As one could expect L1 regression appeared to provide results better than L2, therefore they will be considered further. The cross validation of results using LIVE and CSIQ databases provided slightly ambiguous results. For CSIQ we observed improvement meanwhile tests for LIVE database reveal slight degradation. Fortunately, the optional loss in quality criteria for the worst case of cross validation was slight and can be neglected as it was approx. 1-2% of the measure value, whereas improvement for the TID and CSIQ database was 5 times bigger (5-10%).

When we observe first two criteria (SROCC and COD) improved the OR in all these cases grow a little bit. The explanation for that is in increasing of the COD which is a measure of concentration around the regression curve, so the higher it is, the lower variance of the residuals is; which are used to calculate boundaries for the outlier ratio. Apparently, fine tuning of weights is not able to reduce the outliers while improving overall dispersion of results, therefore tightening the boundaries for the OR would result in increasing the number of the measures classified as *outliers*.

Another interesting (and surprising) observation are the fine results of approximation of MSSIM which outperfoms regular MSSIM - one could favor this version of SSIM computing for its efficiency.

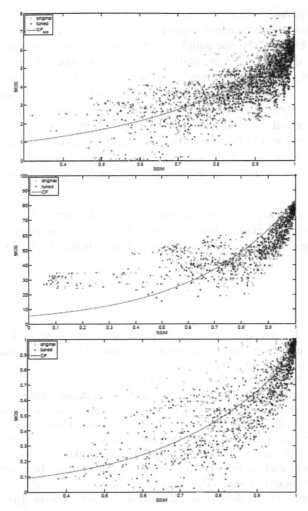

Fig. 4. Scatter plot of original and L1 tuned MSSIM for: TID (a), LIVE (b), CSIQ (c)

Another interesting, side observation is overall resilience of a LIVE database to the tuning. In additional test we tried to tune the SSIM weights to that database but with no success - the improvement of quality criteria was marginal. Apparently the LIVE database seems to be fit to the SSIM measure (or SSIM to the database). This raises a question whether we should use LIVE to evaluate SSIM - luckily the number image quality databases has grown over years so that is not a limitation.

4   Summary

The proposed approach demonstrated its ability to improve performance of the SSIM measure. Its serious advantage is that it allows to estimate weights on basis of the massive human judgments without painstaking collecting human responses or need to deliberate measures' specific parts. On the other hand, estimating weights on the basis of the the rough structure of the measure can also a drawback of proposed method. It is relatively easy to overcome that limitation by posing extended requirements regarding the weights. A prior knowledge of the measure designer can be included into the weight estimation by defining minimization program where one can use constraints for ensuring required properties such as non-negativity or summation of certain weights to one.

Further progress would involve tests using further databases and applying the method to IQA measures of a design similar to SSIM. Another interesting idea to check is to verify if the iterative tuning is able to improve the results.

Acknowledgements. Costume for acquisition of human movement based on IMU sensors with collection, visualization and data analysis software. This project has been supported by Applied Research Programme of NCRD. (project ID 178438 path A)

References

1. Charrier, C., Knoblauch, K., Maloney, L.T., Bovik, A.C., Moorthy, A.K.: Optimizing multiscale ssim for compression via mlds. IEEE Transactions on Image Processing 21(12), 4682–4694 (2012)
2. D'Errico, J.: Optimization tips and tricks (May 2011), http://www.mathworks.com/matlabcentral/fileexchange/8553
3. Kandadai, S., Hardin, J., Creusere, C.: Audio quality assessment using the mean structural similarity measure. In: IEEE International Conference on Acoustics, Speech and Signal Processing, ICASSP 2008, pp. 221–224 (2008), 00024
4. Larson, E.C., Chandler, D.M.: Most apparent distortion: full-reference image quality assessment and the role of strategy. Journal of Electronic Imaging 19(1) (2010)
5. Lissner, I., Preiss, J., Urban, P., Lichtenauer, M.S., Zolliker, P.: Image-difference prediction: From grayscale to color. IEEE Transactions on Image Processing 22(2), 435–446 (2013)
6. Moorthy, A.K., Bovik, A.C.: Perceptually significant spatial pooling techniques for image quality assessment. In: Proc. SPIE 7240, Human Vision and Electronic Imaging XIV, vol. 7240, pp. 724012–724012–11 (2009), 00029
7. Ponomarenko, N., Lukin, V., Zelensky, A., Egiazarian, K., Carli, M., Battisti, F.: Tid2008 a database for evaluation of full reference visual quality assessment metrics. Advances of Modern Radioelectronics 10(4), 30–45 (2009)
8. Rice, J.A.: Mathematical statistics and data analysis, 3rd edn. Duxbury advanced series. Thomson/Brooks/Cole, Belmont (2007)
9. Rouse, D.M., Hemami, S.S.: Understanding and simplifying the structural similarity metric. In: 2008 IEEE Int. Conf. on Image Processing, pp. 1188–1191 (2008)
10. Sheikh, H., Sabir, M., Bovik, A.: A statistical evaluation of recent full reference image quality assessment algorithms. IEEE Transactions on Image Processing 15(11), 3440–3451 (2006)
11. Wang, Z., Shang, X.: Spatial pooling strategies for perceptual image quality assessment. In: 2006 IEEE Int. Conf. on Image Processing, pp. 2945–2948 (2006)

12. Wang, Z., Simoncelli, E., Bovik, A.: Multiscale structural similarity for image quality assessment. In: Conference Records of the 37th Asilomar Conference on Signals, Systems and Computers, vol. 2, pp. 1398–1402. IEEE (2004)
13. Wang, Z., Bovik, A., Sheikh, H., Simoncelli, E.: Image quality assessment: from error visibility to structural similarity. IEEE Transactions on Image Processing 13(4), 600–612 (2004)
14. Wang, Z., Li, Q.: Information content weighting for perceptual image quality assessment. IEEE Transactions on Image Processing 20(5), 1185–1198 (2011)
15. Wang, Z., Lu, L., Bovik, A.C.: Video quality assessment based on structural distortion measurement. Signal Processing: Image Communication 19(2), 121–132 (2004)

Ground Truth and Performance Evaluation of Lane Border Detection

Ali Al-Sarraf[1], Bok-Suk Shin[1], Zezhong Xu[2], and Reinhard Klette[1]

[1] Department of Computer Science
The University of Auckland Auckland, New Zealand
{aals005,r.klette}@auckland.ac.nz
[2] College of Computer Information Engineering
Changzhou Institute of Technology Changzhou, Jiangsu, China
zezhongx@gmail.com

Abstract. Lane-border detection is one of the best-developed modules in vision-based driver assistance systems today. However, there is still a need for further improvement for challenging road and traffic situations, and a need to design tools for quantitative performance evaluation.

This paper discusses and refines a previously published method to generate ground truth for lane markings from recorded video, applies two lane-detection methods to such video data, and then illustrates the proposed performance evaluation by comparing calculated ground truth with detected lane positions. This paper also proposes appropriate performance measures that are required to evaluate the proposed method.

1   Introduction

Vision-based driver assistance systems are already standard modules in modern cars, supported by the availability of high-computing power and low-voltage purpose-designed FPGA solutions, small and accurate cameras, that can fit in any vehicle, and progress in the methodology of computer-vision solutions. Lane border detection, a component of vision-based driver assistance solutions, has been studied for more than twenty years, and there are robust solutions available for road environments where lane markings are clearly visible, such as highways or multi-lane main roads.

Vision-based lane detection supports, for example, lane departure warning, lane keeping, lane centring, and so forth [1]. Despite the many available algorithms and approaches, an ongoing concern [1,9] is the lack of proper ground-truth estimation to evaluate the efficiencies and accuracies.

A common way, how publications validate the accuracy of their approach, is by using their naked eye for the validation. Building a ground-truth data base can become really difficult as roads are not generic even within a single country, let alone internationally. Roads can be well built or not, have proper markings or no marks at all, they can be urban or countryside roads, have solid lane markers or painted dashed lane borders,or differ in many other ways. The environment is only one factor, another factor is the equipment, such as the type of camera used (e.g. image resolution, grey-level or color, bits per pixel, or geometric accuracy).

L.J. Chmielewski et al. (Eds.): ICCVG 2014, LNCS 8671, pp. 66–74, 2014.

The generation of ground truth for lane detection needs to reflect on many parameters, to ensure the creation of a trust-worthy ground truth. Digitally simulated ground truth was created by Revilloud et al. [10] but they found out that, when adapting their lane detection algorithm to their synthetic ground truth, it did not work very well on real-world data as their approach mainly focuses on the ground texture for detecting lines. They stated a need for another solution for ground-truth generation.

There is another obvious solution: to generate ground-truth manually, supported by some graphics routines for drawing lines. However, considering frame rates of at least 25 Hz, and the need to generate ground truth for very long video sequences, this would be a very tedious task.

Borkar et al. [2] developed a technique using time slices and splines to generate ground truth from any type of road image sequence recorded in an *ego-vehicle* (i.e. the vehicle the vision system is operating in). The approach works reasonably well on clearly marked roads, but the involved interaction also comes with the risk of human error and limited usability. The method was easy to re-implement. It works well on long sequences, as long as there are some markings in the frames which identify the lanes. However when selecting points on lane markings and the points are not at the center of the drawn lines, then this may lead to errors.

In this paper, we provide an improvement that makes the ground-truth generation process easier to use, and which also helps to generate ground truth for a diversity of recorded video data. Our solutions use standard image-processing techniques for making the entire process easier, and to reduce the errors in point selections, thus going closer towards a fully automated solution. We also provide novel measures for comparing ground truth with calculated lane borders.

Fig. 1. *Left*: Ground truth and calculated lane markings. *Right*: Magnified window of the image shown on the left. The red lines are calculated ground truth, and the green dots are calculated lane-border positions. Note that algorithms for lane-border detection not necessarily provide curves; it might be just isolated dots.

Figure 1 illustrates the subject of this paper. It shows ground truth together with results applying one lane-detection algorithm which generates isolated points rather than curves as output. A quantitative comparison between ground truth and estimated lane borders requires evaluation measures.

The paper is structured as follows. Section 2 provides a brief explanation of the drawing technique by Borkar et al. and of our improvements. Section 3 discusses how to quantify performance by introducing measures. Section 4 reports about some experiments for illustrating the approach. Section 5 concludes.

2   Ground Truth by Time Slices

Evaluations of computer vision techniques based on available ground truth became a widely accepted approach for improving methods, for identifying issues, and to help to overcome those issues. Current examples are the KITTI benchmark suite [4,7] and some of the sequences on EISATS [3,8]. These are websites offering long video sequences, more than 100 frames each, for testing vision algorithms on recorded road scenes. Such websites provide currently only manually generated ground truth for lane marking in a few frames (e.g. KITTI for about 200 frames). For really challenging video data, so far we can only apply subjective evaluations of algorithmic performances, such as demonstrated by the Robust Vision Challenge at ECCV 2012 [11]. This current situation illustrates the difficulty of providing usable ground truth for extensive lane-detection experiments.

We propose a solution for generating ground-truth data for lane sequences by extending the technique proposed in [2] with the aims of reducing errors in the point-selection step, and of increasing the efficiency of the use of this method.

Ground-truth data for lane sequences is defined by generated curves indicating where the actual lane border is located in an image. The process starts with creating an image called a *time slice* by selecting points from each frame of the given sequence. Next, spline interpolation is applied for those selected points to generate ground truth. See Figure 2.

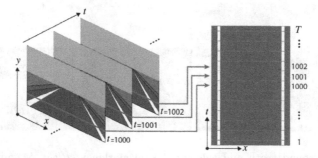

Fig. 2. A time slice is created by using a stack approach which combines single rows of pixels from each frame into one image (i.e. a sequence of rows). Figure follows [2] with modified notation.

For comparing with [2], we use the same two sequences as used in this paper (and made publicly available). The first sequence consists of 1372 frames, each having a resolution of 640×500 pixels, and the second of 400 frames, each having a resolution of 640×480 pixels. For generating $n > 0$ time slices, we extract n rows of pixels from each frame at fixed row locations. A distance between subsequent rows of around 20 to 30 pixels appears to be appropriate for a standard 640×480 VGA image format, and for n, a value between 3 and 5 is reasonable. Each of the n fixed rows, accumulated over time, defines one time slice: the row from Frame 1 goes into the bottom-most row, the row from Frame 2 into the next, and so forth.

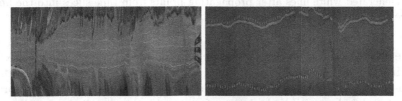

Fig. 3. Samples of two generated time slices for the first sequence. The images have 1372 rows because 1372 frames contributed to each time slice. *Left*: Time slice generated from row 270 (counted from the top, i.e. further away from the ego-vehicle). *Right*: Time slice generated from row 400 (i.e. closer to the ego-vehicle).

Figure 3 shows examples of two time slices calculated from the same image sequence but from two different fixed rows. After creating $n > 0$ different time slices, a number of points is manually selected on the left and right lane borders, and we apply cubic spline interpolation for curve fitting. This generates curves shown in Fig. 4 as white curves in one time slice.

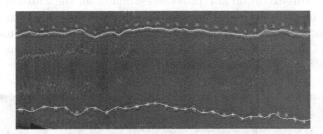

Fig. 4. The white curves are generated by applying curve fitting (interpolation) to manually selected points in the time slice shown on the right in Fig. 3. The interpolated curves follow the lane markings.

After repeating the same curve generation on each of the $n > 0$ time slices, all the created points are propagated from those time slices into corresponding locations (on the fixed rows) in the original frames, thus having n points on each lane border in each frame. The authors of [2] re-apply then curve fitting (by interpolation) once again. This generates the proposed ground truth data for each data sequence. Figure 5 shows ground truth generated this way using our re-implementation of the original algorithm by [2]. The approach is easy and reasonably time-efficient in generating ground truth data on different types of video sequences.

Fig. 5. Generated white lines after propagating points from time slices into the image sequence and interpolating those points, following the original algorithm

However, the crucial problem we experienced is the uncertainty in selecting points in time slices, especially in time slices created by rows far away from the ego-vehicle. These points should ideally be at the center of a lane border. Figures 4 and 5 show visible deviations from an ideal center line.

The index of the fixed row for generating one time slice has impacts on accuracy: the further away from the ego-vehicle, the more likely that manually located points are not supporting ideal ground truth curves being at the center of lane markings.

We added a simple but useful modification, based on tests of various edge detectors on generated time slices. Finally we decided to use the Canny edge detector for detecting left and right edge points for lane markings in time slices and to constrain selected points to midpoints between such left and right edge points. Tracking of pairs of edge points and an automated selection of midpoints leads to improved ground truth generation in recorded frames. Besides an automated point selection, this extension also provides estimates for the width of lane markings (which is used for normalising our evaluation measure; see next section).

Figure 6 shows results of the implementation of the original method (red curves) and of the proposed method (blue curves). The blue curve, i.e. the

Fig. 6. Comparison between original and proposed method. *Top*: Generated ground-truth (red) using the original interactive approach. *Bottom*: Generated ground truth (blue) using our approach, also indicating lane-marking width.

generated ground truth, is at the center of both black border curves, defined for the left and right lane marking; see Fig. 6.

3   Performance Measures

In this section we describe two novel measures for comparing ground truth with calculated lane borders. In each frame, we only consider an interval of relevant rows, with indices between y_{min} and y_{max}. First, we describe a measure for comparing ground truth with detected lane borders also covering algorithms which provide isolated points for lane-border positions. For each row y, with $y_{min} \leq y \leq y_{max}$, we have the following cases for ground truth:

1. Ground truth provides points on a left and a right lane border (case GTB).
2. Ground truth only provides a point on the left border (case GTL).
3. Ground truth only provides a point on the right border (case GTR).
4. Ground truth provides no point in this row y (case GTN).

Analogously, we also have the cases BDB, BDL, BDR, and BDN for *border detection* (BD) by the applied detection algorithm. For example, we may not even see the right border of the lane in which the ego-vehicle is driving in at that moment. We consider cases such as GTL, GTR, and GTN as being defined by the circumstances.

In row y, with $y_{min} \leq y \leq y_{max}$, we use the notation $x_{y,L}^{GT}$ and $x_{y,R}^{GT}$ for detected ground truth points (if they exist at all), and $x_{y,L}^{BD}$ and $x_{y,R}^{BD}$ accordingly for a studied border-detection algorithm. The error $E_{IP}(y,t)$ is defined for row y, with $y_{min} \leq y \leq y_{max}$, and a selected Frame t of the input sequence, using the L_1-norm:

$$
E_{IP}(y,t) = \begin{cases} ||(x_{y,L}^{GT}, x_{y,R}^{GT}) - (x_{y,L}^{BD}, x_{y,R}^{BD})||_1, & \text{if cases BDB and GTB} \\[2mm] ||x_{y,L}^{GT} - x_{y,L}^{BD}||_1, & \text{if cases BDL, and GTL or GTB} \\[2mm] ||x_{y,R}^{GT} - x_{y,R}^{BD}||_1, & \text{if cases BDR, and GTR or GTB} \\[2mm] 0 & \text{otherwise} \end{cases} \tag{1}
$$

Let τ_y be the expected width of the lane marking in row y, provided by our ground-truth generation method. If the value $E_{IP}(y,t)$ is less than the value of τ_y, then we consider this as insignificant deviation from ground truth and replace value $E_{IP}(y,t)$ for this row by zero.

The reason for this normalisation is that lane-detection algorithms typically detect one side of the lane marking, or the center of the lane marking, depending on the methodology used. The use of a value τ was introduced in performance measures in [14] as an a-priori tolerance threshold value, identified with a constant representing the ideal lane-marking width as stated by the Federal Highway Administration (FHA) [15]. This ideal value can be accurate, but not all data sequences have that information available, and it also needs to be considered as a function of row index y. The difference is that we extract τ_y while creating the ground truth data.

The given error measure provides multiple options for measuring inconsistencies between the BD algorithm and the ground truth. We only formally state one option here, defined by the use of only those rows $y_{0,t} < y_{1,t} < \cdots < y_{m_t,t}$, with $y_{\min} \leq y_{i,t} \leq y_{\max}$, for $i = 0, \ldots, m_t$, where we have both GTB and BDB. This gives us the error

$$E_{BD} = \frac{1}{T} \sum_{t=1}^{T} \left[\frac{1}{m_t + 1} \sum_{i=0}^{m_t} E_{IP}(y_{i,t}, t) \right] \tag{2}$$

for a considered method BD for the whole sequence of T frames.

4   Experiments and Discussion

We illustrate a comparison between the proposed ground truth with results of two lane-border detectors using the proposed measure E_{BD}.

The first border detector is an adaptation of the technique described in [6]. This method uses a lane border model, originally proposed in [13], defined by isolated left and right lane border points in one image row, detected by applying a particle filter for each row. The second is a technique proposed in [12] which applies a less restrictive lane border model and a combination of particles defined by multiple image rows, thus also supporting temporary tracking of lane borders while lane markings are actually missing.

We illustrate results for two different data sets, the first sequence of data used by Borkar et al. [2] (see the specification of both sequences given above), and also one sequence from EISATS [3]. See Table 1.

Table 1. Performance results. B1 for Seq #1 of [2], and E1 for EISATS Seq #1

Data	#Frames	Algorithm	GT size	BD size	Coverage	Correct	Misaligned	E_{BD}
B1	1250	[6]	131	30	36.64	63.75	36.25	7.98
B1	1250	[12]	131	30	36.64	79.83	20.16	6.11
E1	325	[6]	131	30	21.37	59.49	40.50	11.44
E1	325	[12]	131	30	21.37	70.23	29.76	6.02

Interestingly, we obtained individual measurements for those sequences (which come with different characteristics, defined by frame resolution, used cameras, and bits per pixel, but also by road conditions, traffic density, lighting, contrast, or weather conditions).

In the table, GT and BD size specify the total numbers of points generated from each sequence (kept constant for both sequences). We provide percentages of correct and misaligned border detections. As a result, the values of measure E_{BD} point out that the method of [12] is outperforming the method of [6] on those two sequences (more clearly on the more challenging EISATS sequence).

5   Conclusions and Future Work

We proposed an improvement to a currently published ground-truth generation method proposed in [2] for lane borders in recorded on-road video data. The addition works well on different types of video sequences, and also for identifying the width of lane border markings.

We defined an appropriate performance measure and applied it to selected lane-border detection algorithms. The evaluation is consistent with statements, for example, in paper [8], that diversities of *situations* requires adaptive selections of techniques for optimizing analysis results. The proposed framework can be used to identify better algorithms which correspond in their performance to a given situation or scenario.

For future work, we would like to test our ground truth method for more BD algorithms, and will also increase the range of considered situations.

References

1. Bar Hillel, A., Lerner, R., Levi, D., Raz, G.: Recent progress in road and lane detection: A survey. Machine Vision Applications, 1–19 (2012)
2. Borkar, A., Hayes, M., Smith, M.T.: An efficient method to generate ground truth for evaluating lane detection systems. In: Proc. IEEE Int. Conf. Acoustics Speech Signal Processing, pp. 1090–1093 (2010)
3. EISATS benchmark data base. The University of Auckland (2013),
   http://www.mi.auckland.ac.nz/EISATS
4. Geiger, A., Lenz, P., Urtasun, R.: Are we ready for autonomous driving? The KITTI Vision Benchmark Suite. In: Proc. IEEE Int. Conf. Computer Vision Pattern Recognition, pp. 3354–3361 (2012)
5. Jiang, R., Klette, R., Vaudrey, T., Wang, S.: New lane model and distance transform for lane detection and tracking. In: Jiang, X., Petkov, N. (eds.) CAIP 2009. LNCS, vol. 5702, pp. 1044–1052. Springer, Heidelberg (2009)
6. Jiang, R., Klette, R., Vaudrey, T., Wang, S.: Lane detection and tracking using a new lane model and distance transform. Machine Vision Applications 22, 721–737 (2011)
7. KITTI vision benchmark suite. Karlsruhe Institute of Technology (2013),
   http://www.cvlibs.net/datasets/kitti/
8. Klette, R., Krüger, N., Vaudrey, T., Pauwels, K., Hulle, M., Morales, S., Kandil, F., Haeusler, R., Pugeault, N., Rabe, C., Lappe, M.: Performance of correspondence algorithms in vision-based driver assistance using an online image sequence database. IEEE Trans. Vehicular Technology 60, 2012–2026 (2011)
9. McCall, J.C., Trivedi, M.M.: Video-based lane estimation and tracking for driver assistance: Survey, system, and evaluation. IEEE Trans. Intelligent Transportation Systems 7, 20–37 (2006)
10. Revilloud, M., Gruyer, D., Pollard, E.: Generator of road marking textures and associated ground truth applied to the evaluation of road marking detection. In: Proc. IEEE Int. Conf. Intelligent Transportation Systems, pp. 933–938 (2012)
11. Robust Vision Challenge at ECCV 2012 (2012),
    http://hci.iwr.uni-heidelberg.de/Static/challenge2012/

12. Shin, B.-S., Tao, J., Klette, R.: A superparticle filter for lane detection (submitted, 2014)
13. Zhou, Y., Xu, R., Hu, X., Ye, Q.: A robust lane detection and tracking method based on computer vision. Measurement Science Technology 17, 736–745 (2006)
14. Borkar, A.: Multi-viewpoint lane detection with applications in driver safety systems. PhD thesis (2011)
15. Federal Highway Administration: Manual Uniform Traffic Control Devices (November 2009), http://mutcd.fhwa.dot.gov/

Development of Methods and Algorithms of Reduction for Image Recognition to Assess the Quality of the Mineral Species in the Mining Industry

Olga E. Baklanova and Olga Ya. Shvets

D.Serikbayev East-Kazakhstan State Technical University
Ust-Kamenogorsk, The Republic of Kazakhstan
{OBaklanova,OShvets}@ektu.kz

Abstract. This paper contains development of methods and algorithms of reduction for image recognition of mineral spices. It is known according to the practice of analyzing graphic pictures that for the majority of the digital images of the real world their size linear decreasing to a certain threshold does not lead to loss of the analyzed information. The main objective of this approach - define a threshold reduction of digital images. Some realizations of this algorithm are presented by defining criterion quantifying the loss of informative of modified image based. Few examples concerning with reduction in the solving of mineral species recognition problems are described and discussed.

Keywords: Reduction for image, Image recognition, Computer vision, Mineral species, Petrographic analysis.

1 Introduction

Petrography is the science that studies the material composition of the rocks. Unlike minerals, rocks are aggregates composed of different minerals [1]. Minerals are homogeneous in composition and structure of the rocks and ores. They are natural chemical compounds resulting from various geological processes. Historically minerals initially determined by color and shape.

Some mining and processing enterprise mixed ore from several fields. In this case it is important to determine the mixing ratio. It is necessary to find a mineral composition of the ore, which can be determined by optical microscopic analysis. In some enterprises, it is implemented manually by technologist-mineralogist.

Nowadays, some complexes micrographs analyzed manually locally in the enter-prise by technologist - mineralogist, or in the center of the head group of companies with the transition to the Internet or other communication channels. Manual analysis has drawbacks such as dependency from psychophysiological properties of laboratory specialist (human factor) and the long duration of treatment of one of the micrograph. But the process of analyzing ore micrographs can be automated and implement it locally in the enterprise, due to the

L.J. Chmielewski et al. (Eds.): ICCVG 2014, LNCS 8671, pp. 75–83, 2014.

fact that subsystem micrographs analysis oriented to samples of a particular ore easier to create than a universal program for quantitative analysis of samples of any material.

In articles [2], [3] the general approaches for image recognition to assess the quality of the mineral species in the mining industry have been considered. In offered work methods and algorithms of preliminary processing of images, in particular problems of a reduction of images are considered.

2   Materials and Methods

2.1   Methods of Automated Acquisition of Mineral Rocks Images

It is required for automated obtaining of micrographs automated microscope containing a motorized specimen stage, a mechanism to change the filters, focusing mechanism, a revolver change lenses [4], [5].

Typically, in this case it is supposed to use the manufacturer's software, which is responsible for the control for motorized units of microscope. Simplified classification of microscopy cameras is shown in Figure 1. Preferably use trinocular microscope with a camera that does not require an optical adapter with a digital interface USB, controlled by a computer and with the TWAIN support.

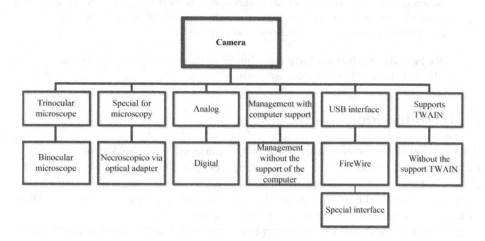

Fig. 1. Classification of microscopy cameras

Thus, the process of obtaining images can pass without operator as in the case of a fully automated microscope and with the participation of the operator. In the case of automated microscope software fully controls the microscope, after getting photo in the memory of a computer program for image analysis starts.

2.2 Methods of Automated Processing of Mineral Rocks Images

Very often different minerals on the micrographs correspond to objects of different types of shapes and colors. This allows the identification of various minerals in the form and color of objects. In some cases, also take into account the polarization of certain minerals sample [6], [7], [8].

In this case, it is necessary to make several pictures, accompanying it by turning the sample. Consider a sample of slag copper anode as an example (Figure 2). Micrographs of this sample were kindly provided Eastern Research Institute of Mining and Metallurgy of Non-ferrous Metals (Kazakhstan, Ust-Kamenogorsk).

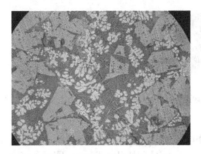

Fig. 2. Micrograph of a sample of slag copper anode, increasing in 500 times

According to experts on microscopy of minerals from Eastern Research Institute of Mining and Metallurgy of Non-ferrous Metals at this picture there is no minerals having dependent on the direction of the plane of polarization of light. In this picture you can detect metallic copper and the following minerals: cuprite Cu_2O, magnetite Fe_3O_4, Delafosse $CuFeO_2$, silicate glass.

Cuprite Cu_2O can be identified as follows: it is characterized by the shape of a round shape, color - it is light gray (sometimes with a slight bluish tint). Figure 3 shows the graphical representation of cuprite.

Fig. 3. Cuprite on micrographs

Fe_3O_4 magnetite on micrographs may also be detected by color and shape. Color of magnetite on micrographs is dark gray. Shape is angular, as expressed by technologists, "octahedral". Figure 4 shows magnetite apart from other minerals picture.

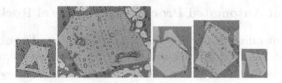

Fig. 4. Magnetite on micrographs

Delafossite $CuFeO_2$ micrographs can allocate to the needle shape and gray (with a brownish tint) color. On Figure 5 it can be seen delafossite on the micrographs.

Fig. 5. Delafossite on micrographs

Metallic copper on the micrographs can be found on the following criteria: color - yellow, shape - round, without flat faces. Figure 6 represents a micrograph metallic copper.

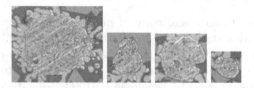

Fig. 6. Metallic copper on micrographs

Silicate glass - is a dark gray mass fills the rest of the space that is left of the other minerals.

These data indicate that for real micrographs slag samples (and some other minerals) it is possible to use automated qualitative assessment of the mineral composition.

After receiving the full image it is often needed to treat it, mainly to simplify further analysis.

2.3 Methods of Reduction for Mineral Rocks Images

The paper presents an approach to quantify the quality loss (informative) digital images with modification of their size. It is known according to the practice of analyzing graphic scenes that for the majority of the digital images of the real world their size linear decreasing to a certain threshold does not lead to loss of the analyzed information. This is possible through a single scaling all informative image objects. This fact can be used in practice to improve the speed of the digital image of mineral rocks recognition algorithms. Reducing the size of the image in N times leads to an increase in processing speed in N^2 times, which greatly increases the efficiency by allowing the use of more "expensive" in terms of time, but better (adequate statement of the problem) algorithms. The main objective of this approach is definition a threshold reduction of digital images. The solution of this problem is possible by defining criterion quantifying the loss of informative modified image. It is not possible due to different dimensions of data to calculate the mean square error between the modified and the original image directly. So, it is necessary to select options for the joint evaluation of digital images, which do not depend on their size [9].

The following reduction methods are implemented in automated rocks recognition system [10]:

− No. There is not interpolation; the raw image from the camera comes to the document. Because of there is no interpolation, you can expect high FPS: nothing hinders them;

− NearestNeighbor - Specifies nearest-neighbor interpolation. The quickest method of interpolation, it is the lowest image quality compared to other interpolation algorithm;

− Bilinear - Specifies bilinear interpolation. Without pre-filtering. This mode is not suitable for shrinking an image below 50 percent of its original size.

− HighQualityBilinear - Specifies high-quality, bilinear interpolation. Pre-filtering is implemented to ensure high-quality shrinking. It is relatively quick method of interpolation. It is quite competitive Preview;

− Bicubic - Specifies bicubic interpolation. Without pre-filtering. This mode is not suitable for shrinking an image below 25 percent of its original size;

− HighQualityBicubic - Specifies high-quality, bicubic interpolation. Pre-filtering is implemented to ensure high-quality shrinking. This mode produces the highest quality transformed images;

− WinScale image scaling algorithm that uses the model of pixels based on the account of their area. This algorithm has low complexity: it uses not more than four pixels of the original image to calculate one pixel of the image. Algorithm has good characteristics - output image is obtained with smooth edges, and used a variable blur.

To shrink an image, groups of pixels in the original image must be mapped to single pixels in the smaller image. The effectiveness of the algorithms that perform these mappings determines the quality of a scaled image. Algorithms that produce higher-quality scaled images tend to require more processing time. In the preceding list, NearestNeighbor is the lowest-quality mode and HighQuality-Bicubic is the highest-quality mode [11]. Quality of algorithm WinScale results is the same as quality of image after bilinear algorithm in condition of comparative complexity [12].

It will be used bicubic interpolation algorithm based on the above for image scaling, which is considered to be the most optimal in terms of a qualitative assessment of the modified image and is used in all GPUs.

We propose two approaches for evaluation of the reduction algorithms in this paper: evaluation of the mean square error variance within a sliding window and reduced the original images and histogram evaluation.

3   Results and Discussion

3.1   Reduction Algorithm Based on Average-Squared Error Estimation Variance

The criterion is based on dividing the image on the same number of areas (non-overlapping windows), according to the selected partition step and calculating the mean square error between the inside of the window variance in brightness for the source and the reduced images.

The algorithm consists of the following steps:

1. The original image is divided into square fields of the same size (the original image grid is applied);
2. It is determined in each region by the average luminance value (luminance of all pixels are added, and the resulting value is divided by the number of pixels);
3. It is calculated for each area according to the formula (1) variance:

$$DF_{k,l} = \frac{1}{N1N2} \sum_{i=1}^{N1} \sum_{j=1}^{N2} (F_{i,j} - FS_{k,l})^2 \qquad (1)$$

where $N1, N2$ - dimension in pixels of the source image, $F_{i,j}$ - the brightness of a pixel for the source image, $FS_{k,l}$ - the average brightness for the source image.

4. The original image is reduced using the HighQualityBicubic algorithm. Then it is calculated for each area according to the formula (2) variance and repeat steps 2 - 3.

$$DG_{k,l} = \frac{1}{M1M2} \sum_{i=1}^{M1} \sum_{j=1}^{M2} (G_{i,j} - GS_{k,l})^2 \qquad (2)$$

where $M1, M2$ - dimension in pixels of the modified image, $G_{i,j}$ - the brightness of a pixel for the modified image, $GS_{k,l}$ - the average brightness for the modified image. Cycle zoom out, at each iteration is fixed to the dispersion. Data are stored in array.

5. It is calculated the loss of informative by the formula (3):

$$\Delta D = \frac{1}{kl} \sum_{i=1}^{k} \sum_{j=1}^{l} (DF_{i,j} - DG_{i,j})^2 \qquad (3)$$

where $DF_{i,j}$ - dispersion is within the window with coordinates (i, j) in the original image, $DG_{i,j}$- variance within the window coordinates on the modified image, I - number of vertical windows, J - the number of windows horizontal . Data is written to the array;

6. It is plotted graphic on data ΔD of dependence loss of quality from down-scaling. It is considered not scaled image has 100% quality. Example of the algorithm is shown on Figure 7.

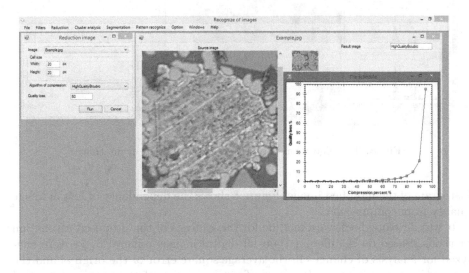

Fig. 7. The algorithm is based on average-squared error estimation variance

3.2 Reduction Algorithm Based on Average-Squared Error Estimation Variance

The method is based on a comparison of "forms" and brightness of the original histogram of the scaled image. Serves as a criterion standard error deviation of the histogram of the original image histogram modified.

Histograms based on each component of the color space, allow us to estimate characteristics of the digital image in terms of forms distribution of color-brightness settings. Power histogram array is the same for any image. This can be used to assess the differences between the original image and scalable. As a criterion is standard error deviation of the original histogram from modified image histogram. Histograms are constructed in relative frequencies, which leads to the differences in the total number of pixels of the original image and scalable:

$$\Delta D = \sqrt{\frac{1}{N} \sum_{i=1}^{N} (HF_i - HG_i)^2)} \qquad (4)$$

where N - array dimension histogram, HF-array relative frequency brightness histogram of the original image, HG - array relative frequency brightness

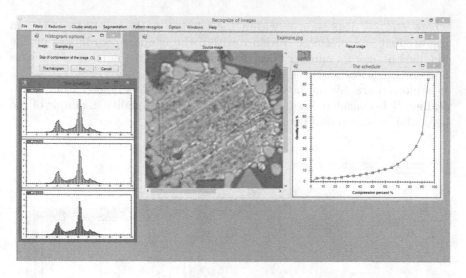

Fig. 8. The algorithm is based on the histogram evaluation

histogram of the modified image. Figure 8 shows the dependence of loss of image quality from compression.

It was developed software module for the analysis of the proposed estimation methods. Based on it different types of digital images mineral rocks were ana-lyzed for analysis of changes in the average square error of the original and the reduced image estimation. It was confirmed viability of the proposed method estimates the loss of information content for all analyzed image.

4   Conclusion

Joint analysis of visual changes "informative" images on the downside increases the value of the criterion. Thus, this fact can be used to automatically calculate the threshold of reduction of the original image. At the same criteria fixed values are translated into a percentage of the loss of information. The original image in the cycle is modified by reducing the size of the step q (in the q = 5 %), at each iteration is fixed to the test. Cycle stops when the zoom is reduced to 0, i.e. Preview "degenerate," and it will match 100 % loss of information. Accordingly, information loss is calculated in percentage, fixed at each reduction step. Further, according to the particular analysis technique selected allowable percentage loss of quality, and hence the limit.

It was developed software module for the analysis of the proposed evaluation method. Based on it different types of digital images mineral rocks were analyzed for analysis of changes in the average square error of the original and the reduced image estimation. It was confirmed viability of the proposed method estimates the loss of information content for all analyzed image.

References

1. Harvey, B., Tracy, R.J.: Petrology: Igneous, Sedimentary, and Metamorphic, 2nd edn. W.H. Freeman, New York (1995)
2. Baklanova, O.E.: Development of algorithms for image recognition needed to assess the quality of the mineral species in the mining industry. In: Abstracts of International Conference Mathematical and Informational Technologies, MIT 2013, Vrnjacka Banja and Budva, September 5-September 14, pp. 63–64 (2013)
3. Baklanova, O.E., Uzdenbaev, Z.S.: Development of methodology for analysis of mineral rocks in the mining industry. In: Joint Issue of the Bulletin of the East Kazakhstan State Technical University and Computer Technology of Institute of Computational Technologies, Siberian Branch of the Russian Academy of Sciences, Part 1, pp. 60–66 (September 2013)
4. Clarke, A.R., Eberhardt, C.N.: Microscopy Techniques for Materials, 459 p. Science Woodhead Publishing, CRC Press (2002)
5. Panteleev, C., Egorova, O., Klykova, E.: Computer microscopy. Technosphere, 304 p. (2005)
6. Farndon, J.: The practical encyclopedia of rocks and minerals. How to Find, Identify, Collect and Maintain the World's best Specimens, with over 1000 Photographs and Artworks. Lorenz Books, London (2006)
7. Chris, P.: Rocks and Minerals. In: Smithsonian Handbooks. Dorling Kindersley, New York (2002)
8. Shaffer, P.R., Herbert, S.Z., Raymond, P.: Rocks, Gems and Minerals, rev. edn. St. Martin's Press, New York (2001)
9. Privalov, O.O., Butenko, L.N.: Algorithm of automatic reduction of digital images of bi-omedical preparations for performance systems auto automated microscopy. In: Modern Science Intensive Technologies: Scientific - Theoretical. Magazine, Moscow, vol. 10, pp. 80–82 (2007)
10. How to: Use Interpolation Mode to Control Image Quality During Scaling, http://msdn.microsoft.com/ru-ru/library/k0fsyd4e(v=vs.110).aspx
11. Interpolation Mode Enumeration, http://msdn.microsoft.com/ru-ru/library/system.drawing.drawing2d.interpolationmode(v=vs.110).aspx
12. Kim, C.-H., Seong, S.-M., Lee, J.-A., Kim, L.-S.: Winscale: An Image-Scaling Algorithm Using an Area Pixel Model. IEEE Transaction on Circuits and Systems for Video Technology 13(6), 549–553 (2003)
13. Gonsalez, R.C., Woods, R.E.: Digital image processing, 3rd edn., 976 p. Pearson Education (2011)

Gaze-Driven Object Tracking
Based on Optical Flow Estimation

Bartosz Bazyluk and Radosław Mantiuk

West Pomeranian University of Technology, Szczecin
Faculty of Computer Science and Information Technology
Żołnierska Str. 49, 71–210 Szczecin, Poland
{bbazyluk,rmantiuk}@wi.zut.edu.pl

Abstract. To efficiently deploy eye tracking within gaze-dependent
image analysis tasks, we present an optical flow-aided extension of the
gaze-driven object tracking technique (GDOT). GDOT assumes that objects in a 3-dimensional space are fixation targets and with high probability computes the fixation directions towards the target observed by the
user. We research whether this technique proves its efficiency for video
footage in 2-dimensional space in which the targets are tracked by optical
flow tracking technique with inaccuracies characteristic for this method.
In the conducted perceptual experiments, we assess efficiency of the gaze-
driven object identification by comparing results with the reference data
where attended objects are known. The GDOT extension reveals higher
errors in comparison to 3D graphics tasks but still outperforms typical
fixation techniques.

1 Introduction

Gaze tracking is a powerful technique which can be applied for the visual saliency analysis. It can indicate the regions of an image that are most frequently
attended by human observer. Gaze data captured by *eye trackers* show how visual space is scanned by the constantly changing gaze to extract information
and build the conscious image of a 3-dimensional scene. Gaze tracking could be
successfully applied in many computer vision application, for example in analysis
of advertisement visibility in movie clips, or in gaze-driven image segmentation.
However, it is disappointing that neither display devices nor image analysis methods make full use of this property of the human visual system (HVS). We argue
that the main reason of this fact is the low accuracy of eye-tracking systems.

Eye trackers capture *gaze direction* indicated by the physical pose of the eye,
in particular location of the pupil centre [1]. The actual *fixation direction* (the
direction consistent with intention of the observer) is determined with the aid
of gaze data that changes over time. Typical fixation detection algorithms are
prone to *accuracy error* of up to two degrees of visual angle [3], which is an
equivalent of 80-pixel distance between the reference fixation point watched by
observer and the fixation point captured by the device (value estimated for a

L.J. Chmielewski et al. (Eds.): ICCVG 2014, LNCS 8671, pp. 84–91, 2014.
© Springer International Publishing Switzerland 2014

typical 22-inch display of 1680x1050 pixel resolution, seen from a distance of 65 cm).

In this work we propose a gaze-tracking system that combines gaze data with information about the image content to greatly improve the accuracy and stability of the contemporary eye trackers. The general purpose fixation detection techniques are not suitable for tracking the moving objects, which are followed with eyes in the *smooth pursuit* movement [9]. To overcome this limitation we use the *gaze-driven object tracking* (GDOT) technique [2], which clearly outperforms the standard fixation detection techniques in this matter. GDOT treats distinct objects in a scene as potential fixation targets and with high probability computes the fixation directions towards the target observed by the viewer. It was demonstrated that this technique can be successfully applied to the depth-of-field effect simulation [10], in tone mapping [6], and as an auxiliary controller in a computer game [2].

In this paper we present a novel application of GDOT in which it is applied to identify visually attended objects in a TV broadcast or other examples of moving pictures. A set of targets (e.g. players in a football game) is tracked by the sparse optical flow-aided method. We use the output from this system as a set of potential attention targets that allow us to compute attention-related statistics, e.g. estimation of the most attended player in the game. The basic difference between the original algorithm and our extension is that GDOT assumes perfect location of the targets. But in the optical flow approach inaccuracies in target positions may occur. We also take into account the cases in which targets go beyond the camera boundaries during footage and must be temporarily or permanently removed from the list of potential targets. We test if this data quality deterioration can be compensated by the regular GDOT routines. We also compare achieved results with efficiency of the typical fixation protocols.

Sect. 2 introduces the main concept of our work, i.e. an optical flow-aided attention tracking system. In Sect. 3 we describe the performed experiments and then discuss their results in Sect. 4. The paper ends with Conclusions.

2   Gaze-Attended Target Identification

The overview of our proposed tracking system is shown in Fig. 1. The optical flow supplies the GDOT module with current positions of the potential targets of attention and eye tracker sends the current gaze positions. The task of GDOT is to select the most likely target of attention for the current time instance.

Proposed Optical Flow-Based Tracking Extension. To use GDOT technique for effective tracking, first a set of potential attention targets has to be provided. In our proposed solution an expert who has the knowledge about scope of the study is responsible for identification and marking of targets. Since our goal is to choose targets that are semantically important for the study and can attract observer's attention, the general purpose automated feature extraction methods may not be used instead. In this work we use re-playable finite video

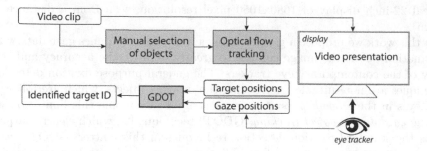

Fig. 1. The design of our gaze-driven target identification system supplied by the optical flow object tracking

clips as stimuli. This allows us to introduce a semi-manual, computer vision-aided framework for target designation and tracking of their movement. In a football match the expert would select game-related visible items like the ball, players, referees, on-screen information like score and TV station logo, as well as other visual attractors like advertisements if they are of interest during study. By marking their position within respective first frames of appearance, an automated tracking procedure can be initiated.

The sparse optical flow estimation is calculated to follow marked targets movement in frame space. To accomplish this task, a frame-to-frame Lucas-Kanade method is used [8]. This well known algorithm considers tracked features to be single pixels, which movement between every two consecutive frames is approximately bound to their local neighbourhoods. This way usually an overdetermined system is produced. It is then solved with a least-squares method.

However tracking the visual features using simple optical flow analysis can be problematic in real-world videos. Such stimuli are often prone to artefacts and general quality issues. Low frame rate together with slow shutter speeds can lead to motion blur which affects sparse flow estimation [7], as well as rapid movement and the natural tendency of moving objects to rotate and occlude each other, often lead to unrecoverable gaps in automatic tracking process. Therefore we found it necessary to implement in our software a way for manual key frame insertion, that would help tracking in these critical moments (e.g. when a quickly moving ball is occluded by players and its tracking cannot be recovered automatically). The expert is also allowed to perform basic linear interpolation of object's path to cater for transient disappearance periods, during which the user's attention can still be bound to the target despite its temporal lack of visibility [9]. These tasks are performed off-line, however implementation of a full real time version is also feasible as long as a reliable automated tracking method can be provided. We consider it to be a part of our future work.

GDOT Algorithm. A small distance between the eye-tracker gaze point and the target is the strongest indicator that an object is attended. The GDOT technique models this indicator as the position probability proportional to the Euclidean distance between the gaze point and targets. If the position consistency becomes unreliable, the object can still be tracked if its velocity is consistent with the smooth pursuit motion of the eye. The velocity computed directly from scan paths (gaze data) is an unreliable measure as it is dominated by the eye-tracker noise, saccades and the tremor of the eye. Fortunately, the smooth pursuit motion operates over longer time periods and thus can be extracted from the noisy data with the help of a low-pass filter. The sum of probabilities is used for the position and velocity consistency because it is likely that either position or velocity is inconsistent even if the target is attended. A naive target tracking algorithm could compute the probability of each target at a given point in time (or at a given frame) and choose the object with the highest probability. This, however, would result in frequent shifts of tracking from one target to another. An elegant way to penalise implausible interpretation of the data without excessive time delay is to model the attention shifts between targets as a Hidden Markov process. Each state in such a process corresponds to tracking a particular target. Since the fixation cannot be too short, the probability of staying in a particular state is usually much higher than the probability of moving to another state (in our case 95% vs. 5%). This way the eye is more likely to keep tracking the same target than to rapidly jump from one target to another. Further details on the GDOT technique can be found in [2].

3   Experiment

The main objective of the performed perceptual experiments was to test the accuracy of the optical flow-based GDOT extension while used with motion picture as stimulus.

Stimuli and Procedure. Three short video clips (18, 29 and 13 seconds long) labelled as A, B and C, each containing a different fragment of a football game, were shown to the observer. In the first case observer was asked to freely watch the match. This training session allowed for familiarisation with the stimuli, procedure and apparatus. For video B, the participant was asked to follow with his eyes a coloured, moving marker associated with either one of the players or the ball (see Fig. 2, left). For video C, the observer was asked to follow the player with the ball (no marker was displayed). The whole experiment was repeated 3 times for each person. For every sequence a manually defined set of potential attention targets was distributed over the scene. The targets were associated with the ball, players, both score and time indicators and the TV station logo (see example in Fig. 2, right). Their positions were tracked during playback using the optical flow-aided technique described in Section 2.

   Each observer sat at a distance of 65 cm from the display (this distance was restricted with a chin rest). The actual experiment was preceded by a 9-point eye tracker calibration. Then, three videos were displayed one by one while eye movements were recorded. In particular, we captured the raw gaze positions and fixation points. The latter were computed by the proprietary eye tracker software based on combination of the Dispersion Threshold Identification (I-DT) [4] and Velocity Threshold Identification (I-VT) [5] fixation detection techniques.

Fig. 2. Left: frame from video B with an example location of the marker. Right: allocation of the potential fixation targets.

Participants and Apparatus. Gaze points were collected from 9 individual observers (aged between 27 and 44 years old, 7 males and 2 females). All participants had normal or corrected to normal vision. No session took longer than 5 minutes. The participants were aware that their gaze is recorded, but were naive about the purpose of experiment.

Our experimental setup consisted of a P-CR Mirametrix S2 eye tracker controlled by proprietary software (version 2.5.1.152). The S2 captured locations of both corneal reflection (the first Purkinje image) and centre of the pupil. The data was collected at the rate of 60 Hz. The eye tracker was positioned under a 24-inch NEC Multisync PA241W LCD display with the screen dimensions of 53x32.5 cm, and the native resolution of 1920x1200 pixels (60Hz). The PC computer (2.8 GHz Intel i7 930 CPU equipped with NVIDIA GeForce 480 GTI 512MB graphics card and 8 GB of RAM, Windows 7 OS) was used to run our evaluation software controlled by MATLAB, and to store the experimental results.

4   Results

We processed the gaze data captured during experiments using the GDOT technique. As a result, the most probable fixation targets were identified for each time instance in the videos. For the videos B and C, also the reference target can be identified because we asked observer to look at the marker of the known position or at the player possessing the ball whose position can also be extracted from the video with some degree of accuracy. Consistency between the reference targets and targets identified by GDOT algorithm gives a measure of its accuracy. We confront the results with the data obtained using raw gaze data and fixation points computed by the eye tracker software. In two latter cases, the closest target to the gaze point/fixation point is assumed to be the identified target.

Quality Metric. We used the error metric introduced by Mantiuk et al. [2]. They noticed that the objective measure of accuracy represented by the difference between reference and captured target poorly corresponds to the subjective experience of using a gaze-contingent application. This measure, called an *error rate*, is the percentage of time a wrong object is tracked. However, in practice minimising the error rate does not necessary improve the perceived quality of the gaze-dependent object identification. This is because the fixation detection algorithms calibrated for a low error rate usually produce rapid changes of fixation from one target to another, which are very distracting. Such unwanted rapid changes can be described by the number of times per second an algorithm changes fixation to a wrong target, which is called *error frequency*.

Accuracy. Fig. 3 compares the error rate and error frequency for three tested techniques. The results were averaged over all observers and repetitions. The proposed GDOT extension has a far superior overall quality when compared to other algorithms, mostly because of the consistency of predictions (low error frequency), but also because it could track longer attended objects (smallest overall error rate).

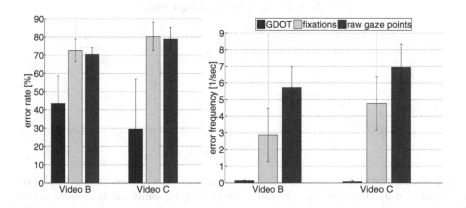

Fig. 3. Average error rate and error frequency for two individual videos

Temporal Characteristic of Object Tracking. The temporal characteristics of each algorithm, shown in Fig. 4, provide an insight into why the GDOT algorithm is judged as significantly better. Plots show the timing of attended object identification, each of them during a single session of the experiment. The reference targets that observers were asked to follow are shown as a red bold dashed line. The blue line is the target identified by the corresponding tracking/fixation algorithm.

The raw gaze data (top plot) resulted in a relatively low error rate. However, raw gaze points also gave an unacceptable level of flickering, resulting in the greatest error frequency. The fixation detection (middle plot) lowers the error

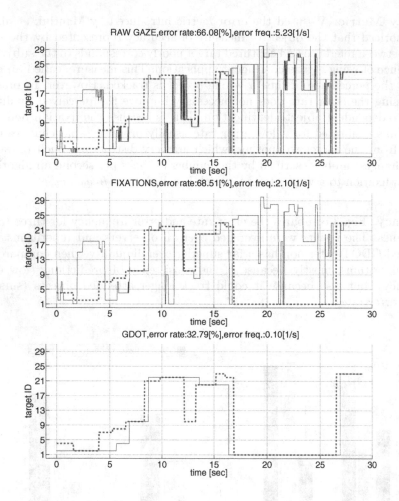

Fig. 4. Target tracking results for an example experimental session (video *B*, observer *paf*, repetition 3). The vertical axis shows IDs of targets, while the horizontal is time. The dashed red lines depict IDs of reference targets, while blue ones show the identified target.

frequency but at the same time gives an unacceptably high error rate. For the majority of sessions the proposed GDOT correctly identified more than 50% of targets for video B and more than 70% for video C (77.21% for an individual session presented in Fig. 4). The dominant source of error were the inaccuracies when switching between targets as well as the delay caused by observers not being able to move their gaze instantaneously when the marker jumped from one object to another. This quite high error value may show that complex video footages which include a high number of fast moving targets with a hard to predict trajectory, still pose a challenge for modern eye tracking because of insufficient device accuracy and its temporal lags.

5 Conclusions

We described a novel use of the GDOT method and proven that it can be successfully used with a video stimuli, if certain features of the motion picture were designated as potential fixation targets and tracked by the optical flow system. As it was shown in the conducted perceptual experiments, GDOT technique outperforms the typical fixation detection techniques in this new field. The overall accuracy is high enough to enable the use of object-oriented gaze and attention tracking in video-based applications.

Acknowledgements. The project was partially funded by the Polish National Science Centre (decision number DEC-2013/09/B/ST6/02270).

References

1. Duchowski, T.A.: Eye Tracking Methodology: Theory and Practice, 2nd edn. Springer (2007)
2. Mantiuk, R., Bazyluk, B., Mantiuk, R.K.: Gaze-dependent Object Tracking for Real Time Rendering. Computer Graphics Forum (Proc. of Eurographics 2013) 32(2), 163–173 (2013)
3. Salvucci, D.D., Goldberg, J.H.: Identifying fixations and saccades in eye-tracking protocols. In: Proceedings of the 2000 Symposium on Eye Tracking Research & Applications (ETRA), New York, pp. 71–78 (2000)
4. Widdel, H.: Operational problems in analysing eye movements. In: Gale, G., Johnson, F. (eds.) Theoretical and Applied Aspects of Eye Movement Research, pp. 21–29. Elsevier Science Publishers B.V. 1, North-Holland (1984)
5. Erkelens, C.J., Vogels, I.M.L.C.: The initial direction and landing position of saccades. Eye Movements Research: Mechanisms, Processes and Applications, pp. 133–144 (1995)
6. Mantiuk, R., Markowski, M.: Gaze-dependent Tone Mapping. In: Kamel, M., Campilho, A. (eds.) ICIAR 2013. LNCS, vol. 7950, pp. 426–433. Springer, Heidelberg (2013)
7. Hailin, J., Favaro, P., Cipolla, R.: Visual tracking in the presence of motion blur. In: Proc. of Computer Vision and Pattern Recognition (CVPR 2005), vol. 2, pp. 18–25 (2005)
8. Lucas, B.D., Kanade, T.: An Iterative Image Registration Technique with an Application to Stereo Vision. In: Proc. of the 7th International Joint Conference on Artificial Intelligence, Canada, vol. 2, pp. 674–679 (1981)
9. Becker, W., Fuchs, A.F.: Prediction in the oculomotor system: smooth pursuit during transient disappearance of a visual target. Experimental Brain Research 57(3), 562–575 (1985)
10. Mantiuk, R., Bazyluk, B., Tomaszewska, A.: Gaze-Dependent Depth-of-Field Effect Rendering in Virtual Environments. In: Ma, M., Fradinho Oliveira, M., Madeiras Pereira, J. (eds.) SGDA 2011. LNCS, vol. 6944, pp. 1–12. Springer, Heidelberg (2011)

Compression of Synthetic-Aperture Radar Images

Marzena Bielecka[1], Andrzej Bielecki[2], and Wojciech Wojdanowski[3]

[1] AGH University of Science and Technology
Faculty of Geology, Geophysics and Environmental Protection
Chair of Geoinformatics and Applied Computer Science
Al. Mickiewicza 30, 30-059, Kraków, Poland
[2] AGH University of Science and Technology, Faculty of Electrical Engineering,
Automation, Computer Science and Biomedical Engineering
Chair of Applied Computer Science
Al. Mickiewicza 30, 30-059, Kraków, Poland
[3] IBM SWG Lab, Kraków, Poland
bielecka@agh.edu.pl, {azbielecki,wuwik34}@gmail.com

Abstract. In this paper the problem of the synthetic-aperture radar images compression is considered. The algorithm of canonical coherent scatterers identification, proposed in [1, 2], based on the analysis of polarimetric signatures, is the starting point of the studies. The question whether the significant dimension reduction of the SAR image matrix preserves the information encoded in the SAR picture or not, is the topic of the paper. It turns out that the compression, by using the Kohonen neural network, allows us to reduce the dimension of the data from 16200-component vector to 100-component vector without losing information. The studies are led in the context of polarimetric data that encode full information about the scatterer. However, there are essential problems with such data processing. Therefore the topic is crucial in the context of the SAR images analysis.

Keywords: SAR, Kohonen neural network, image compression.

1 Introduction

Synthetic-aperture radar (SAR for abbreviation) is the type of a radar that applies a relative motion between an antenna and its target region in order to provide distinctive long-term coherent-signal variations. Although over the past decades extensive research in the area of the segmentation and classification of polarimetric SAR data in the context of outdoor scene analysis have been conducted intensively [6, 12, 17–19, 23], the results are far from satisfactory ones. Among others, the SAR images analysis, based on polarimetric signatures (see [2, 19] for details), is considered. In this method, however, the obtained data has the form of very large matrices. It turned out that the polarimetric signatures pattern analysis, based on artificial neural networks, could be effective [1, 2]. The

L.J. Chmielewski et al. (Eds.): ICCVG 2014, LNCS 8671, pp. 92–99, 2014.

fact that the input vector has a large number of components, over 16000 in the mentioned case, is one of the crucial drawbacks of the method. Therefore, the SAR image compression is a vital issue that has to be solved in order to apply neural methods efficiently. The problem of data amount reduction is, in general, one of the crucial task in data processing and is solved by using various methods [8, 11], especially in the context of SAR images compression[16]. In this paper the SAR images compression is done by using Kohonen neural network [10, 20] is considered.

2   SAR System and Polarimetric Signatures

The SAR is an active coherent system which provides large-scaled two-dimensional images of the Earth surface reflectivity with high spatial and temporal resolutions. The information about polarization of the transmitted and received signal for each pixel of SAR image, is represented by the scattering matrix. The polarimetric signature, that fully describes polarimetric properties of the scatterer, can be calculated on the basis of the scattering matrix. The polarimetric signatures present the scattering power of an object as a function of the ellipticity and orientation angle of both incident and backscattered radar waves. To simplify the visualization of the signatures in the backscattered waves only two components of polarization are taken into consideration. Therefore the polarimetric signatures are represented in two channels: the co- and cross-polarized - Fig.1. In the radar polarimetry there are a few canonical objects which scatter radar waves in a characteristic ways called "scattering mechanisms". These scattering mechanisms include: single bounce scattering (or even bounce), double bounce scattering (or odd bounce), helix scattering (right- and left-oriented helix) and volume scattering. In the case of a single bounce scattering, any radar wave bounces even times from a surface and travels back to the radar. This type of a scattering mechanism can be modeled by trihedral object. Double bounce scattering means that the radar wave scatters odd times and then it goes back to

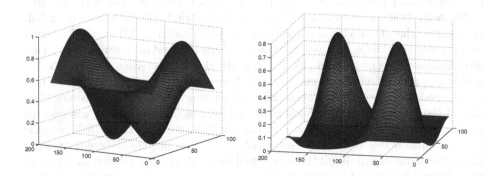

Fig. 1. The dihedral polarimetric signatures: copolarization (left) and crosspolarization (right)

the radar. This scattering mechanism is characteristic for dihedral. Helix scattering is introduced by scattering from a complex man-made structures. It is represented by scattering from left- and right-oriented helix. The latter mechanism - a volume scattering - means that the radar wave is scattered many times from a cloud of thin oriented dipoles. This mechanism is typical for scattering from vegetation. The polarimetric signatures of these canonical objects are mathematically described in the literature [12]. The polarimetric signature which represents incoherent volume scattering is not discussed in this paper.

The polarimetric signatures of real objects, located on the Earth surface, such as buildings, roads, viaducts, forests, fields, water, etc., differ from the canonical ones. The differences are caused by noise, by mixing different scattering types in the area, which is represented in one pixel of radar image or by the inaccuracies of the radar measurement system. The pixels with one dominant scattering mechanism have a polarimetric signature most similar to the corresponding canonical signature of the object. This similarity can be applied to the coherent identification process. The coherent objects are defined as weakly depolarizing scatterers for which one dominant scattering mechanism can be recovered. The coherent objects correspond mostly with man-made targets like buildings, viaducts, bridges, power poles and etc.

Each of polarimetric signatures is represented by a 180×90 matrix. As a result an input vector has got 16200 elements. Therefore, a compression seems to be essential task. This is very crucial in the case of a radar image, whose size is 1024×1024. It gives 1048576 polarimetric signatures for one image and it means that we need 126 gigabytes memory to store it. Therefore, a compression is necessary.

3 SAR Images Analysis - The State of the Art

Image and data classification techniques play an important role in the automatic analysis and interpretation of remote sensing data. However, due to high complexity of measured information from multiple polarimetric channels, this is a challenging problem. Over the past decade, extensive studies in the area of the segmentation and classification of polarimetric SAR data have been led. In general, the classification algorithms for polarimetric SAR can be divided into three main classes in which the classification is based on physical scattering mechanisms inherent in data [15, 24], statistical characteristics of data [13, 23] and image processing techniques [22, 25]. However, any of the existing method is designed directly to the identification of canonical coherent scatterers. The aim of the all mentioned methods is to find groups of pixels which are enough similar to each other. This means also that, by using these methods, it is possible to distinguish between coherent and incoherent pixels but the coherent ones are treated as a one group. In all the mentioned methods the data differs in choice of polarimetric features of a scatterer. One of them is based on the values of signal to clutter ratio [21]. In this method the intensity of studied pixel is compared with the intensity of surrounding pixels (clutter). If the ratio is large i.e. greater than 15 dB, then the pixel is classified as coherent. The biggest disadvantage of this method is the overestimation of the clutter intensity in the urban areas where coherent targets are located very close to each other. The coherent scatterers can be also identified by using the multitemporal analysis of SAR images. In this method small value of amplitude dispersion means that analyzed object is a coherent one [7]. However, for this method the large number of SAR images of the same area is necessary. Another approach to identification of coherent scatterers is based on the entropy analysis [12]. The entropy H, $0 < H < 1$, represents the randomness of a scattering medium between isotropic scattering ($H = 0$) and fully random scattering ($H = 1$). The use of a spatial averaging window, which leads to some reduction of information, is a disadvantage of this method. Therefore, it seems that results obtained by using polarimetric signatures are very promising. This data allows us to distinguish four type of scattering mechanisms in the coherent pixels. A high dimension of data is the only problem.

4   Neural Compression of Polarimetric Signatures

In many applications the high dimensionality of data restricts the choice of data processing methods. A statistical optimal way of dimensionality reduction is to project the data onto a lower-dimensional orthogonal subspace that best preserves the certain properties of the structure of the data set. Two major types of dimension reduction methods: linear and non-linear ones can be distinguished [8, 9]. Principal component analysis (PCA), singular value decomposition (SVD) and factor analysis (FA) are the most widely known linear methods, whereas principle curves and neural networks, including self-organizing maps, are the most popular non-linear ones. However, all of them demand computations which are quite time consuming for the high-dimensional data sets. The self-organizing maps (SOM), called also Kohonen neural networks, were applied in this paper. For the Kohonen map high-dimensional data also means long time of computation but it is possible to reduce it by applying the parallel computations.

The computation was realized by taking advantages of CUDA technology. There were built two Kohonen networks, the one for the co-polarized matrices and the second one for the cross-polarized matrices. Reduction of 16200 element vector to n-dimensional one, in such a way to enable us to retrieve it, was possible with good enough accuracy and it was the aim of the task. In the experiment it turned out that the best results were for n=100. The relatively long time of computations was shortened by using GPU (Graphical Processing Unit), which enabled us to process many tasks in parallel. The networks were trained by using the neural gas algorithm during the first 100 epochs, next the winner takes all (WTA) algorithm was applied. The process of finding the winning neuron, in parallel computation, was carried out on the basis of the, so called, reduction operation. The used sort, which is important in neural gas algorithm, was a bitonic one.

4.1   Results

To check whether the obtained results can be used to further analysis, what in this case means possibility of classification of polarimetric signatures according to their features, the set of 200 elements for co-polarized and 200 elements for cross- polarized matrices was chosen. The data were acquired by TerraSAR-X satellite. In this paper only coherent polarimetric signatures, that constitute four classes: dihedral, trihedral, left and right helix, were analyzed. For the chosen set the classification was performed. Due to the fact, that we know the ideal patterns for each of four considered classes, they can be used as the weights of neurons for the both Kohohnen networks. As a result, the used Kohonen networks are classifiers. It is expected that this network chooses from a given set only these elements that are similar sufficiently to patterns established as its weights [2]. The obtained results are presented in Table 1.

Table 1. The percentage classification efficiency before and after compression

type of polarization	before compression	after compression
dihedral	95	95
lefthelix	100	100
righthelix	95	95
trihedral	100	100

The percentage accuracy of the classification uncompressed and compressed data are shown in columns two and three respectively. It can be observed that although the data was compressed from input having 16200 components into input having only 100 components - see Fig.2, the compression did not decrease the efficiency of the classification accuracy, which remains exactly the same. This means that the raw data, encoded in the aforementioned 180×90 element matrices, is highly redundant. Of course, the carried out compression caused the lost of some information contained in the polarimetric signatures. This can be observed in differences in angles between ideal patterns presented in Table 2. In turn, in Table 3 there are shown angles between real matrices and ideal patterns - one example from every class.

Table 2. Angles between co-polarization matrices before and after compression for patterns

before	dihedral	left	right	trihedral	after	dihedral	left	right	trihedral
dihedral	0	45	45	51	dihedral	0	19	19	20
left	45	0	85	61	left	19	0	36	25
right	45	85	0	61	right	19	36	0	25
trihedral	51	61	61	0	trihedral	19	25	25	0

Table 3. Angles between co-polarization matrices before and after compression for real matrices

class	No.1		No.2		No.3		No.4	
	before	after	before	after	before	after	before	after
dihedral	24.18	6.93	44.95	18.65	44.41	18.12	48.39	17.37
left	44.48	18.82	22.02	5.22	84.91	36.06	64.46	26.41
right	54.42	20.50	82.22	35.99	4.91	1.29	55.51	21.33
trihedral	50.22	17.38	56.74	22.85	60.69	25.00	17.34	8.37

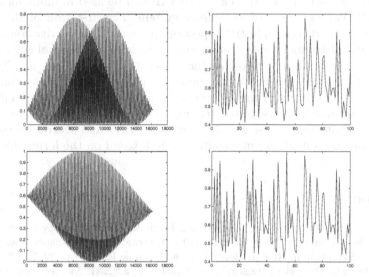

Fig. 2. The cross-polarized polarimetric signatures dihedral type (top): before compression (on the left) and after compression (on the right) and the co-polarized polarimetric signatures dihedral type (bottom): before compression (on the left) and after compression (on the right)

5   Concluding Remarks

The algorithm of canonical coherent scatterers identification, proposed in [2], is based on the analysis of polarimetric signatures. It has given promising results. What is important, in the canonical coherent scatterers identification process, the data are not averaged. It helps us to preserve the spatial information from the image. The recognized canonical coherent scatterers correspond accurately to the man-made structures and that, in turn, allows us to determine precisely the extent of built-up areas. In [1, 2] the Kohonen network was used to the patterns classification only for the canonical scatterers. In order to identify complex real objects, the advanced neural systems, such as ART-type neural networks, are planned to be considered. Thus, the reduction of the input vector is necessary.

Therefore, the question whether the significant dimension reduction preserves the information encoded in the SAR picture, was crucial. In the light of the results, obtained in the experiments described in this paper, the answer is affirmative. This means that the possibility of applying complex neural systems for the SAR analysis, including ART-type networks, is possible.

It should also be mentioned that, potentially, SAR technique can be used in robotics as well. In a such case the pattern analysis has be done in real time and therefore the reduction of its dimension is crucial. As it has been aforementioned, coherent scatterers mainly correspond to artificial man-made targets such as buildings, viaducts, walls, or bridges and the SAT systems are often placed on aircraft boards. Therefore SAR can be used in unmanned aerial vehicles (UAVs) as a part of its sensory system. The first task of the UAVs, used in civil construction industry inspection missions, is the navigation from an initial position to a final position in an unknown three-dimensional environment [14]. Then the robot has to recognize the object, that is inspected, and it has to understand the environment and the object spatial structure in the context of the mission, particularly in the aspects of trajectory planning [3–5]. Therefore the technology which allows us to detect and recognize man-made targets can be an effective-acting part of the visual system of an UAV and also one of the basis of the autonomous flying agent cognitive system based on the formal models of mental processes.

References

1. Porzycka, S., Strzelczyk, J., Bielecka, M., Lesniak, A.: Preliminary pattern recognition in polarimetric signatures. In: IEEE International Geoscience and Remote Sensing Symposium: Remote Sensing for a Dynamic Earth, pp. 22–27 (2012)
2. Bielecka, M., Porzycka-Strzelczyk, S., Strzelczyk, J.: SAR images analysis based on polarimetric signatures. Applied Soft Computing (accepted 2014)
3. Bielecka, M., Skomorowski, M., Bielecki, A.: Fuzzy syntactic approach to pattern recognition and scene analysis. In: Proceedings of the 4th International Conference on Informatics in Control, Automatics and Robotics, ICINCO 2007, ICSO Intelligent Control Systems and Optimization, Robotics and Automation, vol. 1, pp. 29–35 (2007)
4. Bielecki, A., Buratowski, T., Śmigielski, P.: Syntactic algorithm of two-dimensional scene analysis for unmanned flying vehicles. In: Bolc, L., Tadeusiewicz, R., Chmielewski, L.J., Wojciechowski, K. (eds.) ICCVG 2012. LNCS, vol. 7594, pp. 304–312. Springer, Heidelberg (2012)
5. Bielecki, A., Buratowski, T., Śmigielski, P.: Recognition of two-dimensional representation of urban environment for autonomous flying agents. Expert Systems with Applications 40, 3623–3633 (2013)
6. Farmio-Famil, L., Reigber, A., Pottier, E., Boerner, W.M.: Scene characterization using subaperture polarimetric SAR data. IEEE Transactions on Geoscience and Remote Sensing 41, 2264–2276 (2013)
7. Ferretti, A., Prati, C., Rocca, F.: Permanent scatterers in SAR interferometry. IEEE Transaction on Geoscience and Remote Sensing 39, 8–20 (2001)
8. Fodor, I.K.: A Survey of Dimension Reduction Techniques. Lawrence Livermore National Laboratory (2002)

9. Kaski, S.: Data exploration using self-organizing maps. Acta Polytechnica Scandinavica, Mathematics, Computing and Management in Engineering Series 82 (1997)
10. Kohonen, T.: Adaptive, associative and self-organizing functions in neural computing. Applied Optics 26, 4910–4918 (1997)
11. Lech, P., Okarma, K.: Optimization of the fast image Binarization method based on the Monte Carlo approach. Electronics and Electrical Engineering 20, 63–66 (2014)
12. Lee, J.S., Pottier, E.: Polarimetric Radar Imaging. From Basic to Application. CRC Press, Taylor and Francis Group (2009)
13. Lee, J.S., Grunes, M.R., Ainsworth, T., Du, L.J., Schuler, D., Cloude, S.R.: Unsupervised classification using polarimetric decomposition and the complex Wishart classifier. IEEE Transaction on Geoscience and Remote Sensing 37, 2249–2257 (1999)
14. Metni, M., Hamel, T.: A UAV for bridge inspection: Visual servoing control law with orientation limits. Automation in Construction 17, 3–10 (2007)
15. Pottier, E., Lee, J.S.: Unsupervised classification scheme of POLSAR images based on the complex Wishart distribution and the H/A/alpha-Polarimetric decomposition theorem. In: Proc. of the 3rd EUSAR 2000 Conference (2000)
16. Sakarya, F.A., Emek, S.: SAR image compression. In: Proceedings of the 13th Asilomar Conference on Signals, Systems and Computers, vol. 2, pp. 858–862 (1996)
17. Schneider, R.Z., Papathanassiou, K., Hajnsek, I., Moreira, A.: Polarimetric interferometry over urban areas: infromation extraction using coherent scatterers. In: Proceedings of Geoscience and Remote Sensing Symposium (IGARSS 2005), Seoul, Korea, pp. 25–29 (2005)
18. Skingley, J., Rye, A.J.: The Hough transform applied to SAR images for thin line detection. Pattern Recognition Letters 6, 61–67 (1987)
19. Strzelczyk, J., Porzycka-Strzelczyk, S.: Identification of coherent scatterers in SAR images based on the analysis of polarimetric signatures. IEEE Geoscience and Remote Sensing Letters 11, 783–787 (2013)
20. Tadeusiewicz, R.: Neural Networks. Academic Press, Warsaw (1993)
21. Touzi, R., Charbonneau, F.: Characterization of scatterer symmetric scattering using polarimetric SARs. IEEE Transactions on Geoscience and Remote Sensing 40, 2507–2516 (2002)
22. Tan, C.P., Lim, K.S., Ewe, H.T.: Image processing in polarimetric SAR images using a hybrid entropy decomposition and maximum likelihood (EDML). In: Proceedings of International Symposium on Image and Signal Processing and Analysis (ISPA)
23. Wu, Y., Ji, K., Yu, W., Su, Y.: Region-based classification of polarimetric SAR images using Wishart MRF. IEEE Geoscience and Remote Sensing Letters 5, 668–672 (2008)
24. van Zyl, J.J.: Unsupervised classification of scattering mechanisms using radar polarimetry data. IEEE Transactions on Geoscience Remote Sensing 27, 36–45 (1989)
25. Ye, Z., Lu, C.-C.: Wavelet-based unsupervised SAR image segmentation using hidden markov tree models. In: Proceedings of the 16th International Conference on Pattern Recognition, ICPR 2002, vol. 2, p. 20729 (2002)

Feynman-Kac Formula
and Restoration of High ISO Images*

Dariusz Borkowski[1], Adam Jakubowski[1], and Katarzyna Jańczak-Borkowska[2]

[1] Faculty of Mathematics and Computer Science, Nicolaus Copernicus University,
Chopina 12/18, 87-100 Toruń, Poland
{dbor,adjakubo}@mat.umk.pl
[2] Institute of Mathematics and Physics, University of Technology and Life Sciences,
al. prof. S. Kaliskiego 7, 85-789 Bydgoszcz, Poland
kaja@utp.edu.pl

Abstract. In this paper we explore the problem of reconstruction of
RGB images with additive Gaussian noise. In order to solve this problem
we use Feynman-Kac formula and non local means algorithm. Expressing
the problem in stochastic terms allows us to adapt to anisotropic diffusion
the concept of similarity patches used in non local means. This novel
look on the reconstruction is fruitful, gives encouraging results and can
be successfully applied to denoising of high ISO images.

1 Introduction

Let D be a closed rectangular in $\mathbf{R}^2$, $u : D \to \mathbf{R}^n$ be an original image and
$u_0 : D \to \mathbf{R}^n$ be the observed image of the form $u_0 = u + \eta$, where η stands for
a white Gaussian noise (added independently to all coordinates with standard
deviation ρ). We assume that u and u_0 are appropriately regular. We are given
u_0, the problem is to reconstruct u. This is a typical example of an inverse
problem [2].

Various techniques were proposed to tackle this inverse problem. One may
quote the linear filtering, DCT [23], wavelets theory [11], variational methods
[19], stochastic modelling [12, 18] and methods driven by nonlinear diffusion
equation [8, 17, 21, 22]. In another class, one could include methods that take
advantage of the non-local similarity of patches in the image. Among the most
famous, we can name non local means (in short NL-means) [5, 6], BM3D [9, 10,
13], NL-Bayes [14] and K-SVD [1, 15].

In the paper [4] the authors considered the problem of the reconstruction
of grey levels images using anisotropic diffusion expressed in stochastic terms.
This representation allows them to adapt to the reconstruction process the idea
of patches similarity using in NL-means algorithm. This novel look on the reconstruction problem was fruitful and gave very good results for gray images. In
this paper we generalise the results from [4] to colour images and apply proposed
metod to denoising of high ISO images taken from digital cameras.

---

* This research was supported by the National Science Centre (Poland) under decision
number DEC-2012/07/D/ST6/02534.

L.J. Chmielewski et al. (Eds.): ICCVG 2014, LNCS 8671, pp. 100–107, 2014.

2   Feynman-Kac Formula

In order to express the anisotropic diffusion equation $\dfrac{\partial u}{\partial t} = Au$ in stochastic terms, where Au is some diffusion operator, one needs to use the Feynman-Kac formula [16].

Theorem 1 (Feynman-Kac Formula). *Let $u_0 \in C_0^2(\mathbf{R}^n)$ (continuously twice differentiable with compact support) then the function $u(t, x)$ defined by*

$$u(t, x) = \mathbf{E}\left[u_0(X_t)\right] \tag{1}$$

satisfies the diffusion equation $\dfrac{\partial u}{\partial t} = Au$, where X is some stochastic process driven by the operator Au and vice versa this operator determines a stochastic process X.

We do not want to focus on the relationship between Au and X but for us the important information is that the anisotropic diffusion can be expressed in the form of the expected value of some stochastic process.

3   Non Local Means Algorithm

In this section we cite results from [5–7] and for precise definitions and deeper discusion about NL-means algorithm we refer the reader to these articles.

Let $v = \{u_0(i)|i \in I = \mathbf{Z}^2 \cap D\}$ be a discrete noisy image and $\{w(i,j)\}$ be the weights that depend on the similarity between the pixels i and j and satisfy the usual conditions $0 \leq w(i,j) \leq 1$ and $\sum_j w(i,j) = 1$. The reconstructed value $NL(v)(i)$ for a pixel i is defined as a weighted average of all pixels in the image

$$NL(v)(i) = \sum_{j \in I} w(N_i, N_j)v(j).$$

The weight $w(N_i, N_j)$ depends on the similarity of the intensity gray level or colour vectors of neighbourhoods N_i, N_j centred at pixels i and j and can be defined by $w(N_i, N_j) = \frac{1}{Z(i)} \exp\left(-\frac{d(N_i, N_j)}{s^2}\right)$ where $Z(i)$ is the normalising factor $Z(i) = \sum_j \exp\left(-\frac{d(N_i, N_j)}{s^2}\right)$ and $d(N_i, N_j)$ is some measure of distance between intensity gray level or colours vectors of similarity windows. The number s is a parameter that controls the decay of the exponential function.

In [7] the authors proposed to use the following weight function for RGB images:

$$w(B_{i,r}, B_{j,r}) = \exp\left(-\frac{\max\left(\frac{\|B_{i,r} - B_{j,r}\|^2}{3(2r+1)} - 2\rho^2, 0\right)}{s^2}\right),$$

where $B_{i,r}$ means a neighbourhood of a size $(2r + 1) \times (2r + 1)$ RGB pixels centred at i and $\|B_{i,r} - B_{j,r}\|$ is the Euclidean distance between $B_{i,r}$ and $B_{j,r}$.

Fig. 1. Original test images: 512×512 a) Peppers b) Lenna

4   Image Reconstruction of Colour Images Based on Feynman-Kac Formula and Non Local Means

Note that in the case of numerical scheme the Feynman-Kac formula can be written as

$$u(t,x) = \frac{1}{M} \sum_{i=1}^{M} u_0(X_t(\omega_i)),$$

where M is a number of iterations of Monte Carlo method. In particular, for the terminal time $t = T$, for which we get the reconstructed image,

$$u(x) = u(T,x) = \frac{1}{M} \sum_{i=1}^{M} u_0(X_T(\omega_i)).$$

Now we need to construct a stochastic process X driven by a geometry of a colour image. Unfortunately, we can not use the gradient function as it was for grey levels images [4]. And therefore we propose to use the following stochastic process X being a particular case of a general model taken from [3].

Let

$$X_0 = x,$$
$$H_k = \Pi_D \left(X_{k-1} + h \cdot (\Phi_{0,1}, \Phi_{0,1}) \right)$$
$$X_k = \begin{cases} H_k, & \text{if } \Theta, \\ X_{k-1}, & \text{elsewhere,} \end{cases} \qquad k = 1, 2, ..., \tau_m,$$

where $\Pi_D(x)$ denotes a projection of x on the set D and $\Phi_{0,1}$ is a random number generator from the normal distribution with mean 0 and standard deviation 1. By Θ we mean the condition

$$\|(G_\delta * u_0)(H_k) - (G_\delta * u_0)(X_{k-1})\| \le 0.8 \cdot \rho$$

where G_δ is 3×3 Gaussian mask and by τ_m

$$\tau_m = \min\{k; k \ge m \text{ and } \Theta \text{ is true } m \text{ times}\}.$$

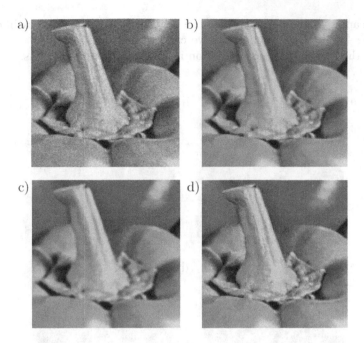

Fig. 2. a) Noisy image $\rho = 10$ b) New method c) Anisotropic diffusion d) NL-means

The interpretation of the process X is the following. First, note that the stochastic process $\tilde{X}$, where $\tilde{X}_0 = x$ and $\tilde{X}_k = \tilde{X}_{k-1} + h \cdot (\Phi_{0,1}, \Phi_{0,1})$ is a discrete approximation of 2-dimensional Wiener process with time step parameter equals h. Modification of this Wiener process by adding the condition Θ ensures that the process X will move to the homogeneous areas. The above construction of X has two important advantages. Firstly, we do not use gradient function or its equivalence for colour images. Secondly, since we can use large value of time step parameter, the process X can be simulated fast (see details in [3]).

Since the process X is considered on the random interval with the terminal time τ_m, the model of stochastic anisotropic diffusion based on Feynman-Kac formula has the following form:

$$u(x) = \sum_{i=1}^{M} \frac{1}{M} u_0(X_{\tau_m(\omega_i)}(\omega_i)), \qquad (2)$$

which means that each pixel $u_0(X_{\tau_m(\omega_i)}(\omega_i))$ is weighted with the same value $\frac{1}{M}$. But since pixels have different colours we may consider them with different weights depending on their neighbourhood. We follow NL-means algorithm and propose to think of weights that depend on patches similarity. Finally, we can introduce a new method of the image restoration based on Feynman-Kac formula

$$u(x) = \frac{1}{Z} \sum_{i=1}^{M} u_0(X_{\tau_m(\omega_i)}(\omega_i)) w(B_{x,r}, B_{X_{\tau_m(\omega_i)}(\omega_i),r}). \qquad (3)$$

The meaning of the parameters in the new method is the same as in original approaches [3, 7]. Very good results we can obtain with $(M, m, h) = (50, 10, 4)$ for which the time of the reconstruction is comparable to NL-means.

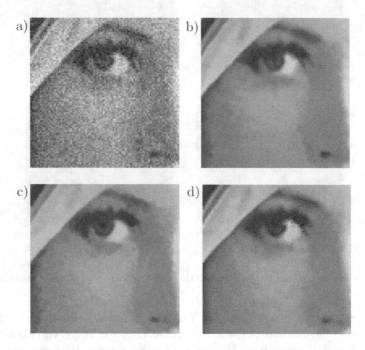

Fig. 3. a) Noisy image $\rho = 30$ b) New method c) Anisotropic diffusion d) NL-means

5   Experimental Results

Some measures of quality for our evaluation experiments regarding new method, non local means algorithm and anisotropic stochastic diffusion are presented in Table 1, Table 2, Fig. 2 and Fig. 3. The results refer to RGB colour images *Lenna* and *Peppers* corrupted (independent all channels) with the Gaussian noise with standard deviation ρ. Noisy images have been reconstructed with using vector analysis in RGB space. The maximum values of Peak Signal to Noise Ratio (in short PSNR) and Structural SIMilarity (in short SSIM) index obtained using tested methods are given in tables. Parameters of SSIM were set to the default values as recommended by [20].

The analysis of the measures of image quality shows that the new method performs better. Moreover, when comparing the figures one can observe that the image created by the new method is visually more pleasant. The reason for this

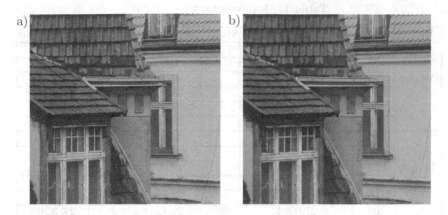

Fig. 4. a) Input high ISO image b) Result of the reconstruction using new method

is that the NL-means approach shows clear evidence of a halo of noise effect around the edges whereas anisotropic diffusion smooth details too much and show of a block image.

The type of high ISO sensor noise produced by a typical digital camera sensor can be modelled as an additive white Gaussian distribution with zero mean and a standard deviation proportional to the value of ISO. In figures Fig. 4., Fig. 5. we see images taken at high ISO value and the result of reconstruction using the new algorithm.

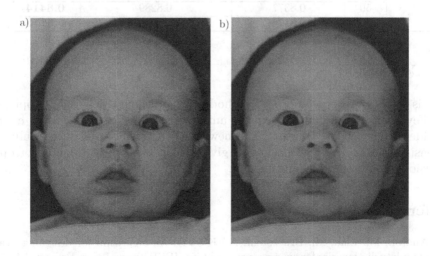

Fig. 5. a) Input high ISO image b) Result of the reconstruction using new method

Table 1. Maximum values of PSNR

Image	Noise ρ	NL-means algorithm	Stoch. anisotropic diffusion	New method
Peppers	10	32.9404	32.3572	**33.1289**
	20	30.2984	30.6057	**31.0984**
	30	27.3031	29.2140	**29.8178**
	40	26.6428	28.1988	**28.6991**
	50	25.9941	27.2549	**27.8611**
	60	25.5353	26.5094	**27.0802**
Lenna	10	34.0127	33.0964	**34.3550**
	20	31.5780	31.1301	**31.8386**
	30	29.6376	29.6041	**30.2871**
	40	28.6433	28.5068	**29.0773**
	50	27.7377	27.5843	**28.1308**
	60	27.0094	26.7234	**27.3205**

Table 2. Maximum values of SSIM

Image	Noise ρ	NL-means algorithm	Stoch. anisotropic diffusion	New method
Peppers	10	0.9536	0.9470	**0.9548**
	20	0.9194	0.9146	**0.9232**
	30	0.8898	0.8866	**0.8994**
	40	0.8645	0.8645	**0.8759**
	50	0.8383	0.8447	**0.8564**
	60	0.8284	0.8229	**0.8362**
Lenna	10	**0.9588**	0.9467	0.9573
	20	0.9224	0.9115	**0.9232**
	30	0.8929	0.8790	**0.8930**
	40	0.8640	0.8528	**0.8648**
	50	0.8377	0.8289	**0.8414**
	60	0.8174	0.8050	**0.8176**

6   Conclusion

In this paper we proposed a new method of digital image denoising. Applying the Feynman-Kac formula to express anisotropic diffusion allows us to adapt the idea from non local means. The new method can be used successfully to reconstruction of high ISO images by giving what is the best from anisotropic diffusion and non local means method.

References

1. Aharon, M., Elad, M., Bruckstein, A.: K-SVD: An algorithm for designing over-complete dictionaries for sparse representation. IEEE Trans. Image Process. 54(11), 4311–4322 (2006)
2. Aubert, G., Kornprobst, P.: Mathematical problems in image processing. Springer, New York (2002)

3. Borkowski, D.: Stochastic approximation to reconstruction of vector-valued images. In: Burduk, R., Jackowski, K., Kurzynski, M., Wozniak, M., Zolnierek, A. (eds.) CORES 2013. AISC, vol. 226, pp. 395–404. Springer, Heidelberg (2013)
4. Borkowski, D., Jańczak-Borkowska, K.: Image restoration using anisotropic stochastic diffusion collaborated with non local means. In: Saeed, K., Chaki, R., Cortesi, A., Wierzchoń, S. (eds.) CISIM 2013. LNCS, vol. 8104, pp. 177–189. Springer, Heidelberg (2013)
5. Buades, A., Coll, B., Morel, J.M.: A non local algorithm for image denoising. IEEE Computer Vision and Pattern Recognition 2, 60–65 (2005)
6. Buades, A., Coll, B., Morel, J.M.: A review of image denoising algorithms, with a new one. Multiscale Model. Simul. 4(2), 490–530 (2006)
7. Buades, A., Coll, B., Morel, J.M.: Non-local means denoising. Image Processing on Line (2011)
8. Catte, F., Lions, P.L., Morel, J.M., Coll, T.: Image selective smoothing and edge detection by nonlinear diffusion. SIAM J. Numer. Anal. 29(1), 182–193 (1992)
9. Dabov, K., Foi, A., Katkovnik, V., Egiazarian, K.: Image denoising by sparse 3D transform-domain collaborative filtering. IEEE Trans. Image Process. 16(8), 2080–2095 (2007)
10. Danielyan, A., Katkovnik, V., Egiazarian, K.: Bm3d frames and variational image deblurring. IEEE Trans. Image Process. 21(4), 1715–1728 (2012)
11. Donoho, D.L., Johnstone, I.M.: Ideal spatial adaptation via wavelet shrinkage. Biometrika 81(3), 425–455 (1994)
12. Geman, S., Geman, D.: Stochastic relaxation, gibbs distributions and the bayesian restoration of images. IEEE Pat. Anal. Mach. Intell. 6, 721–741 (1984)
13. Katkovnik, V., Danielyan, A., Egiazarian, K.: Decoupled inverse and denoising for image deblurring: variational BM3D-frame technique. In: 2011 18th IEEE International Conference on Image Processing (ICIP), pp. 3453–3456 (2011)
14. Lebrun, M., Buades, A., Morel, J.M.: Implementation of the Non-local Bayes image denoising. Image Processing on Line (2011)
15. Mairal, J., Elad, M., Sapiro, G.: Sparse representation for color image restoration. IEEE Trans. Image Process. 17(1), 53–69 (2008)
16. Oksendal, B.: Stochastic differential equations: an introduction with applications, 3rd edn. Springer (1992)
17. Perona, P., Malik, J.: Scale-space and edge detection using anisotropic diffusion. IEEE Trans. Pattern Anal. Mach. Intell. 12(7), 629–639 (1990)
18. Richardson, W.H.: Bayesian-based iterative method of image restoration. JOSA 62(1), 55–59 (1972)
19. Rudin, L.I., Osher, S., Fatemi, E.: Nonlinear total variation based noise removal algorithms. Phys. D 60, 259–268 (1992)
20. Wang, Z., Bovik, A.C., Sheikh, H.R., Simoncelli, E.P.: Image quality assessment: From error visibility to structural similarity. IEEE Trans. Image Process. 13(4), 600–612 (2004)
21. Weickert, J.: Theoretical foundations of anisotropic diffusion in image processing. Computing Supplement 11, 221–236 (1996)
22. Weickert, J.: Coherence-enhancing diffusion filtering. Int. J. Comput. Vision 31(2/3), 111–127 (1999)
23. Yaroslavsky, L.P.: Local adaptive image restoration and enhancement with the use of DFT and DCT in a running window. In: Proceedings of SPIE 2825, pp. 2–13 (1996)

Fusion of Visual and Range Images
for Object Extraction

Sebastian Budzan

Silesian University of Technology, Institute of Automatic Control
Akademicka 16, Gliwice 44-101, Poland
Sebastian.Budzan@polsl.pl

Abstract. This paper proposes a fused vision system using range laser scanner and visual camera for object extraction in mobile systems. Fusion of information gathered from different sources increases the effectiveness of the small objects detection in different scenario, e.g. day, night, outdoor, indoor, sunny or rainy weather. First of all, the algorithm for color images is proposed for extracting objects from the scene. The labelled objects are divided into two classes: background and obstacles, based on the morphological operations and segmentation method. Range laser measurement system is used regardless of the visual images classification to the obstacle and non-obstacle only. After that the size (width, height, depth) of the labelled objects are determined. Then the knowledge rules have been used to classify objects into separate three obstacle classes: small, medium and large.

1 Introduction

Object detection and recognition constitute two fundamental, challenging computer vision problems. Methods that aspire to solve these problems have a wide range of interesting problems and applications such as object segmentation, object tracking, reconstruction of road surfaces, scene parsing, pedestrian classification, autonomous navigation systems and many others. Most of the work has concentrated on systems that operate only on visual input sources like color images and ignores other sensor modalities. The object extraction methods using color images usually are based on the low-level features such as color, intensity or texture. In view of the above fact, in real environment the information about objects in near distance can be achieved by a few types of sensors, like visual camera, laser range scanners, radar, LiDAR, infrared or ultrasound sensors. Compared with color images, range images are less sensitive to changes in illumination or texture, also range scanners provide an attractive source of data in view of their dense and accurate sampling. Fusion of these different modalities could provide reliable and robust solution as multisensory system, with redundant information about current scene. The real-time processing requires that the vision system should be simple, reliable and accurate.

Proposed algorithm is dedicated to an all-terrain vehicles equipped with a semi-active vibration control system. Semi-active vehicle suspension systems,

L.J. Chmielewski et al. (Eds.): ICCVG 2014, LNCS 8671, pp. 108–115, 2014.

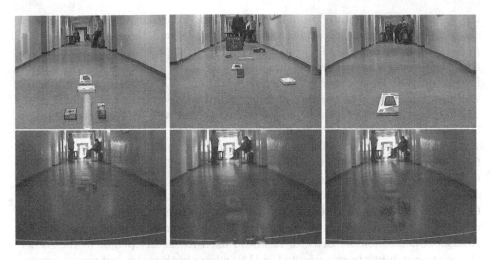

Fig. 1. Correct visual images (top) and images with real disadvantages (bottom) of the sample scene with objects and obstacles

which include magnetorheological dampers [1], are widely used in a vehicle suspension control. The stiffness of the dampers can be evaluated by the control gains based on the solution of continuous time algebraic Riccati equation. Other possibility is to link the gain with information from vision system. The gain of the dampers can be determined on the shape of the road or the shape and dimensions of the obstacles. In this paper visual and range images processing of the scene part has been presented. In Figure 1 several visual images taken during indoor experiments have been presented. Top images have been acquired with correct quality, bottom images shows some disadvantages e.g. poor illumination conditions, blurring effect and reflections on the ground.

2   Related Work

The most popular method for acquiring real world data is imaging using cameras. Initially, only one camera is mounted on the vehicle and the 2D information can be recorded, another configuration requires two cameras to acquire stereo images. Then the 3D point cloud is calculated using epipolar geometry. Dark areas, shadows, reflections are cause of vision systems inability for the extraction high quality object information. With recent advances in 3D imaging cameras, range images have been used for object extraction. Processing color images and especially object extraction has a wide range of applications, such as 3D road surface reconstruction [2], road modelling [3], autonomous robotic object detection [4], object tracking [5], interactive modelling [6], pedestrian detection [7].

A survey of the relevant literature can be found in [8] which shows the results of much research on passive and active object recognition methods. Appearance methods are based on statistical analysis. In Principal Component Analysis [9] the eigenfaces are generated from a set of training images of the specified object class. Then, the similarity between the input image and the eigenfaces is computed. Gould [4] presented the multi-class image segmentation system, where the background and foreground has been extracted, and then the objects in foreground has been classified. Window scanning [10] is based on evaluating well-normalized local histograms of image gradient orientations in a dense grid. The local, small objects can be characterized rather well by the distribution of local intensity gradients or edge directions.

With the development of range sensors, several algorithms have been proposed for detection and classification of real objects. Spinello et al. track the people in 3D point cloud data using a bottom-up top-down people detector [11]. The object detection and localization system based on both color and range images for robots has been presented in [12]. Their method on start removes saturation noise from range images, and then extracts the features of objects. In [13] an AdaBoost head-shoulder detector has been used to classify people in the scene. Other approach has been presented in [14], where both range and vision images separately classify the data first, the classification results are then combined by matching the set of obstacles from laser scanner with the set of obstacles coming from stereo-vision. It is important that such a methods require prior training data.

3   Proposed Method

The range images were collected with a SICK LMS 400 laser scanner mounted forward-looking on the front of a vehicle, 0.5 meter above the ground with a 30-degree angle downwards. This particular model of laser scanner supports up to a 70-degree field-of-view, a measurement resolution of 1 mm, and a maximum scan distance of 3 meters with 0.7 meter death zone. Typically, the scanner has a frequency in the range 180–500 Hz and angular resolution 0.1–1.0 degree. The basic principle of the sensor is to determine the distance to the object by measuring the relative phase of the reflected laser beam. In the experiments the scanner has the angular resolution set to 0.25 degrees and 282 points per scan line. The visual images were collected with AXIS M1011-W: $1/4''$ progressive scan RGB CMOS wireless camera. The camera has a maximum resolution at 640×480 pixels, also has a 30 fps frame rate in all resolutions. The prototype vehicle has been equipped also with real time module sbRIO 9363 from National Instruments, infrared and ultrasound sensors, also encoders mounted on the vehicle wheels to measure distance and velocity, however, after experiments, the infrared and ultrasound sensors information have been not used, because the sensitivity of them for many disturbances e.g. sound noise, light reflections, mounting angle etc. are very high.

The proposed solution presented in Figure 2 can be categorized as a decentralized method, because separately classify the data for both sensors first, the classification results are then combined by a fusion method. Both the sensor types have some practical imperfections such as incomplete and inconsistent

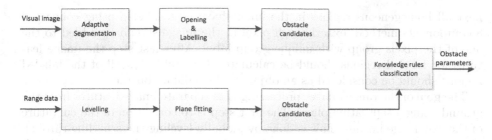

Fig. 2. Block diagram of the proposed solution

data, complex background with different colors and textures, size of the objects, some obscure objects, different illumination condition, also moving vehicle affects sharpness of the visual image.

3.1 Feature Extraction in the Visual and Range Images

Visual image morphological operations are a simple and effective approach to extraction of the objects from the image. The classifier extracts image features from the image using Otsu's thresholding method which utilizes discriminant analysis to find the maximum separability of classes. The method is based on the idea: find the threshold that minimizes the weighted within-class variance. For every possible threshold value, the method evaluates the goodness of this value if used as the threshold. In result, the means of two classes can be separated as far as possible and the variances in both classes will be as minimal as possible. Next, the morphological opening operation (an erosion followed by a dilation) is performed, thus regions of the objects will be connected into homogeneous regions, also most of the gaps in the image will be removed. In the

Table 1. The list of the visual (top) and range (bottom) image features determined by the visual image processing. The unique number of the labeled region is denoted by N.

Parameter Type	Image features
C_v	(x_N, y_N) location of each region center
B_{vl}	(x_{Nbl}, y_{Nbl}) bounding box bottom-left corner coordinates
B_{vr}	(x_{Nbr}, y_{Nbr}) bounding box bottom-right corner coordinates
T_{vl}	(x_{Ntl}, y_{Ntl}) bounding box top-left corner coordinates
T_{vr}	(x_{Ntr}, y_{Ntr}) bounding box top-right corner coordinates
A_v	pixels area of each labeled region
H_r	meters maximum height (depth) of the object
W_r	meters width of the object
O_{rl}	x_{Nl} left outermost point of the object
O_{rr}	x_{Nr} right outermost point of the object

next all homogeneous regions in the image have been labeled using connected 8-components method, exactly each pixel in the image should be added to the one of the pixels group with unique group label. After last step the image features for labeled regions should be calculated (see Table 1). All of the labeled regions should be considered as an object and candidate obstacle.

The goal of the range images processing is to separate image features from the ground using a separating plane. The first step is to correction of the curvature of the raw range images. This is done by globally leveling the scan line through the approximated line from flat raw data. Next, the fitting plane is calculated. This step can be done by calculation of the distances (z-axis) histogram and choosing the highest number of points. By comparing the points distances with those from histogram, image features can be separated into ground and objects (obstacles). All of the points belonging to the fitted plane are removed from the data. In consequence the remaining points are grouped together so that each cluster represents a candidate object and obstacle.

3.2   Fusion of the Sensors Information

Both the results of laser scanner and the results of visual imaging are fused using knowledge based rules. At first, each object is categorized into 1st class: obstacle (OB) or non-obstacle (NOB) objects group. NOB groups is defined as all of the objects, that lie outside the area given by the left and right vehicle bonduary, consequently OB objects lie inside that area. In second step obstacles must be categorized into 2nd class, in much more detailed groups, which can be expressed using three linguistic labels SM (SMall), MI (MIddle), LA (LArge). Each group of the obstacles gives the information for the vehicle control algorithm i.e. SM objects do not change the control parameters, because they will be under and between the vehicle wheels. MI obstacles group contains obstacles that lie exactly on the line produced by the right and/or left vehicle wheel and under the vehicle, in this situations the MI obstacles affects movement of the vehicle in terms of changing the dumpers stiffness. When the height of the obstacle is higher than the bottom of the vehicle the obstacle is categorized as LA obstacle. The above classes can be described by the rules:

- 1st class NOB: $(B_{vl}, B_{vr}, T_{vl}, T_{vr} < V_L$ and $O_{rl}, O_{rr} < V_L)$ or $(B_{vl}, B_{vr}, T_{vl}, T_{vr} > V_R$ and $O_{rl}, O_{rr} > V_R)$
- 1st class OB: $((B_{vl} \geq V_l$ or $T_{vl} \geq V_L)$ and $O_{rl} \geq V_L)$ or $((B_{vr} \leq V_R$ or $T_{vr} \leq V_R)$ and $O_{rr} \leq V_R)$
- 2nd class SM: $(B_{vl}, T_{vl}, O_{rl} > V_L)$ and $(B_{vr}, T_{vr}, O_{rr} < V_R)$ and $H_r < V_H$
- 2nd class MI: $(B_{vl}, T_{vl}, O_{rl} \geq V_L)$ or $(B_{vr}, T_{vr}, O_{rr} \leq V_R)$ and $H_r < V_H$
- 2nd class LA: OB $+ H_r \geq V_H$

Three parameters V_l, V_r and V_H used in above rules should be defined for the vehicle only once. V_l, V_r denotes left and right outermost points and the V_H denote the maximum height of the object in meters. Above rules do not cover the complete relationship of all image features, but they are sufficient to make a final decision.

4 Results

The proposed algorithm has been tested on several acquired datasets. Each dataset consist of about 100 visual images and 1000 range scan lines acquired in 15 seconds while driving at a constant speed. In the experiments 10 objects of dimensions from $8.7 \times 11.0 \times 4.0$ cm to $47.8 \times 56.3 \times 12.2$ cm with different textures, colors and shapes (cubes and cylinders) were used. The objects were placed in various positions and orientations throughout a flat test road.

Fig. 3. Next three frames from visual camera no 11, 12, 13 with projected line (at the bottom) corresponding to the range scan line no 338, 376 and 403

As shown in Figure 3 the visual image contains much more information than one scan line from range scanner, however in the same time the scanner produces 1000 scan lines, when the camera produces only 10 images. Each visual image have been processed according to the section 3.1. The acquired image produces information about position of the object on the x-axis only, height and depth of the object can be measured using range information. The sample results of the most complicated objects configuration and position is presented on Figure 4, where the images after Otsu's tresholding, morphological operations and labeling process are shown. Visual image produces in most cases more obstacle candidates then it should be. Therefore, fusion of the information from the range scanner allows to the current correction and only a few obstacle candidates will be examined at the rules decision step. The Figure 5 shows the processed data from range scanner. First chart (from the left) shows data corresponding to the flat plane without any objects, second one shows maximum height of the nearest

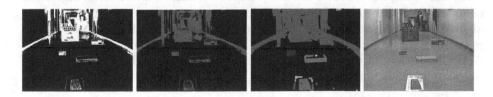

Fig. 4. The acquired scene after visual image processing, after adaptive tresholding, closing and filling the holes, labelling and marked nearest object (from the left)

object seen in the scene. On the last chart the edge of the detected object is presented.

After extracting and detection of the obstacle candidates the rules decision step have been performed. For each tested combination of the objects, the average effectiveness was calculated based on manual selection of the 1st and 2nd class for each object in the scene and simple comparing these nominal classes to the classes obtained by the algorithm. The average effectiveness for tested dataset was about 87%, when the fused algorithm was used. Using range scanner data only produce high effectiveness for low velocity of the vehicle only, thus fusion with visual images gattered from camera allow to increase the velocity. The proposed rules do not cover the complete relationship of all image features, in consequence may cause that some objects with complex texture cannot be categorized correctly.

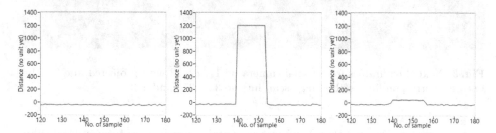

Fig. 5. Scan lines no 336, 337, 343 from the range scanner for the scene presented in figure 3

5   Conclusions

This paper has proposed a real time algorithm for an object extraction in real visual and range images. The proposed algorithm combine adaptive tresholding, morphological operations, filtering, range datasets plane fitting and rules based decision classifier. Some disadvantages have been identified, e.g. dynamic changes in the deflection of the vehicle in the z-axis during acquisition, which may results in removing some of the range scan lines, because differences were about 10 cm. Also the tiny objects can be removed from the range images after plane fitting, what affects directly the total efficiency. There were also limitations for algorithm complexity related with real time module. Therefore in the future some tracking algorithms will be used on the visual image object extraction, because in the proposed algorithm the frames from the video camera are analyzed independly. Also the method of object matching in visual images will be extended to the template matching methods.

Acknowledgment.   The work reported in this paper has been financed by the National Science Centre, decision no. DEC-2011/01/B/ST7/06027.

References

1. Krauze, P., Kasprzyk, J.: Neural network based control of magnetorhelogical quarter-car suspension model. In: 18th IEEE International Conference on Methods and Models in Automation and Robotics, MMAR 2013, Miedzyzdroje, Poland, August 26-29 (2013)
2. Yu, S.-J., Sukumar, S.R., Koschan, A.F., Page, D.L., Abidi, M.A.: 3D reconstruction of road surfaces using an integrated multi-sensory approach. Optics and Lasers in Engineering 45, 808–818 (2007)
3. Matsushita, Y., Miura, J.: On-line road boundary modeling with multiple sensory features, flexible road model, and particle filter. Robotics and Autonomous Systems 59, 274–284 (2011)
4. Gould, S., Baumstarck, P., Quigley, M.: Integrating visual and range data for robotic object detection. In: 18th IEEE International Conference on Methods and Models in Automation and Robotics, MMAR 2013, Miedzyzdroje, Poland, pp. 26–29 (August 2013)
5. Qu Zhonga, Q., Qingqinga, Z., Tengfeia, G.: Moving object tracking based on codebook and particle filter. Procedia Engineering 29, 174–178 (2012)
6. Kima, K., Lepetitb, V., Woo, W.: Real-time interactive modeling and scalable multiple object tracking for AR. Computers and Graphics 36, 945–954 (2012)
7. Premebida, C., Ludwig, O., Nunes, U.: Lidar and vision-based pedestrian detection system. J. Field. Rob. 26, 696–711 (2009)
8. Andreopoulosa, A., Tsotsos, J.K.: 50 Years of object recognition: Directions forward. Computer Vision and Image Understanding 117, 827–891 (2013)
9. Malagon-Borja, L., Fuentes, O.: Object detection using image reconstruction with PCA. Image and Vision Computing 27, 2–9 (2009)
10. Dalal, N., Triggs, B.: Histograms of oriented gradients for human detection. In: IEEE Conference on Computer Vision and Pattern Recognition, pp. 886–893 (2005)
11. Spinello, L., Luber, M., Arras, K.O.: Tracking people in 3d using a bottom-up top-down detector. In: International Conference of Robotics and Automation, pp. 1304–1310 (2011)
12. Das, D., Kobayashi, Y., Kuno, Y.: Multiple object detection and localization using range and color images for service robots. In: ICCAS-SICE International Joint Coference, pp. 3485–3489 (2009)
13. Rapus, M., Munder, S., Baratoff, G., Denzler, J.: Pedestrian recognition using combined low-resolution depth and intensity images. In: IEEE Intelligent Vehicles, pp. 632–636 (2008)
14. Labayrade, R., Royere, C., Gruyer, D., Aubert, D.: Cooperative fusion for multiobstacles detection with use of stereovision and laser scanner. Auton. Rob. 19, 117–140 (2005)

Noise Reduction in Thermal Images

Sebastian Budzan and Roman Wyżgolik

Silesian University of Technology, Institute of Automatic Control
Akademicka 16, 44-100 Gliwice, Poland
{Sebastian.Budzan,Roman.Wyzgolik}@polsl.pl

Abstract. In this cognitive work we focused on investigation of some filters used for image processing in application for noise removal in IR images. In IR imaging the choice of filter depends mainly on the purpose of the processing, e.g. detection of small objects in complex images, edge and contour detection or removal of non-uniformity of the detector array. The performance of the selected noise reduction filters was evaluated using PSNR and RMSE quality measure. The results are shown only for few images from our database which contain over 2000 of IR images.

1 Introduction

IR images (Infra Red images) are used nowadays in several fields of life and new applications are developed every year. Already now IR images are applied in areas like military, industry and medicine. One of the most useful industrial applications of IR imaging is NDT (Non Destructive Testing) of materials [1]. Another example of the use of IR images in medicine, e.g. the measurement of the human body temperature [2]. The importance of IR images applications makes the quality of these IR images critical. The foremost factor which influences the quality of IR images is presence of noise. It is common that the signal-to-noise ratio is low and the contrast of IR images is low as well. These two reasons make the processing of IR images difficult. The sources of a big level of noise are IR sensors and the interference of the signal processing circuit. Depending on the IR sensor technology it may be the problem connected with photoelectric conversion (in photodetectors) or temperature fluctuation noise (in thermal detectors) as well as the influence of manufacturing process [3]. The aforementioned problems cause IR detector non-uniformity, what is revealed by varied response of the pixels. This non-uniformity if not properly corrected, may be the main source of noise in IR images. Also the environmental conditions during the measurement has to be consdiered.

Through the years a lot of methods of noise removal have been examined. Some of them were adopted from traditional image processing, like for example the median filter; some others were converted to improve their influence on IR images, like the center-weighted median filter and methods related to fuzzy logic [4].

The classical methods of noise removal, for example the median filter, can be used in the case of IR images, but the results can be blurred. The reason is the fact that this type of filters has been dedicated to visual image processing, where

L.J. Chmielewski et al. (Eds.): ICCVG 2014, LNCS 8671, pp. 116–123, 2014.

the signal-to-noise ratio is much more bigger than the one for IR images. After using the median filter the important details and small elements can be lost. If the object of interest is very small, in the case of NDT, it can happen that the critical information can be incomprehensible. The reason of this situation is the fact that the median filter has influence on every pixel of the image both the disturbed and the undisturbed. Some of the solutions propose using the median filter combined with other methods to reduce noise and improve filtering. Examples of these other methods can be: statistical test, edge detection kernel or Boolean filter [5–7].

Currently, some successful applications of the wavelet transform can be used to remove noise from IR imaged. This family of methods consists filters with thresholding, shrinkage or even with multi-wavelet transform (for instance SMWT stationary multi-wavelet transform) [8].

During the last years, noise removal methods connected with fuzzy logic have been developed. Examples of this type of methods can be found in [9, 10]. These methods provided good results. The idea of using fuzzy logic is justified by the fact that whereas in classical Boolean algebra, the variables can only take a value true or false, in the case of fuzzy logic every variable can take a value between 0 (totally false) or 1 (totally true). With this approach every pixel of an IR image can be considered as clean in same level and disturbed in some other level in the same time. These values depend on the membership functions, which need to be previously defined. This solution can result much more efficient than the median or Gaussian filter.

2   Discussion

Recent articles on noise reduction in thermal images strongly points out the influence of impulse noise (salt & pepper) on the image quality [4, 11, 12]. In our opinion it is not common in raw thermal images, especially captured by the LWIR (Long Wave InfraRed) cameras with FPA (Focal Plane Array) uncooled microbolometers. However it could be the result of further image processing or transmission. Also authors in their publications overlook the information about the particular IR camera or detector type utilized in their investigations. This information can be very important and helpful. The noise in IR images is not only determined by the detector but also by background and emissivity fluctuations of the object. The real problem we met in raw thermal images is the specific disturbance which occurs in many images, appearing as vertical lines. This occurs particularly, but not only in low contrast images - with object temperature close to the background temperature.The examples of real low-contrast and good-contrast thermal images for the same object is presented in figure 1. Background temperature for both was about 20 °C.

2.1   Noise Source in IR Images

Most popular and cost effective IR cameras are the LWIR equipped with FPA uncooled microbolemeters. The infrared systems based on such the cameras have

Fig. 1. Poor contrast (left) and good contrast (right) IR images. Left: mug of water, temp. about 22 °C, right: mug of water, temp. about 35 °C.

noise of about 80 mK, while the objects of interest (the targets) are typically several Kelvin hotter than their background. In most cases, especially indoor, e.g. room, laboratory, it is achieved and acquired images are with low apparent noise. Outdoor, the IR images acquisition is influenced by environmental conditions and the object temperature can be drastically reduced by atmospheric loss. Especially at long distance, through dust, smoke, or fog. These conditions can greatly reduce the signal to noise ratio of an image.

The important issue is thermal stabilization of the IR camera. As mentioned in introduction, the main source of error in IR images is non-uniformity of FPA. The reason of non-uniformity is different response (gain and offset) of the FPA pixels, due to the fabrication process. Each camera is equipped with NUC (Non Uniformity Correction) procedure, which is automatically preformed during the camera work and is more frequent after the camera is powered on. The time required to stabilize the thermal properties of IR camera can differ according to the camera manufacturer. In our case, thermal images for the investigations presented in this work have been captured with a Wuhan-Guide TP8 IR camera. The camera is equipped with a 384 × 288 pixel uncooled FPA microbolometer. Its spectral range is 8 – 14 μm and thermal sensitivity (resolution) 0.08 °C. The time required for stable response of the camera is more than 75 minutes [2].

3   Noise Removal

A number of noise reduction methods have been proposed. As was mentioned in Introduction many of them were adapted to IR images ground. In conjunction with a number of possible noise sources in IR images, it is difficult to answer the question, what kind of noise is dominant in a particular image. The choice of filter depends mainly on the purpose of the processing, e.g. detection of small objects in complex images, edge and contour detection or removal of non-uniformity of the detector array. After literature survey we choose four representational noise reduction filters in our opinion, i.e. median, fuzzy, density estimation and wavelet transform filters. In figure 2 three examples are shown. First, the sky with five pigeons and pieces of roof, on the second the working bearing is shown and on the last image the plate after NDT (Non-Destructive Testing) procedure with a few circular defects has been presented. The last image shown also the vertical lines of varying widths, which disturbs the image.

Fig. 2. Sample IR images with different type of image details

Median filter reduce the noise from images based on an assumption that signal pixels have high correspondence with their neighbor pixels inside a small area, known as filtering window. Using neighbor information will cause the loss of some thin lines and textures. Small targets and objects often occupy only a few pixels in the IR image, also are surrounded by the pixels with high gradient, thus during filtering process many of them can be replaced by the median pixel and consequently removed from the IR image.

Statistical pattern recognition another reliable technique for noise reduction. It requires the estimation of the probability density function of the data samples [13]. Nonparametric density estimation is based on placing a kernel function on every sample value and on the summation of the values of all kernel function values at each point in the sample space [14]. Using the Gaussian kernel function, the density estimate of the unknown probability density function at x is obtained as a sum of kernel functions placed at each sample x_i

$$p_N(x,h) = \frac{1}{N(h\sqrt{2\pi})^m} \sum_{i=1}^{N} exp(-\frac{\|x - x_i\|^2}{2h^2})$$ (1)

where h is the smoothing parameter (2), $m = 1$, N is a number of pixels in the filtering window.

$$h = 1.06N^{-\frac{1}{5}}\hat{\sigma}$$ (2)

where $\hat{\sigma}$ denotes the approximation of the standard deviation of the samples.

Another possibility is to reduce noise using fuzzy filters. Generally, it processes human knowledge in the absolute values to fuzzy range. In fuzzy filters the similarity degree is calculated with its neighbours to know the similarity level between them. Next, these absolute values are converted to fuzzy values using similarity level, i.e. Small and Large degree of similarity. This similarity level is also known as membership function.

Wavelets are very popular tool for image denoising, because additive noise can be removed while preserving important features of the image. In wavelet denoising the most important is proper thresholding of the coefficients. The idea of thresholding was shown by Donoho and Johnstone [15, 16]. In discrete wavelet analysis image is decomposed into it's approximation and details which represent the low and high-frequency components in the image respectively. High-frequency components contain noise which is reduced through thresholding algorithm. The decomposition is done at few levels using a specific low-pass and high-pass filters. Many publications on wavelets describe this procedure, so we will not describe it here in details. The important is, that after decomposition and wavelet coefficient thresholding, the image is reconstructed with definitely lower level of noise. In this work, we used the Haar wavelet, 4-levels of decomposition, minimax thresholding rule and hard thresholding.

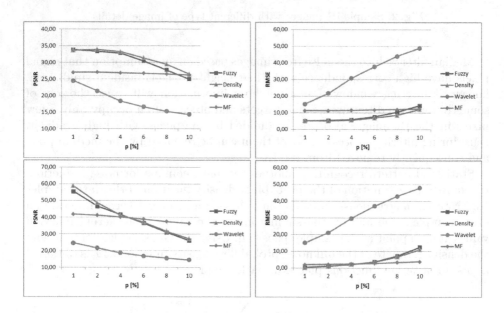

Fig. 3. Results of PSNR and RMSE calculation for small objects (top) and NDT testing (bottom) IR images

The performance of the selected noise reduction filters was evaluated using PSNR and RMSE quality measure. The selected IR images shows most commonly situations during IR images acquiring. First, the impulsive noise reduction filters have been evaluated. The bandwidth for the range of used probabilities $p = 0.01 - 0.1$. In figure 3 the PSNR and RMSE results are shown. Top charts shows results for IR image with five pigeons. Best results we get for Density Estimation filter, especially at lowest noise probability, which is very close to real IR image. Wavelet transform produces poor results, due to poor removal of impulsive noise, but preserves edges of the objects. Figure 4 present IR images

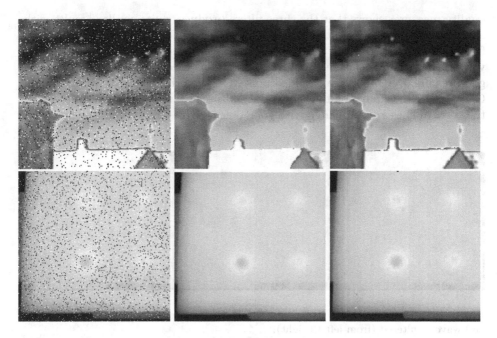

Fig. 4. Results of IR images denoising for noise density $p = 0.04$, noised image, MF filtered, density estimation (from left to right)

after MF and Density Estimation filtering. MF removes the thin lines and small objects of interest and blurs the details at all noise densities. Fuzzy and Density Estimation filters produces similar results and preserves small objects in the image. Small objects e.g. each pigeon, in the IR images can be treated as noise pixels. However, the bottom image after Density Estimation filtering shows poor removal of the vertical lines, which means that these real disturbances are not similar to the impulsive noise. In figure 5 PSNR and RMSE performance for NDT plate are shown. In this experiment IR image was corrupted by the Gaussian noise with variable standard deviation in range 1–10%. Values of the

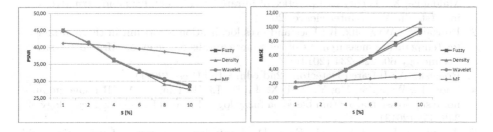

Fig. 5. Results of PSNR (left) and RMSE (right) depending on the gaussian noise standard deviation for NDT plate IR image

quality measures shows that the three filters produces quite similar results with an indication of wavelet filter. The image has a large uniform region, small defects and vertical lines. If we take into consideration only PSNR and RMSE values, then the conclusion should be ambiguous, because MF filter produces good results over the range of added noise. On the other hand, if we take small Gaussian noise value, then the three others filters give us excellent results, where the vertical lines are eliminated with good defects edges preserving (see figure 6).

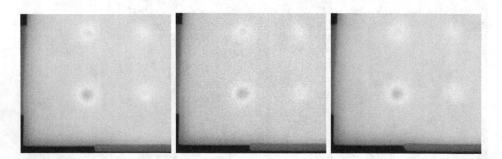

Fig. 6. Results of NDT plate IR images. Original, corrupted by the 4% gaussian noise and wavelet filtered (from left to right).

4   Conclusions

In this paper problem of IR images denoising has been presented. The noise is caused mostly by the IR sensors and influence of the atmosphere. The small objects, which occupy maximum several pixels can be processed as the noise. Results show, that the proposed filters, excluding MF filter can be used not only as classical noise reduction filters, but also as IR images quality enhancement methods. Performed experiments show that noise reduction filters can successfully be applied to the real acquired IR images.

References

1. Maldague, X.: Theory and practice of infrared technology for nondestructive testing, 1st edn. Wiley-Interscience (2001)
2. Budzan, S., Wyżgolik, R.: Face and eyes localization algorithm in thermal images for temperature measurement of the inner canthus of the eyes. Infrared Physics & Technology 60, 225–234 (2013)
3. Rogalski, A.: Infrared Detectors, 2nd edn. CRC Press (2011)
4. Zhou, B., Wang, S., Ma, Y., Mei, X., Li, B., Li, H., Fan, F.: An IR image impulse noise suppression algorithm based on fuzzy logic. Infrared Physics & Technology 60, 346–358 (2013)
5. Aizenberg, I., Butakoff, C., Paliy, D.: Impulsive noise removal using threshold Boolean filtering based on the impulse detecting functions. IEEE Signal Process. Lett. 12(1), 63–66 (2005)

6. Garnett, R., Huegerich, T., Chui, C., He, W.: A universal noise removal algorithm with an impulse detector. IEEE Trans. Image Process. 14(11), 1747–1754 (2005)
7. Pok, G., Liu, Y., Nair, A.S.: Selective removal of impulse noise based on homogeneity level information. IEEE Trans. Image Process. 12(1), 85–92 (2003)
8. Islam, S.M.R., Huang, H., Liao, M., Srinath, N.K.: Image denoising based on wavelet for IR images corrupted by Gaussian, Poisson & Impulse noise. Internationa Jour. of Comp. Scie. and Net. Secur. 6, 59–70 (2013)
9. Schulte, S., De Witte, V., Nachtegael, M., Vand der Weken, D., Kerre, E.E.: Fuzzy random impulse noise reduction method. Fuzzy Set Syst. 158, 270–283 (2007)
10. Nair, M., Raju, G.: A new fuzzy-based decision algorithm for high-density impulse noise removal. Signal, Image and Video Process. 6, 579–595 (2012)
11. Lin, C.L., Kuo, C.W., Lai, C.C., Tsai, M.D., Chang, Y.C., Cheng, H.: A novel approach to fast noise reduction of IR image. Infrared Physics & Technology 54, 1–9 (2011)
12. Lin, C.L.: An approach to improve the quality of IR images of vein-patterns. Sensors 11, 11447–11463 (2011)
13. Silverman, B.W.: Density Estimation for Statistics and Data Analysis. Chapman and Hall, London (1986)
14. Smolka, B., Lukac, R.: Nonparametric Impulsive Noise Removal. In: Campilho, A.C., Kamel, M.S. (eds.) ICIAR 2004. LNCS, vol. 3211, pp. 155–162. Springer, Heidelberg (2004)
15. Donoho, D.L.: De-noising by soft-thresholding. IEEE Trans. on Infor. Theory 41(3), 613–627 (1995)
16. Donoho, D.L., Johnstone, I.M.: Minimax Estimation via Wavelet Shrinkage. The Annals of Statistics 26(3), 879–921 (1998)

Implementation of Advanced Foreground Segmentation Algorithms GMM, ViBE and PBAS in FPGA and GPU – A Comparison

Bartłomiej Bulat, Tomasz Kryjak, and Marek Gorgon

AGH University of Science and Technology
Al. Mickiewicza 30, 30-059, Kraków, Poland
bartek.bulat@gmail.com, {kryjak,mago}@agh.edu.pl

Abstract. The article presents the results of implementing advanced foreground object segmentation algorithms: GMM (Gaussian Mixture Model), ViBE (Visual Background Extractor) and PBAS (Pixel-Based Adaptive Segmenter) on different hardware platforms: CPU, GPU and FPGA. The influence of the architecture on the segmentation accuracy and feasibility to perform real-time video stream processing was analysed. Also the limitations resulting from the specific features of GPU and FPGA were pointed out. Furthermore, the possible use of different platforms in advanced vision systems was discussed.

Keywords: image processing, image analysis, foregorund object segmentation, GMM, ViBE, PBAS, FPGA, GPU.

1 Introduction

Foreground object segmentation is a very important stage in digital video stream processing and analysis systems. It is based on determining and thresholding the differential image between the current frame and the background model. The term background model refers to a representation of the "empty scene" (i.e. without objects of interest). This approach is usually referred to as background subtraction and modelling. A comprehensive review of the most common algorithms is presented in [2].

The most popular method seems to be GMM (Gaussian Mixture Model), which was proposed in 1999 by Stauffer and Grimson [8]. It is constantly developed, modified and improved, and its implementations are available in OpenCV image processing library and Matlab software.

Interesting are also two fairly new proposals ViBE [1] and PBAS [5]. They are based on a similar principle and allow to obtain good segmentation results – according to the *changedetection.net 2012* ranking [4][1]. These three methods will be discussed in this paper.

It is worth to consider, whether working on acceleration of foreground objects segmentation is justified. It should be emphasised that the segmentation is

---

[1] http://www.changedetection.net/

L.J. Chmielewski et al. (Eds.): ICCVG 2014, LNCS 8671, pp. 124–131, 2014.
© Springer International Publishing Switzerland 2014

only one of many elements, beside image pre-processing, connected component labelling, feature extraction, tracking and classification. While properly implemented, a segmentation method can operate in real-time for moderate resolutions on a standard PC. However, the whole vision system can not, particularly for higher resolutions. Thus, the acceleration of some computations in a GPU or FPGA allows to "relive" the CPU and the obtained computing power can be used in other stages of the vision system – usually recognition and classification.

In Section 2 the methods GMM, ViBE and PBAS are very briefly discussed. In Section 3 the used architectures are described. Then, in Section 4 the obtained results are presented and analysed. The article ends with a summary.

2   The Analysed Foreground Segmentation Methods

2.1   GMM

There are two different names of the algorithm [8] used in the literature: GMM (Gaussian Mixture Model) and MOG (Mixture of Gaussians). The background model for a given pixel consists of k Gaussian distributions described by triples: $(\omega_n, \mu_n, \Sigma_n)$, where ω_n – weight, μ_n – average value, Σ_n covariance matrix of the colour components (RGB model). The total number of distributions usually varies between 3-5.

Updating the model requires sorting the distributions, calculating the distances between distributions and the current pixel and an optional update of the distributions parameters. It is worth noting that the computations are independent for each pixel and no neighbourhood operations are involved.

The method was implemented in FPGA several times. In this paper, the results presented in the work [3] are used for comparison. GPU realisations are also described in the literature. In [9] several optimizations were discussed: the use of pinned memory, combining data transfers (memory coalescing), a special organization of the data structure and asynchronous kernels. The modifications made it possible to process more than 30 frames per second, even for HD resolution.

2.2   ViBE

The foreground object segmentation algorithm ViBE (Visual Background Extractor) was proposed by O. Barnich and M. Van Droogenbroeck in 2009 [1]. The background model in ViBE consists of a set of $N = 20$ observed pixel values. The classification is based on calculating the distance between the current pixel and all samples from the model. If at least $\#_{min} = 2$ distances are smaller than a given threshold the pixel is regarded as background. The model is updated by replacing randomly selected samples with the current pixel. Also a neighbourhood update procedure is proposed – a randomly selected sample from a random model in the 3×3 context is updated. To the best knowledge of the authors, a GPU implementation of ViBE has not been described. An FPGA implementation of this algorithm was presented in [7].

2.3 PBAS

The PBAS method [5] is an extension of the approach used in ViBE. Two additional parameters R and T were added to the algorithm. The first defines the threshold for the distance between the current pixel and samples from the model. In contrast to the ViBE, it is determined for each pixel independently. The second parameter specifies the probability of the model update. Also, information about edges was added to the background model. All modifications allowed to obtain slightly better segmentation results than ViBE. On the other hand, the background model of PBAS is larger than ViBE, as additional parameters need to be stored. To the best knowledge of the authors, the GPU implementation of PBAS has not been described. An FPGA implementation of this algorithm was presented in [6].

3 The Used Hardware Platforms

The methods described in Section 2 have been implemented on three platforms: CPU, GPU and FPGA.

General purpose processors are, and will remain for a long time, the most popular platform of implementation for all kinds of algorithms, including video processing. This is due to their vast availability and dissemination of the required programming skills. They are also very versatile, allowing to implement all kinds of algorithms from simple filtering, to machine learning methods. Unfortunately, in image processing tasks CPUs prove to be quite slow, as they are more suitable to perform complex instructions on small or medium datasets, but not simple instructions on huge amounts of data.

Graphic processing units have become a very popular platform for the realisation of parallel computing in recent years, mainly due to changes in architecture (unified shader) and development of CUDA and OpenCL languages. They allow to implement lots of image processing operations: simple filtration and morphological processing, Hough transform, optical flow, analysis and segmentation of MRI images and foreground objects segmentation. It should be noted, however, that the GPU architecture imposes certain restrictions on the implemented algorithms. Firstly, there are no jump instructions. Another problem is the memory model, which makes it difficult to perform operations on shared resources (update necessary in ViBE and PBAS methods). The evaluated algorithms were described in the OpenCL language, which is a cross-platform standard for parallel programming. This allowed to run them on both: multi-core CPU and GPU.

FPGAs are a proven platform for parallel computing, including image processing and analysis. The huge number of logical resources (LUT elements, flip-flops), multipliers and block RAMs allows for the implementation of any type of parallelism (according to Flynn's classification). An important feature of FPGAs is the ability to work in embedded devices – e.g. smart cameras, where image processing and analysis takes place immediately after the acquisition. Furthermore, compared to CPU or GPU, they are characterized by a relatively low energy consumption.

4   The Obtained Results

4.1   Hardware Platforms

In the experiments the following platforms were used:

- a PC (laptop) with Intel®Core™ i7-3632QM (4-cores, 64-bit, nominal freq. 2.2 GHz, maximal 3.2 GHz) and NVIDIA GeForce GT 645M GPU (384 CUDA cores, freq. 710 MHz, PCI-E 3.0),
- ML 605 evaluation board with Virtex 6 FPGA device (XC6VLX240T) from Xilinx (ViBE implementation and in-circuit verification),
- VC 707 evaluation board with Virtex 7 FPGA device (XC7VX485T) from Xilinx (PBAS implementation and in-circuit verification).

4.2   The Impact of Hardware Architecture on Accuracy

The implementation of an algorithm on a platform different than CPU usually requires some modifications. A good example are fixed-point calculations on FPGA devices. For the GMM method realized in OpenCL no changes were required and in the FPGA implementation fixed-point representation was used [3].

However, when implementing ViBE and PBAS on GPU, the neighbourhood update procedure proved to be problematic. The use of shared memory calculations (atomic operations) resulted in poor performance. It was decided, therefore, to modify the algorithm so that the accessing of neighbouring pixels was not required, while maintaining the update functionality. The step, in which for every pixel considered as background a randomly chosen adjacent model was updated, was replaced by the following mechanism. If in the neighbourhood of the considered pixel, at least one pixel labelled as background existed, than a randomly selected sample from the model was replaced by an adjacent value (selected from those regarded as background). This process occurred with a random probability. In addition, it was decided to use a fixed array of pre-generated pseudo-random numbers instead of their runtime generation.

The CIE Lab colourspace was used in the FPGA implementation of the ViBE method [7]. The number of samples in the model was reduced from 35 (CPU, GPU) do 19 (FPGA) due to hardware limitations (bandwidth to external RAM, in which the background model was stored) in the case of PBAS. Also the edges where not used in the model [6]. For both methods, all calculations were performed on fixed-point numbers.

The *changedetection.net 2012* dataset [4] was used to evaluate the impact of the proposed modifications. The obtained foreground masks were compared with manually annotated groundtruths and the parameters TP, TN, FP, FN were calculated. Then a number of common factors: Re (Recall), Sp (Specifity), FPR (False Positive Rate), FNR (False Negative Rate), PWC (Percent Wrong Clasiffication), F (F-measure), Pr (Precision) was computed. A detailed description of the methodology can be found in [6]. As post-processing median filtering

Table 1. Segmentation quality evaluation for different implementations of GMM, ViBE and PBAS methods

	Re	Sp	FPR	FNR	PWC	F	Pr
GMM	0.669	0.987	0.013	0.023	3.286	0.625	0.697
GMM$_{OpenCL}$	0.670	0.987	0.013	0.023	3.279	0.626	0.698
PBAS	0.837	0.922	0.018	0.108	1.994	0.637	0.799
PBAS$_{OpenCL}$	0.816	0.957	0.018	0.118	2.918	0.637	0.793
PBAS$_{FPGA}$	0.797	0.972	0.028	0.202	3.435	0.681	0.699
ViBE	0.723	0.969	0.031	0.012	3.846	0.677	0.761
ViBE$_{OpenCL}$	0.723	0.923	0.037	0.007	3.669	0.572	0.721
ViBE$_{FPGA}$	0.640	0.985	0.015	0.360	3.066	0.680	0.821

with 5×5 window size was used in all cases. The results are summarized in Table 1. The numbers for the GMM$_{FPGA}$ version are not presented, as the authors of paper [3] did not use this dataset for evaluation.

An analysis of the results reveals that modifications related to hardware platform do not significantly affect the segmentation results. In case of ViBE and PBAS, there is a slight deterioration of the parameters associated with the fixed-point representation and limited numbers of samples (PBAS) in the FPGA version.

4.3   Comments Regarding the Implementations

During the implementation of the considered algorithms on the GPU, it turned out that comparing background variants (samples) with the current pixel is quite challenging. Since there is no support for the jump instruction, it is necessary to perform all comparisons (eventually substituted by an empty instruction – *nop*). Therefore, it is impossible to reduce the complexity by dynamically assigning the number of variants in case of the GMM method. The calculations will always be performed for the maximum number of variants ($K = 4$ in the experiments). However, the value is rather small and therefore the adverse effect is minimal.

A similar problem occurs in the case of the ViBE and PBAS methods. The number of variants (samples) is, however, much higher (20 and 35) and the effect is much more apparent. It is worth noting that such problems do not occur in the case of the CPU and FPGA implementations. In the first case, the jump instruction is supported, and in the second the architecture allows to perform all comparisons in parallel.

In the OpenCL language the access to individual memory bytes is slower than to groups of 4, 8 or 16 blocks. One possible solution is to convert the typical RGB format (3 bytes) to $ORGB$ (4 bytes). This results in acceleration, but in the case of processing images from a camera an additional operation is required.

4.4   The Possibility of Real-Time Image Processing

In case of most video systems, real-time processing is very important. Good examples are surveillance of public space or traffic applications. The system operates in real-time when the sequence is processed without any pixel or frame dropping for a given image resolution and number of frames per second (*fps*). Most of contemporary cameras registers 25(30) or 50(60) fps.[2] In this study it was assumed that 25 *fps* is the reference value. The *fps* values for the analysed algorithms and implementations are summarized in Table 2.

Table 2. The number of frames that can be processed by different implementations in one second. 720 HD – resolution 1280×720, 1080 HD – resolution 1920×1080.

	CPU	CPU$_{OpenCL}$	GPU$_{OpenCL}$	FPGA
GMM 720 HD	10	13	63	205
GMM 1080 HD	5	6	27	91
ViBE 720 HD	2	7	3	151
ViBE 1080 HD	1	3	2	67
PBAS 720 HD	2	4	3	125
PBAS 1080 HD	1	2	-	55

The values for all methods in the column FPGA are estimations and were determined using the maximum clock frequency for the designed modules. In case of a working system, a cooperation with external RAM is required (storing the background model). This is often the "bottleneck" of the vision system. FPGA evaluation boards ML605 and VC707 available to the authors allowed to verify the algorithms ViBE for a video stream 640×480 @ 60 *fps* and PBAS for 720×576 @ 50 *fps*. In the first case the resource usage was: flip-flops 12571 (3%)[3], LUT6 9278 (6%), DSP48 3 (1%), BRAM_18 172 20% and in the second: flip-flops 39108 (6%), LUT6 36060 (11%), DSP48 12 (1%), BRAM_18 3 (1%), BRAM_36 248 (24%). The GMM method was verified on a Virtex 4 based platform for 1280×720 @ 20 *fps* video stream by the authors of paper [3]. The resource usage for the algorithm only (no video processing system with external RAM): flip-flops 363 (0.3%), LUT 788 (2%), DSP48 3 (1%), BRAM_18 0 (0%). On the GPU test platform, the PBAS GPU$_{OpenCL}$ version for 1080 HD resolution could not be run due to lack of available memory. It should be pointed out that for FPGA, the number of processed frames per second is independent of the image content and other conditions. For other platforms the *fps* value is an average, which depends on the image content as well as operation of the computer system (e.g. operating system).

Analysis of the results allows to point out a difference between GMM and ViBE/PBAS methods. The first is ideally suited for GPU acceleration ($\times 6$ speedup). The GPU implementation of methods with neighbourhood operations and

---

[2] The number is brackets refer to US video standards.

[3] % of available resources.

large number of samples in the model did not result in any acceleration. It seems that the main issue is the lack of the jump instruction. A further proof is the comparison of the CPU_{OpenCL} and GPU_{OpenCL} versions. The OpenCL implementation evaluated on a CPU turned out to be more efficient for ViBE and PBAS.

FPGA devices provide a wide opportunity to implement parallel computations. However, the bottleneck in this case is the access to external RAM memory resources. Another drawback is also the quite long development time in hardware description languages (i.e. Verilog).

4.5   The Concept of Using GPU and FPGA in a Vision System

The characteristic features of GPU and FPGA devices determine the way how they can be used in a vision system. In the first case, a close cooperation with the CPU within the computer system is necessary. Thus, the GPU could be an accelerator for certain computing tasks such as foreground segmentation.

The advantages of this solution are: the availability of the equipment and its low price, relative ease of programming and high parallel computing performance. In contrast, the main disadvantage is the need to implement data exchange between CPU and GPU. This is especially important in video processing, where the data stream is quite large. The measured transfer time ranges from 4% to 18% of the total computing time for GMM method and is less than 4% for ViBE and PBAS. In addition, the computer system must be equipped with an element responsible for the image acquisition. This could be, for example, a HDMI frame-grabber or network card for IP cameras.

The FPGA cooperating with an external RAM memory module can work independently of a processor system (standalone). Thus, in addition to the use as an accelerator (e.g. FPGA board with PCI-E communication), it can be used in a smart camera and in a configurable frame-grabber (HDMI or Ethernet). Also, the often required video stream decompression (H.264, MJPEG) could also be implemented in FPGA. This approach allows to reduce the required data transfers between different components of the system.

5   Conclusions

The article presents a comparison of three advanced foreground objects segmentation methods: GMM, ViBE and PBAS implemented on CPU, GPU and FPGA. It is shown that the implementation on GPU or FPGA has a very little impact on the segmentation quality, even if some modifications to algorithm were required. The analysis of the calculated *fps* values indicates that the GMM method is better suited for implementation in GPU than ViBE or PBAS. This is due to the relatively small number of distributions (variants) in the model ($K = 4$) and the independent processing of each pixel. The implementation of all methods is possible in FPGA and in all cases allows to obtain a significant acceleration. Here, the main limitation is the fast and wide access to external

RAM resources. FPGAs are more versatile because they can be used as an accelerator, part of smart-camera or an advanced frame-grabber. Also they are more energy efficient. However, they are not so widely available as GPUs and the process of implementation in hardware description language is usually quite time-consuming. In conclusion, before choosing a particular hardware platform to accelerate a segmentation algorithm the following issues should be considered: the computations present in the algorithm (especially involving neighbourhood operations) and the number of variants in the model as well as the architecture of the vision system.

Acknowledgments. The work presented in this paper was supported by AGH Univeristy of Science and Technology project number 11.11.120.612.

References

1. Barnich, O., Van Droogenbroeck, M.: ViBE: A Universal Background Subtraction Algorithm for Video Sequences. IEEE Transactions on Image Processing 20(6), 1709–1724 (2011)
2. Bouwmans, T., Porikli, F., Horferlin, B., Vacavant, A.: Handbook on: Background Modeling and Foreground Detection for Video Surveillance: Traditional and Recent Approaches, Implementations, Benchmarking and Evaluation. Taylor and Francis Group (2014)
3. Genovese, M., Napoli, E.: ASIC and FPGA Implementation of the Gaussian Mixture Model Algorithm for Real-Time Segmentation of High Definition Video. IEEE Transactions on Very Large Scale Integration (VLSI) Systems 22(3), 537–547 (2014)
4. Goyette, N., Jodoin, P., Porikli, F., Konrad, J., Ishwar, P.: Changedetection.net: A new change detection benchmark dataset. In: IEEE Computer Society Conference on Computer Vision and Pattern Recognition Workshops (CVPRW), pp. 1–8 (2012)
5. Hofmann, M., Tiefenbacher, P., Rigoll, G.: Background segmentation with feedback: The Pixel-Based Adaptive Segmenter. In: IEEE Computer Society Conference on Computer Vision and Pattern Recognition Workshops (CVPRW), pp. 38–43 (2012)
6. Kryjak, T., Komorkiewicz, M., Gorgon, M.: Hardware implementation of the PBAS foreground detection method in FPGA. In: Proceedings of the 20th International Conference Mixed Design of Integrated Circuits and Systems (MIXDES), pp. 591–596 (2013)
7. Kryjak, T., Gorgon, M.: Real-time implementation of the ViBE foreground object segmentation algorithm. In: Federated Conference on Computer Science and Information Systems (FedCSIS), pp. 479–484 (2013)
8. Stauffer, C., Grimson, W.E.L.: Adaptive background mixture models for real-time tracking. In: IEEE Computer Society Conference on Computer Vision and Pattern Recognition, vol. 2, pp. xxiii+637+663 (1999)
9. Pham, V., Vo, P., Hung, V.T., Bac, L.H.: GPU Implementation of Extended Gaussian Mixture Model for Background Subtraction. In: IEEE RIVF International Conference on Computing and Communication Technologies, Research, Innovation, and Vision for the Future (RIVF), pp. 1–4 (2010)

A Multi-stage Image Segmentation Framework for Human Detection in Mid Wave Infra-Red (MWIR) Imagery

Ravi Shankar Chekuri[1] and Meghavi Prashnani[2]

[1] IIT Kharagpur, Kharagpur, India
chekurirs@gmail.com
[2] School of Electronics, DAVV, Indore MP, India
meghavi300388@gmail.com

Abstract. Detecting Human objects in Thermal imagery is commonly realized in two steps. The first step is segmentation; it identifies Region of Interest (ROI) in a given image that likely to contain a human target. The second step is Classification; the identified ROI is verified for human objects. Accurate segmentation step can significantly boost classification accuracy. We present a multi-stage image segmentation framework for surveillance applications, to detect human targets present at widely varying ranges in thermal imagery. A temporal median filter is utilized to estimate the background frame from previously sampled frames. Using the estimated background image, clutters are suppressed with K-L Transformation. A box filter is applied on clutter suppressed images for identifying the Region of Interest (ROI) objects. Finally the identified ROIs are subjected to two level segmentation process for accurately extracting the silhouette.

The performance of proposed method is analysed on three thermal Infra-red video sequences containing targets in the range of 500m, 1 km and 1.5 km. This way of demonstrating performance with range is first of its kind in human target detection literature. Experimental results demonstrate that proposed segmentation approach is able to extract human silhouette without loss of significant shape information even for targets at far ranges and with background occlusions.

1   Introduction

Video surveillance is getting more and more importance nowadays. The aim of video-based surveillance is usually to identify and monitor humans. In video-based surveillance systems, human detection is a crucial step. Most existing human activity detection approaches detect human motion in visible spectrum. Sensors operating in the visible spectrum are limited mainly by lighting conditions and presence of shadows. These systems do not work under low light conditions such as night environments without any light.

In contrast to regular camera which records reflected visible light, an Infra-red (IR) camera records electromagnetic radiation emitted by objects in scene as a

L.J. Chmielewski et al. (Eds.): ICCVG 2014, LNCS 8671, pp. 132–144, 2014.
© Springer International Publishing Switzerland 2014

thermal image whose pixel values represent temperature. In a thermal image that consists of humans in a scene, human silhouettes can be easily extracted from the background regardless of lighting conditions and colours of the human surfaces and backgrounds, because the temperatures of human body and background are different in most situations[1]. However the thermal imagery has its own challenges such as low resolution and the "halo effect "that appears around very hot or cold objects [2].

A review of literature on human detection problem indicates that various proposed solutions have been based on the shape, appearance and motion features. These approaches have been demonstrated on colour imagery successfully. However, images sampled from different sensors generally have different characteristics due to the image acquisition process of sensors. Thermal Infra-red imagery has been widely used in surveillance environments, especially for human detection. Researchers proposed and demonstrated the performance of various approaches for human detection in thermal imagery. The approaches are mainly based on thermal contrast and motion [1], thermal image analysis [3], Kinematic models [4], fusion of colour and Infra-red video [5], image registration techniques [6], Identifying hot regions [7] [8], Histograms [9], Background modelling [10], [11], [12].

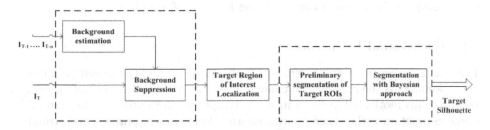

Fig. 1. Proposed multi stage Image segmentation scheme for Human activity detection

We propose an approach for detection of moving human targets from Infra-red imagery based on multi stage segmentation framework. As illustrated in Fig.1 . It consists of three main stages. In the first stage background clutter are subtracted to highlight targets. Next a spatial box filter [13] is applied to localize the target ROI. Then, the target ROI is subjected to a two level segmentation process for accurately extracting the target silhouette.

Our approach is mainly based on motion of the object. The proposed approach adopts a step by step mechanism: first it identifies a ROI from background suppressed image, and then it identifies an object pixel with in ROI. The approach does not use any shape information, and thus it can be used as preprocessing stage before recognition or track tasks. In the Experiments section, the proposed approach is evaluated across three thermal outdoor video sequences, and compared quantitatively with two other Classical approaches. Probability of Detection (P_d) and False targets per frame (FTPF) measures are used for quantifying the performance of proposed approach.

Our main contributions include the following:

1. Design of a multi-stage segmentation framework for human detection in thermal imagery.
2. Propose a background clutter suppression technique based on K-L Transform.
3. Propose a two level segmentation process for extracting target pixels with in ROI

The remainder of paper is organized as follows: Section 2, describes an algorithm for background suppression based on K-L transformation. In Section 3, we describe target ROI extraction based on box filter. Then Section 4, shows how to segment background and target pixels in the given ROI. The experimental evaluation of the approach is presented in Section 5. Finally Section 6, presents conclusion and future work.

2 Background Suppression

Our Proposed background suppression method has two stages; the first stage is estimating the background frame using temporal median filter. Second stage is suppressing the background clutters using K-L transformation.

2.1 Background Estimation

The image frames in video surveillance applications are highly correlated in temporal domain, as the surveillance camera is staring always at same boring background. This motivated authors in using temporal information for background frame estimation rather than spatial information. In our approach to estimate background for image frame I_T which is acquired at time instant 'T', previous 'K' number of frames is considered. i.e. $I_{T-1}......I_{T-K}$ frames. The background is estimated using (1).

$$I_{bg}(m,n) = Median[I_{T-i}(m,n) \,|i=1...K]$$ (1)

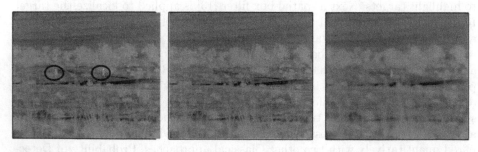

Fig. 2. (a) (b) (c) Visual demonstration of background estimation result using proposed approach in compared to classical median filter

The parameter 'K' is chosen according to the motion of object. The high 'K' can give better estimate of the background. An Example of the background frame extracted by this process is presented in Fig. 2. Fig. 2(a) presents the original frame, Fig. 2(b) presents estimated background frame with proposed approach. For comparison Fig.2(c) give the background frame extracted using classical spatial median filter. Results depicts that proposed method can extract the background effectively.

2.2   Background Suppression Using K-L Transform

In second stage background content is suppressed with the help of estimated background frame. Background content in current frame (I_T) is suppressed by eliminating the correlating information between current frame (I_T) and estimated background frame (I_{bg}). Once correlating information is eliminated the information left out in current frame is minor uncorrelated information. The left out uncorrelated information in residual background suppressed frame can be due to foreground objects introduced, or due to illumination changes or due to sensor noise. In our work the correlating information between current frame and background frame is identified using K-L Transform [15]. K-L transform identifies the new linear subspace for the data set to decorrelate the data. The basis vectors of new sub space define the linear transformation of data. The basis vectors of K-L transform are Eigenvectors of the data covariance matrix. The projection of the data along Eigenvector corresponding to smallest Eigenvalue value identifies the uncorrelated information in the data matrix.

$$C = \frac{1}{M * N} \sum_{m=1}^{M} \sum_{n=1}^{N} (X(m, n) - \overline{X})(X(m, n) - \overline{X})^T \tag{2}$$

$$Y_i = v_i^T X, \quad i = 1, 2..... \tag{3}$$

The background frame (I_{bg}), and current frame (I_T) are transformed to two row vectors, and constitute data matrix $X = [I_{bg}; I_T]$. $\overline{X}$ denotes mean; v_i denotes the Eigen vector; Y_i (i=1,2) denotes the two components of data matrix along the two Eigenvectors of the covariance matrix C; M, N denotes the size of data matrix. An example of background suppressed frame obtained with proposed approach is presented in Fig. 3. Notice the highlighted foreground objects with background suppression.

3   Target ROI Extraction

The background suppressed image contains residual information left out due to foreground objects, illumination changes or due to any moving background like (trees, plants). It is shown in Fig.3(c) the residual image (Background suppressed image) contains foreground objects and moving plants. In our work from the background suppressed images the target ROI is extracted using the double

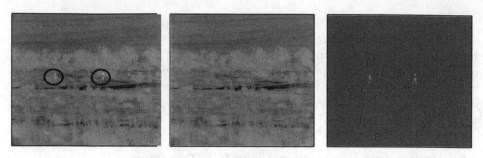

Fig. 3. (a) (b) (c) Background suppression result: (a) Current frame (b) Estimated Background frame (c) Residual image after background subtraction

window box filter [13]. The geometry is generally in the form of hypothesized target region and its immediate neighbourhood. The Rectangular inner window is set slightly higher than the target size. The rectangular outer window is set to cover the neighbourhood area nearly equal to target area. When the rectangular box filter is centred on target, the target region is covered by the inner window and neighbourhood background pixels are covered by the area between inner and outer window. To identify the target ROI, a T-test proposed by [13] is used, with following assumptions.

1. The data set consists of two independent samples one of size n_1 from the inner window and other of size n_2 from outer window.
2. Both inner window and outer window pixels fit a normal distribution. The T-statistic considered in our work is:

$$T = \overline{D}_1 - \overline{D}_2 \tag{4}$$

Where $\overline{D}_1$ and $\overline{D}_2$ are the mean of the two data samples.

$$\overline{D}_1 = \frac{1}{n_1} \sum_{i=1}^{n_1} d_{1i} \tag{5}$$

$$\overline{D}_2 = \frac{1}{n_1} \sum_{i=1}^{n_1} d_{2i} \tag{6}$$

The pixels that resulted high T-statistic measure can contain targets with high probability. An example result of identified ROI, from image presented in Fig.3(c) is shown in Fig.4.

4   Target Silhouette Extraction

As Fig. 4 show, the identified ROIs are not representing shapes of the targets accurately. The extracted ROI is bigger than target region. In this stage, in order to obtain the target silhouette effectively, a two level segmentation approach is

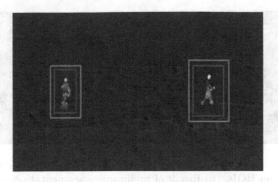

Fig. 4. The ROIs identified using double window box filter, from a background suppressed frame shown in Fig 3(c)

proposed. Application of rectangular box filter on background suppressed images, results ROI regions which are depicted in Fig.4. Having this information we create a spatial residual background model from the pixels which are not related to any of these identified ROIs. This residual background model is used for preliminary shape extraction to roughly segment objects silhouettes from the residual information left in background suppressed images. Then we create a separate appearance model for each object, and refine the silhouette in a Bayesian approach frame-work using the residual and the object appearance (i.e. foreground) models.

4.1 Preliminary Segmentation

Using the pixel values that do not relate to object silhouette, in background suppressed image we create a global residual background model at each time step. In our method this global residual background model $P_r(s)$ is modeled with a finite mixture of Gaussians (MoG), M_r i.e,

$$P_r(s) = \sum_{k=1}^{M_r} \omega_{r,k} P_{r,k}(s) \tag{7}$$

$$= \sum_{k=1}^{M_r} \omega_{r,k}\, \mathcal{N}(x_s|\mu_{r,k},\ \sigma_{r,k}) \tag{8}$$

Where $P_{r,k}(s) = \mathcal{N}(x_s|\mu_{r,k},\ \sigma_{r,k})$ denotes the Gaussian density function, i.e.,

$$P_{r,k}(s) = \frac{1}{\sigma_{r,k}\sqrt{2\pi}} e^{\frac{-(x-\mu_{r,k})^2}{2\sigma_{r,k}}} \tag{9}$$

Fig. 5 demonstrates this process using one frame containing two objects. Red rectangles represent the bounding boxes, and Green rectangles represent the

Fig. 5. (a) (b) (c) Visual demonstration of segmentation processing results for image containing two target ROIs. (b) Result of preliminary segmentation process (c) Result of Second level segmentation process.

bounding boxes enlarged in both directions with 15 %. The pixels outside these boxes are used to form the residual background model at time 't '. Having the set of training samples at time instant 't 'we calculate the maximum likelihood estimate of the global residual MoG model using the expectation- maximization (EM) technique [16]. The estimated residual MoG model $P_r(s)$ can be directly used for foreground pixels identification. However, in this case, the separation is based only on the residual background model and some parts of objects may be misclassified as residual in this process. Using the preliminary segmentation a pixel 'S 'is classified as residual background in either of the two cases:

1. The pixel location is far from the objects.
2. The pixel's value match closely to the residual background model.

Otherwise the pixel is classified as foreground. For the first case, the pixel location far from objects is identified using green bounding boxes. We considered all the pixels outside the green bounding boxes belong to background. In second case we considered pixel 'S'matching the background model if the following inequality holds.

$$\frac{(x_s - \mu_{r,k})}{\sqrt{\sigma_{r,k}}} < Th \tag{10}$$

The output of the preliminary segmentation process on image shown in Fig. 3(c) is demonstrated in Fig. 5(b). White pixels denote the foreground pixels. We can observe the significant part below the head of right object is classified as background, since it matches the residual background information. Similarly we can observe the significant part near stomach of left object is also classified as background. This issue will be addressed in the next section using local appearance models.

4.2   Second Level Segmentation Using Bayesian Approach

The preliminary segmentation process produces object silhouettes with some parts of objects may be misclassified as residual background. In next step, we refine these silhouettes. For refining silhouettes we follow Bayesian approach. For this step statistical information about the a priori and conditional probabilities of the two classes is required. In our case the appearance of a foreground object is modelled by a MoG with the following conditional probability density function:

$$P_f\left(s\right) = \sum_{k=1}^{M_f} \omega_{f,k}\; \mathcal{N}(x_s|\mu_{f,k},\; \sigma_{f,k}) \tag{11}$$

Where we use a smaller number of components in the mixture than we used in the global residual background model. i.e. $M_f < M_r$. To estimate the model parameters we use the pixels within the Red bounding box, which were classified as foreground in the preliminary segmentation step. The parameters of MoG are obtained by EM [16]. We utilize the conditional probability functions of the two classes (residual background and foreground, respectively) at a given pixel S, defined in (8) and (11). The pixel is optimally assigned to a particular class, according to the maximum a posteriori probability. Fig. 5(c) presents the final result obtained using Bayesian approach. We can observe that number of misclassified pixels significantly decreased compared to preliminary segmentation process.

5   Dataset and Experimental Evaluation

To evaluate the performance of the proposed approach, we tested the approach on three challenging thermal video sequences containing human objects at three different ranges. These video sequences are taken from Automatic Target Recognition (ATR) Algorithm development image database, provided by Georgia Tech Applied Research Corporation [17]. The data base contains large set of Mid Wave Infra-red (MWIR) imagery along with target ground truth data. The MWIR imagery is collected using thermal imager with resolution 512×640 pixel. The focal plane array of thermal imager covers a 3.4×2.6 deg fixed FOV. The details of three video sequences used for evaluation of our approach are given in Table 1.

Table 1. Details of Video Recordings used for evaluation of the proposed approach

S.no	Video Recording	Time of the day	Number of frames	Target Range (Km)
1	Cegr01926_0002	Night	623	0.5
2	Cegr01928_0002	Night	623	1
3	Cegr01932_0002	Night	623	1.5

In first video sequence the targets are partially occluded and appeared against heavy background clutter. An image of first video sequence is presented in Fig. 2(a). In second and third video sequences the targets are appeared against less background clutter but at long ranges. To quantify the detection performance two measures are used i.e. true positive rate (TPR) and False target per frame (FTPF).

$$TPR = \frac{\text{\# True detections}}{\text{\# Positive samples}} \tag{12}$$

$$FTPF = \frac{\text{\# False positives}}{\text{\# frames}} \tag{13}$$

The non target ROI regions with size greater than 5 pixels are counted as false positives. Quantitative results are provided by comparing the proposed approach with two classical image segmentation approaches, Running Gaussian averaging Background method [14], and code book approach [18]. Both quantitative and qualitative analysis results are provided to demonstrate the effectiveness of proposed approach.

The averaging background method basically learns the average and standard deviation of each pixel as its model of the background. The codebook approach is one of the prominent detection approaches for outdoor surveillance; it takes inspiration from the techniques of video compression and attempt to form a codebook to represent the background states. The two approaches adopt optimized parameters, with which the corresponding detection results are the best. Table 2 presents the parameter setting for the proposed approach and other two classical segmentation approaches under consideration.

Table 2. Parameter settings for simulation of segmentation methods

S.no	Approach	Parameter settings
1	Averaging background	$\sigma = 5$, and detection threshold of '5'
2	Code book	Min threshold = 0.7 ,Max threshold = 1.3
3	Proposed approach	K = 30 , Th = 2.5, $M_r = 3$, $M_f = 2$ Inner window size: 17 X 36

We manually segment the target regions and take it as ground truth to compare with detection results. Object silhouettes extracted using each segmentation approach is depicted in Fig 6. Extracted silhouettes are shown for each segmentation approach on three different video sequences containing targets at different ranges. Among all the approaches, the proposed approach is showing consistence performance with range. The results demonstrate that, proposed approach able to extract silhouettes in comparable quality with manual segmentation results, even for long range targets. Whereas the averaging background approach, code book approach performed reasonably well at near ranges (500 m, 1 Km), but the performance of these methods is poor for segmenting targets at long ranges (1.5 Km).

The segmented results using Averaging background approach and code book approach have heavy noise, on first video sequence. This noise is mainly contributed due to the movement of plants present in background.

Compared to averaging background approach, code book segmentation approach resulted less noise in segmentation process on first video sequence. This is because of time-series model used by code book approach to each pixel. The segmentation results of proposed approach are very clean on the first video sequence even in the presence of background plant movements. This demonstrates the robustness of proposed segmentation approach to background variations.

Next, we analyse detection performance of three approaches from view point of TPR and FTPF. Table 3 demonstrates the TPR of three segmentation approaches on three video sequences. The proposed approach achieved good TPR even for long range targets. But the TPR of Code book and averaging background approaches reduced significantly for long range targets. Table 4.0 demonstrates the FTPF of three segmentation approaches on three video sequences. The proposed approach is achieved good FTPF on all three video sequences. Whereas the Code book and averaging background methods exhibiting high FTPF on first video sequence containing occlusions and background variations due to plants. On the remaining two video sequences code book and Averaging background approaches exhibiting less FTPF as the targets are appearing against clear background.

To sum up, some qualitative and quantitative experimental comparisons are presented, and the results demonstrate that proposed approach achieved higher TPR and low FTPF. The proposed approach is more robust than two classical

Table 3. True positive rates achieved with the segmentation algorithms on three video sequences

S.no	Scenario Name	Proposed approach	Code book	Averaging Background
1	Cegr01926_0002	0.9671	0.91	0.922
2	Cegr01928_0002	0.9443	0.84	0.82
3	Cegr01932_0002	0.83	0.64	0.69

Table 4. False positive rates (FTPF) achieved with the segmentation algorithms on three video sequences

S.no	Scenario Name	Proposed approach	Code book	Averaging Background
1	Cegr01926_0002	1.1728	4.3	6.5
2	Cegr01928_0002	1.98	3.4	3.2
3	Cegr01932_0002	2.27	3.8	3.67

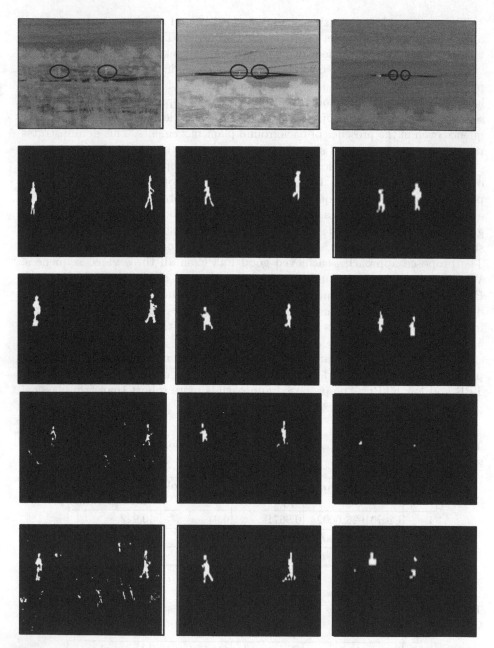

Fig. 6. (a)(b)(c)(d)(e) Visual comparison of segmentation results for three methods across three different video sequences (a)First row presents example images from video sequence 1, 2, and 3; (b)Second row presents the results of manual segmentation process; (c) Third row presents the segmentation results using proposed approach; (d) Fourth row presents segmentation results with code book approach; (e)Fifth row presents segmentation results using averaging background difference approach

segmentation approaches used in video surveillance applications. The proposed approach is capable of segmenting the targets even when targets are partially occluded or even in presence of background variations.

6   Conclusion and Future Work

We present a human target detection approach from thermal imagery using multi stage segmentation framework. The proposed approach uses the temporal information, to effectively estimate the background information and suppresses background using the K-L Transformation. The identified target ROIs will be subjected to two level segmentation process for effectively extracting the target silhouette. The proposed approach does not relies on any prior shape information, so it can be easily adapted for detecting and segmenting any moving targets from thermal imagery with little efforts of fine tuning parameters.

This paper also includes comprehensive qualitative and quantitative experiments across three challenging thermal outdoor video sequences. The comparisons demonstrate the proposed approach is capable of detecting and segmenting the targets present at long ranges and even in presence of occlusions and background variations. However the proposed approach has several limitations. For example as, the target should be moving one, and captured by a static thermal camera. If target is not moving there is possibility that target gets eliminated in background estimation process itself.

The work can be further extended to design a classifier to eliminate the false positives and to recognize human targets. However an image based tracker can also be designed as next stage for continuously tracking human targets in consecutive frames.

References

1. Arlow, H.: Thermal detection contrast of human targets. In: Proc. IEEE International Carnahan Conference on Security Technology, pp. 27–33 (1992)
2. Lin, S.S.: Review: Extending visible band computer vision techniques to infra-red band images. Technical Report, pp. 1-23, University of Pennsylvania, Philadelphia, Pennsylvania (2001)
3. Pavlidis, I., Levine, J., Baukol, P.: Thermal imaging for anxiety detection. In: Proc. IEEE Workshop on Computer Vision Beyond the Visible Spectrum: Methods and Applications, pp. 104–109 (2000)
4. Bhanu, B., Han, J.: Kinematic-based motion analysis in infra-red sequences. In: Proc. IEEE Workshop on Applications of Computer Vision, pp. 208–212 (2002)
5. Nadimi, S., Bhanu, B.: Physical models for moving shadow and object detection in video. IEEE Transactions on Pattern Analysis and Machine Intelligence 26(8), 1079–1087 (2004)
6. Han, J., Bhanu, B.: Fusion of color and infrared video for moving human detection. Pattern Recognition 40(6), 1771–1784, 1079–1087 (2007)
7. Cielnaik, G., Duckett, T.: People Recognition by Mobile Robots. Journal of Intelligent and Fuzzy Systems 15(1), 21–27 (2004)

8. Fang, Y., et al.: A shape -independent method for pedestrian detection with Far-Infrared Images. IEEE Transactions on Vehicular Technology 53(6) (2004)
9. Conaire, C., et al.: Background modelling in Infra-red and Visible spectrum Video for people tracking. In: Proc. of IEEE International Workshop on Object Tracking & Classification Beyond the Visible Spectrum (2005)
10. Zhang, L., Wu, B., Nevita, R.: Pedestrian detection in infrared images based on local shape features. In: Proc. of the IEEE Computer Society Conf on Computer Vision and Pattern Recognition, pp. 1–8 (2007)
11. Stephen, O.H., Amber, F.: Detecting people in IR border surveillance video using scale invariant image moments. In: Proc. SPIE, vol. 7340 (2009)
12. Chen, B.W., Wang, W., Qin, Q.: Infrared target detection based on Fuzzy ART neural network. In: The Second Intl. Conf. on Computational Intelligence and Natural Computing, pp. 240–243. IEEE Computer Society, China (2010)
13. Schachter, B.J.: Target detection strategies. Opt. Eng. 52(4), 041102 (2012)
14. Aldriges, A., et al.: Adaptive Three – Dimensional Spatio-Temporal Filtering Techniques for Infrared Clutter Suppression. In: Proc. of SPIE on Signal and Data Processing of Small Targets, vol. 1481, pp. 110–116.
15. A simple Introduction to the KLT, Springer Praxis Books. Springer, Berlin (2009)
16. Dempster, A.P., et al.: Maximum Likelihood from incomplete data via the EM algorithm. J. Royal Stat. Soc. B 39(1), 1–38 (1977)
17. http://WWW.gtarc.gatech.edu/
18. Wren, C.R., et al.: Real-time tracking of the human body. IEEE Transactions on Pattern Analysis and Machine Intelligence 19(7), 780–785 (1997)

Advantages of Using Object-Specific Knowledge at an Early Processing Stage in the Detection of Trees in LIDAR Data

Leszek J. Chmielewski, Marcin Bator, and Marcin Olejniczak

Warsaw University of Life Sciences (SGGW), Warsaw, Poland
Faculty of Applied Informatics and Mathematics (WZIM)
{leszek_chmielewski,marcin_bator,marcin_olejniczak}@sggw.pl
http://www.wzim.sggw.pl

Abstract. In some imaging setups the following assumptions hold: the objects are opaque and viewed only from one point, their surface is continuous at least piecewise, and the occluding objects are small with respect to the viewed objects. In addition, in the application of our interest the images can be treated similarly to the case of the plane of light. This made it possible to design algorithms with some desired features: the segmentation based on sorting the data according to angle and the version of the object verification method using fuzzy voting with the positive and negative evidence. The algorithms have some opposite and complementary features which could be used in application to LIDAR data in the measurements of trees and forest.

Keywords: Opacity, sorting, angle, Hough transform, voting against, negative evidence, LIDAR, trees, forest, breast-height diameter.

1 Introduction

One of the promising applications of the LIDAR (LIght Detection and Ranging) measurement technique is forestry. There is much literature on the measurements of trees and forest from the air as well as from the surface. Some of the most recent publications are for example [3,12,13,14]. The problem can be also related to depth and distance recovery [6] and surveillance [8].

An important challenge in LIDAR measurements, as it is in the case of all visual techniques, is opacity and occlusion. The repetitive structure of the forest makes it possible to assess the influence of occlusion on the measurement, to some extent [15]. In this paper we shall use occlusion in a positive way, to improve the quality of the results. A new concept of operating on sorted data will be presented. It will help to organise and speed up the calculations and will make it possible to operate on trees in a highly cluttered environment.

The simple observation that the viewed objects are opaque was used in our previous work [5]. In that paper the concept of voting in the Hough transform not only for, but also against the presence of an object was introduced. In the present paper it will be modified, extended and tested.

L.J. Chmielewski et al. (Eds.): ICCVG 2014, LNCS 8671, pp. 145–154, 2014.

The concept of voting for and against has been first proposed in [4]. In the one-point version of the Hough transform the image points potentially belonging to an object voted for its presence, and the neighbouring points voted against, which yielded a well contrasted peak in the accumulator. This concept has been passed over in silence by the publications which cited that paper, however. Our formulation of this problem is entirely different and it directly addresses the shape of the object.

The rest of the paper is organised as follows. In Section 2 the setting in which the measurement problem is considered will be presented. In Sections 3 and 4 two new or modified algorithms designed to detect and measure the tree sections will be described. In the following Section the results from these methods will be shown, and in Section 6 the results will be discussed and the methods will be compared. The last section concludes the paper.

The authors of the sections are as follows: Section 3: M. Bator; Section 4: L. Chmielewski (description, implementation of object detection, visualisation) and M. Olejniczak (modifications to the voting algorithm with respect to [5], implementation of voting); remaining Sections: all the authors.

2   The Measurement Problem

In the present paper we shall try to receive as good results as possible from one horizontal layer of the LIDAR data. In the case of trees the height at which such layer is located will be the breast height (1.3 m) traditionally used in forestry to measure tree stem diameter.

The data were scanned at the stand near Głuchów belonging to the Grójec Forest District, Mazovian Voivodship (Central Poland), with the ground-based FARO LS HE880 LIDAR scanner. The LIDAR is located at the origin of the Cartesian coordinate system. The part of data chosen for presentation in this pilot study extends in the range $x \in [-9.16, 8.18]$ m and $y \in [-4.64, 5.79]$ m and contained 11 trees. The vertical coordinate extends ± 0.01 m around the breast height. The set contains a total of 548 789 points. The data are visible in the Figures 2 and 4 in which the intermediate and final results are shown.

A large number of objects which interfere with the traces of the tree trunks can be seen. These are mainly smaller trees and bushes. The small plants have branches and leaves which are much smaller than the tree trunks of interest, but they form relatively dense clouds of objects that play the role of clutter. Some light rays can transverse the clutter, reflect from the thick trees and come back to the LIDAR. Our algorithms should operate on such noisy data.

The maximum possible diameter of a tree is a parameter to be set for a given forest stand; in the present case it was 40 cm. The minimum tree diameter is traditionally set to 5 to 8 cm, due to that the thinner objects are considered as tree branches rather than stems.

The important assumptions for this kind of images are: the opacity of the objects, the continuity of the surfaces of the objects, the near-vertical shape of the objects of interest, and the cross-section shape close to circular.

3   Algorithm Based on Sorting

In general, the algorithm is aimed at forming subsets from the set of measurement points. Each subset can be a separate tree, if it fulfils the conditions given further.

Initially, the points are transformed to the polar coordinate system $Ol\phi$.

In the below described algorithm, for a pair of points $P_i(l_i, \phi_i)$, $P_j(l_j, \phi_j)$, two conditions related to distance from the origin are used. Point P_i is *considerably farther* from (or *closer* to) the origin than P_j if $l_i - l_j > t_l$ (or $l_j - l_i > t_l$). In the conditions the same threshold can be used. Therefore, the number of parameters of the algorithm is one.

If there are more than one point for a given angle, the farthest one is left and the remaining ones are deleted. This conforms to the assumption on the opacity of objects: if any of the points closer to the LIDAR belonged to a tree, this tree would occlude the farther points, so they could not exist. Therefore, the closer points are noise. They did not occlude the farther points because they could have belonged to small objects from the height slightly different than the farther point. The points which remained are sorted according to angle ϕ.

A new subset is formed, initially containing the first point.

The next point is considered and it becomes the current point. If it is considerably farther from the origin than the previous one, a new (farther) subset is formed, the current point is included into it, and the previous subset is closed. If it is considerably closer, a new (closer) subset is formed and the current point is included into it, but the previous subset is not closed. In the remaining case the current point is included into the current subset.

The following next point is considered (new current one) and the same steps are repeated. If in the previous step a (closer) subset was closed, the current point is compared with the last included point from an open subset. If there are more than one open subsets, the one is used for which the angle difference from the current point to the last included point of the subset is the smallest.

It should be noted that the angle is periodical, so the analysis can lead to including the last analysed points to the first subset formed.

After the subsets are established, each of them is assessed. Too small subsets are rejected (below 75 points). Accepted subsets are processed with the one-point Hough transform for circles [1]. Finally, existence of points behind the circle is checked. This is effective thanks to that the data are sorted.

The clear structure of the algorithm is apparent. However, it properly reflects the assumption of non-transparency and piecewise continuity of objects. It works well if the objects to be detected are larger than those which are considered as noise. No assumptions on the shape of the detected object is made. The continuity of the object's border is captured in a simple way by the parameter t_l which is a measure of difference between an irregularity of one object's surface and a jump between two different objects.

The results are sequenced according to the angle, so they are perfectly suited for further approximation, for example like that in [9].

Fig. 1. Results of segmentation showing regions exceeding the threshold (black) and 180 maxima (crosses)

4   Algorithm Based on Fuzzy Voting for and Against

4.1   Segmentation

This algorithm works on the objects after their detection. Before detection the data are segmented with the fuzzy accumulation algorithm described in [5]. An accumulator with resolution of 0.01×0.01 m fuzzified with a parabolic fuzzification function defined on a mask 21×21 pixels is used. The result is thresholded at $0,001$ of the global maximum value. The thresholded map is shown in Fig. 1. Around each local maximum found, a circular region is selected with the radius equal to the smaller of the two numbers: distance to the nearest maximum and distance to the farthest black point in the current segment. Data belonging to these regions are stored as candidates for objects.

4.2   Detection and Measurement

Object detection is performed as described in [5] with the two-point Hough transform, at the resolution of the accumulator 0.002×0.002 m. The number of trees found is excessive, as shown in Fig. 2. The Hough transform always returns the strongest instance of the object present in the data, irrespectively of how few data support it.

4.3   Voting for and against

The voting scheme has been modified with respect to the version proposed previously in [5]. The shapes of regions to which the positive nad negative votes can belong were changed and their membership functions were adjusted.

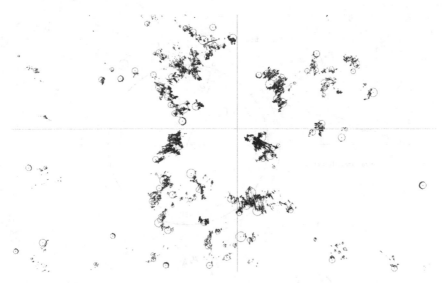

Fig. 2. Results of circle detection before elimination of weakly represented objects: 11 true positives and 169 false positives

The idea is that a point located behind an object contradicts its existence, so it votes *against*. A point in front of an object votes *for* if it is at or near the boundary, and *against*, if it is inside the object.

The conditions of being behind, near the boundary or inside are fuzzy. In Fig. 3 the regions reflecting the notion of *near* are marked with grey signs. Positive and negative signs indicate the voting for and against.

The algorithm operates as follows. The input of a measurement point P to the evidence concerning the circle $s(C, R)$ is considered (Fig. 3a).

To find whether the point is in front or behind the circle, the angle $\angle LCP$ is compared to $\angle LCS$. The line b is the boundary.

In case P is in front, the voting result depends on the location of P with respect to the circle and its neighbourhood limited by the inner and outer circles $s_i(C, R)$, $s_o(C, R)$. Half-width of the ring between them is determined by the position of point D_f on $\overline{CS}$. Between s_i and s_o the vote is positive, inside s_i it is negative, and outside s_o it is zero (*abstention*), according to the function shown in Fig. 3b. The curvilinear fragments were modelled with the sine function. The coordinate related to the function is x_f extending from the centre C outside.

In case P is behind, the voting result depends on its location with respect to the angle $\angle CLS$ and its boundary regions $\angle D_bLS$ (and symmetrically, below a). Outside the angle there is abstention. Between the boundary regions (below line d_b) the vote is strictly against. In the boundary regions, due to the possible error in the determination of radius R, the vote should gradually go down from 0 to -1. The voting function is shown in Fig. 3c. The coordinate related to the function is the angular coordinate x_b going out from the line a.

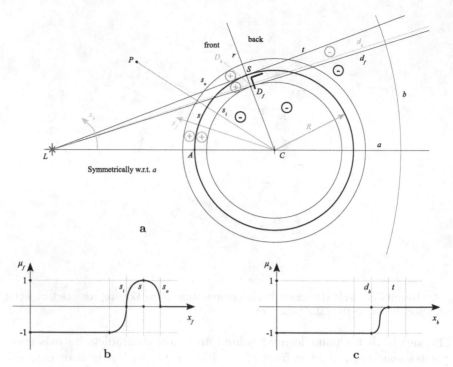

Fig. 3. The layout and notations used in fuzzy voting for and against the circle $s(C, R)$. (a) General layout; (b) voting membership function in front, and (c) behind the circle.

The amount of fuzziness in the process is regulated by the locations of points D_f, D_b. It can be expressed by a parameter $\delta. = |D.S|/|D.C| = |D.S|/R$. Two points D_f and D_b or one D can be used for the front and back.

The votes coming from all the available points P should be counted, separately from the front – for and against, and from the back – against. The number of votes necessary for object acceptance can be set according to the needs of the application, for example, the ratio of front negative votes to the positive ones should be limited and the minimum number of votes should be related to the circle radius. The acceptable number of negative back votes should be very small or zero.

It is interesting why the voting against was overlooked, despite the proposition made in [4], although other voting concepts were developed, including the advanced fuzzy voting schemes. It can be supposed that this was because the negative voting would result in assigning a negative value to the fuzzy membership function, which is in contradiction with the established fuzzy set theory. We pass over this assumption by stating that the negative sign represents only the fact that the given data item belongs to the set of data which contradicts the existence of the object considered.

In the presented method, otherwise than in feature-based methods (e.g. [11]), solely the shape of the object is used to assess the quality of its detection and measurement. It can be treated as an extension of approaches in which the number of votes is compared to the dimensions of the object [10]. It can also be related to methods in which shape is considered as a whole (e.g. [7]).

5   Results

The algorithm with sorting (Section 3) was run with the parameter $t_l = 5$ pixels. The results are shown in Fig. 4a. Additionally to finding the 11 existing trees, two more were found as false positives. The running time, including all the operations: sorting, segmenting and HT was around 1 minute. All the times were checked with a PC with Intel Core i7 3740QM at 2.7 GHz running sequential 32-bit software.

The segmentation (Section 4.1) is a fast calculation and takes several seconds. The detection (Section 4.2) on 180 sets of data took around 25 minutes (the two-point HT has the complexity $O(n^2)$) and gave 180 circles. The algorithm with voting (Section 4.3) was run with $\delta = 0.2$ for both front and back, the number of admissible negative front votes limited to $1/3$ of positive front votes, and the number of back votes (only negative possible) limited to three.

The voting was performed locally, for a given object only with its own data subset as received from the segmentation, and globally, with all the available 0.5 M of data for each object. In the first case the time was less than 5 s, and in the second it was around 20 s.

All the results are shown if Fig. 4.

The sorting algorithm detected all the 11 true objects and two false positives. The voting algorithm with local data rejected 132 objects from the 180 ones found after segmentation, leaving the 11 objects and 37 false positives. The voting algorithm with global data rejected further 34 objects, leaving 11 true positives and 3 false positives. The locations and radii vary between the results of the two algorithms. The false positives found by the two methods are different.

More details on the data and results are available at www.1chmiel.pl/publ/.

6   Discussion

The two compared algorithms use entirely different concepts. However, to construct both of them the facts that the imaged objects are opaque and that the measuring apparatus can observe them from a single, stable point are used.

In the first algorithm based on sorting, the data are greatly reduced before the detection and measurement is done, which minimises the processing time. The shape of the object is not taken into account, so the algorithm is general. It can be used in many applications where small objects in front of the detected objects interfere in the detection process.

The second algorithm works on the detected objects. It verifies the correctness of detection. In the present form it can not be used to improve the true positive rate, but only to remove the false positives. The algorithm can be applied to different shapes of objects by properly designing the functions used.

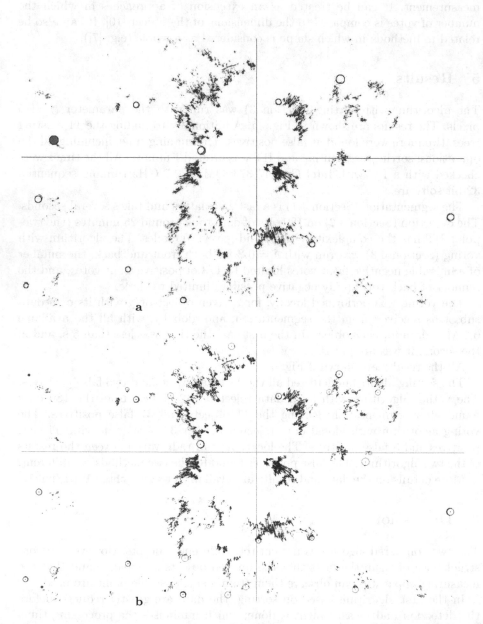

Fig. 4. Results from the algorithms: (**a**) with sorting (Section 3); (**b**) with voting (Section 4), with local and global data. Blue: measuring points; black: circles found by the sorting algorithm and by the global voting algorithm; red inside: false positives; red empty: circles found by the local voting algorithm and not found by the global ones, all false negatives.

Table 1. Comparisons of the properties of the two algorithms used

No.	Property	Sorting	Voting
1	object opacity considered	yes	yes
2	object shape considered	irrelevant	modelled
3	front surface irregularity considered	yes	yes
4	occluding surface irregularity considered	no	yes
5	object detection method	any	any
6	when object measurement is made	after	before
7	globality/locality, natively	global	local
8	globality possible	natively	at some extra cost
9	no. of points that trigger a decision	one	parameterised
10	accuracy, in the example presented	100%	100%
11	specificity, the example presented	82%	73%
12	own speed	fast	fast
13	speed, together with object detection	fast (60 s)	slow (1500 s)

The features of the algorithms are extensively compared in Table 1. The algorithms seem to be complementary in some aspects. For example, the sorting algorithm makes the segmentation quickly, while the initial segmentation is a weak point of the voting algorithm; specific shape is not relevant in the sorting algorithm (positive in case of segmentation), while it is considered in the voting algorithm (positive in object verification). The algorithms can be integrated in the analysis of LIDAR images of trees and in similar applications.

7   Conclusions

Occlusion and noise pose a challenge to the methods of object detection and measurement. The opacity of objects and interfering occluding elements and the fact that the measuring device observes the scene from one point can be used to construct algorithms with desired features.

In the algorithm for data segmentation based on sorting these observations made it possible to achieve high efficiency and generality. The structure of the algorithm is simple and it has from one to three parameters, according to the user's choice, which would simplify its optimisation if necessary.

In the algorithm for object verification based on fuzzy voting, the opacity was used to make it to enable not only positive voting, like in the classical Hough transform and its variants, but also to consider the evidence which can contradict with the existence of an object, thus enabling the rejection of false positive detections. The method can be redesigned for objects with various shapes.

The two presented algorithms could be used together in the frames of the detection of opaque objects in a cluttered environment, including the analysis of trees and forest measured with the LIDAR technology in the presence of bushes and small trees.

Acknowledgements. We wish to thank Krzysztof Stereńczak form the Forest Research Institute and Michał Zasada from the Faculty of Forestry, Warsaw University of Life Sciences (SGGW), for providing the LIDAR data used in the experiments.

References

1. Ballard, D., Brown, C.M.: Computer Vision. Prentice Hall, Englewood Cliffs (1982)
2. Bolc, L., Tadeusiewicz, R., Chmielewski, L.J., Wojciechowski, K. (eds.): ICCVG 2012. LNCS, vol. 7594. Springer, Heidelberg (2012)
3. Brolly, G., Király, G., Czimber, K.: Mapping forest regeneration from terrestrial laser scans. Acta Silvatica et Lignaria Hungarica 9, 135–146 (2014), doi:10.2478/aslh-2013-0011
4. Brown, C.M., Curtiss, M.B., Sher, D.B.: Advanced Hough transform implementations. In: Bundy, A. (ed.) Proc. 8th Int. Joint Conf. Artificial Intelligence, IJCAI 1983, pp. 1081–1085. William Kufmann, Karlsruhe (1983)
5. Chmielewski, L.J., Bator, M.: Hough transform for opaque circles measured from outside and fuzzy voting for and against. In: Bolc, et al. (eds.) [2], pp. 313–320, doi:10.1007/978-3-642-33564-8_38
6. Czúni, L., Csordás, D.: Depth-based indexing and retrieval of photographic images. In: García, N., Salgado, L., Martínez, J.M. (eds.) VLBV 2003. LNCS, vol. 2849, pp. 76–83. Springer, Heidelberg (2003)
7. Frejlichowski, D.: Analysis of four polar shape descriptors properties in an exemplary application. In: Bolc, L., Tadeusiewicz, R., Chmielewski, L.J., Wojciechowski, K. (eds.) ICCVG 2010, Part I. LNCS, vol. 6374, pp. 376–383. Springer, Heidelberg (2010)
8. Frejlichowski, D., Forczmański, P., Nowosielski, A., Gościewska, K., Hofman, R.: SmartMonitor: An approach to simple, intelligent and affordable visual surveillance system. In: Bolc, et al. (eds.) [2], pp. 726–734, doi:10.1007/978-3-642-33564-8_87
9. Kozera, R., Noakes, L., Szmielew, P.: Quartic Orders and Sharpness in Trajectory Estimation for Smooth Cumulative Chord Cubics. In: Chmielewski, L.J., Kozera, R., Shin, B.-S., Wojciechowski, K. (eds.) ICCVG 2014. LNCS, vol. 8671, pp. 9–16. Springer, Heidelberg (2014)
10. Leavers, V.F.: Shape Detection in Computer Vision Using the Hough Transform. Springer, London (1992)
11. Leś, T., Kruk, M., Osowski, S.: Automatic recognition of industrial tools using artificial intelligence approach. Expert Systems with Applications 40(12), 4777–4784 (2013), doi:10.1016/j.eswa.2013.02.030
12. Miścicki, S., Stereńczak, K.: A two-phase inventory method for calculating standing volume and tree-density of forest stands in central Poland based on airborne laser-scanning data. Forest Research Papers 74(2), 127–136 (2013), doi:10.2478/frp-2013-0013
13. Olofsson, K., Holmgren, J., Olsson, H.: Tree stem and height measurements using terrestrial laser scanning and the ransac algorithm. Remote Sensing 6(5), 4323–4344 (2014), doi:10.3390/rs6054323
14. Stereńczak, K., Zasada, M., Brach, M.: The accuracy assessment of DTM generated from LIDAR data for forest area – a case study for scots pine stands in Poland. Baltic Forestry 19(2), 252–262 (2013)
15. Zasada, M., Stereńczak, K., Dudek, W.M., Rybski, A.: Horizon visibility and accuracy of stocking determination on circular sample plots using automated remote measurement techniques. Forest Ecology and Management 302(0), 171–177 (2013), doi:10.1016/j.foreco.2013.03.041

A Modular Workflow Architecture
for Coronary Centerline Extraction
in Computed Tomography Angiography Data

Esteban Correa-Agudelo[1,3], Leonardo Flórez-Valencia[2], Maciej Orkisz[1],
Claire Mouton[1], Eduardo E. Dávila Serrano[1], and Marcela Hernández Hoyos[3]

[1] Université de Lyon, CREATIS; CNRS UMR5220; INSERM U1044; INSA-Lyon
Université Lyon 1, France
{maciej.orkisz,claire.mouton,davila}@creatis.insa-lyon.fr
[2] Grupo Takina, Pontificia Universidad Javeriana, Bogotá, Colombia
florez-l@javeriana.edu.co
[3] Systems and Computing Engineering Department, School of Engineering,
Universidad de los Andes, Bogotá, Colombia
{em.correa20,marc-her}@uniandes.edu.co

Abstract. Efficient and reliable extraction of coronary artery centerline from computed tomography angiography data is a prerequisite for
a variety of medical imaging applications. Many authors have combined
minimum-cost path algorithms and vesselness measures to extract coronary centerlines. We propose a modular decomposition of this extraction process, in order to facilitate the implementation and comparison of
different minimum-cost path strategies allowing users (radiologists and
developers) to focus on subsequent image analysis tasks. Evaluation results show a good overlap ($> 84\%$), and small distances with regard
to reference centerlines (on average, not larger than the voxel size) in
multi-vendor datasets, for two combinations of algorithms that follow
this framework. Therefore, it can serve as a starting point to subsequent
image analysis stages that require coronary centerlines.

Keywords: centerline extraction, vesselness, minimum cost-path algorithms, computed tomography, coronary arteries.

1 Introduction

Efficiently obtaining a reliable coronary artery centerline from computed tomography angiography data is relevant in clinical practice. In the medical imaging
context, centerlines serve as a starting point of segmentation, lesion-detection
and visualization applications. Image processing applications like lumen segmentation, stenosis grading and quantification [1], and curved planar reformatting
reconstruction have successfully used centerlines to review computed tomography angiography data (CTA). In consequence, having reliable centerlines is a
prerequisite for subsequent medical image analysis tasks.

In recent years, a variety of techniques have been proposed and thoroughly
evaluated [2] to extract coronary centerlines in multivendor CTA images. These

L.J. Chmielewski et al. (Eds.): ICCVG 2014, LNCS 8671, pp. 155–162, 2014.

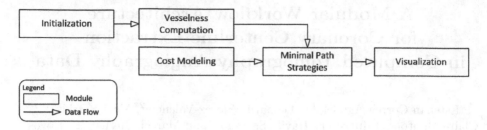

Fig. 1. Minimum-cost path based centerline extraction workflow architecture

can be grouped by the level of user interaction: automatic extraction, minimum user-interaction and interactive. Almost a half of the most successful techniques [3–8] make use of a vesselness measure and a minimum-cost path algorithm to resolve the centerline extraction problem. It is therefore natural to think of a workflow modularization of this process, in order to make the development and comparison tasks easier, speeding up medical imaging projects that involve the centerline extraction process. Hence, this work aims to facilitate the implementation and comparison of different centerline extraction strategies, based on minimum-cost path algorithms, by a workflow modularization. Furthermore, the proposed workflow provides instant feedback to users, reducing time in the centerline extraction task and globally allowing users (radiologists and developers) to focus on the subsequent image analysis stages. For simplicity sake, this paper is focused on the application of this modularized framework to computed tomography angiography data. However, this framework is generic enough to be easily used for a wide class of 3D centerline extraction tasks.

This paper is organized as follows: Section 2 introduces the workflow architecture and modules used in the centerline extraction process. Section 3 describes and validates a combination set of methods that fits the introduced workflow. Finally, section 4 gives the conclusions in terms of the project objective.

2   Workflow Architecture for Centerline Extraction

When analyzing the vessel-centerline extraction methods based on minimum-cost paths, such as [3–8], the following workflow can be defined: First, two seed-points (proximal and distal locations) are typically placed by user interaction. Second, the tubular structures in the image are enhanced by a "vesselness" filter. Third, a path is determined between the seed points, such that the cost of traveling along this path is minimum. This step requires a transformation that translates the vesselness values into costs. Depending on the path-extraction algorithm, the resulting curve may lack the smoothness property required by the visualization module, as well as by subsequent processing steps that exploit the centerline. Therefore, the visualization is preceded by a path refinement.

This workflow has been wrapped in five modules (See Fig. 1): initialization, vesselness computation, cost modeling, minimal path strategies and visualization. For our case of study, initialization and visualization modules remain fixed through the pipeline. Vesselness computation, cost modeling and minimal path strategies can be easily modified, improved or changed using the development framework CreaTools[1] [9] and ITK/VTK image processing libraries.

2.1 Initialization

The initialization module begins by loading CTA data and placing the start and end points into the CTA image. As this requires an interactive definition by the user, a friendly graphical user interface (*GUI*) has been developed for this seed placement task. Currently, this component allows the user to navigate through all image planes of the 3D CTA dataset, to easily edit points (add, remove, export) and to execute the workflow (See Fig. 2).

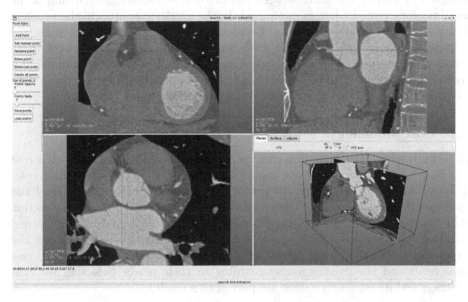

Fig. 2. Seed placement GUI: (*left*) Seed toolbox editor. (*right*) Interactive 3D CTA views. (*bottom*) Execution button. The red spheres represent the start and end-points selected in the artery (source: CreaTools screenshot).

2.2 Vesselness Computation

The extraction of coronary structures is a particularly challenging problem in medical imaging. Coronary vessels exhibit high intensity variability (uneven contrast agent dilution), and are embedded in complex scenes with surrounding structures and tissues with similar intensities. Additionally, voxels located on the central axis of a vessel are not necessarily brighter than other voxels within the lumen, whereas the path extracted should follow the centerline. In this context, vesselness filters are used to highlight the central axis of tube-like patterns,

---

[1] http://www.creatis.insa-lyon.fr/site/en/CreaTools_home

exploiting the local geometry in the image content. Many authors [3, 7, 10–12] have discussed the theoretical properties of their filters, such as the response to different models of vessel profiles, with the aim of distinguishing hyper-intense coronary structures. To date, two built-in multiscale gradient-based vesselness methods are provided in this module [3, 11]. The multiscale feature allows users to set selective vessel radii to fit variable vessel diameters, while getting rid of erroneously connected structures, such as coronary veins or heart chambers.

2.3   Minimum-Cost Path Strategy

The minimal path is the problem of finding the shortest path between two points according to a given metric. In graph theory, the minimum-cost path problem is solved by finding the path between the two vertices such that the sum of the weights of its visited edges is minimized. In the geodesic approach, the problem is solved with a front propagation between the start and end point, using the Eikonal equation (used to model wave propagation), and followed by a back-tracking step to find the optimal path. Literature [2, 7, 8] shows that minimum-cost path algorithms like fast marching or Dijkstra, have successfully been used to deal with the coronary centerline extraction problem described above.

2.4   Cost Modeling

In order to guide the minimum-cost path algorithm through the vessel, a cost function converts the vesselness value of each voxel to a proper positive cost. This conversion process keeps the lowest cost inside the highlighted vessel and increases this cost beyond it. Therefore, the key task is to find the right function that fits the vesselness image dynamics of the CTA image, and has the desired selectivity (sharpness). Our framework has a built-in set of cost functions like exponential, Richard's curve, sigmoids, among others. Users can easily add new ones or extend the existing ones according to their needs. Selecting the cost function and its parametrization are part of this module.

2.5   Visualization

Depending on the actual implementation of the minimal path extraction, the resulting curve is not necessarily smooth, whereas the computation of the curved planar reformatted (CPR) [13] views in the visualization module is based on the use of a Frenet frame sliding along the centerline, and the orientation variations of this frame should be very smooth to provide consistent visualization. Therefore, a Bezier smoothing [14] is applied to the extracted centerline points, and visualization can continue by unrolling the artery creating the CPR view of it. In addition, a 3D volume rendering can be added into this module to facilitate assessment by radiologists. An example of this module is used in an ongoing internal project called CreaCoro. CreaCoro is a GUI built using the CreaTools framework, for the purpose of supporting various research projects in the field of coronary artery segmentation and lesion detection (See Fig. 3).

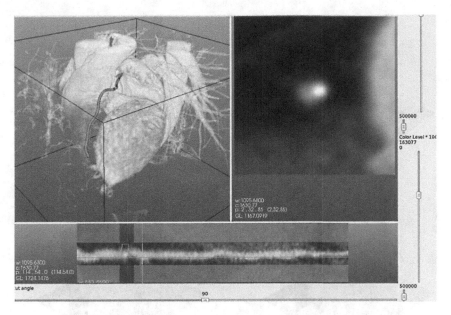

Fig. 3. Current CreaCoro GUI: (*top-left*) 3D volume rendering of a cardiac CT with a coronary artery of interest highlighted. (*top-right*) CPR vessel axial view. (*bottom*) CPR vessel planar view (source: CreaCoro screenshots).

3   Workflow Validation

3.1   Methods

In order to demonstrate the framework ability to track vessel centerlines, the following methods were implemented in the modules related to the extraction task (See Fig. 4). For the vesselness module, two different multi-scale gradient-based vesselness methods were implemented. Method 1, Flux [11] exploits the inward orientation of gradient vectors by computing the gradient flux through the surface of an object. Method 2, is the vesselness proposed in [3], where the image gradient norm at pixel p is evaluated along concentric rays in order to find the best radius that models the vessel as a cylinder. In the shortest path strategy module, the centerline is extracted by a bidirectional Dijkstra [15], which finds the minimum-cost path from the initial seed to a goal seed, running two simultaneous searches: one forward from the starting point, and one backward from the end point, stopping when the two collide. These searches are driven by the vesselness-to-cost converter module. The selected cost function is based on a generalized logistic function applied to a vesselness-based response of the CTA image. Then, the coronary centerline is ready for radiologist's visual assessment and subsequent analysis in the visualization module.

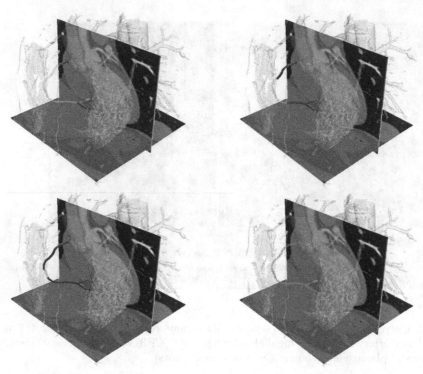

Fig. 4. Graph-based centerline extraction running two simultaneous searches: one forward from the starting point, and one backward from the end point, stopping when the two collide. Blue color represents the fronts advancing within an artery. The extracted centerline is highlighted in red in the bottom-right image (source: CreaTools screenshot).

3.2   Results

Centerline experiments and quantitative analysis were done using the training datasets proposed by the CAT08 challenge [2]. For each patient, consensus centerlines drawn by three experts in four main coronary artery branches are available with their inter-observer variability measures. The extracted centerlines have been sent to the Web-based evaluation framework in order to quantitatively assess them. Four different measures (three for overlap and one for accuracy assessment) were evaluated in this work: overall overlap (**OV**); overlap until first error (**OF**); finally, overlap with the clinically relevant part of the vessel (**OT**). An algorithm score of 100 points is a perfect match between a method and the reference, a score equal to 0 is a total failure in the extraction. The last measure, denoted **AI**, is the average distance from the extracted centerline to the reference one, calculated inside the vessel lumen defined by the locally annotated vessel radius. The scores are calculated in such a way that they indicate if the method does better (> 50 points) or worse (< 50 points), as compared to the observers. Table 1 summarizes the performance of our implementations against

Table 1. Performance comparison extracted from CAT08 web-platform framework

Methods	OV		OF		OT		AI	
	%	score	%	score	%	score	mm	score
Friman et al.	98.5	84.0	83.1	72.8	98.7	84.5	0.23	47.9
Krissian et al.	88.0	67.4	74.2	61.1	88.5	70.0	0.39	29.2
Tek et al.	84.7	46.5	59.5	36.1	86.2	50.3	0.34	35.3
Method 2	**84.4**	**57.8**	**73.8**	**54.2**	**84.9**	**59.4**	**0.40**	**30.1**
Method 1	**84.3**	**60.4**	**65.3**	**50.7**	**84.4**	**59.2**	**0.41**	**29.3**
Metz et al.	91.9	64.5	56.4	45.6	92.5	64.5	0.46	27.9
Dikici et al.	90.8	56.8	48.9	35.6	91.7	55.9	0.46	26.4
Zhang et al.	89.6	51.1	49.9	30.5	90.6	52.4	0.51	24.2

others minimum cost path CAT08 methods. Overall, both versions performed very similarly, which is not surprising, since both vesselness functions are based on similar principles. On average, our implemented methods rank 9-th in the overlapping section and 12-th in the accuracy, in comparison with the CAT08 methods. Visual inspection revealed that most extraction errors occurred near to the ostium. Larger vessel radii could fix this issue, since the vessel radius at ostium is larger (6mm) than the radius range (1mm - 4mm) used by the vesselness filter. Note however that the combinations of new methods that follow the same framework could lead to different results.

4   Conclusions

The contribution of this work is two-fold: first, finding a decomposition of the existing minimum-cost path based methods, so that all can fit the same workflow. Second, the design and implementation of a modular computational framework, in which these methods, as well as new combinations of their components and/or new ones, can be evaluated in a flexible and user-friendly manner. Visualization tools are also provided to support radiologist's interaction and diagnosis. Within this framework, we implemented two example combinations of algorithms, in order to demonstrate its feasibility. These, compared to centerline extraction methods from the CAT08 challenge, were able to track centerline vessels with an accuracy comparable to the experts and similar to the average of state-of-the-art methods. Additional improvements, cost functions and vesselness methods can be implemented and added intuitively, using CreaTools. Eventually, this framework can serve as a starting point to subsequent image analysis stages.

Acknowledgments. This work, performed within the framework of the LABEX PRIMES (ANR-11-LABX-0063) of Université de Lyon, within the program "Investissements d'Avenir" (ANR-11-IDEX-0007) of the French National Research Agency (ANR), has been partly funded by the ECOS Nord Committee grant (*C11S01*), the Administrative Department of Science, Technology and Innovation of Colombia - COLCIENCIAS, and Uniandes Interfacultades (*06-2010*).

References

1. Kirişli, H.A., Schaap, M., Metz, C., Dharampal, A.S., Meijboom, W.B., et al.: Standardized evaluation framework for evaluating coronary artery stenoses detection, stenoses quantification and lumen segmentation algorithms in Computed Tomography Angiography. Med. Image Anal. 17(8), 859–876 (2013)
2. Schaap, M., Metz, C.T., van Walsum, T., van der Giessen, A.G., Weustink, A.C., Mollet, N.R., et al.: Standardized evaluation methodology and reference database for evaluating coronary artery centerline extraction algorithms. Medical Image Analysis 13(5), 701–714 (2009)
3. Gülsün, M.A., Tek, H.: Robust vessel tree modeling. In: Metaxas, D., Axel, L., Fichtinger, G., Székely, G. (eds.) MICCAI 2008, Part I. LNCS, vol. 5241, pp. 602–611. Springer, Heidelberg (2008)
4. Dikici, E., O'Donnell, T., Grady, L., White, R.: Coronary artery centerline tracking using axial symmetries. In: MICCAI Workshop - Grand Challenge Coronary Artery Tracking, New York City, USA (2008)
5. Krissian, K., Bogunovic, H., Pozo, J., Villa-Uriol, M., Frangi, A.: Minimally interactive knowledge-based coronary tracking in CTA using a minimal cost path. In: MICCAI Workshop - Grand Challenge Coronary Artery Tracking, New York City, USA (2008)
6. Zhang, Y., Chen, K., Wong, S.: 3D interactive centerline extraction. In: MICCAI Workshop - Grand Challenge Coronary Artery Tracking, New York City, USA (2008)
7. Friman, O., Kuehnel, C., Peitgen, H.: Coronary centerline extraction using multiple hypothesis tracking and minimal paths. In: MICCAI Workshop - Grand Challenge Coronary Artery Tracking, New York City, USA (2008)
8. Metz, C.T., Schaap, M., Weustink, A.C., Mollet, N.R.A., van Walsum, T., Niessen, W.J.: Coronary centerline extraction from CT coronary angiography images using a minimum cost path approach. Med. Phys. 36(12), 5568–5579 (2009)
9. Dávila Serrano, E.E., Guigues, L., Roux, J.-P., Cervenansky, F., Camarasu-Pop, S., Riveros Reyes, J.G., Flórez-Valencia, L., Hernández Hoyos, M., Orkisz, M.: CreaTools: A framework to develop medical image processing software: Application to simulate pipeline stent deployment in intracranial vessels with aneurysms. In: Bolc, L., Tadeusiewicz, R., Chmielewski, L.J., Wojciechowski, K. (eds.) ICCVG 2012. LNCS, vol. 7594, pp. 55–62. Springer, Heidelberg (2012)
10. Frangi, A.F., Niessen, W.J., Vincken, K.L., Viergever, M.A.: Multiscale vessel enhancement filtering. In: Wells, W.M., Colchester, A.C.F., Delp, S.L. (eds.) MICCAI 1998. LNCS, vol. 1496, pp. 130–137. Springer, Heidelberg (1998)
11. Lesage, D., Angelini, E.D., Bloch, I., Funka-Lea, G.: Design and study of flux-based features for 3D vascular tracking. In: IEEE Int. Symp. Biomed. Imaging: From Nano to Macro, ISBI 2009, Piscataway, NJ, USA, pp. 286–289 (2009)
12. Yang, G., Kitslaar, P., Frenay, M., Broersen, A., Boogers, M.J., Bax, J.J., Reiber, J.H., Dijkstra, J.: Automatic centerline extraction of coronary arteries in coronary computed tomographic angiography. Int. J. Cardiovasc. Imaging 28(4), 921–933 (2012)
13. Kanitsar, A., Fleischmann, D., Wegenkittl, R., Felkel, P., Gröller, M.: CPR - curved planar reformation. In: Visualization 2002, pp. 37–44. IEEE (2002)
14. Bartels, J.C., Beatty, R.H., Barsky, B.A.: Bézier curves, ch. 10, pp. 211–245. Morgan Kaufmann Publishers, Inc. (November 1987)
15. Dijkstra, E.W.: A note on two problems in connexion with graphs. Numerische Mathematik 1(1), 269–271 (1959)

Simulated Holography Based on Stereoscopy and Face Tracking

Łukasz Dąbała and Przemysław Rokita

Institute of Computer Science, Warsaw University of Technology
Nowowiejska 15/19 00-665 Warsaw, Poland
L.Dabala@stud.elka.pw.edu.pl, pro@ii.pw.edu.pl

Abstract. Virtual reality systems are getting more and more popular nowadays. They give user ability to manipulate content without using common hardware controllers such as keyboard or mouse. We propose the method for presenting a stereoscopic content for the user, which uses face tracking technique for changing the position of the viewer on virtual scene. We achieved the impression of holography, where person can see the object from different points of view. At the same time we are creating realistically looking images and assuring interactivity of the system.

1 Introduction

In recent years there was a lot of development in area of virtual reality. These type of systems must constist of at least three elements: a computer, a device for gesture or position tracking and a device that will present information to the user. The most common equipment used for tracking is a simple webcam, which is used in addition to the screen, where results are showed. Because of the fact, that stereoscopic displays are really popular nowadays, such system can be used to deliver this type of content to the user.

There are many possibilites, how to present the stereoscopic content on the screen. Devices, that serve for this purpose are for example shutter glasses, polarized glasses or anaglyph glasses. All of them has its own pros and cons. But screen by itself and equipment for stereo is not everything that should be taken into consideration to create good stereoscopic content. The reason for this will be presented in the background section.

Another thing is view-dependent rendering, which is responsible for changing a view of the scene regarding to the position of the observer. It was used in terms of changing the point from which the whole virtual scene is presented. Everything will be changed and displayed interactively, what is really necessary to assure best experience for the user.

A really important part in our method is a tracking technique, which is based on optical flow. The problem of face tracking is a really complicated and important research area in computer vision. There were many works about this problem and there are plenty of solutions that can work in real-time. Because of that fact, for now we didn't think about developing new technique for face

L.J. Chmielewski et al. (Eds.): ICCVG 2014, LNCS 8671, pp. 163–170, 2014.

tracking. In our case, it was used to find position of the user relatively to the computer screen. It will allow the user to see objects on virtual scene from different perspectives, what leads to the impression of holography.

2 Background and Previous Work

In this section, we provide a background on stereo perception as well as an overview of previous works about view-dependent rendering.

2.1 Stereopsis

Human visual system is a really complicated mechanism. To achieve good perception it combines information from many different cues (for example occlusion, perspective or motion paralax). Stereopsis [8,5] is the most influential one and has a strong impact on viewing experience. Humans, because of the binocular vision, see the environment from two slightly different points, what leads also to the shift of the retinal images. Magnitude of this difference is used to estimate the depth information for the scene. Stereopsis, as a really strong cue, introduces some problems and one of them is visual comfort.

2.2 Visual Discomfort

What can be really annoying for the user during watching 3D content is a visual discomfort, which can be caused by the interplay between the accomodation and vergence cues. Accommodation is mechanism in an eye, which acquires the depth information from work of the muscles responsible for correct light focusing. The vergence cue is getting the same information from the muscles, that are responsible for the eye movements. Because of the fact, that this two mechanisms are connected, there is a possibility, that they will be in disagreement [6]. The conflict between these mechanisms does not happen always and it is tolerated in a small area around the screen called the comfort zone [12]. Really important is that, moving everything to the comfort zone may not be enough to assure a good 3D perception. Both images need to be fused, and this can only happen inside the small region called Panum's fusional area [5, Ch. 14]. Outside of this area, double vision occurs. Visual discomfort can be caused also by differences between left and right image. The phenomena is called binocular rivalry [5, Ch. 12] and in this case, watching such images will lead to constant changes of the view. Such effects are often seen, because of the view-dependent light effects. Of course, if the differences between images are not too big, they can be tolerated by human visual system.

2.3 View-Dependent Systems

There were many previous approaches to constructing systems that will take into consideration position of the user. One of them was a work by Slotbo [13].

He used a system that consisted of two cameras, which were used for tracking the viewer's position to set input for view-dependent rendering. His work showed the possibility that such a system can run in real-time, but without stereoscopic mode. In [4] they developed a system for stereoscopic rendering based on face tracking. They changed a symmetric frustum to asymmetric one to reduce distortions and achieve the most correct 3D perspective of rendered scene, so the perception element was added.

Other types of view-dependent systems are the ones that are using depth sensors. In [18] they proposed a method for improving depth perception by tracking position of the user and creating motion parallax for the rendered image. They showed a set of applications such as box framing and layered video, in which they showed pseudo 3D effects. In [2] they proposed a method for 3D projection of a scene on flat surfaces. They give a user a possibility to explore the scene by walking around.

There were also many systems that are creating the illusion of a 3D depth. An example of such case is a system developed by Pièrard [9]. They proposed a method for 3D illusion by using 2D projectors. Rendered images are projected on the flat surfaces, so the user is not limited to watching content on the screen.

3   Our Method

In this section, we present short description of our method, which is divided in two steps: a rendering part and face tracking.

3.1   Rendering

We want to create as good images as possible and at the same time leave the system responsive for the motion of the user. We tried many types of rendering. First was a simple rendering that uses deferred shading. In this case we considered only diffuse objects, because none of them is able to add details that can cause discomfort. The only thing that can happen is accommodation and vergence conflict. Another type of rendering is raytracing. We use Whitted-style [17] GPU ray-tracer [10], that is using BVH [16] as a speed up for traversal of rays. In both types of rendering we used image based lighting [3] in addition to the pre-computed ambient occlusion [19]. Rays, that are responsible for reflection and refraction, are weighted according to Schlick's approximation [11] to omit costly calculations connected to Fresnel coefficients. Raytracing in comparison to the first method of rendering can add rivalry to the scene. The main reason for this are rays that can change direction, so reflections and refractions. They can hit really different places during stereoscopic rendering, because images for the left and the right eye are rendered from different positions. Nowadays, there were presented some works, that can reduce rivalry in scenes with reflections or refractions. But some of them are really time consuming and because of that reason, for now they are not used in our system. Some results of the rendering are shown on the Fig. 1.

A. Diffuse rendering

B. Anaglyph version of diffuse rendering

C. Raytraced image

D. Anaglyph version of raytraced image

Fig. 1. Results of the rendering methods used in our system

3.2   Face Tracking

Looking at different view-dependent rendering systems, it is easy to come to the conclusion, that everytime some tracking is involved. Knowledge about the user movements is what we are aiming for. This can help us to simulate holography, so the user will be able to watch object from different points of view. Without possibility of face tracking it is impossible to do this, so tracking technique is necessary to adjust the content on the screen.

The most common technique to watch 3D content on the screen is using glasses of different types. We considered anaglyph and row-polarized glasses. But both of them are affecting the possibility to find eyes and tracking them. Sometimes it is even not possible to detect the regions of interest. So to prevent the possibility of not finding features, that can be further used during tracking, we try to detect face and track its position. It is a more robust solution, because it allows user to wear glasses also during detection step.

Solution for face detection (as well as other objects) is a Viola-Johns framework [15]. Detection features are combination of the sequences of rectangles, which are based on Haar wavelets. Each of the rectangles used, consist of regions in two colors: white one and shaded one. The value calculated for every feature is always the difference of the sums of pixels that are inside white regions and shaded ones. Calculating the values for each feature in this way looks rather primitive, but it has one really good advantage over methods like steerable filters, which are more advanced - the rectangular filters by using the method called integral image, can be computed in constant time. Integral image is a method for generating sum of values in a rectangular subset of a grid. In the first step, the summed area table is constructed, where the value in a point (x, y) is a sum of all values that are above and to the left of (x, y). Once the data structure is constructed, every rectangle can be computed by only four table reads. As a learning method AdaBoost was used for both: selecting features and training classifiers. Because the whole system needs to work in real time for detecting the face, cascade classifiers were used. In such a system, there are set of classifiers, where every of them works only on data from the previous one. Because every of the classifiers is limiting the data, detection step is really quick.

After the detection is done, tracking step is needed. There are many techniques that were developed for this reason and they are based on movement or the colour histograms of the object that will be tracked. Because we are interested in movement of the viewer, we involved a tracking technique based on the motion, called Lucas-Kanade optical flow [7]. The method assumes that the flow is constant in a local neighbourhood of the pixel. Method solves equations of optical flow for all the pixels by using the least squares criterion. The method in our system will track specific points, that were found on the detected face. Using this flow, we can change camera origin for the virtual screen in such way, that user can see the object from different perspective. Object is in a center of the virtual sphere and new camera positions will be situated on the surface of this sphere. The only problem in motion that can happen is moving further or closer to the object, because optical flow gives the velocity vectors only in two dimensions. Handling such motion can be done simply by searching differences in face detections sizes in consecutive frames. Of course such difference has to be noticable, because otherwise it can lead to the flickering, what also refers to the horizontal and vertical movements. Errors in finding the face or in the optical flow can lead to the breakdown of the whole system. To prevent optical flow from stopping working, feature points are recalculated, if too many of them were lost. Face detection, because of the movement in depth, is handled directly.

4   Discussion and Result

We have created a system for real-time stereoscopic rendering, which involves viewer's position tracking. View-dependent aspect was studied and developed by many researches before, but in our system, we gave the user an impression of holography, by giving possibility to watch an object from different places. We

Fig. 2. Results of working system, where user can see object from different points of view

tried to improve user's experience by using different methods of rendering. They involve view-dependent effects like reflection and refraction, so user can see even glass objects from different perspective. Some results, where user is watching object from different points of view are shown on Fig. 2.

Our system for simple rendering can work in real-time, but for raytracing it is getting less responsive. The second method of rendering is much more complicated what results in more time needed for creating final images.

Face tracking technique, that we use by now can go wrong. There is a possibility, that it will not detect the face or we will lose followed object. The problem now is that we do not use any other markers, that will help us to keep good tracking path. It can be resolved by adding additional markers for eyes or some other parts of the face, which can make the solution more stable. Stability of the face tracking can be a real problem. We want to reduce noise from the path, because it leads to some fluctuations of the position of the viewed object, what is really annoying for the user. There is only a slight possibility that the input image will have bad quality. For our system the simple camera from laptop is enough, but in bad lighting conditions, the input will have noise. There is a really big possibility, that such corrupted data, will make tracking worse. Of course if tracking or detection go wrong, whole system will give bad results, because it is the main part of it.

In the future we plan to improve the speed of the rendering part, which will help us to handle transparent objects more efficiently. We have not considered visual discomfort, so this is another thing that can be added to our system, as was described in background section. In the case of diffuse rendering there shouldn't be much problems, but with raytracing, things as excessive disparities or rivalry can happen. Recently there were some methods for handling rivalry and preserving the depth of the rendered objects [14,1] and maybe it is worth to add such manipulation to the pipeline. We thought also about adding human head rotations. This type of motion will be able to add another dimension for moving around the screen. Eye tracking is also worth considering.

References

1. Dąbała, Ł., Kellnhofer, P., Ritschel, T., Didyk, P., Templin, K., Myszkowski, K., Rokita, P., Seidel, H.-P.: Manipulating refractive and reflective binocular disparity. Computer Graphics Forum (Proc. Eurographics 2012) 33(2) (2014)
2. Garstka, J., Peters, G.: View-dependent 3d projection using depth-image-based head tracking. In: 8th IEEE International Workshop on Projector Camera Systems, PROCAMS, pp. 52–57 (2011)
3. Greene, N.: Environment mapping and other applications of world projections. IEEE Comp. Graph. and App. 6(11), 21–29 (1986)
4. Nguyen Hoang, A., Tran Hoang, V., Kim, D.: A real-time rendering technique for view-dependent stereoscopy based on face tracking. In: Murgante, B., Misra, S., Carlini, M., Torre, C.M., Nguyen, H.-Q., Taniar, D., Apduhan, B.O., Gervasi, O. (eds.) ICCSA 2013, Part I. LNCS, vol. 7971, pp. 697–707. Springer, Heidelberg (2013)

5. Howard, I.P., Rogers, B.J.: Perceiving in Depth, vol. 2: Stereoscopic Vision. OUP USA (2012)
6. Lambooij, M., IJsselsteijn, W., Fortuin, M., Heynderickx, I.: Visual discomfort and visual fatigue of stereoscopic displays: A review. J. Imag. Sci. and Tech. 53(3), 1–12 (2009)
7. Lucas, B.D., Kanade, T.: An iterative image registration technique with an application to stereo vision. In: Proceedings of the 7th International Joint Conference on Artificial Intelligence, IJCAI 1981, vol. 2, pp. 674–679. Morgan Kaufmann Publishers Inc., San Francisco (1981)
8. Palmer, S.E.: Vision Science: Photons to Phenomenology. The MIT Press (1999)
9. Piérard, S., Pierlot, V., Lejeune, A., Van Droogenbroeck, M.: I-see-3D! An interactive and immersive system that dynamically adapts 2D projections to the location of a user's eyes. In: International Conference on 3D Imaging (IC3D), Liège, Belgium (December 2012)
10. Purcell, T.J., Buck, I., Mark, W.R., Hanrahan, P.: Ray tracing on programmable graphics hardware. ACM Trans. Graph. (Proc. SIGGRAPH) 21(3), 703–712 (2002)
11. Schlick, C.: An inexpensive brdf model for physically-based rendering. Comp. Graph. Forum 13(3), 233–246 (1994)
12. Shibata, T., Kim, J., Hoffman, D.M., Banks, M.S.: The zone of comfort: Predicting visual discomfort with stereo displays. J. Vis. 11(8) (2011)
13. Slotsbo, P.: 3D interactive and view dependent stereo rendering (2004)
14. Templin, K., Didyk, P., Ritschel, T., Myszkowski, K., Seidel, H.-P.: Highlight microdisparity for improved gloss depiction. ACM Trans. Graph. (Proc. SIGGRAPH) 31(4), 92 (2012)
15. Viola, P., Jones, M.: Rapid object detection using a boosted cascade of simple features, pp. 511–518 (2001)
16. Wald, I., Boulos, S., Shirley, P.: Ray tracing deformable scenes using dynamic bounding volume hierarchies. ACM Trans. Graph. 26(1), 6 (2007)
17. Whitted, T.: An improved illumination model for shaded display. ACM SIGGRAPH Computer Graphics 13, 14 (1979)
18. Zhang, C., Yin, Z., Florencio, D.A.F.: Improving depth perception with motion parallax and its application in teleconferencing. In: MMSP, pp. 1–6. IEEE (2009)
19. Zhukov, S., Iones, A., Kronin, G.: An ambient light illumination model. In: Proc. EGSR, pp. 45–55 (1998)

Eye Status Based on Eyelid Detection:
A Driver Assistance System

Michał Daniluk[1], Mahdi Rezaei[2], Radu Nicolescu[2], and Reinhard Klette[2]

[1] Warsaw University of Technology, pl. Politechniki 1, 00-661 Warsaw, Poland
[2] The *.enpeda..* Project, The University of Auckland, New Zealand
mdaniluk123@gmail.com

Abstract. Fatigue and driver drowsiness monitoring is an important subject for designing driver assistance systems. The measurement of eye closure is a fundamental step for driver awareness detection. We propose a method which is based on eyelid detection and the measurement of the distance between the eyelids. First, the face and the eyes of the driver are localized. After extracting the eye region, the proposed algorithm detects eyelids and computes the percentage of eye closure. Experimental results are performed on the BioID database. Our comparisons show that the proposed method outperforms state-of-the-art methods.

1 Introduction and Related Work

Each year more than one million people is killed due to traffic accidents; for example, see the latest report [16] of the *World Health Organisation* (WHO) on road safety. In 2013 more than 1.2 million people died on the world's roads and another 50 million sustained nonfatal injuries as a result of road traffic crashes. The *National Highway Traffic Safety Administration* [1] (NHTSA) conservatively estimates that 100,000 police-reported crashes are the direct result of driver fatigue each year. All these statistics signal that nowadays drivers are often critically distracted and it is essential to develop a system which will detect driver drowsiness and decrease thus the number of car accidents.

In this paper we focus on the problem of detecting driver drowsiness through eye closure analysis to improve road safety. We detect the state of the eyes (open or closed), measure eye closure and compute blink frequency through video sequence analysis. All this information can warn a fatigued driver before a crash happens. Analysis of the driver's eye is a challenge due to the variety of lighting conditions while driving and irregular shape and color of human eyes.

Many techniques have been proposed already to measure the percentage of eye closure, or, at least to detect the eye status as being either open or closed. The analysis of the size of the iris surface [5] can be used to determine the state of the eye (open or closed); this method is based on template matching which has a high computational cost. Another study [2] detects the eyelids and iris using a circular Hough transform. The results of this approach show an accuracy rate of 88.7%, but the reported experiments have not been performed for a publicly available

L.J. Chmielewski et al. (Eds.): ICCVG 2014, LNCS 8671, pp. 171–178, 2014.

dataset. Since the shape of the eye varies for different subjects, the resulting locations are heavily affected by curvature of the eyelid, lighting conditions, and image contrast. The authors of [9] provided an eye-closure measurement method via analyzing the position of the upper and lower eyelids by searching for the change in average image intensity above and below the centre of an already detected eye. The change in image intensity, from dark eye region to light skin region, was captured by a simple vertical integral projection method. The authors report an average median error magnitude of 0.15 and an average 90th percentile error magnitude 0.42 of eye closure, which is unreliable for differentiating eyes into states. The authors of [6] propose eye state-detection that uses statistical features such as sparseness and kurtosis of the histogram from the horizontal edge image of the eye.

We implemented and examined the method proposed in [6] and we noticed that the values of sparseness and kurtosis mainly depend on lighting conditions, and it also varies depending on the subjects. The method is a reasonable solution for determining open or closed eyes, but it is still difficult to measure the degree of eye closure. We also tested a method based on a circular Hough transform which proved to be unstable and worked only on high-resolution images.

Although, most methods are quite robust for non-challenging and normally illuminated scenes, we realized that due to frequent shadows and artificial lighting in day or night scenes, those methods are likely to fail. Furthermore, those methods are not yet tested on public databases, sources are not available, and it is difficult to compare them.

Another approach, which works under challenging lighting conditions, uses a nested cascade of classifiers for open or closed eye-status detection [11]. This detector can not only detect the eye status for frontal faces but also for rotated or tilted head poses in real-time driving applications. The authors obtained a high accuracy (of around 97%) for detecting the eye state, but the efficiency of this method highly depends on the training dataset, as well as on learning parameters.

The rest of this paper is structured as follows. The proposed system is outlined in Section 2. Section 3 provides experiments and obtained result. Section 4 concludes.

2   Proposed Method

The proposed method is based on eyelid detection and measurements of the distance between eyelids. The face and the eyes of a driver are first localized. After extracting the eye region, the proposed algorithm can detect eyelids and computes the percentage of eye closure. In the following sections, each stage of our algorithm is described in detail.

2.1   Face and Eye Detection

The first step of our algorithm is face and eye detection. Our approach uses the object detectors of Viola and Jones [15] and the application of Haar-like features. To determine the presence or absence of Haar-like features, we use *integral images*; see, e.g., [7]. For pixel location $p = (x, y)$, the *integral value*

$$I(p) = \sum_{1 \leq i \leq x \wedge 1 \leq j \leq y} P(i, j) \tag{1}$$

is the sum of all pixel values $P(q)$, where pixel location $q = (i, j)$ is not below, or not to the right of p assuming the origin in the upper left corner of the image carrier.

Considering $p_1, ..., p_4$ as the corners of a rectangle D, the sum of all pixel values for D equals

$$I(D) = I(p_4) + I(p_1) - I(p_2) - I(p_3) \tag{2}$$

See Fig. 1.

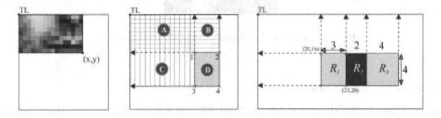

Fig. 1. Calculating integral values for a pixel location (x, y), a rectangle, and a Haar-like feature. Figure by courtesy of the authors of [13].

This technique is then also applied for time-efficient calculation of Haar-like features. Figure 1 illustrates for a Haar-like feature $R_1 R_2 R_3$. Values of contributing regions are weighted by w_i, thus creating a *feature value* for a given *Haar-like feature*. For the shown example, we have

$$I(F_k) = w_1 \cdot I(R_1) - w_2 \cdot I(R_2) + w_3 \cdot I(R_3) \tag{3}$$

The signs of w_i are opposite for light and dark regions.

First, the face is detected in the recorded image. Under non-ideal lighting conditions it is possible that one half of a face is darker than the another side. Inspired from [12] we divide a face into two halves and search for the eye region independently in each of them by adaptively changing detection parameters for the Haar-like object detector.

In order to detect an eyelid, we reduce the eye region of interest. After detection using Haar features, the eye's ROI includes useless information such as the eyebrow and the region between eyebrow and upper eyelid. First, we crop 40% of the upper part of the eye's ROI to remove the eyebrow from the cropped image window. The next step of the algorithm is binarization of the image window using the p-tile thresholding method of [4]. Inspired from [12], we experimentally obtained an adaptive p% value which depends on the intensity value I of the eye region by combining the *mode* M_o and the *mean* value as follows:

$$I = \frac{2}{3} \cdot M_o(E) + \frac{1}{3} \cdot \frac{1}{m} \cdot \sum_{i=1}^{m} E_i \tag{4}$$

Here, E is a eye region, and m is the total number of pixels in E.

After binarization, we detect vertical and horizontal borders in the binary image. Then, we select the largest border region in the image and calculated the bounding box of this region. We obtain a smaller eye region which includes only the iris, pupil, and eyelids. See Fig. 2.

Fig. 2. Example for finding a smaller eye region

2.2   Eyelid Detection

Inspired from [8] we designed our own filters; see Fig. 3, for finding the position of eyelids.

1	...	...	1
-1	...	...	-1
-1	...	...	-1

-1	...	...	-1
1	...	...	1

Filter for upper eyelid   Filter for lower eyelid

Fig. 3. Designed filters for finding eyelids

We used the following two simple facts in developing an algorithm for the detection of eyelids:

1. The upper eyelid is above the lower eyelid.
2. The surrounding region is brighter than the eye.

The eye region is now partitioned into five vertical strips. The filters are applied in each strip; we expect a maximum response at the eyelid position. We use the following median calculation to obtain the estimated position of each eyelid at time t:

$$V(t) = median\{P_1(t), P_2(t), P_3(t), P_4(t), P_5(t)\} \tag{5}$$

where P_i is the estimated position of an eyelid in each strip.

2.3 Calibration

The distance between eyelids depends on the shape of the eye and the distance between camera and face. We apply a calibration procedure during the recording of the first frames to estimate the distance between eyelids for fully open eyes and for closed eyes. During calibration, a user should look into straight into the camera and blink naturally without significant head movements. We experimentally obtained the value for the closed eye in the following way:

$$C = \frac{\frac{f_H}{35} + D[10\% \cdot S]}{2} \tag{6}$$

where f_H is the height of the face, D is a sorted vector of distances between eyelids in the first frames, and S is the size of this vector. We use the following equation to obtain the distance for a fully open eye:

$$O = D[85\% \cdot S] \tag{7}$$

2.4 Measurement of Eye Closure

The eye closure was measured by computing the distance between eyelids for both eyes. Since some people have long eyelashes, the position of lower eyelids moves further down when their eyes are closed. To avoid this problem we assumed that, during blinking, the lower eyelid does not change as much as the upper eyelid, so from the previous frames we obtained

$$L(t) = 3\% \cdot P_{low}(t-5) + 7\% \cdot P_{low}(t-4) + 15\% \cdot P_{low}(t-3) \tag{8}$$
$$+25\% \cdot P_{low}(t-2) + 50\% \cdot P_{low}(t-1)$$

where $P_{low}(t)$ is a position of the lower eyelid at time t. Then, we obtained the position of the lower eyelid using the following equation:

$$P_{low}(t) = \frac{L(t) + P_{low}(t)}{2} \tag{9}$$

To improve our algorithm we assumed that both eyes give us the same information about eye closure. We use the following equation to measure the distance between eyelids. $D_R(t)$ and $D_L(t)$ are the distances between eyelids for the right and left eye at time t, respectively. We have that

$$D(t) = \begin{cases} max(D_R(t), D_L(t)) \text{ if } \frac{D_R(t)+D_L(t)}{2} > C \\ 0 \qquad\qquad \text{ if } \frac{D_R(t)+D_L(t)}{2} \leq C \end{cases} \tag{10}$$

The percentage of eye closure in previous frames supports the confidence for measuring the eye closure in the current frame. We obtained a value of eye closure from previous frames by using the following equation

$$M_p(t) = 3\% \cdot M(t-5) + 7\% \cdot M(t-4) + 15\% \cdot M(t-3) \tag{11}$$
$$+25\% \cdot M(t-2) + 50\% \cdot M(t-1)$$

where $M(t)$ is the percentage of eye closure at time t. We assumed that the difference between the percentage of closure in the current frame and $M_p(t)$ should not be more than 50%. We compute a percentage of eye closure using the following equation:

$$M(t) = \begin{cases} \frac{D_R(t)}{O} \cdot 100 \text{ if } |M_R(t) - M_p(t)| \leq 50\% \wedge |M_L(t) - M_p(t)| > 50\% \\ \frac{D_L(t)}{O} \cdot 100 \text{ if } |M_L(t) - M_p(t)| \leq 50\% \wedge |M_R(t) - M_p(t)| > 50\% \\ \frac{D(t)}{O} \cdot 100 \quad \text{otherwise} \end{cases}$$

(12)

where $M_R(t)$ and $M_L(t)$ are the percentages of right and left eye closures at time t, respectively, and

$$D_L(t) = \begin{cases} D_L(t) \text{ if } D_L(t) > C \\ 0 \quad \text{if } D_L \leq C \end{cases} \tag{13}$$

$$D_R(t) = \begin{cases} D_R(t) \text{ if } D_R(t) > C \\ 0 \quad \text{if } D_R \leq C \end{cases} \tag{14}$$

3   Results

The proposed algorithm was tested on the BioID face database [14] and resulted in better eyelid detection rates than the method reported in [8], which also uses filters to locate positions of eyelids. The BioID face database consists of 1,521 grey-level images with a resolution of 384×286, which were taken under various lighting conditions before complex backgrounds, showing tilted and rotated faces. Our accuracy of eye detection is 97.8%. We analyzed all 1,521 images from the BioID database and marked positions of eyelids on them. We compared the results with true positions of eyelids and assumed that an algorithm gives a *good result* if the distance between eyelids for both eyes fulfils the following constraint:

$$|D_r - D_a| \leq 2 \tag{15}$$

where D_r is the true distance between eyelids and D_a is the calculated distance between eyelids obtained by an algorithm.

The proposed algorithm gives 93.1 % good results of measurement eye closure, compared to Ang Liu's method which gives 88.6 % good results. The *receiver operating characteristic* (ROC) curves for each experiment are shown in Fig. 4. The ROC is important for evaluating different methods for measurement of eye closure, and our proposed method gives better results than the other method.

We also tested the proposed algorithm on our own video sequences [3] under different lighting conditions with several people of different ages. For results for the detected eye status, see Table 1. Videos 1-5 were taken under day light conditions. The proposed algorithm has a good performance under day light conditions. However, analyzing video 6 under dark conditions gave a relatively poor result due to shadows caused by artificial lighting. See Fig. 5 for illustrations.

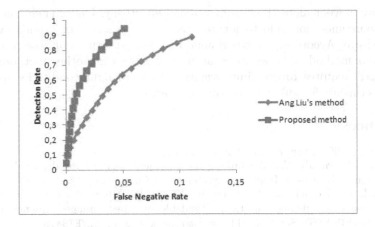

Fig. 4. ROC curve comparison between proposed method and Ang Liu's method

Table 1. Accuracy of the proposed method in terms of detection rate

	Open eye	Closed eye
	Detection rate	
Video 1	99.2%	94.4%
Video 2	99.7%	97.3%
Video 3	97.5%	91.4%
Video 4	99.2%	92.0%
Video 5	98.6%	97.8%
Video 6	96.0%	90.0%

Fig. 5. Results of the proposed method under different lighting conditions

4   Conclusions

In this study, we proposed a driver-monitoring system that can be used to raise a warning alarm in case of driver drowsiness. Accurate measurement of eye closure is a challenging topic in computer vision. Some of the challenges are that various subjects have different shapes of eyes or different lengths of eyelashes, and some use sunglasses while driving. Also, driving conditions are a difficult research context as images even from high-resolution camera might be noisy, which may prevent algorithms from working effectively. Under such conditions we are sometimes not able to locate exactly the position of eyelids even by the naked eye. According to experimental results performed on low resolution images, our method provides more accurate results than other methods. Our method still requires further improvements for dark light conditions and also more experiments for subjects wearing sunglasses.

References

1. NHTSA (2009), http://www.nhtsa.dot.gov/
2. Akrout, B., Mahdi, W.: A blinking measurement method for driver drowsiness detection. Advances in Intelligent Systems and Computing 226, 651–660 (2013)
3. Daniluk, M., Rezaei, M., Nicolescu, R., Klette, R.: Monocular driver monitoring under different lighting conditions. Available in enpeda image sequence analysis test site (EISATS), Set 11 (2014), www.mi.auckland.ac.nz/EISATS
4. Doyle, W.: Operations useful for similarity-invariant pattern recognition. J. ACM 9(2), 259–267 (1962)
5. Horng, W.B., Chen, C.Y., Chang, Y., Fan, C.H.: Driver fatigue detection based on eye tracking and dynamic, template matching. In: Proc. Networking Sensing Control, vol. 1, pp. 7–12 (2004)
6. Jo, J., Jung, H.G., Park, K.R., Kim, J., Lee, S.J.: Vision-based method for detecting driver drowsiness and distraction in driver monitoring system. Optical Engineering 50(12), 127202 (2011)
7. Klette, R.: Concise Computer Vision. Springer, London (2014)
8. Liu, A., Li, Z., Wang, L., Zhao, Y.: A practical driver fatigue detection algorithm based on eye state. In: Proc. Asia Pacific Conf. Postgraduate Research Microelectronics Electronics (PrimeAsia), pp. 235–238 (2010)
9. Malla, A.M., Davidson, P.R., Bones, P.J., Green, R., Jones, R.D.: Automated video-based measurement of eye closure for detecting behavioral microsleep. In: Proc. Engineering Medicine Biology Society (EMBC), pp. 6741–6744 (2010)
10. Omidyeganeh, M., Javadtalab, A., Shirmohammadi, S.: Intelligent driver drowsiness detection through fusion of yawning and eye closure. In: Proc. Virtual Environments Human-Computer Interfaces Measurement Systems (VECIMS), pp. 1–6 (2011)
11. Rezaei, M., Klette, R.: 3D cascade of classifiers for open and closed eye detection in driver distraction monitoring. In: Real, P., Diaz-Pernil, D., Molina-Abril, H., Berciano, A., Kropatsch, W. (eds.) CAIP 2011, Part II. LNCS, vol. 6855, pp. 171–179. Springer, Heidelberg (2011)
12. Rezaei, M., Klette, R.: Adaptive Haar-like classifier for eye status detection under non-ideal lighting conditions. In: Proc. Image Vision Computing New Zealand, pp. 521–526 (2012)
13. Rezaei, M.: Artistic rendering of human portraits paying attention to facial features. In: Brooks, A.L. (ed.) ArtsIT 2011. LNICST, vol. 101, pp. 90–99. Springer, Heidelberg (2012)
14. The BioID face database,
http://www.bioid.com/downloads/facedb/facedatabase.html
15. Viola, P., Jones, M.: Rapid object detection using a boosted cascade of simple features. In: Proc. Computer Vision Pattern Recognition, pp. 511–518 (2001)
16. World Health Organization: WHO global status report on road safety 2013: supporting a decade of action (2013)

Automatic Assessment of Skull Circumference in Craniosynostosis

Anna Fabijańska[1], Tomasz Węgliński[1], Jarosław Gocławski[1],
Wanda Mikołajczyk-Wieczorek[2], Krzysztof Zakrzewski[2],
and Emilia Nowosławska[2]

[1] Łódź University of Technology, Institute of Applied Computer Science
18/22 Stefanowskiego Str., 90-924 Łódź, Poland
anna.fabijanska@p.lodz.pl
[2] Polish Mother's Memorial Hospital - Research Institute
281/289 Rzgowska St., Łódź, Poland
krzysztof.zakrzewski_xl.@wp.pl

Abstract. The premature fusion of one or more calvarias sutures of the infant's skull causes a common pediatric disease called craniosynostosis. This condition causes a serious deformation of the head shape and may produce a noticeable disorder in the neuropsychological development of a child and can be treated only by a surgery. The fused sutures are typically confirmed by the computed tomography (CT) imaging. The surgical outcome and overall progress of the treatment is assessed based on a clinical judgment and an additional manual measurement of the head circumference (HC) index. The research presented in this paper considered the problem of an automatic calculation of the HC index based on CT scans. In particular, algorithms for the skull segmentation, determination of the head central sagittal plane and skull landmarks used for the calculation of the HC indices are introduced.

Keywords: image processing, image analysis, craniosynostosis, head circumference.

1 Introduction

Craniosynostosis is a common pediatric disease which affects about 1 in 2500 individuals [1]. It is caused by the premature fusion of one or more calvarias sutures of the skull [2,3].

In the early stages of life, the sutures of the child's skull are partially opened what allows a normal skull and brain growth. However, if one or more sutures are prematurely fused, the brain is forced to grow in different directions. This causes head shape deformations and the possible risk of the increased intracranial brain, causing a noticeable disorder in the neuropsychological development of a child. There are several types of craniosynostosis, depending on which sutures are prematurely closed. The most common ones are: the *scaphocephaly*, which manifest itself as a long narrow head and the *trigonocephaly* detected as a midline forehead ridge and frontotemporal narrowing[1].

L.J. Chmielewski et al. (Eds.): ICCVG 2014, LNCS 8671, pp. 179–186, 2014.

The fused sutures are typically confirmed by the computed tomography (CT) imaging. CT scan allows to assess the type of synostosis and plan the surgical reconstruction of the skull, which is the only possibility of the disease treatment. The main objective of the surgery is to reopen the cranial sutures and create the arbitrary skull gaps to allow the proper brain development. Figure 1 presents a CT scan of the craniosynostosic brain before (Fig. 1a) and after the surgical correction (Fig. 1b).

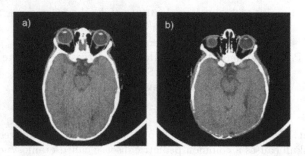

Fig. 1. CT scan of craniosynostosic brain a) before and b) after the surgical correction of the skull

The craniosystosis is assessed using two main parameters namely: *cephalic index* (CI) and *head circumference* (HC) [4]. These are usually calculated before and (periodically) after the surgery and allow to confirm the proper brain growth and monitor the overall progress of the treatment. Recently, the measurement of both: CI and HC indices is performed manually what has a limited accuracy and repeatability. Additionally, HC determination requires physical contact with a patient, what can be difficult, especially after the surgery. Therefore, there is a need of a development of image processing and analysis algorithms which will automate assessment of craniosynostosis.

The ongoing research in the field of image processing and analysis consider a few of problems related to the pre- and postoperative control of the craniosynostosic patients. The recent research is mainly focused on 3D modelling of the skull [5,6], classifying craniosynostosis head shapes [7], evaluation of changes in holes dimensions [8] and estimation of the intracranial volume [9,10]. However, to the best of our knowledge, no research has been conducted on the problem of an automatic calculation of cephalic and head circumference indices.

Having in mind the above mentioned facts, this paper proposes a method for an automatic determination of HC index from volumetric CT scans. The method can be used to assess the skull circumference without a physical contact with a patient. This allows the neurosurgeons to diagnose the progress of the treatment based on the historical CT data, independently from the time and the location of their acquisition. Additionally, the method can be used to calculate HC index for different types of craniosynostosis, even if the skull is partially discontinuous due to the surgery. The method is described in detail in the following section.

2   Proposed Approach

2.1   Preprocessing

In this work CT datasets are regarded. These consist of Z slices, $X \times Y$ pixels each. The slices are stacked and compose a volumetric image. These images however cannot be directly put into a regular pixel grid. It's because the distance between slices d_z is usually different from a pixel dimensions (d_x, d_y, where: $d_x = d_y$). In order to ensure uniform processing, an image data is firstly regularized via linear interpolation. In particular, based on image information from the existing slices, a volumetric image of the slice thickness equal to pixel dimensions d_x is build.

2.2   Skull Segmentation

In the input CT images voxel intensities L are coded as signed integers and represent Hounsfield units. Therefore, a skull I is easily extracted by a simple thresholding. In particular, it is the largest connected component build from voxels of intensities L higher than 700 HU (see Eq. 1).

$$I(x, y, z) = \{1 : L(x, y, z) > 700\} \tag{1}$$

2.3   Determination of the Central Sagittal Plane

The first step of the circumference measurement is a positioning skull in line with the central sagittal plane (CSP) of an input image. This is obtained in two steps: rotation and translation of a skull image I, described by Equations 2 and 3 respectively.

$$I_2 = rot(-\alpha, I) \tag{2}$$

$$I_3 = trans(d, I_2) \tag{3}$$

where α is a skull orientation angle and d is a distance between the central sagittal planes of the skull and the input image.

The angle α of skull orientation is the angle between the central sagittal planes of the input image and the skull. The reflection of the skull about its symmetry plane produces approximately identical object. Therefore, in order to find the orientation angle α, the image of skull I is firstly reflected about the CSP of the input image and then rotated around this plane. The rotation angle ϕ for which 3D cross-correlation between the original and the reflected, rotated image of the skull is maximal, is twice as big as the orientation angle (i.e. $\alpha = \phi/2$).

This procedure is explained in Figures 2 and 3. Figure 2 sketches the idea of correlating the original and the rotated, reflected image. Figure 3 presents a sample slice of the skull, its reflection about the CSP of an input image and the position for which the 3D cross-correlation of images is maximal.

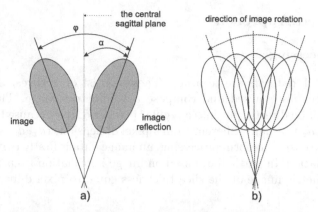

Fig. 2. Skull orientation determination; a) a skull and its reflection; b) a skull rotation

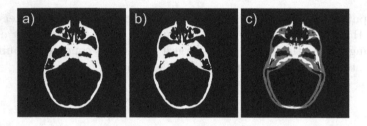

Fig. 3. Determination of the maximal correlation between images of skull; a) a sample slice; b) a reflection about the CSP of image; c) the highest correlated images

After the angle α is found, image I_2 (see Eq. 2) is aligned symmetrically about the central sagittal plane of an image. In order to find translation d (see Eq. 3) image I_2 is again reflected about its CSP. Next, both image I_2 and its reflection are gradually and symmetrically translated towards the centre of the image (see Fig. 4 and 5). Translation which maximizes 3D cross-correlation between the translated image I_2 and its reflection defines d.

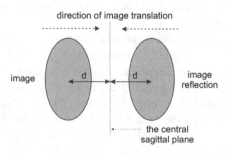

Fig. 4. The idea of determination of a skull translation

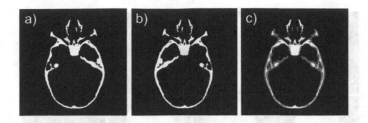

Fig. 5. Determination of the maximal correlation between images of skull; a) a sample slice; b) reflection about the CSP of an image; c) the highest correlated images

2.4   Determination of Skull Landmarks

A head circumference is a measurement taken around the largest part of a skull and includes two landmarks, i.e. *glabella* and *maximal occipital point*. The first one is the most-front point of a skull while the latter is the most-back point of a skull. Let us regard, that an input image is put in the Cartesian coordinate system where plane $x = X/2$ is the central sagittal plane of a skull. In such a case, a skull landmarks can be found based on the image created on the CSP i.e. $x = X/2$. Regarding symbols from Figure 6, *glabella* is a skull voxel on a plane $x = X/2$ with the lowest y coordinate, while *maximal occipital point* is a skull voxel on a plane $x = X/2$ with the highest y coordinate.

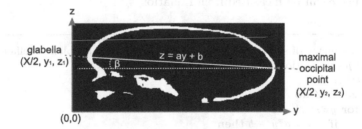

Fig. 6. Skull landmarks

Coordinates $(X/2, y_1, z_1)$ and $(X/2, y_2, z_2)$ of the regarded landmarks define a plane for measuring skull circumference. The plane equation is $z = ay + b$, where: $a = \frac{z_2-z_1}{y_2-y_1}$ and $b = \frac{y_2z_1-y_1z_2}{y_2-y_1}$.

It is difficult to measure a skull circumference directly on a plane $z = ay + b$. It is because the plane for measuring circumference is not parallel to the plane of CT slice and the measurement must be performed across slices. Therefore, firstly its projection p on a plane $z = z_2$ is found in accordance with an Algorithm 1. Projection image is used to find a skull outline and its length. The length is next rescaled to recompense shape deformation due to projection.

In the regarded problem skulls may not be complete and some its parts may be missing (eq. due to vault remodelling). Therefore, finding a skull outline requires the additional processing. Firstly, head region h (Fig. 7b) and the skull s

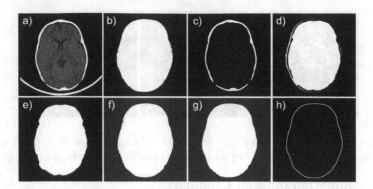

Fig. 7. Skull circumference measurement; a) image projection onto z plane; b) head mask; c) skull projection onto z plane; d) head mask XOR skull; e) brain mask; f) brain mask AND skull; g) previous image after hole filling and closing; h) edge of skull

(Fig. 7c) are found based on the projection image (Fig. 7a). In these steps thresholding is applied. The following operations include: h XOR s (Fig. 7d), morphological opening (Fig. 7e), adding image of skull (Fig. 7f) and hole filling followed by the morphological closing (Fig 7g). The result is the skull outline (Fig. 7h), which is represented by a 1-pixel width 8-connected line. In such a case, skull circumference c can be measured from Equation 4.

Data: *in* - image of skull; X, Y, Z - image dimensions; a, b - plane coefficients
Result: p - projection
for *x=1:1:X* **do**
 for *z=1:1:Z* **do**
  for *y=1:1:Y* **do**
   if $z == a*y + b$ **then**
   | p(y, x) = in(y, x, z)
   end
  end
 end
end

Algorithm 1: Projecting a plane $z = ay + b$ onto a plane $z = z_2$

$$c = \frac{(n + m\sqrt{2})d_x}{cos\beta} \tag{4}$$

where: n is the number of pairs of outline pixels connected by an edge, m is the number of pairs of outline pixels connected by a corner, d_x is a pixel dimension and $\beta = atan(|a|)$ is an angle between planes $z = ay + b$ and $z = z_2$ (see Fig. 6).

3 Results

The results of head circumference measurement in 10 sample cases are given in Table 1 (series: *auto*) and compared with the manual measurements performed by the specialist (series: *manual*). The manual measurement has been done using The Medical Imaging Interaction Toolkit (MITK), in particular the *measurement-path* tool. Additionally, in the last row the absolute error of the automatic measurement is given (in %). The cases were sorted due to the error value.

Table 1. The results of the head circumference measurement (in *cm*)

Case ID	1	2	3	4	5	6	7	8	9	10
auto	49.48	49.51	49.41	50.80	51.56	46.59	46.96	51.91	43.75	51.23
manual	49.23	49.11	49.84	50.19	50.90	45.89	46.24	50.91	42.87	49.85
error [%]	0.50	0.82	0.87	1.21	1.34	1.52	1.55	1.96	2.05	2.75

Results presented in Table 1 clearly show, that the introduced approach to a skull circumference measurement was successful in all the regarded cases. Results of the manual and the automatic measurements are very close and the measurement error does not exceed 3%. In the case of the considered problem this accuracy is sufficient.

In most of the considered cases the skull circumference determined automatically was higher than the circumference determined manually. The difference is caused by the fact, that in the case of manual measurement head circumference was approximated by a path build from straight lines. Unfortunately, there were no historical measurements of a skull circumference performed manually in physical contact with a child which could be used as a reference

4 Conclusions

In this paper a technique for a skull circumference measurement was introduced. The method is dedicated to CT volumetric scans and performs measurements automatically, without a user interaction. As a result, the circumference measurement is objective. It is not influenced by a manual selection of skull landmarks which can vary depending on a specialist. Additionally, the method does not require a physical contact with a child and may be used for monitoring changes of skull dimensions based on the historical CT scans, acquired in different moments at different sites. Another advantage of the introduced approach is its resistance to a skull discontinuity. As a result it can be successfully applied for a skull circumference measurement in the postoperative craniosystosis, where some parts of skull are removed during the corrective surgery.

Acknowledgements. This research was funded by the Ministry of Science and Higher Education of Poland from founds for science in years 2013-2015 in a framework of Iuventus Plus Programme (project no. IP 2012 011272).

References

1. Lajeunie, E., Le Merrer, M., Marchac, C., Renier, D.: Genetic study of scapho-cepaly. Am. J. Med. Gene. 62, 282–285 (1996)
2. Cohen, M.M., MacLean, M.C.: Craniosynostosis: Diagnosis, Evaluation, and Management, 2nd edn. Oxford University Press, Oxford (2000)
3. Marieb, E.N., Hoehn, K.: Human Anatomy and Physiology. Pearson Benjamin Cummings. San Francisco (2007)
4. Thompson, D.N.P., Britto, J.: The clinical management of craniosynostosis, pp. 12–44. Mac Keith Press, London (2004)
5. Wolański, W., Larysz, D., Gzik, M., Kawlewska, E.: Modeling and biomechanical analysis of craniosynostosis correction with the use of finite element method. Int. J. Numer. Meth. Biomed. Engng. 2013 29, 916–925 (2013)
6. Gzik, M., Wolański, W., Tejszerska, D., Gzik-Zroska, B., Koźlak, M., Larysz, D., Mandera, M.: Application of 3D modeling and modern visualization technique to neurosurgical trigonocephaly correction in children. World Congress on Medical Physics and Biomedical Engineering, IFMBE Proceedings 25(9), 68–71 (2009)
7. Lin, H.J., Ruiz-Correa, S., Shapiro, L.G., Speltz, M.L., Cunningham, M.L., Sze, R.W.: Predicting Neuropsychological Development from Skull Imaging. In: EMBS Annual International Conference, New York City, USA (2006)
8. Teng, C.C., Shapiro, L., Hopper, R.A., Halen, J.V.: Pediatric Cranial Defect Surface Analysis For Craniosynostosis Postoperation CT Images. Biomedical Imaging: From Nano to Macro, 620–623 (2008)
9. Jensen, R.R., Thorup, S.S., Paulsen, R.R., Darvann, T.A., Hermann, N.V., Larsen, P., Kreiborg, S., Larsen, R.: Genus zero graph segmentation: Estimation of intracranial volume. Pattern Recognition Letters (in print, 2014)
10. de Oliveira, M.E., Hallila, H., Ritvanen, A., Buchler, P., Paulasto, M., Hukki, J.: Postoperative Evaluation of Surgery f or Craniosynostosis Based on Image Registration Techniques. In: 32nd Annual International Conference of the IEEE EMBS, pp. 5620–5623 (2010)

Performance Evaluation of Binary Descriptors of Local Features

Jan Figat, Tomasz Kornuta, and Włodzimierz Kasprzak

Warsaw University of Technology, Institute of Control and Computation Eng.
Nowowiejska 15/19 00-665 Warsaw, Poland
{J.Figat,T.Kornuta,W.Kasprzak}@ia.pw.edu.pl

Abstract. The article is devoted to the evaluation of performance of image features with binary descriptors for the purpose of their utilization in recognition of objects by service robots. In the conducted experiments we used the dataset and followed the methodology proposed by Mikolajczyk and Schmid. The performance analysis takes into account the discriminative power of a combination of keypoint detector and feature descriptor, as well as time consumption.

Keywords: performance evaluation, image features, binary descriptors, SIFT, FAST, BRIEF, BRISK, ORB, FREAK.

1 Motivation of the Work

The recently observed progress in service robotics would not be possible without the progress in the recognition of everyday objects. Our two-handed robot Velma posses an active head equipped with a pair of RGB cameras and a pair of vertically mounted Kinect sensors. Such a perception subsystem enables the robot to acquire point clouds constituting its environment. We developed a process of generation of 3D object models consisting of two types of point clouds: a dense colour point cloud (used mainly for visualisation) and a sparse feature cloud (used for recognition). Currently our object recognition process relies on SIFT (Scale Invariant Feature Transform) [1] features transformed into a feature cloud on the basis of additional depth information. We have chosen SIFT because it is one of the most valued feature.

However, the recent advent in image features turned our attention to features possessing binary descriptors. The advantage of utilization of those type of features is simple: reduced time consumption. This is achieved due to the fact that instead of computation of all gradients for each pixel in the patch, binary descriptors are encoded on the basis of comparison of intensity of pairs of selected pixels. Additionally, the comparison between the binary descriptors is much faster from the classical HOG-like descriptors because it bases on the Hamming distance, which can be computed by summing the bits being result of the XOR operation between the two compared binary strings. Hence utilization of such a feature in the process of a real-time recognition of objects by a service

L.J. Chmielewski et al. (Eds.): ICCVG 2014, LNCS 8671, pp. 187–194, 2014.

robot is highly desirable. With several types of features currently present in order to select the one that fits best to our needs we examined their properties and compared their discriminative power. In this paper we present the results of such a performance evaluation.

2   Local Features with Binary Descriptors

Typically, a local feature consists of a detector (which detects stable keypoints) and a descriptor (characterising its neighbourhood). BRIEF (Binary Robust Independent Elementary Features) [2] offers a binary descriptor, without the proposal of its own method of detection of keypoints, thus typically it is combined with FAST (Features from Accelerated Segment Test) [3] detector. The BRIEF descriptor usually contains 128, 256 or 512 bits whereas the size is equal to the number of analysed pairs of pixels of analysed patch. Hence the number influences both the speed rate and discriminative power. The descriptor is sensitive to noise, because for each pixel of a given pair it considers only the point intensity, disregarding the neighbouring pixels. This sensitivity can be reduced by prior smoothing of the image and typically Gaussian filter is used. BRIEF does not have a constant sampling pattern. Instead pairs of pixels used for building of the descriptor are randomly selected. The authors proposed five methods of determination of the point pairs and pointed that the best results were achieved with the use of random selection with Gaussian distribution.

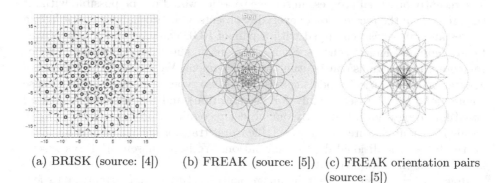

(a) BRISK (source: [4])   (b) FREAK (source: [5])   (c) FREAK orientation pairs
                                                          (source: [5])

Fig. 1. Sampling patterns

ORB (Oriented FAST and Rotated BRIEF) [6] is similar to BRIEF with added rotation and scaling invariance. Besides, instead of using a randomly selected pairs, ORB learns the optimal set of sampling pairs using machine learning techniques. ORB uses FAST to find keypoints. Additionally, it builds image pyramid to achieve scale robustness. The rotation invariance is obtained by using moments, which are computed in a circular-shaped patch around the center of its mass. Sampling pairs should have two properties: they should be uncorrelated and the chosen set of pairs should be characterized with possibly maximal variance (it will make the feature more discriminative). To fulfil those needs, ORB runs a greedy search among all pairs following a predefined binary tests.

The BRISK (Binary Robust Invariant Scalable Keypoints) [4] descriptor is using a hand-crafted sampling pattern, composed out of concentric rings, with more points on outer rings. Fig. 1a presents BRISK sampling pattern with 60 sampling points. The small blue circles represent the sampling points locations, whereas the radiuses of red dashed circles are correspond to the standard deviation of the Gaussian kernel used to smooth the intensity values at the sampling points. Two types of sampling-point pairs are distinguished: short-distance and long-distance ones. Authors proposed to set the thresholds of distances depending on the scale in which keypoint was detected. BRISK also possess an orientation compensation mechanism.

The FREAK (Fast Retina Keypoint) [5] descriptor, similarly to BRISK, uses an encoded sampling pattern (fig. 1b). This pattern uses overlapping concentric circles with more points on inner rings. Each circle represents a sensitive field. In order to achieve the rotation invariance, FREAK samples pairs with symmetric sensitive fields with respect to the patch center, as shown on fig. 1c. FREAK is also similar to ORB by learning the optimal set of sampling pairs. First it creates a set of pairs mimicking the saccadic search (human retina movements) and subsequently uses machine learning to select subset possessing the most discriminative power.

3   Performance Evaluation

3.1   Dataset

Our methodology of evaluation of performance of image features follows the work of Mikolajczyk and Schmid [7] and, besides others, we decided to use their image dataset. The dataset used contains images subjected to six different distortions (image transformations), namely: blurring, change of viewpoint (rotation), change of scale, JPEG compression, change in illumination. It is divided into eight images subsets, as presented in fig. 2. Those subsets are named bikes, trees, graffiti, wall, bark, boat, lueven and UBC respectively. Each of such a subsets consists of six images: one considered as basic image and five being more and more distorted. Additionally, the distorted images are supplemented with files containing homography between the basic image and considered one.

3.2   Performance Evaluation

Fig. 3 presents the developed process for evaluation of performance of image features. For each image of a given pair (containing basic and distorted images) we first detect keypoints with a given detector and subsequently extract the associated descriptors.

Fig. 2. Dataset used in the performance evaluation [7]

Next features from those two sets are compared in order to find the best matches. The knowledge of the proper homography between the two analysed images enables us to transform the positions of features extracted from the distorted image into the equivalent position in basic image. We treat this as a ground truth and reject all correspondences with difference in image positions being grater than a given parameter. We checked the results for distance being equal to 1, 2, 3, 4 and 5 pixels and noticed that the most optimal results were obtained for the distance equal to 2, so during further experiments set the distance to 2.

During the experiments we also measured the time of keypoint detection, descriptor extractor and feature matching. In our implementation we used the OpenCV [8] library (version 2.4.8) running on a PC with a quadcore Phenom II 965 processor and 4GB RAM, under control of Ubuntu 12.0.4 OS.

3.3   Results of Experiments

First set of tests was performed for all of the abovedescribed binary descriptors, basing on exactly the same set of keypoints. Because our goal was to find a combination of detector and descriptor giving better (or at least not behaving much worse) then the featured currently used in our tasks, we applied the SIFT detector for localization of keypoints and measured the SIFT descriptor performance, treating it as a reference. Results of comparison of the percentage of correctly found correspondences with keypoints localized by SIFT detector are presented inin fig. 4a. In this case SIFT performance simply dominates binary descriptors.

Next, we decided to conduct the same experiments for default detectors (using FAST of those features that do not have their own, special detectors i.e. BRIEF and FREAK). Fig. 4b presents results of such a comparison. We can observe that the best results were obtained once again for SIFT, however in several cases ORB acted almost as good, and sometimes even better.

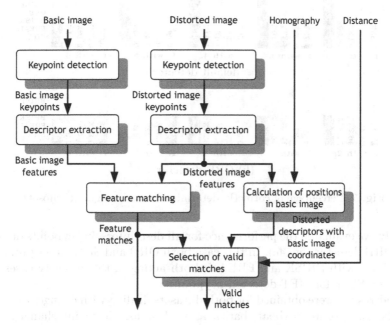

Fig. 3. Process of evaluation of features

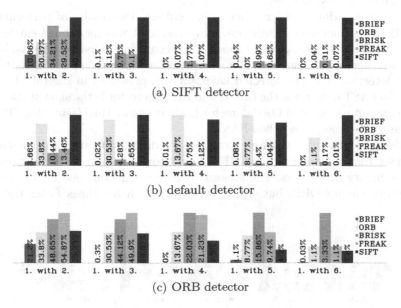

Fig. 4. Percentage of correctly determined matches (boat subset)

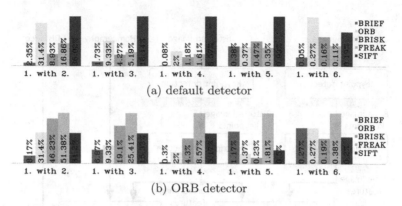

Fig. 5. Percentage of correctly determined matches (graffiti subset)

Finally, we evaluated the performance for all descriptors on keypoints detected by the ORB detector (fig. 4c). In this case both ORB and SIFT descriptors were overwhelmed with BRISK and FREAK, both acting in the majority cases even better then SIFT for SIFT-detected keypoints.

Similar results were obtained for both datasets dealing with changes of a zoom with additional rotation (boat, bark), as well as for viewpoint changes (wall, graffiti). In particular, for graffiti images the best results were obtained for ORB detector with FREAK, beating all other combinations (fig. 5b). In case of the wall subset the combination of ORB detector with FREAK descriptor also appeared to be one of the best (fig. 6a).

It is worth noting that for other image subsets the results of performation evaluation were not that unanimous. However, as it was mentioned earlier, we are seeking features for a given purpose, i.e. recognition of indoor objects, hence robustness against blurring or image compression is not so important to us.

The detection time per detected keypoint was presented in the tab. 1. As it shows the FAST detector is the fastest and SIFT detector is the slowest. Besides, it is important to note that ORB detector is almost twice time faster then BRISK but almost 20 times slower then FAST.

In the tab. 1 the time feature extraction per detected feature was shown. As we can see the extraction time for SIFT descriptor was far more time-consuming then for binary descriptors. The longest feature extraction time for the binary descriptors was for ORB, but still it was more then ten times faster then for SIFT.

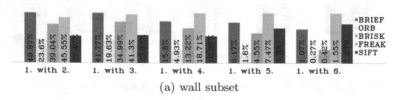

Fig. 6. Percentage of correctly determined matches for ORB detector

Table 1. Average feature detection and extraction times (boat images)

Detector	Detection time [μs]
FAST	0.87857
ORB	16.39273
BRISK	30.63530
SIFT	229.67313

Descriptor	Extraction time [μs]
BRIEF	7,42990
ORB	14.5747
BRISK	9.60987
FREAK	9.09653
SIFT	174.44800

(a) Average keypoint detection time   (b) Average descriptor extraction time

Table 2. Average detection and extraction time for boat images

Detector	Descriptor	Average time per feature point [μs]
FAST	BRIEF	8.30847
ORB	ORB	30.96741
BRISK	BRISK	39.30988
ORB	BRISK	27.95955
FAST	FREAK	11.33364
ORB	FREAK	32.42584
SIFT	SIFT	404.12113

The decision to choose an appropriate descriptor with detector was based on both the time of operation as well as the needs of our research. From the tab. 2 it can be seen that FREAK with ORB detector is a little bit slower than BRISK with ORB detector, but more than ten times faster than the SIFT with SIFT detector.

3.4   Conclusions

The results obtained for ORB detector with FREAK descriptor were much better than for others descriptors, especially for the viewpoint changes. Surprisingly, these results were event better then for classical SIFT detector and descriptor combination. For the zoom with rotation changes, combination of ORB detector with FREAK descriptor seemed to be a little bit worse than ORB wit BRISK, whereas for the point of view changes the results were much better than the performance of the other descriptors. Additionally, in comparison to SIFT, the time consumption for combination of ORB with FREAK is one order of magnitude smaller (tab. 2). Therefore, we decided that a combination of ORB detector with FREAK descriptor fits best to our needs.

4   Summary

The article was devoted to the evaluation of performance of local features with binary descriptors. We evaluated the features with binary descriptors, taking

SIFT as ground truth. Comparison was made for several combinations of detectors and descriptors. Aside of the discriminative performance of features we analysed the time consumption for various combinations of keypoint detectors and extraction of descriptors. As a result we have chosen ORB detector and FREAK descriptor, which seem to be the best for the purpose of recognition of everyday objects in the indoor environment.

In our future work will plan to use the selected combination in the object recognition and generation of 3D models of objects. Aside of that, during the experiments it appeared that the chosen dataset does not entirely fulfil our needs. In particular, distortions such as blur or JPEG compression are not important for service robots performing manipulation tasks, but instead systematic studies of rotation (viewpoint change), scaling, occlusions and object damages (due to e.g. scratches resulting from repeated grasping of objects with a robot gripper) would be required. The last one we find especially interesting.

Acknowledgments. The authors acknowledge the support of European Union within the RAPP project funded by the 7th Framework Programme (Collaborative Project FP7-ICT 610947). The authors would also like to thank to Łukasz Jendrzejek and Karol Koniuszewski for help with the implementation and initial experiments.

References

1. Lowe, D.G.: Distinctive image features from scale-invariant keypoints. International Journal of Computer Vision 60(2), 91–110 (2004)
2. Calonder, M., Lepetit, V., Strecha, C., Fua, P.: BRIEF: Binary Robust Independent Elementary Features. In: Daniilidis, K., Maragos, P., Paragios, N. (eds.) ECCV 2010, Part IV. LNCS, vol. 6314, pp. 778–792. Springer, Heidelberg (2010)
3. Rosten, E., Drummond, T.: Machine learning for high-speed corner detection. In: Leonardis, A., Bischof, H., Pinz, A. (eds.) ECCV 2006, Part I. LNCS, vol. 3951, pp. 430–443. Springer, Heidelberg (2006)
4. Leutenegger, S., Chli, M., Siegwart, R.Y.: Brisk: Binary robust invariant scalable keypoints. In: 2011 IEEE International Conference on Computer Vision (ICCV), pp. 2548–2555. IEEE (2011)
5. Alahi, A., Ortiz, R., Vandergheynst, P.: FREAK: Fast Retina Keypoint. In: 2012 IEEE Conference on Computer Vision and Pattern Recognition (CVPR), pp. 510–517. IEEE (2012)
6. Rublee, E., Rabaud, V., Konolige, K., Bradski, G.: Orb: an efficient alternative to sift or surf. In: 2011 IEEE International Conference on Computer Vision (ICCV), pp. 2564–2571. IEEE (2011)
7. Mikolajczyk, K., Schmid, C.: A performance evaluation of local descriptors. IEEE Transactions on Pattern Analysis and Machine Intelligence 27(10), 1615–1630 (2005)
8. Bradski, G., Kaehler, A.: Learning OpenCV: Computer Vision with the OpenCV Library, 1st edn. O'Reilly (September 2008)

Characteristics of Bottom-Up Parsable edNLC Graph Languages for Syntactic Pattern Recognition

Mariusz Flasiński[1] and Zofia Flasińska[2]

[1] IT Systems Department, Jagiellonian University
ul. prof. St. Łojasiewicza 4, Kraków 30-348, Poland
Mariusz.Flasinski@uj.edu.pl
[2] Luxoft Poland, ul. Krakowska 280, Zabierzów 32-080, Poland

Abstract. Further results of research into graph grammar-based parsing for syntactic pattern recognition (*Pattern Recognition*: 21, 623-629 (1988); 23, 765-774 (1990); 26, 1-16 (1993); 43, 2249-2264 (2010), *Comput. Vision Graph. Image Process.* 47, 1-21 (1989), *Theoret. Comp. Sci.* 201, 189-231 (1998)) are presented in the paper. The bottom-up parsable ETPR(k) subclass of well-known edNLC graph grammars is defined.

1 Introduction

Although graph grammars are the strongest generative formalism applied for a description of structural visual patterns [14], their use for syntactic pattern recognition is still not satisfactory. It is caused by a hard (i.e. PSPACE-complete or NP-complete) membership problem for classes of graph grammars interesting from the application point of view [21]. Therefore, in spite of the fact that the first mathematical models of graph automata were proposed in the late 1960s [1] only a few graph parsing algorithms have been defined for almost 60 years [19, 2, 13, 4, 16, 20, 17, 3, 18, 22, 23].

Graph grammars of the class edNLC introduced by Janssens and Rozenberg [15] are a very strong formalism for visual patterns' generation. Therefore, an extensive fundamental research into defining parsable subclasses of edNLC languages has been led since the late 1980s and it has resulted in defining efficient parsers, $O(n^2)$, for ETPL(k) subclass of these languages [5–8, 10]. The ETPL(k)grammars have been used in such syntactic pattern recognition application areas as: scene analysis [5], the vision subsystem of an industrial robot control system [8], pattern recognition of mechanical parts in the CAD/CAM integration system [9], recognition of Polish Sign Language [11]. Visual patterns have been represented with the help of a family of IE-graphs [5] generated by ETPL(k) grammars as it is shown in Fig. 1.

Although ETPL(k) grammars are a very strong generative/discriminative formalism some graph languages cannot be described by this class (see [10], Theorem 4). It is caused by the fact that ETPL(k) languages are top-down parsable,

L.J. Chmielewski et al. (Eds.): ICCVG 2014, LNCS 8671, pp. 195–202, 2014.

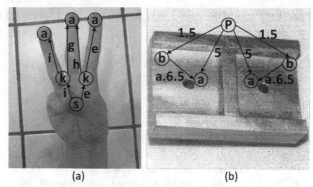

(a)   (b)

Fig. 1. Applications of ETPL(k) grammars in (a) Polish Sign Language recognition [11] and (b) pattern recognition of mechanical parts [9]

whereas a bottom-up syntax analyzer would be strong enough. Therefore, a research into defining a bottom-up parsable subclass of edNLC grammars has been started recently. Its first results are presented in the paper.

2   Preliminaries

Let us begin with definitions of: directed node- and edge-labelled graph (EDG graph) and edNLC graph grammar, which generates such graphs [15].

Definition 1. A *directed node- and edge-labelled graph, EDG graph,* over Σ and Γ is a quintuple $H = (V, E, \Sigma, \Gamma, \phi)$, where V is a finite, non-empty set of nodes, Σ is a finite, non-empty set of node labels, Γ is a finite, non-empty set of edge labels, E is a set of edges of the form (v, λ, w), where $v, w \in V, \lambda \in \Gamma$, $\phi : V \longrightarrow \Sigma$ is the node-labelling function.

Definition 2. An *edge-labelled directed Node Label Controlled, edNLC, graph grammar* is a quintuple $G = (\Sigma, \Delta, \Gamma, P, Z)$, where Σ is a finite, non-empty set of node labels, $\Delta \subseteq \Sigma$ is a set of terminal node labels, Γ is a finite, non-empty set of edge labels, P is a finite set of productions of the form (l, D, C), in which $l \in \Sigma, D$ is an EDG graph, $C : \Gamma \times \{in, out\} \longrightarrow 2^{\Sigma \times \Sigma \times \Gamma \times \{in,out\}}$ is the embedding transformation, Z is the EDG starting graph (axiom).

In order to define a bottom-up parsable subclass of edNLC grammars, we will have to order both nodes and edges of graphs generated, similarly as we have made it for top-down parsable ETPL(k) subclass [5, 6, 8]. For such ordering we should assume certain properties concerning EDG graphs. As it has been shown in a variety of computer vision applications of parsable ETPL(k) grammars [5–9, 11], these assumptions do not restrict a descriptive power of these grammars and they can be fulfilled easily. Firstly, we assume that a relation of simple ordering can be imposed on the set of edge labels, i.e. $\Gamma = \{\gamma_1, \ldots, \gamma_k : \gamma_1 < \ldots \gamma_k\}$. Secondly, we assume that for each edge label (which represents some spatial relation) we can define an inverse edge label (which represents a symmetric spatial relation). In other words, for each $\lambda \in \Gamma$ there exists $\lambda^{-1} \in \Gamma$ such that edges $(v, \lambda, w) \in E$ and $(w, \lambda^{-1}, v) \in E$ represent the same relation. (We call them *semantically equivalent*, e.g. "up" and "down" , "right" and "left" [8].) The last assumption says that we should be able to define some principle/rule that allows us to identify, in an unambiguous way, an object (of a scene) or a feature (of an object) in an image, which is distinguished in such a sense that a graph node representing it will be indexed with 1. Such a "starting" node is called the *S-node* of the graph [5, 8].

3   Reversely Indexed Edge-unambiguous Graph

As we have mentioned it, in order to define an efficiently parsable subclass of edNLC grammars, we have to transform EDG graph into a graph such that its nodes and edges are ordered in an unambiguous way. We cannot use IE graphs (Indexed Edge-unambiguous graphs) introduced in [5, 8], because their indexing is suitable for top-down parsing, whereas we want to define a bottom-up parsable subclass of edNLC grammars. Therefore, we will define a way of indexing, which is proper for bottom-up parsing with the following algorithm. Let us assume that the algorithm uses the *stack* data structure (with standard operations *push*, *pop*, *empty*) for storing graph nodes. We begin with defining procedures and functions of the algorithm.

- **function** *choose_S_node(G)* : *S_node* - the function identifies and returns the S-node of the graph G.
- **procedure** *assign_index(v, index)* - the procedure assigns *index* to node v.
- **function** *assign_indices(G, v, index, stack)* : *numb_of_neighbors* - the function assigns indices in the increasing order to all neighbors (being not indexed yet) of v according to relation $<$ in the set of edge labels. Then, the function pushes the neighbors of v to the *stack* in that order. (The last indexed neighbor is on the top of the stack.) The function returns the number of indexed nodes.
- **procedure** *reverse_edges(G, v)* - the procedure reverses each edge coming into v, if it goes out from a node having a greater index than v.

Algorithm 1 (generating RIE graph)

```
current_index := 1;
v₀ := choose_S_node(G);
assign_index(v₀, current_index);
stack.push(v₀);
while not stack_empty() do
        begin
        v := stack.pop();
        numb_of_neighbors := assign_indices(G, v, current_index, stack);
        reverse_edges(G, v);
        current_index := current_index + number_of_neighbors;
        end;
```

Definition 3. A *reversely indexed edge-unambiguous graph, RIE graph,* over Σ and Γ is a quintuple $g = (V, E, \Sigma, \Gamma, \phi)$, where V is a *finite, non-empty set of nodes* that indices have been ascribed to according to Algorithm 1, E is a *set of edges* of the form (v, λ, w), where $v, w \in V, \lambda \in \Gamma$, such that index of v is less than index of w, Σ, Γ and ϕ are defined as in Definition 1.

A graph shown in Fig. 2 is an example of an RIE graph. We define levels in an RIE graph in the following way. The *n-th level* of an RIE graph g corresponds to the n-th level of its spanning directed tree t, such that the S-node of g corresponds to the root of t and t is generated according to the Breadth First Search (BFS) rule.

We will introduce a characteristic description of an RIE graph in an analogical way as it is made for IE graphs generated by top-down parsable ETPL(k) grammars [5, 6, 8]. Firstly, we define a *characteristic description of a node* (indexed with) k, which is a quadruple: $n(k), r, (e_1 \ldots e_r), (i_1 \ldots i_r)$, where n is a label of the node k, r is the out-degree of k (an out-degree of the node designates the number of edges going out from this node), $(i_1 \ldots i_r)$ is a string of node indices, to which edges going out from k come (in increasing order), $(e_1 \ldots e_r)$ is a string of edge labels ordered in such a way that an edge having a label e_x comes into a node having an index i_x. For example: $w(2), 4, (h\ f\ d\ e), (3\ 7\ 8\ 9)$ is a characteristic description of a node indexed with 2 of a graph shown in Fig. 2.

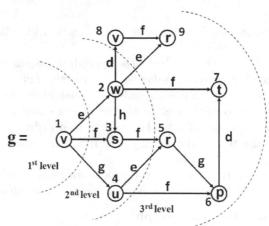

Fig. 2. An example of an RIE graph

A string of characteristic descriptions of succeeding nodes of a graph is called a *characteristic description of a graph*. Usually, we represent it in the matrix-like form. For example:

$v(1)$	$w(2)$	$s(3)$	$u(4)$	$r(5)$	$p(6)$	$t(7)$	$v(8)$	$r(9)$
3	4	1	2	1	1	0	1	0
$e\ f\ g$	$h\ f\ d\ e$	f	$e\ f$	g	d	$-$	f	$-$
2 3 4	3 7 8 9	5	5 6	6	7	$-$	9	$-$

is a characteristic description of a graph g shown in Fig. 2.

4   ETPR(k) Graph Grammar

Efficiently (top-down) parsable ETPL(k) subclass of edNLC grammars [5, 6, 8] have been defined by an analogy to the well-known (top-down parsable) LL(k) subclass of (string) context-free grammars. Since constructing an efficiently bottom-up parsable subclass of edNLC grammars is our goal, we use the same methodological paradigm and we define this subclass by an analogy to the well-known (bottom-up parsable) LR(k) subclass of (string) context-free grammars. We make it by imposing a series of constraints on a class edNLC.

First of all, we limit the depth of the right-hand side graphs of productions as follows.

Definition 4. Let $G = (\Sigma, \Delta, \Gamma, P, Z)$ be an *edNLC* graph grammar. The grammar G is called a *TLP-RIE graph grammar* (abbrev. from Two-Level Productions), if the following conditions are fulfilled.

1. P is a finite set of productions of the form (l, D, C), where: (a) $l \in \Sigma$, (b) D is the *RIE* graph having the characteristic description:

$$
\begin{array}{ccccccc}
n_1(1) & n_2(2) & \ldots & n_m(m) & \quad or \quad & n_1(1), & where\ n_i(i) \\
r_1 & r_2 & \ldots & r_m & & 0 & r_i \\
E_1 & E_2 & \ldots & E_m & & - & E_i \\
I_1 & I_2 & \ldots & I_m & & - & I_i
\end{array}
$$

is a characteristic description of the node $i, i = 1, \ldots, m, n_1 \in \Delta$, $i, i = 2, \ldots, m$ is the node of the second level,
(c) $C : \Gamma \times \{in, out\} \longrightarrow 2^{\Sigma \times \Sigma \times \Gamma \times \{in, out\}}$ is the embedding transformation.

2. Z is an *RIE* graph such that its characteristic description satisfies the condition defined in point 1(b).

Secondly, we restrict a way of deriving a graph to the one determined by the simple ordering imposed on the resulting graph by the following two definitions.

Definition 5. A TLP-RIE graph grammar G is called a *closed TLP-RIE graph grammar G*, if for each derivation of this grammar

$$
Z = g_0 \underset{G}{\Longrightarrow} g_1 \underset{G}{\Longrightarrow} \ldots \underset{G}{\Longrightarrow} g_n
$$

a graph $g_i, i = 0, \ldots, n$ is an *RIE* graph.

Definition 6. Let there be given a derivation of a closed TLP-RIE grammar G:

$$
Z = g_0 \underset{G}{\Longrightarrow} g_1 \underset{G}{\Longrightarrow} \ldots \underset{G}{\Longrightarrow} g_n.
$$

The derivation is called a *regular right-hand side derivation* (denoted $\underset{rr(G)}{\Longrightarrow}$), if:
(1) for each $i = 0, \ldots, n-1$ we apply a production for a node having the greatest index in a graph g_i,
(2) node indices do not change during a derivation.

A closed TLP-RIE graph grammar, which generates graphs according to the regular right-hand side derivation is called a *closed TLPO-RIE graph grammar* (abbrev. from Two-Level Production-Ordered).

Now, we define a notion analogical to a notion of a *handle* in the (standard) compiler construction theory. It allows us to extract two-level subgraphs of an analyzed graph, which are matched against right-hand sides of productions during bottom-up parsing [5, 6, 8].

Definition 7. Let g be an RIE graph, l - a node of g defined by a characteristic description $n(l), r, e_1 \ldots e_r, i_1 \ldots i_r$. A subgraph h of the graph g consisting of node l, nodes having indices $i_{a+1}, i_{a+2}, \ldots, i_{a+m}, a \geq 0, a + m \leq r$, and edges connecting the nodes: $l, i_{a+1}, i_{a+2}, \ldots, i_{a+m}$ is called an *m-successors two-level graph originated in the node l and beginning with the (i_{a+1})th successor*. The subgraph h is denoted $h = m - TL(g, l, i_{a+1})$. By $0 - TL(g, l, -)$ we denote the subgraph of g consisting only of node l.

Finally, we can define a parsable PR(k) graph grammar in an analogical way as it is made for parsable LR(k) string grammars.

Definition 8. Let $G = (\Sigma, \Delta, \Gamma, P, Z)$ be a closed TLPO-RIE graph grammar. The grammar G is called a *PR(k)* (Production-ordered k-Right nodes unambiguous) *graph grammar* if the following condition is fulfilled. Let

$$Z \xrightarrow[rr(G)]{*} X_1 A X_2 \xRightarrow[rr(G)]{} X_1 g X_2,$$

$$Z \xrightarrow[rr(G)]{*} X_3 B X_4 \xRightarrow[rr(G)]{} X_1 g X_5$$

$$\text{and } k - TL(X_2, 1, 2) = k - TL(X_5, 1, 2),$$

where $\xrightarrow[rr(G)]{*}$ is the transitive and reflexive closure of $\xRightarrow[rr(G)]{}$, A, B are characteristic descriptions of certain nodes, X_1, X_2, X_3, X_4, X_5 are substrings of characteristic descriptions, g is the right-hand side of a production: $A \longrightarrow g$. Then: $\qquad X_1 = X_3 \ , \quad A = B \ , \quad X_4 = X_5 \ .$

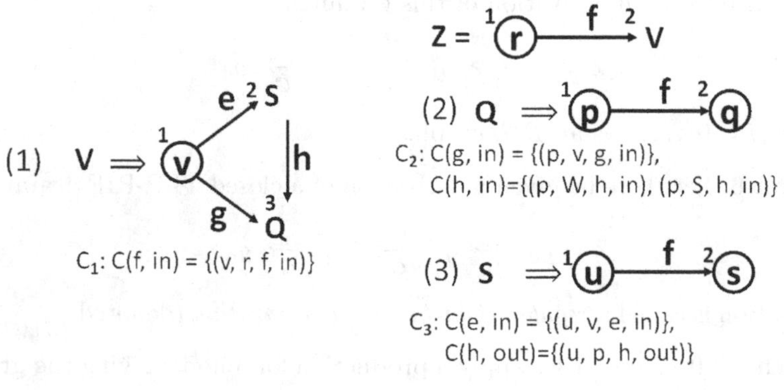

Fig. 3. An example of ETPR(k) productions

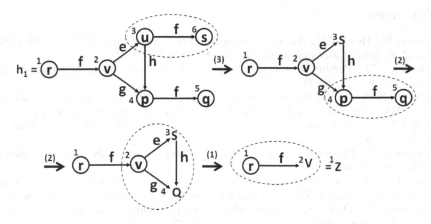

Fig. 4. An example of an ETPR(k) parser analysis

A notion of a *property of preserving a potential previous context* has been introduced for ETPL(k) grammars in [5, 8]. It says that the embedding transformation has to preserve the edge context for nodes having less indices than the node the production is applied for. In order to define a deterministic bottom-up parsing scheme we require that this property holds for PR(k) grammars as well.

Definition 9. A PR(k) graph grammar G is called an *ETPR(k)* (Embedding Transformation - preserving Production-ordered k-Right nodes unambiguous, *graph grammar*, if it has a property of preserving a potential previous context.

5   Concluding Remarks

For a deterministic ETPR(k) subclass of edNLC graph grammars constructed in a previous section a bottom-up parser has been implemented [12]. The ETPR(k) parser analyzes RIE graphs in an analogical way as the well-known bottom-up LR(k) parser for string languages. Let us consider the axiom and first three ETPR(k) productions shown in Fig. 3. An example of a parsing process is shown in Fig. 4. The parser identifies *handles* in the form of k-TL graphs (marked with dashed ovals) successively. Then it matches them to right-hand sides of productions and performs reductions to proper left-hand sides.

As we have mentioned it in Introduction, a bottom-up parsable ETPR(k) subclass of edNLC grammars can generate some graph languages that ETPL(k) cannot (see [10], Theorem 4). On the other hand, the ETPR(k) parsing scheme is as efficient, $O(n^2)$, ([12], Theorem 2.2) as the ETPL(k) one. It means that generative/discriminative possibilities of edNLC graph grammars in the area of syntactic pattern recognition have been enhanced with the model introduced in this paper.

References

1. Blum, M., Hewitt, C.: Automata on a two-dimensional tape. In: Proc. 8th IEEE Conf. Switching Automaton Theory, pp. 155–160 (1968)
2. Brayer, J.M.: Parsing of web grammars. In: Proc. IEEE Workshop Data Descr. Long Beach, CA (1977)
3. Bunke, H.O., Haller, B.: A parser for context free plex grammars. In: Nagl, M. (ed.) WG 1989. LNCS, vol. 411, pp. 136–150. Springer, Heidelberg (1990)
4. Della Vigna, P., Ghezzi, C.: Context-free graph grammars. Inform. Control 37, 207–233 (1978)
5. Flasiński, M.: Parsing of edNLC-graph grammars for scene analysis. Pattern Recognition 21, 623–629 (1988)
6. Flasiński, M.: Characteristics of edNLC - graph grammars for syntactic pattern recognition. Comput. Vision Graphics Image Process., CVGIP 47, 1–21 (1989)
7. Flasiński, M.: Distorted pattern analysis with the help of Nodel Label Controlled graph languages. Pattern Recognition 23, 765–774 (1990)
8. Flasiński, M.: On the parsing of deterministic graph languages for syntactic pattern recognition. Pattern Recognition 26, 1–16 (1993)
9. Flasiński, M.: Use of graph grammars for the description of mechanical parts. Computer Aided Design 27, 403–433 (1995)
10. Flasiński, M.: Power properties of NLC graph grammars with a polynomial membership problem. Theoretical Computer Science 201, 189–231 (1998)
11. Flasiński, M., Myśliński, S.: On the use of graph parsing for recognition of isolated hand postures of Polish Sign Language. Pattern Recognition 43, 2249–2264 (2010)
12. Flasińska, Z.: Bottom-up parser for edNLC graph grammars, MSc Thesis, AGH University of Science and Technology, Cracow (2013)
13. Franck, R.: A class of linearly parsable graph grammars. Acta. Inform. 10, 175–201 (1978)
14. Fu, K.S.: Syntactic Pattern Recognition and Applications. Prentice Hall, Englewood Cliffs (1982)
15. Janssens, D., Rozenberg, G.: On the structure of node-label-controlled graph languages. Inform. Sci. 20, 191–216 (1980)
16. Kaul, M.: Parsing of graphs in linear time. In: Ehrig, H., Nagl, M., Rozenberg, G. (eds.) Graph Grammars 1982. LNCS, vol. 153, pp. 206–218. Springer, Heidelberg (1983)
17. Lautemann, C.: Efficient algorithms on context-free graph languages. In: Lepistö, T., Salomaa, A. (eds.) ICALP 1988. LNCS, vol. 317, pp. 362–378. Springer, Heidelberg (1988)
18. Peng, K.J., Yamamoto, T., Aoki, Y.: A new parsing scheme for plex grammars. Pattern Recognition 23, 393–402 (1990)
19. Rosenfeld, A., Milgram, D.L.: Web automata and web grammars. Machine Intell 7, 307–324 (1972)
20. Shi, Q.Y., Fu, K.S.: Parsing and translation of attributed expansive graph languages for scene analysis. IEEE Trans. Pattern Analysis Mach. Intell., PAMI 5, 472–485 (1983)
21. Turan, G.: On the complexity of graph grammars. Techn. Rep. Automata Theory Research Group, Szeged (1982)
22. Wills, L.M.: Using attributed graph parsing to recognize clichés in programs. In: Cuny, J., Engels, G., Ehrig, H., Rozenberg, G. (eds.) Graph Grammars 1994. LNCS, vol. 1073, pp. 170–184. Springer, Heidelberg (1996)
23. Zhang, D.Q., Zhang, K., Cao, J.: A context-sensitive graph grammar formalism for the specification of visual languages. Computer J. 44, 186–200 (2001)

Comparing Clothing Styles by Means of Computer Vision Methods

Paweł Forczmański[1], Piotr Czapiewski[1], Dariusz Frejlichowski[1],
Krzysztof Okarma[2], and Radosław Hofman[3]

[1] West Pomeranian University of Technology, Szczecin
Faculty of Computer Science and Information Technology
Żołnierska 49, 71–210 Szczecin, Poland
{pforczmanski,pczapiewski,dfrejlichowski}@wi.zut.edu.pl
[2] West Pomeranian University of Technology, Szczecin
Faculty of Electrical Engineering
26. Kwietnia 10, 71–126 Szczecin, Poland
okarma@zut.edu.pl
[3] FireFrog Media sp. z o.o. Jeleniogórska 16, 60–179 Poznań, Poland
radekh@fire-frog.pl

Abstract. The paper deals with a problem of comparing and retrieving visual data representing various clothing styles. Proposed solution joins several sophisticated computer vision methods, such as face detection using AdaBoost strategy, human body segmentation and decomposition using pictorial structures and appearance models, together with visual descriptors employing simplified dominant color descriptor. The input images do not necessary have to be taken in controlled environment, so the flexibility of the system is high. The proposed algorithm makes it possible to compare images presenting humans and retrieve images with similar clothing style. The potential application is the area of social network services, mostly recommendation web-based systems, that help people choose clothes and share with clothing ideas. Developed algorithm has been tested on 650 images gathered from various social media in the Internet and showed high accuracy rate.

1 Introduction

1.1 Motivation

Current observations of humans activities in the Internet show, that the most of the interest is focused at social networking services, as platforms to build social networks or social relations among people. Those people share their interests and activities, and move them from real-life zone into virtual one. Social network sites are varied but one of the most common features is the incorporation of photo and video sharing. On the other hand, the progress in the e-commerce area makes it possible to develop new applications that may in future change many real-life activities. One of such activities is shopping. Although there are many spheres of shopping activities, i.e. buying electronic devices, that can be

L.J. Chmielewski et al. (Eds.): ICCVG 2014, LNCS 8671, pp. 203–211, 2014.

performed successfully on the web, there are also some that are not easy to perform. One of the examples is buying clothes. The problem is the lack of physical contact with products and difficulty with finding proper things. It comes from the variety of styles, materials, sizes and their combinations. An automatic computer system that may be able to compare clothes based on different criteria is highly desirable.

1.2 Previous Works

Previous research dealing with fashion and clothing focuses on computer vision methods applied to fashion images, on semantic attributes describing clothes, or on both. In [1] a HCI system has been proposed acting as a "responsive mirror", aimed at creating interactive experience for cloth fitting in a real-life shop. The system is focused on tracking human pose, recognizing the clothes and finding similar ones using both color and fashion features. The algorithm for body parts and clothes detection relies on simple bounding boxes and heuristic proportion boxes and requires the images to be taken in a controlled environment. Also, only one type of clothes (shirts) and the features specific to it are analysed.

An approach to recognizing clothing characteristics of one group of clothes (coats and jackets) has been proposed in [2]. Certain binary attributes regarding to fashion were defined and a classifier was used to recognize them in the images. Searching for similar clothes is based on the extracted semantic attributes and disregards colours or visual patterns. Images are taken from clothing retail sites and contain single elements of clothing on the clean background.

In [3] unconstrained images were analysed, with pose detection and recognition of attributes describing clothes, however, only for upper-body clothes. In other works the clothing information was used as an additional context information for person identification or other monitoring and retrieval tasks [4,5,6].

All of the above deal with only single garment at a time, disregarding clothes composition. Also, features specific to certain types of clothes are analysed, making it difficult to create an universal solution to find similar fashion compositions.

2 Algorithm Description

The algorithm consists of several stages: (i) human body detection, (ii) body decomposition, (iii) visual descriptors calculation, and (iv) comparison and retrieval. The general scheme of processing is presented in the following figure (Fig. 1). The detailed description of all stages is given further in the paper.

Human body part detectors are a common way to handle the variability in appearance in high-level computer vision problems, such as detection and semantic segmentation [7,8,9]. Identifying its parts, however, remains an open question. Anatomical parts, such as arms and legs, are difficult to detect reliably because parallel lines are common in natural images. In contrast, a visual conjunction such as "half of a frontal face and a left shoulder" may be a perfectly good discriminative visual pattern. For the purposes of this study, it is assumed that the input image includes a human figure, which, in ideal situation, satisfies the following conditions:

1. person is standing, upright posture, facing towards the camera;
2. whole human silhouette is visible, oriented vertically;
3. natural pose, hands lowered along the trunk;
4. area of a figure covers no less than 40% of the total image area;
5. ambient illumination;
6. uniform background with a low degree of complexity;
7. spatial resolution of the image – at least 320×240 pixels;
8. only one dominant figure is visible in the image.

Above conditions allow for effective detection of human silhouette and lead to the successful extraction of interesting elements in the outfit. In the case of non-compliance with such conditions, the procedure may give erroneous or ambiguous results, which will reduce the effectiveness of the comparison stage.

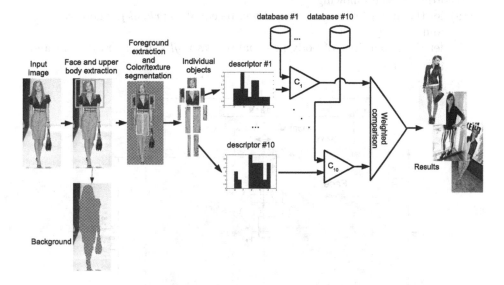

Fig. 1. The general scheme of processing, divided into the most significant stages

2.1   Initial Processing

The initial processing is aimed at detecting human silhouettes. As an input, an image is entered, which does not necessary have to contain humans. In order to determine the presence of a human being, a face detector based on Viola-Jones approach [10] is used. While the accuracy of this detector relies strongly on the learning database, in our case, we employ Haar-like features calculated on frontal and profile portraits for two independent classifiers. We use an implementation of the algorithm which is a part of OpenCV library. Then, using typical human body proportions, an area containing upper part of a body is selected.

As not all images presenting humans are suitable for the subsequent stages of processing, a verification stage is introduced. It is aimed at evaluating sizes and positions of detected human figures, in order to select silhouettes that are suitable for garment extraction. It employs calculating selected proportions and position specific heuristic. Therefore, in the initial processing stage we perform the following actions:

1. detect frontal faces and profiles, remember their positions and dimensions, discard areas smaller than 20×20 pixels;
2. accept faces located in the upper area of the input image (see Fig.2);
3. eliminate repetitive areas in accordance with the principle, that detected objects must be separated by a minimum of 100 pixels (areas that do not meet this condition are rejected, except the first one);
4. denote the upper left corner of the face bounding box as (xp, yp) and its dimensions as xs (height) and ys (width);
5. extrapolate the upper body part on a basis of the face position and size according to the following:
   (a) let the upper left corner of the body be equal to (xk, yk), where $xk = \frac{xs}{2}$ and $yk = yp - ys$;
   (b) let the dimensions of body be equal to $xks \times yks$, where $xks = 3xs$ and $yks = 3ys$.

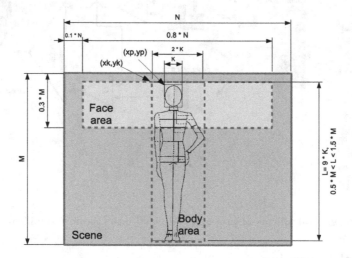

Fig. 2. Assumptions related to the position and size of head and whole body

2.2   Human Body Segmentation and Decomposition

The next stage employs a number of approaches that allows for automated detection of human body in the image, segmenting it from the background (regardless of the context and content of the scene) and then decomposing it into sub-areas containing independent body parts associated with specific garment. Firstly, a watershed algorithm [11] is used for human body segmentation. It starts from the area detected at the above stage (upper body part). Then it applies an algorithm presented in [12] and [13]. It uses two observations: (i) relative to the reference frame (face or upper-body part detected earlier), some parts of the human body have rather stable location (e.g. the torso is typically below the face); (ii) the appearance models of different body parts are statistically related. For example, the lower arms of a person are colored either like the torso (clothing) or like the face (skin). This implies that the appearance of some parts can be predicted from the appearance of other parts. Such assumptions lead to a very successful segmentation. At the prototype stage we employed software components published at [14]. It allows for articulated human pose estimation in still images. The algorithm [12] is designed to operate in uncontrolled images with difficult illumination conditions and cluttered backgrounds. The only assumption the algorithm makes is that people are upright (i.e. their head is above their torso) and they are seen approximately from a frontal viewpoint.

As an output we get a set of line segments indicating location, size and orientation of the body parts, which are later used to calculate visual descriptors responsible for specific garment (see Fig. 3. As it can be seen from these examples, in most cases, the silhouettes were located and divided into parts in a satisfactory manner. Minor errors are due to the difficulty of segmentation (caused probably by similar hue values of the body and the background).

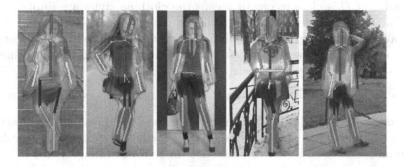

Fig. 3. Exemplary segmentation results

2.3   Visual Descriptors Calculation

Each of the extracted clothing components can be described by a variety of color and texture descriptors. According to our observations, the characteristics related to texture and other visual aspects are not so important, or are not visible in the low resolution images published on the Internet. In our case we use a simplified dominant color descriptor, adopted from MPEG-7 standard [15].

There are 10 components of human body, we are focused on, namely: face, torso, upper arms, lower arms, thighs and lower legs. In effect we create a feature vector, which is used for comparison. Color descriptor is calculated for every input object in the RGB color space. In the first step we perform a conversion from RGB to HSV representation, in order to reduce between-channel correlation.

Then we perform color quantization, in order to reduce the number of colors and create a histogram with 72 bins.

Finally, the values in histogram are sorted in the decreasing order and the first 8 bins are left unchanged, while the other are zeroed. Next, the values in output histogram are normalized to one by dividing them by a sum of all values. The final feature vector is created as a concatenation of all 10 single vectors, leading to a sparse 720-element vector, with at most 80 values greater than zero.

2.4 Similarity Estimation

In practice, some of the garment elements are more important than others. Therefore, as a result of experimental evaluation and as an observation of segmentation errors, we use the following weights w_k associated with the body elements: torso: $w_1 = 0.4$, upper arms: $w_2 = w_3 = 0.1$, thighs: $w_4 = w_5 = 0.1$, lower arms: $w_6 = w_7 = 0.05$, lower legs: $w_8 = w_9 = 0.05$, face $w_{10} = 0$.

The comparison of two descriptors related to two silhouettes H_A and H_B belonging to analyzed images A and B is performed by histogram intersection:

$$D(A, B) = \sum_{k=1}^{10} \sum_{i=1}^{72} w_k * min(H_A(i, k), H_B(i, k)). \tag{1}$$

If the value of D is close to one, it means the clothing styles are similar, while D tending to zero suggests different styles, in terms of dominant colors.

The above approach gives a possibility to compare clothing elements regarding their geometrical transformations (scaling and rotation). It is also invariant to some extent to cropping and noising.

The strategy responsible for evaluation of the results is one of the following:

– the decision on similarity is taken on the basis of the threshold, (i.e. $t = 0.5$). In a situation where the overall similarity coefficient exceeds the threshold, the images are considered to be similar (in terms clothing styles);
– we retrieve the images from the reference database on the basis of decreasing similarity coefficients and select first two or three objects.

In the results section shown later, we show the effects of the second strategy, as it fits most to human expectations.

3 Experiments

During our experiments we collected 650 images containing humans (500 women and 150 men), that satisfied conditions described in the introductory part of the paper. The images were gathered from various social network websites and were not processed in any way.

From the 500 images of women, the face detection algorithm selected 417 images (83%), while for 150 males, this rate was equal to 110 (73%). In other cases,

Fig. 4. Exemplary results of style retrieval (the first image in each row is a query while the rest are the retrieved ones). The similarity coefficients in each row are equal to 0.55, 0.54, 0.53; 0.53, 0.49, 0.46; 0.52, 0.45, 0.43; 0.41, 0.40, 0.39; 0.53, 0.48, 0.39; 0.61, 0.51, 0.16, respectively).

face was not detected or its position was not consistent with the initial assumptions. Further, for the selected images, the visual descriptors were calculated and compared.

Sample detailed results of the comparison are presented in subsequent images (Fig. 4). The first image is the query, while the next three images were considered to be similar and arranged in order of decreasing similarity.

Analysis of the results leads to the conclusion that in the case of good segmentation and proper position and orientation of the photographed person, the procedure of detecting and segmenting parts of the body responsible for specific areas of the garment is possible. Errors in segmentation mainly included erroneously detected arms and legs, which suggests that the greatest attention should be paid to the recognition of the body, arms and thighs.

4   Summary

This chapter presented an algorithm for comparing sets of compositionally selected garment. It uses several advanced computer vision algorithms, including face detection algorithm, verifying the size and position of the figure, segmented from the background, and the detection of individual body parts. On the basis of these data an efficient color descriptor based on the MPEG-7 and an effective method of comparing descriptors have been proposed. In the section describing the results of experimental studies much space is devoted to the practical implementation of this algorithm, which may be important for solving the problems related to this project.

Acknowledgements. The project Construction of innovative recommendation based on users' styles system prototype: FireStyle (original title: Zbudowanie prototypu innowacyjnego systemu rekomendacji zgodnych ze stylami uzytkowników: FireStyle) is the project co-founded by European Union (project number: UDA-POIG.01.04.00-30-196/12, value: 14.949.474,00 PLN, EU contribution: 7.879.581,50 PLN, realization period: 01.2013-10.2014). European funds – for the development of innovative economy (Fundusze Europejskie – dla rozwoju innowacyjnej gospodarki).

References

1. Zhang, W., Begole, B., Chu, M., Liu, J., Yee, N.: Real-time clothes comparison based on multi-view vision. In: Second ACM/IEEE International Conference on Distributed Smart Cameras, ICDSC 2008, pp. 1–10. IEEE (2008)
2. Di, W., Wah, C., Bhardwaj, A., Piramuthu, R., Sundaresan, N.: Style Finder: Fine-Grained Clothing Style Detection and Retrieval. In: IEEE Conference on Computer Vision and Pattern Recognition Workshops, CVPRW 2013, pp. 8–13. IEEE (2013)
3. Chen, H., Gallagher, A., Girod, B.: Describing clothing by semantic attributes. In: Fitzgibbon, A., Lazebnik, S., Perona, P., Sato, Y., Schmid, C. (eds.) ECCV 2012, Part III. LNCS, vol. 7574, pp. 609–623. Springer, Heidelberg (2012)

4. Anguelov, D., Lee, K., Gokturk, S.B., Sumengen, B.: Contextual identity recognition in personal photo albums. In: IEEE Conference on Computer Vision and Pattern Recognition, CVPR 2007, pp. 1–7. IEEE (2007)
5. Song, Y., Leung, T.: Context-aided human recognition – clustering. In: Leonardis, A., Bischof, H., Pinz, A. (eds.) ECCV 2006. LNCS, vol. 3953, pp. 382–395. Springer, Heidelberg (2006)
6. Liu, S., Song, Z., Liu, G., Xu, C., Lu, H., Yan, S.: Street-to-shop: Cross-scenario clothing retrieval via parts alignment and auxiliary set. In: IEEE Conference on Computer Vision and Pattern Recognition, CVPR 2012, pp. 3330–3337. IEEE (2012)
7. Zisserman, A.: Human Pose Estimation in images and videos, http://www.di.ens.fr/willow/events/cvml2010/materials/INRIA_summer_school_2010_Andrew_human_pose.pdf
8. Ramanan, D., Forsyth, D.A., Zisserman, A.: Tracking People by Learning their Appearance. IEEE Transactions on Pattern Analysis and Machine Intelligence 29, 65–81 (2007)
9. Ramanan, D.: Part-based Models for Finding People and Estimating Their Pose. In: Moeslund, T., Hilton, A., Krüger, V., Sigal, L. (eds.) Visual Analysis of Humans, pp. 199–223. Springer, London (2011)
10. Viola, P., Jones, M.: Rapid object detection using a boosted cascade of simple features. In: IEEE Conference on Computer Vision and Pattern Recognition, CVPR 2001, pp. I-511–I-518. IEEE (2001)
11. Roerdink, J., Meijster, A.: The Watershed Transform: Defnitions. Algorithms and Parallelization Strategies Fundamenta Informaticae 41, 187–228 (2001)
12. Eichner, M., Ferrari, V.: Better Appearance Models for Pictorial Structures. In: Proceedings of British Machine Vision Conference (2009)
13. Eichner, M., Marin-Jimenez, M., Zisserman, A., Ferrari, V.: Articulated Human Pose Estimation and Search in (Almost) Unconstrained Still Images. Technical Report No. 272. ETH Zurich, D-ITET, BIWI (2010)
14. Human Pose estimation page, http://groups.inf.ed.ac.uk/calvin/articulated_human_pose_estimation_code/
15. Yamada, A., Pickering, M., Jeannin, S., Cieplinski, L., Jens, R.O., Kim, M.: MPEG-7 Visual Part of Experimentation Model Version 9.0 - Part 3 Dominant Color. ISO/IEC JTC1/SC29/WG11/N3914 (2001)

Adaptive and Quality-Aware Storage of JPEG Files in the Web Environment

Paweł Forczmański and Radosław Mantiuk

West Pomeranian University of Technology
Szczecin, Faculty of Computer Science and Information Technology
Żołnierska Str. 49, 71–210 Szczecin, Poland
{pforczmanski,rmantiuk}@wi.zut.edu.pl

Abstract. The paper presents a concept, implementation and results of experiments conducted on an online image archiving system which performs JPEG/JFIF compression of user-submitted files. The compression level is chosen automatically based on the quality loss assessment. During development a comparative survey of ten image quality measures, including Mean Squared Error (MSE), Image Fidelity (IF) and Structural Similarity Index (SSIM), has been carried out in order to evaluate their performance in relation to colour image JFIF compression. Furthermore, an Edge Intensity Measure (EIM) has been proposed as a solution to identify images with low edge intensity, whose quality loss is almost universally assessed incorrectly. Finally, an algorithm for determining the most suitable level of compression of a given image has been designed and implemented, incorporating the three image quality measures and the EIM. The proposed algorithm stores the typical JFIF/JPEG files with much higher quality than most of the popular web-based systems, yet without high computing overhead and high image quality deterioration.

1 Introduction and Motivation

The Internet-based systems allow to gather, store, archive and present digital images. However, the number of such images and a limited storage space leads to a problem of optimal, adaptive, and quality aware compression. One can observe, that most of Internet-based systems employ some sort of lossy compression mechanisms that make it possible to store large number of acceptable-quality photographs without very high requirements for disk space. They also impose various restrictions on the user, i.e. maximal spatial resolution, maximal file size and the total number of images. However, such restrictions concern often a trade-off between quality and data volume. Moreover, all photographs stored by such sites are treated the same, no matter what they present and what characteristics they feature.

The general idea behind this work is a web-based system that makes it possible to store images in the most popular JPEG/JFIF lossy compression format, yet taking into consideration image content and predefined output quality. In

L.J. Chmielewski et al. (Eds.): ICCVG 2014, LNCS 8671, pp. 212–219, 2014.

effect, images are stored with a highest possible quality, yet with lossy compression (without high storage space requirements). Such images are often used in web-based print services, where a quality is a main issue. It is crucial for any application involving digital photographs (i.e. biometric travel documents [1]).

In order to achieve good quality with highest possible compression rate, we propose to use a set of objective quality measures together with a developed heuristics. All these elements are employed to reduce a number of re-compression stages on the way to the optimal (or sub-optimal) compression ratio. Hence, the images with low details are compressed with higher rate, while images featuring high number of details are compressed in a less aggressive manner.

The paper is organized as follows. In the beginning, several interesting objective image quality metrics are presented. Then, an algorithm aimed at choosing an optimal (or sub-optimal) JPEG compression factor adapted to input image is presented. Finally, some results on benchmark datasets and concluding remarks are provided.

2 Objective Image Quality Assessment

Objective Image Quality Metrics (IQM) deliver quantised assessment of the perceptual quality of images. Two features of IQMs are especially desirable in our framework: they provide automatic quality testing, and judge image deterioration from a human visual system (HVS) perspective. IQMs are specialised in predicting the level of annoyance caused by globally present artefacts such as image blockiness, noise, or blur that arise in compression and broadcasting applications [2], i.e. also in JPEG compression employed in our system. They deliver results comparable with a quality value, which is derived in mean opinion score (MOS) experiments with human observers [3]. In other words, in applications like our JPEG-based compression storage, the objective metrics are comparable to the subjective quality assessment performed during time consuming perceptual experiments [4].

There are a number of IQMs that prove their effectiveness, like SSIM [5], HDRVDP [6], Visual Information Fidelity [2], and others. The latest approach in development of IQM takes into account the machine learning techniques in which various image feature descriptors like the SSIM index, computer vision bag-of-visual worlds, Spearman correlation and many others are used to assess the perceptual difference [7]. For more in depth information on the image quality problem we refer the reader to the textbooks [2,8], and survey papers [9,10]. In following section we briefly present the objective image quality metrics applied in our quality-aware JPEG storage framework.

Root Mean Squared Error. (MSE) directly measures the difference of pixel intensity. This metric is not suitable for assessment of image quality because the reported difference is weakly correlated with the error perceived by a human [11]. However, because of its simplicity, RMSE is often used in compression system and we evaluate its performance to give a background for comparison.

Image Fidelity (IF) metric is comparable to MSE:

$$IF(x,y) = 1 - \frac{\sum_{i=1}^{N}(x_i - y_i)^2}{\sum_{i=1}^{N} x_i^2} = 1 - \frac{N \cdot MSE(x,y)}{\sum_{i=1}^{N} x_i^2}, \qquad (1)$$

where x_i and y_i are values of the corresponding i-th pixels, and N denotes number of pixels in the image. However, MSE is scaled by the reference pixel value, resulting in the relative measure of difference between two pixels.

Structural Similarity Index Metric. (SSIM) [2,5] detects structural changes in the image. The SSIM is an extension of *Universal Image Quality* (UIQ)[12], however it gives more stable results. It is sensitive to difference in the mean intensity and contrast but the main factors are local correlations of pixel values. These dependencies carry information about the structure of the objects and reveal structural image difference. The SSIM metric is computed as a measure of difference between two windows x and y of size $N \times N$ pixels (8×8 in our setup):

$$SSIM(x,y) = \frac{(2\mu_x\mu_y + c_1)(2\sigma_{xy} + c_2)}{(\mu_x^2 + \mu_y^2 + c_1)(\sigma_x^2 + \sigma_y^2 + c_2))}, \qquad (2)$$

where μ_x and μ_y are averages, and σ_x and σ_y are variances of x and y windows, respectively. σ_{xy} is a covariance of x and y. The c_1 and c_2 variables stabilise the division with weak denominator and equal to $c_1 = (k_1 L)^2$, $c_2 = (k_2 L)^2$ for $k_1 = 0.01$ and $k_2 = 0.03$. L denotes the range of pixel values ($L = 2^{number\ of\ bits\ per\ pixel} - 1$). The resultant SSIM index is a decimal value between -1 and 1. Value 1 is reachable for two identical windows.

In the experiments we convert RGB pixel values to luminance and compute difference in the luminance space. Generally, IQMs are not suitable for colour processing and only preliminary research was done in this matter [13,14]. The main solution is to convert the RGB value to a perceptual colour space taking into account viewing conditions, image appearance phenomena, chromatic adaptation, etc. We address this issue for future work.

3   Developed Algorithm

3.1   Compression-vs-Quality Model

In order to develop a model, which will be used to predict an image quality (in terms of IQM) knowing only its JPEG compression quality parameter, we analysed the results published in [15]. The LIVE dataset, described there, consists of 29 original, uncompressed images.

Firstly, we performed a procedure of JPEG compression on all those images, changing compression quality (Q parameter) from 5 to 100, where lower Q values stand for higher compression rate. Then, we estimated the objective quality of output images, using several IQMs. The results of such evaluation, normalized to $< 0, 1 >$, are presented in Fig. 1. As it can be seen, almost all measures, except Maximum Difference MD, Structural Content SC and Normalized Cross-Correlation NCC are monotonic functions. Moreover, MD, SC and NCC are

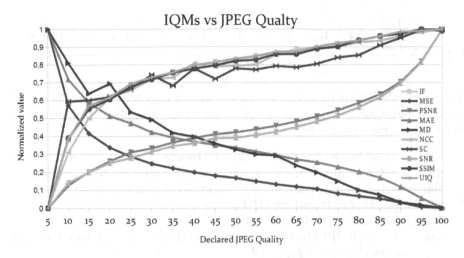

Fig. 1. The objective quality measures as a function of compression quality

highly variable in the range of very high and very low compression. On the other hand, the rest of measures is almost linear in range (30, 80), which can be helpful in developing a linear model of compression quality prediction.

The second set of initial experiments was aimed at evaluation of Mean Opinion Scores (MOS) in terms of JPEG compression and objective image quality measurements, on a basis of extended LIVE dataset [15]. The results show, that MOS for LIVE images is within a range (20, 80), where lower values are responsible for good image quality. Unfortunately, no measure can be approximated with a straight line. Hence, it makes it difficult to create a linear model of such relation. It can also be observed, that Mean Absolute Error MAE, Structural Content SC, Peak Signal-to-Noise Ratio PSNR and Signal-to-Noise Ratio SNR have a very high variance, which also has a negative influence on the developed model. The only usable (in terms of our model) are SSIM, UIQ (very similar), MSE, MD and IF.

Since there is no single measure, that can be employed, as a result of our investigations, for further application, we have chosen MSE, IF and SSIM as a basis for a compression-vs-quality model.

3.2   Processing Stages

Since typical image quality metrics fail in case of images with high detail level, the algorithm of quality estimation relies strongly on the edge intensity E in the analysed (grayscale) image $I(x, y)$ of size $M \times N$ pixels. This metric is inspired by Image Activity Measure presented in [16] and calculated for JPEG2000 files. In our case we apply it in a different manner. Firstly, we estimate Edge Intensity Measure E(I) using Laplace filtering, based on the following formula:

$$E(I) = \frac{\sum\limits_{x=2}^{M-1} \sum\limits_{y=2}^{N-1} (I(x-1,y) + I(x+1,y) + I(x,y-1) + I(x,y+1) - 4I(x,y))^2}{(M-2)(N-2)}$$

(3)

We do not calculate it for image's borders, since it may introduce artifacts and influence the result. Hence, the complete list of steps applied to image being processed are presented below:

1. take an input image I being an reference (uncompressed) object of the highest possible quality. If the input image is a compressed object (i.e. JPEG-compressed) it may not necessary lead to the optimal compression;
2. calculate $E(I)$, $IF(I)$ and $SSIM(I)$;
3. if $E(I) < 150$, then set $E(I) = 150$;
4. compress I with JPEG/JFIF algorithm, setting its quality to 60 and 80; hence we get two copies I_{60} and I_{80};
5. calculate $MSE(I_{60})$, $IF(I_{60})$, and $SSIM(I_{60})$ together with $MSE(I_{80})$, $IF(I_{80})$, and $SSIM(I_{80})$;
6. using linear interpolation between above points we build a linear model described as lines $y = ax + b$, one for each quality measure, where y is a quality measure estimate $(MSE, IF, SSIM)$ at the compression quality x, and:

$$a_{MSE} = \frac{MSE_{60} - MSE_{80}}{20}; \quad b_{MSE} = MSE_{60} - 60a_{MSE};$$

(4)

$$a_{IF} = \frac{IF_{60} - IF_{80}}{20}; \quad b_{IF} = IF_{60} - 60a_{IF};$$

(5)

$$a_{SSIM} = \frac{SSIM_{60} - SSIM_{80}}{20}; \quad b_{SIM} = SSIM60 - 60a_{SSIM};$$

(6)

7. if the directional coefficient a is equal to zero (in all cases) or lower than zero in case of IF and SSIM, or greater than zero in case of MSE, the algorithm ends (since by decreasing compression factor we can not have a decrease in the images' quality);
8. set the minimal and maximal quality parameters of JPEG algorithm: $k_{min} = 30$ and $k_{max} = 100$, respectively;
9. using above linear model, estimate the highest quality parameter (the minimal compression factor) k, for which the minimal quality thresholds are met. The quality of I_k is acceptable, if one of the following is satisfied:
   (a) $MSE(I_k) < MSE_{min} \wedge IF(I_k) > IF_{min} \wedge SSIM(I_k) > SSIM_{opt}$;
   (b) $MSE(I_k) < MSE_{opt} \wedge IF(I_k) > IF_{opt} \wedge SSIM(I_k) > SSIM_{min}$;
   where the thresholds MSE_{min}, MSE_{opt}, IF_{min}, IF_{opt}, $SSIM_{min}$ and $SSMI_{opt}$ are presented in Tab. 1.
10. the main loop: while $k_{min} < k_{max}$ do:
    (a) Compress an image, create a copy I_k with compression quality k.
    (b) Check the quality thresholds.

Table 1. Quality thresholds obtained at the experimental stage

Measure	min	opt
MSE	100	$25 - \frac{1500}{E(I)}$
IF	0.9965	$0.9985 + \frac{0.21}{E(I)}$
$SSIM$	0.99	$0.9975 + \frac{0.345}{E(I)}$

(c) If the quality is acceptable (see p.9), set $k_{max} = k$ and decrement the compression quality $k = k - 1$ (increase the compression factor).

(d) In other case, increment $k = k + 1$, and set $k_{min} = k$.

11. In the end, k_{min} is the lowest quality coefficient, which satisfies quality requirements.

Remark 1: If the compression quality coefficient are equal to 60 or 80, there is no need of performing renewed compression and quality estimation steps in the main loop.

Remark 2: If the compression quality coefficient is lower than 30, there is no need of performing quality estimation, since further compression (with lower quality coefficient) may not lead to a significantly lower size of file.

4 Experiments

4.1 Datasets

Analysis of the effectiveness of chosen method was carried out using two sets of test images: LIVE image database created at University of Texas/Austin [15,3,5] and our own WMC database developed independently with the use of published images on Wikimedia Commons. The LIVE dataset consists of 29 images stored in bitmap format, which dimensions are not greater than 768 x 512 pixels. The reference images present different content (i.e. landscapes, portraits, macro photographs) and feature variable intensity, contrast and quality. The other dataset, namely WMC, contains 30 images stored in JPEG format, with dimensions close to 1024×768 pixels. They were collected from Wikimedia Commons on order to increase the diversity of original LIVE images. They present night landscapes, astrophotography, maps and scanned documents.

4.2 Results

The mean quality measures for original LIVE and WMC images compressed by our approach and the JPEG compression quality factors $Q = 70$, 75, and 80 are presented in the Tab. 2. Additionally, in Tab. 3 the information about data volume and compression ratios is provided.

The compression ratio averaged over all images is equal to 39.1%, which is better than the JPEG compression with Q=75 but worse than for Q=70. This result was achieved with comparable image quality computed based on SSIM and

Table 2. Quality measures for LIVE and WMC images

Data-set	EIM	Ours MSE	SSIM	IF	Q = 70 MSE	SSIM	IF	Q = 75 MSE	SSIM	IF	Q = 80 MSE	SSIM	IF
LIVE	1822	27.8	0.9969	0.999	38.9	0.9952	0.9983	33.6	0.996	0.9986	27.3	0.9969	0.9989
WMC	1269	28.6	0.9978	0.9991	34.2	0.9966	0.9983	30.2	0.9971	0.9986	25.5	0.9978	0.9989
Joint	1541	28.2	0.9973	0.999	36.5	0.9959	0.9983	31.9	0.9966	0.9986	26.4	0.9974	0.9989

Table 3. Data volumes and compression ratios (as a proportion of compressed-to-original filesize)

Dataset	No. files	$\sum$ [kB]	mean [kB]	Ours $\sum$ [kB]	ratio	Q = 70 $\sum$ [kB]	ratio	Q = 75 $\sum$ [kB]	ratio	Q = 80 $\sum$ [kB]	ratio
LIVE	29	5706	197	2297	40.3%	1789	31.4%	1971	34.5%	2253	39.5%
WMC	30	8903	297	3420	38.4%	3726	41.9%	3963	44.5%	4231	47.5%
Joint	59	14609	248	5717	39.1%	5516	37.8%	5934	40.6%	6484	44.4%

IF. At the same time, the mean quality is not much lower, than in case of $Q = 80$. It means, that we obtained better quality with lower filesize in comparision to the standard approach.

The general observation is that the usage of our adaptive and content-aware compression leads to actual savings in storage space without strong quality degradation. When we averaged compression quality varying for individual images, the achieved quality Q was equal to 72.6.

The closer look unveils, that the higher compression ratio was observed for WMC database. It is probably because of the higher complexity (in terms of edges intensity) than in case of LIVE. The other aspect, especially important for practical implementation is that in most cases (83% and 63% of images, for LIVE and WMC, respectively) the adaptive compression algorithm ends after only two iterations.

5   Conclusions

We have presented an algorithm of adaptive and quality-aware JPEG compression aimed at Internet storage sites. It allows to compress images in much more efficient manner, taking into consideration the content of images. Basing on the observation, that 'smooth' images can be compressed stronger, while 'edgy' images have to be compressed weaker, we have chosen a set of image quality metrics, that allow to estimate (predict) image quality before it is compressed. Further, for an input image, the algorithm searches for the JPEG compression quality parameter, that guarantees acceptable quality (after compression). A comparison with traditional JPEG compression shows, that our method saves storage space while preserving higher image quality.

The application area includes all social networks sites, that gather digital images. Effective compression is in their case very important and still open issue.

The future works would include adding more perception-alike algorithms of image quality assessment, as well as including more sophisticated algorithms of image complexity identification (especially in case of naturally noised images).

Acknowledgement. The experimental results presented in this paper are a part of Bachelor's Thesis prepared under a supervision of Paweł Forczmański by Gerard Cybe at The Faculty of Computer Science and Information Technology, West Pomeranian University of Technology, Szczecin in 2014.

References

1. Forczmański, P.: Web system for biometric verification of facial portraits. Perspective Technologies and Methods in MEMS Design. In: Proceedings of the 6th International Conference Memstech 2010, Lviv, Ukraine, pp. 152–157 (2010)
2. Wang, Z., Bovik, A.C.: Modern Image Quality Assessment. Morgan & Claypool Publishers (2006)
3. Sheikh, H., Sabir, M., Bovik, A.: A statistical evaluation of recent full reference image quality assessment algorithms. IEEE Trans. on Image Processing 15(11), 3440–3451 (2006)
4. Mantiuk, R.K., Tomaszewska, A., Mantiuk, R.: Comparison of four subjective methods for image quality assessment. Computer Graphics Forum 31(8), 2478–2491 (2012)
5. Wang, Z., Bovik, A.C., Sheikh, H.R., Simoncelli, E.P.: Image Quality Assessment: From Error Visibility To Structural Similarity. IEEE Transactions on Image Processing 13(4), 600–612 (2004)
6. Mantiuk, R., Kim, K.J., Rempel, A.G., Heidrich, W.: HDR-VDP-2: a calibrated visual metric for visibility and quality predictions in all luminance conditions. In: Proc. of SIGGRAPH 2011, pp. 1–14 (2011)
7. Cadik, M., Herzog, R., Mantiuk, R., Mantiuk, R., Myszkowski, K., Seidel, H.P.: Learning to Predict Localized Distortions in Rendered Images. Computer Graphics Forum (Proc. of Pacific Graphics 2013) 32(7), 401–410 (2013)
8. Wu, H., Rao, K.: Digital Video Image Quality and Perceptual Coding. CRC Press (2005)
9. Lin, W., Kuo, C.-C.J.: Perceptual visual quality metrics: A survey. JVCIR, 297–312 (2011)
10. Pedersen, M., Hardeberg, J.: Full-Reference Image Quality Metrics: Classification and Evaluation. Foundations and Trends in Computer Graphics and Vision, vol. 7(1), pp. 1–80 (2011)
11. Wang, Z., Bovik, A.C.: Mean Squared Error: Love It or Leave It? IEEE Signal Processing Magazine 26, 98–117 (2009)
12. Wang, Z., Bovik, A.C.: A Universal Image Quality Index. IEEE Signal Processing Letters 9(3), 81–84 (2002)
13. Okarma, K.: Colour Image Quality Assessment Using Structural Similarity Index and Singular Value Decomposition. In: Bolc, L., Kulikowski, J.L., Wojciechowski, K. (eds.) ICCVG 2008. LNCS, vol. 5337, pp. 55–65. Springer, Heidelberg (2009)
14. Lissner, I., Preiss, J., Urban, P., Lichtenauer, M.S., Zolliker, P.: Image-difference prediction: From grayscale to color. IEEE Transactions on Image Processing 22(2), 435–446 (2013)
15. Sheikh, H.R., Wang, Z., Cormack, L., Bovik, A.C.: Live Image Quality Assessment Database (2003), http://Live.Ece.Utexas.Edu/Research/Quality (accessed October 26, 2013)
16. Li, L., Wang, Z.-S.: Compression Quality Prediction Model For JPEG2000. IEEE Transactions On Image Processing 19(2), 384–398 (2010)

Human Detection for a Video Surveillance Applied in the 'SmartMonitor' System

Dariusz Frejlichowski[1], Katarzyna Gościewska[1,2],
Paweł Forczmański[1], and Radosław Hofman[2]

[1] West Pomeranian University of Technology, Szczecin
Faculty of Computer Science and Information Technology
Żołnierska 52, 71-210, Szczecin, Poland
{dfrejlichowski,pforczmanski}@wi.zut.edu.pl
[2] Smart Monitor sp. z o.o., Niemierzyńska 17a, 71-441, Szczecin, Poland
{katarzyna.gosciewska,radekh}@smartmonitor.pl

Abstract. Human detection is one of the key and crucial tasks in video
surveillance systems and is important for the purpose of object tracking,
fall detection, human gait analysis or abnormal event detection. This
paper concerns the application of two classifiers for human detection in
the 'SmartMonitor' system — an intelligent security system based on
image analysis. The classifiers are based on the Histogram of Oriented
Gradients (HOG) descriptor and simple Haar-like features. The paper
provides a brief description of the main system characteristics, discusses
the problem of human detection and includes some results of the experiments performed using various parameters of HOG and Haar classifiers
that were trained using benchmark databases and tested using appropriate video sequences. The paper aims at investigating the effectiveness
and performance of both methods applied separately before incorporating them into the 'SmartMonitor' system's video processing model.

1 Introduction

'SmartMonitor' is an intelligent security system combining the functionalities of
alarm, home automation and video surveillance systems. It monitors the scene,
detects objects and events, records captured images and reacts to certain situations in a way pre-specified by a user. The detection of objects and events is
based on the Video Content Analysis algorithms which analyse a video stream
in a real-time. The results of this analysis are a base for system response which
may include sending an e-mail or a text message, triggering an alarm in a form
of a siren or a light signal or sending a signal to controlled devices. The type
of system response depends on the individual user requirements and the system
working conditions. The customizability, an autonomous operation and automatic reaction are the key advantages of the system.

The core element of the system is a central unit built of electronic components typical for the PCs, and installed software. Other important devices
include cameras and various sensors (detectors) providing data to the system

L.J. Chmielewski et al. (Eds.): ICCVG 2014, LNCS 8671, pp. 220–227, 2014.
© Springer International Publishing Switzerland 2014

and controlled devices receiving signals from the system during an automatic response or sent by a user. At present, 'SmartMonitor' is a complete solution coming to the market, targeted to increase the safety of the individuals and their assets. The possible applications of the system include protection against unauthorised intrusion, supervision over ill persons and crime detection. The exemplary installation locations are buildings, such as houses, apartments, small businesses, caring houses for elderly people, as well as building surroundings, especially near entrances and windows, but also gardens, backyards or parking spaces. Since 2011, the 'SmartMonitor' system has been presented in several papers. In 2012 the initial approach was described in [1], and a more developed version was presented in [2]. Furthermore, we investigated individual problems, such as foreground region extraction based on background model [3] in 2012 and artefacts removal [4] in 2013. In 2014, 'SmartMonitor' has been described in [5] as a solution applied for the protection of ill and elderly people.

In the 'SmartMonitor' system, human detection is the part of the software responsible for video content analysis, called a video processing model, where main elements are: background modelling based on Gaussian Mixture Models, human detection based on Haar and HOG classifiers, and Mean-Shift tracking. Both classifiers are adaptive human silhouette classifiers based on a cascading approach. Their main task is to reject moving objects that are not under interest of the system and leave only human silhouettes. This in turn will speed up calculations on tracking step.

The main goal of the paper is to investigate real performance of human detection based on Haar and HOG classifiers separately. The paper is organized as follows: the second section discusses the problem of human detection. The third section contains experimental conditions and results, and the last section concludes the paper.

2 Human Detection Using Haar and HOG Classifiers

The task of human detection may be very challenging due to varying conditions in the scene, e.g. lighting or weather, and variations in appearance of objects — shape, size, clothing, poses or number. Human detection aims at determining whether a given image (or a part of it) includes a human or not. Since this type of classification step precedes tracking in a video surveillance system, it enables reducing the number of objects subjected to it. Besides tracking, human detection is also an important step in other approaches such as behaviour understanding [6], abnormal behaviour detection in crowd [7], fall detection [8] or people counting [9,10]. The detection process itself involves two steps: the first one is to detect a moving object and the second is the classification. Objects can be detected using background subtraction, optical flow or spatio-temporal filtering techniques, and classified with respect to various features like motion, texture and shape of object [11].

In the paper, the focus is put on Haar and HOG classifiers. Haar classifier uses simple Haar-like features proposed by Viola et al. in [12] and Adaboost learning technique. Individual Haar-like features are weak classifiers, therefore they are combined in a cascade using Adaboost algorithm that selects the most appropriate weak classifiers and assigns their weights. During training, features are selected in order to reject negative objects at early stage of recognition, what reduces the number of calculations. During classification, subsequent features of an object are calculated only if the answer of the previous feature is equal to the learned value. Otherwise, the object is rejected [12].

HOG was proposed by Dalal and Triggs in [13]. It is a descriptor which uses previously defined patterns and feature vectors for object detection. The deriviation of HOG representation includes several steps. Firstly, gamma and colour normalization are performed, and oriented gradients are calculated using directional filters (detection of vertical and horizontal edges). Then, the length and orientation of gradients are calculated. Furthermore, an image is divided into cells and frequencies of oriented gradients are calculated for each cell. In the next step, cells are grouped into larger overlapping blocks (square, rectangular or in the polar-logarithmic coordinates) and normalized separately. The final HOG representation is obtained by concatenating oriented histograms of all blocks. The representation is invariant to translation within an image plane — directional gradients and histogram do not change despite an object's position change.

Haar and HOG approaches are extensively reported in the literature and used in various applications, also combined with other techniques or modified. Leinhart and Maydt [14] extended the original object detection framework proposed by Viola et al. by adding a set of 45-degree rotated features and deriving a new post-optimization procedure. Pavani et al. [15] proposed other extension of Haar-like features by assigning optimal weights to the feature rectangles in order to increase the non-object discrimination ability. Hoang et al. [16] proposed the feature description method for rapid human detection that uses modified parallelogram-shaped Haar-like features. Authors of [17] use Haar-like features and particle filter for automatic multiple human detection and tracking in varying conditions. Zhu et al. [18] proposed the integration of HOG features and the cascade-of-rejectors approach for fast human detection. HOG blocks are of varying size and Adaboost is used for feature selection. In [19] an algorithm combining HOG as a local feature, head contour as a global feature and Adaboost algorithm to learn classifier is presented. Conde et al. [20] proposed a new method for human detection, namely HoGG, which is based on HOG and Gabor filters. This approach proved to be efficient regardless of environmental conditions.

3   Experimental Conditions and Results

The main goal of the experiments was to investigate the real effectiveness and performance of each classifier as a binary human/non-human classifier. Therefore, we assumed that the foreground extraction stage and the information about consecutive frames are not taken into account, and only an individual frame is processed at the particular moment. Such conditions should be especially considered in case of low frame-rate Closed Circuit Television, i.e. IP cameras in wireless environment. As a result of the classifier, a list of areas that belong to a human is obtained. In the experiments we utilise Haar and HOG classifiers with various operating parameters: input image size (640 × 360 pixels or smaller), image scaling factor (1.1, 1.2, 1.3), Canny pruning (1 — with or 0 — without), number of detections in adjacent regions indicating the threshold above which the location is considered to be a correctly classified object (1, 2 or 3), minimum size of the object (5 × 20 pixels), maximum size of the object (210 × 80 pixels). The database used for testing was the benchmark prepared by us which consists of video sequences containing real scenes recorded in home environment and its surroundings. For training, we used commonly applied benchmark databases in the following manner: HOG classifier trained on the Daimler-Chrysler database [21,22] (HOG-Daimler), HOG classifier trained on the default OpenCV database (HOG-Default) and Haar classifier trained on the default OpenCV database (Haar-Default). During the experiments we have tested above combinations of classifier and training database using various video sequences. We focused on scaling factor (1.1, 1.2, 1.3) and Canny pruning (0, 1) in case of HOG classifier, and scaling factor (1.1, 1.2) and a number of adjacent regions (1, 2, 3) in case of Haar classifier. In the paper we give a description of the results obtained for one exemplary video sequence. We provide corresponding pictorial results in Fig. 1-3 showing detection results for all above combinations and an exemplary video frame. Each figure contains six images, and each image illustrates a result of the classifier operating with different parameters. The resulting images were evaluated visually in respect of accuracy and correctness of human detection.

The discussed video sequence was recorded in the garden. The camera was located about three meters above the ground. High level of MPEG-4 compression resulted in a strong noise. There is also a background noise caused by moving leaves and grass as well as changes in illumination due to sun shining through the clouds. In the first experiment, the HOG classifier trained on Daimler-Chrysler was tested. Unfortunately, despite the lack of foreground objects, a large number of false regions was detected, among which the least in case of scaling factor equal to 1.3. These false detections result from background movements and strong brightness gradients. The human figure which appeared in the subsequent frames was correctly detected but false detections remained (see Fig. 1). The use of Canny pruning did not improve the results (see the second row in Fig. 1).

In the second experiment, the HOG classifier trained on default OpenCV database was tested. There were no falsely detected regions in the scene without moving objects. The classifier is not able to detect a moving object which is partially occluded or is located too far from the camera. It is caused by a specific training database that does not take such situations into account. In the opposite case, i.e. a larger size and fully visible object, the classifier appropriately detects it for 1.1 and 1.2 scaling factors. The use of Canny pruning did not improve the results. An exemplary result is illustrated in Fig. 2.

The last experiment concerned the examination of Haar classifier trained on the default OpenCV database. Due to strong brightness gradients a small number

Fig. 1. Results of HOG-Daimler classifier, a person in the center of the frame

Fig. 2. Results of HOG-Default classifier, a person present in the scene

of false detections occurred, among which the least in case of 1.2 scaling factor. The classifier did not detect a partially occluded object. In turn, a full human silhouette was detected appropriately regardless the scaling factor, as can be seen on example in Fig. 3. However, in some cases, there was a small number of false detections present. Haar classifier is also not able to deal with very small objects located too far from the camera, but is faster than HOG classifier. An exemplary result is illustrated in Fig. 3.

Some performance tests were also done in order to investigate the speed of particular classifiers implemented using C/C++ and OpenCV (see Table 1), and combined in Matlab environment. It is not obvious, which classifier is the best. However, when considering classification accuracy, the most preferred solution is the HOG classifier with a sufficiently large training database and using 1.1 scaling factor without Canny pruning. The classification accuracy is very good for the objects of an appropriate size. The observations proved high efficiency

Fig. 3. Results of Haar-Default classifier, a correctly detected person

Table 1. Results of performance tests — average time in milliseconds per frame

	HOG-default			Haar		
Scaling factor	1.1	1.2	1.3	1.1	1.2	1.3
With Canny pruning	316 ms	240 ms	169 ms	280 ms	164 ms	117 ms
Without Canny pruning	301 ms	195 ms	184 ms	220 ms	148 ms	111 ms

of the HOG classifier. In turn, Haar classifier does not give a large number of false detections and its computational cost is low. Moreover, there were some classification errors caused by false detections resulting from the similarity between regions and template, false detections due to an inadequate scale of the searched object, lack of information about regions with moving objects or lack of region limitation to limit the area of interest. These errors can be eliminated using moving object detection and tracking before object classification.

Taking the above information into account, we decided to combine Haar and HOG classifiers, and precede human detection with moving object extraction using background subtraction technique to reduce the searched area. The idea of combining both classifiers is based on the cascading approach. A cascade consists of several video stream processing steps and the main steps are background modelling for foreground binary mask extraction, morphological operations, the selection of geometrically appropriate objects and finally the classification. Some aspects of joining Haar-based and HOG-based classifiers which reduce the number of false alarms are also presented in [23].

4   Summary and Conclusions

Human detection in video and static images is especially important for automated video surveillance and has recently attracted many researchers. It concerns detecting moving object within the image scene and classifying whether it is a human or not. In the paper, two human silhouette classifiers which are based on Haar-like features and Histogram of Oriented Gradients were presented and experimentally tested to be applied in the 'SmartMonitor' system. It is an intelligent security system based on Video Content Analysis algorithms that is able to analyse captured video streams and react to the detected objects and events based on specific rules and without human intervention. Since the solution focuses on such working scenarios as intrusion detection or supervision over ill person including fall detection, a human detection is an important step in its video processing model. During the experiments both classifiers were trained on benchmark databases and tested on prepared by us video sequences. It turned out that the analysed approaches individually have their advantages and disadvantages, hence we decided to use a combination of them. Focusing on choosing appropriate parameters for human detection, the best results were obtained for HOG classifier with 1.1 scaling factor and without the Canny pruning step.

Acknowledgments. The project *"Innovative security system based on image analysis–"SmartMonitor" prototype construction"* (original title: *Budowa prototypu innowacyjnego systemu bezpieczeństwa opartego o analize obrazu – "Smart-Monitor"*) is a project co-founded by European Union (EU) (project number PL: UDA-POIG.01.04.00-32-008/10-02, Value: 9.996.604 PLN, EU contribution: 5.848.560 PLN, realization period: 07.2011–04.2013). *European Funds–for the development of innovative economy (Fundusze Europejskie—dla rozwoju innowacyjnej gospodarki).*

References

1. Frejlichowski, D., Forczmański, P., Nowosielski, A., Gościewska, K., Hofman, R.: SmartMonitor: An Approach to Simple, Intelligent and Affordable Visual Surveillance System. In: Bolc, L., Tadeusiewicz, R., Chmielewski, L.J., Wojciechowski, K. (eds.) ICCVG 2012. LNCS, vol. 7594, pp. 726–734. Springer, Heidelberg (2012)
2. Frejlichowski, D., Gościewska, K., Forczmański, P., Nowosielski, A., Hofman, R.: SmartMonitor: recent progress in the development of an innovative visual surveillance system. J. of Theoretical and Applied Computer Science 6(3), 28–35 (2012)
3. Frejlichowski, D., Gościewska, K., Forczmański, P., Nowosielski, A., Hofman, R.: Extraction of the Foreground Regions by Means of the Adaptive Background Modelling Based on Various Colour Components for a Visual Surveillance System. In: Kott, L. (ed.) ICALP 1986. LNCS, vol. 226, pp. 351–360. Springer, Heidelberg (1986)
4. Frejlichowski, D., Gościewska, K., Forczmański, P., Nowosielski, A., Hofman, R.: The Removal of False Detections from Foreground Regions Extracted Using Adaptive Background Modelling for a Visual Surveillance System. In: Saeed, K., Chaki, R., Cortesi, A., Wierzchoń, S. (eds.) CISIM 2013. LNCS, vol. 8104, pp. 253–264. Springer, Heidelberg (2013)
5. Frejlichowski, D., Gościewska, K., Forczmański, P., Hofman, R.: "SmartMonitor" — An Intelligent Security System for the Protection of Individuals and Small Properties with the Possibility of Home Automation. Sensors 14, 9922–9948 (2014)
6. Borges, P.V.K., Conci, N., Cavallaro, A.: Video-Based Human Behavior Understanding: A Survey. IEEE T. Circ. Syst. Vid. 23(11), 1993–2008 (2013)
7. Zhang, D., Peng, H., Haibin, Y., Lu, Y.: Crowd Abnormal Behavior Detection Based on Machine Learning. Information Technology Journal 12, 1199–1205 (2013)

8. Vishwakarma, V., Mandal, C., Sural, S.: Automatic Detection of Human Fall in Video. In: Ghosh, A., De, R.K., Pal, S.K. (eds.) PReMI 2007. LNCS, vol. 4815, pp. 616–623. Springer, Heidelberg (2007)

9. Hou, Y.-L., Pang, G.K.H.: People Counting and Human Detection in a Challenging Situation. IEEE T. Syst. Man Cy. A 41(1), 24–33 (2011)

10. Karpagavalli, P., Ramprasad, A.V.: Estimating the Density of the People and Counting the number of people in a crowd environment for human safety. In: 2013 International Conference on Communications and Signal Processing (ICCSP), pp. 663–667 (2013)

11. Paul, M., Haque, S.M.E., Chakraborty, S.: Human detection in surveillance video and its applications — a review. EURASIP Journal on Advanced in Signal Processing 2013(1), 1–16 (2013)

12. Viola, P., Jones, M.: Rapid Object Detection Using a Boosted Cascade of Simple Features. In: IEEE Computer Society Conference on Computer Vision and Pattern Recognition (CVPR), vol. 1, pp. 511–518 (2001)

13. Dalal, N., Triggs, B.: Histograms of oriented gradients for human detection. In: IEEE Computer Society Conference on Computer Vision and Pattern Recognition, vol. 1, pp. 886–893 (2005)

14. Lienhart, R., Maydt, J.: An extended set of Haar-like features for rapid object detection. In: Proceedings of 2002 International Conference on Image Processing, vol. 1, pp. I-900–I-903 (2002)

15. Pavani, S.-K., Delgado, D., Frangi, A.F.: Haar-like features with optimally weighted rectangles for rapid object detection. Pattern Recogn. 43, 160–172 (2010)

16. Hoang, V.-D., Le, M.-H., Jo, K.-H.: Fast human detection based on parallelogram haar-like features. In: IECON 2012 – 38th Annual Conference on IEEE Industrial Electronics Society, pp. 4220–4225 (2012)

17. Kushwaha, A.K.S., Sharma, C.M., Khare, M., Srivastava, R.K., Khare, A.: Automatic multiple human detection and tracking for visual surveillance system. In: 2012 International Conference on Informatics, Electronics & Vision (ICIEV), pp. 326–331 (2012)

18. Zhu, Q., Avidan, S., Yeh, M.-C., Cheng, K.-T.: Fast Human Detection Using Cascade of Histograms of Oriented Gradients. In: Proceeding of the 2006 IEEE Computer Society Conference on Computer Vision and Pattern Recognition, pp. 1491–1498 (2006)

19. Huang, S.-S., Tsai, H.-M., Hsiao, P.-Y., Tu, M.-Q., Jian, E.-L.: Combining Histograms of Oriented Gradients with Global Feature for Human Detection. In: Lee, K.-T., Tsai, W.-H., Liao, H.-Y.M., Chen, T., Hsieh, J.-W., Tseng, C.-C. (eds.) MMM 2011 Part II. LNCS, vol. 6524, pp. 208–218. Springer, Heidelberg (2011)

20. Conde, C., Moctezuma, D., De Diego, I.M., Cabello, E.: HoGG: Gabor and HoG-based human detection for surveillance in non-controlled environments. Neurocomputing 100, 19–30 (2013)

21. Keller, C.G., Enzweiler, M., Gavrila, D.M.: A New Benchmark for Stereo-Based Pedestrian Detection. In: 2011 IEEE Intelligent Vehicles Symposium (IV), pp. 691–696 (2011)

22. Kim, J., Han, Y., Hahn, H.: Human Detection using Projected Edge Feature. World Academy of Science, Engineering and Technology, International Science Index 60 5(12), 1672–1675 (2011)

23. Forczmański, P., Seweryn, M.: Surveillance Video Stream Analysis Using Adaptive Background Model and Object Recognition. In: Bolc, L., Tadeusiewicz, R., Chmielewski, L.J., Wojciechowski, K. (eds.) ICCVG 2010, Part I. LNCS, vol. 6374, pp. 114–121. Springer, Heidelberg (2010)

Egomotion Estimation
by Point-Cloud Back-Mapping

Haokun Geng, Radu Nicolescu, and Reinhard Klette

Department of Computer Science, University of Auckland, New Zealand
hgen001@aucklanduni.ac.nz

Abstract. We consider egomotion estimation in the context of driver-
assistance systems. In order to estimate the actual vehicle movement we
only apply stereo cameras (and not any additional sensor). The paper
proposes a visual odometry method by back-mapping clouds of reconstructed 3D points. Our method, called *stereo-vision point-cloud back
mapping method* (sPBM), aims at minimizing 3D back-projection errors. We report about extensive experiments for sPBM. At this stage we
consider accuracy as being the first priority; optimizing run-time performance will need to be considered later. Accurately estimated motion
among subsequent frames of a recorded video sequence can then be used,
for example, for 3D roadside reconstruction.

1 Introduction and Related Work

Computer vision techniques are widely used for solving problems that require extensive and precise geometric calculations. For example, driver-assistance
systems (DAS) in the automotive industry require solutions of such problems.
Computers are trained to listen, to see, and to sense the road geometry and the
dynamic traffic environment. DAS are designed to provide comfort with safety,
to assist drivers to follow traffic instructions, and to deal with road incidents. For
instance, DAS should avoid that a sudden turn results in a pedestrian accident,
or a braking manoeuvre in a collision. Demands for computer vision involved in
DAS are increasing in future towards holistic scene understanding.

Motion data can be obtained by multiple types of sensors, including inertial
measurement units (IMU), global positioning system (GPS) units, radar sensors,
cameras, or laser range-scanners. Stereo cameras offer in principle economy and
robustness, but require more advances in vision methodologies. Camera-based
ego-motion estimation (also known as *visual odometry*) is the method we use to
determine the trajectory of the *ego-vehicle* (i.e. the vehicle where the cameras are
operating in). It is the first step of a whole pipeline of processes for understanding
the road environment. Computationally it is an expensive task that requires
massive observations and calculations. It estimates positional and directional
data from input image pairs recorded at speeds of 25 Hz or more.

Nister et al. [13] firstly introduced visual odometry in 2004; it estimates odometry information based on recorded stereo image pairs only, not using other data
as, e.g., the vehicles' yaw rate or speed. An advantage of visual odometry is

L.J. Chmielewski et al. (Eds.): ICCVG 2014, LNCS 8671, pp. 228–235, 2014.

that it avoids the influence of motion estimation errors in other sensors, e.g. the influence of mechanical issues such as wheel slips, or the still existing inaccuracy of (cost-efficient) GPS or IMU sensors. Scaramuzza et al. [16] suggest that visual odometry methods usually lead to a smaller relative position error (in a range between 0.1% to 2% of actual motion), compared to traditional wheel odometry methods. [10] presents a vision-based ego-motion application used in Mars exploration rovers; it demonstrated the great capability of this technology on another planet for the first time. With these advantages and examples, vision-based ego-motion analysis proves itself as being a valuable navigation technology, and a potential feature of mobile computer vision applications.

This paper presents a novel vision-based ego-motion estimation method. 3D point clouds are calculated based on generated disparity maps. In this paper we apply an *iterative semi-global stereo matching* (iSGM) method as introduced in [7] in 2012; see also [8] for a description of the iSGM algorithm.

Due to the types of used video input data, existing visual odometry methods can be divided into three main categories: monocular, stereo, and omnidirectional. Each of the three types is designed for particular problem domains. For solving our problem, we choose to focus on stereo-vision methods. A solid mathematical foundation of for navigation using stereo-vision methods has been published in [11,12].

Following those basic contributions, various studies have been carried out, from 2D-to-2D matching to 2D-to-3D registration, and finally to 3D-to-3D motion estimation. A method for solving a 3D-to-3D point registration problem was presented in [6]. The given algorithm estimates the stereo cameras' 3D rigid transformation by directly taking the disparity images as the input. [14] defined concepts of two-frame motion field estimation; the paper demonstrated a novel approach for calculating 3-dimensional scene flow data using a Kalman filter and parallel implementations.

Visual odometry depends on feature detection. A good feature detector is a critical factor for improving the estimation results. [17] carefully evaluated a number of popular 2D feature detectors; the results showed that the *oriented BRIEF* (ORB) detector (see [15] for its implementation and, e.g., [8] for a definition) gave the best results among all available (in mid 2013) detectors in OpenCV when also requesting time efficiency. Rotation invariance and noise resistance of the ORB detector comes close to SIFT performance, but at a much better time efficiency of ORB compared to SIFT.

The iterative closest point (ICP) method is typically used to find the translation and rotation between two clouds of points by minimising geometric differences between them. This algorithm was firstly implemented in 1992 by Besl and McKay; see [3]. The authors of [5] report an improved extension of the popular ICP algorithm using a least trimmed squares (LTS) approach.

The Kalman filter is a tool for minimising estimation errors caused by white noise of input data; it effectively improves both the robustness and the regularity (smoothness) of calculated trajectories. The authors of [1] designed a robust ego-motion algorithm with an extended Kalman filter for 3D position and velocity estimation; they continued their work and successfully implemented a head-wearable stereo system with real-time ego-motion estimation capability reported in [2].

In our proposed method, we consider the pair-wise registration task to be a linear problem, since the time interval between every two input frames is relatively small (approximately 0.03 seconds). Our method is different from other existing work with respect to three aspects. First, it uses a motion layer to remove all the moving features between every two frames. Second, it applies a segmentation-cut method to minimise typical errors occurring in stereo matching. Third, it measures a number of local transformations with calculated weights, in order to sum up an accurate global transformation.

2 Ego-motion Estimation Method

A stereo-cameras system is mounted inside the car just behind the rear mirror.[1] Our proposed method consists of the following main components: 2D feature matching, 3D feature triangulation and mapping, motion estimation, and noise minimising with a Kalman filter.

2.1 Disparity Smoothness Issues

Stereo matching applies a data cost and a continuity cost function [8] when calculating the location difference (i.e. the *disparity*) between a pair of corresponding pixels in the left and right image. Our method of choice is iSGM (see [7]) for generating the disparity maps of recorded stereo frames. Calculated disparity maps generally contain noise, miss-match errors, and gaps (due to occlusions and low confidence). In order to improve the availability of dense and accurate disparity data, we implemented an "aggressive" method for smoothing disparity values for any given tracked feature.

For any subsequences of subsequent s frames (we use $s = 5$ in the formula below and experiments), the disparity value of a traced feature is bound by the following rules:

$$d_{(k \cdots k+5)} = \begin{cases} -1 & \text{if } d_{\triangle total} < |d_k - d_{k+5}| \\ k \cdot C_d \cdot + d_0 & \text{if } d_{\triangle total} \geq |d_k - d_{k+5}| \end{cases} \tag{1}$$

where C_d is the mean value of changes in disparity values among considered subsequences of length s. We consider a linear model for the ego-vehicle's motion.

In order to minimise the errors (or uncertainties) for different estimation scenarios, we propose a feature selection scheme. Features with a smaller disparity are put into a candidate set for estimating rotational measurements. Features with larger disparity values are used to calculate the translational component of the ego-vehicle's motion. The scheme uses a threshold (to create the two candidate sets) which is the median value of disparities of all detected features.

---

[1] In our test system, the cameras record sequences as 12-bit grey-level images at 30 Hz with a dimension (width times height) of 2046 × 1080 pixels for both the left and right images.

2.2   From Local to Global Transformations

There is a common observation for any reconstructed cloud of 3D points: the white noise is mainly distributed along the Z-axis. In order to minimise the errors, we segment those clouds of 3D points and smooth disparities. For any set of 3D points on a local (triangulated) segment, we specify two values: (1) The depth value d_{edge} of its nearest edge element, and (2) the smallest depth value $d_{smallest}$ inside the segmented region. Based on those two values, we then calculate a smoothed depth value to replace a measured value as follows:

$$Z_{smooth} = Z_{edge} - (\frac{Z_{edge} - Z_{smallest}}{d_{edge} + d_{smallest}}) \cdot d_{edge} \tag{2}$$

A pair of local segments (between subsequent frames) generates a local transformation. Every local transformation has a weight for finally defining the global transformation. The weight is obtained as follows:

$$\omega(x, \mu, \sigma) = \frac{1}{\sigma\sqrt{2\pi}} e^{-\frac{(x-\mu)^2}{2\sigma^2}} \tag{3}$$

where $\mu = 0$, $\sigma = 150$, and x is the distance to the cameras within an assumed range of $(0, 150]$ meters. The global transformation is then defined by

$$T_{global} = \sum (\omega_x \cdot T_{local}) / \sum \omega_x \tag{4}$$

Improved translation and rotation parameters $(\mathbf{R}, \mathbf{t})$ can be obtained by applying least-square optimization with two sorted sets of n matched features from Frame k (feature $m_{k,i}$) to Frame $k + 1$ (feature $m_{k+1,i}$):

$$E = \arg \min_{(\mathbf{R},\mathbf{t})} \sum_{i=1}^{n} |P(m_{k+1,i}) - P(\mathbf{R}_{k,i} \cdot m_{k,i} - \mathbf{t}_{k,i})| \tag{5}$$

The projection function $P(m_k)$ is defined as follows:

$$P(m_k) = \frac{f \cdot b}{d} \cdot [u, v, 1]^\top = [X, Y, Z]^\top \tag{6}$$

for a feature m_k detected at (u, v) in the input image. Here, f is the focal length of the corresponding camera, b is the length of the baseline, and d is the disparity value of the given feature.

2.3   Extended Kalman Filter

In order to minimise the Gaussian noise in the estimation of the ego-vehicle's motion, we propose to use an iterated extended Kalman filter (IEKF) to solve this problem. As introduced by Julier et al [9], an IEKF is designed for filtering noise in nonlinear calculations, but it is also reliable for solving problems that are almost linear. Since the time interval between each two subsequent frames is relatively small, which is defining an nonlinear problem but "almost" linear.

Process Model. The process model of our method follows the general form

$$\mathbf{x}_k = \begin{bmatrix} \mathbf{A}_k & 0 \\ 0 & \mathbf{A}_k \end{bmatrix} \cdot \mathbf{x}_{k-1} + \mathbf{B}_k^\top + \mathbf{n}_k \tag{7}$$

of a Kalman filter where the state vector $\mathbf{x}_k$ contains the camera's pose given by world coordinates (X, Y, Z) and Euler angles φ, θ, and ψ, extended by changes (X', Y', Z') and φ', θ', and ψ'. The Euler angles are calculated for pitch, roll, and yaw. For calculating the current state vector $\mathbf{x}_k$, we combine the positional and directional data into a state-transformation matrix as follows:

$$\mathbf{A}_k = \begin{bmatrix} 1 & 0 & 0 & \Delta t & 0 & 0 \\ 0 & 1 & 0 & 0 & \Delta t & 0 \\ 0 & 0 & 1 & 0 & 0 & \Delta t \\ 1 & 0 & 0 & \Delta t & 0 & 0 \\ 0 & 1 & 0 & 0 & \Delta t & 0 \\ 0 & 0 & 1 & 0 & 0 & \Delta t \end{bmatrix} \tag{8}$$

Vector $\mathbf{B}_k$ is the optimal control-input of the Kalman filter.

Measurement Model. A measurement is the observed camera translation and its rotation. As we assumed a linear model, the new translation and rotation is directly obtained by our ICP method. Thus, the relation between the current state vector $\mathbf{x}_k$ and the measurement state vector $\mathbf{z}_k$ is described as follows:

$$\mathbf{z}_k = \mathbf{H} \cdot \mathbf{x}_k + \mathbf{n}_k = \begin{bmatrix} \mathbf{I}_6 & 0 \\ 0 & \mathbf{I}_6 \end{bmatrix} \cdot \mathbf{x}_k + \mathbf{n}_k \tag{9}$$

where $\mathbf{R}_x$, $\mathbf{R}_y$, and $\mathbf{R}_z$ are the rotation matrices calculated from the three relevant Euler angles. The variable $\mathbf{n}_k$ represents the measurement error assumed to be Gaussian noise with zero-mean.

An implemented Kalman filter consists of two major steps in one calculation: prediction and correction. In the prediction step, it predicts the projections of the current state vector to the next state, in order to obtain a so-called 'priori' estimation. In the correction step, it measures the optimal Kalman gain, then updates the 'posteriori' state based on the calculated Kalman gain.

Prediction. Between every two frames, it is required to estimate a *priori* state vector $\tilde{\mathbf{x}}_{k+1|k}$:

$$\tilde{\mathbf{x}}_{k+1|k} = \mathbf{A}_k \cdot \tilde{\mathbf{x}}_k + \mathbf{B}_k \tag{10}$$

and a *priori* projection noise covariance matrix $\mathbf{P}_{k+1|k}$:

$$\mathbf{P}_{k+1|k} = \mathbf{A}_k \cdot \mathbf{P}_k \cdot \mathbf{A}_k^\top + \mathbf{Q}_k \tag{11}$$

Variable $\mathbf{Q}_k$ is the covariance of the uncertainty in the measurement.

Correction. First we calculate the Kalman gain for the next state based on Equ. (9).

$$\mathbf{K}_{k+1} = \mathbf{P}_{k+1|k} \cdot \mathbf{H}_{k+1}^{\top} \cdot (\mathbf{H}_{k+1} \cdot \mathbf{P}_{k+1|k} \cdot \mathbf{H}_{k+1}^{\top} + \mathbf{R}_k)^{-1} \qquad (12)$$

Variable $\mathbf{R}_k$ is the covariance of white noise $\mathbf{n}_k$ in the observational data, the residual covariance $\tilde{\mathbf{n}}_{k+1}$ can be measured as follows:

$$\tilde{\mathbf{n}}_{k+1} = \mathbf{z}_{k+1} - \mathbf{H}_{k+1} \cdot \tilde{\mathbf{x}}_{k+1|k} \qquad (13)$$

Finally, we update the '*posteriori*' state vector:

$$\tilde{\mathbf{x}}_{k+1|k+1} = \tilde{\mathbf{x}}_{k+1|k} + \mathbf{K}_{k+1} \cdot \tilde{\mathbf{n}}_{k+1} \qquad (14)$$

and the '*posteriori*' projection noise covariance matrix:

$$\mathbf{P}_{k+1|k+1} = (\mathbf{I} - \mathbf{K}_{k+1} \cdot \mathbf{H}_{k+1}) \cdot \mathbf{P}_{k+1|k} \qquad (15)$$

3   Results and Evaluation

The evaluation is carried out following camera calibration, which also provides the cameras intrinsic parameters, and time-synchronised stereo-pair video recording. In this paper we report about a sequence of 1,246 stereo frames recorded at 30 Hz; see Fig. 1. The calibrated focal length is 2908.86 pixels, the baseline length is 0.338903 m. Frame dimensions are 2046×1080 pixels. The proposed method is implemented in C++ with OpenCV and PCL technology on a standard laptop computer. The tracked features are estimated using the Lucas-Kanade algorithm; see, e.g. [4,8].

Fig. 1. *Left*: Subsequence when driving straight. *Right*: Subsequence while driving around a roundabout.

Figure 2 presents a dense 3D reconstruction of street segments with the shown camera trajectory. Figure 3 and Fig. 4 show the tracked features' incremental registration in the scene. We measure the re-projection error, frame by frame, in order to evaluate the accuracy of the ego-motion estimation. The result shows that the mean of the re-projection errors for these two subsequences are all under 2 pixels, which is acceptable for driver-assistance purposes, but possibly not yet ideal for the very challenging road-side reconstruction as pioneered in [18].

Due to currently (still) non-availability of sources for previously published ego-motion algorithms (e.g. for [2]) it remains a future project to compare results.

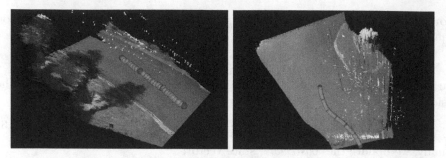

Fig. 2. Estimated camera trajectory with corresponding 3D road reconstruction. *Left*: Driving-straight subsequence. *Right*: Roundabout subsequence.

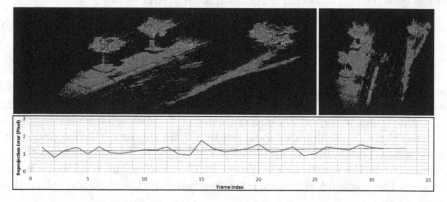

Fig. 3. Tracked features in a 3D representation for the driving-straight subsequence

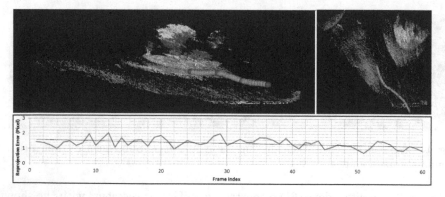

Fig. 4. Tracked features in a 3D representation for the roundabout subsequence

4　Conclusions

The reason why we choose an ICP-based method is that it has the potential to be extended for adding or removing non-static objects in a traffic scene, and for mapping changes of road environments over time. As a next step, a 3D feature outlier removal scheme will be designed and implemented for more accurate estimation. As mentioned before, one type of sensors alone (here: stereo cameras) might solve the problem under various conditions, but combining gathered data with those recorded by another sensor (e.g., a GPS unit) is expected to improve the robustness of our proposed method. The ultimate goal is to estimate accurate ego-motion of the vehicle for all circumstances when driving a car, so that it could provide a solid foundation for higher-order applications of the driver assistance system such as holistic traffic scene understanding.

References

1. Badino, H., Franke, U., Rabe, C., Gehrig, S.: Stereo vision-based detection of moving objects under strong camera motion. In: Proc. Int. Conf. Computer Vision Theory Applications, pp. 25–28 (2006)
2. Badino, H., Kanade, T.: A head-wearable short-baseline stereo system for the simultaneous estimation of structure and motion. In: Proc. Conf. Machine Vision Applications (2011)
3. Besl, P.J., McKay, N.D.: A method for registration of 3-D shapes. IEEE Trans. Pattern Analysis Machine Intelligence 14(2), 239–256 (1992)
4. Bouguet, J.Y.: Pyramidal implementation of the Lucas Kanade feature tracker description of the algorithm. Intel Corporation, Microprocessor Research Labs, USA (2000)
5. Chetverikov, D., Svirko, D., Stepanov, D., Krsek, P.: The trimmed iterative closest point algorithm. In: Proc. ICPR, vol. 3, pp. 545–548 (2002)
6. Demirdjian, D., Darrell, T.: Motion estimation from disparity images. In: Proc. ICCV, vol. 1, pp. 213–218 (2001)
7. Hermann, S., Klette, R.: Iterative semi-global matching for robust driver assistance systems. In: Lee, K.M., Matsushita, Y., Rehg, J.M., Hu, Z. (eds.) ACCV 2012, Part III. LNCS, vol. 7726, pp. 465–478. Springer, Heidelberg (2013)
8. Klette, R.: Concise Computer Vision. Springer, London (2014)
9. Julier, S.J., Uhlmann, J.K.: Unscented filtering and nonlinear estimation. Proc. IEEE 92(3), 401–422 (2004)
10. Maimone, M., Cheng, Y., Matthies, L.: Two years of visual odometry on the Mars exploration rovers. J. Field Robotics 24, 169–186 (2007)
11. Matthies, L., Shafer, S.: Error modeling in stereo navigation. IEEE J. Robotics Automation 3, 239–248 (1987)
12. Matthies, L.: Dynamic stereo vision. Ph.D. dissertation, Carnegie Mellon University (1989)
13. Nister, D., Naroditsky, O., Bergen, J.: Visual odometry. In: Proc. ICVPR, pp. 652–659 (2004)
14. Rabe, C., Müller, T., Wedel, A., Franke, U.: Dense, robust, and accurate motion field estimation from stereo image sequences in real-time. In: Daniilidis, K., Maragos, P., Paragios, N. (eds.) ECCV 2010, Part IV. LNCS, vol. 6314, pp. 582–595. Springer, Heidelberg (2010)
15. Rublee, E., Rabaud, V., Konolige, K., Bradski, G.: ORB: an efficient alternative to SIFT or SURF. In: Proc. ICCV, pp. 2564–2571 (2011)
16. Scaramuzza, D., Fraundorfer, F.: Visual odometry tutorial. Robotics Automation Magazine 18(4), 80–92 (2011)
17. Song, Z., Klette, R.: Robustness of point feature detection. In: Wilson, R., Hancock, E., Bors, A., Smith, W. (eds.) CAIP 2013, Part II. LNCS, vol. 8048, pp. 91–99. Springer, Heidelberg (2013)
18. Zeng, Y., Klette, R.: Multi-run 3D streetside reconstruction from a vehicle. In: Wilson, R., Hancock, E., Bors, A., Smith, W. (eds.) CAIP 2013, Part I. LNCS, vol. 8047, pp. 580–588. Springer, Heidelberg (2013)

Tracking People in Video Sequences
by Clustering Feature Motion Paths

Adam Gudyś[1,2], Jakub Rosner[1,2], Jakub Segen[1],
Konrad Wojciechowski[1], and Marek Kulbacki[1]

[1] Polish-Japanese Institute of Information Technology
Koszykowa 86, 02-008 Warsaw, Poland
[2] Silesian University of Technology, Institute of Informatics
Akademicka 16, 44-100 Gliwice, Poland
mk@pjwstk.edu.pl

Abstract. Methods of tracking human motion in video sequences can be used to count people, identify pedestrian traffic patterns, analyze behavior statistics of shoppers, or as a preliminary step in the analysis and recognition of a person's actions and behavior. A novel method for tracking multiple people in a video sequence is presented, based on clustering the motion paths of local features in images. It extends and improves the earlier tracking method based on clustering motion paths, by using the SURF detector and descriptor to identify, compare, and link the local features between video frames, instead of the characteristic points in bounding contours. A special care was put into the implementation to minimize time and memory requirements of the procedure, which allows it to process a 1080p video sequence in real-time on a dual processor workstation. The correctness of the procedure has been confirmed by experiments on synthetic and real video data.

1   Introduction

Tracking peoples motion is an important issue in intelligent video analysis. It is applied e.g., for counting people in a monitored area, determining time spent in the area by individual persons, or identifying patterns in a human traffic [13,8]. It can be also used as a preliminary step for more detailed analysis performed by video surveillance systems, such as learning and recognition of human actions [6], which is the subject of ongoing research.

The problem of people tracking has been widely investigated in the literature and many approaches have been proposed for this purpose. Some of them are based on the simplification that there is only a single silhouette at video sequence. For instance [10] matched moving objects to the 3D-model of a walking person. The problem with this approach is that the model is restricted to the videos of people walking parallel to the image plane with constant velocity and without occlusions. The different strategy was used by [12]. It employed detection of motion areas using intensity features and iterative merging of them on the basis of direction of motion. Some other researches utilized moving light display images of

L.J. Chmielewski et al. (Eds.): ICCVG 2014, LNCS 8671, pp. 236–245, 2014.

people [9]. Tracking-by-detection approach used in recent work combines object detection with data association methods, such as conditional random field [5] or minimization of energy function [1]. Other data association methods use Markov-Chain Monte-Carlo Data Association (MCMCDA) [3]. These methods are costly and not always appropriate for online processing.

The basic of the presented study is an algorithm introduced by [11]. It is based on feature paths, i.e., sequences of matching feature points across consecutive video frames. It employs the fact that paths corresponding to a motion of a single object are close to each other spatially and overlap in time. Therefore, the paths are clustered in a way that each cluster gathers elements corresponding to a single person. The clustering is updated incrementally in every frame as feature paths extend. In the original study feature points were extracted as corners in bounding contours. In the presented algorithm they are calculated with a use of SURF algorithm [2], which gives more robust features than contour corners. Extracting clean contours may be difficult, but when they are available, both types of features can be used to directly enhance the method from [11]. As previously, clusters are scanned for possible merges. This is especially beneficial at the beginning of a motion when there are few short paths and there is a significant probability of several paths from the same object to be assigned to different clusters. Cluster merging allows this fragmentation to be reduced.

All aforementioned steps, i.e., extension and assignment of paths as well as update of clusters are repeated in consecutive frames. One of our goals was to make the system capable to work in real time on long video sequences. Hence, a special effort was put to reduce time and memory requirements of the procedure. As a result, the algorithm is able to process in real time 1080p video sequence on a workstation equipped with dual hexa-core central processors. The main parameters of the algorithm concern an approximate size of a persons silhouette at the analyzed video and are the most important factors determining sensitivity and specificity of the method: too small values result in some silhouettes being undetected, too large cause groups of people to be clustered as one. The presence prior knowledge is, however, a typical requirement for performing successful video analysis.

2   Path Generation

Path creation process bases on matching similar pixels on consecutive frames. Pixels are selected using SURF detector. Detector recognises characteristic pixels on the image (feature points) and creates vectors (descriptors), identifying them using information about sibling pixels. Pixels having most similar descriptors on consecutive video frames are recognised as matching points and form feature paths. To express matching formally, let be given points x and y from frames X and Y, respectively. Point x matches point y ($x \simeq y$) iff:

1. $\sim \exists_{z \in Y}(\rho(x, z) < \rho(x, y))$,
2. $\rho(x, y) < \tau$,
3. $\varphi(x, y) < T$,

where ρ a metric in the descriptor space, φ is a metric in the image space, τ and T are some thresholds given as algorithm parameters. A path in a sequence of video frames $V^1, V^2, \ldots, V^k$ is a sequence of pixels $p^1, p^2, \ldots, p^k$ such that $p^1 \in V^b$ and $\forall_{i>1} \left((\exists p^i \in V^{b+i} : p^i \simeq p^{i-j} \Rightarrow j < \delta) \vee p^i = \Gamma \right)$, where Γ indicates a gap and means that no pixel belongs to a path in a current frame; δ is a maximum gap length. Gaps could be extrapolated or just omitted in the next part of the described method.

The path generation procedure begins with detecting all feature points in the first frame of the sequence. Then, for each consecutive frame the algorithm: (a) finds feature points, (b) performs assignment of those points with points from the previous frame to detect matches, and (c) adds to each path a matching point or a gap, if no match has been found. If the gap is longer than threshold δ, a new path is created.

Making an assignment is a crucial issue for path creation procedure. Let $d^1, d^2, \ldots, d^n$ and $g^1, g^2, \ldots, g^k$ be pixels from frames D and G, respectively. Assignment matrix $A = [a_{ij} \in \{0, 1\}]_{n \times k}$ is a matrix in which each row and each column contains at most one "1" such that $a_{ij} = 1 \Leftrightarrow d^i \simeq g^j$. For solving assignment problem, Hungarian algorithm is used [7]. Because of its structure, conditions (2) and (3) of matching relation are not checked. After Hungarian assignment matrix is created, all matching (in Hungarian algorithm sense) pixels has to be examined for fulfilling these conditions. Threshold T is not defined explicitly. Due to gap existence, permissible distance between matching points grows. This is why another parameter was introduced: a velocity v. The threshold is altered according to the formula $T = v(L+1)$ with L being a current gap length.

As stated previously, the resulting feature paths are input to the clustering procedure. For this purpose the path representation has to be extended. Path P is now defined as $(P^1, P^2, \ldots, P^l, c)$, where l is a path length, P^i represent i-th path point described by spatio-temporal coordinates (x, y, t) and tangential coordinates (u, v). Vector $c = (c_x, c_y)$ is the mean spatial displacement of the path from its associated cluster. For convenience let $P_{\text{component}}$ indicate a specified component of path P, e.g., P_x^i denotes x coordinate of i-th path point. The tangential coordinates are computed as a difference of outputs of backward filter B and forward filter F:

$$\left(P_u^i, P_v^i \right) = \left(B_x^i - F_x^i, B_y^i - F_y^i \right), i = 1 \ldots l. \tag{1}$$

The filters for x coordinate are given as (the definition for y is analogous):

$$B_x^i = \begin{cases} B_x^{i+1} + \alpha(P_x^i - B_x^{i+1}), & \text{for } i < l \\ P_x^i, & \text{for } i = l \end{cases}$$

$$F_x^i = \begin{cases} F_x^{i-1} + \alpha(P_x^i - F_x^{i-1}), & \text{for } i > 1 \\ P_x^i, & \text{for } i = 1 \end{cases}$$

3   Path Clustering

The cluster representation is analogous to that of a path, with additional parameters describing group properties. A cluster Z is defined as $(Z^1, Z^2, \ldots, Z^k, b, e, N)$, where k is the length of the cluster and Z^i represent i-th cluster point described by the spatio-temporal coordinates (x, y, t), tangential coordinates (u, v), and the number of feature points n contributing to it. The pair $b = (b_x, b_y)$ indicates the mean spatial displacement of cluster points to points of paths contributing to a cluster. The pair $e = (e_x, e_y)$ indicates the variance of this displacement. The value N represents the total number of paths contributing to a cluster. Analogously to paths, $Z_{\text{component}}$ notation is employed.

Path clusters are updated incrementally as input paths are extended. Let P be the path that was extended in the current frame to length l. If l exceeds a threshold $l_{\min}$, it is checked whether P has a cluster associated with it. Let us assume that there is such cluster Z of length k. Two cases may occur. The first one is when $Z_t^k \neq P_t^l$, i.e., the cluster has to be extended, which is done according to the following equations (the expression for y is analogous to x):

$$Z_x^{k+1} = P_x^l - P_{c_x} \tag{2}$$

$$Z_t^{k+1} = k + 1, \tag{3}$$

$$Z_n^{k+1} = 1. \tag{4}$$

The second possible situation when $Z_t^k = P_t^l$, that is, the cluster has to be updated as presented below (the expression for y is analogous to x):

$$Z_x^{k'} = \frac{Z_x^k Z_n^k + P_x^l - P_{c_x}}{Z_n^{k'}} \tag{5}$$

$$Z_n^{k'} = Z_n^k + 1. \tag{6}$$

If there is no cluster associated with the path, the algorithm founds the closest one. The distance between cluster Z and the path P consists of two components, spatial d and tangential $d\tau$. Let $\hat{Z}$ and $\hat{P}$ be the sequences of Z and P points overlapping in time, i.e., $\hat{Z}_t^i = \hat{P}_t^i$, for all $i = 1 \ldots L$, where L is the overlap length. The spatial distance component is computed as follows:

$$d(Z, P) = \frac{1}{L} \left(\sum_{i=1}^{L} (\hat{P}_x^i - \hat{Z}_x^i)^2 + \sum_{i=1}^{L} (\hat{P}_y^i - \hat{Z}_y^i)^2 \right), \tag{7}$$

while the tangential component is expressed as

$$d\tau(Z, P) = \frac{\sum_{i=1}^{L} (\hat{P}_u^i - \hat{Z}_u^i)^2 + \sum_{i=1}^{L} (\hat{P}_v^i - \hat{Z}_v^i)^2}{\min \left(\sum_{i=1}^{L} ((\hat{P}_u^i)^2 + (\hat{P}_v^i)^2), \sum_{i=1}^{L} ((\hat{Z}_u^i)^2 + (\hat{Z}_v^i)^2) \right) + 2L}. \tag{8}$$

The total distance computation proceeds only when both d and $d\tau$ components are below thresholds d_{assign} and $d\tau_{\text{assign}}$. If so, the components are joined according to the equation

$$D(Z, P) = \frac{\max(Z'_{e_x}, \delta_x)}{\rho_x^2} + \frac{\max(Z'_{e_y}, \delta_y)}{\rho_y^2} + \frac{d\tau(Z, P)}{\rho_\tau^2}, \tag{9}$$

where ρ_x, ρ_y, ρ_τ are weighting factors, Z' denotes cluster Z after the assignment and (δ_x, δ_y) are squared differences between mean displacement (P_{c_x}, P_{c_y}) of P from Z and mean displacement of other paths assigned to the cluster (Z_{b_x}, Z_{b_y}). Below the formulations for x are given, the calculations for y are analogous.

$$P_{c_x} = \frac{1}{L} \sum_{i=1}^{L} (\hat{P}_x^i - \hat{Z}_x^i), \tag{10}$$

$$\delta_x = (P_{c_x} - Z_{b_x})^2. \tag{11}$$

The components of Z' are calculated as

$$Z'_{b_x} = \frac{Z_{b_x} Z_N + P_{c_x}}{Z_N + 1}, \tag{12}$$

$$Z'_{e_x} = \frac{(Z_{e_x} + Z_{b_x}^2) Z_N + P_{c_x}^2}{Z_N + 1} - (Z'_{b_x})^2. \tag{13}$$

When cluster Z minimizing distance $D(Z, P)$ is selected, it is replaced by its updated version Z' with cluster points being recalculated as follows:

$$\hat{Z}'^i_x = \frac{Z_{b_x} Z_n + P_{c_x}}{\hat{Z}_n^i + 1}, \tag{14}$$

$$\hat{Z}'^i_n = \hat{Z}_n^i + 1, \tag{15}$$

for $i = 1 \ldots L$. Points from P which are not contained in the overlapping part $\hat{P}$ are inserted to Z analogously as in the cluster extension phase.

After all paths in a frame are analyzed, the algorithm checks for possible merges between clusters. This is done with a use of greedy heuristics which iterates over all clusters on the list and finds the closest cluster from following ones. The distance $D(Z, W)$ between clusters Z and W is computed on the basis of spatial and tangential components d and $d\tau$. The components are calculated as previously, with an exception that cluster $\hat{Z}'$ is formed by assigning to it all paths from W. Analogously to the path-cluster distance, D is computed only when d and $d\tau$ are below thresholds d_{merge} and $d\tau_{\mathrm{merge}}$, respectively.

4   Experimental Results

4.1   Simulated Data

Synthetic video sequence consisted of several circles moving on a two dimensional plane. It was assumed that each circle has a single path attached in its center (Fig. 1). A file with path information was also generated synthetically. There were four main algorithm parameters to be tested in the procedure: spatial and

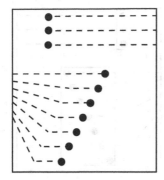

Fig. 1. Synthetic dataset consisting of moving circles, each with a path attached to its center (a dashed line)

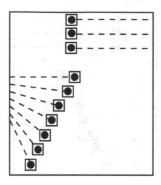

Fig. 2. Setting thresholds to 0 results in each path falling into a separate cluster (a rectangle)

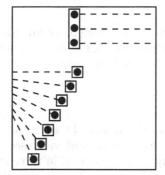

Fig. 3. Increasing spatial distance threshold in path assignment procedure allows parallel paths to be clustered together

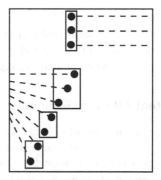

Fig. 4. Non-zero value of tangential distance threshold in path assignment procedure allows non-parallel paths to be clustered

tangential distance thresholds in path assignment (d_{assign}, $d\tau_{\mathrm{assign}}$) and spatial and tangential distance thresholds in cluster merging (d_{merge}, $d\tau_{\mathrm{merge}}$).

At the beginning of the experimental phase all these parameters were set to 0, which are the most restrictive values (only identical paths are clustered together in this scenario). According to the expectations, for each path separate cluster was created and no merges were observed throughout the whole video sequence (Fig. 2). In the second test we increased value of spatial distance threshold d_{assign}which allowed parallel paths to be clustered together. The higher value of threshold parameter, the more distant paths fell into same cluster. However, as tangential threshold $d\tau_{\mathrm{assign}}$was 0, non-parallel paths were always assigned to separate clusters (Fig. 3). In the next step, the spatial distance threshold for path assignment was set to infinity, so only tangential component was significant. Then we started to increase tangential distance threshold observing that the angle between paths allowing them to fall into single cluster also increases, thus procedure operates correctly (Fig. 4). The last synthetic experiments proved

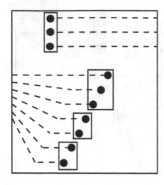 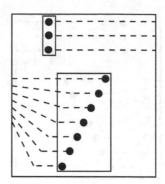

Fig. 5. Zero thresholds in cluster merging procedure prevent clusters from being joined.

Fig. 6. Non-zero thresholds in the merging procedure allow existing clusters to be joined in further video frames.

that increasing values of distance thresholds in cluster merging procedure allowed clusters to be joined in further steps of the procedure (Fig. 5, Fig. 6). To conclude, the algorithm was shown to work properly on the synthetic data.

4.2   Real Life Experiments

The aim of the second experimental part was to check how the algorithm performs in the real life scenario. For this purpose we used a short video sequence captured on Bytom Market Square. The sequence was processed in three steps. At first motion areas were extracted with a use of background separation. Then, feature points were generated by SURF algorithm and used for paths construction. Finally, the clustering procedure was executed. The clustering parameters

Fig. 7. Path clustering procedure applied on a video sequence from Bytom Market Square. Black lines indicate paths, white lines join cluster centers over consecutive frames, white rectangles are cluster contours in the current frame.

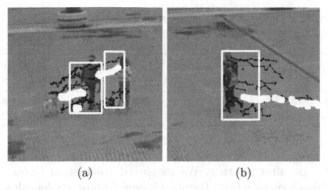

(a)   (b)

Fig. 8. Close-ups of groups of walking people. Too low distances between silhouettes prevents them from being properly identified by the clustering algorithm (b).

Fig. 9. Path clusters projected to the world reference frame

were tuned to detect most accurately human silhouettes on the examined sequence. Algorithm results can be seen in Fig. 7 and Fig. 8. Sequences of path and cluster points are represented as black and white lines, respectively. Additionally, for each cluster a rectangular border around assigned path points from the current frame is shown. As one can see, the algorithm works properly–each person is represented by a separate cluster. Of course, if spatial distance between two people is smaller than the assumed thresholds, it may happen that several silhouettes are gathered in the same cluster (Fig. 8.b). This behaviour is, however, expected for the presented algorithm.

As the camera used for acquiring video sequence at Market Square is calibrated with respect to the world reference frame, clusters can be projected to the map as shown in Fig. 9.

4.3   Time and Memory Considerations

As stated previously, the system is intended to operate in real time. Currently, background separation, path generation and path clustering are executed

Table 1. Execution times in minutes of tracking algorithm stages on the example sequence of 45,000 frames

	Background separation	Path generation	Path clustering	Total
Serial	165	94	6	265
Parallel (12 threads)	13	8	6	27

independently one after another. We measured calculation times of all these stages on a video sequence from Bytom Market Square. Its length was approximately 37 minutes and it consisted of 45,000 frames in 1080p resolution. The procedure was run on a workstation with dual Intel Xeon X5650 CPU (12 physical cores with hyper-threading clocked at 2.67GHz) and 48GB of RAM. At first, all stages were run sequentially in a single thread. As shown in Table 1, the total execution time was 265 minutes which is much longer the length of the video sequence. The conclusion is that the computational power of a single CPU core is insufficient for processing sequence in real time. However, when two first stages, i.e. background separation and path generation are distributed across 12 threads, the total execution time decreases to 27 minutes meaning that the time of the sequence analysis is shorter than the sequence itself. Therefore, the algorithm can be pipelined and used for the real-time video processing which was one of the goals of the presented research.

Another issue related to the analysis of long sequences are memory requirements. Namely, the representation of path clusters should be as compact as possible in order to reduce overhead related to dumping clusters to a hard drive. The amount of memory allocated by the application after processing 45,000 frames is approximately 1.8GB. Therefore, on a machine equipped with 8GB of memory, which is a standard nowadays, one can expect clusters to be backed up on the HDD every two hours. Therefore, the overhead related to transferring data from memory to the hard drive is negligible.

5   Conclusions

In the paper we present a new method for tracking people's motion at the video sequence, based on clustering feature paths. After separating the moving foreground from the stationary background, paths are constructed from feature points extracted with the SURF detector. These paths are superior to paths built with characteristic points of bounding contours in previously published methods. The overlapping paths are clustered and the resulting clusters correlate well with moving people (or similar size objects). The effectiveness of the algorithm has been tested on synthetic and real-life datasets. As the system is intended to operate in real time, time and memory requirements were carefully concerned. Experiments show that the entire method executed on dual-processor workstation is able to process in real time 1080p video sequence. The presented method is used in a system for analysis and recognition of human actions (under investigation). It can also be used for counting people in monitored area or identifying patterns of human traffic. Quantitative comparison of the presented method with other results, based on common metrics such as [4], will be an extension of this work.

Acknowledgements. This project has been supported by Applied Research Programme of the National Centre for Research and Development (project ID 178438 path A).

References

1. Andriyenko, A., Schindler, K., Roth, S.: Discrete-Continuous Optimization for Multi-Target Tracking. In: Proc. of CVPR 2012, pp. 1926–1933 (2012)
2. Bay, H., Tuytelaars, T., Van Gool, L.: Surf: Speeded up robust features. In: Leonardis, A., Bischof, H., Pinz, A. (eds.) ECCV 2006, Part I. LNCS, vol. 3951, pp. 404–417. Springer, Heidelberg (2006)
3. Benfold, B., Reid, I.: Stable Multi-Target Tracking in Real-Time Surveillance Video. In: Proc. of CVPR 2011, pp. 3457–3464 (2011)
4. Bernardin, K., Stiefelhagen, R.: Evaluating Multiple Object Tracking Performance: The CLEAR MOT Metrics. EURASIP J. Image Video Process., Article ID 246309 (2008)
5. Milan, A., Schindler, K., Roth, S.: Detection- and Trajectory-Level Exclusion in Multiple Object Tracking. In: Proc. of CVPR 2013, pp. 3682–3689 (2013)
6. Moeslund, T.B., Hilton, A., Krüger, V.: A survey of advances in vision-based human motion capture and analysis. Comput. Vis. Image Und. 104(2), 90–126 (2006)
7. Munkres, J.: Algorithms for the Assignment and Transportation Problems. SIAM J. Appl. Math. 5(1), 32–38 (1957)
8. Rabaud, V., Belongie, S.: Counting crowded moving objects. In: Proc. of CVPR 2006, pp. 705–711 (2006)
9. Rashid, R.F.: Towards a system for the interpretation of moving light displays. IEEE T. Pattern Anal. 6, 574–581 (1980)
10. Rohr, K.: Towards model-based recognition of human movements in image sequences. CVGIP: Image Understanding 59(1), 94–115 (1994)
11. Segen, J., Pingali, S.G.: A camera-based system for tracking people in real time. In: Proc. of ICPR 1996, pp. 63–67 (1996)
12. Shio, A., Sklansky, J.: Segmentation of people in motion. In: Proc. of IEEE Workshop on Visual Motion 1991, pp. 325–332 (1991)
13. Yang, D.B., Gonzalez-Banos, H.H., Guibas, L.J.: Counting people in crowds with a real-time network of simple image sensors. In: Proc. of ICCV 2003, pp. 122–129 (2003)

Multiple Instances Detection in RGBD Images

Zuzana Haladová and Elena Šikudová

Faculty of Mathematics, Physics and Informatics
Comenius University, Bratislava, Slovakia
haladova@fmph.uniba.sk, sikudova@sccg.sk

Abstract. Object instances detection and registration is the area closely connected to augmented reality. Only correctly detected and registered real world object can be used to register the real and virtual world for the purpose of displaying the augmented information. Although detection and registration methods are well studied, little attention is paid to the situation where multiple instances of objects are present in the scene and need to be augmented (e.g. a table full of fliers, several exemplars of historical coins in the museum, etc.). In this paper we propose a new method for multiple instances of object detection in cluttered scenes using local features and Hough-based voting.

1 Introduction

Since the beginning of the new century the growing popularity of markerless augmented reality applications inspired the research in the area of object instances detection, registration and tracking. The usage of common daily objects or specially developed fliers or magazines as AR markers became more popular than traditional ARtoolkit-like black and white patterns. Although there are many different methods for object instance detection emerging every year, very little attention is paid to the case where multiple instances of the same object are present. In this work we review existing methods of multiple instances detection and propose a new method for grayscale images and RGBD images overcoming the limitations of previous methods. The overview of the proposed method can be seen on figure 1.

When dealing with the visual (ARToolkit-like) markers or when we add non-visual markers, the correspondence is not an issue. On the other hand in the case of markerless object detection utilizing local features, it is not easy to determine how many instances of one object are present in the image.

In the area of multiple object instances detection we can identify 2 basic strategies. One approach is to first segment the image and then recognize and register all the segmented objects. The segmentation can be done in the image domain or in case of the RGBD data in the depth. This method however deals with the not yet fully solved problem of the segmentation of objects in cluttered scenes. The problem of segmentation in the depth domain can occur when e.g. objects lie side by side on the same plane. The second method estimates the number and the position of the object instances based on the clustering of

L.J. Chmielewski et al. (Eds.): ICCVG 2014, LNCS 8671, pp. 246–253, 2014.

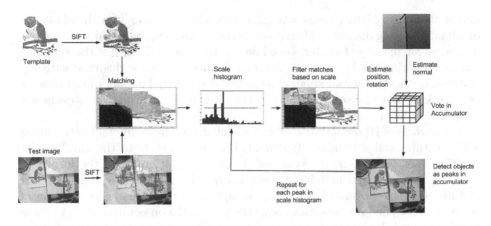

Fig. 1. Overview of the registration process

the detected points, the iterative RANSAC and/or Hough based voting [8]. The basic clustering of features approach is inefficient in case of more complex scenes with very close or overlapping objects. Although the greedy method which iteratively finds the best-matching instance, removes the corresponding features and finds another instance using RANSAC approach to compute homography is extensively used, it was proved to be inefficient for robust multiple instances object detection in [3]. Although we will not focus on the object class detection, the utilization of Hough based voting is known also in this domain [11].

2   Important Existing Approaches

The most significant work in this area was done in [1–5]. The authors of [1–3] focus on the segmentation of multiple instances of a low-textured object on a conveyor belt. In the first step they extract the SIFT [7] features, divide the image into P regions and match features using the second-nearest neighbour filtering. In every region they search for instances of one object with marked control points (the vertices of the object contour). For every matched feature they find the positions of the control points and use the mean-shift algorithm to cluster the control points positions and estimate the final positions as the center of the clusters. The authors utilize the color similarity measure to distinguish overlaying segmented objects with the overlap larger than 30% percent. The main limitation of this method is that all instances have to be of one object of the same scale without perspective deformations.

In [5] the authors propose a method for detection and localization of multiple objects and multiple instances of objects. In the training phase they acquire a video sequence containing the objects to be recognized and annotate and segment them manually. Then they use PCA-SIFT [6] to find the keypoints and store their descriptors and relative location towards the annotated object's center. In the recognition phase, they compute the PCA-SIFT keypoints in the image and match them using linear nearest neighbor search with estimated threshold for maximal matching distance. Then every keypoint correctly matched with the object votes for the object center, based on the rotation and scale of the keypoint estimated during SIFT detection. Afterwards these votes are clustered with agglomerative clustering and small clusters are discarded. The main limitation of this work is that the scale of the objects must be known and all objects are supposed to be of same size.

The authors of [4] use a sparse object model created from different views using SIFT features and a bundle adjustment. For every feature in the database its position on the sparse model is stored. In the recognition phase the local features are extracted and matched for every object in the database. The matched features are then clustered in the (x, y) image space. For each cluster a subset of points is chosen and a hypothesis about the pose of the object according to these points is stated. If the number of consistent points is bigger than a threshold, a new object instance is created and its pose is refined using all consistent points. This process is repeated until there is not enough points left or the number of iterations is reached. Then all instances with similar position and orientation from different clusters are merged. The scale is corrected using the ratio of standard deviation of all pairwise distances within the test and train images and the rotation is done aligning the principal components of test and train data. The main limitation of this work is that the preprocessing phase is time consuming and there is a necessity to photograph the object from different positions.

Based on these previous works and their limitations we decided to construct 2 methods for multiple objects detection. One utilizes only grayscale images, and the second one also the depth information from the RGBD sensor.

3   2D Approach

Our 2D method detects multiple instances of objects of different scales, orientation and possible out of plain rotation in grayscale images. We utilize the SIFT features, because they posses, together with the position of the feature, the information about the scale σ and rotation θ. The scale information is derived from the detector's scale-space pyramid as the octave in which the keypoint is detected. The rotation of the feature is estimated as dominant orientation of the gradient in the neighborhood of the interesting point. The size of the neighborhood is determined by the previously estimated scale. In the training phase of our method we build the database of the objects to be recognized. We then compute the SIFT features (interesting points, IP) and store their descriptors, scale and rotation in the database.

The recognition is performed as follows (see figure 1). We extract the SIFT features from a test image and store their descriptors, rotation θ, scale σ and position. We match the features with the database and estimate the closest features based on the Euclidean distance of the descriptors. There are 3 commonly used methods to filter the estimated matches: second nearest neighbor, double check and threshold. We propose a new method for matches filtering called **the**

scale ratio $- r$. To filter the matches we firstly compute the ratios of the scale of test image features σ and the scale of their corresponding database image (template) features σ' as follows

$$r = \frac{\sigma}{\sigma'}.$$

Then we create the histogram of these scale ratios. We look for the peaks of the histogram. A peak in the histogram has both neighboring bin values lower and its height is bigger than a threshold. Then we iterate over the peaks in the histogram. In every iteration we take the scale ratio, select only the features having this scale ratio and proceed as follows.

We create a 3D accumulator, where we store the votes for center points of the objects in the test images. The 3 dimensions of the accumulator are the x and y coordinates of the image and the rotation α of the object. The coordinates of the center point are estimated from the SIFT orientations of the matched IPs A and A' as follows

$$S = A + r.\mathbf{M}_{rot}(\alpha).\mathbf{v},$$

where r is the scale ratio. Vector

$$\mathbf{v} = A' - S'$$

is the vector from the IP A' to the center point S' of the template. Matrix

$$\mathbf{M}_{rot}(\alpha) = \begin{bmatrix} \cos\alpha & \sin\alpha \\ -\sin\alpha & \cos\alpha \end{bmatrix}$$

is the rotation matrix and α is the rotation of the object

$$\alpha = (\theta - \theta') \mod 2\pi,$$

where θ and θ' are the SIFT orientations of the matched IPs A and A'.

For every feature point which votes in the accumulator we store the ID of the corresponding accumulator bin. The peaks of the accumulator represent the position of centers and the rotation of the objects from the database found in the test image. To determine the peaks of the accumulator we use the threshold p on the height of the peak. To estimate the correct position of objects in the image even if the out of the plain rotation of the objects is present we can compute the homography transformation between the matched points from the test image and the database objects. We need at least 3 corresponding pairs to compute the affine homography. For every peak in the accumulator we take the feature pairs from test and template images that voted in the bin and compute the homography.

We can compute the homography using two approaches. We can use all point pairs assuming that all matches were correct or we can utilize the RANSAC approach [9]. Then the homography can be used to compute the correct positions of the object corners (4 in the case of rectangle). To check the correctness of the computed corner positions we compare the area of the detected object to the area of the template object scaled according to scale ratio. If the difference is within the threshold we draw the final contour of the object.

Although the RANSAC approach is extensively used in the registration of object instances in the image, it fails to detect more than one instance even if it is used in iterative manner. In our work we utilize it only for estimation of the transformation of pairs belonging to one instance. This is ensured by the voting in the accumulator.

4   RGBD Approach

Since the emerge of the Kinect sensor in 2010, RGBD sensors became affordable and very popular in computer vision tasks. We decided to utilize the depth information produced by this sensor for our multiple instances detection approach. The first steps are similar to the previous approach, we extract the interesting points and compute their descriptors using SIFT approach and match them with the database. We can then filter the matches based on their scale ratio, similarly to previous approach or proceed without filtering.

Another filtering can be done by checking the consistency of the scale ratio and the ratio of the depth of the point from test image and the template image. Then we will iterate over the point pairs and vote in the 3D accumulator. We decided to use the 3D accumulator (2D subsampled image space + rotation) instead of 4D accumulator (3D subsampled space + rotation). In the 3D accumulator we vote for the projections of the objects centers (S) onto the image space. To determine the correct vote for each point pair, we compute the vector $\mathbf{v}$ from the point A to the center S' in the template space. Then we estimate the normal vector $\mathbf{n}_p$ at the point A from the depth data as follows.

First, the points in the sphere neighborhood of A with diameter $d = 10$ are extracted. In the next step the principal component analysis (PCA) of the extracted points is computed. Next, the cross product of the first two principal components (eigenvectors corresponding to two largest eigenvalues) is computed. The cross product is the normal vector of the plane of the object in the 3D space. Next we estimate the position of the center of the object in 3D S'' lying on the object plane P defined by the computed normal vector and point A. The center of the object S'' is computed as

$$S'' = A + r.\mathbf{K}_{rot}(\beta, \mathbf{s}).\mathbf{M}_{rot}(\alpha).\mathbf{v},$$

where matrix

$$\mathbf{K}_{rot}(\beta, \mathbf{s}) =$$
$$= \begin{bmatrix} \cos\beta + s_x^2(1 - \cos\beta) & s_x s_y(1 - \cos\beta) - s_z\sin\beta & s_x s_z(1 - \cos\beta) + s_y\sin\beta \\ s_y s_x(1 - \cos\beta) + s_z\sin\beta & \cos\beta + s_y^2(1 - \cos\beta) & s_y s_z(1 - \cos\beta) - s_x\sin\beta \\ s_z s_x(1 - \cos\beta) - s_y\sin\beta & s_z s_y(1 - \cos\beta) + s_x\sin\beta & \cos\beta + s_z^2(1 - \cos\beta) \end{bmatrix}$$

is the rotation matrix, and angle

$$\beta = \arccos\left(\frac{\mathbf{n}_p \cdot \mathbf{n}_l}{\|\mathbf{n}_p\| \|\mathbf{n}_l\|}\right)$$

is the angle between n_p and normal vector of the image plane $n_l = [0, 0, 1]$ and vector

$$\mathbf{s} = \mathbf{n}_p \times \mathbf{n}_l$$

is the direction vector of the line defined as the intersection of the object and image plane.

Then the new center S is the projection of the center S'' to the image space. We have to have in mind that our 3D accumulator does not posses the information about the z coordinate of the S'' point nor the normal vector of the plane. To properly register the detected object on the image we store the average normal vector of the points which voted in the corresponding accumulator bin.

5 Results

In our previous work we have tested our 2D method on 30 artificial images and achieved 98% precision and 97% recall.

In this paper we evaluate our methods on 30 real world images captured by Primesense RD1.09 sensor in a cluttered environment. To acquire the images from the device we used the OpenNI 2 SDK. Images contain up to 5 instances of the object and were taken as a keyframes of the video sequence acquired in the cluttered office environment. The examples of the images with corresponding depth images can be seen in figure 2. We refer to the evaluation of our 2D method on RGB images as the Test 1. Test 2 refers to the evaluation of the RGBD method on RGB + depth images.

Fig. 2. Examples of images (RGB + depth) used in Test 1 and Test 2

To evaluate our method we have manually annotated the objects on all created images. We marked the 4 corners of the objects and saved their (ground truth) coordinates. In the evaluation process we have tested the distance of the detected and true positions of each corner of the object. The detected object is considered a correct detection (CD) if there exists a ground truth object whose corners are within a given threshold from the detected corner positions

$$CD = \begin{cases} 1 & \exists G \, \forall i \in \{1, \dots 4\} : d(G_i, D_i) < T_{pix}, \\ 0 & \text{otherwise}, \end{cases}$$

where G_i is the i-th corner of the ground truth object, D_i is the i-th corner of the detected object and $T_{pix} = 10$ is the threshold. The proposed method was tested for different values of the accumulator threshold p and the values of precision and recall were computed for each value of p.

The precision/recall curves for different values of p, for both tests can be seen in figure 3. The examples of the processed images with correct detections can be seen on figure 4.

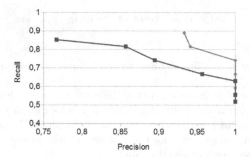

Fig. 3. Precision/recall curve for Test 1 (blue) and Test 2 (orange)

Fig. 4. Examples of correct detections in Test 1 (red) and Test 2 (blue)

6   Conclusions and Discussion

We have proposed a new approach for multiple instances detection in images. We have decided to overcome the limitations of previous state of the art methods – the time consuming pre-processing phase and the fact that all objects has to be of the same known scale without perspective distortions. In our methods we use the SIFT local features, but any scale and rotationally invariant methods that can extract the scale and the rotation of the features can be utilized. SIFT was chosen as it provided the highest precision in the tests in our previous work. To speed up the process it is possible to utilize the GPU version of the SIFT [10]. Our method was tested on rectangular template objects however the generalization to polygonal objects can be easily performed, since the features vote for the central point of the object and its orientation in the accumulator. Generalization for non-planar 3D objects is possible with the extension of the template database with photographs of the objects from different sides. Our approach was tested on real-world images containing instances of just one template object. The extension to instances of multiple template objects in one image is in iterative manner processing every object from the template database. Based on the validation we can state that our 2D method works with 85% precision (81% recall) on real images. The proposed 3D method works with 93% precision (89% recall) on real world RGBD data.

Currently, we are testing the proposed RGBD method using data acquired from the Kinect 2 sensor. The sensor is based on the time of flight technology and therefore does not have problems connected to fixed baseline. The depth maps are improved compared to Kinect Xbox 360 or Primesense RD1.09.

This paper was supported by the operational program ASFEU project "COMENIANA - metódy a prostriedky digitalizácie a prezentácie 3D objektov kultúrneho dedičstva", ITMS: 26240220077, which is co-financed from resources of European regional development fund. It was also partially funded by Comenius University grant for young researchers UK/164/2014.

References

1. Piccinini, P., Prati, A., Cucchiara, R.: SIFT-based segmentation of multiple instances of low-textured objects. In: International Conference on Machine Vision (ICMV), Hong Kong, pp. 28–30 (2010)
2. Piccinini, P., Prati, A., Cucchiara, R.: A fast multi-model approach for object duplicate extraction. In: Workshop on Applications of Computer Vision, pp. 1–6 (2009)
3. Piccinini, P., Prati, A., Cucchiara, R.: Real-time object detection and localization with SIFT-based clustering. Image and Vision Computing 8(30), 573–587 (2012)
4. Collet, A., Berenson, D., Srinivasa, S.S., Ferguson, D.: Object recognition and full pose registration from a single image for robotic manipulation. In: IEEE International Conference on Robotics and Automation, pp. 48–55 (2009)
5. Zickler, S., Veloso, M.M.: Detection and Localization of Multiple Objects. In: 6th IEEE-RAS International Conference on Humanoid Robots, pp. 20–25 (2006)
6. Ke, Y., Sukthankar, R.: PCA – SIFT: A more distinctive representation for local image descriptors. In: IEEE Computer Society Conference on Computer Vision and Pattern Recognition, pp. 500–506 (2004)
7. Lowe, D.: Distinctive Image Features from Scale-Invariant Keypoints. International Journal of Computer Vision 60(2), 91–110 (2004)
8. Ballard, D.H.: Generalizing the Hough transform to detect arbitrary shapes. Pattern Recognition 13(2), 111–122 (1981)
9. Fischler, M.A., Bolles, R.C.: Random sample consensus: a paradigm for model fitting with applications to image analysis and automated cartography. Communications of the ACM 24(6), 381–395 (1981)
10. Sinha, S.N., Frahm, J., Pollefeys, M., Genc, Y.: Feature tracking and matching in video using programmable graphics hardware. Machine Vision and Applications 22(1), 201–217 (2011)
11. Mikolajczyk, K., Bastian, L., Bernt, S.: Multiple object class detection with a generative model. In: IEEE Computer Society Conference on Computer Vision and Pattern Recognition, vol. 1 (2006)

Superpixel Based Retinal Area Detection
in SLO Images

Muhammad Salman Haleem[1], Liangxiu Han[1], Jano van Hemert[2],
Baihua li[1], and Alan Fleming[2]

[1] School of Computing, Mathematics and Digital Technology,
Manchester Metropolitan University, Chester Street, Manchester, M1 5GD, UK
[2] Optos plc, Queensferry House, Carnegie Business Campus, Enterprise Way,
Dunfermline, KY11 8GR, UK
muhammad.s.haleem2@stu.mmu.ac.uk, {l.han,b,li}@mmu.ac.uk,
{jvanhemert,afleming}@optos.com

Abstract. Distinguishing true retinal area from artefacts in SLO images
is a challenging task, which is the first important step towards computer-
aided disease diagnosis. In this paper, we have developed a new method
based on superpixel feature analysis and classification approaches for
determination of retinal area scanned by Scanning Laser Ophthalmo-
scope(SLO). Our prototype has achieved the accuracy of 90% on healthy
as well as diseased retinal images. To the best of our knowledge, this is
the first work on retinal area detection in SLO images.

Keywords: Scanning Laser Ophthalmoscope, fundus imaging, retinal
image analysis, retinal artefacts extraction.

1   Introduction

Early detection and treatment of retinal eye diseases is critical to avoid pre-
ventable vision loss. Conventionally, retinal disease identification techniques are
based on manual observations. Patients are imaged using a fundus camera or
a Scanning Laser Ophthalmoscope (SLO). Optometrists and ophthalmologists
often rely on image operations such as change of contrast and zooming to interpret these images and diagnose results based on their own experience and
domain knowledge. Automated analysis of retinal images has the potential to
reduce the time that the clinicians need to spend looking at images which can
expect more patients to be screened and more consistent diagnoses can be given
in a time efficient manner.

The 2-dimensional retinal scans obtained from imaging instruments (e.g. fundus camera, SLO) may contain structures other than retinal area; collectively
regarded as artefacts. Exclusion of artefacts is important as a pre-processing step
before detection of eye diseases. SLO has the widest FOV with over 200 degrees
angle internal to the eye, which equates to over 82% of the retina visible unlike
conventional fundus imaging, which can capture only 45 degrees. An example
of result of both instruments is shown in Fig. 1. Due to the wide FOV of SLO

L.J. Chmielewski et al. (Eds.): ICCVG 2014, LNCS 8671, pp. 254–261, 2014.

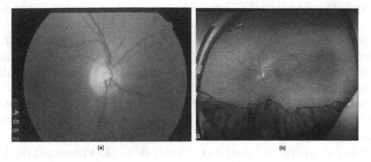

Fig. 1. An example of (a) a fundus image and (b) an SLO image annotated with true retinal area and Optic Nerve Head

images, extraneous objects such as the eyelashes, eyelids and dust on optical surfaces may appear bright and in focus. Therefore, automatic segmentation of these artefacts from SLO imaged retina is not a trivial task. The purpose of performing this study is to develop a method that can differentiate between retinal area and any artefacts present on ultra-wide field SLO images in order to segment out true retinal area.

To the best of our knowledge, there is no existing work to differentiate between retinal area and the artefacts. The main purpose of carrying out this study is to determine those features which can be used to distinguish between true retinal area and the artefacts. In this work, we have developed a new method to automatically extract out artefacts from SLO retinal scans which can be distinguished from retinal area using relevant image based superpixels. In order to make image analysis computationally efficient on high resolution SLO images, we have represented different small regions of SLO images as pixels. Our prototype has achieved the accuracy of 90% on healthy as well as diseased retinal images.

The rest of this paper is organised as follows: Section 2 introduces previous work for feature determination of fundus images, Section 3 discusses our proposed method, Section 4 provides the quantitative and visual results of our proposed method and Section 5 concludes the method with future work.

2   Literature Survey

There are several image based features which have been represent different retinal structures in fundus images such as colour, illumination, intensity, skewness, texture, histogram, sharpness etc [4,14,5]. For reducing computational complexity, grid analysis containing small patches of the image has been proposed. [4] and the mean response of each feature aggregated over each patch was taken into account. The features of Region of Interest (ROI) of anatomical structures such as Optic Nerve Head (ONH) and Fovea have also been analyzed [10]. The features included structural similarity index, area and visual descriptor etc. Instead of grid analysis, the fundus retinal image have been divided into different irregular shaped subregions [13]. Some of the main features calculated for these subregions are Gaussian and its gradient, Difference of Gaussian etc.

Our current methodology is focused on using textural information to distinguish among retinal area and the artefacts. We divided each SLO image into small regions called superpixels. Superpixels represent the image in small meaningful regions and each region is equivalent to a pixel. The feature vector is calculated for each superpixel rather than pixel for high computational efficiency. For classification, we only used selected features so as to reduce the classification time. Since previously stated methods are applied on fundus images, our method is a first step for superpixel based image analysis in SLO images. The details of the methods are discussed in the following section.

3   Methodology

Our methodology is based on following steps:

- Image Preprocessing
- Superpixels Generation
- Feature Generation and Selection
- Classification

3.1   Image Preprocessing

Images were normalized by applying a Gamma (γ) adjustment to bring the mean image intensity to a target value. γ was calculated using

$$\gamma = \frac{log_{10}(\mu_{target}) - log_{10}(255)}{log_{10}(\mu_{orig}) - log_{10}(255)} \tag{1}$$

where μ_{orig} is mean intensity of the original image and μ_{target} is mean intensity of the target image Finally, the Gamma adjustment of the image is given by Equation 2.

$$I_{norm} = (\frac{I}{255})^{\gamma}, \tag{2}$$

3.2   Superpixels Generation

Previously, the superpixels have been generated for analyzing anatomical structures and retinal changes in fundus images [3,13]. For superpixel determination, Watershed approach is the quickest way for subregion determination. However, in order to avoid data redundancy, the superpixel generation method used in our methodology is Simple Linear Iterative Clustering (SLIC) [2], which was proved to be efficient in terms of computational time, region compactness and adherence. In SLIC, the image is sampled with initial clusters in a regular grid space. In the next step, each image pixel is associated with a nearest cluster centre within the search region, which is twice of the size of grid interval. The distance vector is calculated in terms of intensity values and pixel positions. After assigning each pixel to the nearest centre, an updating step adjusts the cluster centres to the mean of pixels in this group. The residual error is then calculated between new cluster centre and previous cluster centre. Such iterations continue until the error convergences.

3.3   Feature Generation and Selection

After the generation of superpixels, the next step is to analyze their features. Due to textural difference between artefacts and retinal area observed in Fig. 1, one of the possible choices is the use of Haralick features [6] or Grey Level Co-occurrence Matrix (GLCM) analysis. GLCM analysis has been used for determining different regions in fundus retinal image [9]. It calculates second order statistics of an image using pixel adjacency. There are four angles for observing the pixel adjacency i.e. $\theta = 0°, 45°, 90°, 135°$. The mean value in each direction was taken for each Haralick features. Also, Gaussian filter bank has been one of the most discriminative features for image based segmentation in fundus images [8,13]. Gaussian filter bank includes Gaussian $\mathcal{N}(\sigma)$, its two first order derivatives i.e. $\mathcal{N}_x(\sigma)$ and $\mathcal{N}_y(\sigma)$ and three second order derivatives i.e. $\mathcal{N}_{xx}(\sigma)$, $\mathcal{N}_{xy}(\sigma)$ and $\mathcal{N}_{yy}(\sigma)$ in horizontal(x) and vertical(y) directions. The filter bank is applied at scales $\sigma = 1, 2, 4, 8, 16$.

We initially combined the Haralick features and Gaussian features and determined the classification power. The features are calculated for red and green channels (blue channel is zero in SLO images) and classification power was calculated using *Area Under the Curve* (AUC) [11]. AUC is taken using 5-fold cross validation on the training set. The classification power of complete feature set (40 Haralick and 60 Gaussian) is shown in Fig. 2(c). The feature vector of such a high dimension will affect the classification process in terms of computational efficiency therefore we decided to reduce its dimensionality.

Table 1. Haralick Features [6]

Feature Name	Equation	Feature Name	Equation
acorr	$\sum_i \sum_j ijp(i,j)$	I_μ	$\dfrac{\sum_i \sum_j I_s(i,j)}{N_s}$ (Superpixel mean)
corr	$\dfrac{\sum_i \sum_j (ij)p(i,j) - \mu_x \mu_y}{\sigma_x \sigma_y}$	H_{diff}	$-\sum_{i=0}^{N_g-1} p_{x-y} log(p_{x-y}(i))$
IM_1	$(1 - exp[-2.0(H_{xy} - H)])^{0.5}$	μ_{sum}	$\sum_{i=2}^{2N_g} ip_{x+y}(i)$
H_{sum}	$-\sum_{i=2}^{2N_g} p_{x+y} log(p_{x+y}(i))$	σ_{sos}	$\sum_i \sum_j (i - \mu)^2 p(i,j)$
σ_{sum}	$\sum_{i=2}^{2N_g} (i - H_{sum})p_{x+y}(i)$	H	$-\sum_i \sum_j p(i,j) log(p(i,j))$

$p_{x+y}(k) = \sum_{i=1}^{N_g} \sum_{j=1}^{N_g} p(i,j), k = i + j - 1 = 1, 2, ..., 2N_g$ and $p_{x-y}(k) = \sum_{i=1}^{N_g} \sum_{j=1}^{N_g} p(i,j), k = |i - j| + 1 = 1, ..., N_g$, $H_{xy} = -\sum_i \sum_j p_x(i)p_y(j) log(p_x(i)p_y(j))$

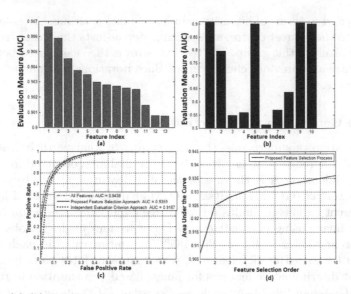

Fig. 2. (a),(b) Results of Independent Evaluation Criterion of IEC selected features and proposed feature set respectively. (c) Comparison of Classification power of all feature sets in terms of AUC and (d) Our feature selection process. The x-axis of both (b) and (d) is same and details mentioned in Table 2.

Table 2. Feature Selection Order of Fig. 2

	Feature Symbols
Fig. 2(a)	$\mathcal{N}_R(16)$, μ_{sumR}, $\mathcal{N}_R(8)$, σ_{sumR}, $\mathcal{N}_R(4)$, $\mathcal{N}_R(2)$, $\mathcal{N}_R(1)$, $\mathcal{N}_{yyR}(1)$, $I_{\mu R}$, $\mathcal{N}_{xxR}(1)$, $\mathcal{N}_{yyR}(2)$, $acorr_R$, σ_{sosR}
Fig. 2(b)(d)	$\mathcal{N}_R(16)$, σ_{sosG}, IM_{1G}, $\mathcal{N}_{yR}(16)$, $acorr_R$, H_{sumR}, H_{diffR}, $corr_R$, μ_{sumR}, $\mathcal{N}_{yyR}(1)$

In order to reduce the dimension as well as keeping eye on which features can be the part of feature set while having the classification power near to complete feature set, we used the following approach: From available set of features, the feature with highest AUC is selected. The next selected feature when combined with first selected feature, it will give highest AUC compared to other non-selected features. The process (shown in Fig. 2(d)) selected 10 features since AUC showed small improvement beyond it.

The classification performance of proposed feature set was compared with feature set selected using Independent Evaluation Criterion (IEC) [7]. This approach ranks the features based on their Individual Classification Performance (ICP). We used AUC as evaluation criterion and selected the features with ICP greater than 0.9. The ICP of 13 selected features under the criterion is presented in Fig. 2(a). We also evaluated ICP of the features selected by our proposed approach as shown in Fig. 2(b). The x-axis information of Fig. 2(a)(b) and (d) is presented in Table 2. The details of symbolic representation of Table 2 is presented in Table 1.

Compared to results in Fig. 2(a), ICP of most of the features in our proposed feature set were even below 0.8. Yet, the feature set was able to perform better with classification performance nearer to complete feature set (Fig. 2(c)). Also, unlike [8] and [13], Haralick features dominated in proposed feature set. The main drawback of Haralick features is its low computational efficiency in terms of pixel wise calculation but since we are using superpixels, the drawback has been addressed.

4   Classifier Construction and Experimental Evaluation

The main purpose of determining the feature set was determination of retinal boundary which can include large part of retinal area while keeping the artefacts out. Therefore, we constructed a classifier using Artificial Neural Networks [12] which takes training samples as inputs and determines the model that best fits to training samples using non-linear regression. The model was trained and tested for each of mentioned feature set so as to determine classification accuracy.

Table 3. Average Accuracies

Features Set	D_S	D_P
Proposed Feature Selection	90.81	92.00%
Independent Evaluation Criterion	89.61	90.29%

The images for training and testing have been obtained from Optos [1] acquired using their ultra-wide field SLO. Each image has a dimension of 3072 × 3900 and composed of only red and green channel. The dataset is composed of healthy and diseased retinal images; most of the diseased retinal images are from Diabetic Retinopathy patients. The system has been trained with 28 images and tested against 76 images. For training purpose, retinal mask covering the retinal area was applied after superpixel determination. The superpixels were assigned the class of retinal area or artefacts depending upon majority of pixels belonging to particular class.

The retinal area detection accuracy is determined using Dice Coefficient is the degree of overlap between the system output and the annotation mask obtained from the clinicians. The Dice Coefficient can be defined as in equation 3:

$$D(A, B) = \frac{2|A \cap B|}{|A| + |B|} \tag{3}$$

where A and B are the segmented images surrounded by model boundary and annotations from the ophthalmologists respectively, $|.|$ represents the area of the region, and ∩ denotes the intersection. Its value varies between 0 and 1 where a higher value indicates higher degree of overlap. The average superpixel classification accuracy D_S and retinal area segmentation accuracy D_P was calculated across both feature set and the results are shown in Table 3. As hypothesized on training set, the features selected by our proposed approach performed better on the test set as well. Some of the visual results on the test set are shown in Figure 3.

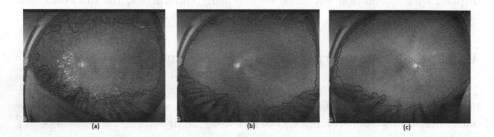

Fig. 3. Visual results of retina detector framework

5   Conclusion

Distinguishing true retinal area from artefacts in SLO images is a challenging task, which is also the first important step towards computer-aided disease diagnosis. In this work, we have proposed image based feature set for automatic detection of retinal area in SLO images. We have used superpixels to represent different irregular regions in a compact way and reduce the computing cost. A classifier has been built based on selected features to extract out true retinal area. The experimental evaluation result shows that image based features proposed by our methodology achieves an accuracy of 92% in segmentation of retinal area from SLO image.

Since most artefacts detection methods have been applied previously to the fundus images, our method serves as a first step towards the processing of ultra-widefield SLO images. Moreover, a complete retinal scan is possible if the retina is imaged from different angles using an ultra-widefield SLO and then montaging the resulting image. Montaging can be possible only if the artefacts are removed before.

References

1. http://www.optos.com
2. Achanta, R., Shaji, A., Smith, K., Lucchi, A., Fua, P., Süsstrunk, S.: Slic superpixels compared to state-of-the-art superpixel methods. IEEE Transactions on Pattern Analysis and Machine Intelligence 34 (2011)

3. Cheng, J., Liu, J., Xu, Y., Yin, F., Wong, D., Tan, N.M., Tao, D., Cheng, C.Y., Aung, T., Wong, T.Y.: Superpixel classification based optic disc and optic cup segmentation for glaucoma screening. IEEE Transactions on Medical Imaging 32, 1019–1032 (2013)
4. Davis, H., Russell, S., Barriga, E., Abramoff, M., Soliz, P.: Vision-based, real-time retinal image quality assessment. In: 22nd IEEE International Symposium on Computer-Based Medical Systems, pp. 1–6 (2009)
5. Haleem, M.S., Han, L., Hemert, J.V., Li, B.: Automatic extraction of retinal features from colour retinal images for glaucoma diagnosis: A review. Computerized Medical Imaging and Graphics 37, 581–596 (2013)
6. Haralick, R.M., Shanmugam, K., Dinstein, I.: Textural features for image classification. IEEE Transactions on Systems, Man and Cybernetics 3 (1973)
7. Liu, H., Motoda, H. (eds.): Feature Selection for Knowledge Discovery and Data Mining. Kluwer Academic Publishers Norwell, MA (1998)
8. Lupascu, C.A., Tegolo, D., Trucco, E.: Fabc: Retinal vessel segmentation using adaboost. IEEE Transactions on Information Technology in Biomedicine 14, 1267–1274 (2010)
9. Muramatsu, C., Hatanaka, Y., Sawada, A., Yamamoto, T., Fujita, H.: Computerized detection of peripapillary chorioretinal atrophy by texture analysis. In: Conference Proceedings IEEE Engineering in Medicine and Biology Society, pp. 5947–5950 (2011)
10. Pires, R., Jelinek, H., Wainer, J., Rocha, A.: Retinal image quality analysis for automatic diabetic retinopathy detection. In: 25th SIBGRAPI Conference on Graphics, Patterns and Images (SIBGRAPI), pp. 229–236 (2012)
11. Serrano, A.J., Soria, E., Martin, J.D., Magdalena, R., Gomez, J.: Feature selection using roc curves on classification problems. In: The International Joint Conference on Neural Networks (IJCNN), pp. 1–6 (2010)
12. Smola, A., Vishwanathan, S.: Introduction to Machine Learning. Cambridge University Press (2008)
13. Tang, L., Niemeijer, M., Reinhardt, J., Garvin, M.: Splat feature classification with application to retinal hemorrhage detection in fundus images. IEEE Transactions on Medical Imaging 32, 364–375 (2013)
14. Yu, H., Agurto, C., Barriga, S., Nemeth, S.C., Soliz, P., Zamora, G.: Automated image quality evaluation of retinal fundus photographs in diabetic retinopathy screening. In: IEEE Southwest Symposium on Image Analysis and Interpretation (SSIAI), pp. 125–128 (2012)

Automated Traffic Analysis in Aerial Images

Tom Hößler and Tom Landgraf

Fraunhofer IVI, Zeunerstr. 38, 01069 Dresden, Germany
Tom.Hoessler@ivi.fraunhofer.de

Abstract. Wide range traffic monitoring for the tracking of overtaking manoeuvres is an issue of current research. The collected data will allow the updating of a model which describes overtaking manoeuvres depending on various boundary conditions. The model is used for road planning, e.g. recommendations may be provided to decide where driving on the oncoming traffic lane cannot be allowed due to traffic safety. The necessary update of the model requires wide area traffic observation. This challenging task has been solved by recording aerial image sequences in combination with an automated image analysis.

1 Introduction

The model of overtaking manoeuvres describes the average car drivers' overtaking behaviour. This leads to recommendations for road planning in order to increase traffic safety [1]. However the current model is largely based on studies from the 1980s. The used input variables are obsolete because of the recent development of vehicles. Hence, the model has to be updated using traffic observation.

The state of the art ground based monitoring captures a limited range and the recorded vehicles may cover or overlap each other [2]. Using several cameras to reduce this effect is very complex and expensive. Therefore, wide range traffic monitoring is required which provides a satisfying resolution of time and geometry and allows the distinction of the vehicles recorded. Unmanned aerial vehicles (UAV) are a new measuring approach and capable platforms for this task because they create new opportunities for acquisition of measurement data and photography in areas which are difficult to access.

For this reason, the **Ho**vering **R**emote Controlled **U**ltra-light **S**ensor Platform (HORUS) was developed at the Fraunhofer Institute for Transportation and Infrastructure Systems IVI in Dresden. This UAV can be used as technology platform, for measurements and for taking samples because it is compact with a high payload. HORUS provides a good platform especially for wide range traffic monitoring because it can be equipped with a high-resolution camera.

Within the interdisciplinary research project "Aktualisierung des Überholmodells auf Landstraßen" of the German Federal Highway Research Institute, the Institute of Transport Planning and Road Traffic of the TU Dresden and the Fraunhofer Institute for Transportation and Infrastructure Systems in cooperation with the Airclip GmbH a new application was developed. In this context, HORUS is used to take aerial sequences of overtaking on country roads.

L.J. Chmielewski et al. (Eds.): ICCVG 2014, LNCS 8671, pp. 262–269, 2014.

This paper presents the measuring system HORUS and focuses on the determination of the world coordinates of the recorded vehicles including camera calibration and deriving measurement uncertainties. Finally, the developed algorithm for an automated analysis of the aerial image sequences is outlined.

2 Measuring System

The measuring system consists of the sensor platform HORUS and a high-resolution camera. HORUS can be operated with 4, 8 or 12 rotors depending on the required payload and flight time. The 1.0 m × 1.3 m wide copter uses the GPS to fly independently and to keep a defined position during the measurement. The maximum flying height is approximately 250 m due to legal restrictions. The H-shaped geometry of the frame allows any arrangement of the payloads and flight batteries as well as the rapid exchange of different sensor modules. For the acquisition of aerial image sequences HORUS is equipped with a camera mount which actively balances the pitch and roll motions of the copter. Hence, the camera angle maintains constant.

The camera GoPro Hero3 Black Edition is used here because it combines a very high optical resolution with low weight and easy usability. Furthermore, its fisheye lens provides a wide field of view. The recorded data are saved with 15 fps and 3840 × 2160 pixels. Figure 1 shows the octocopter HORUS and the mounted camera GoPro Hero3 Black Edition.

This measuring system satisfies the following requirements for a successful recording of overtaking on selected routes [1]:

1. continuous recording of time and distance travelled by all participants of the overtaking manoeuvres as well as derived velocities and accelerations,
2. visibility of large section lengths of at least 600 m and
3. imperceptible measurement not affecting the drivers.

Fig. 1. Octocopter HORUS with Bottom Mounted Camera

3   Calculation of Vehicle Positions from Images

It is necessary to transform measured image coordinates into world coordinates, because the trajectories of the vehicles are to be determined. For this purpose, an appropriate model containing all projection equations is formulated and the measurement uncertainties are calculated [3]. Camera calibration is necessary in order to estimate the camera parameters.

3.1   Measurement Uncertainty of Calculated Vehicle Positions

Transferring the image to world coordinates requires a geometric calibration. For the calculation of the uncertainty this mathematical model is analysed according to the specifications of DIN 1319 [4] (equivalent to the Guide to the Expression of Uncertainty in Measurement - GUM). The result is the dispersion of the measured world coordinates.

In this regard, an implicit measurement equation

$$F(X, Y) = O \tag{1}$$

is used because it expresses the interdependence of all input and output variables combined to the column vectors X and Y. The column vector O is a zero vector.

The uncertainty matrix U_x contains the common and the individual uncertainty components of all input variables. The output uncertainty matrix U_y follows according to

$$U_y = Q U_x Q^T \tag{2}$$

with

$$Q = -F_y^{-1} F_x, \tag{3}$$

where F_x and F_y are the derivatives of the model equation (1) with respect to all input and output variables respectively. For a detailed calculation of the transformation of image into world coordinates depending on 22 input variables see [3].

3.2   Camera Calibration

The camera parameters, which are separated in extrinsic and intrinsic parameters, have to be determined because they are used in the implicit projection model (1). The extrinsic camera parameters are the translation vector and the rotation matrix specifying the transformation between the camera coordinate system and the superordinate world coordinate system. They result from the measuring arrangement. The intrinsic camera parameters characterize the geometric and digital characteristics of the viewing camera defining the projection into the image coordinate system [5]. The intrinsic camera parameters are estimated by camera calibration.

Because of the fisheye lens a ray's incidence angle is different from its accordant reflection angle. In contrast to central perspective projection the rays

Table 1. Comparison of Different Geometric Models Using the Standard Deviation of
Unit Weight $\hat{\sigma}_0$

Geometric Model	$\hat{\sigma}_0$ in Pixel
Central Perspective Model	2.20
Equidistant Model	0.10
Equisolid-Angle Model	0.12
Orthographic Model	0.50
Stereographic Model	0.14

are refracted in the direction of the optical axis. Thus, four different geometric
models used for fisheye camera modelling [6] were applied in the calibration process. The models are extended by a set of additional parameters to compensate
for systematic effects such as radial symmetric distortion and the decentering
distortion [7] as well as affinity and shear [8].

The camera calibration was performed at the Institute of Photogrammetry
and Remote Sensing of the TU Dresden where a specially arranged calibration
room has been established for the analysis of the geometric models of fisheye
lenses. 141 control points are distributed and their coordinates have been determined with an uncertainty between 0.02 mm and 0.23 mm [6]. In order to
estimate the intrinsic camera parameters, images were taken in the hemispherical calibration room and the calculation of a spatial resection has been conducted
with sub-pixel accuracy.

Table 1 shows the resulting standard deviation of unit weight $\hat{\sigma}_0$ as a criterion for the suitability of the geometric model for the camera-lens combination
tested [6]. The smaller the value of the standard deviation of unit weight $\hat{\sigma}_0$,
the greater the precision achieved. As expected, the accuracy is worst applying
the central perspective projection. The equidistant projection model delivers the
best precision [3]. Its standard deviation of unit weight of 0.1 pixel is very satisfying because remaining residuals could already partly reflect the influence of
the control point accuracy [6].

3.3   Examplary Uncertainty Calculation

Since most of the overtaking manoeuvres take place in the centre of the observed road section, Table 2 shows corresponding exemplary values used for the
input variables and their measurement uncertainties [3]. These data follow from
previous measurements such as camera calibration and practical assumptions.
The uncertainty shares describe the square influence of a particular uncertainty
on the output variable X which characterizes the world coordinate in parallel
with the captured road. However, the algorithms are not limited to this special
case. The extrinsic camera parameters shown consist of the translation vector
$(X_0, Y_0, Z_0)^T$, the angles ω, φ, κ defining pitch, roll and yaw of the camera and
the ground plane Z_P. Further input variables are the intrinsic camera parameters
estimated by camera calibration and the image coordinates x', y'.

Table 2. Calculation Example for the Measurement Uncertainty for the Image Centre

Variable	Value	Uncertainty	Unit	Uncertainty Share
X_0	0	0.5	m	< 1%
Y_0	0	0.5	m	< 1%
Z_0	250	2	m	< 5%
Z_P	0	2	m	< 5%
ω	5°	1°		< 1%
φ	0	1°		> 90%
κ	0	0.5°		< 1%
Intrinsic Parameters				< 1%
x'	0	0.2	μm	< 1%
y'	0	0.2	μm	< 1%
Results: X	0	4.4	m	
Y	20	5	m	

Considering the flying height of 250 m and the length of the observed road section of 800 m, the world coordinates could be determined with low measurement uncertainties. This fact facilitates the further evaluation and the formulation of the model of overtaking manoeuvres.

The extrinsic camera parameters, especially the roll angle φ with an uncertainty share of more than 90%, are obviously decisive for the uncertainty of the output variable X which is between 4.4 m in the centre and about 17 m at the edge of the aerial image. Thus, if a higher accuracy of the output variable is required, it is necessary to reduce the uncertainty of the extrinsic parameter φ. A decrease of the uncertainty of the roll angle φ by e.g. 50% reduces the uncertainty of the world coordinate X by about 45%. This could be realized by a more efficient hardware stabilization of the HORUS.

Another way to increase the accuracy of the input variables is the use of at least three control points with known world coordinates which do not lie on a straight line [10]. Since the intrinsic camera parameters are known, the extrinsic camera parameters may be determined for each frame by a spatial resection. However, a disadvantage of this method is the increased computational complexity.

4   Automated Image Processing Algorithm for Vehicle Detection and Tracking

This section provides an overview of the developed image processing algorithm determining and tracking the positions of vehicles in the world coordinate system of the aerial images. Because of the large evaluated data set containing more than 130 aerial image sequences, about 15 minutes each, until now extensive automation and fast processing is required. A special feature is the detection of vehicles, corresponding to small objects of about 30×10 pixels in the images, despite illumination changes, shadows and slight camera movements.

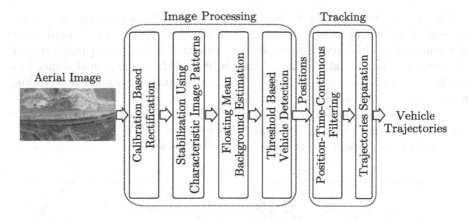

Fig. 2. Schematic Algorithm of the Automated Analysis of the Aerial Images

The automated analysis of the aerial images is performed as the schema in Fig.2 shows. Using methods of image processing, which were realized in the integrated development environment for machine vision HALCON, the positions for all vehicles in each frame can be determined. The post-processing tracking removes fault detections and combines the single image positions to the required trajectories [3].

After the rectification and transformation into world coordinates of each recorded image, stabilization is necessary to compensate for the movements remaining from the camera stabilization of HORUS. The basis for an automated detection of moving vehicles is the subsequent estimated background which does not contain any moving objects. It must be continuously adapted to the changing environmental conditions such as changes in brightness. An established method of background estimation is the calculation of an moving average [9]. Assuming that vehicles are the only moving objects recorded, their position can be determined by subtracting each image from the background image. The vehicles are segmented automatically by thresholding and edited by morphological operations.

The positions which were stored independently for each image are assigned to the respective vehicles in a post-process. The filtering deletes coordinates that cannot be assigned to any vehicle. Assuming that a vehicle travels a short distance during the time interval between two frames, trajectories are predicted and the most likely positions of a particular vehicle are found. The resulting trajectories characterize the movement of vehicles on the recorded road and can be further processed, e.g. by calculating the derivatives to gain velocity and acceleration, to formulate a model describing overtaking manoeuvres.

For further analysis of overtaking manoeuvres especially the X-component of the observed movement is interesting because within the scope of this work the selected roads are in parallel with the X-axis. Figure 3 shows an exemplary time course of the X-positions of detected vehicles. The discrete entries are not assigned to the particular vehicles and obviously contain errors.

The result after tracking is shown in Fig. 4. Each curve of one colour documents the movement of a particular vehicle along the captured road. Since the gradient of the curve represents the velocity, an overtaking manoeuvre is characterized by the intersection of two curves of the same signed slope. This can be used for automated overtaking detection. Figure 4 contains an overtaking manoeuvre at $t = 9.5\,\mathrm{s}$.

Since the world coordinates X and Y of all recorded vehicles are stored, the vehicle movement in the entire ground plane captured can be investigated. Thus, the analysis of intersections or curves is possible as well.

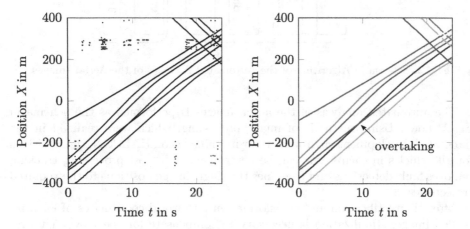

Fig. 3. Positions of Detected Vehicles   **Fig. 4.** Positions of Tracked Vehicles

5   Summary and Outlook

The developed sensor system comprising UAV measuring platform HORUS provides a novel approach for traffic monitoring. In contrast to the recent ground based systems a wide area up to 800 metres can be monitored with one sensor system in a cost-effective way. A further advantage is the implicit time-synchronized data. With the help of the autonomous flight module of HORUS and the developed image processing the UAV-based measuring process is almost completely automated and therefore easy to operate.

The time accuracy and the uncertainty of the measured world coordinates are sufficient in order to determine the positions of recorded vehicles as well as derived velocities and accelerations in the context of research on overtaking manoeuvres. Consequently, the automated analysis of aerial images presented in this paper in combination with the innovative measurement system HORUS is an efficient tool for the analysis of overtaking manoeuvres. The ability is proven by the successful analysis of more than 600 recorded image sequences.

Since the algorithms are not restricted to straight roads the automated aerial based vehicle monitoring can be realized for curves or intersection areas as well.

The detection of all vehicles recorded allows the identification of further parameters of transport planning, such as the traffic volume, which provides information about the quality, efficiency and safety of traffic flow and is used in road design. Therefore many issues of traffic monitoring and planning are covered.

The modular design of the presented algorithms facilitates further developments: Automation can be further increased e.g. by alternative image stabilization without the manual selection of reference patterns. In this regard, the use of at least three signalized control points with known coordinates is possible. If they are not located on a straight line, a spatial resection provides the extrinsic camera parameters for each frame [10].

Acknowledgement. These investigations were accomplished within the scope of the interdisciplinary project 02.0336/2012/BGB financed by the German Federal Highway Research Institute.

References

1. Lippold, C., Vetters, A., Steinert, F.: Aktualisierung des Überholmodells auf Landstraßen - I. Zwischenbericht. TU Dresden (2013)
2. Leich, A.: Ein Beitrag zur Realisierung der videobasierten weiträumigen Verkehrsbeobachtung. PhD Thesis, TU Dresden (2006)
3. Hößler, T.: Automatische Auswertung von Überholvorgängen aus Luftbildaufnahmen der Flugdrohne HORUS. Diplomarbeit, TU Dresden (2014)
4. DIN 1319-4: Grundlagen der Messtechnik - Auswertung von Messungen, Messunsicherheit. Beuth (1999)
5. Trucco, E., Verri, A.: Introductory techniques for 3-D computer vision. Prentice Hall (1998)
6. Schneider, D., Schwalbe, E., Maas, H.-G.: Validation of geometric models for fisheye lenses. ISPRS Journal of Photogrammetry and Remote Sensing 64(3), 259–266 (2009)
7. Brown, D.C.: Close-range camera calibration. Photogrammetric Engineering 37(8), 855–866 (1971)
8. El-Hakim, S.F.: Real-time image meteorology with CCD cameras. Photogrammetric Engineering and Remote Sensing 52(11), 1757–1766 (1986)
9. Döge, K.-P.: Videodetektion im Straßenverkehr, Oldenburg (2013)
10. Luhmann, T.: Nahbereichsphotogrammetrie - Grundlagen, Methoden und Anwendungen. Wichmann (2010)

Unsupervised Detector Adaptation
by Joint Dataset Feature Learning

Kyaw Kyaw Htike and David Hogg

School of Computing, University of Leeds, Leeds, UK
{sckkh,d.c.hogg}@leeds.ac.uk

Abstract. Object detection is an important step in automated scene understanding. Training state-of-the-art object detectors typically require manual annotation of training data which can be labor-intensive. In this paper, we propose a novel algorithm to automatically adapt a pedestrian detector trained on a generic image dataset to a video in an unsupervised way using joint dataset deep feature learning. Our approach does not require any background subtraction or tracking in the video. Experiments on two challenging video datasets show that our algorithm is effective and outperforms the state-of-the-art approach.

1 Introduction

Object detection has received a lot of attention in the field of Computer Vision. Pedestrians are one of the most common object categories in natural scenes. Most state-of-the-art pedestrian detectors are trained in a supervised fashion using large publicly available generic datasets [1,2].

However, it has been recently shown that every dataset has an inherent bias [11]. This implies that a pedestrian detector that has been specifically trained for (and is tuned to) a specific scene would do better than a generic detector for *that* scene. In fact, it has been shown that generic detectors often exhibit unsatisfactory performance when applied to scenes that differ from the original training data in some ways (such as image resolution, camera angle, illumination conditions and image compression effects) [2].

We tackle this problem by formulating a novel *unsupervised domain adaptation* framework that starts with a readily available *generic* image dataset and automatically adapt it to a target video (of a particular scene) without requiring any annotation in the target scene, thereby generating a *scene-specific* pedestrian detector.

Domain adaptation for object detectors is a relatively new area. Most state-of-the-art research use some variations of an iterative self-training algorithm [12,7]. Unfortunately, self-training carries the risk of classifier *drifting*. In this paper, we investigate a different approach: domain adaptation purely by exploiting the *manifold property* of data.

High dimensional visual data usually exist in a nonlinear manifold that has a much smaller number of dimensions than the original data. This manifold can be

L.J. Chmielewski et al. (Eds.): ICCVG 2014, LNCS 8671, pp. 270–277, 2014.

learnt using unsupervised approaches. The most relevant works to our research in this area are [6,5]. Gopalan *et al.* [6] propose building intermediate representations between source and target domains by using geodesic flows. However, their approach requires sampling a finite number of subspaces and tuning many parameters such as the number of intermediate representations.

Gong *et al.* [5] improved on [6] by giving a kernel version of [6]. However both [6,5] are dealing with only image data for both source and target domains and *not* videos. For videos, unique challenges are present such as the largely imbalanced nature of positive and negative data. Moreover, their approach does *not* learn deep representations required for manifolds that are highly non-linear.

In this paper we propose, using state-of-the-art deep learning, to learn the nonlinear manifold spanned by the union of the source image dataset and the sampled data of the target video. The intuition is that by learning a representation in that manifold and training a classifier on data in that representation, the resulting detector would generalize well for the target scene. This can then be used as a scene-specific detector.

Contributions. We make the following novel contributions:

1. An algorithm that adapts a pedestrian detector from an *image* dataset to a *video* using only the manifold assumption.
2. An application of state-of-the-art deep feature learning for detector adaptation in *videos* and showing its effectiveness. Furthermore, instead of starting with raw pixel values (as in standard deep learning), our approach takes as input, features such as Histogram of Oriented Gradients (HOGs) [1].
3. For videos, due to huge class imbalance, random sampling of data will result in almost all samples to be from non-pedestrian class. We propose a simple and effective biased sampling approach to minimize this problem.
4. A technique to automatically set the deep network structure with no tuning.
5. The integration of all of the above components into a system.

2   Proposed Approach

2.1   Overview

The overview of the algorithm is illustrated in Fig. 1. The algorithm is made up of two stages: (1) unsupervised deep feature learning (no supervision labels used) and (2) non-linear projection and classifier training (with labelled data). We use HOGs as the base features (before learning higher non-linear representations). In Fig. 1, we have omitted the HOG feature extraction for clarity. Our algorithm can work with any type of base features and classifier combination. However, for simplicity, we use HOGs and a linear Support Vector Machine (SVM) respectively.

Let the generic pedestrian dataset $\mathcal{G} = \{G_{\text{pos}}, G_{\text{neg}}\}$ be a set of fixed-sized pedestrian and non-pedestrian patches, $G_{\text{pos}} = \{p_1^+, p_2^+, \ldots, p_{N_1}^+\}$ and $G_{\text{neg}} = \{p_1^-, p_2^-, \ldots, p_{N_2}^-\}$ respectively where N_1 is number of pedestrian patches and

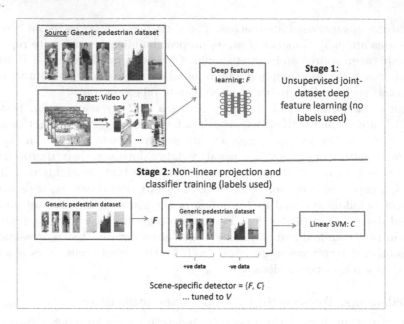

Fig. 1. Overview of the proposed algorithm

N_2 is the number of non-pedestrian patches. Let the target video be $\mathcal{V} = \{I_1, I_2, \ldots, I_M\}$ where M is the number of frames in $\mathcal{V}$. Furthermore, let the $\mathcal{H}$ be the function to extract base features on a given image patch.

Algorithm 1 describes the detector adaptation process. The patches obtained from the generic dataset $\mathcal{G}$ are combined with the patches sampled from the target video $\mathcal{V}$. The sampling technique is detailed in Algorithm 2. After obtaining all the patches $\mathbf{D}_{\mathrm{patches}}$, we extract HOG features from each of them, producing a feature vector for each patch. These feature vectors are input to the deep learning algorithm described in Algorithm 3. The deep learning algorithm produces, as output, a function $\mathcal{H}$ which takes in a HOG feature vector and produces a feature vector of much smaller dimension by projecting the HOG feature vector onto the learnt manifold. We then project all the HOG features of the positive and negative data of the generic dataset into this space and train a linear SVM.

Algorithm 1. Detector adaptation overview

Input: $\mathcal{G}, \mathcal{V}, \mathcal{H}$
Output: Scene-specific detector = $\{\mathcal{F}, \mathcal{C}\}$
1: $\mathbf{D}_{\mathrm{patches}} \leftarrow \mathcal{G}$
2: $S \leftarrow \mathrm{SamplePatchesFromVideo}(\mathcal{V}, \mathcal{G}, \mathcal{H})$
3: $\mathbf{D}_{\mathrm{patches}} \leftarrow \mathbf{D}_{\mathrm{patches}} \cup S$
4: $\mathbf{D} \leftarrow \mathcal{H}(\mathbf{D}_{\mathrm{patches}})$
5: $\mathcal{F} = \mathrm{LearnDeepFeatures}(\mathbf{D})$
6: $\mathcal{C} = \mathrm{TrainSVM}(\mathcal{F}(\mathcal{H}(G_{\mathrm{pos}})), \mathcal{F}(\mathcal{H}(G_{\mathrm{neg}})))$
7: **return** $\{\mathcal{F}, \mathcal{C}\}$

Algorithm 2. Biased sampling of patches from video

Input: $\mathcal{V}, \mathcal{G}, \mathcal{H}$
Output: Sampled patches, $\mathbf{D}_{\text{patches}}$
  1: $C = \text{TrainSVM}(\mathcal{H}(G_{\text{pos}}), \mathcal{H}(G_{\text{neg}}))$
  2: Sample N frames from $\mathcal{V}$.
  3: Run sliding-window detector with C on the N sampled frames
  4: $\mathbf{D}_{\text{patches}} \leftarrow$ positive detections from detector
  5: **return** $\mathbf{D}_{\text{patches}}$

Algorithm 3. Deep Feature Learning

Input: HOG features, $\mathbf{D}$
Output: Learnt non-linear projection function, $\mathcal{F}$
  1: Apply PCA on $\mathbf{D}$ and keep 99% variance
  2: $\mathbf{D} \leftarrow$ Project $\mathbf{D}$ onto principal component space
  3: ndimsIn $\leftarrow$ number of dimensions of $\mathbf{D}$
  4: Estimate intrinsic dimension of $\mathbf{D}$ using [8]
  5: ndimsOut $\leftarrow$ Estimated intrinsic dimension
  6: $\mathcal{A} \leftarrow$ SetUpAutoEncoder(ndimsIn, ndimsOut)
  7: $\mathcal{A} \leftarrow$ initialise $\mathcal{A}$ using [4]
  8: $\mathcal{A} \leftarrow$ Min LossFunc($\mathcal{A}, \mathbf{D}$) using mini-batch L-BFGS
  9: $\mathcal{F} \leftarrow$ Remove the decoder part of $\mathcal{A}$
 10: **return** $\mathcal{F}$

2.2   Sampling Representative Data from Video

Although we are not concerned with any supervision labels during the feature learning stage, we would like to get a mixture of both pedestrian and non-pedestrian patches from the video. However, naive random sampling of pedestrian-sized patches from video in the space of multi-scale sliding windows would result in pedestrian patches being sampled only with extremely low probability. Therefore, we propose a biased sampling strategy as given in Algorithm 2.

2.3   Deep Feature Learning

In order to learn deep non-linear features, we use a deep autoencoder. We do not use any layer-wise stacked pre-training for initialization since recent research [10,9] has shown that one of the main problems with deep networks is *pathological curvature* which looks like local optima to 1st-order optimization techniques such as gradient descent, but not to 2nd-order optimization methods.

Therefore, combined with a sensible weight initialization proposed in [4], we use the limited-memory version of Broyden Fletcher Goldfarb Shanno (L-BFGS) algorithm which is an approximated 2nd-order method. This also has the added advantage that there is no need to set or tune the learning rate. We use mini-batch training for efficiency and robustness. The formal description is given in Algorithm 3 and explained below.

Data Normalization & Intrinsic Dimensionality Estimation. We first perform PCA and keep 99% of the total variance to condition the data for faster convergence during subsequent deep learning. After projecting the data using PCA coefficients, we estimate the intrinsic dimensionality of the data using [8].

Setting up the deep autoencoder architecture & initialization. The architecture is shown in Fig. 2. Note that the network structure is obtained automatically and systematically and we do not have to manually tune it. After the network has been set up, we randomly initialize it using the method in [4].

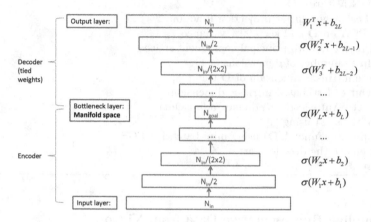

Fig. 2. The deep autoencoder architecture. N_{in} is the number of data dimensions after normalization. N_{goal} is the automatically estimated intrinsic dimensionality. Each hidden layer has half of the number of hidden neurons as its previous layer and this is repeated until N_{goal} is reached. After that, the decoding layers is mirrored to the encoding layers. The encoding and decoding parts are symmetric and weights are tied (but not the biases). All hidden layers have hyperbolic tangent nonlinearity activation (represented by $\sigma(\bullet)$). There are a total of L hidden nonlinear layers in the encoder (which produces a total of $2L$ layers feed-forward neural network).

Network optimization. In order to train the autoencoder, the network in Fig. 2 can be mathematically written as a smooth differentiable multivariate loss function which should be minimized. This is given in Equation 1; m refers to the number of data in each mini-batch, W_j is affine projection matrix for layer j, $x^{(i)}$ is a column vector of data point i and b_j is a vector of bias for layer j.

$$\underset{\substack{W_1,...,W_L, \\ b_1,...,b_{2L}}}{\arg\min} \quad \frac{1}{2m} \sum_{i=1}^{m} \left\{ \left\| \sum_{j=1}^{L} \sigma(W_j x^{(i)} + b_j) + \sum_{j=L+1}^{2L-1} \sigma(W_{(2L-j+1)}^T x^{(i)} + b_j) + \right. \right.$$

$$\left. \left. W_1^T x^{(i)} + b_{(2L)} - x^{(i)} \right\|_2^2 \right\} \tag{1}$$

Removing the decoding part. After training the deep network, the decoder part is no longer needed and is thus removed. We now have a deep non-linear projection function $\mathcal{F}$ with the number of projection layers given by L.

2.4 Training Scene-Specific Detector

We use the learnt encoder, $\mathcal{F}$, to project the generic dataset $\mathcal{G}$ and train a SVM on these features. This is illustrated in Fig. 3.

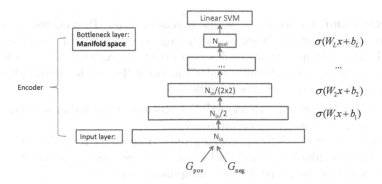

Fig. 3. Training the scene-specific detector

3 Experimental Results

Datasets. INRIA pedestrian dataset [1] is used as the source dataset. We evaluate on two target datasets: CUHK Square (a 60 mins video) and MIT Traffic (90 mins) [12]. Frame samples are shown in Fig. 4. Each dataset is divided into two halves: the 1st half is used for unsupervised detector adaptation and the 2nd half for quantitative evaluation. These datasets are very challenging: they vary greatly from the INRIA dataset in terms of resolution, camera angle and poses.

Fig. 4. A frame sampled from the CUHK video (left) and from the MIT video (right)

Deep learning parameters. For CUHK experiments, the layer sizes for encoder part of the deep network are found to be $\mathcal{E} = [1498, 749, 375, 187, 94, 35]$. The decoder layer sizes are $\mathcal{D} = [94, 187, 375, 749, 1498]$. The complete layer sizes for the whole network is therefore given by $\mathcal{R} = [\mathcal{E}, \mathcal{D}]$. The first and last elements of $\mathcal{R}$ correspond to input and output layer sizes respectively (*i.e.* the number of dimensions after PCA projection) and the ones in the middle are hidden layers. In this case, 35 is the size of the bottleneck layer. For MIT, $\mathcal{E} = [1536, 768, 384, 192, 96, 48, 23]$. Mini-batch size for training is fixed at 1000 for both CUHK and MIT.

Evaluation and discussion. We use precision-recall (PR) curves in order to compare the performance. Detection bounding boxes are scored according to the PASCAL 50% overlap criteria [3]. Average Precision (AP) is calculated for each PR curve by integrating the area under the curve. For each target dataset, we perform 3 different types of experiments:

1. `Generic`: The detector (HOG+SVM) trained on INRIA dataset. This is the baseline *without* any domain adaptation.
2. `Geodesic(CVPR12)`: The approach proposed by Gong *et al.* [5]. We use the code made available by them and extend it to be applicable to video.
3. `Proposed`: Our proposed detector adaptation algorithm.

The PR curves are shown in Fig. 5 and the corresponding APs are shown in Table 1. As can be seen, our algorithm (`Proposed`) outperforms the baseline (`Generic`) and the state-of-art (`Geodesic`) in both datasets. For CUHK, `Proposed` achieves almost twice the AP of baseline (0.6880 vs. 0.3554), whereas `Geodesic` has less improvement over the baseline (0.5286 vs. 0.3554). Interestingly, for MIT, `Geodesic` performs worse than the baseline whereas `Proposed` clearly improves over the baseline and attains an AP which is around 1.5 times that of the baseline. This suggests that for the MIT traffic dataset, which is a more difficult dataset than the CUHK dataset (partly due to much lower resolution), the state-of-the-art `Geodesic` fails to improve over the baseline whereas

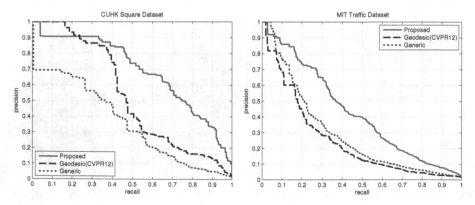

Fig. 5. Detection precision-recall curves

Table 1. Average precision results

	CUHK (AP)	MIT (AP)
Generic	0.3554	0.2883
Geodesic(CVPR12) [5]	0.5286	0.2460
Proposed	**0.6880**	**0.4292**

our approach, due to unsupervised learning of deep non-linear features and the resulting implicit manifold regularization, achieves much better results.

4 Conclusion

In this paper, we propose an algorithm to automatically generate a scene-specific pedestrian detector that is tuned to a particular scene by unsupervised domain adaptation of a generic detector. Our algorithm learns the underlying manifold where both the generic and the target dataset jointly reside and a detector is trained in this space, implicitly regularized to perform well on the target scene. Evaluation on two public video datasets show the effectiveness of our approach.

References

1. Dalal, N., Triggs, B.: Histograms of oriented gradients for human detection. In: CVPR (1), pp. 886–893 (2005)
2. Dollár, P., Wojek, C., Schiele, B., Perona, P.: Pedestrian detection: A benchmark. In: CVPR, pp. 304–311 (2009)
3. Everingham, M., Gool, L.J.V., Williams, C.K.I., Winn, J.M., Zisserman, A.: The pascal visual object classes (voc) challenge. International Journal of Computer Vision 88(2), 303–338 (2010)
4. Glorot, X., Bengio, Y.: Understanding the difficulty of training deep feedforward neural networks. In: International Conference on Artificial Intelligence and Statistics, pp. 249–256 (2010)
5. Gong, B., Shi, Y., Sha, F., Grauman, K.: Geodesic flow kernel for unsupervised domain adaptation. In: CVPR, pp. 2066–2073 (2012)
6. Gopalan, R., Li, R., Chellappa, R.: Domain adaptation for object recognition: An unsupervised approach. In: ICCV, pp. 999–1006 (2011)
7. Tang, K., Ramanathan, V., Fei-Fei, L., Koller, D.: Shifting weights: Adapting object detectors from image to video. In: Neural Information Processing Systems (NIPS) (2012)
8. Levina, E., Bickel, P.J.: Maximum likelihood estimation of intrinsic dimension. In: Advances in Neural Information Processing Systems, pp. 777–784 (2004)
9. Martens, J.: Deep learning via hessian-free optimization. In: Proceedings of the 27th International Conference on Machine Learning (ICML 2010), pp. 735–742 (2010)
10. Ngiam, J., Coates, A., Lahiri, A., Prochnow, B., Ng, A., Le, Q.V.: On optimization methods for deep learning. In: Proceedings of the 28th International Conference on Machine Learning (ICML 2011), pp. 265–272 (2011)
11. Torralba, A., Efros, A.A.: Unbiased look at dataset bias. In: 2011 IEEE Conference on Computer Vision and Pattern Recognition (CVPR), pp. 1521–1528. IEEE (2011)
12. Wang, M., Li, W., Wang, X.: Transferring a generic pedestrian detector towards specific scenes. In: CVPR, pp. 3274–3281 (2012)

True Zoom with Cylindrical Light Feld System

Kurmi Indrajit, K.S. Venkatesh, and Gupta Sumana

IIT Kanpur, Electrical Enggineering Department
Kalyanpur, Kanur, Uttar Pradesh, India
{indrajit,venkats,sumana}@iitk.ac.in

Abstract. Light fields are a computational photography technique which allow features like refocusing and novel view synthesis. The previous work in light fields either have sampling bias or have a very complex acquisition setup. Here, we acquire a light field using a simple cylindrical arrangement of cameras. Our acquisition setup is simpler to implement where there is need to capture a large field of view. The parameterization we present uniformly samples the environment in the horizontal direction. Zooming options provided in traditional cameras either tend to change the relative sizes of the objects in an image(optical zoom) or introduce pixelation effect(digital zoom). We propose as well as demonstrate an approach that we have named "true zoom" that produces a significantly superior and realistic zooming effect.

Keywords: Computational Photography, Light field, Zoom.

1 Introduction

In 1996 Levoy [1] and Gortler [2] implemented 2PP (Two plane parameterization). The 2PP has certain shortcomings such as nonuniform sampling [4] and an inability to capture large environments. Hence there has been a lot of work done for alternative parameterizations. Some of the parameterizations proposed are spherical light fields [3], two sphere parameterization [4] and sphere plane parameterization [4]. While these parameterizations give uniform sampling, they are too complex for practical implementation.

The rest of the paper is organized as follows. Section 2 shows our system parameterization, its acquisition setup and the process of novel view synthesis using our system. Section 3 demonstrates an application of novel view synthesis i.e. true zoom. We demonstrate its superiority over other available zooming techniques [5] [6].

2 Cylindrical Light Field System

We present a parameterization that carries out uniform sampling of the light field in the horizontal direction. The parameterization also has a simple acquisition setup, simple enough for actual implementation.

L.J. Chmielewski et al. (Eds.): ICCVG 2014, LNCS 8671, pp. 278–285, 2014.
© Springer International Publishing Switzerland 2014

Parametrization. The parameterization uses cylindrical surfaces for both the directional surface (camera surface) and the focal surface. The directional surface parameterizes the direction of the light ray. The intersection of any light ray with this surface gives us two parameters (θ, h) where θ is the azimuth angle of the intersection and h is height of the intersection over the $z = 0$ surface. For the discrete case(finite no. of cameras), this also signifies or determines the position of the nearest camera. The focal surface can also be parameterized in a similar way. Thus any ray L is parameterized as $L(\theta_d, h_d, \theta_f, h_f)$ for the continuous case as shown in Figure 1 where the subscripts d and f denote the directional and focal surfaces respectively.

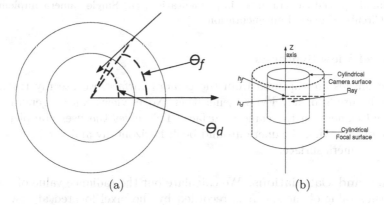

(a)   (b)

Fig. 1. Parameterization of Cylindrical light field system: (a) Top view of the parameterization; (b) Side view of the parameterization

The light field cannot be captured continuously due to practical limitation. Hence, in the discrete case, the parameters are uniformly sampled. The number and position of cameras determine the sampling of the camera surface parameters. The other two(focal surface) parameters can be discretized by either properly sampling the two parameters at the focal surface or at the imaging plane of each camera which is sandwiched between the camera and focal surfaces. The two parameters in an imaging plane parameterization are (r, c) where r denotes the row no. and c denotes the column no. of the imaging plane of the respective camera. Thus, any ray which passes through these two cylindrical surfaces, shall be parameterized as $L(\theta, h, r, c)$ for the discrete case(finite camera count) and as $L(\theta_d, h_d, \theta_f, h_f)$ for the continuous case(a continuum of cameras).

Acquisition System Setup. We have not physically implemented the acquisition set up but have shown it is indeed practically viable. Instead we have resorted to an artificial environment generated using C++ and Open GL. This allows us to create synthetic scenes which can then be (observed) using arbitrarily parameterized cameras. The virtual objects are placed at different depths and are then imaged using virtual cameras located at position of our choosing and with individual focal length as required. We, propose three different ways for implementing the setup for real scenes as shown in Figure 2.

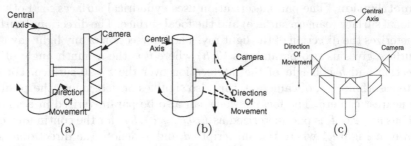

Fig. 2. Arrangement of cameras for implementing Cylindrical light field system: (a) Longitudinally placed camera array implementation; (b) Single camera implementation; (c) Circular Camera Implementation.

2.1   Novel View Synthesis

Once the images are captured from the camera surface, we use ray tracing as shown in Figure 3 for novel view generation. Novel views can be generated for any virtual camera on the camera surface. This gives the user complete freedom to move the virtual camera around both horizontally and vertically on the cylindrical camera surface.

Approach and Calculations. We calculate out the radiance value of the ray R (Intensity value of the ray R is recorded by the pixel located at row r and column c) that would be captured by our novel camera situated at angle θ_v and height h_v. For each pixel in the virtual camera, contributions are made from several of the real cameras in the vicinity. In the Figure 3 we show an example of ray tracing from just one real camera. Let the contributing pixel of the real camera be (r_1, c_1). The effective radiance of ray R striking (r, c) of the virtual camera is linear combination of the contributions of several surrounding real cameras.

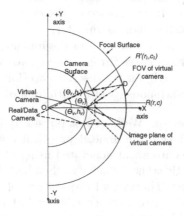

Fig. 3. Ray tracing for cylindrical light field system

Results

Here we demonstrate the results of the novel view generated using our proposed system. The results are shown for four different cases of image rendering.The original real cameras are placed on a cylindrical surface with a spacing of 1 unit in elevation and 10° in azimuth. The diameter of cylindrical surface is 4 unit. Uniform weighting is used for interpolating values from multiple cameras. The ghosting effect seen in Figure 4(c) and 4(d) is a form of out of focus blur but is seen instead as a series of ghost due to discretization of the blur function in turn caused by the finite number of cameras [7].

| (a) | (b) | (c) | (d) |

Fig. 4. Novel view synthesis: (a) Near-point single camera interpolation; (b) Mid-point single camera interpolation; (c) Near-point multiple camera interpolation; (d) Mid-point multiple camera interpolation

3   True Zoom

Novel view synthesis can be used in various places, such as for giving special effects in movies like "Matrix", live sports and to give a virtual tour of the scene. Here we present yet another use of virtual view synthesis by using it to improve upon the zooming effects produced by a normal camera. At present available cameras give a user two kinds of zooming options: digital zoom and optical zoom.

Digital zoom is the process of coming up with a reasonable approximation of what color a pixel might have been, had it been actually captured. Various algorithms [5] [6] have been developed so as to do precisely that. While some algorithms are unquestionably better than others, the truth is that all of these algorithms are still only producing "educated guesses"; they are not able to determine actually what color a pixel is since that pixel does not exist in reality.

For capturing images, cameras employ perspective projection which can be described as below

$$x = f * X/Z \tag{1}$$
$$y = f * Y/Z \tag{2}$$

where f denotes focal length of the camera, x and y denote 2D coordinates on the image. X, Y, Z are 3D coordinates of the point. Optical zoom is a process of changing the focal length of the camera. This also changes the cameras field of view. Note that there is no movement of either the camera or the subject. Hence it can be said that optical zoom uses the imaging process to its benefit for implementing the optical zoom effect. Optical zoom is performed by physically moving the camera's lenses to change their effective focal length. While optical zoom maintains the resolution of the original image and hence is better than the digital zoom, still it does not bring the observer any closer to or any farther from the object or scenes.

3.1   True Zoom for Cylindrical Light Field System

In the case of true zoom, we place the virtual camera nearer or farther from the scenes. These results in virtually bringing the observer closer or farther to the scenes. The objects in the scene are projected back on to the imaging plane according to their new depth relative to the virtual camera as shown in the Figure 5(a) and 5(b).

$$x = f * X/(Z - changeddistance) \qquad (3)$$

$$y = f * Y/(Z - changeddistance) \qquad (4)$$

Thus we see that each X and Y coordinates of the point in 3D, are transformed onto the imaging plane according to their new depth from the virtual camera center and hence this approach represents zoom in the true sense of the word. This approach maintains the same field of view as the original camera.

Approach and Calculations. The true zoom implementation for a cylindrical light field is shown in Figures 5(a) and 5(b). For capturing the true zoomed view of the scene, the virtual camera is placed facing radially outward at the desired location. Subsequently ray tracing is applied for scene generation in this camera in the usual manner.

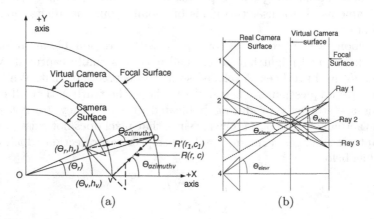

Fig. 5. Implementing True Zoom for Cylindrical Light Field system

3.2   Results

Here we show the results of the true zoomed views generated using our proposed system.

a)   b)   c)   d)

Fig. 6. True Zoom In: Real cameras at 4 unit distance and virtual camera at 8 unit distance, both at 10° apart; (a) Real Camera Image; (b) Optical zoom 2x Zoom In; (c) True zoom 2x Zoom In; (d) Result obtained using model

Analysis of Results. Figure 3.2 and 3.2, show objects being clipped at the bottom for the optical zoom in view compared to the true zoom and virtual model view. In Figure 8 A depicts this difference between optical zoom and true zoom. For objects at different depths, the effects are seen to differ due to a change in the field of view in the optical zoom case. For the zoom out case, the field of view of the camera in the case of optical zoom increases too much compared to the field of view of the original camera and hence gives an inappropriate result. This effect can be clearly seen for the outward looking case in Figure 3.2 and Figure 8.

a)   b)   c)   d)

Fig. 7. True Zoom out: Real cameras at 4 unit distance and virtual camera at 2 unit distance, both at 10° apart; (a) Real Camera Image; (b) Optical zoom 2x Zoom out; (c) True zoom 2x Zoom out; (d) Result obtained using model

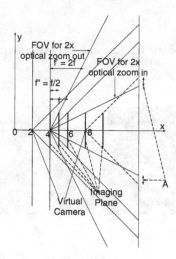

Fig. 8. Analysis of Results

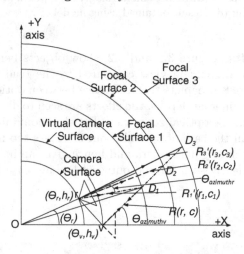

Fig. 9. Change of position of focal surface for cylindrical light field system

3.3   Refocusing of True Zoomed Image

We have shown that objects around the focal surface remain in the focus and the objects distant from the focal surface are blurred. This property of the focal surface is used for refocusing i.e. once the image is taken we can then later on change the focal surface position depending upon the objects in the image, which we want to focus upon and emphasize. The same ray R for the virtual camera is reconstructed using different sets of the rays R_1', R_2', R_3' from the real cameras as we change the position of the focal surface. By changing the real ray from which the virtual camera ray is reconstructed we change the range of objects which will be seen in focus.

(a)   (b)   (c)

Fig. 10. True zoom refocusing:Real cameras at 4 unit distance and virtual camera at 8 unit distance; (a) True zoom with Front object in focus by keeping focal surface at 15 unit; (b) True zoom with back object in focus by keeping focal surface at 25 unit; (c) True zoom with background in focus by keeping focal surface at 100 unit

We utilize this property and implement true zoom simultaneously and create true zoomed image with varying focal surface position. The implementation of this property for our system is shown in the Figure 9. The user gets to create images with zoom and can refocus the image as desired at the same time.

4   Conclusion

We have presented a cylindrical light field system and have also proposed its acquisition setup. The acquisition setup is easier to implement for real environments than setups proposed in the past. The results have been demonstrated only for synthetic scenes. We introduce true zoom as an application of novel view synthesis. True zoom gives the user the true sensation of zooming as it brings the user closer to or farther from the scenes. We have demonstrated refocusing of true zoomed images where the user is given the capability to true zoom as well as refocus the scene simultaneously.

References

1. Marc, L., Pat, H.: Light field rendering. In: SIGGRAPH 1996 (1996)
2. Gortler, S.J., Grzeszczuk, R., Szeliski, R., Cohen, M.F.: The Lumigraph. In: SIGGRAPH 1996 (1996)
3. Ihm, I., Park, S., Kyoung, R.: Rendering of Spherical Light Fields. In: Proc. Pacific Graphics 1997, pp. 59–68 (1997)
4. Emilio, C., Apostolos, L., Don, F.: Uniformly Sampled Light Fields, Phd. Thesis, University of Texas at Austin (1998)
5. Almira, J.M., Romero, A.E.: Image zooming based on sampling theorems. Technical report, University of Barcelona (2011)
6. Lan, Y.C.: Adaptive Digital Zoom Techniques Based on Hypothesized Boundary. Technical report, Nanyang Technological University, Singapore (2011)
7. Chai, J.-X., Tong, X., Chan, S.-C., Shum, H.-Y.: Plenoptic Sampling. In: SIGGRAPH 2000 (2000)

Identification of Products on Shop-Racks by Morphological Preprocessing and Feature-Based Detection

Marcin Iwanowski[1], Bartłomiej Zieliński[1],
Grzegorz Sarwas[2], and Sebastian Stygar[2]

[1] Institute of Control and Industrial Electronics
Warsaw University of Technology
ul. Koszykowa 75; 00-662 Warszawa Poland
{iwanowski,zielinsb}@ee.pw.edu.pl
[2] Lingaro Sp.z o.o.
ul. Puławska 99a; 02-595 Warszawa Poland
{grzegorz.sarwas,sebastian.stygar}@lingaro.com

Abstract. In this paper we describe the method allowing the identification of products on the shop-racks. This method consists of two steps: morphological preprocessing where the image of the rack is segmented in order to find the split-lines between products; and recognition step where, based on the segmentation results, the feature-point approach is used to identify the products. In the proposed method, thanks to novel preprocessing step, we reduce the search-space to possible locations obtained as results of segmentation.

1 Introduction

Thanks to the rapidly growing computer vision application possibilities, the vision systems appear as a supporting technologies in various areas. One of them is supervision of shop-racks in view of investigating the location and identification of particular products. The latter can be further used e.g. by producers to analyze the sale strategies. In this paper we present a novel method allowing the identification of products on shop-racks. It consists of two steps. In the first one the image of the rack is segmented in order to find the boundaries between products. This step is based on the morphological image processing. In the second step, starting from the segmentation results, the products are identified with use of a feature-point approach. The novelty of the method consists in the preprocessing step that precedes the product identification. Usual approach to finding objects within an image by means of the feature-point approach consists in matching previously calculated feature-vectors of reference objects with feature-vector computed for the examined image. In our method the preprocessing step divides the search-space into separate regions where the products can possibly be located.

L.J. Chmielewski et al. (Eds.): ICCVG 2014, LNCS 8671, pp. 286–293, 2014.

The preprocessing step is based mostly on morphological operators [2,6,10]. It allows for finding the split-lines that separate shelves and products on them. Each of these two kinds of split-lines is detected using similar generic algorithm, but with different parameters. The detection of shelves is performed based on the processing of the gradient computed along 'y' axis of the image coordinate system, while the split-lines between products—along the 'x' axis. The split-lines, being the result of preprocessing step, form bounding boxes of particular products or groups of products located on a shelf.

The second step of the proposed method is the feature-point based product identification. It makes use of the above bounding boxes to focus the search of product templates on the most prospective image areas. In the current study the SIFT feature extractor [7,8] is used. Finally, the RANSAC algorithm [1] is applied to match the feature points located inside each bounding box with the feature point sets of template products stored in the database. This way products are recognized.

The paper consists of 6 sections. In section 2 the preprocessing step is described. Section 3 is focused on the feature-point-based identification. In section 4 the results are described. Section 5 and 6 are acknowledgments and conclusions, respectively.

2 Morphological Preprocessing

2.1 Algorithm Overview

The aim of this step of processing is to segment the input image of the shop-rack in order to find the places where particular products are located. An example of such segmentation of image shown in Fig. 1(a) is given in Fig. 1(b). It is important to mention that in our case the segmentation does not refer to finding the accurate boundaries of objects (as most of image segmentation techniques does). It is oriented here towards extraction of the bounding boxes inside which the products are located. We use here an important property of images under consideration. Namely, the visibility of meaningful horizontal and vertical lines. The former, spread across the whole image refer to shelves, while the latter to the boundaries of objects[1]. The horizontal and vertical boundaries are shown in Figs. 1(c) and (d), respectively.

In order to find the bounding boxes the following three-step algorithm is proposed, that is applied for the detection of both horizontal and vertical lines.

1. *Directional gradient computation* The input image is a rgb-color one. Since the color of directional details may differ from one object to another, the information on particular, chosen colors cannot be used. On the contrary, the full-color information should be used instead. Consequently, the boundaries

---

[1] We assume here that the products are characterized by "regular" shapes, which means in this case that they are close to rectangular. It is true for the vast majority of the real cases.

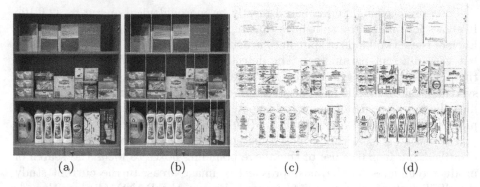

(a)   (b)   (c)   (d)

Fig. 1. Input image (a), segmented image (b), horizontal boundaries (c), vertical boundaries (d)

are detected on each color channel separately and, in the next step, all three results are combined together by computing their sum, which is the final gray-tone image containing the information on the boundaries. In order to find the boundaries on particular channels, morphological gradients [2,6,10] are computed.

2. *Gradient filtering* The image with boundaries is further processed in order to remove all irrelevant ones i.e. boundaries not reflecting the real object bounding boxes. The filtering depends on the direction, but in all cases it is based on the morphological approach [2,3,6,10]. The choice of filtering method depends on the direction but in both cases (horizontal and vertical) the filtering algorithm should not introduce blurring on one hand, and should remove irrelevant boundaries on the other.

3. *Line detection* The filtered gradient consists of meaningful boundaries. In the case of horizontal boundaries, they refer to shelves. In the vertical case they should be located between object located on these shelves. Since the product on each shelf are distributed individually, the vertical boundaries differ from one shelf to another as shown in Fig. 1(b). The line detection is performed based on the projection of the filtered gradient on one of the axes. The horizontal boundaries are projected on the 'y' axis, while the vertical ones— on the 'x' axis of the image coordinate system. The projection is computed as a sum of pixels values in each line or column, respectively. This reduces the two-dimensional image into a vector. The intensity of filtered directional gradients is thus reflected to the value of vector elements. To detect lines of given length l, the threshold on the vector values should be set up as l. Final position of lines is than computed as the average indexes (coordinates) of regions on the projection vector that are above the threshold.

The above algorithm is applied both to shelf detection and to the detection of product vertical boundaries. The details of these two particular cases are described below.

2.2   Shelf Detection

In this case the horizontal lines are detected. To extract them, the morphological gradient by erosion with vertical linear structuring element is computed for each color component. The final boundaries are obtained as a sum of all three gradients:

$$i_2 = (i_r - \varepsilon_V(i_r)) + (i_g - \varepsilon_V(i_g)) + (i_b - \varepsilon_V(i_b)), \tag{1}$$

where i_r, i_g, i_b stand for the red, green, and blue components of the input image, respectively; ε_V for the morphological erosion with vertical structuring element, and i_2 for the output image. The image shown in Fig. 1(c) is the negative of i_2 computed for i as shown in Fig. 1(a).

The above gradient consists of lines of different length. Those which are important from the point of view of the final goal (which in this case is shelf detection) are spread from left to the right image boundary. In order to properly detect them, the others—shorter— should be filtered out. The filtering in this case consist of the following operations. At first, the short lines are removed using the opening filter with the horizontal linear structuring element. The length of this element should be chosen as longer than the longest horizontal non-shelf boundaries i.e. boundaries of products put on the shelves. Next, in order to improve the visibility of boundaries the image is dilated with disk-shaped structuring element. This step is particularly important in case of the photographs of racks where the camera is slightly rotated. In such a case the horizontal gradient line is split into several segments shifted by one pixel along the 'y' axis. The shape extension provided by the dilation allows to "glue" these shifted lines and the create finally single line going along the whole image. These operations may be described as:

$$i_3 = \delta_O\left(\gamma_H(i_2)\right), \tag{2}$$

where γ_H stands for the opening (erosion followed by dilation) with horizontal structuring element, and δ_O stands for dilation with disk structuring element. The image shown in Fig. 2(a) presents the opening result of Fig. 1(c), image Fig. 2(b) is the result of dilation (i_3).

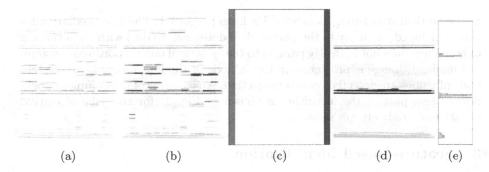

| (a) | (b) | (c) | (d) | (e) |

Fig. 2. Filtering: opening (a), dilation (b), boundary masks: left and right (c), final result (d) and profile (e)

In order to precisely find the shelves, the image i_3 is further processed using the morphological reconstruction approach. The idea of this filtering step is to extract from the i_3 image only those lines that starts near the left boundary of the image and ends near the right one. To extract such lines two image boundary masks are used, containing only the left and right image boundary pixels. In fact, instead of just a boundary pixels, we consider a mask that covers a certain area along the 'x' axis equal approx. to 10% of the total width of the image (see Fig. 2(c)). The final image, shown in Fig. 2(d), is thus computed as:

$$i_4 = \min\left(R_{i_3}(m_L), R_{i_3}(m_R)\right), \qquad (3)$$

where $R_a(b)$ stands for the morphological reconstruction [3] of mask image a from markers b, "min" stands for the point-wise image minimum, m_L and m_R for the left and right boundary mask, respectively. Finally, the profile of the i_4 is calculated as a vector of sums of pixel values along 'x' axis (see Fig. 2(e)). The final position of split lines referring to shelves are computed as described in the previous section.

2.3 Product Vertical Boundaries Detection

The detection of product vertical boundaries is performed within the frames of the same generic algorithm. Prior to start the algorithm the input image of shop-rack is split into separate images of shelves using the split-lines detected in the previous step (shelf detection) – one image per shelf. Let now j be the image with a single shelf. We start with the computation of its gradient, that in this case is based on the following formula (sum of component-wise morphological horizontal gradients):

$$j_2 = (\delta_H(j_r) - \varepsilon_H(j_r)) + (\delta_H(j_g) - \varepsilon_H(j_g)) + (\delta_H(j_b) - \varepsilon_H(j_b)), \qquad (4)$$

where j_r, j_g, j_b stand for the color components of the color single-shelf image. The gradient image is next filtered to remove irrelevant (too short) gradient lines using the following combination of operators:

$$j_3 = \gamma_{V2}\left(\delta_O\left(\gamma_{V1}(j_2)\right)\right), \qquad (5)$$

where vertical structuring element $V2$ is longer than $V1$. The intermediary dilation is included, similarly to the case of shelf detection, to deal with the situation of boundary lines not perfectly parallel to the 'y' axis of image coordinate system.

Finally, j_3 image is projected on the 'x' axis of the image coordinate system and split-lines are detected on this projection. An example of the complete workflow of this part of the algorithm is shown in Fig. 3 (for the sake of clarity, negative of gradients are shown).

3   Feature-Based Identification

There exist many feature-based methods of image object matching. In this research the well-known SIFT approach [7,8] is evaluated in order to recognize

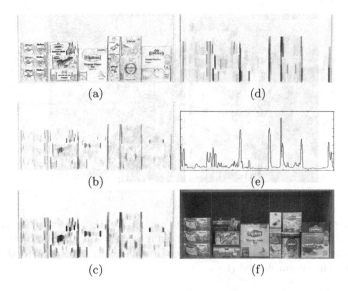

(a)   (d)

(b)   (e)

(c)   (f)

Fig. 3. Shelf processing: gradient (a), opening γ_{V1} (b), dilation δ_O (c), opening γ_{V2} (d), projection (e), final cuts superimposed on the input image (f)

products placed on shop-racks. SIFT is a descriptor which is invariant to scaling, translation, rotation, as well as robust against moderate affine transformations and illumination alterations. The method takes advantage of a set of interest points extracted from an image. The points robustly represent local image characteristics. It is possible to match corresponding points in two images and, therefore, identify objects. This is done by comparing the interest points detected from a data set of reference pattern images with the points extracted from an image under examination. The search for corresponding key-points might be performed in different ways. In our research RANSAC [1] algorithm has been used.

The product recognition was performed within bounding boxes detected in the preprocessing step, which delimited the area where particular object was positioned. For every bounding box an adjustment between SIFT key-points in the box and SIFT key-points of patterns was searched. Patterns for which at least N points or $p\%$ of the total number of SIFT interest points have been matched with the points of detected box were admitted to further consideration. Then, for each pattern's matched points in the examined box a convex hull was calculated. Patterns which convex hulls did not intersect with the other ones were assumed to be recognized and their SIFT key-points were removed from the box. On the other hand, if any convex hulls did intersect, from corresponding patterns the one that had the most points matched was marked as recognized. The box examination was performed until no pattern exceeded required threshold $p\%$ or N matches. Patterns which convex hulls did not intersect with the other ones were assumed to be recognized and their SIFT key-points were removed from the box, as shown in Fig. 3.

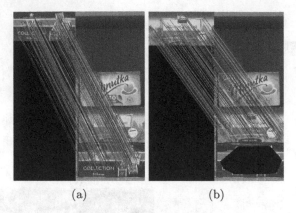

(a)   (b)

Fig. 4. Example of object recognition. After identifying the object with the greatest number of matches (a), all the key-points within a convex hull spanned by the matched points are removed from the examined image and the next pattern with the greatest number of matches is considered (b).

4   Results

In order to verify the usefulness of presented approach it has been subjected to experiments. They have been evaluated on a data set of images depicting model shop-racks. Every image contained around 20 different objects, size of image was 3000x4000 pixels. The objects—some of which were visually very similar, as they differed only with little details—have been randomly positioned on shelves. In order to make the recognition task more difficult, there were 40 pattern images, so that the pattern data set contained images absent from the examined shop-rack images.

In the course of experiments the following values of constants have been set. The SIFT matching sensitivity factors equaled $p = 15\%$ and $N = 20$. SIFT descriptors D_a and D_b are matched when the distance $d(D_a, D_b) \cdot t$, where t stands for a threshold, is not greater than the distance of D_a to all the other descriptors. In other words, t expresses acceptable difference between the best match and the other matches. Lowe's recommendation was $t = 1.5$. However, in our research it turned out that greater values prove to decrease false positive matches and, therefore, yield better identification results. The optimal threshold evaluated in the experiments equaled $t = 2$.

In terms of computational complexity the proposed method has been compared with straightforward approach where a whole image was treated as a single bounding box. In both cases the most time consuming operation was matching the interest points, which took, respectively, 80% and 93% of total calculation time. In real-life applications, when a lot more patterns are considered, these numbers would obviously be even more overwhelming. The advantage of presented method is that the matching is performed approximately 1.72 times faster.

5 Conclusions

In the paper, the method for identifying products on the shop-racks was presented. It consist of two steps: morphological preprocessing and SIFT-based identification step. Thanks to the preprocessing step, the search-space for SIFT-feature points was reduced to bounding boxes detected. Results obtained for examined set of images have been very promising. For correctly detected bounding boxes, perfect—namely 100%—object detection has been achieved. It is worth mentioning, that even very similar objects (i.e. differing with a small details) have been properly recognized. Moreover, the presented approach computational complexity is significantly reduced in comparison with straightforward one, in which patterns are being tried to match within a whole image.

Acknowledgments. This work was co-financed by the European Union within European Regional Development Fund, through grant Innovative Economy POIG.01.04.00-14-129/12.

References

1. Fischler, M.A., Bolles, R.C.: Random sample consensus: A paradigm for model fitting with applications to image analysis and automated cartography. Graphics and Image Processing 24(4) (1981)
2. Serra, J.: Image analysis and mathematical morphology, vol. 1. Academic Press (1983)
3. Vincent, L.: Morphological grayscale reconstruction in image analysis: applications and efficient algorithms. IEEE Trans. on Image Processing 2(2) (April 1993)
4. Mojsilovic, B., Rogowitz, A.: Capturing image semantics with low-level descriptors. In: Proceedings of the 2001 International Conference on Image Processing, vol. 1, pp. 18–21 (2001)
5. Mikolajczyk, K., Schmid, C.: Scale and Affine Invariant Interest Point Detectors. International Journal of Computer Vision 60(1), 63–86 (2004)
6. Soille, P.: Morphological image analysis. Springer (1999, 2004)
7. Lowe, D.G.: Object recognition from local scale-invariant features. In: Proceedings of the International Conference on Computer Vision, vol. 2, pp. 1150–1157
8. Lowe, D.G.: Distinctive Image Features from Scale-Invariant Keypoints. International Journal of Computer Vision 60(2), 91–110 (2004)
9. Mikolajczyk, K., Schmid, C.: A Performance Evaluation of Local Descriptors. IEEE Transactions on Pattern Analysis and Machine Intelligence 27(10) (2005)
10. Iwanowski, M.: Metody morfologiczne w przetwarzaniu obrazow cyfrowych. EXIT (2009)

Computer Simulation of the SWI Protocol in Nuclear Magnetic Resonance Imaging

Grzegorz Izydorczyk and Artur Klepaczko

Łódź University of Technology, Institute of Electronics
90-924 Łódź, ul. Wólczańska 211/215
izydorczyk.grzegorz@gmail.com, aklepaczko@p.lodz.pl

Abstract. In this paper a design of a computer simulator of susceptibility weighted imaging (SWI) protocol is presented. The ultimate application of the proposed system is to provide a framework for quantitative validation of SWI image processing algorithms. SWI is based on field non-uniformity caused by local susceptibility distribution and thus resulting in both measured signal phase shift and faster decay of transverse magnetization vector. The designed system accounts for both of these effects. Obtained simulated images demonstrate correctness of the results for simple objects, proving the propriety of the model.

1 Introduction

Magnetic resonance imaging (MRI) is currently a key diagnostic technology allowing for non-invasive visualization of soft tissues inside a human body. Within the MRI setting, susceptibility weighted imaging (SWI) is a relatively new concept [1] with the major application in venography. SWI is based on the effect of susceptibility-driven magnetic field perturbations leading to both – MR signal phase and magnitude local alterations. The current challanges in SWI processing embrace vein segmentation and detection of anomalies in the vessel system [2].

However, medical image processing methods require validation, i.e. evaluation of their accuracy and potential limits. Unfortunately, maintenance and operation of the MRI equipment is expensive and thus hardly available for experiments. In consequence, acquisition of real test images e.g. with the use of phantoms is significantly hampered. This brings a need for computer simulation which allows quantitative comparison of the processing results with the underlying ground-truth models. The described system enables formation of synthetic SWI images and as such it provides a framework for validation of SWI processing algorithms.

Since 1984, when the first one-dimensional MRI simulator was designed [3], a multiple of different approaches has been introduced [4–8]. Acceleration of processor clocks brought new possibilities to simulate with both higher precision and resolution. However only a few simulators account for magnetic field perturbations, allowing for susceptibility weighted imaging protocol simulation. The one suggested by Yoder [5] involved magnetic field inhomogeneities in numerical

L.J. Chmielewski et al. (Eds.): ICCVG 2014, LNCS 8671, pp. 294–301, 2014.

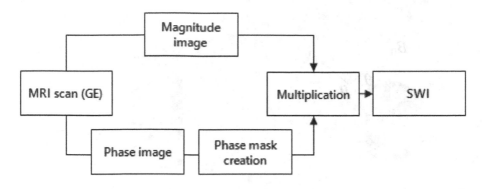

Fig. 1. SWI protocol data flow

calculation of magnetization vector evolution by implementation of convolution kernel. Later proposed SIMRI [6] implemented discrete time solution of Bloch equation and allowed for handling different field inhomogeneities along with T2* effects of Lorentz distribution. Yet another one, JEMRIS [7] solves the problem numerically, based on its mathematical description, thus leading to more accurate results, especially in case of time varying systems.

Proposed simulator, based on the SIMRI solution, estimates magnetic field perturbations induced by known geometries, thus making it dedicated for SWI.

2 Materials and Methods

2.1 Susceptibility Weighted Imaging

The SWI protocol (Fig. 1) begins with typical Gradient Echo (GE) sequence, which results in complex signal consisting of magnitude and phase components [9]. The latter one is usually biased with phase wraps and strong nonlinearities around tissue boundaries, making post-processing unavoidable [10]. High-pass filtered phase values are then transformed into the range [0,1] according to a chosen map function, e.g. negative (eq. 1) or triangular (eq. 2) mask:

$$f(\boldsymbol{r}) = \begin{cases} \frac{\pi+\varphi(\boldsymbol{r})}{\pi} & -\pi < \varphi(\boldsymbol{r}) < 0 \\ 1 & 0 \leq \varphi(\boldsymbol{r}) < \pi \end{cases} \tag{1}$$

$$f(\boldsymbol{r}) = \begin{cases} \frac{\pi+\varphi(\boldsymbol{r})}{\pi} & -\pi < \varphi(\boldsymbol{r}) < 0 \\ \frac{\pi-\varphi(\boldsymbol{r})}{\pi} & 0 \leq \varphi(\boldsymbol{r}) < \pi \end{cases} \tag{2}$$

Received weights are finally used to decrease brightness of corresponding voxels in magnitude image. As a result, an image of enhanced tissue contrast is obtained thanks to phase jump on varying tissues boundaries.

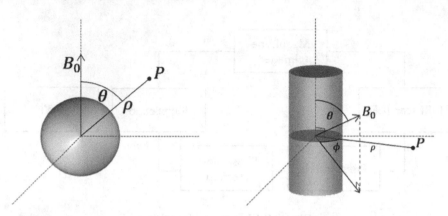

Fig. 2. Models of a sphere and long cylinder, both of radius R

2.2 MRI Simulation

The designed simulator implements a 3D spoiled gradient echo sequence using a discrete time solution of Bloch equation, as described in [11]. It is assumed that the flow is fully compensated and thus it does not introduce additional phase errors. Evolution of magnetization vector M in position r at time $t + \Delta t$ can be expressed as a product of previous magnetization value, rotation matrix corresponding to spin precession $\mathbf{R}_{\mathrm{prec}}$ and matrix of relaxation factors $\mathbf{R}_{\mathrm{relax}}$ (eq. 3), both being a function of magnetic field perturbations $\Delta B(r)$.

$$M(r, t + \Delta t) = M(r,t)\mathbf{R}_{\mathrm{prec}}(r)\mathbf{R}_{\mathrm{relax}}(r) \tag{3}$$

The time-independent perturbations are assumed to result from magnetic susceptibility alone. For known echo time (TE) parameter of GE sequence, phase component of the MRI signal $\varphi(r)$ can be estimated according to

$$\varphi(r) = \gamma \Delta B(r) TE. \tag{4}$$

In case of simple geometries such as sphere or long cylinder (Fig.2), which can model a tumor or a venous vessel, respectively, magnetic field perturbations can be evaluated analytically (eq. 5 and 6).

$$\Delta B(\rho) = \begin{cases} 0 & \rho < R \\ \frac{\Delta \chi}{3} B_0 \frac{R^3}{\rho^3}(3\cos^2\theta - 1) & \rho > R \end{cases}, \tag{5}$$

$$\Delta B(\rho) = \begin{cases} \frac{\Delta \chi}{6} B_0 (3\cos^2\theta - 1) & \rho < R \\ \frac{\Delta \chi}{2} B_0 \frac{R^2}{\rho^2}\sin^2\theta\cos 2\phi & \rho > R \end{cases}, \tag{6}$$

where ρ is the distance from the center of a sphere or the long axis of a cylinder, respectively, while angles θ and ϕ are defined as indicated in the Fig. 2.

In GE based sequences, spins at echo time do not rephase completely and as a result transverse component of magnetization vector decays faster, what is known as T2* effect. If a given voxel consists of N subvoxels, each described with magnetic field perturbations $\Delta B_i'$ and average perturbation over the voxel is ΔB, additional signal decay $d(t)$ caused by intravoxel magnetization differences can be expressed by

$$d(t) \cong d(TE) = \frac{1}{N}\sqrt{\left(\sum_i \cos\vartheta_i\right)^2 + \left(\sum_i \sin\vartheta_i\right)^2} \qquad (7)$$

where ϑ_i corresponds to the additional phase shift and is equal to

$$\vartheta_i = \gamma(\Delta B_i' - \Delta B)TE. \qquad (8)$$

3   Results

In order to verify operation, several structures of well-defined susceptibility distribution were taken into consideration, modeled with real-life properties and tested under typical SWI sequence parameters (3 T, $TE = 17$ ms, $TR = 46$ ms, $FA = 10°$), i.e. muscular venous vessel of 4 mm diameter and a spherical blood carrying tumor of 100 μm radius. Applied relaxation rates and proton density parameters are collected in Table 1.

Table 1. Relaxation rates and proton density (PD) parameters

Tissue	1.5 T		3 T		PD
	T1 [ms]	T2 [ms]	T1 [ms]	T2 [ms]	[a.u.]
Muscle	1130	35	1420	33	79
Venous vessel	1440	122	1930	32	72
Gray matter	1124	95	1820	99	70

3.1   Muscular Venous Vessel

Simulation was performed with cubic voxels of size $0.25 \times 0.25 \times 0.25$ mm, whereas magnetic field perturbations were approximated using eight times denser mesh in each direction, corresponding to averaging over 512 samples.

Distribution of magnetic field perturbations depicted in Fig. 3 follows the equation (5), providing clearly visible darker area inside the vein and influencing the surroundings in a complex manner. Depending on the orientation, local differences in magnetic field can be either negative (dark pixels) in the plane perpendicular to direction of the main magnetic field or positive (bright pixels) in the plane containing main magnetic field vector.

Applied homodyne-based high-pass filtering resulted in successful suppression of phase gradients in case of central slices but failed close to the field boundaries. Nonetheless, even with imperfect filtration it was possible to minimize gradient artifacts with the aid of negative mask function (Fig. 4).

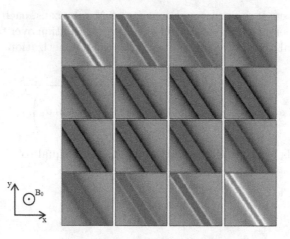

Fig. 3. Magnetic susceptibility driven field perturbations around a long cylinder in each slice along Z axis

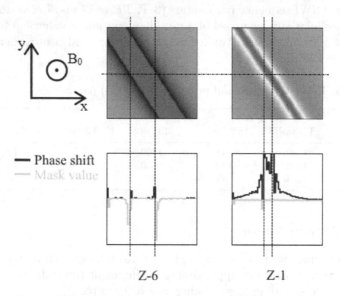

Fig. 4. Phase values with corresponding mask profiles gathered along X axis for two slices along B_0 direction and passing through the center of a voxel

Comparison of the number of mask multiplications indicates remarkable improvement of contrast between venous vessel and the surroundings (see Fig. 5), clearly exposing vessel walls. With further increase of the number of multiplications, contrast becomes stronger leading to overestimation of vessel dimensions and fake wall inside the venous vessel close to the region boundary. Four multiplications provided visually the best trade-off between contrast and distortions.

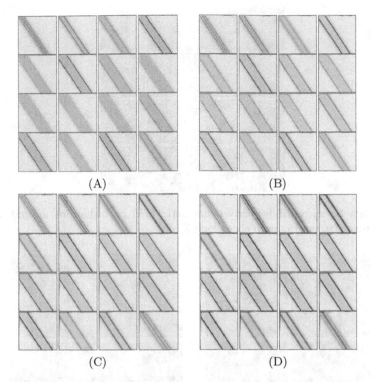

(A)   (B)

(C)   (D)

Fig. 5. Comparison of images using gradient echo (A) and SWI protocols: using 4 (B), 8 (C) and 16 (D) multiplications

3.2   Brain Blood Carrying Tumor

Another structure of well defined influence on magnetic field distribution is sphere, which can be used to model blood carrying tumor. In this case simulation was performed for $0.125 \times 0.125 \times 0.125$ mm voxel size, whereas magnetic field perturbations were estimated over 512 samples per voxel, as in the previous case. MRI signal has been biased with Gaussian noise of standard deviation of $\sigma = 1.2 \cdot 10^{-3}$ in each channel separately.

Despite tiny dimensions of the investigated object and no perturbations inside of it, the sphere is clearly visible itself due to the external field alterations, being both negative in the plane perpendicular to the direction of main magnetic field and positive in the plain containing vector of main magnetic field (Fig. 6).

During phase image post-processing triangular mask was applied. This allowed to enhance contrast on the basis of both positive and negative phase shifts, resulting in almost uniform dark interior of a tumor. In order to remove noise, before further processing both magnitude and phase components were processed with 3×3 median filter for each slice. As a result (Fig. 7), strong blurring of the magnitude image can be noticed, whereas the phase one remains almost intact, allowing for noise removal without losing phase information, hence the great benefit of susceptibility weighted imaging technique.

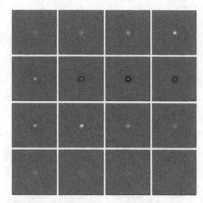

Fig. 6. Magnetic susceptibility driven magnetic field perturbations around a blood carrying tumor (sphere) in each slice along Z axis

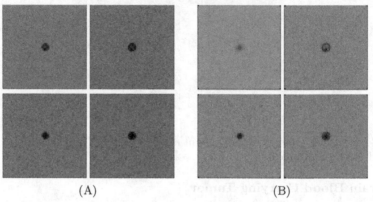

(A)   (B)

Fig. 7. SWI images obtained with minimum intensity projection over 16 slices under 3 T main magnetic field using triangular mask with 0, 1, 4, 8 multiplications and noise of $\sigma = 1.2 \cdot 10^{-3}$ without (A) and with 3×3 median filter (B)

4   Summary

The proposed system allows for SWI protocol simulation. It accounts for local field perturbations due to the susceptibility distribution and takes advantage of subvoxel field estimation to evaluate faster signal decay known as T2* relaxation.

Visual resemblance of synthetic images comprising known geometries indicates correctness of the obtained results. However, a comparison between the real phantom and the outcome of proposed simulator of some simple object should be evaluated in order to verify its operation.

Intravoxel field perturbations introduce explicit difference into an MR image. Phase shifts on tissue boundaries leads to the enhancement of the image contrast. Moreover, as susceptibility driven magnetic field perturbations occur not only in space occupied by an object but also in its surroundings, SWI technique allows to reveal tiny structures, even of subvoxel dimensions. Therefore, simulation of susceptibility based effects should cover perturbations not only on the voxel-but also subvoxel-level. The proposed algorithm of T2* effect estimation is based on the assumption that magnetization vector after RF pulse is approximately constant over the voxel, which is not true when strong field perturbations are present inside of it. Under such circumstances, evolution of magnetization vector evaluated over denser grid than it comes from the image resolution may lead to more realistic results.

Acknowledgments. This paper was supported by the Polish National Science Centre under grant no. 2013/08/M/ST7/00943.

References

1. Haacke, E.M., Reichenbach, J.R. (eds.): Susceptibility Weighted Imaging in MRI: basic Concepts and Clinical Applications. Wiley-Blackwell, New Jersey (2011)
2. Klepaczko, A., Kociński, M., Materka, A.: Quantitative description of 3D vascularity images: texture-based approach and its verification through cluster analysis. Pattern Analysis and Applications 14(4), 415–424 (2011)
3. Bittoun, J., Tacquin, J., Sauzade, M.: A computer algorithm for the simulation of any nuclear magnetic resonance (NMR) imaging method. J. Magn. Reson. Imaging 3, 363–376 (1984)
4. Kwan, R.S., Evans, A., Pike, G.: MRI simulation-based evaluation of image-processing and classification methods. IEEE Transactions on Medical Imaging 18(11), 1085–1097 (1999)
5. Yoder, D.A., Zhao, Y., Paschal, C.B., Fitzpatric, J.M.: MRI simulator with object-specific field map calculations. Magnetic Resonance Imaging 22, 315–328 (2004)
6. Benoit-Cattin, H., Collewet, G., Belaroussi, B., Saint-Jalmes, H., Odet, C.: The SIMRI project: a versatile and interactive MRI simulator. Journal of Magnetic Resonance 173, 97–115 (2005)
7. Stoecker, T., Vahedipour, K., Pflugfelder, D., Shah, N.J.: High-performance computing mri simulations. Magnetic Resonance in Medicine 64(1), 186–193 (2010)
8. Klepaczko, A., Szczypiński, P., Dwojakowski, G., Strzelecki, M., Materka, A.: Computer simulation of magnetic resonance angiography imaging: Model description and validation. PLoS ONE 9(4), e93689 (2014)
9. Haacke, E.M., Brown, R.W., Thompson, M.R., Venkatesan, R.: Magnetic resonance imaging: physical principles and sequence design. Wiely-Loss, New York (1999)
10. Schenck, J.: The role of magnetic susceptibility in magnetic resonance imaging: MRI magnetic compatibility of the first and second kinds. Med. Phys. 23, 815–850 (1996)
11. Liang, Z.P., Lauterbur, P.C.: Principles of Magnetic Resonance Imaging: A Signal Processing Perspective. IEEE Press, New York (2000)

SETh: The Method for Long-Term Object Tracking

Karol Jedrasiak[1], Mariusz Andrzejczak[2], and Aleksander Nawrat[1]

[1] Institute of Automatic Control, Silesian University of Technology
Akademicka 16, 44-100 Gliwice, Poland
[2] Ośrodek Badawczo-Rozwojowy Urządzeń Mechanicznych "OBRUM" sp. z o.o.
ul. Toszecka 102, 44-117 Gliwice, Poland
{karol.jedrasiak}@polsl.pl

Abstract. The article presents a novel long-term object tracking method called SETh. It is an adaptive tracking by detection method which allows near real-time tracking within challenging sequences. The algorithm consists of three stages: detection, verification and learning. In order to measure the performance of the method a video data set consisting of more than a hundred videos was created and manually labelled by a human. Quality of the tracking by SETh was compared against five state-of-the-art methods. The presented method achieved results comparable and mostly exceeding the existing methods, which proves its capability for real life applications like e.g. vision-based control of UAVs.

Keywords: object tracking, long-term tracking, adaptive, image processing.

1 Introduction

The modern world is full of cameras placed in supermarkets, banks, or on the streets. Each of these cameras record movies in the form of a compressed image sequence. A huge number of recorded information makes it impossible to be verified by human. Therefore there is a need for an automatic method of analysis of the sequences. One of the main issues associated with this problem is the problem of tracking objects in image sequences. For a human it is considered a simple task, but for machine it is rather a complicated process because of the need for the extraction of the data from the image.

Currently, algorithms for tracking objects of interest between the individual frames have reached a certain level of maturity allowing accurate tracking of the objects under the assumption that the objects does not change its shape and appearance. Such restrictions are not met in real scenarios therefore the existing algorithms for long-term tracking are disappointing. Changes in the appearance of the tracked object requires a certain way of updating detection module to the new conditions. Development of a new method for long-term objects tracking is motivated by the fact that less than one percent of the recorded surveillance video is ever watched [1,2]. The use of automated analysis of recorded material

L.J. Chmielewski et al. (Eds.): ICCVG 2014, LNCS 8671, pp. 302–315, 2014.

is particularly important in the crises situations, such as terrorist attacks. For example, a review of video material of bombings in Dubai in 2010 by a human lasted for several weeks, where the automatic analysis of materials of attack in Boston lasted only three days. The article presents a novel object tracking method which is computationally straightforward and performs in near real-time. It consists of three consecutive phases: detection, verification and learning in a way inspired by semi-supervised methods. The proposed approach and the developed algorithms were verified using a comprehensive set of prepared test sequences consisting of both synthetic and real scenes.

2 Literature Review

Term "method for object tracking" is defined as any method aimed to estimate the trajectory of a moving object being tracked in a sequence of images. The task of the tracker is to assign consistent labels to the tracked object in a sequence of consecutive frames [3]. Object tracking is, however, complex, e.g. due to the following problems [4]: the loss of information caused by projection of the 3D world on a 2D one; noise in the images; complex motion of objects; loose or articulated nature of the shape of objects; partial or complete occlusion of the tracked object; complicated shape of objects; changes in scene illumination; time constraints related to the real-time processing.

Visual tracking is considered one of the fundamental problems in computer vision. It is used in e.g. vision surveillance, human-computer interactions, navigation of unmanned objects, or issues related to the expanded reality [5]. Some tracking applications assume that the tracked object is known in advance, which allows to use the knowledge during the process of designing the tracking method. However, majority of the methods allows to track any object determined during the algorithm work time [4].

Below are presented some of the object tracking methods considered as the state-of-the-art reference methods. One of the most popular algorithms for tracking of the visual features is the algorithm called the Lukas-Kanade Tracker (KLT) [6]. The algorithm allows tracking features between subsequent images of the sequence. KLT can be divided into two main phases: detection of features and tracking. Detection of characteristic points is usually implemented using the autocorrelation method, e.g. Harris corner detector. Localization of feature points is found by identifying for each of the points the translation vector that minimizes the difference between the measure computed within a rectangular window centered around analyzed in pixels.

TLD method [7] (*Tracking-Learning-Detection*) is able to unequivocal state whether the defined in the first frame of a sequence tracked object is within the cam-era view or not. TLD method assumes that the long-term tracking of objects should consist of three phases: tracking, learning and detection. Tracking is realized by the Median-flow-tracker [8]. The task of the detection is independent of the tracking. NCC was used for the purpose. The detector can commit two types of errors: false positive and false negative. The task of the learning element is the observation of the tracker and detector and estimation on the basis error of detection and generation of new training samples in order to reduce the impact of the identified errors in the future.

FRAGtrack algorithm [9] assumes that the tracked object is represented by multiple image fragments. Each fragment vote regarding the probable position and the scale level of the tracked object by comparing the histogram of their area to the histogram of the tracked object from the first frame. The approach based on voting allows to track during partial occlusion or changes in pose of the tracked object. The authors emphasize that the proposed method is characterized by the constant computational complexity regardless of the size of the object being tracked.

VTD tracking method [4] according to the authors allows to track objects at the same time changing the appearance and character of the movement. The solution assumes the division of tracking tasks in two stages: defining the model of observa-tion and tracking its movement. Sparse PCA is calculated on a set of basic patterns of motion and appearance features. Tracking is also composed of a number of tracking compound elements where each of them realize tracking of different type of object changes. Results returned by tracking elements are further combined into one by usage of IMCMC (*Interactive Markov Chain Monte Carlo*).

The authors in [10] note that the tracking methods based on detection are largely based on a classifier, which task is to distinguish an object from its background. Even small errors in tracking element can cause the erroneous determination of training samples of the classifier and in the result cause a drift of the solution. The authors present the solution where they use the method called MIL Track (*Multiple Instance Learning Tracking*) instead of the typical supervised learning.

3   SETh

Among many groups of different methods of tracking one of the most convenient for the user with simultaneously some of the best tracking results is the group of tracking by detection [11, 12]. Typically, the object of interest is visible in the frame for considerable amount of time. However, there is a high probability that in a non-zero time the object is outside the view of the camera. It is assumed that in the first frame of a sequence a rectangular area of interest for tracked object is selected and the aim of the tracking algorithm is to detect the object of interest in successive frames of a sequence or to specify that the object is not visible in the image. Stream processing is done frame by frame, and the process time can be infinitely long. Thus defined tracking is known as long-term tracking [7]. Long-term tracking is difficult due to, e.g. problem of determining whether an object is within the field of view of the camera. This problem belongs to the complex ones, as the tracked object at that time could change the position, orientation, or appearance, therefore its appearance known from the first frame of the sequence may become obsolete [13]. As another important problem we can identify resistance of the tracking algorithm to changes in a camera position, lighting conditions, partial and total occlusion and moving background and finally, reducing the time of processing. The long-term tracking is widely considered as a combination of two phases: tracking and detection [7].

The proposed algorithm is derived from the family of methods of tracking by de-tection, generalized by updating the model of both tracked object and its closest sur-roundings. The developed algorithm for long-term tracking, SETh, is based on many years of experience and researches of the author [14, 15, 16].

The algorithm is initialized, and then executed sequentially in three successive phases: detection, verification, and learning. SETh algorithm is used to determine the position of the object being tracked or unequivocal statement that the object is not visible in the image. The algorithm allows tracking in a manner inspired by the semi-supervised methods, i.e., the operator in the first frame to track of the sequence indi-cates the area of interest containing the object to be tracked. In subsequent frames of the sequence the task of the algorithm is to track the position of the object without any additional information.

Fig. 1. Algorithm overview schema

During the detection step the goal is to detect features in the image, and then assign them to the appropriate labels: object, background or indeterminate features. The result of this step are sets: Θ – features of the object, Ω – features of the background and Υ – unrecognized features so far.

An important element of the presented algorithm is a method for detection of features. The ideal detector is defined as possibly computationally simple method for finding the areas of the image possible to detect reproducibly regardless of the change in the point of view of the camera and at the same time resistant to all possible types of transformation. Currently, the closest to the prescribed requirements and with shortest computation time is BRISK detector [17]. Therefore, it was decided to use it as an element of the proposed long-term tracking algorithm. BRISK is insensitive to scaling and rotation due to the addition of local maxima search step not only in image space, but also the in the scale space.

Detected features have to be described by a descriptor that allows them to be uniquely compared. Description of the detected features should provide plenty uniqueness of the description, be computed efficiently and allows to timely and accurately compare the descriptor with a large set of data. All these advantages are met by FREAK descriptor described in [18]. FREAK was created based on the inspiration of information processes occurring in the human retina. FREAK descriptor is an efficient way to describe the feature by a cascade of binary string numbers calculated on the basis of differences in brightness in the area similar to the human retina sampling area. The sampling pattern which is used is circular and the points closer to the center have a higher density distribution. The density of occurrence decreases exponentially with the distance from the center of the feature which is described. Binary string of FREAK descriptor F (1) is a one-bit sequence coding differences in Gaussian function (DoG):

$$F = \sum_{0 \leqslant a \leqslant N} 2^a T(P_a), \tag{1}$$

$$T(P_a) = \begin{cases} 1, & (I(P_a^{r_1})) > 0, \\ 0, & otherwise, \end{cases} \tag{2}$$

where P_a is a pair of receptive fields, and N is the desired length of the descriptor, $I(P_a^{r_1})$ is a smooth function of a Gaussian brightness value of the first pair of reception field P_a. Combinations of several tens of pairs of fields result in the thousands of possible pairs of which 512 are selected by the decorrelation.

According to the scheme of the algorithm detected and described features have to be assigned to Θ, Ω and Υ sets on the basis of comparisons with the features of the object from the previous frame of the tracked object Θ' and the background Ω'.

The main objective of the verification phase is the selection of the correct position of the object, from the proposed by the stage of detection, and to determine the certainty level m_F. Simplified schema of the verification phase is shown in fig. 2.

Features belonging to a group with confidence level above the thresholds γ_1 and γ_2 are passed on to the stage of learning which update the model for binary classification of features between the object and the background. If there were not enough features detected during the detection phase, an alternative calculations are made in order to face the problem.

The detected features are labeled as object contained in the set Θ may indicate multiple localizations of the object being tracked. The observed scene may contain more than one object identical to the tracked. In addition, the detected characteristic points in the face of noise can be detected incorrectly. For this reason, the detection and matching of characteristic points is insufficient to determine the correct position of the object.

It is therefore required to specify unknown number of areas in a way resistance to noise and outliers. It is assumed that incorrect matches are distant from each other in Euclidean distance sense. For the purpose an unsupervised learning method DBSCAN was used [19]. The following parameter values were chosen: $Min_{pts} = 3$, because a group of three points can be described by the minimal area rectangle; $E_{ps} = 61$, as suggested in a research paper of FLIR company [20], where measured the minimal number of pixels sufficient for recognition of a person from the distance of 45 meters. Discovered N groups g in a set Θ were labeled Θ_{tym}. The tracked object is labeled using Feret box with a center in a point $c(x, y)$ in a first frame of sequence, so in each successive frame the detected

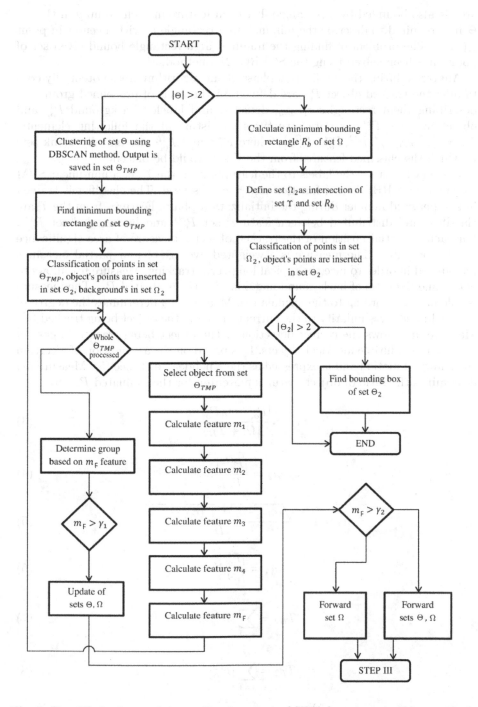

Fig. 2. Simplified schema of the verification stage of SETh long-term tracking method

area is also bounded by a rectangle. For each feature in each group g in the set Θ it is required to describe the minimal area rectangle r_i with a center in point $c_i(x, y)$. The problem of finding the minimal area rectangle bound given set of points has been solved using the SGPRC [21] method.

Analyzed during the verification phase of the algorithm areas potentially containing the tracked object P_{o_i} are defined on the basis of predefined groups g_i, describing them rectangles r_i, r_{ib}, detected and labeled background $P_{o_i}^{\Omega}$ and object features $P_{o_i}^{\Theta}$, as data structures consisting of the following elements: $P_{o_i} = \{r_i, r_{ib}, P_{o_i}^{\Theta}, P_{o_i}^{\Omega}, P_{o_i}^{\Theta_2}, P_{o_i}^{\Omega_2}\}$, where $P_{o_i}^{\Theta_2}$ and $P_{o_i}^{\Omega_2}$ are initially blank sets in which the classified features from the Υ set would be placed.

In order to attach the labels to the features from the Υ set a non-linear SVM classifier with RBF kernel function and $\gamma = 3$ is used. The classifier is trained in a supervised manner during the initialization phase. Features from the Υ are classified and distributed between features set $P_{o_i}^{\Theta_2}$ and background set $P_{o_i}^{\Omega_2}$. For each potential position of the tracked object a measure of area significance m_F is computed. The measure is a weighted average of four partial measures introduced in order to face the typical long-term tracking. Measure m_1 allows to determine the ratio of background matching for the evaluated P_{o_i}. The measure is calculated according to the formula (3). Measure m_2 determines the degree of the evaluated P_{o_i} similarity to the current model of the object being tracked (4). Measure m_3 allows the correct detection of the object being tracked in case of detection of multiple identical objects. It is based on the assumption of a certain continuity of motion and is expressed as the Euclidean distance (5). Measure m_4 determines the ratio of object features matching for the evaluated P_{o_i} (6).

$$m_1 = \frac{|P_{o_i}^{\Omega}| + ||P_{o_i}^{\Omega_2}|}{|\Omega| + T_{B2}}, \tag{3}$$

$$m_2 = \frac{|P_{o_i}^{\Theta_2}|}{T_{T2}}, \tag{4}$$

$$m_3 = 1 - \frac{\sqrt{(c_{ix} - c_x)^2 + (c_{iy} - c_y)^2}}{L}, \tag{5}$$

$$m_4 = \frac{|P_{o_i}^{\Theta}|}{|\Theta|}, \tag{6}$$

$$T_{B2} = \sum_{i=1}^{N} |P_{o_i}^{\Omega_2}|, \tag{7}$$

$$T_{T2} = \sum_{i=1}^{N} |P_{o_i}^{\Theta_2}|, \tag{8}$$

$$L = \sum_{i=1}^{N} \sqrt{(c_{ix} - x_x)^2 + (x_{iy} - c_y)^2}. \tag{9}$$

The values of all measurements were normalized to a closed interval from zero to one. For this purpose the following auxiliary variables (7, 8, 9) were introduced. The final measure m_F is calculated in accordance to the following formula: $m_F = \alpha m_1 + \beta m_2 + \gamma m_3 + \delta m_4$, where $\alpha, \beta, \gamma, \delta$ are the weight coefficients of each partial measure. In the study the following coefficient values were used: $\alpha = 0.3, \beta = 0.1, \gamma = 0.1, \delta = 0.5$. The values α and δ were as greater in order to emphasize the significance of the feature descriptors matching with respect to additional heuristics.

The tracked object is considered to be the potential object P_{o_i} characterized by the highest value of the final measure m_F. If the value of the final measurement is above the cut-off γ_1 we assume that one can update the sets of object Θ' and background Ω' features. Experimentally determined value $\gamma_1 = 0.3$. In addition, it is recognized that above this cut-off background features are further passed to the learning phase of the algorithm. The significance level m_F above the cut-off γ_2 is considered reliably and above it all the object and background features are further passed to the learning phase of the algorithm. Experimentally determined value of γ_2 is 0.7.

Alternatively, if there are no more than two features in the set Θ we suggest to conduct countermeasure based on the background features matching. The procedure is based on the observation that a moving object on the stage is not fully independent. Its presence affects the other elements of the scene by changing the reflection of light, generating shadows, shielding some area from rain, etc. Classically this phenomenon is seen as negative, hindering the process of object tracking. Here however, we assume that there is the tracked object visible in the image, however due to dynamic change of appearance the matching process didnt succeed but there is still a possibility that the object is within the best matched background area of interest. In order to point out the localization, we classify the features within the matched area and treat the result as a temporary good hint.

The long-term tracking requires updating a representation of the object being tracked in order to ensure its quality in the face of changes occurring in appearance of the object. Goal of the learning phase is to iteratively build a model representation of the tracked object based on consecutive frames of the video stream. Features within Θ' and Ω' sets selected during verification phase are used to teach nonlinear kernel SVM classifier with RBF kernel with γ selected as three.

4   Tests

An important problem from the point of view of the effectiveness of tracking algorithms is the method for evaluating the acquired results. There are applications of both the qualitative and quantitative analysis. The following measures were inspired by the known from the literature measures [7, 22, 23]. Used measures are based on the sequence length L, determined by the human expert reference ground truth labeled R_G, area of interest computed by the tracking method labeled R_W, the number of correct indications τ_P, such frames as the value $\epsilon_{OR} > 50\%$, the total number of indications labeled τ. There is used a measure of compliance called overlap ratio defined as the weighted ratio between the R_W and R_G areas called ε_{OR} (10), measure of the ratio of the number of correct indications to the length of the sequence is denoted by ε_{SR} (11), measure of the location error calculated as the Euclidean distance between the center of the R_W and R_G denoted by ε_{LO} (12), average error value computed as an arithmetic mean of localization error, labeled as ε_{ALO} (13).

$$\varepsilon_{OR} = 2\frac{|R_G \cap R_W|}{|R_G| + |R_W|}, \tag{10}$$

$$\varepsilon_{SR} = \frac{\tau_P}{L}, \tag{11}$$

$$\varepsilon_{LO} = sqrt(R_{Gx} - R_{Wx})^2 + (R_{Gy} - R_{Wy})^2, \tag{12}$$

$$\varepsilon_{ALO} = \frac{1}{L}\sum_{i=1}^{L}\varepsilon_{LO_i}. \tag{13}$$

Acquired results by the proposed long-term tracking method SETh were compared against reference methods. For comparisons the publicly available for research purposes implementations of the selected methods were used. There were five state-of-the-art reference methods selected for comparison: Lukas Kanade Tracker, labeled in results as KLT; Tracking-Learning-Detection, labeled in results as TLD; FRAGTrack, labeled in results as FRAG; Visual Tracking Decomposition, labeled in results as VTD; Multiple Instance Learning Tracking, labeled in results as MIL Track.

Due to the limitations of length of the article only selected representative test re-sults are presented from a set of total 102 test sequences. There have been hand annotated over 25'500 frames. All sequences are documented and the data set has been made available to the public [24].

The calculations were performed on a personal computer with an Intel Core i5 2.4 GHz, 8GB RAM, graphics card NVIDIA GeForce GT 525 M and 64-bit operating system Windows 7 Professional.

The acquired results of comparison of tracking quality of SETh and reference state-of-the-art method are presented in fig. 3. It can be observed that presented SETh method was able to track the object during the whole sequence. It is worth to mention that other methods lost their target and had problems with tracking reinitialization. Computed measures (fig. 4) present that both the highest localization precision and the lowest average error were scored by presented SETh method. Second result is taken by VTD and surprisingly the last place was reserved for TLD method.

In the fig. 5. visual results of object tracking during car driving are presented. The camera was attached to the head of the driver (*glasses*). It can be observed that all tracking methods except the proposed SETh and TLD methods failed.

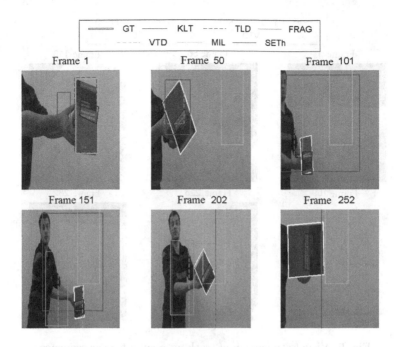

Fig. 3. Visual comparison of tracking results for rts sequence

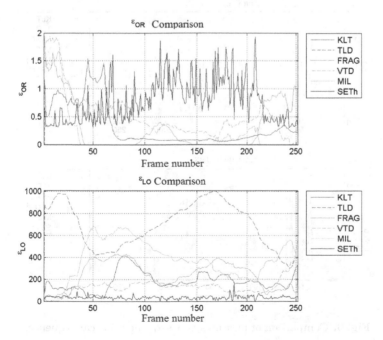

Fig. 4. Comparison of measures test sequences for rts sequence

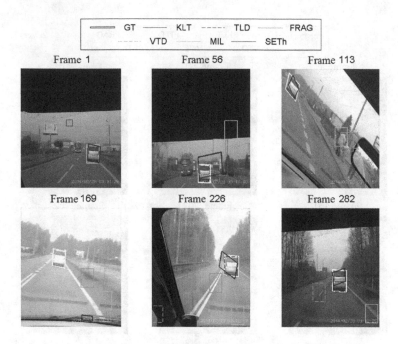

Fig. 5. Visual comparison of tracking results for car sequence

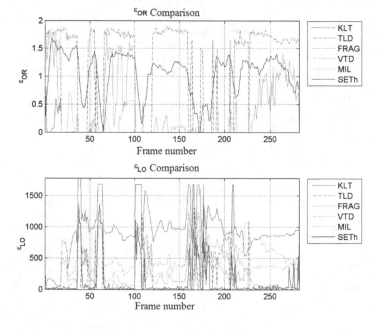

Fig. 6. Comparison of measures test sequences for car sequence.

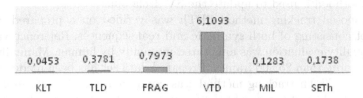

Fig. 7. Column performance comparison of the selected state-of-the-art tracking methods

It is worth to notice that the presented SETh method is invariant to rotation and scale. However, it is vulnerable to low contrast and visible in the frame 169. It can be observed that regardless the short error in tracking the proposed method was able to correctly reinitialize tracking.

Computed measures for the car sequence are presented in the fig. 6. It can be no-ticed that the best results as supposed were acquired by SETh and TLD methods, which are able to reinitialize tracking after failure.

The proposed SETh method was compared in terms of computation time against the five reference state-of-the-art methods. The computed average time of processing is presented in the fig. 7. KLT method was able to compute its output in real-time without any further optimizations. The rest of the methods achieved similar results in the range starting from 100 ms to 1000 ms. Indisputably the worst time of computa-tion, which was over 6000 ms was scored by VTD method. It is worth to mention that video sequences used for measurements were 1280x720 pixels.

5   Conclusions

The article presents a novel method for long-term object tracking named SETh. The solution performs in a near real-time consecutive phases: detection, verifi-cation and learning. The proposed tracking method begins with the detection of visual fea-tures using BRISK detector and describing them using FREAK descriptor. The described features are compared with a set of known features of the object of interest and then clustered by an unsupervised method in order to determine the amount and areas potentially containing the object. Groups of features labeled as object are used to determine the region of interest - the potential area of object which surroundings are compared against the features labeled as background. Utilization during tracking not only objects features but background features as well, allows to increase the quality of tracking of objects characterized by changeable appearance. The object or background labels are attached to unspecified labels within the potential object's area using binary nonlinear SVM. For each potential object final measure consisting of four par-tial measures is computed. Final measurement value is double thresholded. The tracked object is assumed to be a potential object characterized by a highest value of final measure. The feature points within selected tracked object's area and neighborhood is used to update the SVM classifier.

The proposed tracking method SETh was verified on a prepared comprehensive set consisting of both synthetic and real sequences. Reference value for tracking quality evaluation was annotated manually by human. Manually annotated were more than 25'500 frames. Prepared data set has been made available to the public. SETh tracking method was compared with five state-of-the-art methods and achieved comparable or superior results, suggesting that it is possible to apply it in real-life applications e.g. visual-based control of UAVs [25] or tracking pedestrians [26].

Acknowledgement. This work has been supported by Applied Research Programme of the National Centre for Research and Development as a project ID 178438 path A – Costume for acquisition of human movement based on IMU sensors with collection, visualization and data analysis software.

References

1. Pritch, A.Y., Ratovitch, S., Hendel, A., Peleg, S.: Clustered Synopsis of Surveillance Video. In: Sixth IEEE International Conference on Advanced Video and Signal Based Surveillance. IEEE (2009)
2. Pritch, Y., Rav-Acha, A., Peleg, S.: Video Synopsis. The Hebrew University of Jerusalem
3. Yilmaz, A., Li, X., Shah, M.: Contour based object tracking with occlusion handling in video acquired using mobile cameras. IEEE Trans. Patt. Analy. Mach. Intell. 26(11), 1531–1536 (2004)
4. Kwon, J., Lee, K.M.: Visual tracking decomposition. In: Computer Vision and Pattern Recognition (CVPR) (2010)
5. Wu, A.: Towards Linear-Time Incremental Structure from Motion. In: IEEE International Conference on 3D Vision, pp. 127–134 (2013)
6. Tomasi, C., Kanade, T.: Detection and Tracking of Point Features. Carnegie Mellon University Technical Report CMU-CS-91-132 (1991)
7. Kalal, Z., Mikolajczyk, K., Matas, J.: Tracking-learning-detection. IEEE Transactions on Pattern Analysis and Machine Intelligence 34, 1409–1422 (2012)
8. Kalal, Z., MikolajczykK., M.J.: Forward-Backward Error: Automatic Detection of Tracking Failures. In: International Conference on Pattern Recognition, pp. 23–26 (2010)
9. Adam, A., Rivlin, E., Shimshoni, I.: Robust fragments-based tracking using the integral histogram. In: 2006 IEEE Computer Society Conference on Computer Vision and Pattern Recognition, vol. 1 (2006)
10. Babenko, B., Yang, M.H., Belongie, S.: Robust object tracking with online multiple instance learning. IEEE Transactions on Pattern Analysis and Machine Intelligence 33(8), 1619–1632 (2011)
11. Breitenstein, M.D., Reichlin, F., Leibe, B., Koller-Meier, E., Gool, L.V.: Robust Tracking-by-Detection Using a Detector Confidence Particle Filter. In: Proc. IEEE 12th Intl Conf. Computer Vision (2009)
12. Grabner, H., Bischof, H.: On-line boosting and vision. In: CVPR (2006)

13. Grabner, H., Leistner, C., Bischof, H.: Semi-Supervised On-Line Boosting for Robust Tracking. In: Forsyth, D., Torr, P., Zisserman, A. (eds.) ECCV 2008, Part I. LNCS, vol. 5302, pp. 234–247. Springer, Heidelberg (2008)
14. Jedrasiak, K., Nawrat, A.: Fast color recognition algorithm for robotics. Problemy Eksploatacji, Maintenance Problems (Quarterly), 69–76 (2008)
15. Nawrat, A., Jedrasiak, K.: SETh system spatio-temporal object tracking using combined color and motion feature. Advanced robotics, control and advanced manufacturing systems. In: Proceedings of the 9th WSEAS International Conference on Robotics, Control and Manufacturing Technology (ROCOM 2009), pp. 67–72 (2009)
16. Jędrasiak, K., Nawrat, A.: Image recognition technique for unmanned aerial vehicles. In: Bolc, L., Kulikowski, J.L., Wojciechowski, K. (eds.) ICCVG 2008. LNCS, vol. 5337, pp. 391–399. Springer, Heidelberg (2009)
17. Leutenegger, S., Chli, M., Siegwart, R.: Brisk: Binary robust invariant scalable keypoints. In: ICCV 2011, pp. 2548–2555 (2010)
18. Alahi, A., Ortiz, R., Vandergheynst, P.: FREAK: Fast Retina Keypoint. In: IEEE Conference on Computer Vision and Pattern Recognition (2012)
19. Ester, M., Kriegel, H.P., Sander, J., Xu, X.: A Density-Based Algorithm for Discovering Clusters in Large Spatial Databases with Noise. In: Proceedings of the 2nd International Conference on Knowledge Discovery and Data Mining (KDD 1996), pp. 226–231 (1996)
20. FLIR, http://www.flir.com/PL (access on March 5, 2014)
21. Toussaint, G.T.: Solving geometric problems with the rotating calipers. Proc. IEEE Melecon 83, A10 (1983)
22. Oron, S., Bar-Hillel, A., Levi, D., Avidan, S.: Locally Orderless Tracking. In: IEEE Conference on Computer Vision and Pattern Recognition (CVPR) (2012)
23. Morzy, T.: Eksploracja Danych Metody i Algorytmy. Wydawnictwo Naukowe PWN, Warszawa (2013)
24. Results, https://www.dropbox.com/sh/v705ac32e8006z7/s1ezUqplcE
25. Iwaneczko, P., Jędrasiak, K., Daniec, K., Nawrat, A.: A Prototype of Unmanned Aerial Vehicle for Image Acquisition. In: Bolc, L., Tadeusiewicz, R., Chmielewski, L.J., Wojciechowski, K. (eds.) ICCVG 2012. LNCS, vol. 7594, pp. 87–94. Springer, Heidelberg (2012)
26. Jędrasiak, K., Nawrat, A., Daniec, K., Koteras, R., Mikulski, M., Grzejszczak, T.: A Prototype Device for Concealed Weapon Detection Using IR and CMOS Cameras Fast Image Fusion. In: Bolc, L., Tadeusiewicz, R., Chmielewski, L.J., Wojciechowski, K. (eds.) ICCVG 2012. LNCS, vol. 7594, pp. 423–432. Springer, Heidelberg (2012)

Human Activity Interpretation Using Evenly Distributed Points on the Human Hull

Łukasz Kamiński, Krzysztof Kowalak,
Paweł Gardziński, and Sławomir Maćkowiak

Poznań University of Technology, Poland
{lkaminski,kkowalak,pgardzinski,smack}@multimedia.edu.pl
http://www.multimedia.edu.pl

Abstract. In this paper, a human activity recognition system which automatically detects human behaviors in video is presented. The solution presented in this paper uses a directed graphical model with proposed by the authors Evenly Distributed Points (EDP) method. The experimental results prove efficient representation of the human activity and high score of recognition.

1 Introduction

Behavior understanding and activity recognition using visual surveillance involves the most advanced and complex research in the field of image processing, computer vision and artificial intelligence. The system developed at Poznań University of Technology exploited a directed graphical model based on propagation nets, a subset of dynamic Bayesian networks approaches, to model the behaviors together with Evenly Distributed Points (EDP) method.

There are various representations commonly used for activity understanding, including object-based features, pixel-based features and other feature representations. Object-based representation constructs a set of features for each object in a video based on an assumption that individual objects can be segmented reasonably well for event reasoning. These features include trajectory or blob-level descriptors such as bounding box and shape. Among these features, a trajectory-based feature is commonly employed to represent the motion history of a target in a scene [3,4].

Following the paradigm of object-based representation, there are also attempts to exploit multiple abstract levels of features in a unified framework. For example, Park and Trivedi [5] introduce a framework that switches between trajectory-based features (e.g. velocity and position) and blob-based features (e.g. aspect ratio of bounding box and height) based on the visual quality of detected objects. The system proposed by Poznań University of Technology belongs to the above mentioned category of representation and is a subset of Bayesian networks [2,15]. In the proposed solution, the characteristic features of a human body placed on the human hull and the information about tracking these points are combined together.

L.J. Chmielewski et al. (Eds.): ICCVG 2014, LNCS 8671, pp. 316–323, 2014.

Detailed review of other approaches such as Petri nets, syntactic approaches or rule-based approaches can be found in a survey by Turaga et al. [1].

This paper is divided into 4 main sections. Section 2 presents the behavior description and provides detailed explanation on the Evenly Distributed Points on the human hull. Section 3 presents behavior testing system and explains required blocks of video processing. Section 4 presents the assumptions of the experiments and achieved results for exemplary behavior that is a *call for help*.

2 Behavior Description

Let us consider a system based on a single stationary camera that records a scene. Events that happen in that scene can be interpreted (on the frame level) as a sequence of states in time (Fig. 1). Subsequently, those states can be described using the entire picture captured by the camera. However, that amount of information is not necessary, therefore feature extraction techniques are recommended. SIFT (Scale Invariant Feature Transform), Haar-like features and HOG (Histogram of Oriented Gradients) [6] belong to the most popular techniques for feature detection and description. Nevertheless, results shown in the latter paragraph prove that method described in this paper gives equally good results as the above mentioned methods and requires less computational effort. Proposed approach creates key body points on a human hull that can be used to detect human behavior as well.

The behavior of a person can be described by a set of trajectories of characteristic points, as shown in Fig. 2. A set of characteristic points at a given time defines a pose. A set of poses defined for consecutive time points or a set of time vectors for individual points forms a descriptor. Therefore, there are two possible ways to describe a behavior:

- Time-cut interpreted as a sequence of poses in time,
- Space-cut interpreted as a set of trajectories of tracked characteristic points.

In this paper we employ the Time-cut interpretation which correlates to HMM as a representation model.

The set of points to define a pose may have different configuration for different types of behavior to be detected. In other words, for each type of behavior, a

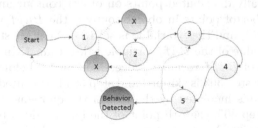

Fig. 1. Behavior as a sequence of poses (states)

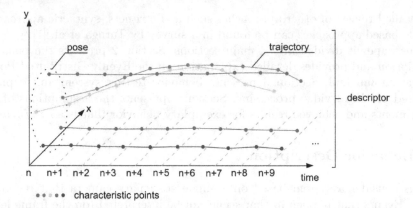

Fig. 2. Example of a behavior as a set of poses, characteristic points form trajectories in time. Trajectory acquired from $Calling for help$ behavior.

set of points is generated having a configuration different from the set of points for another type of behavior. For consecutive frames, the positions of points belonging to the Time-cut set are traced and form poses.

The method of selection of points proposed by the authors is called Evenly Distributed Points (EDP). Proposed approach is based on selection of evenly spread, arbitrary number of points from the hull. This kind of approach allows for gradual selection of the level of hull mapping. The method has been depicted in Fig. 3, wherein the following references refer to:

- *Step*- step of selection of consecutive points;
- *Buff*- a buffer storing reminder of a division in order to minimize an error caused by calculations on integer numbers. It is a case when the *Step* is not an integer;
- *rest(lPktKont/lPkt)*- a function calculating a reminder of a division.

The selected hull points define a pose descriptor of the hull (typically of a silhouette of a person) in a given video frame and are buffered in an output vector as shown in Fig. 3.

More specifically, the procedure in Fig. 3 starts from step 301, where the *Step* variable is set as value of *lPktKont/lPkt*, wherein *lPkt* denotes chosen number of equally distributed points on object contour and *lPktKont* denotes a total number of points in object contour, the *Buff* variable is set to *rest(lPktKont/lPkt)* and the i variable is set to 0. Next, at step 302, it is verified whether the value of the *Buff* variable is less than 1. In case it is not, at step 303 the value of *Buff* variable is decreased by 1.0 before moving to step 304. Otherwise, the step 303 is skipped and step 304 is executed where the value of the Buff variable is increased by the rest of the quotient (*lPktKont/lPkt*). Subsequently, at step 305, the i-th point of the hull is added to an output vector as a selected point. Next, at step 306, the variable i is set to a value of

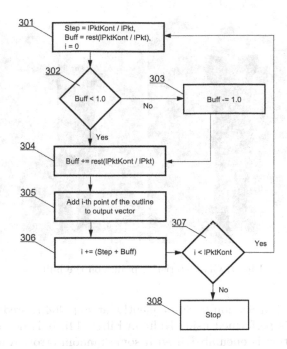

Fig. 3. Evenly Distributed Points - algorithm block diagram

$Step + Buff$. Next, it is verified 307 whether i is lower that $lPktKont$ and in case it is the process returns to step 301 in order to process the next point or otherwise the procedure ends at step 308.

3   Behavior Detection System

Figure 5 presents the human activity recognition system according to the proposed solution. The method is utilized for analyzing behavior in an intelligent surveillance system. The system is feasible to provide a series of consecutive images (start point 401) of an area under surveillance for consecutive time points.

Presented system uses a single stationary camera. With this assumption, in majority of cases some part of scene contains a static background, which carries redundant information. Therefore, a background subtraction algorithm is used to extract foreground image (e.g. active areas, moving objects) during step 402. From the available algorithms improved adaptive Gaussian Mixture Model (GMM) for background subtraction [13] has been chosen. It is assumed, that the background model is updated during processing of each frame. This results in the best fit of the background model to changing conditions in the scene. To eliminate shadows of the tracked objects, the algorithm described in [12] which is also used during the step 402 is applied. Next step of the algorithm after shadow elimination is characteristic points extraction (step 403) that generates a set of points defining each moving silhouette on an image. This algorithm was

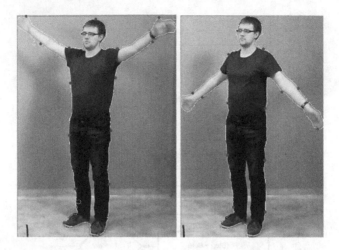

Fig. 4. Characteristics points on the hull

described in detail in Section 2. Subsequently, at step 404 a prediction of positions of objects is performed using Kalman Filter [14]. It is necessary because object segmentation is encumbered with some random error. Kalman filtering effectively smoothest trajectories of moving objects. This results in an increase of the accuracy of prediction. Each tracked object has its own Kalman Filter, so that at step 405 the generated trajectories of points for said moving silhouettes can be compared with reference database records of predefined behaviors. The system can use multiple descriptors of the same behavior and enables creation of various combinations of trajectories.

The comparison is performed by calculating the Euclidean distance for pairs of corresponding points. Each pose descriptor (set of characteristic points for a currently processed pose) shall fit within a predetermined range. For example, assuming that 4 points of a person are traced (e.g. two palms and two feet), the characteristic point designated as the "right palm" must be for each frame located in a distance D not larger than δ from the reference right hand for each behavior, namely:

$$D = \sqrt{(x_{obs} - x_{ref})^2 + (y_{obs} - y_{ref})^2} \tag{1}$$
$$D \leq \delta$$

wherein x_{obs}, y_{obs} designate the position of characteristic points (note: these are not spatial coordinates) and x_{ref}, y_{ref} designate corresponding reference values. Fulfilling the above equation allows a transition to the subsequent state (pose) in a descriptor. Obviously, being in the x state implies the information of visiting a series of previous states (poses) of the analyzed behavior. Thresholds δ were chosen through calibration process with the validation of sequences set. More details about calibration process can be found in Section 4. Thresholds are necessary to deal with different body shapes of humans.

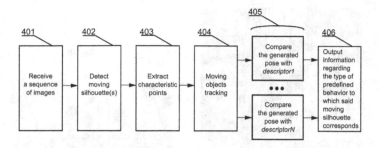

Fig. 5. General diagram of descriptors testing system

4 Experimental Results

The experiments were performed for many different behaviors, such as *Faint*, *Fall*, *Fight*, *StomachPain* and *Crouch*. In our experiments all sequences in resolution 640x480 were divided with respect to the subjects into a training set (9 persons), a validation set (8 persons) and a test set (9 persons). The classifiers were trained on the training set while the validation set was used to optimize the parameters of each method (δ parameter mentioned in Section 3). The recognition results were obtained on the test set. Authors were looking for well-known databases needed to perform experiments but commonly used test sequences doesn't meet required conditions. This paper contains results concerning *Callforhelp* behavior.

The efficiency of recognition was analyzed. To evaluate classification algorithms here the precision and recall performance metrics were used that are defined as follows:

$$precision = \frac{TP}{TP + FP} \tag{2}$$

$$recall = \frac{TP}{TP + FN} \tag{3}$$

where TP is the set of true positives, FP is the set of false positives and FN is the set of false negatives.

The effectiveness of the proposed approach was validated using three descriptors that consisted of varied number of states (10, 18 and 36 states) and eight descriptors that represented different realizations of the same human activity with 24 states, together 9 persons from test set.

The experiments were conducted in two steps. In the first step all eleven above mentioned descriptors were tested separately. The results obtained for these descriptors fluctuated between 32% and 79% recall ratio. Subsequently, in the second step the tests concerned varied number of combinations of two or more descriptors. This approach allowed to obtain much better results. Acquired results fluctuated between 58% and 100% recall ratio. These experiments showed that the increase in number of descriptors results in higher recall ratio. The recognition results are presented on Figs. 6, 7 and 8.

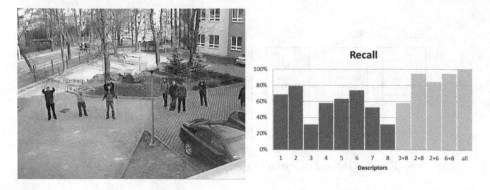

Fig. 6. Left figure: visual evaluation results. Right figure: human activity recognition system evaluation results for eight different descriptors (and their combinations) representing the same human activity.

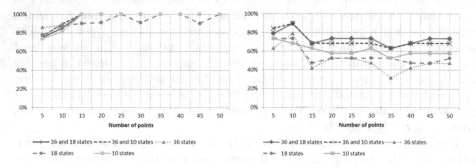

Fig. 7. Human activity recognition evaluation results for descriptors depending on the different number of states, precision (left), recall (right) parameters

5   Conclusions

In this paper, a novel system for human activity recognition from monocular video is proposed. The proposed system is a complex solution which incorporates several techniques which are used to detect moving objects, track them and recognize their activities. This system uses evenly distributed points on human hull which are used in classification process. The results prove that the proposed solution achieves higher detection efficiency with higher accuracy for simultaneous usage of various descriptors while being robust to different weather conditions and behavior realizations. Moreover, the experiment results show that some work regarding characteristic points distribution and their relation to the specific behaviors is worth further research in the proposed approach.

Acknowledgement. Research project was supported by the National Science Centre, Poland according to the Grant no. 4775/B/T02/2011/40.

References

1. Turaga, P., Chellappa, R., Subrahmanian, V.S., Udrea, O.: Machine recognition of human activities - a survey. IEEE Transactions on Circuits and Systems for Video Technology 18(11), 1473–1488 (2008)
2. Du, Y., Chen, F., Xu, W., Li, Y.: Recognizing interaction activities using dynamic Bayesian network. In: International Conference on Pattern Recogntion, pp. 618–621 (2006)
3. Fu, Z., Hu, W., Tan, T.: Similarity based vehicle trajectory clustering and anomaly detection. In: International Conference on Image Processing, pp. 602–605 (2005)
4. Johnson, N., Hogg, D.C.: Learning the distribution of object trajectories for event recognition. Image and Vision Computing 14(8), 609–615 (1996)
5. Park, S., Trivedi, M.M.: A two-stage multi-view analysis framework for human activity and interactions. In: IEEE Workshop on Motion and Video Computing (2007)
6. Dalal, N., Triggs, B.: Histograms of Oriented Gradients for Human Detection. In: IEEE Computer Society Conference on Computer Vision and Pattern Recognition, Montbonnot, France (2005)
7. Wai Lee, M., Nevatia, R.: Body Part Detection for Human Pose Estimation and Tracking. In: IEEE Workshop on Motion and Video Computing (WMVC 2007) (2007)
8. Zhao, L.: Dressed Human Modeling, Detection, and Parts Localization. The Robotics Institute, Carnegie Mellon University, Pittsburgh (2001)
9. Corvee, E., Bremond, F.: Body Parts Detection for People Tracking Using Trees of Histogram of Oriented Gradient Descriptors. In: AVSS 7th IEEE International Conference on Audio Video and Signal Based Surveillance (2010)
10. Mikolajczyk, K., Schmid, C., Zisserman, A.: Human Detection Based on a Probabilistic Assembly of Robust Part Detectors. In: Pajdla, T., Matas, J(G.) (eds.) ECCV 2004. LNCS, vol. 3021, pp. 69–82. Springer, Heidelberg (2004)
11. Lao, W., Han, J., de With, P.H.N.: Fast Detection and Modeling of Human-Body Parts from Monocular Video. In: Perales, F.J., Fisher, R.B. (eds.) AMDO 2008. LNCS, vol. 5098, pp. 380–389. Springer, Heidelberg (2008)
12. Cucchiara, R., Grana, C., Neri, G., Piccardi, M., Prati, A.: The Sakbot System for Moving Object Detection and Tracking. In: Video-Based Surveillance Systems Computer Vision and Distributed Processing, pp. 145–157 (2001)
13. Zivkovic, Z.: Improved Adaptive Gaussian Mixture Model for Background Subtraction. In: Proceedings of ICPR (2004)
14. Welch, G., Bishop, G.: An Introduction to the Kalman Filter. TR 95-041 Department of Computer Science University of North Carolina at Chapel Hill (2006)
15. Gong, S., Xiang, T.: Recognition of group activities using dynamic probabilistic networks. In: IEEE International Conference on Computer Vision, pp. 742–749 (2003)

Person Detection and Head Tracking to Detect Falls in Depth Maps

Michał Kępski[2] and Bogdan Kwolek[1]

[1] AGH University of Science and Technology, 30 Mickiewicza Av.
30-059 Kraków, Poland
bkw@agh.edu.pl
[2] University of Rzeszów, 16c Rejtana Av., 35-959 Rzeszów, Poland
mkepski@univ.rzeszow.pl

Abstract. We present a system for fall detection in which the fall hypothesis, generated on the basis of accelerometric data, is validated by k-NN based classifier operating on depth features. We show that validation of the alarms in such a way leads to lower ratio of false alarms. We demonstrate the detection performance of the system using publicly available data. We discuss algorithms for person detection in images acquired by both a static and an active depth sensor. The head is modeled in 3D by an ellipsoid that is matched to point clouds, and which is also projected into 2D, where it is matched to edges in the depth maps.

1 Introduction

Visual motion analysis aims to detect and track objects, and more generally, to understand their behaviors from image sequences. With the ubiquitous availability of low-cost cameras and their increasing importance in a wide range of real-world applications such as visual surveillance, human-machine interfaces, etc., it is becoming increasingly important to automatically analyze and understand human activities and behaviors [12]. The aim of human activity recognition is an automated analysis (or interpretation) of ongoing events and their context from video data. Its applications include surveillance systems [11], patient monitoring systems [7], and a variety of systems that involve interactions between persons and electronic devices such as human-computer interfaces [5].

Automatic recognition of anomalous human activities and falls in an indoor setting from video sequences is currently an active research topic [6]. Falls are a major cause of injury for older people and a significant obstacle in independent living of the seniors. They are one of the top causes of injury-related hospital admissions in people aged 65 years and over. Thus, significant attention has been devoted to develop an efficient system for human fall detection [6].

The most common method for fall detection consists in use of a tri-axial accelerometer. However, fall detectors using only accelerometers generate too much false alarms. In this work we demonstrate that accelerometer-based fall hypothesis can be authenticated reliably by a classifier operating on features representing a person in lying pose. We show that such authentication leads

L.J. Chmielewski et al. (Eds.): ICCVG 2014, LNCS 8671, pp. 324–331, 2014.
© Springer International Publishing Switzerland 2014

to better fall detection performance, particularly to lower ratio of false positive alarms. In a scenario with a static camera, the extraction of the person is achieved through dynamic background subtraction [2,10], whereas in scenarios with an active camera, he/she is extracted using depth region growing. Because in the course of performing common activities of daily living (ADLs), such as moving a chair, other scene elements of objects, e.g. in the considered example the chair, can be separated from the background apart from the person, we track also the head of the person undergoing monitoring. Thanks to the head tracking, a controller responsible for steering of the pan-tilt head with the camera is able to keep the person in the central or specified part of the image.

The head tracking techniques have already been applied in fall detection [8]. However, on the basis of monocular cameras it is not easy to achieve long-term head tracking. As demonstrated in [4,9], the head tracking supported by the depth maps is far more reliable. Thus, in this work the head is tracked in range maps, which indicate calibrated depth in the scene, rather than a measure of intensity or color. The depth maps were acquired by the Kinect sensor.

2   Overview of the System

A potential fall is indicated when the signal upper peak value (UPV) from the accelerometer, see inertial measurement unit (IMU) block on Fig. 1, is greater than 2.5 g. If such an event happen, the system determines the depth connected components on the depth images, delineates the person and computes the features, which are then fed to a classifier. Given the extracted in advance equation describing the floor, the distance between the person's gravity center and the floor is calculated by a procedure in a block called feature extraction, see Fig. 1. The person is extracted on the basis of a depth reference image, which is updated whenever the person moves or the scene changes. If two or more connected components of sufficient area are extracted, or alternatively the area of the connected component representing the person is too large according to its distance to the camera, the system starts tracking of the head. The tracking begins on the oldest frame in the circular buffer.

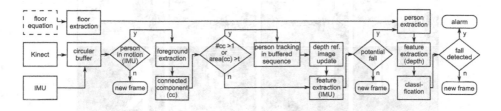

Fig. 1. Flowchart of the fall detection system

3   Person Detection in Depth Maps

3.1   Human Detection in Depth Maps from a Stationary Camera

The person is detected on the basis of a scene reference image, which is extracted in advance and then updated on-line. In the depth reference image each pixel assumes the median value of several pixels values from the past images. Given the sorted lists of pixels the depth reference image can be updated quickly by removing the oldest pixels and updating the sorted lists with the pixels from the current depth image and then extracting the median value. We found that for typical human motions, good results can be obtained using 13 consecutive depth images. For Kinect acquiring the images at 25 Hz we take every fifteenth image.

Figure 2 illustrates some images with the segmented person, which were obtained using the discussed technique. In the image #400 the person closed the door, which then appears on the binary image being a difference map between the current depth image and the depth reference image. As we can see, in frame 650, owing to adaptation of the depth reference image, the door disappears on the binary image. In frame 800 we can see a chair, which has been previously moved, and which disappears in frame 1000. As we can observe, the updated depth reference image allows us to extract the person's silhouette in the depth images. In order to eliminate small objects the depth connected components were extracted. Afterwards, small artifacts were eliminated. Otherwise, the depth images can be cleaned using morphological erosion. When the person does not move, the depth reference image is not updated.

In the detection mode the foreground objects are extracted through differencing the current image from such a depth reference map. Afterwards, the foreground object is determined through extracting the largest connected component in the thresholded difference map.

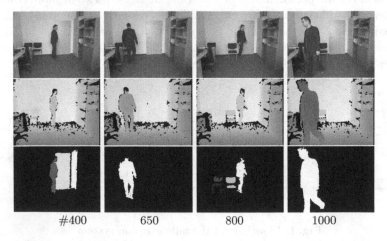

#400   650   800   1000

Fig. 2. Delineation of person using depth reference image. RGB images (upper row), depth (middle row) and binary images depicting the delineated person (bottom row)

3.2 Human Detection in Depth Map Sequences from Active Camera

In the considered scenario with an active camera, the person to be delineated in a scene moves around, while the pan-tilt unit rotates the camera to keep the subject in the central part of the depth map. Two degrees of freedom pan-tilt unit has been used to rotate the Kinect. The pursuing a moving subject is accomplished by a series of correcting saccades to the positions of the detected object in the depth maps. The object position is given as the centroid of the delineated area. The control goal of the pursuit is to hold the subject as close as possible to the central part of the depth map. This is achieved by two PID controllers, which were tuned manually to provide the assumed response time.

Region growing is a technique to separate objects or object segments from unordered pixels. The developed depth region growing starts with selecting a seed point in the current frame as an initial growing region of the whole depth region belonging to the person. Assuming that there is a common depth region between depth regions belonging to a person in two consecutive frames, such seed region is determined using the **and** operator between the previously delineated depth region belonging to person and the current depth map. The algorithm then seeks all neighboring pixels of the current region. The selected pixels are then sorted according to their depth similarities and stored in the list of candidate pixels. The depth similarity is the Euclidean distance between the depth values of a pixel from the candidate list and its closest pixel from the current region. The depth similarity is used in an examination whether a neighboring pixel around a region pixel is allowed to be included in the region. In our implementation the person region may not grow to a very large region away from a seed point. Given the location of the person in the scene as well as the distance of his/her head to the sensor we calculate the expected area of the person. The images in middle row of Fig. 4 depict some examples of the segmented person.

4 Head Tracking in Depth Maps

Since in the course of performing ADLs, other scene elements of objects can be separated from the background apart from the person, we track also the head of the person undergoing monitoring. As demonstrated in [8], the information about the head location can be very useful cue in fall detection.

The head is tracked using particle filtering (PF) [1]. Particle filters approximate the posterior distribution over the states with a set of particles $\mathbf{x} = (\mathbf{x}^{(1)}, \mathbf{x}^{(2)}, \ldots, \mathbf{x}^{(m)})$, where each of which has an associated importance weight $w^{(j)} \in \mathcal{R}^+$. In each time step, the particles are propagated further by the motion model $p(\mathbf{x}_k|\mathbf{x}_{k-1})$. Subsequently, the importance weights are updated on the basis of the observation model $p(\mathbf{z}_k|\mathbf{x}_k)$.

The head is modeled by an ellipsoid. The observation model combines fitness score between the ellipsoid and point clouds, and fitness score between the projected ellipsoid and the edges on the depth map. A distance of a point (x, y, z) to an ellipsoid, parameterized by axes of length a, b, c is calculated as follows:

$$d = \sqrt{\frac{(x - x_0)^2}{a^2} + \frac{(y - y_0)^2}{b^2} + \frac{(z - z_0)^2}{c^2}} - 1 \tag{1}$$

The degree of membership of the point to the ellipsoid is determined as follows:

$$m = 1 - \frac{d}{t} \tag{2}$$

where t is a threshold, which was determined experimentally. The ellipsoid fitness score is determined in the following manner:

$$f_1 = \sum_{(x,y,z) \in S} m(x, y, z) \tag{3}$$

where $S(x_0, y_0, z_0)$ denotes a set of points belonging to the head and its surround. The ellipsoid is then projected onto 2D plane using the (Kinect) camera model. For each pixel (u, v) contained in the ellipse E we calculate matching of the ellipse with the edges on the depth map as follows:

$$p = \begin{cases} D_e(u, v) \cdot (5 - D_d(u, v)), & D_d(u, v) < 5 \\ 0, & D_d(u, v) \geq 5 \end{cases} \tag{4}$$

where $D_e(u, v) \in 0, 1$ is pixel value in binary edge image and $D_d(u, v)$ is pixel value in an edge distance image. The ellipse fitness score is calculated as follows:

$$f_2 = \sum_{(u,v) \in E} p(u, v) \tag{5}$$

The head likelihood is calculated as follows:

$$p(\mathbf{z}_k^{(i)} | \mathbf{x}_k^{(i)}) = \frac{1}{\sqrt{2\pi\sigma^2}} \exp\left(-\frac{f_1 \cdot f_2}{2\sigma^2}\right) \tag{6}$$

From time $k - 1$ to k all particles are propagated according to: $\mathbf{x}_k^{(i)} = \mathbf{x}_{k-1}^{(i)} + \delta^{(i)}$, where $\delta^{(i)} = \mathcal{N}(0, \Sigma)$. Figure 3 shows sample tracking results which were obtained by a particle filter consisting of 500 particles. The head tracking was done on the same sequence as in Fig. 2. The state vector consists of 3D location, and pitch and roll angles. As we can observe, owing to the tracking, the head

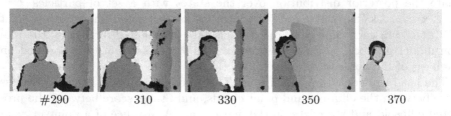

#290   310   330   350   370

Fig. 3. Head tracking in depth maps acquired by a static camera, see Fig. 2

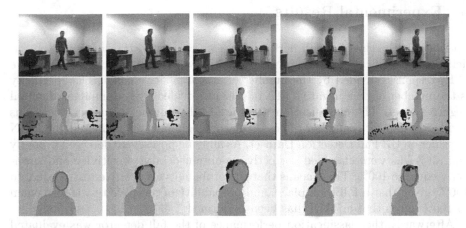

Fig. 4. Head tracking in depth maps acquired by an active camera. RGB images (upper row), segmented person (middle row), the ellipse overlaid on depth map (bottom row)

can be delineated from the background, even if some foreground objects appear in the person segmented image, see frame #400 in Fig. 2.

Figure 4 shows sample tracking results, which were obtained on images acquired by the active camera. The segmented person by depth region growing is marked by green.

5   Lying Pose Recognition

A dataset consisting of images with normal activities like walking, sitting down, crouching down and lying has been composed in order to evaluate a k-NN classifier responsible for examination whether a person is lying on the floor. In total 312 images were selected from UR Fall Detection Dataset[1] and another image sequences, which were recorded in typical rooms, like office, classroom, etc. The discussed dataset consists of 202 images with typical ADLs, whereas 110 images depict a person lying on the floor. The following features were extracted from such a collection of depth images [3]:

- h/w - a ratio of width to height of the person's bounding box
- h/h_{max} - a ratio expressing the height of the person's surrounding box in the current frame to the person's height
- D - the distance of the person centroid to the floor
- $max(\sigma_x, \sigma_z)$ - standard deviation from the centroid for the abscissa and the applicate, respectively.

---

[1] http://fenix.univ.rzeszow.pl/~mkepski/ds/uf.html

6   Experimental Results

To examine the classification performances we calculated the sensitivity, specificity, and classification accuracy. The sensitivity is the number of true positive (TP) responses divided by the number of actual positive cases. The specificity is the number of true negative (TN) decisions divided by the number of actual negative cases. The classification accuracy is the number of correct decisions divided by the total number of cases. At the beginning we evaluated the k-NN classifier on UR Fall Detection Dataset. As all lying poses were detected properly and all ADLs were classified correctly we obtained both sensitivity and specificity equal to 100%. That means that the probability of positive test is equal to 100%, given that a fall took place, and probability of negative test is also equal to 100%, given that an ADL has been performed.

Afterwards, the classification performance of the fall detector was evaluated on 10-fold cross-validation using dataset consisting of 402 negative examples and 210 positive examples. The results, which were obtained by the k-NN (for k=5) classifier are shown in Tab. 1. As we can observe, the specificity and precision of the classifier is equal to 100%.

Table 1. Performance of lying pose classification

			True	
		Fall	No Fall	
k-NN	Fall	208	0	Accuracy=99.67%
	No fall	2	402	Precision=100.0%
		Sens.=99.05% Spec.=100.0%

The system was tested with simulated-falls performed by young volunteers onto crash mats. The accelerometer was worn near the pelvis. Five volunteers attended in the tests and evaluations of our system. Intentional falls were performed in home towards a carpet with thickness of about 2 cm. Each individual performed ADLs like walking, sitting, crouching down, leaning down/picking up objects from the floor, lying on a bed. As expected, using only the accelerometer the number of false alarms was considerable. Experimental results demonstrated that most of them were successfully validated by depth image-based lying pose detector. In a scenario with the static camera, the verification of the fall can be achieved at low computational cost as the depth image processing is performed when the module processing the data from the accelerometer indicates a potential fall. Moreover, the accelerometer delivers information, which image should be processed to recognize the lying pose of the person. A comprehensive evaluation showed that the system has high accuracy of fall detection and very low level of false alarms.

7   Conclusions

In this paper we discussed a system for fall detection, which uses accelerometric and depth data. The fall hypothesis generated on the basis of accelerometric data is authenticated by depth map processing module. In maps acquired by a static camera, the person is delineated on the basis of depth reference image, whereas in images from an active camera, he/she is segmented using region growing. Since the foreground objects may appear in the segmented images we also perform head tracking. The head tracking contributes towards better localization of the person, particularly when the active camera is utilized. Given the segmented person, the algorithm extracts features, which are then used by k-NN classifier responsible for recognizing the lying pose. Owing to the use of k-NN classifier the ratio of false alarm is much lower in comparison to a fall detector using only accelerometric data. We demonstrated the detection performance of the classifier on publicly available dataset. It achieves 100% specificity and precision.

Acknowledgments. This study was supported by the National Science Center (NCN) within the research project N N516 483240.

References

1. Isard, M., Blake, A.: CONDENSATION - conditional density propagation for visual tracking. Int. J. Computer Vision 29(1), 5–28 (1998)
2. Kepski, M., Kwolek, B., Austvoll, I.: Fuzzy inference-based reliable fall detection using Kinect and accelerometer. In: Rutkowski, L., Korytkowski, M., Scherer, R., Tadeusiewicz, R., Zadeh, L.A., Zurada, J.M. (eds.) ICAISC 2012, Part I. LNCS, vol. 7267, pp. 266–273. Springer, Heidelberg (2012)
3. Kepski, M., Kwolek, B.: Unobtrusive fall detection at home using kinect sensor. In: Wilson, R., Hancock, E., Bors, A., Smith, W. (eds.) CAIP 2013, Part I. LNCS, vol. 8047, pp. 457–464. Springer, Heidelberg (2013)
4. Kwolek, B.: Face tracking system based on color, stereovision and elliptical shape features. In: IEEE Conf. on Adv. Video and Signal Based Surveill., pp. 21–26 (2003)
5. Kwolek, B.: Visual system for tracking and interpreting selected human actions. Journal of WSCG 11(2), 274–281 (2003)
6. Mubashir, M., Shao, L., Seed, L.: A survey on fall detection: Principles and approaches. Neurocomputing 100, 144–152 (2013), special issue: Behaviours in video
7. Nait-Charif, H., McKenna, S.J.: Activity summarisation and fall detection in a supportive home environment. In: Int. Conf. on Pattern Rec., pp. 4:323–4:326 (2004)
8. Rougier, C., Meunier, J., St-Arnaud, A., Rousseau, J.: Monocular 3D head tracking to detect falls of elderly people. In: 28th Annual Int. Conf. of the IEEE Engineering in Medicine and Biology Society, EMBS 2006, pp. 6384–6387 (2006)
9. Russakoff, D.B., Herman, M.: Head tracking using stereo. Mach. Vision Appl. 13(3), 164–173 (2002)
10. Stone, E., Skubic, M.: Fall detection in homes of older adults using the Microsoft Kinect. IEEE J. of Biomedical and Health Informatics (2014)
11. Vishwakarma, S., Agrawal, A.: A survey on activity recognition and behavior understanding in video surveillance. Vis. Comput. 29, 983–1009 (2013)
12. Weinland, D., Ronfard, R., Boyer, E.: A survey of vision-based methods for action representation, segmentation and recognition. CVIU 115(2), 224–241 (2011)

Interactive Vine:
Build Communicative Relationship

Young Mi Kim

GSAIM, Chung-Ang University
221 Huksuk-dong, Dongjak-gu, 156-756,
Seoul, Korea (R.O.K)
ymkimlab@naver.com

Abstract. This research proposes the graphic system based on the computer vision technology using fingertips. It is the integrated system of graphic to the part that tracked the fingertips after reading the images of hands combined with artistic concept. This work of art being introduced is a graphic expression based on the screen and interactive media art for modern people who experience absence of communication and personal relationships that became estranged socially. Upon putting hand on the manufacture interactive table, it extracts the fingertips as feature points through adaptively suitable oval extraction method considering geometric features of hands. To project the graphic in the input image of camera, precise extraction and tracking technology of feature points of fingertips are important, and this thesis is about the explanation of that technology.

Keywords: Interactive media art, Interactive Vine, Art technology, Hand feature detection.

1   Background

In proposed work of art, concrete wall was substituted for the wall of mind people have. Modern people live with their closed mind due to the stress coming from busy schedule, conflicts happening in personal relationship, hurt they experienced in the past. Although they desire for the communication, they live on their life giving it up for they dont know the approach method for communication and rest of mind. This work of art noted this problem. This work of art aims to provide the foundation which people can communicate more closely with the aid of technology. Accordingly, approach as an interactive art to change the severance wall into communication wall was presented. Warmth of warm hand of two people put on the table is delivered to Ivy, and gives the sensation that it extends towards wall with that strength. Superficially, it is correct that graphic is printed out extracting the fingertips. Sensationally, however, it is the sensation that conveys the warmth and heart in hands towards each other to the table.

L.J. Chmielewski et al. (Eds.): ICCVG 2014, LNCS 8671, pp. 332–337, 2014.
© Springer International Publishing Switzerland 2014

2   Design

Configuration is largely composed of wall, hand, vine and heart. The table and wall has role as a screen, and hand as an input image, vine as an output pattern, heart is the form of final output. The upper face of table is made of acrylic, thus enabling images of projector under the table to project through it. Table is adhered to the wall so as to form one screen that table and wall are connected. The L-form screen is made when seen from side view. Two projectors in total are used, and one is under the table, and the other one prints out facing the wall. To precisely detect the images of hands put on the table, camera is installed in the center of the upper face of the table.

Fig. 1. Position that the fingertips are towards the wall

Like in Fig 1, when two people put one of their hands on the table, 5 ivy branches, total 10 of them are generated and towards the wall alternating. (formation of human relation) Without any fixed form, branches alternate each other randomly. (communication) Design and size of leaves differ according to the shape and size of accessors hands, big leaves are generated in the case of big hands and small leaves are generated in the case of small hands like that of females or childrens. Graphic of interactive table differ depending on the approach method, say for example, if fingertips are towards the wall like in Fig 1, free curve form of ivy is formed regarding it as the first step for the communication. In Fig 2, if two people stand in the direction they could face each other and put their hands on the table, the fingertips become towards each other. It was

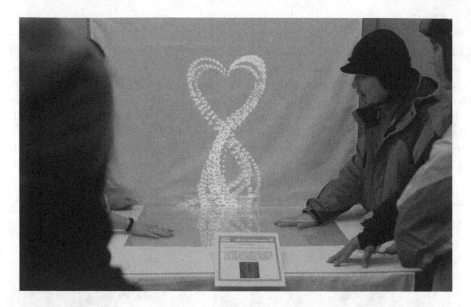

Fig. 2. Position that fingertips are towards each other(Exhibition)[1]

programmed to enlarge the heart shape as the hands become closer putting the hands stretching out to each other as a meaning of the relationship development between two people.[2]

3   Fingertips Tracking System Which Applied in Interactive Table Preparation

Proposed system is a tracking system of fingertips pt on the table based on the geometric features of hands. It is difficult to acquire enough information for estimating the three dimensional movement from users bare hands. Thus, to acquire enough feature points in the hand, 5 fingertips are defined as feature points. It is supposed that fingertips can be distinguished clearly keeping the position that users hands are spread and located near the vertical direction of camera when hands of users are extracted from input images in order to find 5 fingertips accurately. On the basis of center points of palm and directional component of hands that possess information about geometric features of hands, fingertips are individually distinguish and used in tracking fingertips measuring similarity between consecutive images. First, from the images acquired from camera, hands domain is extracted using the information of skin color which are HSV and RGB color.

Extracted hands domain is classified into interested area and directional vector which indicates direction of hands and center of palm are calculated. With the aid of curvature that each pixel forming the contour of hands has, candidates for fingerprints are detected. Applying adaptive optimal oval detection method

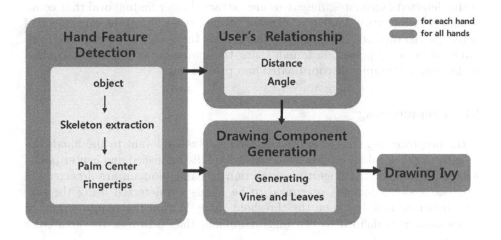

Fig. 3. Diagram

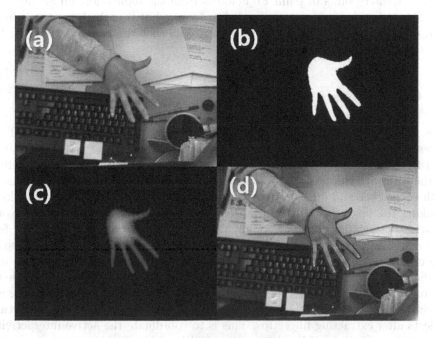

Fig. 4. Input image and result of extraction of adaptive hand domain. (a)Input image (b)Extraction of hand domain (c)Application of distance transform method (d)Pc, center points of palm detected.

to the detected candidates, fingertips are extracted after finding oval that counteracts each fingertip. And in a series of frames, considering the movement of fingertips and distance each fingertip forms from the center point of palm, optimal corresponding points are found. Using the movement of fingertips acquired in this way, ivy graphic is coordinated and printed out.

3.1 Preprocessing

In the preprocessing step to extract fingertips, pixels relevant to the hands domain from the acquired images from camera are distinguished and center points of palm needed for the fingertips extraction in hands domain are detected. In proposed system, domains presumed to be hands are detected using the skin color information[3] based on the threshold value. Within the acquired images, hands domain is defined as the biggest domain that possesses the skin color information.

Fig 4(a) is the input images acquired from camera and Fig 4(b) is the result of production of binarization images after extracting hands domain using the input images. Center points of palm Pc is found from the hands domain acquired in this step using distance transform.[4] Fig 4(c) and 2(d) each shows the images that distance transform was applied and results that center points of palm Pc was detected.

4   Conclusions

The research of arts in this thesis replaced the wall in the mind caused by absence of communication in this era to the actual wall. And ivy climbing the wall freely is personified as the step to the communication. The ivy, extending to the wall with the warmth of hand put on the manufactured table, alternates with each other and opens a door towards communication. Here, a technology tracking the fingertips and printing out the graphic was used. It is the work of arts that relationship and communication between two people can be felt depending on the direction of fingertips put on the interactive table. Through the creative exhibition of HCI(Human-Computer Interaction), evaluation and verification of works of arts were conducted. Further, many people were able to assume the attention and expectations about communication. Afterwards, we intend to develop this to the research of augmented reality coordinating virtual objects after extracting fingertips. This is to coordinate the active interactivity not under restrictions of hand movements with arts.

References

1. Youngmi, K., Heesun, C., Joosoo, C.: HCI 2010 Open Creativity. In: 15th Human Computer Interface, p. 32. Repubilc of Korea (2011)

2. Kim, Y.-M., Choi, H., Choi, J.-S.: Hand Ivy: Hand Feature Detection for an Advanced Interactive Tabletop. In: Dickmann, L., Volkmann, G., Malaka, R., Boll, S., Krüger, A., Olivier, P. (eds.) SG 2011. LNCS, vol. 6815, pp. 199–202. Springer, Heidelberg (2011)
3. Gasparini, F., Schettini, R.: Skin Segmentation using Multiple Thresholding. In: Proc. SPIE, vol. 6061, pp. 60610F-1–60610F-8 (2006)
4. Borgefors, G.: Distance Transformations in Digital Images. In: ICVGIP, vol. 34, pp. 344–371 (1986)
5. Interactive Vine Movie, http://youtu.be/7GGrq_6uPxY

Conjugate Gradient in Noisy Photometric Stereo

Ryszard Kozera[1] and Felicja Okulicka-Dłużewska[2]

[1] Warsaw University of Life Sciences-SGGW, Faculty of Applied Informatics and Mathematics
Nowoursynowska str. 159, 02-776 Warsaw, Poland
ryszard.kozera@gmail.com
[2] Warsaw University of Technology, Faculty of Mathematics and Information Science
Koszykowa str. 75, 00-662 Warsaw, Poland
f.okulicka@mini.pw.edu.pl

Abstract. This paper discusses the problem of reconstructing the Lambertian surface from noisy three-light source Photometric Stereo. In the continuous image setting the shape recovery process is divided into two steps: an algebraic one (gradient computation) and analytical one (gradient integration). The digitized case with added noise has it discrete analogue in which also perturbed gradient from three noisy images is first computed. Generically such non-integrable vector field is subsequently rectified to the "closest" integrable one. Finally, numerical integration scheme yields the unknown surface. The process of vector field rectification is reduced to the corresponding linear optimization task of very high dimension (comparable with the image resolution). Standard methods based on matrix pseudo-inversion suffer from heavy computation due to the necessity of large matrix inversion. A possible alternative is to set up an iterative scheme based on local snapshots' optimizations (e.g. 2D-Leap-Frog). Another approach which is proposed in this paper is solving the above global optimization scheme by Conjugate Gradient with no inversion of matrices of large dimension. The experimental results from this paper show that the application of Conjugate Gradient forms a computationally feasible alternative in denoising Photometric Stereo.

Keywords: Shape Reconstruction, Photometric Stereo, noise removal, Conjugate Gradient, numerical computation.

1 Introduction

A classical *shape-from-shading problem* relies on reconstructing the unknown illuminated shape S from its image [5, 14]. Mathematically the shape-from-shading problem is modelled by the so-called *image irradiance equation* [5]:

$$R(n_1(x,y,z), n_2(x,y,z), n_3(x,y,z)) = E(x,y), \tag{1}$$

where function R is called *a reflectance map* which governs surface reflecting properties depending on surface normal $n = (n_1, n_2, n_3)$. As different surfaces S have different reflectance properties there is a big variety of R. The function E from (1) measures the intensity of the reflected light at image point $(x,y) \in \Omega$ and forms one component of the available data. The second given component is a distant light-source direction $p = (p_1, p_2, p_3)$. In case when surface $S = graph(u)$ coincides with the graph of the

L.J. Chmielewski et al. (Eds.): ICCVG 2014, LNCS 8671, pp. 338–346, 2014.

unknown function $u : \Omega \to \mathbb{R}^2$ the surface normal is $n = \pm(u_x(x,y), u_y(x,y), -1)$ (we choose the positive sign). In general reflectance map R is difficult to be determined. However, for certain materials it can be estimated by using optics law [5]. One of such class of surfaces is the so-called family of *Lambertian surfaces* for which R is proportional to the $cos(\alpha)$, where α is the angle between the normal n and light-source illumination direction p (light-source is assumed here to be positioned at infinity). The latter implies that image irradiance equation (1) for Lambertian surface takes the following special form [5, 6]:

$$\frac{p_1 u_x(x,y) + p_2 u_y(x,y) - p_3}{\sqrt{p_1^2 + p_2^2 + p_3^2}\sqrt{u_x^2(x,y) + u_y^2(x,y) + 1}} = E(x,y). \tag{2}$$

It turns out that generically problem (2) for a single light-source illumination is *ill-posed* [5, 10]. There are some conditions under which such deficiency can be removed [1, 7–10, 15]. Namely one of possible approaches to disambiguate (2) is to admit more illuminations enforcing extra constraints on reconstruction problem (2). This technique is called *Photometric Stereo*, where the unknown surface S is illuminated from multiple linearly independent distant light-source directions [5, 7, 8, 15]. It is proved that the three-light source Photometric Stereo is sufficient for exact surface S reconstruction (modulo its vertical shift) - see [5, 7]. The reconstruction process is split here into two independent steps, namely an *algebraic* and then an *analytical* step. More specifically three image irradiance equations (for light-source directions p, q, r):

$$\frac{\langle n|p \rangle}{||n|| \cdot ||p||} = E_p(x,y), \quad \frac{\langle n|q \rangle}{||n|| \cdot ||q||} = E_q(x,y), \quad \frac{\langle n|r \rangle}{||n|| \cdot ||r||} = E_r(x,y), \tag{3}$$

yield unique gradient $(\nabla u)(x,y) = (f_1(x,y,E_p,E_q,E_r,p,q,r), f_2(x,y,E_p,E_q,E_r,p,q,r))$ - here $\langle \cdot | \cdot \rangle$ and $|| \cdot ||$ denote standard dot product and the norm in $\mathbb{R}^n$. Indeed the following holds [5, 7]:

Theorem 1. *The system (3) gives a unique gradient (u_x, u_y) over $\Omega = \Omega_1 \cap \Omega_2 \cap \Omega_3$:*

$$u_x = \frac{(q_2 r_3 - q_3 r_2)E_p||p|| + (p_3 r_2 - p_2 r_3)E_q||q|| + (p_2 q_3 - p_3 q_2)E_r||r||}{(q_2 r_1 - q_1 r_2)E_p||p|| + (p_1 r_2 - p_2 r_1)E_q||q|| + (p_2 q_1 - p_1 q_2)E_r||r||},$$
$$\tag{4}$$
$$u_y = \frac{(q_3 r_1 - q_1 r_3)E_p||p|| + (p_1 r_3 - p_3 r_1)E_q||q|| + (p_3 q_1 - p_1 q_3)E_r||r||}{(q_2 r_1 - q_1 r_2)E_p||p|| + (p_1 r_2 - p_2 r_1)E_q||q|| + (p_2 q_1 - p_1 q_2)E_r||r||},$$

for $p = (p_1, p_2, p_3)$, $q = (q_1, q_2, q_3)$ and $r = (r_1, r_2, r_3)$ linearly independent.

In the next analytical step the vector field (4) is integrated subject to the satisfaction of the so-called *integrability condition*:

$$\int_{\gamma_c} u_x dx + u_y dy = 0, \tag{5}$$

for each piecewise smooth closed curve $\gamma_c \subset \Omega$. Subsequently the function u is computed by (modulo constant $u(x_0, y_0)$):

$$u(x,y) = u(x_0,y_0) + \int_0^T [u_x(\gamma_1(t),\gamma_2(t))\dot{\gamma}_1(t) + u_y(\gamma_1(t),\gamma_2(t))\dot{\gamma}_2(t)]dt,$$

for $\gamma : [0,T] \to \mathbb{R}^2$, where $\gamma \in V_{x_0,y_0} = \{\gamma \in C^1 : \gamma \subset \Omega$ is compact and joins (x,y) with fixed (x_0,y_0) from $\Omega\}$. This procedure recovers the unknown surface S from three images E_p, E_q and E_r under the admission of their continuity. In practice any real input image is built from pixels (a digitized form of the ideal continuous image). In addition, the camera introduces some extra errors. Both those components are integrated here and are treated as a Gaussian noise. The later produces vector field v which almost surely violates the integrability condition (5). Therefore the above shape reconstruction scheme from noisy Photometric Stereo requires a prior rectification of non-integrable vector field v to enforce its integrability.

2 Image Pixelization

A digitized analogue of the integrability condition (5) can be established for each four adjacent pixels of image Ω (see [11, 12]). Here one integrates over polygonal curve γ_a (i.e. along vertical and/or horizontal closed paths) which joins the centers of four adjacent pixels (an atomic discrete integrability condition). Once all of such atomic paths' integrals vanish it is easy to show that integral (5) is also nullified along arbitrary polygonal curve (a full discrete integrability condition). Recall the forward-difference derivative approximations:

$$v_x[i,k] \approx \frac{u[i+1,k]-u[i,k]}{\Delta x}, k = j,j+1, \quad v_y[l,j] \approx \frac{u[l,j+1]-u[l,j]}{\Delta y}, l = i,i+1. \quad (6)$$

We impose the family of linear constraints on noisy vector fields $v = (v_1,v_2)$ computed at each (i,j)-pixel from (4). This provides a linear system of equations usually not satisfied by the noisy vector field v. For four adjacent pixels $\tilde{p}[i,j], \tilde{p}[i+1,j], \tilde{p}[i+1,j+1], \tilde{p}[i,j+1]$, where $\tilde{p}[i,j] = (x[i],y[j])$ the equation (5) reads:

$$\int_{\tilde{p}[i,j]}^{\tilde{p}[i+1,j]} v_x dx + \int_{\tilde{p}[i+1,j]}^{\tilde{p}[i+1,j+1]} v_y dy + \int_{\tilde{p}[i+1,j+1]}^{\tilde{p}[i,j+1]} v_x dx + \int_{\tilde{p}[i,j+1]}^{\tilde{p}[i,j]} v_y dy = 0. \quad (7)$$

Applying the derivatives approximations (6) to (7) leads to the linear homogenous equation:

$$v_x[i,j]\Delta x + v_y[i+1,j]\Delta y - v_x[i,j+1]\Delta x - v_y[i,j]\Delta y = 0.$$

Repeating the last procedure to all four adjacent pixels from image Ω gives the corresponding homogenous system of equations abbreviated here as $L(\hat{v}) = 0$. Obviously for noisy vector field v we obtain $L(v) \neq 0$. In a strive to search for $\hat{v}_{opt}$ satisfying $L(\hat{v}_{opt}) = 0$ which is the "closest" to v we reduce the noise by finding the minimum of the following convex cost function:

$$I_Q(\hat{v}_{opt}) = \min_{\hat{v} \in V_I} \Sigma_{i,j}\{(\hat{v}_x[i,j] - v_x[i,j])^2 + (\hat{v}_y[i,j] - v_y[i,j])^2\}, \quad (8)$$

where: $V_I = \{\hat{v} \in \mathbb{R}^m : L(\hat{v}) = 0, \ L : \mathbb{R}^m \to \mathbb{R}^n\}$. It is well known that a unique solution $\hat{v}_{opt} \in V_I$ to (8) is given by the pseudo-inversion of L (see [10]):

$$\hat{v}_{opt} = v - L^T(LL^T)^{-1}(L(v)). \quad (9)$$

Visibly formula (9) requires the inversion of the big matrix LL^T which involves heavy computations not always plausible for standard computer hardware. One option is to resort to the Leap-Frog-like schemes using overlapping snapshot local optimizations [11–13] which can be handled (though with long execution time) by standard computers. Another option is to use the iterative methods to solve $(LL^T)(x) = b$ not relying on matrix inversion. Among such iterative methods (either stationary or non-stationary) we choose one of the non-stationary Krylov's method, namely a Conjugate Gradient (CG method) [16, 18]. CG algorithm not only theoretically always converges to the solution of $(LL^T)(x) = b$ but also is the fastest among the remaining Krylov's methods [16, 18]. Recall that CG scheme is limited to the symmetric and positive definite matrices which coincidentally is satisfied by the matrix LL^T.

3 Numerical Procedure

We reduce the noise in the non-integrable field v (computed from (4) with noisy images E_p, E_q, E_r) using (9). The inverse of the matrix LL^T is not calculated as it requires the additional memory allocation. Indeed although the matrix LL^T is sparse (it has only five non-zeros in each row) its inverse however is dense occupying large memory allocation. We follow now the CG procedure to calculate the optimal integrable vector field $\hat{v}_{opt}$ according to:

1. calculate $b = L(v)$
2. solve $(LL^T)(x) = b$ by CG iterative method
3. calculate $\hat{v}_{opt} = v - L^T(x)$.

Theoretically, all Krylov's algorithms always converge in at most $m_1 = n$ steps, where n is the dimension of the matrix of iteration [16, 18]. The stopping condition for CG algorithm admits $||r^i|| = ||LL^T(x^i) - b|| \leq \varepsilon$, where r^i is the residuum and x^i is the approximation of the solution of $(LL^T)(x) = b$ calculated in i-th step.

4 Numerical Experiments

Remarkably our numerical experiments are possible to be performed on standard PC machine with processor Intel Core, CPU 3.00 GHz, 4.00 GB RAM. As the matrix LL^T has only few non zeros in each row placed regularly and forming the static pattern it is not necessary to keep the whole matrix LL^T in the memory. Exploiting such static pattern of LL^T it is sufficient to write the proper formula for matrix-vector multiplication. Recall that $LL^T \in M_{n \times n}(\mathbb{R})$ where n is the number of atomic four adjacent pixels loops. In the Tables 1-3 the number of iterations for the CG is presented for different shapes. Numerical experiments show that the number of iterations in our problems falls within the range $\mathcal{O}(\sqrt{n})$ while the theoretical bound of the number of iterations is much worse i.e. of order n (see [16, 18]). Therefore the calculations conducted for the special matrix LL^T with the aid of CG method offers fast computational tool for denoising vector fields in Photometric Stereo. We present now some experiments for reconstruction of the unknown surface S from noisy three-source Photometric Stereo. Note that the ideal images

Table 1. Tests for S_1 reconstructions from E_p, E_q and E_r with noise $\mathcal{N}(0.0, 0.02)$ and the stopping condition $\|r_i\| < 10^{-15}$

Number of pixels	16	32	64	128	256	512
LL^T dimension	256	1024	4096	16384	65536	262144
Number of CG iterations	16	32	64	128	366	761
$\|S_{1,\hat{v}_{1,opt}} - S_1\|$	1.73	3.20	6.40	12.24	23.34	48.00
$\frac{\|S_{1,\hat{v}_{1,opt}} - S_1\|}{\|S_1\|}$	0.098	0.091	0.090	0.086	0.082	0.080

Fig. 1. Noiseless digitized images E_p, E_q and E_r for Lambertian surface S_1

Fig. 2. Noisy digitized images E_p, E_q and E_r for surface S_1 with noise $\mathcal{N}(0.0, 0.02)$

are generated here synthetically from the analytical formulas of u applied to Lambertian model (2). Subsequently Gaussian noise is added to all three images E_p, E_q and E_r. For simplicity we also assume that all images are acquired over entire $\Omega = [0,1] \times [0,1]$ (in case when $cos(\alpha) < 0$ we still admit the Lambertian model).

Example 1. Let $S_1 = graph(u_1)$, where $u_1(x,y) = x^2 + y^2 + x*y$ is defined over $(x,y) \in \Omega = [0,1] \times [0,1]$. The light-source directions are: $p = (0,0,-1)$, $q = (0.0, \sqrt{9}, -\frac{1}{\sqrt{2}}) = (0.0, 0.333333, -0.707107)$ and $r = (\frac{1}{\sqrt{7}}, 0.0, -\frac{1}{\sqrt{2}}) = (0.377964, 0.0, -0.707107)$. The results for CG procedure are presented in Table 1. The noiseless digitized images E_p, E_q and E_r of S_1 (see Figure 1) can be compared with the corresponding noisy images (see Figure 2). The reconstructed surfaces: $S_{1,v}$ (without rectification) and $S_{1,\hat{v}_{opt}}$ (with rectification) from v (noise level is here again $\mathcal{N}(0.0, 0.02)$) together with the ideal surface S_1 are shown in Figure 3.

Example 2. Let $S_2 = graph(u_2)$, where $u_2(x,y) = (0.75 + \frac{1}{3} * (1 - tanh((x+y-2)^2 + (x-y)^2 - \frac{25}{3}))$ is defined over $(x,y) \in \Omega = [0,1] \times [0,1]$. The light-source directions are: $p = (0,0,-1)$, $q = (1 - \sqrt{3}, 0, -1 - \sqrt{3})/(2\sqrt{2}) = (-0.258819, 0.0, -0.965926)$,

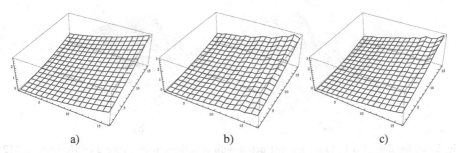

a)   b)   c)

Fig. 3. a) Ideal S_1, reconstructed as b) $S_{1,v}$ without and c) $S_{1,\hat{v}_{opt}}$ with rectification of v (noise $\mathcal{N}(0.0, 0.02)$)

Table 2. Tests for S_2 reconstructions from E_p, E_q and E_r with noise $\mathcal{N}(0.0, 0.02)$ and the stopping condition $||r_i|| < 10^{-10}$

Number of pixels	16	32	64	128	512
Number of CG iterations	16	32	64	128	512
$||S_{2,\hat{v}_{opt}} - S_2||$	11	22	41	83	340
$\frac{||S_{2,\hat{v}_{opt}} - S_2||}{||S_2||}$	0.56	0.56	0.55	0.57	0.58

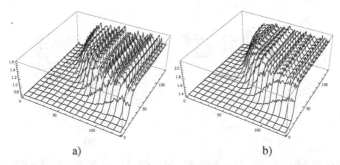

a)   b)

Fig. 4. S_2 reconstructed as a) $S_{2,v}$ without and b) $S_{2,\hat{v}_{opt}}$ with rectification of v (noise $\mathcal{N}(0.0, 0.02)$)

$r = (\frac{1}{2} \sin \frac{\pi}{24}, \frac{\sqrt{3}}{2} \sin \frac{\pi}{24}, -\cos \frac{\pi}{24}) = (0.0652631, 0.113039, -0.991445)$. The test results for CG procedure are presented in Table 2. The most time consuming case for 512 pixels needs about five hours for CG iterations. For small number of pixels: 16, 32, 64 the calculations are quick - namely they only last few minutes on standard PC. The reconstructed surfaces: $S_{2,v}$ (without rectification) and $S_{2,\hat{v}_{opt}}$ (with rectification) from v for 128 pixels (noise level is here $\mathcal{N}(0.0, 0.02)$) are shown in Figure 4. The Figure 5 permits to see the ideal graph S_2 and reconstructed $S_{2,\hat{v}_{2,opt}}$ for 512 number of pixels.

Example 3. Let $S_3 = graph(u_3)$, where $u_3(x,y) = \frac{1}{x^2+y^2+3xy}$ is defined over $(x,y) \in \Omega = [0,1] \times [0,1]$. The test results for CG procedure are presented in Table 3. The reconstructed surfaces: $S_{3,v}$ (without rectification) and $S_{3,\hat{v}_{opt}}$ (with rectification) from v for 32 pixels (noise level is here $\mathcal{N}(0.0, 0.02)$) are shown in Figure 4.

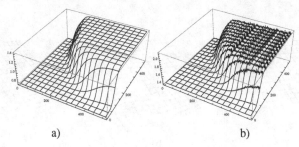

a)   b)

Fig. 5. a) Ideal S_2 and b) $S_{2,\hat{v}_{opt}}$ reconstructed with rectification of v (noise $\mathcal{N}(0.0, 0.02)$, 512 pixels)

Table 3. Tests for S_3 reconstructions from E_p, E_q and E_r with noise $\mathcal{N}(0.0, 0.02)$ and the stopping condition $||r_i|| < 10^{-10}$

Number of pixels	16	32	64	128	512
Number of CG iterations	16	32	64	128	512
$||S_{3,\hat{v}_{3,opt}} - S_3||$	33	65	41	83	340
$\frac{||S_{3,\hat{v}_{3,opt}} - S_3||}{||S_3||}$	0.58	0.56	0.55	0.57	0.58

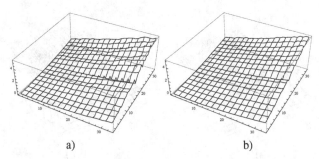

a)   b)

Fig. 6. S_3 reconstructed as a) $S_{3,v}$ without and b) $S_{3,\hat{v}_{opt}}$ with rectification of v (noise $\mathcal{N}(0.0, 0.02)$)

4.1 Numerical Complexity

Two methods of solving the equation $(LL^T)(x) = b$ are considered here - *direct* and *iterative* [3]. The most commonly used direct method is based on the decomposition of the symmetric banded matrix $LL^T = \tilde{L}\tilde{L}^T$ where the matrix $\tilde{L}$ is banded lower triangular and generally denser than the lower part of LL^T. Two systems of equations should then be solved: $\tilde{L}(y) = b$ and $\tilde{L}^T(x) = y$. This method requires the allocation of the symmetric matrix with the width of the band equal to $n_b = \mathcal{O}(\sqrt{m})$, where m is the number of unknowns. Thus the memory complexity for $LL^T \in M_{n \times n}(\mathbb{R})$ is of order $\mathcal{O}(n \cdot n_b) = \mathcal{O}(n \cdot \sqrt{m})$. The time complexity of the decomposition is measured by the number of floating numbers operations and is equal $\mathcal{O}(n \cdot n_b^2) = \mathcal{O}(n \cdot m)$ (see [3]). The solution of two triangular sets of equations needs the $\mathcal{O}(n \cdot n_b) = \mathcal{O}(n \cdot \sqrt{m})$ operations. The whole direct algorithm has the time complexity $\mathcal{O}(n \cdot (m + \sqrt{m}))$. Notice that

$m > n$. The CG method applied here does not require the memory allocation for matrix LL^T i.e. its memory complexity is equal zero. The time complexity for CG, where the number of iterations falls within the range $\mathcal{O}(\sqrt{n})$ and there are only few non-zeros in each row of matrix, is $\mathcal{O}(n^{\frac{3}{2}})$. Both are visibly smaller than for the direct method. In fact the biggest experimental test calculated using CG algorithm on our machine cannot be calculated on the same computer by direct method. In addition the iterative method is prone for easier parallel implementation. Even more during the parallel execution the communication takes less time as the iterative methods rely on sending the solution vectors only while the direct methods need additionally the sending of the matrix parts by parts.

5 Conclusions

As shown the CG algorithm offers a computationally feasible method for reconstructing the surface S in noisy three light-source Photometric Stereo. The sparsity and regularity of operator L leads to the possibility of computing problem (9) without requirements of allocating big matrices in the machine memory. In addition, for operators enforcing integration the CG algorithm converges in a small number of iterations comparing the size of the problem. CG application gives the possibility of algorithm extensions into a parallelization or into a distributed computation. CG computed $\hat{v}_{opt}$ can also provide a good initial guess for the non-linear optimization schemes [13] derived for noisy Photometric Stereo. More discussion on depth recovery from noisy vector field can also be found in [2, 4, 17, 19, 20].

References

1. Brooks, M.J., Chojnacki, W., Kozera, R.: Impossible and ambiguous shading patterns. Int. J. Comp. Vision 7(2), 119–126 (1992)
2. Castelán, M., Hancock, E.R.: Imposing integrability in geometric shape-from-shading. In: Sanfeliu, A., Ruiz-Shulcloper, J. (eds.) CIARP 2003. LNCS, vol. 2905, pp. 196–203. Springer, Heidelberg (2003)
3. Golub, G.H., Van Loan, C.F.: Matrix Computations, 4th edn. (2013)
4. Frankot, R.T., Chellappa, R.: A method of enforcing integrability in shape from shading algorithms. IEEE Trans. Patt. Rec. Machine Intell. 10(4), 439–451 (1988)
5. Horn, B.K.P.: Robot Vision. McGraw-Hill, New York (1986)
6. Horn, B.K.P., Brooks, M.J.: Shape from Shading. MIT Press, Cambridge
7. Kozera, R.: Existence and uniqueness in Photometric Stereo. Appl. Math. Comput. 44(1), 1–104 (1991)
8. Kozera, R.: On shape recovery from two shading patterns. Int. J. Patt. Rec. Art. Intel. 6(4), 673–698 (1992)
9. Kozera, R.: On complete integrals and uniqueness in shape from shading. Appl. Math. Comput. 73(1), 1–37 (1995)
10. Kozera, R.: Uniqueness in shape from shading revisited. J. Math. Imag. Vision 7, 123–138 (1997)
11. Noakes, L., Kozera, R.: The 2-D leap-frog: Integrability, noise, and digitization. In: Bertrand, G., Imiya, A., Klette, R. (eds.) Digital and Image Geometry. LNCS, vol. 2243, pp. 352–364. Springer, Heidelberg (2002)

12. Noakes, L., Kozera, R.: Denoising images: Non-linear leap-frog for shape and light-source recovery. In: Asano, T., Klette, R., Ronse, C. (eds.) Geometry, Morphology, and Computational Imaging. LNCS, vol. 2616, pp. 419–436. Springer, Heidelberg (2003)
13. Noakes, L., Kozera, R.: Nonlinearities and noise reduction in 3-source Photometric Stereo. J. Math. Imag. Vision 18(3), 119–127 (2003)
14. Oliensis, J.: Uniqueness in shape from shading. Int. J. Comp. Vision 6(2), 75–104 (1991)
15. Onn, R., Bruckstein, A.: Uniqueness in shape from shading. Int. J. Comp. Vision 5(1), 105–113 (1990)
16. Saad, Y.: Iterative Methods for Sparse Linear Systems. SIAM (2003)
17. Simchony, T., Chellappa, R., Shao, M.: Direct analytical methods for solving Poisson equations in computer vision problems. IEEE Trans. Patt. Rec. Machine Intell. 12(5), 435–446 (1990)
18. van der Vorst, H.A.: Iterative Krylov Methods for Large Linear Systems. Cambridge Monographs on Applied and Computational Mathematics (2009)
19. Wei, T., Klette, R.: On depth recovery from gradient vector field. In: Bhattacharaya, B.B., Sur-Kolay, S., Nandy, S.C., Bagch, A. (eds.) Algorithms. in Architectures and Information Systems Security, pp. 765–797 (2009)
20. Wöhler, C.: 3D Computer Vision: Efficient Methods and Applications. Springer, Heidelberg (2009)

Model Based Approach
for Melanoma Segmentation

Karol Kropidłowski[1], Marcin Kociołek[1],
Michał Strzelecki[1], and Dariusz Czubiński[2]

[1] Institute of Electronics, Łódź University of Technology
Wólczańska 211/215, 90-924 Łódź, Poland
[2] DerMed Training Center Piotrkowska 48, 90-265 Łódź, Poland
karolkropidlowski@wp.pl

Abstract. There is no suitable golden standard for assessment and comparison of segmentation methods applied to skin lesions images. Thus there is a need for development of image analysis techniques that satisfy at least subjective criteria defined by dermatologists. We present a model based approach for melanocytic image segmentation as a tool to improve computer aided diagnosis. During the research it was necessary to correct non-uniform image illumination caused by dermatoscope lightning. The correction algorithm based on dermatoscope light intensity estimation was used. The proposed segmentation method is based on histogram skin modeling. Preliminary test results are promising, for the analyzed melanoma images mean Jaccard index of 89.48% and mean sensitivity of 92.45% were obtained (when compared to expert assessment).

1 Introduction

The malignant melanoma [1] is a malignant tumor of the skin, mucous membranes or the uveitis. It is dangerous because it grows fast and easily metastasizes. Late detection of the malignant melanoma is responsible for 75% of deaths associated with skin cancers. Annually over 77 thousand people die from malignant melanoma worldwide. (14-th place in neoplastic disease,
http://www.worldlifeexpectancy.com/world-rankings-total-deaths). This cancer arises from the cells that produce melanin pigment (called melanocytes) and are further transformed into malignant ones. Ultraviolet radiation is considered to be the main cause for the malignant mutation.

Prognosis depends on tumor type and the development of skin lesion inside the tissue. Two scales are used for malignancy evaluation, the five-point Clark scale [1] and the four-point Breslow scale [1]. Both scales take into account only the depth of invasion. For lesser malignant tumors the cure rate is over 90%, if diagnosed early.

Due to the rapid course of the disease, early diagnosis is an important factor that increases chances of successful cure. Computer analysis and image processing are effective tools supporting quantitative medical diagnosis [2]. Therefore it is appropriate to develop computer based methods for dermatological images

L.J. Chmielewski et al. (Eds.): ICCVG 2014, LNCS 8671, pp. 347–355, 2014.

analysis. This can objectify, accelerate and improve the efficiency of melanoma diagnosis.

The segmentation is a very important step in the computer aided diagnosis. Precise segmentation is needed for further automated analysis which will lead to an accurate diagnosis of the malignant melanoma.

The problem of skin lesion image segmentation has been raised often in literature in the past several years. Work [3] contains extensive overview of methods used in melanoma segmentation. The authors used methods such as thresholding [4], the Otsu method [4], the adaptive method [3], gradient based methods [3], fuzzy C-means [5], gradient vector flow [3], adaptive snake [3], Expectation Maximization Level Set Method [3], Fuzzy-Based Split-and-Merge Algorithm [3]. The conducted trials show that the best methods are adaptive snake, expectation-maximization and level-set.

Another group of methods for melanoma and non-melanoma image segmentation was evaluated in [6]. Methods such as Garnavis method [7], statistical region merging [8], k-means [9], unsupervised segmentation of color-texture regions [10], and the dermatologist-like method [11]. The best results were obtained by means of Garnavi and dermatologist like methods. Althought plenty of methods used in dermatoscopy images segmentation, none of them is golden standard for assessment and comparison of the segmentation methods. Thus there is a need for development of image analysis techniques that satisfy at least subjective criteria defined by dermatologists.

In article [15] complete system of melanoma diagnosis is presented. The system combines pre-processing operations such as contrast increase, segmentation using histogram triangulation, post-processing, ABCD feature extraction and computation of Total Dermatoscopy Score and classification. Based on the author research system achieved 92% accuracy.

The aim of this paper is to present a new segmentation approach for images that contain melanocytic nevuss. The proposed method utilizes skin model based on histograms in the RGB color space. Such a method is similar to the background identification concept shown in [12]. The effectiveness of the proposed method was quantitatively compared to other known in approaches, such as thresholding [4], the Otsu method [4], the adaptive method [3] and level set [13].

The structure of the work is as follows. The second chapter presents short overview of current methods of melanoma image analysis. The third chapter contains description of the analyzed images and the proposed segmentation method. The fourth chapter presents some tests of the proposed method. The sixth chapter contains the discussion of test results. The last chapter sums up the paper.

2   Materials and Methods

The material in our work constitutes 40 digital images of skin lesions (Fig.1).

The images contain malignant melanoma and non-malignant nevi. Our acquisition system consist of a digital camera (Nikon D90) equipped with the dermatoscope (Heine Delta 20). Images were recorded in the RGB format

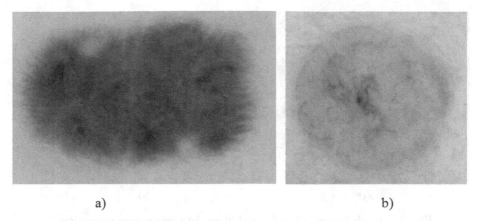

a)   b)

Fig. 1. Melanoma nevus (a), and non melanoma nevus (b)

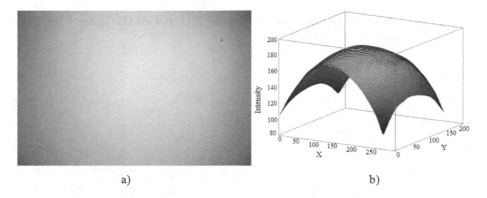

a)   b)

Fig. 2. The image of the white test plate obtained by means of the acquisition system (a). The Illumination model of the dermatoscope (b).

(16 bits per channel). The resolution of images is 2848 x 4288 pixels. Field of view (FOV) covers an area of 10 by 15 mm. Original image files were saved as Nikon Electronic Format (NEF). For analysis all files were converted to 24 bit bitmaps (8 bits per channel). For all 40 images, a trained dermatologist manually created masks outlined investigated nevi for evaluation of the tested segmentation methods (Fig.8).

Examination of the images shows that the FOV is not uniformly illuminated. Corners of the FOV are slightly darker than the center. Such characteristic of the image can affect segmentation results for methods which utilize thresholding. In order to estimate the illumination characteristic, the image of a uniformly white test plate was acquired (Fig 2a). Based on the test plate image, the dermatoscope illumination model was estimated (Fig. 2b).

This model was used to correct the skin lesion images. Each image was corrected by adding the inverted illumination model. Fig. 3 shows example of an image before and after the correction.

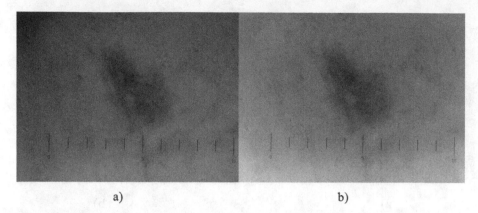

a)   b)

Fig. 3. Sample image before (a) and after (b) illumination correction.

The Fig. 4 shows an intensity profile for the 11th row of the image from Fig. 3 before and after the correction.

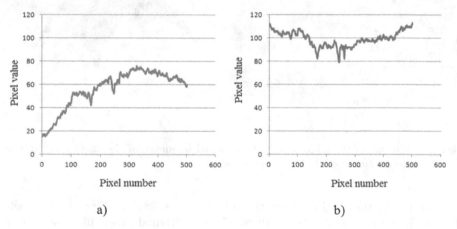

a)   b)

Fig. 4. The intensity profile for the 11th row of image from fig. 3 before (a) and after (b) the illumination correction.

The analyzed images might contain some artificial objects in the FOV, such the scale on a dermatoscope lens or a color phantom (as shown in Fig. 3). Such objects can affect the segmentation results. To avoid them, image regions containing healthy skin and skin lesion only were marked manually for further analysis.

2.1   Simple Skin Modeling

In order to segment the skin lesion images the Simple Skin Modeling (SSM) algorithm was proposed, as shown in Fig. 5.

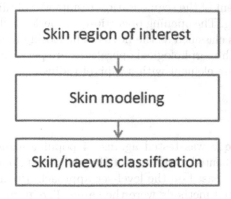

Fig. 5. The SSM segmentation algorithm

The SSM is a semiautomatic method. In the first step the user marks a region (or regions) containing the healthy skin. Four such regions are shown in Fig.6.

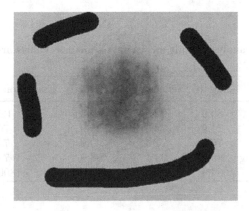

Fig. 6. Four regions of the healthy skin marked on the sample image

In the next step algorithm scans the image pixels in the selected skin area and finds the lowest minimum and the highest maximum intensity values for each color channel (R,G,B channels are used). Those three ranges constitute the assumed simple skin model.

The last step of the procedure is to classify all pixels of the image. If all RGB intensities of given pixel fall between the minimum and the maximum ranges, such pixel is classified as the healthy skin, otherwise it belongs to the nevus. Thus as a result of the above algorithm two regions (healthy skin and nevus) are obtained.

Further improvement of the segmentation results was obtained using morphological post-processing. The opening operation was performed in order to remove small groups of pixels classified as the nevus. The closing removes small holes in the nevus region. Both morphological operations are performed by means of the disc shaped structuring element with a 5 pixel radius.

3   Results

The proposed technique was tested against 4 popular segmentation methods. Three of them implemented variations of thresholding (global, adaptive, Otsu) while the last one was based on the level-set approach. Pre and post processing operations for all tested methods were the same. The ground true images were obtained based on manual segmentation performed by the dermatologist. Sample segmentation results for all investigated methods are shown in the Fig. 7.

Three parameters were used to evaluate robustness of the above methods: the Jaccard index [14], the sensitivity and the specificity. Averaged values of evaluated parameters obtained for all 40 test images are shown in Table 1. Additionally, the execution times needed for each investigated segmentation method were measured (PC Intel Mobile Core 2 Duo T9400, 2.53GHz) and presented in Table 1.

Table 1. Averaged analysis result for 40 nevus images. Values are given in percent

Method	Jaccard	Sensitivity	Specificity	Execution time [ms]
SSM	89,5	92,5	99,3	125
Adaptive	71,9	72,3	99,9	76
Otsu	76,7	77,4	99,6	74
Thresholding	89,8	93,1	98,9	73
Level Set	84,4	91,8	98,0	180000

4   Discussion

The SSM along with the global threshold outperforms the Otsu and the level set methods according to the Jaccard index and the sensitivity. The specificity was almost the same for all tested approaches. The thresholding is slightly better in terms of the Jaccard index and the sensitivity when compared to the SSM, however the latter provider higher specificity. The global thresholding requires a manual selection of threshold to ensure the best segmentation. According to computation times all methods except the level set are executed in a fraction of a second.

The proposed simple skin model method requires an interaction from the user. This interaction involves marking a reference region of healthy skin. For

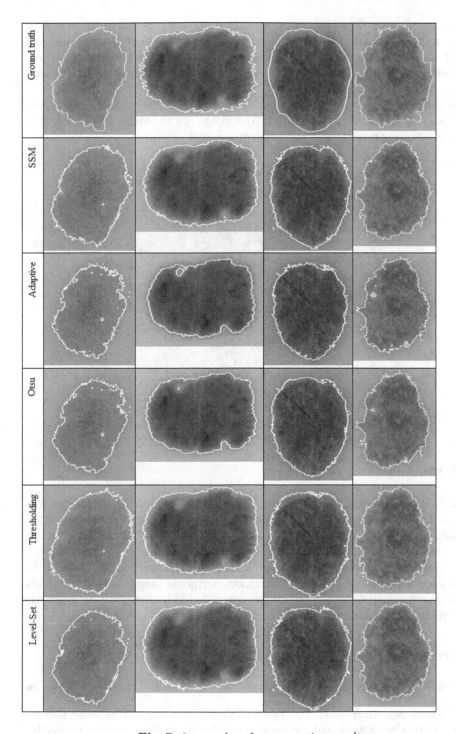

Fig. 7. 4 examples of segmentation results

the application of a skin lesion analysis this is not a big problem, as usually a limited number of lesions is analyzed during a dermatological examination of a patient so the marking of the skin region will not extend the examination time. The clear advantage of the SSM method is the lack of parameters which need setting during the image analysis.

Limitations of SSM and other tested methods are the segmentation artifacts introduced by the presence of hairs in the image, as shown in Fig. 8. Further works will concentrate on hair and artifact removal.

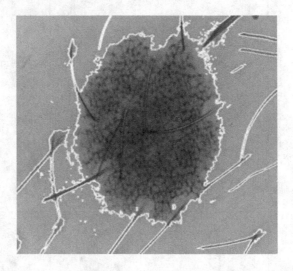

Fig. 8. A segmentation affected due to presence of hairs

5 Summary

A simple and efficient method for the segmentation of skin lesion images was presented. The SSM algorithm was tested against other popular segmentation methods which are reported in the literature. Conducted tests demonstrated the robustness of the SSM method. It is also simple and does not require definition of additional parameters. Further improvements of the method are possible to obtain even better accuracy. The research on melanoma image analysis methods will be continued, to develop a reliable computer based tool supporting diagnosis of the malignant melanoma.

References

1. Jablonska, S., Chorzelski, T.: Choroby skory, Wydawnictwo Lekarskie, Warsaw (in Polish 2004)
2. Strzelecki, M., Szczypinski, P., Materka, A., Klepaczko, A.: A software tool for automatic classification and segmentation of 2D/3D medical images. Nuclear Instruments & Methods In Physics Research A 702, 137–140 (2013)

3. Silveira, M., Nascimento, J.C., Marques, J.S., Maral, A.R.S., Mendona, T., Yamauchi, S., Maeda, J., Rozeira, J.: Comparison of Segmentation Methods for Melanoma Diagnosis in Dermoscopy Images. IEEE Journal of Selected Topics in Signal Processing 3(1), 35–45 (2009)
4. Gonzalez, R.C., Woods, R.E.: Digital Image Processing. Pearson International Edition
5. Beuren, A.T., Pinheiro, R.J.G., Facon, J.: Color approach of melanoma lesion segmentation. In: IWSSIP 2012, Vienna, Austria, April 11-13, pp. 284–287 (2012) ISBN 978-3-200-02328-4
6. Norton, K.-A., Iyatomi, H., Celebi, M.E., Ishizaki, S., Sawada, M., Suzaki, R., Kobayashi, K., Tanaka, M., Ogawa, K.: Three-phase general border detection method for dermoscopy images using non-uniform illumination correction. Skin Research and Technology 18, 290–300 (2012), doi:10.1111/j.1600-0846.2011.00569.x
7. Garnavi, R., Aldeen, M., Celebi, M.E., Varigos, G., Finch, S.: Border detection in dermoscopy images using hybrid thresholding on optimized color channels. Computerized Medical Imaging and Graphics 35, 105–115 (2011)
8. Celebi, M.E., Kingravi, H.A., Iyatomi, H., Aslandogan, Y.A., Stoecker, W.V., Moss, R.H., Malters, J.M., Grichnik, J.M., Marghoob, A.A., Rabinovitz, H.S., Menzies, S.W.: Border detection in dermoscopy images using statistical region Mering. Skin Research and Technology 14, 347–353 (2008)
9. Zhou, H., Chen, M., Gass, R., Ferris, L., Drogowski, L., Rehg, J.M.: Spatially constrained segmentation of dermoscopy images. In: The 5th IEEE International Symposium on ISBI 2008, pp. 800–803 (2008)
10. Celebi, M.E., Aslandogan, Y.A., Stoecker, W.V., Iyatomi, H., Oka, H., Chen, X.: Unsupervised border detection in dermoscopy images. Skin Research and Technology 13, 454–462 (2007)
11. Iyatomi, H., Oka, H., Saito, M., Miyake, A., Kimoto, M., Yamagami, J., Kobayashi, S., Tanikawa, A., Hagiwara, M., Ogawa, K., Argenziano, G., Soyer, H.P., Tanaka, M.: Quantitative assessment of tumour extraction from dermoscopy images and evaluation of computer - based extraction methods for an automatic melanoma diagnostic system. Melanoma Research 16, 183–190 (2006)
12. Chalfoun, J., Kociolek, M., Dima, A., Halter, M., Cardone, A., Peskin, A., Bajcsy, P., Brady, M.: Segmenting time-lapse phase contrast images of adjacent NIH 3T3 cells. Journal of Microscopy 249(1), 41–52 (2013)
13. Chan, T.F., Vese, L.A.: Active Contours Without Edges. IEEE Transactions on Image Processing 10(2), 266–277 (2001)
14. Tan, P.N., Steinbach, M., Kumar, V.: Introduction to Data Mining. Addison-Wesley (2005)
15. Smaoui, N., Bessassi, S.: A developed system for melanoma diagnosis. International Journal of Computer Vision and Signal Processing 3(1), 10–17 (2013)

DTW-Based Gait Recognition from Recovered 3-D Joint Angles and Inter-ankle Distance

Tomasz Krzeszowski[3], Adam Switonski[2,4], Bogdan Kwolek[1],
Henryk Josinski[4], and Konrad Wojciechowski[2,4]

[1] AGH University of Science and Technology
30 Mickiewicza Av., 30-059 Krakow, Poland
[2] Polish-Japanese Institute of Information Technology
Al. Legionów 2, 41-902 Bytom, Poland
[3] Rzeszów University of Technology
Al. Powst. Warszawy 12, 35-959 Rzeszów, Poland
[4] Silesian University of Technology
Akademicka 16, 44-100 Gliwice, Poland
tkrzeszo@prz.edu.pl, {aswitonski,kwojciechowski}@pjwstk.edu.pl,
bkw@agh.edu.pl, henryk.josinski@polsl.pl

Abstract. We present a view independent approach for 3D human gait recognition. The identification of the person is done on the basis of motion estimated by our marker-less 3D motion tracking algorithm. We show tracking performance using ground-truth data acquired by Vicon motion capture system. The identification is achieved by dynamic time warping using both joint angles and inter-joint distances. We show how to calculate approximate Euclidean distance metric between two sets of Euler angles. We compare the correctly classified ratio obtained by DTW built on unit quaternion distance metric and such an Euler angle distance metric. We then show that combining the rotation distances with inter-ankle distances and other person attributes like height leads to considerably better correctly classified ratio.

1 Introduction

Gait is an attractive biometric feature for human identification at a distance [2]. Compared with other biometric modalities, such as face or iris, gait has many advantages since the identification techniques are non-contact, non-invasive, perceivable at a larger distance and do not require cooperation of the individual.

The existing methods for gait recognition can be divided in two main categories: appearance-based (model-free) and model-based [9]. Appearance-based gait recognition approaches consider gait as a holistic pattern, where the full-body of a human subject is represented by silhouettes or contours. Model-based approaches identify individuals on the basis of kinematic characteristics of the walking manner. Model based approaches fit a model to human body and represent gait using the parameters of the model that are estimated over time. Model based approaches are more complex and computationally more expensive than

L.J. Chmielewski et al. (Eds.): ICCVG 2014, LNCS 8671, pp. 356–363, 2014.
© Springer International Publishing Switzerland 2014

model free approaches. Thus, the majority of the approaches are based on appearance and rely on analysis of image sequences acquired by a single camera. The main limitation of such approaches is that they can perform the recognition from a specific viewpoint. To achieve view-independent person identification, Jean et al. [4] proposed an approach to determine view-normalized body part trajectories. However, as reported by Yu et al. [15], the appearance-based methods are view dependent and perform best when a side view is used.

The use of 3D gait analysis dates back to the nineties of the last century [1]. In 3D gait recognition the human body structures are modeled explicitly, often with support of the gait biomechanics [14]. As a result, they are far more resistant to view changes than 2D approaches. In [12] 3D markers locations were used to extract joint-angle trajectories. The recognition was achieved using dynamic time warping on the normalized joint-angle information and nearest neighbor classifier with Euclidean distance. It was evaluated on two walking databases of 18 people and over 150 walk instances. In [13], an approach relying on matching 3D motion models to images, and then tracking and restoring the motion parameters is proposed. The system was evaluated on datasets with four people, i.e. 2 women and 2 men walking at 9 different speeds ranging from 3 to 7 km/h by increments of 0.5 km/h. The motion models were derived on the basis of Vicon motion capture system (moCap). Recently, in [3] a multi-camera based gait recognition method has been developed to overcome the non-frontal pose problem. The recognition was done using the recovered 3D human joints.

Despite its attractive features, gait-based person identification is still far from being ready to be deployed in practice. What limits the use of gait recognition systems in real-world scenarios is the impact of lots of covariate factors, which affect the dynamics of the gait. The most important covariate factors include camera setup (viewpoint), lightning, walking surface, footwear and clothing, carrying conditions. Thus, most of gait analysis techniques, particularly neglecting 3D information, are unable to reliably match gait signatures from differing viewpoints, but also in case of different walking surface, different clothing. Moreover, they are also strongly dependant on the ability of the background segmentation and require accurate delineation between the subject and the background.

In this work, 3D-joint angles and locations are estimated on the basis of marker-less human motion tracking. They are inferred with the help of a 3D human model. The estimation takes place on video sequences acquired by four calibrated and synchronized cameras. We show the tracking performance of the motion tracking algorithm using ground-truth data acquired by a commercial motion capture system from Vicon Nexus. The person identification is done on the basis of dynamic time warping (DTW) using both joint angles and inter-joint distances. We show how to calculate approximate Euclidean distance metric between two sets of Euler angles. We compare the correctly classified ratio obtained by DTW built on unit quaternion distance metric and such an Euler angle distance metric. We then show that combining the rotation distances with the inter-ankle distances and other person attributes like height leads to considerably better correctly classified ratio of the person identification system.

2   Articulated Motion Tracking

The purpose of motion capture systems is to measure the motion of bony segments during various activities of the performer. Optical marker motion capture
(marker-based) relies on attaching reflective markers to be tracked using standard computer-vision techniques. One of the most popular commercially available systems is provided by Vicon. The Vicon system relies on infrared cameras
and artificial reflective markers. The markers are attached to predefined body
parts of a human subject. The markers reflect the light signal, which is emitted
and then registered by a set of infrared cameras surrounding the subject. The
data from each camera consisting of 2D coordinates of each recognized marker
position is matched and then used by the triangulation algorithm, which computes the 3D position and the label of each visible marker. The motion data are
stored in the C3D format, in which each frame of information is represented as
a list consisting of Cartesian x, y, z coordinates for each marker. The motions
are stored in ASF/AMC format with 19 defined segments, see also the skeleton
on Fig. 1. They are calculated on the basis of 39 markers.

Most approaches for marker-less 3D motion tracking use a human body model
to guide the pose estimation process, as the use of a model greatly increases the
accuracy and robustness of the pose recovery. In our system [6], the articulated
model of the human body is built on kinematic chain with 11 segments. Such a
3D model consists of truncated cones that model the pelvis, torso/head, upper
and lower arm and legs, see Fig. 1. Its configuration is defined by 26 DOF and it
is determined by position and orientation of the pelvis in the global coordinate
system and the relative angles between the connected limbs. Each truncated
cone is projected into 2D image plane via perspective projection. In this way we
attain the image of the 3D model in a given configuration, which can then be
matched to the person extracted through image analysis. A modified Particle
Swarm Optimization (APSO) algorithm is used to estimate the 3D motion [5].
The motion is inferred using four calibrated and synchronized cameras.

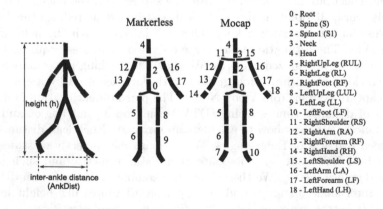

Fig. 1. Human attributes and joints used in gait recognition

3   DTW on Joint Rotations and Geometric Relations

Dynamic time warping (DTW) [10] is algorithm for assessment the similarity between two temporal sequences, which may vary in time or speed. DTW is often used in motion analysis [7]. The similarities in walking patterns could be measured by DTW, even if one person was walking faster than the other, or if there were accelerations and decelerations during the movements. It determines an optimal match between two given sequences and returns distance-like measure between sequences. The sequences are warped non-linearly in the time dimension to match each other as closely as possible.

In the DTW algorithm, two motions R and R' of length N and M frames, respectively, are compared using local cost measure c. By evaluating c for all possible pairs of data we get a cost matrix C of size $N \times M$, which contains the matching costs. To find the best match between the given sequences we should find a path through the grid, which minimizes the total distance between them. The alignment minimizing the cost is represented by a so-called warping path, which, under certain constraints, optimally allocates the frame indices of the first motion with the frame indices of the second motion. Such optimal path can be found in $O(NM)$ using dynamic programming.

The natural way for representing human motion is to encode the rotations of each bone around three axes. One possible alternative is to utilize unit quaternions for encoding joint rotations. Quaternion-based pose distance is often used in DTW-based motion comparison [11]. However, quaternions can represent only rotations around a line through the origin of the coordinate system. As pointed out in [8], geometric relations between body key points are very important motion features. Thus, in our DTW-based algorithm for gait recognition we employ both individual distances between corresponding joint rotations as well as geometric relations between body parts.

Assume that B is a set of bones that are directed away from the root of the kinematic chain. The minimum angle between two angles $\Delta(\theta, \theta')$ was computed as follows: $\Delta(\theta, \theta') = \pi - ||\theta - \theta'| - \pi|$. The approximate measure of the distance between the two joint rotations is the sum of each of the Euler angle differences: $\rho_\theta = \sqrt{\Delta(\theta, \theta')^2 + \Delta(\phi, \phi')^2 + \Delta(\eta, \eta')^2}$. The local cost measure is equal to sum of the approximate distances between each two corresponding joint rotations: $c_\theta = \sum_{b \in B} \rho_\theta(b)$. For DTW employing both individual distances between corresponding joint rotations, geometric relations between body parts, and other body features, their weighted 3D Euclidean distance terms are included in the objective function: $c_{pose} = w_1 c_\theta + w_2(|h - h'| + |AnkDist - AnkDist'|)$, where h denotes persons's height, $AnkDist$ stands for inter-ankle distance, $w_1 = 57.3$ and $w_2 = 1.7$.

The quaternion based pose distance between two human poses has been calculated as sum of terms expressing distances between unit quaternions: $c_{quat} = \sum_{b \in B} 2/\pi \arccos(\langle q_b, q_b' \rangle)$, where $\langle \cdot, \cdot \rangle$ stands for standard dot product in $\mathbb{R}^4$. The term $\arccos(\langle q_b, q_b' \rangle)$ is known as the geodesic distance of the real three-dimensional projective space, which assumes it maximal value equal to $\pi/2$ for the case that q_b and q_b' are orthogonal.

4   Experimental Results

The marker-less motion tracking system was evaluated on video sequences with 22 walking individuals. In each sequence the same actor performed two walks, consisting in following a virtual line joining two opposite cameras and following a virtual line joining two nonconsecutive laboratory corners. The first subsequence is referred to as 'straight', whereas the second one is called 'diagonal'. Given the estimated pose, the model was projected to 2D plane and then overlaid on the images. Figure 2 depicts some results that were obtained for person 1 in a straight walk. The degree of overlap of the projected 3D body model with the performer's silhouette reflects the accuracy of motion tracking. The results were obtained by APSO consisting of 300 particles and executing 20 iterations per frame.

Fig. 2. 3D human body tracking in sequence p1s2. Shown are results in frames #0, 20, 40, 60, 80, 100. The left sub-images are seen from view 1, the right ones - view 2.

In Table 1 are shown some quantitative results that were obtained using the discussed image sequences. Given the human pose estimated by marker-less system, as well as the locations of physical markers, the virtual markers were generated on the 3D model utilized in marker-less moCap. The errors were calculated using the locations of the markers recovered by marker-based moCap system and locations of the virtual markers estimated by our marker-less moCap system. For each frame they were computed as average Euclidean distance between corresponding physical and virtual markers. For each sequence they were then averaged over ten runs of the APSO with unlike initializations.

Table 2 presents correctly classified ratio (CCR) that was obtained by DTW built on angle distance metrics only. It demonstrates the CCRs, which were

Table 1. Average errors for $M = 39$ markers in four image sequences. The images from sequence p1s2 are depicted on Fig. 2.

	#particles	it.	Seq. p1s1 error [mm]	Seq. p1s2 error [mm]	Seq. p2s1 error [mm]	Seq. p2s2 error [mm]
APSO	100	10	60.0±42.9	51.3±25.5	59.8±30.4	55.8±23.2
	100	20	50.1±29.3	47.6±21.5	57.8±24.7	55.4±20.3
	300	10	48.4±29.9	48.4±24.7	58.5±26.6	56.2±20.5
	300	20	44.9±22.1	45.0±19.9	56.3±22.1	54.1±17.4

Table 2. CCR obtained by DTW built on angle distance metrics

	System	Metrics	Rank 1 CCR	[%]	Rank 2 CCR	[%]	Rank 3 CCR	[%]
crossval	Motion	Euclid.	199	86.5	216	93.9	223	97.0
		Manhattan	202	87.8	217	94.3	222	96.5
		Quat. geod.	197	85.6	217	94.3	224	97.4
	moCap	Euclid.	230	100	230	100	230	100
		Manhattan	230	100	230	100	230	100
		Quat. geod.	230	100	230	100	230	100

Table 3. CCR obtained by DTW using angle distance, inter-ankle distance and height

	System	Metrics	Rank 1 CCR	[%]	Rank 2 CCR	[%]	Rank 3 CCR	[%]
crossval	Motion	Euclid.	222	96.5	229	99.6	230	100
		Manhattan	223	97.0	227	98.7	230	100
	moCap	Euclid.	230	100	230	100	230	100
		Manhattan	230	100	230	100	230	100
sep. test/val	Motion	Euclid.	93	80.2	106	91.4	112	96.5
		Manhattan	93	80.2	105	90.5	112	96.5
	moCap	Euclid.	114	98.3	230	100	230	100
		Manhattan	115	99.1	230	100	230	100

achieved using data from both maker-based and marker-less motion capture systems. At the beginning we evaluated CCR in 10-fold evaluation using approximate Euclidean and Manhattan distance metrics between sets of Euler angles as well as quaternion geodesic distance. As we can observe, the DTW built on approximate Euclidean and Manhattan distances gave better CCR scores than DTW operating on geodesic quaternion distances. The CCR that was obtained using data from marker-based moCap is perfect.

Table 3 shows CCR that was obtained using 3-D joint angles, inter-ankle distance and height, recovered by our marker-less moCap system. As we can observe, the CCR ratio is much higher in comparison to CCR, which was obtained by DTW operating on rotation information only. Thanks to the use of the approximate angle metrics together with joint-to-joint distances and other human attributes like height we achieved considerably better identification performance. We calculated also CCR using separated test and validation data. As we can notice, for marker-less system, the CCR obtained on separate test and validation data is smaller in comparison to CCR, which was obtained in the 10-fold cross-validation.

Figure 3 depicts the confusion matrix both for DTW operating on rotation data only and rotation data together with inter-ankle distances and height. As we can see, the distance between joints as well as person attributes like height lead to far better identification scores.

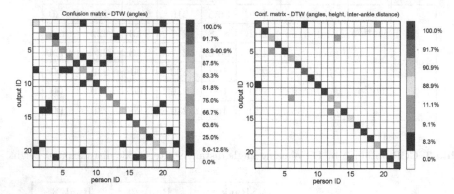

Fig. 3. Confusion matrix for DTW operating on angles only (left), DTW built on angles, inter-ankle distances, and height (right)

Figure 4 illustrates the warping paths for LeftUpLeg joints as well as inter-ankle distance, see Fig. 1, which were obtained for person 1 and 2. The discussed figure demonstrates that both angles and inter-joints distances contribute towards better identification performance.

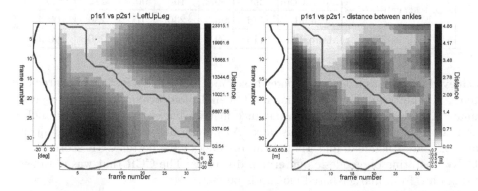

Fig. 4. Warping paths for a joint angle (left) and inter-ankle distance (right)

5   Conclusions

In DTW-based comparison of motion sequences the standard approach consists in the use of quaternions. However, the quaternions can not be utilized to measure the inter-joints distances. In order to comprise such inter-joints distances as well as other human attributes we proposed to use approximate Euclidean distance metric between two sets of Euler angles in dynamic time warping. Owing to the use of such a metric we can combine the rotations with inter-joint distances and other features. We demonstrated that the combined features allow us to obtain better classification scores.

Acknowledgment. This work has been partially supported by the Polish Ministry of Science and Higher Education within a grant for young researchers U-529/DS/M and the National Science Center (NCN) within the research projects N N516 483240 and DEC-2011/01/B/ST6/06988.

References

1. Areblad, M., Nigg, B., Ekstrand, J., Olsson, K., Ekström, H.: Three-dimensional measurement of rearfoot motion during running. J. Biom. 23(9), 933–940 (1990)
2. Boulgouris, N., Hatzinakos, D., Plataniotis, K.: Gait recognition: a challenging signal processing technology for biometric identification. Signal Proc. Magazine, 78–90 (2005)
3. Gu, J., Ding, X., Wang, S., Wu, Y.: Action and gait recognition from recovered 3-D human joints. IEEE Trans. Sys. Man Cyber. Part B 40(4), 1021–1033 (2010)
4. Jean, F., Albu, A.B., Bergevin, R.: Towards view-invariant gait modeling: Computing view-normalized body part trajectories. Pattern Recogn 42(11) (November 2009)
5. Krzeszowski, T., Kwolek, B., Wojciechowski, K., Josinski, H.: Markerless articulated human body tracking for gait analysis and recognition. Machine Graphics & Vision 20(3), 267–281 (2011)
6. Krzeszowski, T., Kwolek, B., Michalczuk, A., Świtoński, A., Josiński, H.: View independent human gait recognition using markerless 3D human motion capture. In: Bolc, L., Tadeusiewicz, R., Chmielewski, L.J., Wojciechowski, K. (eds.) ICCVG 2012. LNCS, vol. 7594, pp. 491–500. Springer, Heidelberg (2012)
7. Kulbacki, M., Bak, A.: Unsupervised learning motion models using dynamic time warping. In: Intelligent Information Systems. Advances in Soft Computing, vol. 17, pp. 217–226. Physica-Verlag HD (2002)
8. Müller, M., Röder, T., Clausen, M.: Efficient content-based retrieval of motion capture data. ACM Trans. Graph. 24(3), 677–685 (2005)
9. Nixon, M.S., Carter, J.: Automatic recognition by gait. Proc. of the IEEE 94(11), 2013–2024 (2006)
10. Sakoe, H., Chiba, S.: Dynamic programming algorithm optimization for spoken word recognition. IEEE Trans. on Acoustics, Speech and Signal Processing 26(1), 43–49 (1978)
11. Switonski, A., Polanski, A., Wojciechowski, K.: Human identification based on the reduced kinematic data of the gait. Int. Sym. Sig. Pr. Anal., 650–655 (2011)
12. Tanawongsuwan, R., Bobick, A.: Gait recognition from time-normalized joint-angle trajectories in the walking plane. In: CVPR, vol. 2, pp. 726–731 (2001)
13. Urtasun, R., Fua, P.: 3D tracking for gait characterization and recognition. In: Proc. of IEEE Int. Conf. on Automatic Face and Gesture Rec., pp. 17–22 (2004)
14. Yam, C., Nixon, M.S., Carter, J.N.: Automated person recognition by walking and running via model-based approaches. Pattern Rec. 37(5), 1057–1072 (2004)
15. Yu, S., Tan, D., Tan, T.: Modelling the effect of view angle variation on appearance-based gait recognition. In: Narayanan, P.J., Nayar, S.K., Shum, H.-Y. (eds.) ACCV 2006. LNCS, vol. 3851, pp. 807–816. Springer, Heidelberg (2006)

Collaborative Tool for Annotation of Synovitis and Assessment in Ultrasound Images

Marek Kulbacki[1], Jakub Segen[1], Piotr Habela[1], Mateusz Janiak[1],
Wojciech Knieć[1], Marcin Fojcik[2], Paweł Mielnik[3], and Konrad Wojciechowski[1]

[1] Polish-Japanese Institute of Information Technology
Koszykowa 86, 02-008 Warsaw, Poland
[2] Sogn og Fjordane University College
Vievegen 2, 6812 Førde, Norway
[3] Revmatologisk Avdeling, Førde sentralsjukehus
Svanehaugvegen 2, 6812 Førde, Norway
mk@pjwstk.edu.pl

Abstract. We present a cloud based collaborative tool intended for organization and unification of USG data and annotation of features useful for discovery of synovitis. The Annotation Editor can be used to outline anatomical features in an ultrasound images such as joint and bones, and identify regions of synovitis and level of synovitis activity. The software will be used by medical personnel for building reference database of annotated ultrasound images. This database will be the source of training and testing data in a system of automated assessment of synovitis activity. System supports collaborative use and management of the database from multiple locations. Semiquantitative ultrasound is a reliable and widely used method of assessing synovitis. Presently used manual assessment needs trained medical personnel and the result can be affected by a human error. A proposed system that can automatically assess the activity of synovitis would eliminate human dependent discrepancies and reduce time and the cost of evaluation.

Keywords: Synovitis, Medical Image Annotation, Ultrasonography, Medical Databases, Modern Diagnostics.

1 Introduction

Chronic arthritis is a heterogeneous group of diseases characterized by longlasting inflammation of joints. They can influence the patients general condition and involve other organs besides joints. Prevalence of chronic arthritis can be estimated up to 1.5% of population. The most frequent is rheumatoid arthritis with estimated prevalence from 0.5 to 1.0% of population. Accurate measurement of disease activity is crucial to provide an adequate treatment and care to the patients, and medical ultrasound examination provides useful information regarding this activity. Medical ultrasound examination is a method of visualization of the human body structures with high frequency acoustic waves. Power Doppler method uses Doppler effect to measure and visualize blood circulation

L.J. Chmielewski et al. (Eds.): ICCVG 2014, LNCS 8671, pp. 364–373, 2014.

in tissues. Ultrasound examination with power Doppler is a validated method of assessing joint inflammation [1]. The procedure is standardized and different projections can be used to visualize joints and joint inflammation, but most frequently dorsal medial line is used in joints of the hand. Both quantitative and semiquantitative methods of activity measurement were evaluated in clinical praxis [2,3]. Both were considered reliable and repeatable. When quantitative methods measure directly different parameters such as intensity of Doppler signal, semiquantitative method evaluates ultrasound image. The second one is performed by a human examiner. The examiner estimates the synovitis activity based on experience or standardized atlases. The result is registered as a number from 0 to 3, where 0 means no inflammation and 3 the highest possible inflammation activity. Level of arthritis in USG without PD is achieved with estimation of dark grey/black area (hypoechoic) over the joint. Measured area corresponds to area of synovitis (Fig. 1 top). In USG with PD the this level is estimated according to intensity and area with a visible flow in small blood around the field of synovitis (Fig. 1 bottom).

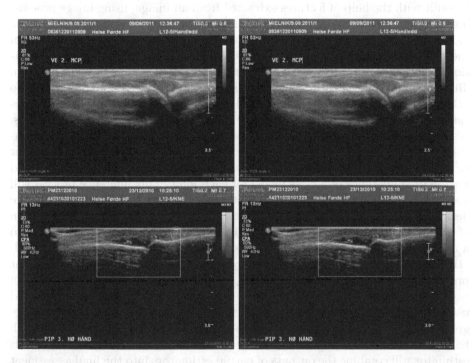

Fig. 1. Images of selected joint without and with outlined synovitis region: classic USG (top), USG with PD (bottom)

Semiquantitative method is more often used in clinical praxis and scientific studies [2]. Possible discrepancies between different examiners and different examinations can influence results in this method [4]. A software system with automated synovitis assessments would reduce human dependent discrepancies in synovitis evaluation, which would improve the quality of results from large multicenter studies, where comparability of assessments from different sources is essential. It would also reduce the time and cost of large scale medical trials and help in everyday clinical practice. A project MEDUSA, summarized in Section 1.1, has been undertaken towards the development of such a system. A tool for ultrasound image data organization and annotation, which is a critical part of MEDUSA, is described in the reminder of this paper.

1.1   The Goal - Synovitis Estimator

Manually prepared annotations are necessary to construct a synovitis estimator - an adaptable function, that will be trained to assess a degree of synovitis activity from an ultrasound image of a joint using machine learning methods. The estimator will be trained using ultrasound images of joints along with their synovitis assessment activity scores provided by expert examiners, with the aim for the estimator to approximate the average expert score. The estimator will be built with the help of features extracted from an image, using image processing methods. While many common techniques of image based recognition use global features that preserve only a small part of image information, a goal of the proposed approach is to use as much as possible of the relevant information from images in a form that is invariant to transformations resulting from different probe placements, joint articulations, and interpatient differences. To achieve this goal we use an articulated model containing the image features that are related to parts of the skeleton, such as the bone edges and joints. A method of registration appropriate for articulated models, such as the Constellation method, graphcuts optimization [5], Laplacian eigenfunctions [6], or stochastic graphs [7], are the basis of a learning algorithm that will be used for the final inference of a class model for each joint. This inference process will use a supervised learning approach that relies on annotations identifying the desired features, added to the test images by trained examiners. Registration of an image of a joint with a class model will, in effect, bring the image into a common frame of reference. The measurements performed on the image relative to the class model will have reduced variability with respect to different probe placements and joint articulations, and after intensity normalization, with respect to interpatient differences. The synovitis estimator will be constructed using methods of learning multivariate functions, such as the multivariate regression. For a greater reliability, multiple partial estimators will be used, each based on a different type of image measurement. The final, integrated synovitis estimator will combine the outputs of partial estimators into the final assessment score using a method such as boosting [8]. To collect representative training sets required for analyses of USG images and assessment of synovitis activity stage and gather rheumatologists, annotators and researchers distributed geographically we developed collaborative environment for organization and processing of USG data.

1.2   Medical Data Collection and Feature Selection

Ultrasound images are collected in standard measurement procedure from the patients with chronic arthritis during routine visits at the rheumatology department of Helse Førde. Preliminary analyses are conducted by trained, experienced medical personnel. In the next step group of trained medical students adds manually annotations representing joint structure and inflammatory level. Annotations added to the images by a trained examiner will identify and mark in each image selected anatomical features such as bones and joints, outline the regions that show inflammation and add to the image the human scores of the degree of synovitis (Fig. 2). These annotations verified by experts are training sets necessary for analyses of USG images and assessment of synovitis activity stage. To reduce bias associated with different joint anatomy we limited measurements and assessments to metacarpo-phalangeal joints (MCP) and proximal intra-phalangeal joints (PIP), what results in the occurrence of 20 different joints.

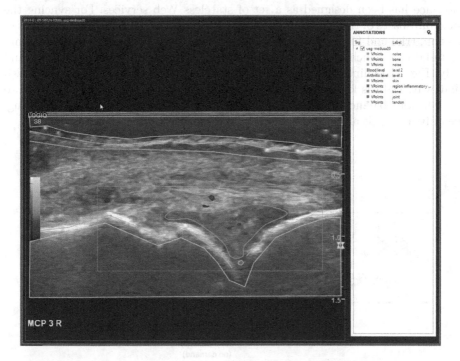

Fig. 2. Annotations of anatomical features and synovitis region and level

2   System Architecture

According to given requirements, the proposed solution is based on client-server model. For performance reasons and flexibility C++ programming language was chosen. Software is able to run in multiplatform environment in particular Linux and Windows platforms with possible extensions to mobile platforms (tablets and smartphones data browsing and inter-user communication). Client application has modular structure, that enables a simple extension of its capabilities with dedicated plugin system. Main requirements of hand ultrasonography image server and its remote access and annotation by a client were motivated by the following considerations:

- The resources on the cloud available to search and download by remote clients;
- Consistent data set in the face of multiple distributed data providers and annotators;
- Consistent authorization mechanism for the data access and updating;
- Uniform data, identifiable and easily transformable for the purpose of prospective integration with another kinds of medical data.

To simplify the design and to allow for partially offline use of the tools, the system interface has been designed as a set of stateless Web services. For syncing the local databases of the client applications with the system, incremental bundles of session, trial and file metadata are served accordingly to a last sync timestamp. Metadata are synchronized separately and data files are downloaded on demand only (Fig. 3). Online collaboration on the trial annotation process is also realized that way. Data is kept under the control of a database management system to ease the load balancing and backups. Raw USG data is not the subject of editing: we only add, edit and delete metadata and annotations.

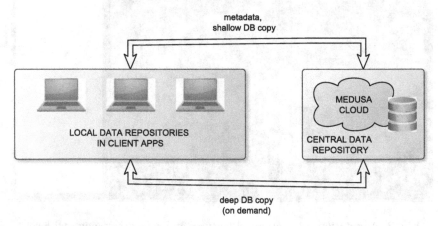

Fig. 3. Data Synchronization between Central Data Repository and Local Data Repository

The developed prototype demonstrates features that benefit medical informatics systems. It provides centralized storage for medical data and their descriptions and exchange of data between users, giving them possibility to consult specific cases. Local repository is ciphered and the access to remote storage is limited only to verified/registered users. Users are able to filter the data according to given criteria and manage filters themselves. This stage supports browsing, viewing, processing and comparing data records. Client application is modular and use intuitive data flow from sources to sinks to easily swap and extend data processing modules [9]. Data processors can perform appropriate data manipulations such as filtering and transforming images or feature detection. Finally data sinks are placed where data flow results would be permanently stored allowing to browse such data and use it in further work. Such data flow allows grouping of elements, performing some more general steps and use that structures separately as templates. It is also possible to save and restore the structure of the processed objects. Such structure could be also exchanged between platform users for discussion of particular data flow application and testing.

2.1   Annotation Editor

The architecture of Annotation Editor is based on previously developed Motion Data Editor [10], that was originally designed to support physicians in viewing medical data for diagnosis of various human movement disorders. The Annotation Editor is an application dedicated to medical and technical staff working with USG images. It's main goal is to support medical teams in collecting USG images, annotating them in the direction of inflammatory level with well-defined image areas and verification of proposed annotations and other attributes. These goals were achieved by a composition of a standalone application (supplied with medical data browser and editor) and dedicated medical images database. Annotation Editor introduces simple, yet complete procedure for annotations state

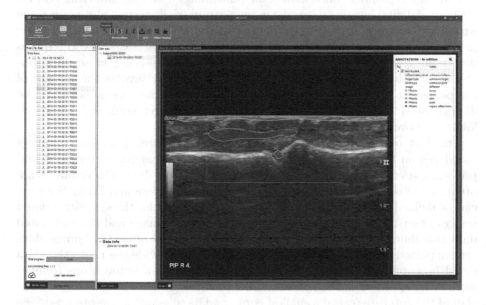

Fig. 4. Annotation Editor User Interface

change based on a simple state machine mechanism. Current USG systems in hospitals provides data in DICOM format. Although it is a standard its very inconvenient for the use in distributed environment, where each operation involving raw image data is a time consuming process. Annotation Editor supports and can import DICOM files but uses PNG format for image processing. PNG format thanks to lossless compression is about 20 times more efficient than original DICOM data. For metadata such as annotations and other descriptive data we chosen XML format. Client application has also custom User Interface with access to different spaces: Data Providers, Viewers, Annotators, Validators (Fig. 4). It organizes data according to the hierarchy Lab > Session > Trial > File. That structure represents the core content of the system (session and trial is only required and visible to the client). But this is the whole structure necessary when we gather data from hospital and process multiple trials. The annotation dictionary provides the building blocks for creating trial annotations. Session groups and User groups are introduced to ease the management of the larger number of users with their various roles and possibly, also a varying access of the data made available to them.

2.2 Database

The database component of the system (Fig. 5) depends on rather conventional technological solutions involving common protocols and data formats used by a stateless service oriented interface layer [11]. This allows for integration with various client platforms while maintaining a uniform mechanism for user identification and authorization. Although the primary role of the component is to provide the repository functionality for publishing, updating, browsing and retrieving of digital imaging data, the usage pattern of the system also poses some workflow management challenges. Those two characteristics, data and workflow management, are interrelated. Even the simplest data access scenario requires determining the user role and their privileges, resource being in an appropriate state of its lifecycle, and, on the other hand, may involve the update of the persistent data. Two conceptual layers of the system's functionality can be distinguished: data collection, unification, storage and retrieval, and online collaboration over the stored data.

The first of the aforementioned layers requires agreeing on and applying standards on the data formats, image properties and naming conventions and providing selected users with the privilege of submitting data. The resources are organized into a generic hierarchy that distinguishes Sessions and Trials. Subjects can be defined on per-session basis, though are not used for the synovitis related images described here. Each Trial represents a single image and the associated data containing its description. Both the publishing and retrieval of image data are supported by the set of services that effectively provide the respective data cloud functionality. However, to assure the capability of autonomous (offline) work of an application, the operations for bulk download of a lightweight snapshot of the database (called a shallow copy) and its subsequent timestamp-driven updates have been provided. Multiple provider users are allowed and, based on

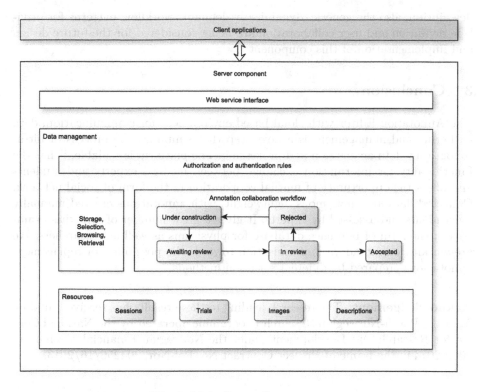

Fig. 5. Main Server Components

the origin and purpose of the data and assignment of a session to particular session groups (as well as users to user groups) the access control is maintained. The second layer can be described as online collaboration over the imaging data. Here, although each particular step is performed through a stateless service operation call, a coordination of the work and the consistency of parallel access needs to be assured. Hence the necessary data is stored together with resources being processed that indicate their current state of processing and its performers. The current status of work, on annotating a USG image, can be described as a simple state machine that describes a particular annotation and consists of the following states: 1 under construction, 2 awaiting review, 3 under review, 4 approved, 0 rejected, where the rejected annotation can be restored to the state 1 again by its original author (annotator). The roles involved in the process are Student retrieves and analyzes image; provides an annotation, and Doctor reviews the annotation. The annotations that have been approved become visible to all the users having the read privileges of the respective sessions. The need of providing the aforementioned functionality requires going beyond the existing publish-assign privileges-browse-retrieve scenario. The aforementioned use case illustrates the fact that the generic repositories of imaging data like the one described here can potentially be a subject of many types of similar collaboration processes and hence, in addition of generic structure for resource repository and description, also the generic, dynamically definable workflow patterns for privilege definition and user collaboration are being considered for the future design and implementation of this component.

3   Conclusion

The Annotation Editor with cloud based environment for communication, data gathering and management is a next step that simplifies the process of ultrasonography data acquisition and processing. The platform is scalable, it has the functionality for information exchange between medical experts and students and offers the opportunity of mutual cooperation in the form of social network. Collected data are anonymous, lightweight, with annotations created manually by students and assessed by experts. It gives a great number of synovitis examples in the form of reference database for physicians as well as researchers. We are working on metadata uniformisation towards the possibility of replacement annotations prepared by different selection methods.

Acknowledgement. The research leading to these results has received funding from the Polish-Norwegian Research Programme operated by the National Centre for Research and Development under the Norwegian Financial Mechanism 2009-2014 in the frame of Project Contract No. Pol-Nor/204256/16/2013.

References

1. Østergaard, M., Szkudlarek, M.: Ultrasonography: a valid method for assessing rheumatoid arthritis? Arthritis Rheum. Arthritis Rheum. 52(3), 681–686 (2005)
2. Kamishima, T., Tanimura, K., Henmi, M., Narita, A., Sakamoto, F., Terae, S., Shirato, H.: Power Doppler ultrasound of rheumatoid synovitis: quantification of vascular signal and analysis of interobserver variability. Skeletal Radiol 38(5), 467–472 (2009)
3. Kamishima, T., Sagawa, A., Tanimura, K., Shimizu, M., Matsuhashi, M., Shinohara, M., Hagiwara, H., Henmi, M., Narita, A., Terae, S., Shirato, H.: Semiquantitative analysis of rheumatoid finger joint synovitis using power Doppler ultrasonography: when to perform follow-up study after treatment consisting mainly of antitumor necrosis factor alpha agent. Skeletal Radiol 39(5), 457–465 (2010)
4. Albrecht, K., Muller-Ladner, U., Strunk, J.: Quantification of the synovial perfusion in rheumatoid arthritis using Doppler ultrasonography. Clinical and experimental rheumatology 25(4), 630 (2007)
5. Chang, W., Zwicker, M.: Automatic Registration for Articulated Shapes. In: Computer Graphics Forum (Proc. SGP 2008), vol. 27, p. 5 (2008)
6. Mateus, D., Horaud, R.P., Knossow, D., Cuzzolin, F., Boyer, E.: Articulated shape matching using laplacian eigenfunctions and unsupervised point registration. In: Proc. IEEE CVPR (June 2008)
7. Segen, J.: Inference of Stochastic Graph Models for 2D and 3D Shape. In: Proc. of NATO Adv. Res. Workshop on Shape in Picture, Driebergen, Netherlands (September 1992)

8. Schapire, R.E.: The Boosting Approach to Machine Learning: An Overview. In: Workshop on Nonlinear Estimation and Classification, Berkeley, CA. Mathematical Sciences Research Institute(MSRI) (2003)
9. Janiak, M., Kulbacki, M., Knieć, W., Nowacki, J.P., Drabik, A.: Data Flow Processing Framework For Multimodal Data Environment Software. In: ICCSE 2014, New Delhi, India (2014)
10. Kulbacki, M., Janiak, M., Knieć, W.: Motion Data Editor Software Architecture Oriented on Efficient and General Purpose Data Analysis. ACIIDS (2), 545–554 (2014)
11. Filipowicz, W., Habela, P., Kaczmarski, K., Kulbacki, M.: A Generic Approach to Design and Querying of Multipurpose Human Motion Database. ICCVG (1), 105–113 (2010)

The Detection of Horizontal Lines Based on the Monte Carlo Reduced Resolution Images

Piotr Lech

West Pomeranian University of Technology, Szczecin
Department of Signal Processing and Multimedia Engineering
26. Kwietnia 10, 71-126 Szczecin, Poland
piotr.lech@zut.edu.pl

Abstract. This paper presents the idea of fast algorithm for detecting horizontal lines in digital images. For this algorithm a dedicated procedure of data size reduction is proposed which utilizes the Monte Carlo method for preparation of lower size images from original High Definition ones. This approach is proposed for real-time, embedded systems or steering the mobile robot based on image analysis. The presented method is similar to downgrading the image resolution. The nearly real-time algorithm has been tested on real image data sets obtained from the mobile robot camera.

Keywords: image analysis, Monte Carlo method, downgrading image resolution.

1 Introduction

Image-based line detection is an important problem for mobile robot navigation [1]. On the base of detected lines, a robot is also able to acquire information that would be useful for construction of an environment map. Typically, the equation of the most dominant straight line in an image is calculated during the line extraction process, as illustrated in Fig. 1. Too many designated lines hinders their classification and causes the increase of the calculation time. The critical point of computations in the routine of vision data processing is the point where the computer has to decide which pixels may correspond to the line. At the end of this process, the initial camera image is converted to its binary representation where some of pixels represent lines and some others represent a free space (background). Some popular approaches used to achieve this result are based on edge detectors, such as Sobel or Canny, or applying pixel intensity based thresholding e.g. Otsu [7] or fast Otsu [3,4] method. Unfortunately, all the histogram based methods of image thresholding are time consuming. A good way for speeding up the calculations is reducing the amount of analyzed data. The presented method is similar to decreasing the image resolution. Each image is divided into blocks. For each block the reduction of the number of pixels has been applied. It is considered as a base for estimation of the new value of pixel and such prepared image is used an the input for the edge detector.

L.J. Chmielewski et al. (Eds.): ICCVG 2014, LNCS 8671, pp. 374–381, 2014.

Fig. 1. The original HD image (left) and the result of Canny lines detector (right)

Fig. 1 illustrates the problem of generation of superfluous information (too large number of detected lines) for high resolution images. Changing the edge detection algorithm from Canny to Sobel filtering does not improve this situation.

The main objective of the proposed algorithm is the reduction of the computational effort related to classical line detectors. This objective is achieved by the reduction of image resolution and using conventional line detection algorithms. This approach allows the use of classical algorithms if the native image resolution is too big for processing and its change is not allowed. It is possible to use this method as a hybrid solution where some of the tasks are performed for low resolution representation and some others for full resolution images. These operations can be completely separated as they are related to different algorithms. In some cases, the access to the full resolution images may be used only for the correction or refinement of results.

2   Downgrading the Image Resolution

The idea of downgrading the image resolution is based on the Monte Carlo method (MMC) prepared to randomly selected pixels from the original image. The image is divided into blocks of predefined size (e.g. 9×9 pixels). Each

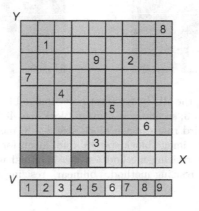

Fig. 2. Visualization of creation of the Monte Carlo representation of a block

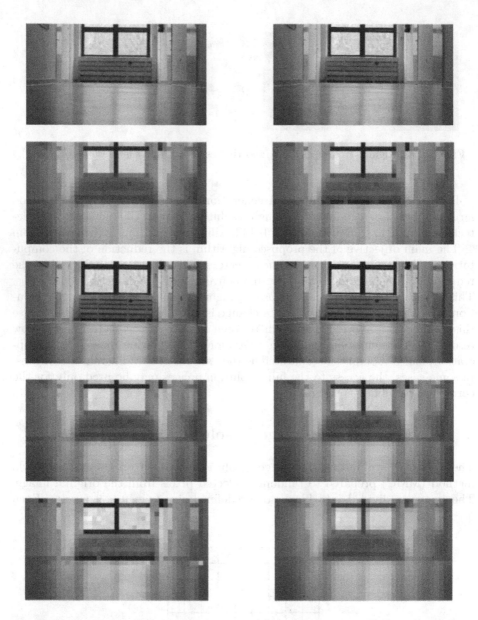

Fig. 3. Result of resizing the HD image (first row - image block size 8×8: MMC mean $n = 3$, MMC median $n = 3$; second row - image block size 48×48: MMC mean $n = 7$, MMC median $n = 7$; third row - image block size 8×8: mean for all pixels, median for all pixels; fourth row - image block size 48×48: mean for all pixels, median for all pixels, fifth row - classic resizing method for size identical with images created from block 48×48: "nearest" resizing method, "bilinear" resizing method)

block is converted into vector of size n (where n is the number of draws). Fig. 2 presents the vector obtained for $n = 9$ draws. This vector is equivalent to the Monte Carlo image representation corresponding to the block.

The new pixel is created from the MMC vector in two ways:

- as the mean vector value (MMC mean),
- as the median of vector value (MMC median).

All of the estimated pixels corresponding to blocks from the source image are stored in the new low density image (denoted as the MMC image). The result of the tests for creating new downgraded image from the original "corridor" HD image is presented in Fig. 3. The results of applying two popular classical methods of image resizing ("nearest" and "bilinear") are shown in the last row of Fig. 3. In the nearest neighbor interpolation the output pixel is assigned to the value of the pixel that the point falls within. No other pixels are taken into account. For the bilinear interpolation - the output pixel value is a weighted average of pixels in the nearest 2-by-2 neighborhood.

Table 1. Normalized computation times of downgrade image resolulution

Downgrade method	Blok 8 × 8	Blok 48 × 48
Mean for all pixels	0.86	0.85
Median for all pixels	0.90	0.88
MMC mean, n =3	0.70	0.60
MMC median, n=7	0.78	0.68
Nearest-neighbor interpolation	0.80	0.70
Bilinear interpolation	1	0.9

3   The Essence of the Monte Carlo Method in Image Processing

For a static image of a scene a constant value can be defined, which is the result of counting the samples fulfilling given logical condition. Such condition can be the fact of belonging of an image sample to a given level of luminance or a position in image or other defined condition.

Stored values are equal to:

- 0 - ("zeros") for the samples which don't satisfy the condition,
- 1 - ("ones") for the samples which satisfy the condition.

As the result of entire image analysis its binary equivalent is obtained. Binary image keeps the quantitative information for the objects' features defined by the logical condition, which can be calculated by counting the number of all "ones" in the image:

$$\hat{L} = m \qquad (1)$$

where :

- m – total number of "ones" in the image.

The simplest way to accelerate the algorithm is decreasing the number of analysed samples. The procedure used in experiment begins with copying all the samples of binary image into one-dimensional vector. Each sample is numbered from 1 to N, where N is the total number of samples in analyzed scene. Then n independent numbers are generated, which denote the numbers of randomly chosen elements in the vector. For all randomly chosen samples the total number of "ones" (k) is then calculated.

Estimated number of samples which are equal to 1 obtained in the MMC experiment is:

$$\hat{L}_{MMC} = \frac{k}{n} \cdot N \qquad (2)$$

where:

- k – number of "ones" in randomly chosen samples,
- n – total number of draws,
- N – total number of samples in the entire scene.

The error of estimation is equal to:

$$\varepsilon_\alpha = \frac{u_\alpha}{\sqrt{n}} \cdot \sqrt{\frac{K}{N} \cdot \left(1 - \frac{K}{N}\right)} \qquad (3)$$

where:

- K – total number of "ones" in the entire image,
- u_α – the value denoting two-sided critical range.

4   The Horizontal Line Detector

A popular approach used to achieve lines extracting from images is the application of edge detectors, such as Sobel or Canny filters. The morphology and the median filter or the Hough Transform and line classification can be used for selecting horizontal lines [6].

The test algorithm consists of several steps:

1. the HD image resolution change to low resolution (tested with MMC median and MMC mean method for different size of blocks and number of samples n),
2. edge detecting (tested for Sobel and Canny algorithms),
3. horizontal line filtering by the median filter with mask [1h] (tested for different h e.g. 3,7,11).

The developed algorithms were tested on the basis of image sequences obtained from the HD camera installed on a mobile robot platform (open source based - Mobot Explorer A1). The task set for the implementation of the

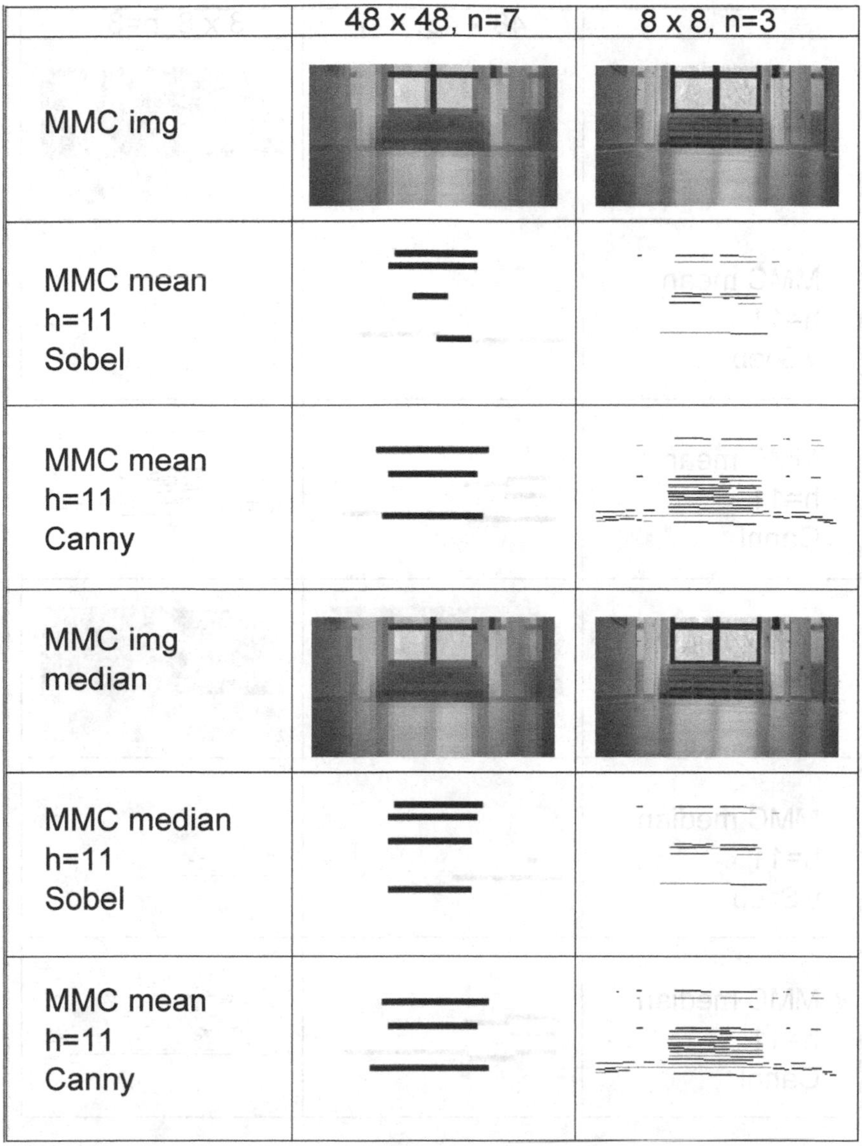

	48 x 48, n=7	8 x 8, n=3
MMC img		
MMC mean h=11 Sobel		
MMC mean h=11 Canny		
MMC img median		
MMC median h=11 Sobel		
MMC mean h=11 Canny		

Fig. 4. Result obtained for all steps of algorithm for the "corridor" image

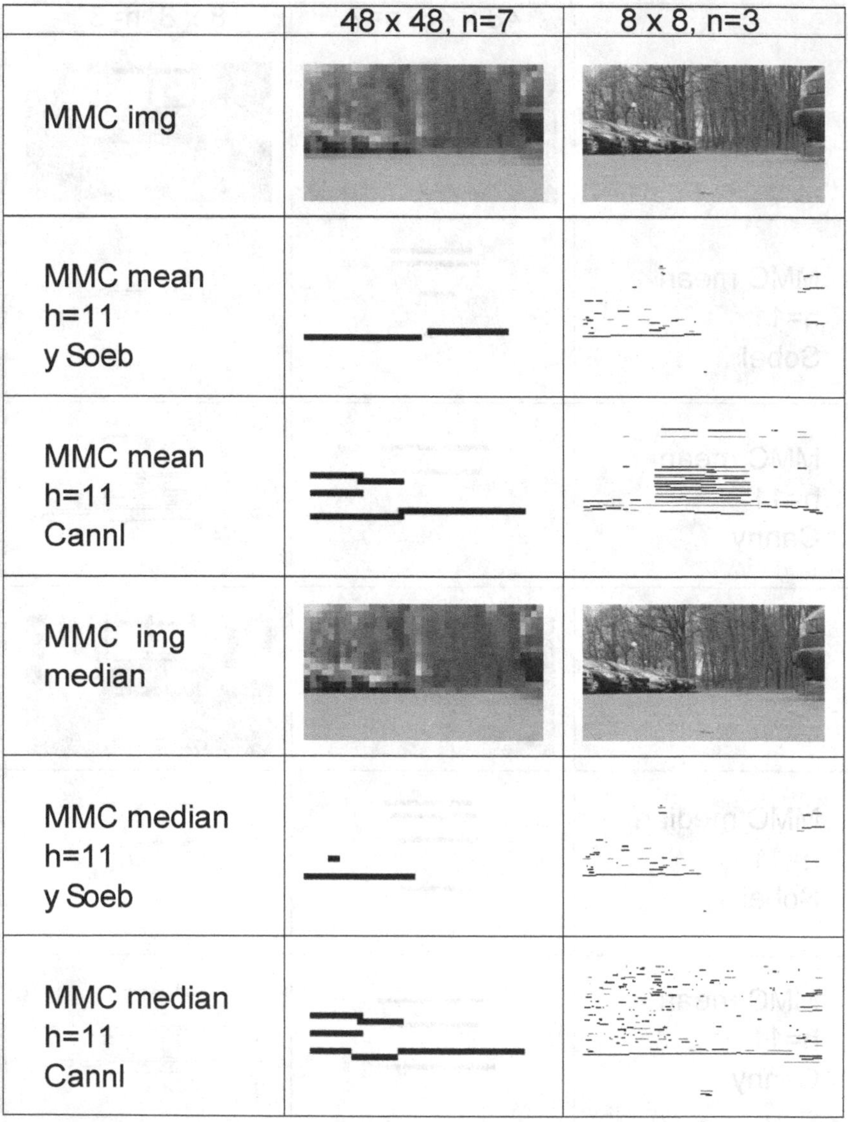

	48 x 48, n=7	8 x 8, n=3
MMC img		
MMC mean h=11 y Soeb		
MMC mean h=11 Cannl		
MMC img median		
MMC median h=11 y Soeb		
MMC median h=11 Cannl		

Fig. 5. Result obtained for all steps of algorithm for the "outdoor" image

detection of the horizontal line defines the maximum feasible range of the robot movement [2].

In the experiment presented above the algorithm (with additional morphological image cleaning step) was used to detect the horizontal line. In previous tests, it was observed that in the cases studied the longest line determined by the filter is also the line defining the potential range of motion of the robot.

The presented method of establishing the scope of robot motion is currently in the preliminary stage of development and requires testing in different environments. Nevertheless, it is well suited to illustrate the effects of the extraction of the horizontal line using the fast Monte Carlo method.

5   Conclusions

The proposed method of reduction the resolution of images is interesting because of the simple implementation and low computational complexity. This method can be very useful, inter alia, for the detection lines or shapes. It can also be used for fast Track-Before-Detect algorithms [5]. In the future, capabilities of the proposed methods in SLAM algorithms applied for mobile robots will be considered.

References

1. Cui, X.-N., Kim, Y.-G., Kim, H.: Floor Segmentation by Computing Plane Normals from Image Motion Fields for Visual Navigation. International Journal of Control, Automation, and Systems 7(5), 788–798 (2009)
2. Fazl-Ersi, E., Tsotsos, J.K.: Region Classification for Robust Floor Detection in Indoor Environments. In: Kamel, M., Campilho, A. (eds.) ICIAR 2009. LNCS, vol. 5627, pp. 717–726. Springer, Heidelberg (2009)
3. Lech, P., Okarma, K.: Optimization of the fast image binarization method based on the Monte Carlo approach. Elektronika Ir Elektrotechnika 20(4), 63–66 (2014)
4. Lech, P., Okarma, K., Tecław, M.: A fast histogram estimation based on the Monte Carlo method for image binarization. In: Choras, R.S. (ed.) Image Processing and Communications Challenges 5. AISC, vol. 233, pp. 73–80. Springer, Heidelberg (2014)
5. Mazurek, P.: Optimization of Bayesian Track-Before-Detect algorithms for GPGPUs implementations. Przeglad Elektrotechniczny 86(7), 187–189 (2010)
6. McDonald, J.B., Franz, J., Shorten, R.: Application of the Hough Transform to Lane Detection in Motorway Driving Scenarios. In: Proc. Irish Signals and Systems Conference, pp. 340–345 (2001)
7. Otsu, N.: A threshold selection method from gray-level histograms. IEEE Trans. Systems, Man and Cybernetics 9(1), 62–66 (1979)

Fast Histogram Based Image Binarization Using the Monte Carlo Threshold Estimation

Piotr Lech and Krzysztof Okarma

West Pomeranian University of Technology, Szczecin
Faculty of Electrical Engineering
Department of Signal Processing and Multimedia Engineering
26. Kwietnia 10, 71-126 Szczecin, Poland
{piotr.lech,krzysztof.okarma}@zut.edu.pl

Abstract. In the paper the idea of universal fast image binarization method is discussed which utilizes the histogram estimation using the Monte Carlo approach. Proposed reduction of the computational burden dependent on the number of analyzed pixels may be useful especially in real-time and embedded systems with limited amount of memory and processing power. An additional advantage of such simplified approach is relatively easy implementation independently on the used programming language.

The experimental results obtained for some typical benchmark datasets used in DIBCO contests, confirm the effectiveness and usefulness of the proposed approach for popular histogram based image binarization algorithms. As shown by presented results, the proposed method can also be useful as a pre-processing step for the Optical Character Recognition systems.

Keywords: image binarization, thresholding, Monte Carlo method.

1 Introduction

Analysis of binary images plays an important role in computer vision systems applied in various areas of science and technology. Some well-known examples may be related to Optical Character Recognition (OCR) systems, wide applications of mathematical morphology [4] or shape analysis methods applied for image recognition purposes [3] as well as in biomedical analysis [12]. Another interesting area of its applications is related to low cost embedded systems applied for vision based self-navigation of autonomous mobile robots e.g. line-followers.

Classical algorithms of image binarization are based on the analysis of the image histogram which is typically determined using the time-consuming analysis of the whole image. Such approach may be a significant limitation in many applications where high resolution images are processed, especially in real-time video systems. A good example is also the document binarization being still an active area of research, both for machine printed and handwritten documents, especially historical ones containing many distortions [10,14].

L.J. Chmielewski et al. (Eds.): ICCVG 2014, LNCS 8671, pp. 382–390, 2014.
© Springer International Publishing Switzerland 2014

Considering the necessity of full image analysis as one of the main draw-backs of the histogram based image binarization algorithms, the reduction of the amount of analyzed pixels seems to be an interesting solution. Nevertheless, obtained results of such estimation should be compared with "ground truth" results which are unknown in many situations.

2   Methods Used for Verification of Image Binarization Algorithms

The knowledge of the "ground truth" binary images is absolutely essential for the verification of correctness of the binarization results. Some of the most valu-able datasets which can be used for this purposes are images used during the Document Image Binarization Contests (DIBCO) organized by a group of Greek researchers. Every two years the contest is related to handwritten images and is organized in conjunction with the International Conference on Frontiers in Handwriting Recognition (ICFHR).

The comparison of the results obtained using various algorithms with availa-ble "ground truth" images should be made not only by simple comparison of threshold values, since the threshold error may influence on the resulting binary image in different ways. Considering the fact that existing full-reference image quality metrics are typically dedicated for grayscale images, there are only a few binary image quality assessment methods which could be applied for comparison of binarization results. Nevertheless, some recently proposed metrics e.g. based on Border Distance [16] or Binary Structure Information [2], are not very po-pular and some other metrics such as PSNR or metrics based on Precision and Recall are typically applied. One of such typical metrics is F-Measure which is calculated as follows:

$$FM = 2 \cdot \frac{RC \cdot PR}{RC + PR} \cdot 100\% , \tag{1}$$

where Recall (RC) and Precision (PR) are calculated as the ratios of true posi-tives to the sum of true positives and false negatives and true positives to the sum of all positives respectively.

Some other distance-based evaluation measures which are typically used are known as Distance Reciprocal Distortion (DRD) [8] and Misclassification Penalty Metric (MPM). Typical metrics applied for the evaluation of binarization results, including pseudo-FMeasure based on pseudo-Recall and pseudo-Precision, are described in the article [9].

3   The Idea of Simplified Balanced Histogram Thresholding

One of the simplest methods of binarization based on the histogram analysis is known as Balanced Histogram Thresholding (BHT) [1]. Since the method is based on the equalization of weights of two classes represented in the image histogram by pixels on both sides of the threshold, it is very easy for implementation. Nevertheless, the obtained results are usually unsatisfactory for images with dominant background (or foreground).

Considering the statistical properties of the Monte Carlo method, based on the random choice of the limited number of samples using the pseudo-random numbers generator with uniform distribution, similar threshold value can also be obtained for reduced number of analyzed pixels. Therefore, the BHT algorithm has been chosen as the first one for the experimental verification of validity of such an approach. According to the Monte Carlo method, the pixels for the analysis are randomly chosen in the way providing their uniform distribution on the image plane. Since the probability of choosing of the pixel located on the left and on the right side of the threshold is similar, even a significant decrease of the number of drawn pixels should lead to quite precise estimation of the threshold value. More detailed description of the Monte Carlo method for fast image analysis purposes and its statistical properties can be found in the paper [11].

4   Proposed Method of Threshold Estimation

The idea of the reduction of the number of analyzed pixels in order to approximate the histogram's shape can be applied for any histogram based thresholding algorithm. Since various kinds of such methods have been proposed for image binarization, three representative ones have been chosen for the experiments. The first algorithm, based on the time-consuming entropy analysis, has been proposed by Kapur [5]. Threshold value is chosen so that the between-class entropy is maximized. Due to the high computational effort of this method, a reduction of the number of analyzed pixels would be highly desirable.

The second algorithm taken into consideration is the well-known Otsu method based on the assumption that the optimum threshold should separate the foreground and background pixels so that their intra-class variance is minimal which is equivalent to maximization of the inter-class variance [13]. Some preliminary results obtained using the Monte Carlo method applied for the fast Otsu binarization, although without the comparison with some other algorithms, have been presented in the papers [6,7].

Another considered algorithm is unimodal thresholding proposed by Rosin [15] due to its potential usefulness for text recognition purposes for low fill factor values (images with dominant background and relatively small areas occupied by text). The algorithm is based on finding the maximum deviation as the threshold is chosen in the point located furthest from the line connecting the peak and the end of the histogram. Since one of the assumptions of this method is the domination of the dark pixels in the image, the proper thresholding of the test images from the H-DIBCO 2010 and H-DIBCO 2012 datasets (containing dark text on brighter background) used in the experiments, require flipping of the histogram (or calculations on the negatives of the test images).

5   Experimental Results

The experiments have been conducted using the images contained in H-DIBCO 2010 and H-DIBCO 2012 datasets containing 10 and 14 images with handwritten text and their "ground truth" binary images respectively. Four thresholding algorithms considered in the paper have been applied for all images in their "classical" versions analyzing the full histogram as well as applying the Monte Carlo method for various number of samples. Exemplary images H03 (chosen as a typical one) and H06 (a "hard" one) from the H-DIBCO 2012 database with their binary "ground truth" images are presented in Figs. 1 and 2 respectively.

The results of the evaluation metrics obtained for two exemplary images, being considered as representative for both datasets, using the various number

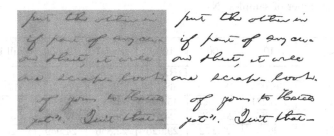

Fig. 1. Original H03 image from H-DIBCO 2012 dataset (left) and the "ground truth" binary image (right)

Table 1. Obtained results of the binarization evaluation metrics for the H03 image using various number of samples (N)

Method \ N	10	100	1000	10000	Full image
DRD					
BHT	220.963	245.073	220.963	245.073	245.073
Kapur	245.070	72.129	170.004	9.981	8.843
Rosin	220.963	31.538	27.015	14.786	12.957
Otsu	7.608	4.783	6.514	5.248	5.248
MPM					
BHT	0.182	0.206	0.182	0.206	0.206
Kapur	0.207	0.041	0.005	0.002	0.002
Rosin	0.182	0.013	0.010	0.004	0.004
Otsu	$3.10 \cdot 10^{-4}$	$6.67 \cdot 10^{-4}$	0.0013	$8.51 \cdot 10^{-4}$	$8.51 \cdot 10^{-4}$
F-Measure					
BHT	23.119	21.363	23.119	21.363	21.363
Kapur	21.363	47.052	76.870	83.910	85.190
Rosin	23.119	65.754	68.832	78.944	80.755
Otsu	82.679	90.033	87.966	89.516	89.516

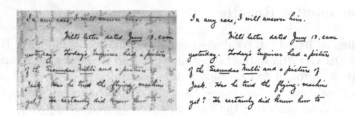

Fig. 2. Original H06 image from H-DIBCO 2012 dataset (left) and the "ground truth" binary image (right)

Table 2. Obtained results of the binarization evaluation metrics for the H06 image using various number of samples (N)

Method \ N	10	100	1000	10000	100000	Full image
DRD						
BHT	298.076	183.511	168.271	178.011	178.011	178.011
Kapur	168.271	137.245	45.999	11.841	6.833	7.772
Rosin	36.287	202.673	124.723	29.796	39.269	37.786
Otsu	196.63	27.172	29.625	22.856	24.949	23.902
MPM						
BHT	0.406	0.265	0.245	0.258	0.258	0.258
Kapur	0.245	0.199	0.068	0.017	0.009	0.011
Rosin	0.054	0.290	0.182	0.071	0.058	0.056
Otsu	0.283	0.041	0.044	0.034	0.037	0.035
F-Measure						
BHT	15.314	22.541	24.056	23.065	23.065	23.065
Kapur	24.056	27.880	52.552	78.864	84.900	83.730
Rosin	58.043	20.890	29.796	51.603	56.237	57.121
Otsu	21.383	64.386	62.535	67.905	66.143	67.012

of samples randomly chosen for analysis using the Monte Carlo method are presented in Tables 1 and 2. The binarization results achieved using such determined threshold values are presented in Figs. 3 and 4 where the bottom rows contain the images obtained using the original binarization methods. The chosen numbers of analyzed pixels are equivalent to relatively small percentages of both images since their resolution is 1709×1371 pixels for the H03 image and 1499×939 pixels for the H06 one. Even drawing the 100000 samples the analysis is conducted for about 4-7% of the total number of pixels.

Fig. 3. Exemplary experimental results obtained for H03 image from H-DIBCO 2012 dataset using the Monte Carlo method with various number of samples (from the top: 10, 100, 1000 and 10000) and full image analysis (bottom row) applied for BHT, Kapur, Rosin and Otsu methods (from left to right respectively)

6   Conclusions

Presented results verify the validity of the proposed approach for various image binarization algorithms. Due to a significant reduction of computational demands of the histogram calculation such methods may be very useful for many applications where the fast binarization plays an important role e.g. navigation of mobile robots or data preprocessing for the OCR applications. As has been verified for both test datasets, the results comparable with the application of full image analysis can be obtained for all methods analyzing not more than 10% of the total number of pixels. It is worth to notice that the images in H-DIBCO databases are some of the most demanding in view of their binarization so even better results can be obtained for smaller number of randomly chosen pixels from some more typical images containing less distortions.

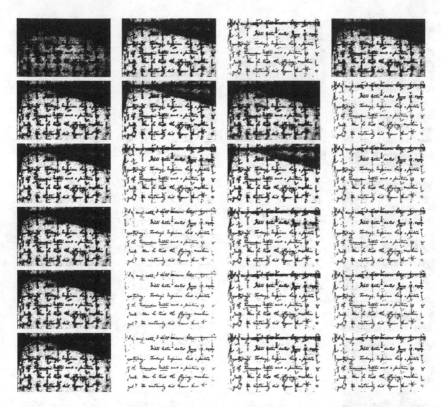

Fig. 4. Exemplary experimental results obtained for H06 image from H-DIBCO 2012 dataset using the Monte Carlo method with various number of samples (from the top: 10, 100, 1000, 10000 and 100000) and full image analysis (bottom row) applied for BHT, Kapur, Rosin and Otsu methods (from left to right respectively)

Since some of image binarization methods provide worse results for specific types of images, the application of the Monte Carlo method gives additionally a chance to obtain different threshold values which may be more accurate for specific images. Such situation has taken place for the H03 image using 100 pixels for the Monte Carlo based Otsu method leading to slightly better results than for the "classical" Otsu method as illustrated in Table 1. For the same image a similar phenomenon can be observed for lower performance BHT method using 10 and 1000 randomly chosen pixels for the analysis as well as for the H06 image (1000 samples for the BHT algorithm and 100000 pixels for Kapur thresholding).

For some methods (e.g. Rosin thresholding) a non-monotonic changes of performance metrics for different number of samples can be noticed resulting from the specific character of the statistical Monte Carlo method as a more monotonic dependence can be achieved for multiple repetitions of experiments. Especially for extremely low number of samples the obtained threshold values may significantly differ from the ground truth. One the other hand, for some images even for significantly reduced number of samples (e.g. 10 pixels) the difference between them may be quite small although a verification by an additional statistical experiment is recommended in such cases.

Considering such phenomenon, our future research will focus on the investigation of properties of a combined thresholding method based on the fast Monte Carlo approach applied to different histogram based image binarization algorithms.

References

1. dos Anjos, A., Shahbazkia, H.: Bi-level image thresholding - a fast method. In: Encarnação, P., Veloso, A. (eds.) BIOSIGNALS, pp. 70–76. INSTICC - Institute for Systems and Technologies of Information, Control and Communication (2008)
2. Chou, C.H., Hsu, Y.H.: Image quality assessment based on binary structure information. In: Proc. 7th Int. Conf. Computational Intelligence and Security (CIS), pp. 1136–1140 (2011)
3. Frejlichowski, D., Forczmański, P.: General shape analysis applied to stamps retrieval from scanned documents. In: Dicheva, D., Dochev, D. (eds.) AIMSA 2010. LNCS, vol. 6304, pp. 251–260. Springer, Heidelberg (2010)
4. Iwanowski, M.: Morphological classification of binary image pixels. Machine Graphics and Vision 18(2), 155–173 (2009)
5. Kapur, J., Sahoo, P., Wong, A.: A new method for gray-level picture thresholding using the entropy of the histogram. Computer Vision, Graphics, and Image Processing 29(3), 273–285 (1985)
6. Lech, P., Okarma, K.: Optimization of the fast image binarization method based on the Monte Carlo approach. Elektronika Ir Elektrotechnika 20(4), 63–66 (2014)
7. Lech, P., Okarma, K., Tecław, M.: A fast histogram estimation based on the Monte Carlo method for image binarization. In: Choraś, R.S. (ed.) Image Processing and Communications Challenges 5. AISC, vol. 233, pp. 73–80. Springer, Heidelberg (2014)
8. Lu, H., Kot, A., Shi, Y.: Distance-reciprocal distortion measure for binary document images. IEEE Signal Processing Letters 11(2), 228–231 (2004)
9. Ntirogiannis, K., Gatos, B., Pratikakis, I.: Performance evaluation methodology for historical document image binarization. IEEE Trans. Image Processing 22(2), 595–609 (2013)
10. Ntirogiannis, K., Gatos, B., Pratikakis, I.: A combined approach for the binarization of handwritten document images. Pattern Recognition Letters 35, 3–15 (2014); frontiers in Handwriting Processing
11. Okarma, K., Lech, P.: Application of the Monte Carlo preliminary image analysis and classification method for the automatic reservation of parking space. Machine Graphics and Vision 18(4), 439–452 (2009)
12. Oszutowska–Mazurek, D., Mazurek, P., Sycz, K., Waker–Wójciuk, G.: Adaptive windowed threshold for box counting algorithm in cytoscreening applications. In: Choraś, R.S. (ed.) Image Processing and Communications Challenges 5. AISC, vol. 233, pp. 3–12. Springer, Heidelberg (2014)
13. Otsu, N.: A threshold selection method from gray-level histograms. IEEE Trans. Systems, Man and Cybernetics 9(1), 62–66 (1979)

14. Pratikakis, I., Gatos, B., Ntirogiannis, K.: ICDAR 2013 Document Image Binarization Contest (DIBCO 2013). In: Proc. 12th Int. Conf. Document Analysis and Recognition ICDAR, pp. 1471–1476 (2013)
15. Rosin, P.L.: Unimodal thresholding. Pattern Recognition 34(11), 2083–2096 (2001)
16. Zhang, F., Cao, K., Zhang, J.L.: A simple quality evaluation method of binary images based on border distance. Optik - International Journal for Light and Electron Optics 122(14), 1236–1239 (2011)

Stereo Refinement for Photo Editing

Dongwei Liu and Reinhard Klette

The .enpeda.. Project, Department of Computer Science
The University of Auckland, New Zealand
dliu697@aucklanduni.ac.nz, r.keltte@auckland.ac.nz

Abstract. We present a method for refining depth information generated by a stereo-matching algorithm with the goal to provide depth-aware photo-effect applications. Our key idea is to use structural features of the base image to enhance the depth information. Our method pre-processes the original disparity map by revising the sky region and removing incorrect data (on the left-side of the disparity map) caused by occlusion. The base image is mean-shift segmented. A median filter is applied on the disparity map within each segment. Invalid step-edges in the disparity map are removed by a joint bilateral filter. Experiments show that our method can revise holes, inaccurate object edges, speckle noises, and invalid step-edges from the given depth information. Results illustrate the applicability for photo editing.

Keywords: stereo vision, stereo refinement, photo editing.

1 Introduction

Photography is an art that maps a real-world 3D scene into a planar photo. During this process, the depth information of the scene is lost. Various impressive 3D rendering techniques can be applied to photos if depth information is available, for example out-of-focus blur [19], addition of smoke or haze [20,6], or relighting.

Depth from a single 2D picture would be convenient but is an unsolvable problem in general. Studies in this area either apply constraints on the scene or rely on massive human interaction [3,15].

Depth sensors are more reliable, such as *binocular stereo* [5,7], structured lighting as used in the *Kinect* [11], *depth from defocus (DFD)* [16,17], or a *light field camera* [14]. Binocular stereo is the common sensor used for outdoor scenes, and the underlying methodology is close to human visual cognition. Generated depth maps when using stereo vision are still imperfect for photo editing, even when using a top-performing stereo matcher such as iSGM [8], for the following three reasons:

First, depth values for some pixels are unavailable in a photo, represented by *holes* in the depth map (see Fig. 1, green frame). Those holes can be due to occlusion, which is inherent for stereo vision, or to low confidence in stereo matching. For object detection or distance measurement tasks, such holes can be tolerated to some extent, but for photo editing a dense depth map is needed.

L.J. Chmielewski et al. (Eds.): ICCVG 2014, LNCS 8671, pp. 391–399, 2014.

Second, the depth map may include speckle noise (see Fig. 1, red frame), and inaccurate object edges. The issue is especially noticeable for objects with a detailed geometry, for example for tree crowns (see Fig. 1, blue frame). For photo editing, even slight mismatches on some clearly visible edges introduce visual discomfort.

Third, the depth map may involve invalid step-edges. Stereo matching methods detect *disparity* between base and match images. The disparity is measured in integers. The depth of a point is inversely proportional to its disparity value. Thus, depth does not change smoothly when only using integer disparities. For example, if the disparity values of two adjacent pixels are 2 and 1, their depth varies by factor 2. This issue also causes visual discomfort during photo editing.

Fig. 1. The result of stereo matching is imperfect for photo editing. *Left:* Base image. *Right:* Depth map generated by iSGM [8] overlayed with the base image. See *blue frame* for inaccurate edges, *green frame* for holes, and *red frame* for speckle noise.

We observe that for photo editing, the depth map should have little "collision" with human visual cognition of the base image. On the other hand, 100% accurate depth information is also not necessary. Informally speaking, a depth map needs to look "plausible". Based on this observation, we present a novel depth-refinement method to solve the three problems mentioned above. The key idea is to use structural features of the base image to enhance the depth map.

Our process takes as input a stereo pair. We generate an enhanced disparity map, fit for photo editing. The process includes four steps. First we pre-process a given disparity map in which the disparity in the sky region gets revised, and incorrect information on the left side of the base image (caused by occlusion) is removed. Then, we mean-shift segment the base image. Notable object edges are detected during segmentation. Later, we run a median filter on the disparity map within each segment. In this step, holes on the disparity map are "fixed", disparities around object edges are revised, and minor speckle noise is also removed. At last, before converting the disparity map into a depth map, a joint bilateral filter is employed to remove invalid step-edges.

The rest of the paper is structured as follows. In Section 2 we recall algorithms as used in our method. Section 3 provides details for our depth-refinement method. Experimental results are shown and discussed in Section 4. Section 5 concludes.

2   Basic Concepts and Notations

This section briefly recalls algorithms as used in our approach.

Stereo Matching. Research on stereo matching has a long history already. Good performing algorithms are, for example, based on belief propagation [5] or on *semi-global matching* (SGM) [7]. A variant of SGM, *iterative SGM* (iSGM) [8], was winning the Robust Vision Challenge at ECCV 2012, and we use iSGM in this paper. Stereo matching aims at solving an ill-posed problem (to identify exactly one matching pixel in a match image starting with one pixel in a base image [9]. Difficulties for solving this problem arise for many reasons, and one is occlusion. Algorithms (including iSGM) use a smoothness constraint which also causes "blurred" disparities at occlusion edges. For our purpose we like to "sharpen" at those edges; for this reason we "merge" results of iSGM with segmentation results in the base image.

Mean-Shift Image Segmentation. *Mean-shift segmentation* [4] is an iterative steepest-ascent method that detects peaks in the density function defined in a feature space; e.g., see [9]. Mean-shift requires to specify a window of defined size, and weights on this window (the kernel) in feature space.

Median Filter and Bilateral Filter. We also apply the median and bilateral filter, which are both known as edge-protecting image smoothing fmethods. The *median filter* is a nonlinear operation which runs through an image I and replaces each pixel value $I(p)$ by the median value of neighboring pixels within a $(2k + 1) \times (2k + 1)$ window W_p:

$$I_{median}(p) = \text{median}\{I(p_i) : p_i \in W_p\} \tag{1}$$

The *bilateral filter* [18], also known as "surface blur", is a selective mean filter for image smoothing or noise reduction. The filter does a weighted average for each pixel p in image I in a window W_p considering both spatial distance and color intensity distance of pixels:

$$I_{bilateral}(p) = \frac{1}{\omega_p} \sum_{p_i \in W_p} I(p_i) \cdot f_c(\|I(p_i) - I(p)\|) \cdot f_s(\|p_i - p\|) \tag{2}$$

where f_c is the kernel for color-intensity distances of pixels, f_s is the kernel for the spatial distance of pixels, ω_p is a normalization parameter defined by

$$\omega_p = \sum_{p_i \in W_p} f_c(\|I(p_i) - I(p)\|) \cdot f_s(\|p_i - p\|) \tag{3}$$

Here, f_c and f_s can be Gaussian functions. A variation of a bilateral filter has been developed for depth refinement, called *joint bilateral filter* [12,10]. This filter uses the original color image I to specify the kernel, and then refines the corresponding depth map D:

$$D_{J\_bilateral}(p) = \frac{1}{\omega_p} \sum_{p_i \in W_p} D(p_i) \cdot f_c(\|I(p_i) - I(p)\|) \cdot f_s(\|p_i - p\|) \tag{4}$$

3 Depth Refinement

Given a pair of rectified stereo images, base image I_L and match image I_R, we calculate a disparity map D_0 using a stereo matching method, where D_0 is given in coordinates of I_L defined on Ω.

3.1 Sky Region and Left-Side Occlusions

Sky is typically shown in landscape photographs. Since a sky region is often large and has little texture, the stereo matching results in such a region are often not accurate. We detect the sky region in I_L, and set the corresponding values in D_0 uniformly to 0, which marks the sky region as being at infinity.

Blue sky and cloud regions have both high values in the blue channel of I_L. Thus, we define a pixel p is a *sky pixel* if p is in the upper half of I_L, and its blue channel value $B(p)$ is larger than a threshold T_{sky}:

$$D(p) = 0 \quad \text{if} \quad p \in \Omega_{upper} \wedge B(p) > T_{sky} \tag{5}$$

We used $T_{sky} = 0.8 \cdot G_{max}$ in our experiments, where G_{max} is the maximum level in each color channel of I_L.

Due to the nature of stereo vision, a part of the scene on the left-side (in Ω_{left}) of image I_L is not included in I_R.[1] Thus, accurate depth information of this region cannot be generated by stereo matching. In general, a usual practice is to discard I_L on Ω_{left}. For photography this operation may destroy the composition of an artwork. Thus, we aim at repairing data in Ω_{left} by given information.

We remove erroneous information in Ω_{left}; resulting gaps are repaired by the process discussed in Section 3.3. If the disparity value at a pixel $p \in \Omega_{left}$ deviates significantly from the median value of the row, we identify it as being an outlier, and invalidate the value of $D(p)$:

$$D(p) = \text{NA} \quad \text{if} \quad p \in \Omega_{left} \wedge |D(p) - \text{median}(\text{Row}_y)| > T_{outlier} \tag{6}$$

where $p = (x, y)$ and Row_y denotes all the disparity values in row y.[2] We denote the pre-processed disparity map as D_1.

3.2 Image Segmentation

For analyzing the structural features of I_L, we employ mean-shift image segmentation which clusters the pixels of I_L into a family **S** of segments. Figure 2, top-right, shows a segmentation result. Each segment is labeled constantly with its mean color.

In the segmentation procedure, we convert I_L from RGB into the Lab color space which is closer to human visual cognition principles. Then we run mean-shift on the 3D feature space formed by the Lab color values using a uniform

---

[1] We select Ω_{left} to be the left 10% of Ω.
[2] We decided for threshold $T_{outlier} = 0.3 \cdot d_{max}$, where d_{max} is the maximum disparity.

Fig. 2. Disparity refinement. *Upper row:* Base image and mean-shift segmentation result. *Bottom row:* Original disparity map, sky region and left-side occlusions processed, and final result.

kernel function. The window size $2k + 1$ is selected to be $0.125 \cdot G_{max} - 1$ which is a reasonable window size due to our experiments (a smaller value clusters the image into more segments, and clearly visible edges should also not be ignored). Generally we prefer over-segmentation to under-segmentation.

Compared with region-based segmentation methods [2] or a superpixel technique [1], mean-shift appears to be better at detecting complex edges, and even discontinuous objects.

3.3   Holes, Speckle Noises, and Inaccurate Edges

Similar to the joint bilateral filter, we define *joint median filter* to be a median filter applied on a disparity map D with a family $\mathbf{S}$ of segments as masks:

$$D_{J\_median}(p) = \text{median}\{D(p_i): \ p_i \in W_p \cap S_p\} \tag{7}$$

Here W_p is a window arround p, $S_p \in \mathbf{S}$ is the segment which contains pixel p.

We use the joint median filter as the main step of our refinement. The size of the window W_p is leaved as a user parameters, which should be decided according to the scale of the inaccurate edges and speckle noises.

Due to the large size of holes, the joint median filter may not cover all the unavailable pixels unless using a very large W_p, which may lead to over-smoothed result and low efficiency. Thus, we first run the joint median filter on every pixel in D_1, and then run the filter iteratively on those pixels still unavailable until all the holes are fixed. The processed depth map is denoted as D_2.

Taking advantage of the image segments $\mathbf{S}$ which represent the edge information of the base image I_L, inaccurate depth information around object edges and speckle noise are revised by the voting mechanism of median filter. See Fig. 2.

Note that joint bilateral filter does not discard invalid information (e.g. inaccurate edges or speckle noise). Instead, it spread inaccurate values to adjacent regions. In another words, joint bilateral filter is impressible to outliers. This effect is shown in Section 4. In contract, our joint median filter is robuster on outliers if the window W_p has sufficient size.

3.4   Invalid Step-Edges

A step-edge in the depth map is *invalid* iff it does not correspond to an actual depth discontinuity in the scene.

The disparity map D is converted into depth map d by the following formula:

$$d(p) = \frac{f \cdot b}{D(p) + \Delta}, \ D(p) \in \mathbb{N} \tag{8}$$

where Δ is a small value to avoid divisor to be zero, f is the focal length, and b is the base distance.

Since $D(p) \in \mathbb{N}$, the depth value $d(p)$ does not transit smoothly. Median filter does not create new value, so it does not remove those invalid step-edges in D_2. Thus, we employ the joint bilateral filter mentioned in (4), which remove this issue while keep valid edge sharp. We use Gaussian kernel and Euclidean metric for both spatial distance and color intensity distance. The filtered result is noted as D_3.

Though the joint bilateral filter may spread inaccurate information, it works well as an edge-protecting smooth filter on D_2, where inaccurate information has been revised.

4   Experiments

We test our refinement method on the disparity maps generated by iSGM [8]. The original resolution of the images in Fig. 2, 3, and 4 is 2400 × 1600. The refinement window W_p is set to be 80 × 80.

Fig. 3. Comparison between joint bilateral refinement and our method. From left to right: base image, original disparity map, joint bilateral filter result, our result.

Figure 3 compares the original disparity maps, the results of joint bilateral filter, and our results. Our method can generate dense disparity maps with clear object edges. Compared with joint bilateral filter, our method is robuster on outliers (for example, the speckle noise on the ground regions and the inaccurate tree crown edges). Our method also achieves correct disparity on sky regions, and avoids the interference of left-side inaccurate information caused by occlusion.

To test the usability of our result in photo editing, we implement two simple depth-award photo effects: darken the foreground or background of a photo. See Fig. 4. The darken effect change smoothly and naturally along depth. The edges of objects (like tree crowns) also feels natural and comfortable under the darken effect. Our results meet the demand of depth-award photo effects.

Fig. 4. Application examples: darken the foreground or background of the photos shown in fig. 3, using our refined disparity map

We also test our method on standard examples provided by *Middlebury Stereo Vision Page* [13], see Fig. 5. The resolution of the upper and lower examples are 434×383 and 384×288, respectively. We set the refinement window W_p to be 15×15. The refined disparity maps are better than the original disparity maps, but not perfect compared with the ground truths. We infer that this issue is induced by the low resolution input data. The core mechanism of our method is a selective median filter, which is reliable only on a large refinement window. However, the low resolution input data limits the size of the window. This is a limitation of our method.

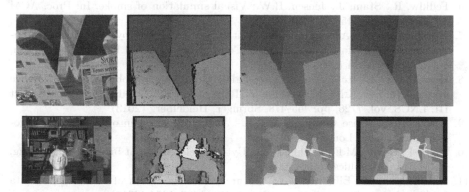

Fig. 5. Results on *Middlebury Stereo Vision Page* data set [13]. From left to right: base image, original disparity map, our refined result, ground truth.

5 Conclusions

In this paper we present a stereo refinement method for photo editing. The input is a stereo pair. We calculate the disparity map and pre-process it by revising the sky region and by removing incorrect data on the left of the disparity map. Then, the base image is mean-shift segmented in order to detect edge information. Later, a median filter is applied on the disparity map within each segment. Finally, invalid step-edges in the disparity map are removed by a joint bilateral filter.

Experiments show that our method can revise holes, inaccurate object edges, speckle noise, and invalid step-edges from disparity maps generated by a stereo matcher. The results are suitable for photo editing.

Acknowledgment. The authors thank Simon Hermann for providing the lib of iSGM stereo matcher, and Sandino Morales for a source code of mean-shift segmentation. This paper is supported by China Scholarship council.

References

1. Achanta, R., Shaji, A., Smith, K., Lucchi, A., Fua, P., Susstrunk, S.: SLIC superpixels compared to state-of-the-art superpixel methods. IEEE Trans. Pattern Analysis Machine Intelligence 34, 2274–2282 (2012)
2. Deng, Y., Manjunath, B.S.: Unsupervised segmentation of color-texture regions in images and video. IEEE Trans. Pattern Analysis Machine Intelligence 23, 800–810 (2001)
3. Fattal, R.: Single image dehazing. ACM Trans. Graphics 27(72) (2008)
4. Fukunaga, K., Hostetler, L.D.: The estimation of the gradient of a density function, with applications in pattern recognition. IEEE Trans. Information Theory 21, 32–40 (1975)
5. Felzenszwalb, P.F., Huttenlocher, D.P.: Efficient belief propagation for early vision. Int. J. Computer Vision 70, 41–54 (2006)
6. Fedkiw, R., Stam, J., Jensen, H.W.: Visual simulation of smoke. In: Proc. ACM SIGGRAPH, pp. 15–22 (2001)
7. Hirschmüller, H.: Accurate and efficient stereo processing by semi-global matching and mutual information. In: Proc. Computer Vision and Pattern Recognition, vol. 2, pp. 807–814 (2005)
8. Hermann, S., Klette, R.: Iterative semi-global matching for robust driver assistance systems. In: Lee, K.M., Matsushita, Y., Rehg, J.M., Hu, Z. (eds.) ACCV 2012, Part III. LNCS, vol. 7726, pp. 465–478. Springer, Heidelberg (2013)
9. Klette, R.: Concise Computer Vision - An Introduction into Theory and Algorithms. Springer, London (2014)
10. Kopf, J., Cohen, M.F., Lischinski, D., Uyttendaele, M.: Joint bilateral upsampling. ACM Tran. Graphics 26(96) (2007)
11. Khoshelham, K., Elberink, S.-O.: Accuracy and resolution of Kinect depth data for indoor mapping applications. Sensors 12, 1437–1454 (2012)
12. Matsuo, T., Fukushima, N., Ishibashi, Y.: Weighted joint bilateral filter with slope depth compensation filter for depth map refinement. In: Proc. Int. Conf. Computer Vision Theory Applications (2013)

13. Middlebury Stereo Vision Page, http://vision.middlebury.edu/stereo/data/
14. Ng, R., Levoy, M., Brédif, M., Duval, G., Horowitz, M., Hanrahan, P.: Light field photography with a hand–held plenoptic camera. Computer Science Technical Report 2(11) (2005)
15. Oh, B.M., Chen, M., Dorsey, J., Durand, F.: Image-based modeling and photo editing. In: Proc. ACM SIGGRAPH, pp. 433–442 (2001)
16. Schechner, Y.Y., Kiryati, N.: Depth from defocus vs. stereo: How different really are they? Int. J. Computer Vision 39, 141–162 (2000)
17. Subbarao, M., Surya, G.: Depth from defocus: a spatial domain approach. Int. J. Computer Vision 13, 271–294 (1994)
18. Tomasi, C., Manduchi, R.: Bilateral filtering for gray and color image. In: Proc. Int. Conf. Computer Vision, pp. 839–846 (1998)
19. Wu, J., Zheng, C., Hu, X., Wang, Y., Zhang, L.: Realistic rendering of bokeh effect based on optical aberrations. The Visual Computer 26, 555–563 (2010)
20. Zhou, K., Hou, Q., Gong, M., Snyder, J., Guo, B., Shum, H.-Y.: Fogshop: Real-time design and rendering of inhomogeneous, single-scattering media. In: Proc. Pacific Conf. Computer Graphics Applications, pp. 116–125 (2007)

Depth Map's 2D Histogram Assisted Occlusion Handling in Video Object Tracking

Adam Łuczak, Sławomir Maćkowiak, and Jakub Siast

Poznań University of Technology, Poland
{aluczak,smack,jsiast}@multimedia.edu.pl
http://www.multimedia.edu.pl

Abstract. The paper describes new algorithm for automatic video object tracking. Proposed architecture consists of two loops of Kalman filter. In the loop of the tracking process, the information achieved from video and from 2D histogram based on depth map is used. Two loops work simultaneously and the parameters between the loops are interchanged when the occlusion occurs. The 2D histogram representation of the depth map has unique properties that can be used to improve the tracking eficiency especially in the case of occlusions of the objects in the image. Experimental results prove that the proposed system can accurately track multiple objects in complex scenes.

1 Introduction

Accurately tracking of moving objects within monitored scenes is crucial to a range of surveillance tasks. There are many effective methods of detecting and tracking objects, many analyses have been conducted to improve object tracking technique accuracy. Comprehensive literature survey of object tracking is presented in [1]. Another comprehensive survey was also produced by [2,3]. Techniques used in object tracking are categorized on the basis of the used type of objects and used motion representations. The most significant challenge in video object tracking is the frequent problem of occlusion. During occlusion, an ambiguity occurs in occluded object features. The tracking methods must be capable to resolve the individuality of the objects involved in the occlusion, when the occlusion takes place.

In real situation 3 types of the occlusion occur: *i*) a self-occlusion when one part of the object occludes another, *ii*) an inter-object occlusion when two objects being track occlude another object, *iii*) and occlusion by the background when a structure in the background occludes the tracked objects.

In this paper, a new technique to deal with the second type of the occlusions using the information contained in the depth maps is presented.

Depth maps create new opportunities to improve the algorithms of analysis of 3D scene, also in the video object tracking. New video acquisition systems often use the stereo cameras that allow the calculation of the depth map - an image that contains information about the distance of the points from the lens.

L.J. Chmielewski et al. (Eds.): ICCVG 2014, LNCS 8671, pp. 400–408, 2014.
© Springer International Publishing Switzerland 2014

Until recently, the depth map estimation algorithms were very complex, time-consuming and generated depth maps of poor quality. For depth estimation a global optimization algorithm like Belief propagation or Graph cuts has been used. Nowadays, the local cost aggregation methods are used instead of global optimization [5]. For example Winner-Takes-All (WTA) algorithm with low complexity gives better results than the old solutions. WTA algorithm is also suitable for hardware implementations. Moreover, increasingly are also available stereoscopic cameras with depth map estimation support. Some of the hardware or even software solutions allow obtaining a depth map in real time [6-9]. For example the Bumblebee stereo camera system offered by Point Grey Research [11] is able to produce a depth map in real time. Despite significant progress in algorithms of depth maps estimation, they still are not perfect. Main problems arise when the scene consists some semi-transparent objects, light reflections, occlusions or obscuring objects. On the other hand, even not perfect depth maps contain reach information about 3D scene. It is still possible to obtain information about the object distance from the camera lenses. Such information can help us properly measure of scaling or distance for tracked objects (e.g. car or person, etc.)[10]. The authors consider the use of depth maps to improve the efficiency of the tracking when inter-object occlusions occur.

This paper is divided into 4 main sections. Section 2 presents a novel idea of 2D histogram of depth map. Section 3 presents a new video object tracking algorithm that uses the information from 2D histogram of depth map in the tracking process. In the section 4 the assumptions of the experiments and achieved results for object tracking under the occlusions conditions are presented.

2 2D Histogram of Depth Map

Luminance of each pixel in a depth map is interpreted as a normalized disparity. Usually depth maps with 256 disparity levels are used. The proposed 2D histogram is a graphical representation of disparity values distribution in a depth map. For a depth map with resolution $J \times K$ pixels we build the 2D histogram with resolution $J \times 256$. Each column of the 2D histogram is a 1D histogram with 256 bins corresponding to 256 disparity levels. This 1D histogram for column j ($j \subset \langle 1; J \rangle$) is calculated for j-th column of the depth map.

The proposed 2D histogram is defined as (1):

$$2D\ histogram = DH = \begin{bmatrix} L(0,1) & \cdots & L(0,J) \\ \vdots & \ddots & \vdots \\ L(255,1) & \cdots & L(255,J) \end{bmatrix} \frac{255}{K} \tag{1}$$

where $L(i,j)$ is a number of pixels in j-th column of a depth map that have disparity value of i. K is a number of pixels in a single depth map column. The 2D histogram values are normalized to range $\langle 0, 255 \rangle$. Fig.1 presents a depth map and its 2D histogram.

Considering a picture from Fig. 1 c and associated 2D histogram from Fig.1 b we can see that three people from a center part of a picture are represented in a 2D depth histogram as a three separated aggregations of lighter pixels.

Depth map with camera parameters represents information about three dimensional scene. In presented algorithm for 2D histogram calculation a depth map is treated as a two dimensional picture. No information about perspective are exploited. The presented technique has two useful properties. First is a low computational complexity. Second, horizontal coordinate of an tracked objects in a picture are the same as horizontal coordinate of its representation in 2D histogram. With this property associating an objects in a sequence and in a 2D histogram is simplified.

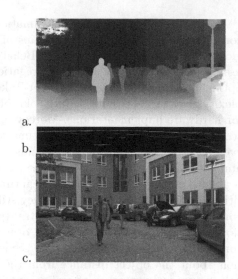

a.

b.

c.

Fig. 1. a. Depth map and b. 2D histogram associated with c. a frame 282 from *Poznan Car Park* sequence

What is very important, partly obscured objects are still easy distinguishable on a 2D histogram. Of course, object cannot be recognised properly even using depth map due to the occlusion, but the information about the position in space of not obscured part is still correct.

3   Tracking Approach Assisted by the Information from 2D Histogram of Depth Map

Occlusions are predicted by checking pairs of bounding boxes at predicted positions. Suspending the update phase for any length of time, however, is problematic since motions (particularly of people) can rapidly evolve. A recent simple but effective approach is to track the boundaries of bounding boxes separately which results in at least some updating evidence recovered for a substantial proportion of the occlusion event.

The proposed video object tracking architecture is presented in Figure 2. The tracker consists of two Kalman Filter loops. The first loop works on consecutive frames of the video. This is a typical implementation of a system for object detection and tracking based on the segmentation and classification of moving pixels in the scene. Motion detection processes locate blobs (connected regions of moving pixels) to create a candidate list of observations of the current active scene objects. Normally these blobs are recovered by pixel differencing against the reference frame of the static scene, usually attributed with their bounding box.

The Tracker module is implemented using a two-step approach: prediction and update. In the prediction step of the procedure, position of the objects tracked in previous frames are projected to the current frame according to trajectory models. Next, in the Data Association step predicted positions of objects are confrontated with list of candidate observations i.e. objects from Object Detection phase. Corresponding objects and observations are found.

The second loop is a fresh approach in the tracking systems. This loop works on 2D histogram of disparity map (a depth map). In this domain, the process locates moving regions and creates a candidate list of observations of objects. In the concept, the algorithm defines the moving blobs in two-dimensional space of the histogram. When two or more objects occlude one another it can still be possible to separate objects in 2D histogram. The only prerequisitive is that the objects have a different assiociated depth. If that condition is fulfilled the object will be represented in 2D histogram of depth map as separated blobs. This makes segmenting the object blob during occlusion easier.

In order to apply the Kalman filter, the process should be described by the following linear equations:

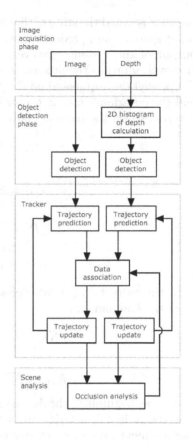

Fig. 2. Tracking architecture

$$\overline{x_{I_k}} = A_I \widehat{x_{I_{(k-1)}}} + B_I u_{I_{(k-1)}} \tag{2}$$

$$\overline{x_{D_k}} = A_D \widehat{x_{D_{(k-1)}}} + B_D u_{D_{(k-1)}} \tag{3}$$

$$z_{I_k} = H_I x_{I_k} + \nu_{I_k} \tag{4}$$

$$z_{D_k} = H_D x_{D_k} + \nu_{D_k} \tag{5}$$

The equations (2) and (4) concern the loop in video domain, (3) and (5) concern the loop in the 2D histogram of the depth domain. The (2) and (3) equations are called the equations of state or process models, while the (4) and (5) are the measurement models. In the above equations, A, B, H are matrices,where A_I and A_D are the state-transition models for image and depth equations, H_I and H_D are the observation models for image and depth equations, B_I and B_D are the control-input models for image and depth equations, the vector x is called the state of the system, the vector contains information from the input system, e.g., predetermined speed of the objects. Vector z is the measured output of the system. However, u and ν mean a noise (standard deviations). However, u means the process noise whereas ν is the measurement noise. During the prediction step, based on the previous x statea new value of x is determined, and the covariance matrix Q_I for image and Q_D for the depth. These values are determined on the basis of above equations.

$$Q_I = E[u_{I_{(k-1)}}(u_{I_{(k-1)}})^T] \tag{6}$$

$$Q_D = E[u_{D_{(k-1)}}(u_{D_{(k-1)}})^T] \tag{7}$$

$$\overline{P_{I_k}} = A_I P_{I_{(k-1)}} A_I^T + Q_I \tag{8}$$

$$\overline{P_{D_k}} = A_D P_{D_{(k-1)}} A_D^T + Q_D \tag{9}$$

In the correction (update) phase we set the variable K, hereinafter referred to as the Kalman gain.

$$K_{I_k} = \overline{P_{I_k}} H_I^T (H_I \overline{P_{I_k}} H_I^T + R)^{-1} \tag{10}$$

$$K_{D_k} = \overline{P_{D_k}} H_D^T (H_D \overline{P_{D_k}} H_D^T + R)^{-1} \tag{11}$$

At the beginning, the Kalman gain is determined. If we look at the way how the K is calculated, (10) and (11), we come to the conclusion that if the measurement noises are greater which here is represented by the covariance R, the value of K is lower. Here we come to the heart of the proposal. In the case of a small value of K_{I_k} (for the object tracking in the video, it indicates the occlusion existance) and when the second parameter for the depth loop K_{D_k} is greater than δ_D (the Kalman gain does not indicate the measurement error, no occlusion exist) the R_I covariance matrix should be replaced by the R_D covariance matrix (12). The parameter δ is used to control the interchange between parameters R_I and R_D. Its value was chosen experimentally. Motion object segmentation in the 2D histogram of depth map gives more precise information about the object moving trajectory. Due to the different values and measurement representation between image and depth, the covariance matrix can not be used directly but scaling is required. The measurement in the 2D histogram of the disparity is more reliable, the standard deviation and the R_D has the lower values.

Vice versa, the covariance matrix R_I in the case of a small value K_{D_k} should be replaced by the scaled value of R_I. Only of course if the K_{I_k} is greater than δ_I.

$$\text{If } K_{I_k} \leq \delta_I \cap K_{D_k} > \delta_D \text{ then } R_I = R_D scale,$$
$$\text{and if } K_{D_k} \leq \delta_D \text{ then } R_D = R_I \frac{1}{scale}. \tag{12}$$

From (4) and (5) the position of the detected blobs in the image and 2D histogram of the depth map (from the measurement phase) z_{I_k} and z_{D_k} are calculated. For two-dimensional space:

$$H_I = H_D = \begin{bmatrix} 1 & 0 & 0 & 0 \\ 0 & 1 & 0 & 0 \end{bmatrix} \tag{13}$$

After the measurement process the new values of the process state for image and 2D histogram domain are calculated (14)(15), the values of the covariance matrices R_I and R_D are updated.

$$\widehat{x_{I_k}} = \overline{x_{I_k}} + K_{I_k}[z_{I_k} - H_I \overline{x_{I_k}}] \tag{14}$$

$$\widehat{x_{D_k}} = \overline{x_{D_k}} + K_{D_k}[z_{D_k} - H_D \overline{x_{D_k}}] \tag{15}$$

$$P_{I_k} = [1 - K_{I_k} H_I] \overline{P_{I_k}} \tag{16}$$

$$P_{D_k} = [1 - K_{D_k} H_D] \overline{P_{D_k}} \tag{17}$$

$$R_I = E[\nu_{I_{(k-1)}} (\nu_{I_{(k-1)}})^T] \tag{18}$$

$$R_D = E[\nu_{D_{(k-1)}} (\nu_{D_{(k-1)}})^T] \tag{19}$$

4   Experimental Results

The final versions of the proposed system architecture to object tracking have been obtained by extensive iterative experiments in the scope of this paper. Proposed two-loops Kalman filter tracking algorithm has been implemented. Here, we report the experimental results that allow to estimate the overall efficiency of the object detection under the occlusions condition. This is done using subjective and objective tests on two MPEG MVD test sequences (1920 x 1080 resolution - *Poznan Car Park, Poznan Street*). More extensive test for other MVD sequences are planed when depth maps will be available.

Table 1. Experimental results

Sequence	Tracking mode	Total frames	Frames with occlusions	Accuracy [frames]	Accuracy [%]
Poznan Car Park	without DM	150	98	93	62%
	with DM	150	98	138	92%
Poznan Street	without DM	130	35	98	75%
	with DM	130	35	121	93%

Fig. 3. Tracking algorithm results for frames numberr 223, 254, 282, 299, and 315 of *Poznan Car Park* sequence (a bounding boxes of detected moving objects achieved for the tracking system with and without information from depth)
a. the case of the tracking algorithm without the information from the depth maps.
b. the information used in the proposed solution to gain the efficiency of the detection.
c. the case of the proposed tracking algorithm (the two-loops Kalman filter solution exploiting video and 2D histogram of a depth map).

The experiments were divided into 2 steps. First test was done for architecture with one-loop Kalman filter. The information from 2D histogram of depth map has not been used at this moment. The moving object blobs are detected with HOG features and SVM classification process. The second step of the experiment use the full proposed approach (detection and tracking object on the video and detection and tracking information on the 2D histogram of the depth map). The results of the detection for both steps are presented in the Table 1. As shown on the Fig.3, also subjective tests prove that the proposed solution achieves more efficiency than classic method exploiting only video information (one-loop architecture). The average gain of the efficiency of object tracking under the occlusions is more than 24% for all frames of the sequence, moreover the gain of the efficiency for the frames when the occlusions occur only is higher than 85%.

5   Conclusions

In this paper, a novel idea of the system to track the objects in video sequence has been presented. In the paper the architecure of the tracking system, which exploits the information from the depth has been proposed. Proposed method combines well known Kalman filter based tracking method and 2D histogram of depth map. This architecture has been tested under the scenarios where different occlusion situations were present. This original approach results in significant improvement of accuracy of objects' tracking. Moreover, by adding a depth map and 2D histogram to tracking algorithms their functionality has been enriched.

Acknowledgement. Research project was supported by the National Science Centre, Poland according to the Grant no. 4775/B/T02/2011/40.

References

1. Pulford, G.W.: Taxonomy of multiple target tracking methods. IEE Proceedings Radar, Sonar and Navigation 152(5), 291–304 (2005)
2. Yilmaz, A., Javed, O., Shah, M.: Object tracking: A survey. ACM Computing Surveys (CSUR) 38(4), 1–45 (2006)
3. Turaga, P., Chellappa, R., Subrahmanian, V.S., Udrea, O.: Machine recognition of human activities - a survey. IEEE Transactions on Circuits and Systems for Video Technology 18(11), 1473–1488 (2008)
4. Du, Y., Chen, F., Xu, W., Li, Y.: Recognizing interaction activities using dynamic Bayesian network. In: International Conference on Pattern Recogntion, pp. 618–621 (2006)
5. Scharstein, D., Szeliski, R.: Middlebury Stereo Vision Page, http://vision.middlebury.edu/stereo/ (online December 1, 2013)
6. Yongtae, K., Jiyoung, K., Wanghoon, S.-K.-H.: Fast Disparity and Motion Estimation for Multi-view Video Coding. IEEE Transactions on Consumer Electronics 53(2), 712–719 (2007)
7. Wu, D., Zhang, H., Li, X., Qian, L.: Depth Map Generation Algorithm for Multi-view Video. In: 2013 Fifth International Conference on Computational and Information Sciences (ICCIS), Shiyang, China (2013)
8. Lee, L.S.H., Sharma, S.: Real-time disparity estimation algorithm for stereo camera systems. IEEE Transactions on Consumer Electronics 57(3), 1018–1026 (2011)

9. Han, H., Han, X., Yang, F.: An improved gradient-based dense stereo correspondence algorithm using guided filter. International Journal for Light and Electron Optics 125(1), 115–120 (accepted for publication, 2014)
10. Claps, A., Reyes, M., Escalera, S.: Multi-modal user identification and object recognition surveillance system. Pattern Recognition Letters 34(7), 799–808 (2013) ISSN 0167-8655
11. Scharstein, D., Szeliski, R.: Middlebury Stereo Vision Page, http://vision.middlebury.edu/stereo/ (online December 1, 2013)

Novel Approach to Noise Reduction in Ultrasound Images Based on Geodesic Paths

Krystyna Malik, Bernadetta Machala, and Bogdan Smolka

Silesian University of Technology, Gliwice, Poland
{krystyna.malik,bernadetta.machala,bogdan.smolka}@polsl.pl

Abstract. In this paper a new method of multiplicative noise reduction in ultrasound images is proposed. The novel technique is a modification of the bilateral denosing scheme, which takes into account the similarity of pixels and their spatial distance. The filter output is calculated as a weighted average of the pixels which are in the neighborhood relation with the center of the filtering window, and the weights are functions of the minimal connection costs between surounding pixels. Experimental results show that the proposed method yields significantly better results than the other techniques in case of ultrasound images contaminated by medium and strong multiplicative noise disturbances.

1   Introduction

Ultrasound imaging is one of the most widely used technique in medical diagnosis. The application of ultrasound has greatly expanded over the past couple of decades, because this technique is non-invasive, safer, less expensive and simpler to use than other medical imaging techniques. Unfortunately, the quality of a medical ultrasonic image is often degraded by multiplicative noise, also known as speckle noise [1, 2].

Speckle is a random granular pattern produced mainly by multiplicative noise, that strongly degrades the visual evaluation in ultrasound images. It is an undesirable property because it affects image edges and fine details, and decreases the image contrast, diminishes the image fidelity and affects its diagnostic value. Speckle noise can also mask small but very often diagnostically significant image features, and it reduces the efficiency of detection and recognition of the anatomical structures in medical images.

Therefore, in medical ultrasound image processing, the reduction of speckle noise with preservation of edges and image details plays a crucial role for the diagnosis. Through the years, many denoising techniques have been proposed and current approaches fall into three categories including adaptive local filters, anisotropic diffusion based methods, and wavelet techniques [1–4].

In this work a new approach to the problem of noise removal in ultrasound images is presented. The proposed filtering design is a modification of the bilateral filter [5]. The concept of the presented denosing scheme was proposed in [6] and was applied to noise removal in color images contaminated by mixed Gaussian

L.J. Chmielewski et al. (Eds.): ICCVG 2014, LNCS 8671, pp. 409–417, 2014.

and impulsive noise. However, performed research showed that this method can be also used for denoising of grayscale images contaminated with multiplicative noise.

2 Bilateral Filter

The Bilateral filter (BF) is a nonlinear noise reducing technique, which smoothes images while preserving their edges and details [5,7]. In this method the intensity value of each pixel in an image is replaced by a weighted sum of the pixels' intensities in a filtering window. The weights depend on the spatial distance as well as on the intensity difference between the central pixel and other pixels in the filtering window. A new value at a pixel location x is calculated as follows

$$J(x) = \frac{1}{Z} \sum_{y \in \mathcal{N}_x} w(x, y) I(y), \quad Z = \sum_{y \in \mathcal{N}_x} w(x, y), \tag{1}$$

where $\mathcal{N}_x$ is the local neighborhood of x and $w(x, y)$ is the weight assigned to pixel at location y which belongs to $\mathcal{N}_x$. The weight assigned to a pixel at $y \in \mathcal{N}_x$ is defined as $w(x, y) = w_S(x, y) \cdot w_I(x, y)$. This weight is a result of a multiplication of two components $w_S(x, y) = \exp\left(-\|x - y\|^2 / 2\sigma_S^2\right)$ and $w_I(x, y) = \exp\left(-\|I(x) - I(y)\|^2 / 2\sigma_I^2\right)$,

where $\|\cdot\|$ denotes the Euclidean distance between x and y in the image domain, σ_S and σ_I are weighting parameters in the *Spatial* and *Intensity* domains respectively.

Figure 1, explains the construction of the bilateral filter. The central pixel is transformed using a sliding filtering window, which includes the analyzed pixel and its neighbors. The analyzed pixel is the central pixel of the mask. First, the array of spatial distances between the central pixel and the rest of pixels of the window is created (see Fig. 1b). Afterwards another array containing the information about absolute intensity difference between the central pixel and its neighbors is calculated as shown in Fig. 1c.

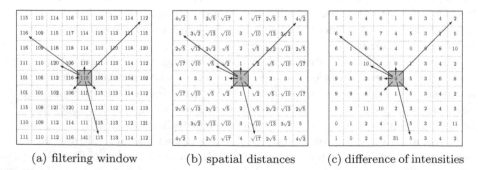

(a) filtering window   (b) spatial distances   (c) difference of intensities

Fig. 1. An example illustrating the construction of the bilateral filter

The bilateral filter is a highly efficient noise reducing scheme, however it has severe problems to remove the noisy pixels. If the central pixel of the local filtering window is corrupted and in the close neighborhood of this pixel is located another noisy pixel, which possess similar intensities as the analyzed pixel, then the weights $w_I(\boldsymbol{x}, \boldsymbol{y})$ are relatively high, which leads to the preservation of the contaminated pixel. Therefore, we present and discuss a modification of the filter which alleviates this problem.

3   Proposed Noise Reduction Method

The proposed Geodesic Bilateral Filter (GBF) like the bilateral filter changes the value of each pixel by a weighted average of the samples in a local neighborhood. The concept of the GBF is based on assigning each pixel from the filtering window an optimal digital path which connects them with the central pixel. The filter output is the weighted average of the pixels in a local neighborhood and the weights depend on the minimum connection cost assigned to each pixel in the local neighborhood.

For the calculation of the weights, we treat the image as a graph and utilize the Dijkstra's algorithm for finding the optimal connections between the pixels, where the graph weights are simply the absolute differences between adjacent pixels intensities. The Dijkstra's algorithm was implemented assuming 8-neighborhood crossing costs between pixels, which is calculated as the difference in the intensity of neighboring pixels. The central pixel is denoted as $\boldsymbol{x}$, the other pixels in the neighborhood pixel $\boldsymbol{x}$ are denoted by $\boldsymbol{x}_k, (k = 1, 2, .., 8)$ and connection cost $c(\boldsymbol{x}, \boldsymbol{x}_k)$ is the difference of intensity between pixels, and is calculated as $c(\boldsymbol{x}, \boldsymbol{x}_k) = |I(\boldsymbol{x}) - I(\boldsymbol{x}_k)|$.

For the analyzed neighborhood, an array C is created. The array includes the crossing cost between central pixel and its neighbors. Initially $C(\boldsymbol{x}) = 0$ and $C(\boldsymbol{y}) = \infty$ for all other pixels, which indicates that the pixel has unassigned cost value. First, the cost of crossing between the central pixel and its neighbors is computed (Fig. 2a). Then, the algorithm assigns to each pixel in the window the lowest cost relative to the central pixel (Fig. 2b) and creates the path with minimum cost function value (Fig. 2c). Finally, the array C includes the shortest paths for all pixels in the window. The computational complexity of the proposed method, using a small filtering window, is similar to the computational complexity of BF.

The weight of the GBF depends on the cost function, which determines the cost of the crossing from the central pixel at position $\boldsymbol{x}$ to each pixel in the local neighborhood $\mathcal{N}_{\boldsymbol{x}}$ is defined as: $w(\boldsymbol{x}, \boldsymbol{y}) = \exp\left(-C(\boldsymbol{x}, \boldsymbol{y})^2/h^2\right)$, where h is a parameter of weight and $C(\boldsymbol{x}, \boldsymbol{y})$ is cost function.

The cost function assigned to $\boldsymbol{y}$ is the minimum total cost of the optimal paths between $\boldsymbol{x}$ and $\boldsymbol{y}$, $C(\boldsymbol{x}, \boldsymbol{y}) = \sum_{i=1}^{m} |I(\boldsymbol{x}_i) - I(\boldsymbol{x}_{i-1})|$, where $\boldsymbol{x}_0 = \boldsymbol{x}$ is the origin vertex of the minimum cost path, $\boldsymbol{x}_m = \boldsymbol{y}$ is the destination vertex and m is the number of the optimum path segments.

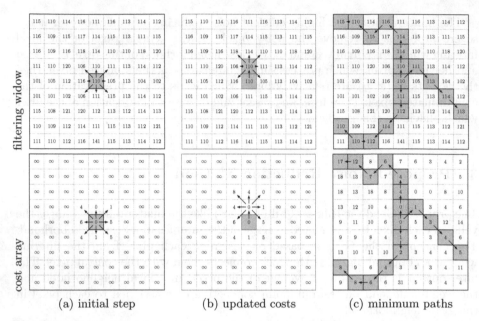

| | (a) initial step | (b) updated costs | (c) minimum paths |

Fig. 2. An illustration of the creation of minimum paths connecting pixels with the central element of filtering window

The new value of the pixel is calculated from

$$\widetilde{J}(\boldsymbol{x}) = \frac{1}{Z} \sum_{\boldsymbol{y} \in \mathcal{N}_{\boldsymbol{x}}} w(\boldsymbol{x}, \boldsymbol{y}) I(\boldsymbol{y}), \quad Z = \sum_{\boldsymbol{y} \in \mathcal{N}_{\boldsymbol{x}}} w(\boldsymbol{x}, \boldsymbol{y}). \tag{2}$$

4   Experiments

The Geodesic Bilateral Filter was compared with other speckle noise reduction techniques in terms of the visual quality of the restored image and also in terms of objective quality measures. In this work 13 different speckle reduction algorithm have been tested. We used for the comparison following filters: Lee statistic filter (LSF) [8], Kuan filter (KF) [8], Frost filter (FF) [9], Wiener filter (WF) [10], Bilateral filter (BF), Anisotropic Diffusion (AD) [11,12], Speckle Reduction Anisotropic Diffusion (SRAD) [13], VisuShrink (VS) [14], SureShrink (SS) [15], BayesShrink (BS) [16].

To quantiatively evaluate the denoising methods we used 15 quality metrics: Peak Signal to Noise Ratio (PSNR) [17], Signal to Noise Ratio (SNR) [17], Root Mean Square Error (RMSE) [17], Normalized Mean Square Error (NMSE) [18], Laplacian Mean Squared Error (LMSE) [18], Mean Absolute Error (MAE) [19], Maximum Difference (MD) [18], Normalized Cross-Correlation (NC) [18], Coefficient of Correlation (CoC) [17], Normalized Absolute Error (NAE) [18], Universal Quality Index (UQI) [20], Quality Index based on Local Variance (QILV) [21], Structural Content (SC) [18], Mean Structural Similarity Quality Index (MSSIM) [22], Speckle Reduction Score (SRS) [4].

For the purposes of the research two types of speckle noise were modeled: multiplicative noise model, denoted as MG, in which the Gaussian distribution is used. The noisy pixels $I(\boldsymbol{x})$ are defined as: $I(\boldsymbol{x}) = O(\boldsymbol{x}) + O(\boldsymbol{x}) \cdot \delta = O(\boldsymbol{x})(1+\delta)$.

The structure of the second model denoted as MU is similar. It differs only in the definition of the variable δ, which is uniformly distributed random variable. The gray test images depicted in Fig. 3 were contaminated by two types of multiplicative noise with intensities described by the standard deviation of the respective distribution ranging from 0.1 to 0.3.

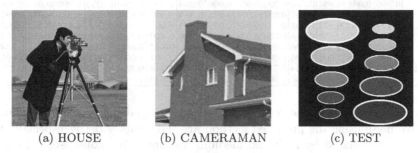

(a) HOUSE   (b) CAMERAMAN   (c) TEST

Fig. 3. Gray test images used in the experiments

The control parameters were selected experimentally to obtain optimal results in terms of the PSNR quality coefficient. The comparison of the efficiency of the proposed GBF with the other speckle reduction techniques are summarized in Tab. 1. Efficacy results from various image quality metrics obtained for test image MU_{20} are summarized in Tab. 2.

Table 1. Comparison of PSNR values for images contaminated by MG and MU noise restored by the GBF and competing techniques

Images	Noise	GBF	MF	LSF	KF	FF	WF	BLPF	BF	AD	SRAD	VS	SS	BS
House	MG_{10}	34.68	32.07	33.86	33.86	30.75	33.38	33.83	33.06	**34.99**	30.30	33.61	33.31	33.27
	MG_{20}	**30.93**	26.45	28.49	28.49	25.26	27.93	28.25	24.81	30.21	30.10	29.63	29.71	29.04
	MG_{30}	**28.16**	23.14	25.13	25.11	22.04	24.73	24.84	19.84	26.83	27.60	26.65	26.72	26.17
	MU_{10}	34.37	30.23	33.74	33.70	30.63	33.58	33.70	32.74	**34.87**	30.25	33.62	33.28	33.07
	MU_{20}	**30.47**	24.43	28.24	28.24	25.02	27.66	27.98	23.75	29.98	30.05	29.41	29.55	28.92
	MU_{30}	**27.34**	21.16	24.90	24.87	21.86	24.55	24.63	19.01	26.54	27.34	26.40	26.46	26.20
Cameraman	MG_{10}	32.45	31.43	32.14	32.14	30.53	32.23	**32.84**	32.39	32.41	28.40	30.93	30.28	32.07
	MG_{20}	**28.83**	26.65	28.16	28.16	25.37	25.68	28.02	25.11	27.84	28.19	27.78	27.45	28.10
	MG_{30}	**26.74**	23.55	25.35	25.35	22.24	22.33	24.98	19.71	24.86	26.59	25.84	25.60	25.84
	MU_{10}	32.15	30.12	32.15	32.15	30.55	32.64	**32.86**	32.32	32.43	28.44	30.90	30.11	32.27
	MU_{20}	**28.47**	24.94	28.16	28.15	25.33	26.15	28.00	24.52	27.83	28.21	27.80	27.41	28.18
	MU_{30}	**26.34**	21.65	25.22	25.22	22.07	22.53	24.87	18.86	24.73	26.87	25.75	25.52	25.83
Test	MG_{10}	**36.09**	30.64	23.22	23.11	23.21	33.11	28.02	35.41	28.41	24.00	29.48	30.18	28.03
	MG_{20}	**29.85**	26.67	22.41	22.31	22.08	26.31	24.61	26.77	24.41	23.43	24.23	25.29	23.55
	MG_{30}	**25.63**	23.78	21.38	21.33	20.76	22.22	22.45	21.66	22.37	22.75	21.22	22.57	20.68
	MU_{10}	**35.18**	29.89	23.20	23.09	23.20	33.08	27.94	34.88	28.33	23.81	29.42	30.13	27.99
	MU_{20}	**29.34**	25.55	22.34	22.26	22.02	26.37	24.52	26.38	24.29	23.18	23.97	25.18	23.41
	MU_{30}	**24.98**	22.48	21.22	21.17	20.61	22.21	22.15	21.35	22.16	22.50	21.07	22.41	20.58

Table 2. Comparison of image quality metrics, (Cameraman MU$_{20}$)

Metric	Noise	GBF	MF	LSF	KF	FF	WF	BLPF	BF	AD	SRAD	VS	SS	BS
PSNR	22.18	**28.83**	26.65	28.16	28.16	25.37	25.68	27.45	28.02	25.11	27.84	20.34	27.78	28.10
SNR	16.55	**23.19**	21.02	22.53	22.53	19.74	20.05	21.82	22.39	19.48	22.21	14.71	22.15	22.46
RMSE	19.85	**9.23**	11.86	9.97	9.97	13.73	13.26	10.81	10.12	14.15	10.34	24.52	10.41	10.04
NMSE	0.022	**0.005**	0.008	0.006	0.006	0.011	0.01	0.007	0.006	0.011	0.006	0.034	0.006	0.006
LMSE	39.06	1.586	4.282	1.754	1.754	21.65	10.01	0.856	0.895	16.48	1.594	**58.48**	0.908	1.147
MAE	14.02	**6.298**	8.424	7.138	7.138	9.860	8.941	7.383	7.277	9.805	7.437	17.96	7.335	7.339
MD	122	102	95	79	79	88	126	112	**74**	126	76	149	103	77
NC	0.999	0.988	0.994	0.995	0.995	0.996	0.996	0.994	0.997	0.994	0.9953	0.997	0.995	0.996
CoC	0.953	**0.989**	0.982	0.987	0.987	0.976	0.978	0.985	0.987	0.975	0.986	0.934	0.986	0.987
NAE	0.119	**0.053**	0.072	0.061	0.061	0.084	0.076	0.063	0.062	0.083	0.063	0.152	0.062	0.062
UQI	0.300	0.352	0.353	0.388	0.388	0.334	0.369	0.306	**0.407**	0.308	0.397	0.204	0.31	0.354
Qilv	0.639	0.806	0.932	0.896	0.896	0.877	0.901	0.84	**0.957**	0.896	0.918	0.476	0.854	0.957
SC	0.980	1.019	1.004	1.006	1.006	0.997	0.998	1.006	1.001	1.001	1.004	**0.974**	1.005	1.002
MSSIM	0.674	**0.806**	0.705	0.744	0.744	0.721	0.700	0.755	0.715	0.734	0.725	0.579	0.751	0.737
SRS	26.32	1.279	3.020	1.306	1.306	15.60	7.006	0.647	0.640	12.09	1.156	**33.87**	0.682	0.845

As can be observed, the results obtained for images contaminated by multiplicative noise using the proposed method are significantly better especially for images contaminated by high and medium multiplicative noise levels. Figures 4 and 5 present the visual comparison of image restoration techniques using real ultrasound images. As can be observed using the proposed algorithm, the

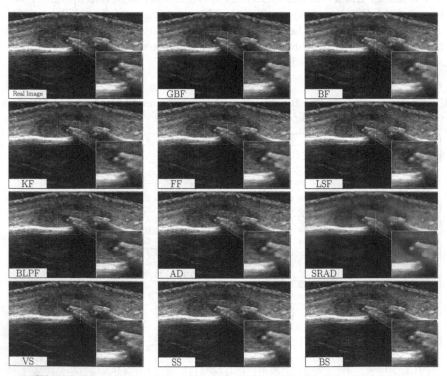

Fig. 4. Comparison of the effciency of the GBF with other techniques

filtering output is visually much better than the results obtained by other techniques. The image is smoothed, the edges are well preserved, it contains more details and is visually more pleasing.

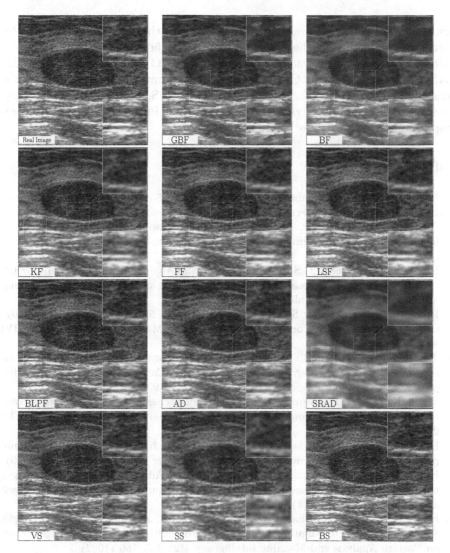

Fig. 5. Comparison of the effciency of the GBF with other techniques.

5   Conclusions

The results of the performed experiments indicate that very good restoration quality has been achieved using the proposed filtering design for images contaminated by medium and strong multiplicative noise. The new filtering method yields significantly better results in comparison with other denoising methods both in terms of subjective and objective restoration quality measures. The beneficial feature of the GBF is the removal of noise with preservation of edges and image details.

Acknowledgment. This work was supported by the Polish Norwegian Research Programme under the Project Pol-Nor/204256/16/2013. This work was performed using the infrastructure supported by POIG.02.03.01-24-099/13 grant: "GCONiI - Upper-Silesian Center for Scientific Computation". In Fig. 4 the ultrasound image created for MEDUSA project at Section for Rheumatology; Department for Neurology, the Rheumatology and Physical Medicine, Central Hospital, Forde, Norway has been used.

References

1. Michailovich, O., Tannenbaum, A.: Despeckling of medical ultrasound images. IEEE Trans. Ultrason., Ferroelect., Freq. Contr. 53, 64–78 (2006)
2. Sarode, M., Deshmukh, P.: Reduction of speckle noise and image enhancement of images using filtering technique. International Journal of Advancements in Technology 2(1), 30–38 (2011)
3. Loizou, C.P., Pattichis, C.S.: Despeckle Filtering Algorithms and Software for Ultrasound Imaging. Synthesis Lectures on Algorithms and Software in Engineering. Morgan and Claypool Publishers (2008)
4. Rosa, R., Monteiro, F.C.: Speckle ultrasound image filtering: Performance analysis and comparison. In: Computational Vision and Medical Image Processing IV: VIPIMAGE (2013)
5. Tomasi, C., Manduchi, R.: Bilateral filtering for gray and color images. In: Proceedings of the Sixth International Conference on Computer Vision, ICCV 1998, p. 839. IEEE Computer Society, Washington, DC (1998)
6. Malik, K., Smolka, B.: Improved bilateral filtering scheme for noise removal in color images. In: The International Conference on Informatics and Applications (ICIA 2012) (2012)
7. Paris, S., Durand, F.: A fast approximation of the bilateral filter using a signal processing approach. International Journal Computer Vision 81(1), 24–52 (2009)
8. Kuan, D.T., Sawchuk, A., Strand, T.C., Chavel, P.: Adaptive restoration of images with speckle. IEEE Transactions on Speckle ultrasound image Acoustics, Speech and Signal Processing 35(3), 373–383 (1987)
9. Frost, V.S., Stiles, J.A., Shanmugan, K.S., Holtzman, J.: A model for radar images and its application to adaptive digital filtering of multiplicative noise. IEEE Trans. on Pattern Analysis and Machine Intelligence 4(2), 157–166 (1982)
10. Jin, F., Fieguth, P., Winger, L., Jernigan, E.: Adaptive wiener filtering of noisy images and image sequences. In: International Conference on Image Processing, ICIP 2003, vol. 3, pp. 349–352 (2003)
11. Perona, P., Malik, J.: Scale-space and edge detection using anisotropic diffusion. IEEE Trans. on Pattern Analysis and Machine Intelligence 12, 629–639 (1990)
12. Zhi, X., Wang, T.: An anisotropic diffusion filter for ultrasonic speckle reduction. In: 5th International Conference on Visual Information Engineering, VIE 2008, pp. 327–330 (2008)

13. Yu, Y., Acton, S.T.: Speckle reducing anisotropic diffusion. IEEE Transactions on Image Processing 11(11), 1260–1270 (2002)
14. Donoho, D.L., Johnstone, I.M.: Ideal spatial adaptation by wavelet shrinkage. Biometrika 81, 425–455 (1994)
15. Donoho, D.L., Johnstone, I.M.: Adapting to unknown smoothness via wavelet shrinkage. Journal of the American Statistical Association, 1200–1224 (1995)
16. Chang, S.G., Yu, B., Vetterli, M.: Adaptive wavelet thresholding for image denoising and compression. IEEE Transactions on Image Processing 9(9), 1532–1546 (2000)
17. Prakash, K.B., Babu, R.V., VenuGopal, B.: Image independent filter for removal of speckle noise. International Journal of Computer Science Issues 8(5) (2011)
18. Eskicioglu, A.M., Fisher, P.S.: Image quality measures and their performance. IEEE Transactions on Communications 43(12), 2959–2965 (1995)
19. Avcibas, I., Sankur, B., Sayood, K.: Statistical evaluation of image quality measures. Journal of Electronic Imaging 11, 206–223 (2002)
20. Wang, Z., Bovik, A.C.: A universal image quality index. IEEE Signal Processing Letters (3), 81–84 (2002)
21. Aja-Fernandez, S., Estepar, R.S.J., Alberola-Lopez, C., Westin, C.-F.: Image quality assessment based on local variance. In: 28th Annual International Conference of the IEEE on Engineering in Medicine and Biology Society, EMBS 2006, pp. 4815–4818. IEEE (2006)
22. Wang, Z., Bovik, A.C., Sheikh, H.R., Simoncelli, E.P.: Image quality assessment: From error measurement to structural similarity. IEEE Transactions on Image Processing 13, 600–612 (2004)

Binarisation of Colour Map Images through Extraction of Regions

Sayan Mandal[1], Samit Biswas[1], Amit Kumar Das[1], and Bhabatosh Chanda[2]

[1] CST Department, Indian Institute of Engineering Science and Technology, Shibpur
mesayaan@gmail.com,{samit,amit}@cs.becs.ac.in
[2] ECS Unit, Indian Statistical Institute, Kolkata, India
chanda@isical.ac.in

Abstract. Methods to convert colour images to binary form are already reported in the literature. However, these methods are inadequate for binary conversion of complex documents such as maps due to large intensity variations in different regions and entangled texts with lines representing borders, rivers, roads and other similar components. This paper proposes a new binary conversion technique, for coloured land map images, by extracting the regions and analysing the hue, saturation spread and within class 'kurtosis'. This is a region-wise adaptive algorithm which copes up with the sharp changes of the discriminating features on different regions. Here, local regions are selected as clusters having the same hues and saturation. These regions are individually converted to binary form using the spread of their degree of within class kurtosis. The individual regions are finally combined. Our experiments include 446 colour maps from the map image database created for this purpose and made freely available at $http://code.google.com/p/lmidb$.

1 Introduction

Scanned paper maps are among the most complex documents to extract information, such as texts, from them. Backgrounds of maps are cluttered with colours of different states, countries, districts and also of roadways, railways, streams. The texts are drawn in various colours, orientations, fonts and profusely entangled with other landmarks. Algorithms using global threshold fail to extract text by converting such documents to binary form due to the large change in colour intensity. In certain maps, the background of a particular area (say a state or city) is darker than the texts in the same map at some other area. In such cases, global threshold algorithms (e.g., [10]) fail to produce an acceptable image in binary form. In general those global algorithms produce indiscriminate large patches of regions. Local threshold algorithms, which consider pixel and their neighbours (e.g.,[9]), produce unsatisfactory results too as they do not consider the relative change in intensity. An example of a coloured land map (as shown in Fig. 1) and corresponding results in binary obtained using Otsu [10] and Niblack [9] algorithms endorse our observation. As both global and local algorithms fail to address map threshold problem, we propose a region based adaptive algorithm. This is achieved by restricting the analysis of the global algorithm to a

L.J. Chmielewski et al. (Eds.): ICCVG 2014, LNCS 8671, pp. 418–427, 2014.
© Springer International Publishing Switzerland 2014

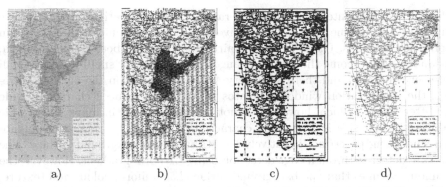

Fig. 1. a) Input; Binarised images using b) Otsu [10], c) Niblack [9], d) Gatos [3]

local region and threshold is based on it. The proposed technique performs a binary conversion on a local region automatically selected on the basis of their colour spread and finally combines the regions together. Regions are selected by identifying the dominant colour bands present in the map from its hue and saturation value analysis. All such colour bands are separately converted to binary, using the spread of the 'kurtosis' to get the regions present in the map, such as any particular country, state or district. The extracted regions stitched together is the desired map image in binary. The region selection and conversion of map documents to binary lead to further analysis that can be immensely instrumental in knowing the geographical change in historical perspective. It also has applications in GPS technology and map study and analysis.

2   Related Work

This section contains a reasonable selection of methods, which are already reported in literature, for conversion to binary in general and document image conversion to binary in particular. For completeness even the techniques applied to gray level images have also been included.

Otsu [10] is a popular global thresholding method. The application of such a technique to map image produces poor binarisation with the possibility of large regions converted to black (Fig. 1). Niblack's [9] algorithm uses a local threshold.It tends to produce a large amount of noise in the background areas and it does not consider the relative change in illuminations. For maps, it suffers from the basic problem of using a local threshold, i.e., providing unnecessary details in the converted binary images like unrecognisable thickened texts and lines along with dark sparks when the image has indistinguishable histogram.

The Method proposed by Sauvola [12] shows excellent threshold for text documents, however, it produces several artefacts for map image documents. It is an improvement over the Niblack where the threshold adaptively changes with the contrast of the image, which takes care of the relative change in illumination. However, in case of maps, some of the lines with different shades of gray and relatively less intensity value are erased. Gatos [3] method is an iterative binarisation technique that follows Sauvola to choose an initial threshold. On application to maps, Gatos produces fairly good results, better than Sauvola, but unable to overcome the sudden changes in intensity for small regions (small states or countries) and there are jittery artefacts present in the output. Moreover, the interpolation window in Gatos is suggested to be 2 characters wide for better results; which, however, cannot be implemented in maps where wide variation in text size is a common characteristic. Lu et. al. [7] uses a polynomial smoothing procedure iteratively to estimate the background surface. The texts are detected through edge detection using L1-norm gradient. However, the technique assumes that the background surface has uniform colour and texture, thus it is not concrete for all cases. The methods proposed by [6] as well as Sauvola's have been identified to be the best threshold techniques for degraded documents in a comparative study by Sezgin and Sankur [13]. Like Otsu [10], the algorithms assume background and foreground as normally distributed. The algorithms maximises the likelihood of the joint distribution of the gray image.

Wolf's algorithm[15] is a further improvement over Sauvola aimed to extract text from multimedia documents. Wolf aims to improve the result where the gray levels of the text and non-text are significantly closer. It normalises the contrast of the whole image and calculate the threshold on its basis. However, since it is normalised over the entire image, any speck of dark blob or uneven illumination would affect the entire image. Feng [1] suggests another local gray-level algorithm that calculates the mean, minimum and standard deviation around a window covering 1-2 characters. To negate the effects of uneven illumination, another secondary window is considered, larger in size, which contains the former window, where from they get the dynamic range of gray level standard deviation in that region. Then they set the window size to tolerate the subtle change in illumination. The technique works better than Wolf's algorithm, as it takes the second window locally rather than the whole image. However, the paper suggests to tune the parameters empirically and therefore its application in varied cases remains questionable. Ramírez-Ortegón et al. [8] binarised images based on edge detection and gray histograms. They consider the fact that the background in a certain region is darker than the text intensity in the same image and name such pixels as transition pixels. Then they compute the mean and variance of such pixels so as to determine the threshold.

Kherada et. al. [5] separated coloured texts for shadowed, reflective and specular background into RGB channels and for each of these channels applied a fixed point ICA algorithm to extract text from the background and then got the binary image by applying [10]. The channel containing maximum information of foreground text is considered. The technique, does not consider images having high saturation where more than one channel can contain high information. Also, since the threshold is global, sudden changes in shade cannot be handled.

Thillou and Gosselin [14] binarised coloured documents by calculating an initial threshold by Otsu or Sauvola (depending on whether the background is clean or complex) to remove useless parts of the image. This is followed by an unsupervised K means colour clustering (with K=3). Background is selected as the cluster having biggest rate of occurrence. An Euclidean distance with both mean color pixel of the cluster and mean color of the skeleton is performed for both the two remaining clusters. The cluster with the smallest distance is considered as the main textual part.The algorithm fails if the foreground concentration is higher than background. Also, it depends widely on the selection of the initial threshold.

Utilisation of local and global features, for better binary conversion, have been proposed by Ramírez et. al. [8] and Feng [1]. In [8] documents have been converted to binary by using threshold values using edge detection based on some hybrid of local and global characteristics. The drawback of [8] is the *a priory* assumption of the smooth variation of both the background and foreground. Similarly, the work by Feng [1] employs a hybrid technique by considering two windows, where the size of the larger window is empirically decided. However, the window being essentially rectangular may not produce good results in the case of maps and certain other documents where the intensity variation is abrupt between non-linear polygons representing distinct regions.

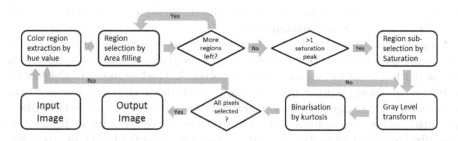

Fig. 2. Overview of the proposed approach

3   The Proposed Method

The proposed method primarily exploits two aspects for better binarisation. First, the selected window takes the shape of a uniform colour region (usually, a non-linear polygon; see Fig. 4b) which is formed automatically during run time. Second, kurtosis spread measure, forms cubical curve for regions having uniform colour intensities selected in the first step. This provides better and definite threshold than variance or skew even for noisy images. We start with the RGB colour image as input and convert it to HSI. During each pass of the algorithm, one area having a particular colour in the map is extracted and binarised. Each such area forms a different country, state, district or city. After all the areas have been binarised, they are stitched to give the full binarised map. The proposed method is depicted in Fig. 2 and details of some important steps, excluding pre-processing to remove salt and pepper noise, are in order.

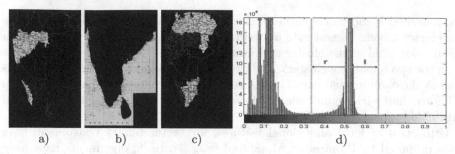

Fig. 3. a), b), c) Colour regions extracted from Fig. 1(a). d) Hue plot of Fig. 1a. The red dots indicate the mode, the green line indicate the spread of one maxima with 'r' and 'l' as the right and left spread.

3.1 Extraction of Colour Regions by Hue Value Analysis

In brief the selection of each colour region (data points) is explained as follows:

Step 1. Consider each pixel (i, j) individually from the input colour image P. It consists of HSI values such as $P_H(i, j)$, $P_S(i, j)$, and $P_I(i, j)$. Use another matrix E of the same size as P whose elements are binary-flags. These flags are used if the corresponding pixel in P is already marked for a colour region or not. Initially all cells in E are marked as 0.

Step 2. As we intend to find the number of colour bands present, we primarily work with the hue value of the image. The histogram for the hue range of the map is plotted and from it the modes are noted. As the hue measure gives us the dominant wavelength present in the colour, each mode suggests a colour band present. Any particular colour does not possess the same hue value throughout the entire image due to imperfection in printing or scanning itself. In fact, the same pixel would differ in its hue value during different scans by the same scanner under the same condition. We, therefore get a spread of each colour over a small range of hue values. In order to compute this range of hue values, we take the standard deviation from each mode as the spread of that colour band.

For each colour band, let hue attribute of a mode be M_p and the spread from the peak be r to the right and l to the left. This is determined by calculating the minima between two modes. The spreads to the left and to the right of the minima are the right spread of the left mode and the left spread of the right mode, respectively (Fig.4d). We extract the region having the same colour band in another matrix P_m; where:

$$
P_m(i', j') = \begin{cases} P(i', j') & \text{if} \begin{cases} E(i', j') = 0 \ (non\ flagged) \\ \wedge P_H(i', j') \in [M_p - l, M_p + r] \end{cases} \\ 0 & \text{Otherwise} \end{cases}
$$

Step 3. The resulting region, P_m in the previous step is basically a single or a group of regions, belonging to either the same state, district etc. or to different states having the same colour (Fig. 3b, c and d). Some other lines or dots which might be present in other parts of the map having same hue and representing rail line, river may also appear. Store these regions of same colour for further use in P_m^r *where* P_m^r contains the pixels modified in this pass.

Step 4. Select the next mode from the hue histogram and iterate through step 2 and 3 till all the regions are extracted.

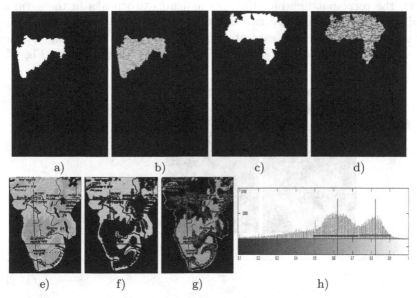

Fig. 4. Region extraction through area filling a,c) Biggest region selection of Fig. 3b and Fig. 3d; b,d) Corresponding region of the map, found in a and c;e,f,g)Separation of regions by saturation spread; h) Saturation plot for Fig. 4e

3.2 Region Selection through Area Filling Algorithm and Saturation Spread

For each iteration, P_m^r stores the regions having similar colour intensity. This includes several chunks of regions as well as fine lines of the same colour which may be present in the other regions as rail lines, roads, symbols etc. On this image, we apply the area filling algorithm which gives us the biggest region as one unified region (Fig. 4a, c). The pixels selected in the area filling pass are marked in the previously defined matrix E. Modify all cells in E as follows:

$$E(i',j') = \begin{cases} E(i',j') + 1 \ (flagged) & \text{if } P(i,j) \neq 0 \\ 0 & \text{Otherwise} \end{cases}$$

We iterate to find the next biggest region and continue till all enclosed regions have been collected. On getting each such region, we pick their corresponding pixel values (marked in E in this pass) in the original image to extract one distinct region (Fig. 4b,d). The set of pixels marked in this pass is stored in a separate array E_m^r for future verification (see section 4).

For physical maps, certain regions selected through the hue spread may have a change in colour saturation to indicate depth, density or contour of the region. For such regions, we carry out a further refinement by taking the plot for the saturation value of the region selected. For regions having uniform hue, (Fig. 4b, d) the saturation plot gives a single mode. However, for the images given in Fig. 4e, the corresponding plot(Fig. 4h) indicates two peaks in the saturation plot distribution as there are two distinct saturation values present (i.e. two tinge of orange). We further extract each of these regions by taking the modes from the saturation plot and corresponding spread from each mode (Fig. 4f, g).

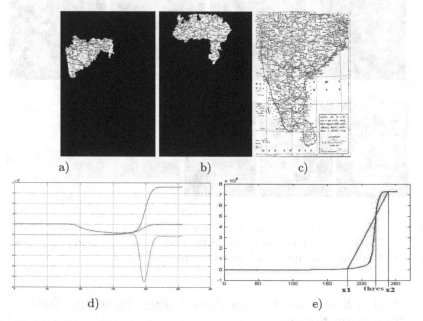

Fig. 5. Globalised binarisation through Kurtosis spread calculation. Threshold of a) Fig. 4b; b) Fig. 4d; c) Final image after post processing d)comparison,red: variance,green:skew,blue:kurtosis. e)Kurtosis spread and threshold calculation.

3.3   Binarisation through Kurtosis Spread Calculation

The resulting regions got from the previous subsection is basically a set of non-linear polygons (see Fig. 4b and d). Consider the original pixel value for each of these regions individually and compute the within class kurtosis (T_h) of their intensity. The mean intensity having highest change in within class kurtosis is the threshold for that colour region under consideration. In brief the kurtosis spread computation for a colour region is given below:

Step 1. Consider the intensity of each colour region P_m having P_x pixels and its histogram (H). Compute cumulative frequency (q) and the mean (v) as shown below:

$$q = \sum_{i=1}^{g} H_i ; v = \frac{\sum_{i=1}^{g} H_i * i}{q}$$

where g is the maximum gray level within the selected region. Initialize, another array $Q = \{\Phi\}$; where Q will contain the binarised regions.

Step 2. For each gray level (t), compute cumulative frequency (q_t) up to t, foreground mean (μ_t) and background mean (μ_b):

$$q_t = \sum_{i=1}^{t} H_i ; \ \mu_t = \begin{cases} \frac{\sum_{i=1}^{t} H_i * i}{q_t} & \text{if } q_t \neq 0 \\ 0 & \text{Otherwise} \end{cases} ; \ \mu_b = \begin{cases} \frac{v - \mu_t}{q - q_t} & \text{if } (q - q_t) \neq 0 \\ 0 & \text{Otherwise} \end{cases}$$

Step 3. Use (μ_t) and (μ_b) to compute the foreground kurtosis spread $(L1)$ and the background kurtosis spread $(L2)$. Finally, we estimate the within-class kurtosis (T_h) using $(L1)$ and $(L2)$ as follows:

$$L1 = \begin{cases} \frac{\sum_{c=1}^{t} (c - \mu_t)^4 * H(c)}{q_t} & \text{if } q_t \neq 0 \\ 0 & \text{Otherwise} \end{cases} \quad L2 = \begin{cases} \frac{\sum_{d=t+1}^{g} (d - \mu_b)^4 * H(d)}{q - q_t} & \text{if } (q - q_t) \neq 0 \\ 0 & \text{Otherwise} \end{cases}$$

T_h, the within class kurtosis at t is given by:
$T_h = L1 * \frac{q_t}{P_x} + L2 * \frac{q - q_t}{P_x}$;

The plot for T_h for all values of t from 1 to g (choose g=256) is given in Fig. 5e. The two points $x1$ and $x2$ are found on the basis of the maximum changes in gradient from constant to positive and from positive to constant. Finally, the mean between $x1$ and $x2$ is the selected final threshold (see Fig. 5e). Based on this threshold, we binarise the region to form the result in Fig. 5 a,b and store it in 'R'.

Finally, store all these regions in $Q = Q \bigcup R$; so Q is final binarised map image.

Table 1. Performance evaluation of different binarisation methods w.r.t the parameters used in [4] for a) map image binarisation b) document image binarisation

Methods	F-Measure	PSNR	NRM	MPM (x100)	Methods	F-Measure	PSNR	NRM (x10)	MPM (x1000)
Niblack [9]	46.52	6.76	0.19	4.92	Niblack [9]	95.83	16.61	0.57	0.77
Gatos [3]	82.52	13.68	0.09	0.36	Gatos [3]	96.68	19.52	0.12	0.23
Lu [7]	62.67	9.63	0.07	0.85	Lu [7]	93.16	20.37	0.22	0.39
Ramirez [11]	67.21	10.44	0.05	0.81	Ramirez [11]	94.62	17.95	0.50	0.14
Otsu [10]	69.77	11.40	0.05	0.64	Otsu [10]	96.70	19.56	0.12	0.36
mSauvola [2]	76.47	12.94	0.08	0.40	mSauvola [2]	66.93	9.68	0.18	9.00
Sauvola [12]	81.62	15.71	0.11	0.07	Sauvola [12]	96.55	19.30	0.18	0.33
Our Technique	88.42	16.24	0.03	0.07	Our Technique	96.60	19.47	0.09	0.13

a.   b.

4   Dataset Details and Experimental Results

The plot for within class kurtosis along with within class variance and skew has been shown in Fig. 5d. The shape of the plot for within class variance and skew for regions having constant intensities are essentially parabolic in nature. Whereas Kurtosis spread provides a cubical curve which has higher discriminating capabilities.

We check the final modified matrix E to find that all the cells have flag equal to 1. This implies that all the pixels in the image have been selected into one and only one region and that they have been binarised i.e., if there are 'n' regions extracted in the map and $E^r_{m_i}$ indicates the pixels selected in any i-th region, then:

$$E^r_{m_1} \bigcup E^r_{m_2} \bigcup ... \bigcup E^r_{m_n} = P \ \ and \ \ E^r_{m_i} \cap E^r_{m_j} = \phi \ \ \forall i,j \in E \wedge i \neq j$$

As there is no publicly available map image dataset we have created our own by collecting maps (scanned at 200 and 300 dpi) from Atlases of Indic scripts (Bangla, Hindi) and English. Topographic and tourist maps are also collected. The ground truth has been created by selecting regions of different intensities and threshold values manually. The database and the corresponding ground truth, containing binarised images, can be freely accessed from $http: // code. google. com/ p/ lmidb$.

DIBCO (Document Image Binarisation Contest) 2009 [4] parameters such as, F-Measure, NRM, MPM, PSNR, have been used for measuring the performance of our approach with respect to some of the popularly used binarisation methods used for document images.

The results of binarisation on map images using the benchmark dataset employing well known binarisation algorithms and the proposed approach are listed in table 1. For all the stated parameters, the results obtained using the proposed method have been far more promising than the existing techniques. The efficacy of the proposed method is also tested on document images other than the maps using the dataset (http://users.iit.demokritos.gr/ bgat/DIBCO2009/ benchmark/). The results (see table 1) are comparable or better than most of the competing methods.

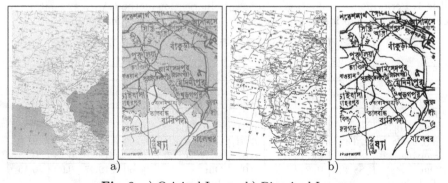

a)   b)

Fig. 6. a) Original Image; b) Binarised Image

5   Conclusion

In this work it is shown that the fully automated binarisation of land map is possible avoiding unwanted artifacts in a wide variety of scanned land map images. Use of hue and saturation spread to help classify different regions of the scanned map images is proposed and verified through this work with the endorsement of the benefits of using adaptive non-linear polygon shaped window and measure of kurtosis instead of mean/variance.

At present we are fine tuning our method to adapt it for better binarisation of any complex document. Furthermore, it may not be out of place to mention the benefits accrued from identification of regions for the purpose of binarisation. For example, information on the land elevation; location and areas of land and water bodies, national and international boundaries etc. are available from the identified regions and may be used for further processing.

References

1. Feng, M.-L., Tan, Y.-P.: Contrast adaptive binarization of low quality document images
2. Graud, T., Lazzara, G.: Efficient multiscale sauvola's binarization. International Journal of Document Analysis and Recognition (2013)
3. Gatos, B., Pratikakis, I., Perantonis, S.J.: Adaptive degraded document image binarization. Pattern Recognition (2006)
4. Gatos, B., Ntirogiannis, K., Pratikakis, I.: Icdar 2009 document image binarization contest (dibco 2009). In: ICDAR, pp. 1375–1382 (2009)
5. Kherada, S., Namboodiri, A.M.: An ica based approach for complex color scene text binarization
6. Kittler, J., Illingworth, J.: Minimum error thresholding. Pattern Recognition (1986)
7. Lu, S., Su, B., Tan, C.L.: Document image binarization using background estimation and stroke edges. IJDAR 13(4), 303–314 (2010)
8. Ramírez-Ortegón, M.A., Tapia, E., Ramirez-Ramirez, L.L., Rojas, R., Cuevas, E.: Transition pixel: A concept for binarization based on edge detection and gray-intensity histograms. Pattern Recognition (2010)
9. Niblack, W.: An introduction to image processing. Prentice-Hall, Englewood Cliffs (1986)
10. Otsu, N.: A tlreshold selection method from gray-level histograms. IEEE Transactions on Systrems, Man, and Cybernetics (1979)
11. Ramírez-Ortegón, M.A., Tapia, E., Ramírez-Ramírez, L.L., Rojas, R., Cuevas, E.: Transition pixel: A concept for binarization based on edge detection and gray-intensity histograms. Pattern Recognition 43, 1233–1243 (2010)
12. Sauvola, J.J., Pietikainen, M.: Adaptive document image binarization. Pattern Recognition 33(2), 225–236 (2000)
13. Sezgin, M., Sankur, B.: Survey over image thresholding techniques and quantitative performance evaluation. Journal of Electronic Imaging (2004)
14. Thillou, B., Gosselin, C.: Color binarization for complex camera-based images. In: Color Imaging X: Processing, Hardcopy, and Applications
15. Wolf, C., Jolion, J.-M.: Extraction and recognition of artificial text in multimedia documents. Pattern Analysis and Applications (2003)

Directional Filter and the Viterbi Algorithm for Line Following Robots

Przemysław Mazurek

West–Pomeranian University of Technology, Szczecin
Department of Signal Processing and Multimedia Engineering
26–Kwietnia 10 St. 71126 Szczecin, Poland
przemyslaw.mazurek@zut.edu.pl

Abstract. The line estimation algorithm dedicated to line following robots is proposed in this paper. The line estimation is based on the Viterbi algorithm and directional filtering using moving average filter. Two cases of system are compared using Monte Carlo approach – with proposed directional filter and without this filter. The performance is measured using comparison of cumulative errors for horizontal direction. The results shows 20% improvements for Gaussian noise standard deviation 0.3 − 0.9 range, for proposed solution in comparison to the Viterbi algorithm alone approach.

Keywords: Dynamic Programming, Tracking, Image Processing, Viterbi Algorithm.

1 Introduction

Line following robots are applied for components delivery in manufactures [1], especially. They are also applied in many contests in robotics and for educational purposes, because they could be very simple and cheap. The line following robot uses linear sensor (1D) or camera (2D) and very high line–to–background contrast is assumed typically. Even two light sensors with simple logic [2] for the line recognition could be applied for such intentional assumption. Real application of line following robots requires more robust image processing algorithms and pattern recognition techniques. The line could be deteriorated and lighting conditions could be variable. Locally variable lighting conditions, and noises related to the deteriorated background and real line as well as false lines are the sources of low quality of acquired image. The positive signal of line and dark background are assumed (or opposite mapping). The application of the camera allows the line estimation (tracking) but low–quality image requires robust image processing and tracking algorithms. The line width could be variable due to deterioration as well as low contrast that are shown in example in Section 4. Both problems are considered in this paper and the solution is provided.

L.J. Chmielewski et al. (Eds.): ICCVG 2014, LNCS 8671, pp. 428–435, 2014.

1.1   Related Works

The idea of line following robots is quite old [3]. The area of applications related to harvesting and similar task, where the line is not specified directly, is considered in [4]. Hough Transform approach for highly deteriorated line is considered in [5] for the road lane estimation as well as in agricultural application [6]. The application of LIDAR for the acquisition of 3D structures for line estimation is considered in [7]. The application of Monte Carlo sampling of image space is considered in [8].

1.2   Content and Contribution of the Paper

The problem of the line tracking with variable width and very–low contrast at the edge or below of edge of visibility by human is considered in this paper. Such assumption requires very robust algorithm, that will work very well even if the line or lighting conditions are significantly better. It allows the application of the proposed algorithm for scenarios, where the line is not intentionally added, so image existing line could be used, also. The line could be hidden in the image noise and the line width could be variable, due to deterioration. Multiple (false) lines that are parallel to the correct line may be image disturbance sources also.

In this paper the Viterbi algorithm [9] for line following robots is applied and briefly described in Section 2. The application of the directional filtering for image preprocessing is proposed in Section 3. The boundary possibilities of the line estimation are estimated using numerical experiments based on Monte Carlo approach in Section 4. Such assumptions allow the testing of many cases that are not available in small real image databases. The discussion is provided in Section 5 and the final conclusions are formulated in Section 6.

2   The Viterbi Algorithm for Line Estimation

The Viterbi algorithm is the dynamic programming algorithm that could be applied for the line tracking. Acquired image is analyzed, starting from the bottom row. The pixels may correspond to the nodes (states) of the trellis. Appropriate transitions between nodes of two following rows are related to the possible transitions. This is defined by the Markov transition matrix and probabilities of transition could be assigned. Five transitions with equal probabilities in this paper (Fig. 1) are assumed. The number of transitions depends on the line model.

The selection of the best path in the trellis corresponding to the most probable line is based on the local and global choice. Tracking process starts from the first (bottom) row ($n = 1$) and the local costs $d_{n,x}^{n+1,x}$ are computed for all paths allowed by trellis to the second row ($n = 2$), where x is the position in horizontal direction. The local cost could be defined as a sum of the pixel values and highest values correspond to the possible line and should be preferred (local choice). The local cost for particular local path is added to the node value V of the previous row n, and projected to the next row $n + 1$:

$$V_{n+1,x} = \max \left(V_{n,x+g} + d_{n,x+g}^{n+1,x} \right), \tag{1}$$

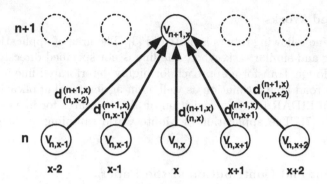

Fig. 1. Local paths in example trellis

where the transitions are defined using the following set:

$$g \in \{-2, -1, 0, +1, +2\}, \tag{2}$$

and the starting condition is:

$$V_{n=1,.} = 0 \tag{3}$$

The selection of the best path to the particular node is preserved additionally:

$$L_n^{n+1,x} = \arg\max_g \left(V_{n,x+g} + d_{n,x+g}^{n+1,x}\right), \tag{4}$$

where L denotes local transition. The projection of the values is executed n_{max} times. The depth of the projection (n_{max}) influences the estimation results, but this it is not considered in this paper.

After reaching of the n_{max} row in first phase (forward phase), the second phase is started (backward phase). The maximal value P_{opt} for n_{max} selects the most probable path, starting from the last row:

$$P_{opt} = \max\left(V_{n=n_{max},.}\right), \tag{5}$$

that selects $x_{n=n_{max}}$ node:

$$x_{n=n_{max}} = \max_x \left(V_{n=n_{max},x}\right). \tag{6}$$

The following recursive formula finds path in trellis (backward):

$$x_{n-1} = x_n + L_{n-1}^{n,x}, \tag{7}$$

for successively decremented row numbers:

$$n = n_{max}, \cdots, 2. \tag{8}$$

The transition between first and second row for specific starting point x_1 is the result of the Viterbi algorithm - part of the estimated trajectory. Overall process is repeated using moving window approach for the input image. Obtained estimation result of the Viterbi algorithm could be used in next processing steps, but it is not recommended. First forward–backward calculation could give wrong result and may propagate wrong result to next calculations if first result is reused in next computations. This property is related to the typical problems of initialization of recursive processing algorithms.

3   Directional Filtering for Preprocessing

Image processing of acquired image could improve performance of tracking algorithm and is allowed for the TBD (Track–Before–Detect) approach [10,11]. Proposed filtering technique is based on directional MA (Moving Average) filter. This is low computation cost FIR (Finite Impulse Response) filter, that is applied in vertical direction. The overall schematic of the proposed system is shown in Fig. 2.

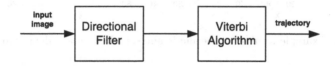

Fig. 2. Schematic of line tracking system with directional filtering

The directional MA filter uses simple formula:

$$Y(x,y) = \frac{1}{N} \sum_{i=0}^{N-1} X(x, y+i),$$ (9)

where $N-1$ is the filter order applied for vertical dimension (y) only. The X and Y variables are input and output images respectively. Such filter is dedicated to the line that is vertical or slightly sloped. General case of line with sharp turns is not considered is this paper. It is sufficient for many practical cases, but not for the specific robot following contests where the line could change direction in any way.

The aim of the filter application is the noise suppression [12], with reduced influence on the vertical edges, so blurring in horizontal direction is not recommended. This suppression is mostly independent on line and the background. The idea of directional filtering is the basis of the TBD systems based on e.g. velocity filters and local Hough Transform [13].

4   Results

An example input image and result of processing for directional filtering are shown in Fig. 3.

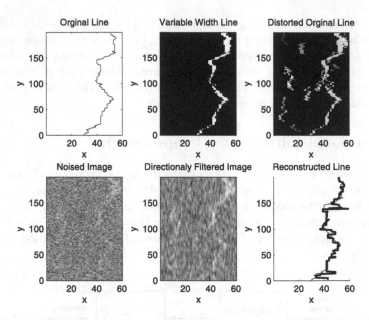

Fig. 3. Example results for specific image – high standard deviation 1.2

Monte Carlo approach is applied for the performance analysis under heavy distortions (multiple additional lines with similar spatial properties). Two systems are compared: without directional filtering and with directional filtering, for exactly the same input images. Monte Carlo tests uses 300 testing scenarios for particular standard deviation (std) and filter length (N). The $n_{max} = 60$, line width from $\langle 1 - 5 \rangle$ pixel range (probability of direction change is 0.1), line direction change with 0.25 probability are assumed for Markov g–set. Line length in y direction is $L_y = 200$. Cumulative errors $(Cerr)$ for both cases could be compared for the performance measurements. The pair of measurements $\{Cerr_{withfilter}, Cerr_{withoutfilter}\}$ marked by the point bellow line with slope 45° (equal error boundary) has better estimation result for system with directional filtering, and the point above this line has better estimation result for system without directional filtering (Fig. 4). The slope of regression line for multiple tests could be criterion of improvement for different filter orders.

The regression line $E_{withfilter} = f(E_{withoutfilter})$ could be modeled using the following formula:

$$E_{withfilter} = a_1 E_{withoutfilter} + a_0, \tag{10}$$

and a_0 is very low value and could be omitted in regression fit. The values of $a_1 < 1$ are indicators of better performance of system with directional filtering. Mean error $\bar{E}$ for position in horizontal direction is:

$$\bar{E}_{withfilter} = a_1 \bar{E}_{withoutfilter} = E_{withfilter}/L_y. \tag{11}$$

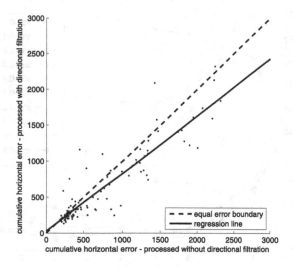

Fig. 4. Example results for Monte Carlo test for standard deviation 0.8

The highest value is about $2500/L_y = 12.5$ pixel and typical value is about $500/L_y = 2.5$ pixel for cases shown in 4. Results for different standard deviations and orders of directional filter are show in Fig. 5.

5   Discussion

The results that are shown in Fig. 5 depict better performance of system with directional filtering – values $a_1 < 1$ is related to the reduction of position errors according to formula (11). Low–valued noise distortions (standard deviation < 0.3) cases are better processed with the use of system without directional filtering. This is the result of line blurring introduced by filter. Larger noise is the main source of the position errors so filtering adds blurring to the line and background area, reducing errors. Larger noise gives about 20% reduction of the position errors in horizontal direction, which is related to $a_1 \approx 0.8$ value. Small minimum could be observed for filter order $3 - 7$ range and higher standard deviations (Fig. 5). Such filters orders are optimal and increasing order reduces performance due to line direction changes. Grayscale image could be used by the Viterbi algorithm so Euclidean metric is used. This is much better solution in comparison to the binary images processing. The Viterbi algorithm is one of the TBD (Track–Before–Detect) algorithms and allows the processing of signals hidden in noise. TBD processing assumes raw signal processing that has superior performance over conventional Detection and Tracking approach, that uses threshold algorithm. The obtained system is a kind of hierarchical TBD system [12]. Additional improvement of obtained results could be achieved using the estimated line filtering [14].

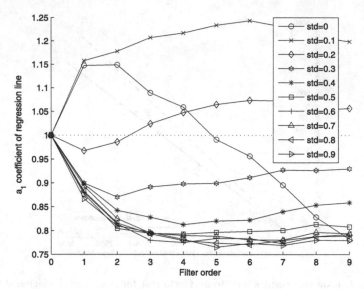

Fig. 5. Example results for Monte Carlo test for different standard deviations and orders of directional filter

6   Conclusions

Proposed directional filtering for the Viterbi algorithm input image preprocessing improves the estimation of lines. Such approach could be applied not only for the line following robots, but also in medical image processing for example [15]. Proposed approach extends possibilities of the application of the Viterbi based TBD algorithm by the application of the directional filtering that could be also considered as first TBD algorithm. The direction changes of the line is supported by the Markov model [16] processed by the Viterbi algorithm. Another preprocessing schemes could be applied for different types of lines [17,18].

The implementation of proposed algorithm does not requires high computation power and typical microcontrollers or DSP (Digital Signal Processors) could be applied for the real–time processing. Some DSP's have hardware unit or dedicated instructions for the acceleration of implementation of the Viterbi algorithm, that could be considered also. The direction filtering could be implemented using vertical instructions that are supported by all SIMD (Single–Instruction Multiple–Data) processors including VLIW (Very Long Instruction Word), additionally. Recursive processing of directional MA filers should be considered for the efficient implementation.

Acknowledgment. This work is supported by the UE EFRR ZPORR project Z/2.32/I/1.3.1/267/05 "Szczecin University of Technology – Research and Education Center of Modern Multimedia Technologies" (Poland).

References

1. Horan, B., Najdovski, Z., Black, T., Nahavandi, S., Crothers, P.: Oztug mobile robot for manufacturing transportation. In: IEEE International Conference on Systems, Man and Cybernetics (SMC 2011), pp. 3554–3560 (2011)
2. Hasan, K., Nahid, A., Mamun, A.: Implementation of autonomous line follower robot. In: IEEE/OSA/IAPR International Conference on Informatics, Electronics & Vision, pp. 865–869 (2012)
3. Ishikawa, S., Kuwamoto, H., Ozawa, S.: Visual navigation of an autonomous vehicle using white line recognition. IEEE Transaction on Pattern Analysis and Machine Intelligent 10(5), 743–749 (1988)
4. Ollis, M.: Perception Algorithms for a Harvesting Robot. CMU-RI-TR-97-43, Carnegie Mellon University (1997)
5. Taubel, G., Yang, J.S.: A lane departure warning system based on the integration of the optical flow and Hough transform methods. In: 2013 10th IEEE International Conference on Control and Automation (ICCA), Hangzhou, China, June 12-14, pp. 1352–1357 (2013)
6. Astrand, B., Baerveldt, A.: A vision-based row-following system for agricultural field machinery. Mechatronics 15(2), 251–269 (2005)
7. Zhang, J., Chambers, A., Maeta, S., Bergerman, M., Singh, S.: 3d perception for accurate row following: Methodology and results. In: 2013 IEEE/RSJ International Conference on Intelligent Robots and Systems (IROS), Tokyo, Japan, November 3-7, pp. 5306–5313 (2013)
8. Okarma, K., Lech, P.: A fast image analysis for the line tracking robots. In: Rutkowski, L., Scherer, R., Tadeusiewicz, R., Zadeh, L.A., Zurada, J.M. (eds.) ICAISC 2010, Part II. LNCS, vol. 6114, pp. 329–336. Springer, Heidelberg (2010)
9. Viterbi, A.: Error bounds for convolutional codes and an asymptotically optimum decoding algorithm. IEEE Transactions on Information Theory 13(2), 260–269 (1967)
10. Stone, L., Barlow, C., Corwin, T.: Bayesian Multiple Target Tracking. Artech House (1999)
11. Mazurek, P.: Optimization of bayesian track-before-detect algorithms for GPGPUs implementations. Electrical Review R. 86(7), 187–189 (2010)
12. Mazurek, P.: Hierarchical track-before-detect algorithm for tracking of amplitude modulated signals. In: Choraś, R.S. (ed.) Image Processing and Communications Challenges 3. AISC, vol. 102, pp. 511–518. Springer, Heidelberg (2011)
13. Blackman, S., Popoli, R.: Design and Analysis of Modern Tracking Systems. Artech House (1999)
14. Frejlichowski, D.: Application of the curvature scale space descriptor to the problem of general shape analysis. Electrical Review 88(10 B), 209–212 (2012)
15. Scott, T.A., Nilanjan, R.: Biomedical Image Analysis: Tracking. Morgan & Claypool (2005)
16. Mazurek, P.: Code reordering using local random extraction and insertion (LREI) operator for GPGPU-based track-before-detect systems. Soft Computing 18(6), 1095–1106 (2013)
17. Mazurek, P.: Comparison of different measurement spaces for spatio-temporal recurrent track-before-detect algorithm. In: Choraś, R.S. (ed.) Image Processing and Communications Challenges 3. AISC, vol. 102, pp. 157–164. Springer, Heidelberg (2011)
18. Mazurek, P.: Preprocessing using maximal autocovariance for spatio-temporal track-before-detect algorithm. In: Choras, R.S. (ed.) Image Processing and Communications Challenges 5. AISC, vol. 233, pp. 45–54. Springer, Heidelberg (2014)

Automated Visual Perception-Based Web Browser Rendering Results Comparison with Multi-part Fragment Image Matching

Julian Myrcha and Przemysław Rokita

Institute of Computer Science, Warsaw Uniwersity of Technology
Nowowiejska 15/19, 00-665 Warsaw, Poland
P.Rokita@ii.pw.edu.pl

Abstract. A difference measurement method for similar web pages is proposed. Displaying same html documents on a different browsers or different browser versions may produce different results, when compared as images. They may be visually indistinguishable or may visually differ. There are many factors causing that differences. There are ones - as advertisements introduced or changed randomly by some sites, which should be handled accordingly. The proposed method automatically register different part of compared images and employ VDP method to produce visual difference map and compute difference coefficients. Obtained results shows, that it is possible properly compare web pages even if part of them change sizes causing translation of the resulting content. Proposed system was realised as a part of the automated testing environment suited to perform regression tests for browser engines.

1 Introduction

There are more and more information prepared and distributed using web pages. They are created using growing number of tools and technologies. We have also new HTML standards. On the other hand there is also big shift on the hardware side - computers are no longer the only device suitable to display web pages. We have now smart-phones, tablets and even tv-sets capable to display web content. That devices has own version of browsers, tailored to their capabilities. Fast growing and changing market causes need for new versions of browsers - for both computer and smart-phones to accommodate new features.

As a part of verification if newly developed browser engine is bug-free, there is a need to compare results produced by that new browser engine with reference results obtained from previous versions or competing browsers. Such comparisons may be done in two steps, from computationally simple to more expensive:

- DOM - extract and compare Document Object Model Tree
- Compare rendered pages as images

First approach may be much faster, but is difficult for different browser engines - structure of the tree is similar, but detailed information varies. It could be

L.J. Chmielewski et al. (Eds.): ICCVG 2014, LNCS 8671, pp. 436–445, 2014.
© Springer International Publishing Switzerland 2014

employed for the same family of browsers. As building DOM Tree is a first stage of displaying page content, even identical DOM do not guarantee same viewable results. This directs us towards the second solution. Comparing snapshot of the page we could be sure, that we could obtain proper solutions.

1.1 Related Work

Selected topic is similar, but not identical to widely discussed problem of establishing similarity between different web pages [1, 5, 13]. It was analysed in the context of searching and building a query. Most of the sources concentrates on analysing structure of the HTML document [1]. Having that one could predict visual structure of the page. Although for analysing similarity this is proper approach, for pages which do not differ in the source it could not be employed.

Part of the work is related to distinguishing noticeable differences in the image - see Section 2.2.

1.2 Plan of Paper

The paper is organised as follows. Section 2 presents ideas and tools used in the presented algorithm. Section 3 describes proposed method. Section 4 presents results of the experiments. Section 5 presents conclusions and future work.

2 Preliminaries

In this section we will briefly describe ideas which are basis for our work. To properly measure similarities between almost the same page we need two tools: image registration techniques and visual difference measure.

2.1 Image Registration

First step in every image comparison is a image registration [3][18]. We could use correlation to map entire images - this assumes that they are only rigidly misaligned. It could be computed both in spatial and frequency domain which gives us performance boost. This methods fails, if images were structurally changed - see Fig. 1.

The second approach is to use point mapping. This solution may be considered globally - with the same drawback as correlation method, but it could also be applied locally [3]. In such situation image registration is given not with the single global transformation but is specified by a set of local transformations, for given piece of source image. This approach provides much better results in case when regions on the image moves. On the other hand complexity and computational cost grows enormously.

There is also third approach, when we model distortion not as transformations of rigid objects, but we treat it as transformation of elastic model. That approach work well for medic images, but do not behave well for images of documents.

Fig. 1. Input images: Firefox (a) and Chrome (b)

In case of document image registration available sources treat both document images as continuous area [6, 7, 11, 12, 17] concentrating on other possible distortions like slope, skewing, perspective distortion and other. Our distortions are much simpler - it is mainly shifts potion of the image, but we give up assumption about document image being continuous. Also source of the images is different - digital opposed to scans - which simplifies computations.

2.2 Visual Difference

Having two registered images, crop to the same size, we could try to decide if images are the same. The simplest situation is when images are binary the same, which implies visual identity.are Very often it is slightly different - images are visually the same or almost the same, but their digital representation differ. It is common and desired for image compression - although lossy compression did not enable recovery exact image, restored version is suitable if is visually almost the same.

There were many approaches to compare images. Historically most used PSNR is known to be inadequate in most situations, may be used only to roughly compare distortions made to the same image in the same way - e.g for compression method comparison. This shows visual visibility of changes only approximately.

Problem of visual recognition of changes on two images were widely discussed [8, 4, 9, 10, 2, 14–16]. Two widely recognized solutions are the Visual Difference Predictor [4] and the Visual Difference Metric [9]. They were compared in [2].

3 Proposed Method

Web pages are documents, but unlike other documents have several specific features. Our method takes several assumptions, which are appropriate for most, but not all web pages. We exclude web pages containing only text - it is not severe restriction for today web pages, when even simplest one contains some logos or icons.

3.1 Assumptions

- Pages must contains some icons or images.
- Pages must be scaled accordingly - icons or images should have same size.
- We accept pages with different sizes - comparison will be done for common part of them.
- We accept changes in structure of the page, causes by introduction of advertisements.
- Process must be fully automatic.

Fig. 2. Blocks shown on input images: Firefox (a) and Chrome (b)

3.2 The Method

Our method consists of following steps, described below:

Find Starting Points Candidates for Point Mapping Registration. First using sliding window which size is 1/16 size of the screen we adaptively compute histogram, from which we get most frequent colour and assign create background mask. Then we convert both pages from RGB to YUV colour space. Then local variance is computed on both images. This selects pixels which can be icons or images. For each connected pixels segment is created, with bounding x and y coordinates. Very small segments are dropped immediately (they are from text letter) and remaining segments are verified with several features - aspect ratio, filling inside bounding box, background pixels filling inside bounding box. From segments satisfying such conditions first biggest 32 is selected for matching purposes - see Fig. 3.

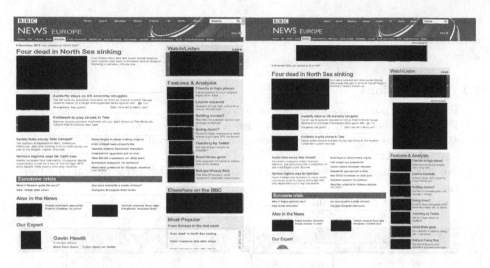

Fig. 3. Images shown on input page shots: Firefox (a) and Chrome (b)

Register Rigid Parts of Screen. Having selected best candidates from both images, matching process is starting. We first sort candidates according to Y axis. Then starting from lowest coordinate in the first set we look for best match in the second set. For each found match we check order of the matched segments in the second image and remove those matches, which are not growing linearly - see Fig. 4.

Recreate Second Image Using Movements Defined by Registrations. Matches found in previous step are used to recreate image using painters method - see Fig. 5. As is visible on that figure, sometimes content visible on reference page is not visible on test page - it is pushed out. In that situation recreation that part of page could not be performed.

Crop Images to the Same Size. Above process removes from second image those areas, which are not existing on first image - mainly inserted blocks with adds. Only changes which resulted in pushing content down or right are removed - if page is only different then such changes are preserved for the next stage. Now we could crop reference image and restored one to the same size, based on the content.

Compute Structure Difference Coefficients. Percentage of the cropped area on the both images to their full area gives us first part of the result.

$$SD_R = \frac{Cropped_R}{Entire_R}$$

$$SD_T = \frac{Cropped_T}{Entire_T}$$

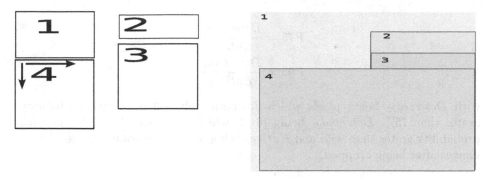

Fig. 4. Order of selected segments and their matching to second image (a) Painters method of recreating second image (b)

Fig. 5. Second image recreated with painter method

with SD being structure difference of the image, *Cropped* being an area of the cropped pixels and *Entire* being an area of the full image.

Compute VDP Difference Coefficients. Main step is to compute VDP map [4] between reference and restored second image. Number of pixels with different probability of change detection form the most important part of the result.

$$P75 = \frac{Detected_{75}}{Entire_c}$$

$$P95 = \frac{Detected_{95}}{Entire_c}$$

with $Detected_{75}$ being pixels which are noticeably different with probability grater than 75%, $Detected_{95}$ being pixels which are noticeably different with probability grater than 95% and $Entire_c$ being area of the common size of both images after being cropped.

Compute Binary Changed Pixels. This parameter is not directly taken to the final assessment, but we compute it as a verification for visual coefficients. It is simply a number of pixels which are represented by different colour values on reference and rebuild test image.

$$BC = \frac{Changed}{Entire_c}$$

It is obvious that it must be bigger than $P75$, but it is interesting how much bigger it is.

Total Results. This parameter is simply a sum of structure difference and non-zero VDP for the common image.

$$total = SD_R + SD_T + P75$$

It treats portions for both images which were not compared as being different and sum it with visually different part found on compared images.

4   Experiments

We have tested our method on the test set, containing 48 screen pairs from very different sites, in European languages and in Chinese characters. For Web pages presented in this paper results are in Tab. 1.

Table 1. Change coefficients computed for images presented in this paper

parameter	value	description
P75	11.86%	pixels with 75% probability of change detection
P95	10.76%	pixels with 95% probability of change detection
BC	20.19%	real binary changed pixels
R resolution	994x1200	Reference (Firefox) image resolution
SD_R	0%	number of ignored pixels in reference image
T resolution	1262x1262	Test (Chrome) image resolution
SD_T	25.11%	number of ignored pixels in test image
total	36.97%	total results

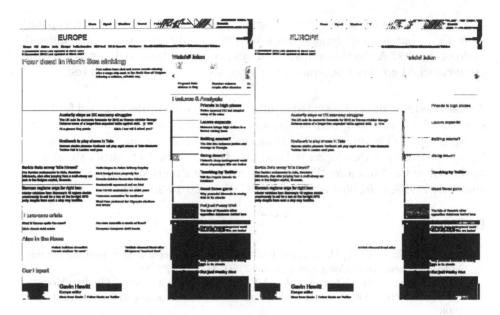

Fig. 6. Error pixels extracted from difference map constructed on registered image - (a) simple pixel differences (b) VDP map

It behave well in all situations, when page have contained suitable number images or iconographic. As you see on Fig. 6, images are points of registrations - so if render engines produce same results, but only slightly shifted (as you see on same texts) it is still marked as difference.

This may require second phase of fine-tuned registration to precisely register text areas, which may reduce misalignment even greater. Although it may work for some test cases, for more then half in our test sets changes were in the texts, so this step does not provide the expected profit. This issue - small movements, which are invisible to the observer - should be covered by better visual difference measure, than VDP method used.

There are also noticeable artefacts in the bottom and right bottom of the page. It is caused by the fact, that some of the content was pushed of the page by the advertisements. It could be simply solved by means of an artificial cut-off bottom of the image with offset equal to the largest part movement in the reconstructed image. As that movement may concern only single column (in our case it is right column) removal of the rest - where may be interesting artefacts - is not reasonable.

5   Summary

We have developed a working system for fully automatic comparison of the web pages, regardless of changes in the structure caused by emerging ads. The use of VDP method yielded as taking into account the perceptual capabilities of the observer to notice the differences in comparable areas. Prepared tool is capable to verify in batch mode large amount of tests, producing easy to comprehend table of results. A developer may then simply concentrate only on tests with significant bad coefficients, which greatly reduces costs of regression tests.

Acknowledgements. Presented results are based on a project carried for Samsung Electronics Poland, entitled "Automated Web Browser Rendering Results Comparison". This project was co-financed by the European Union from the European Regional Development Fund and the state budget within the Activity 1.4-4.1 of the Innovation Economy Operational Program - projects reference numbers: POIG.01.04.00-14-199/09, POIG.01.04.00-14-200/09.

References

1. Alpuente, M., Romero, D.: A visual technique for web pages comparison. Electronic Notes in Theoretical Computer Science 235(C), 3–18 (2009)
2. Li, B., Meyer, G.W., Klassen, R.V.: A Comparison of Two Image Quality Models. In: Proc. SPIE 3299, Human Vision and Electronic Imaging III, p. 98 (July 17, 1998)
3. Brown, L.G.: A survey of image registration techniques. ACM Comput. Surv. (December 1992)
4. Daly, S.: The visible differences predictor: an algorithm for the assessment of image fidelity. In: Watson, A.B. (ed.) Digital Images and Human Vision, pp. 179–206. MIT Press, Cambridge (1993)
5. Eglin, V., Bres, S.: Document page similarity based on layout visual saliency: Application to query by example and document classification. In: ICDAR 2003: Proceedings of the Seventh International Conference on Document Analysis and Recognition, Washington, DC, USA, p. 1208. IEEE Computer Society (2003)
6. Gopalakrishnan, G., Kumar, B., Narayanan, A., Mullick, R.: A Fast Piece-wise Deformable Method for Multi-Modality Image Registration. In: Proceedings of the 34th Applied Imagery and Pattern Recognition Workshop (AIPR 2005) (2005)
7. Isgrò, F., Pilu, M.: A fast and robust image registration method based on an early consensus paradigm. Pattern Recogn. Lett. (June 2004)
8. Lin, W., Jay Kuo, C.: -C.: Perceptual visual quality metrics: A survey. Journal of Visual Communication and Image Representation 22(4), 297–312 (2011)
9. Lubin, J.: A visual discrimination model for imaging system design and evaluation. In: Vision Models For Target Detection And Recognition, pp. 245–283. World Scientific Publishing Company (1995)
10. Mantiuk, R., Kim, K.J., Rempel, A.G., Heidrich, W.: HDR-VDP-2: a calibrated visual metric for visibility and quality predictions in all luminance conditions. ACM Trans. Graph 30, 40:1–40:14 (2011)
11. Peng, H., Long, F., Siu, W.-C., Chi, Z., Feng, D.D.: Document image matching based on component blocks. In: Proceedings of the ICIP 2000 (2000)
12. Sun, C., Cai, R.: Document Image Registration Using Geometric Invariance and Hausdorff Distance. In: Proceedings of the 2009 First International Workshop on Education Technology and Computer Science, vol. 02 (2009)
13. Takama, Y., Mitsuhashi, N.: Visual Similarity Comparison for Web Page Retrieval. In: Proceedings of the 2005 IEEE/WIC/ACM International Conference on Web Intelligence (WI 2005) (2005)

14. Tolhurst, D.J., Ripamonti, C., Párraga, C.A., Lovell, P.G., Troscianko, T.: A multiresolution color model for visual difference prediction. In: Proceedings of the 2nd Symposium on Applied Perception in Graphics and Visualization, pp. 135–138.
15. Gao, X., Lu, W., Tao, D., Li, X.: Image quality assessment and human visual system. In: Proc. SPIE 7744, Visual Communications and Image Processing (2010)
16. Yee, Y.H., Newman, A.: A perceptual metric for production testing. In: ACM SIGGRAPH 2004 Sketches (2004)
17. Zhu, Y., Dai, R., Xiao, B., Wang, C.: Document Image Registration Based on Geometric Invariant and Contour Matching. In: Proceedings of the International Conference on Computational Intelligence and Multimedia Applications (ICCIMA 2007), vol. 03 (2007)
18. Zitová, B., Flusser, J.: Image registration methods: a survey. Image and Vision Computing 21(11), 977–1000 (2003)

Texture Analysis for Identifying Heterogeneity in Medical Images

Jakub Nalepa[1,5], Janusz Szymanek[5], Michael P. Hayball[2,3],
Stephen J. Brown[3], Balaji Ganeshan[2,4], and Kenneth Miles[4]

[1] Silesian University of Technology, Poland
jakub.nalepa@polsl.pl
[2] TexRAD Ltd, UK
{mike,balaji}@texrad.co.uk
[3] Cambridge Computed Imaging, UK
{mike.hayball,stephen.brown}@cambridge-imaging.co.uk
[4] University College London, UK
{b.ganeshan,kenneth.miles}@ucl.ac.uk
[5] Future Processing, Poland
{jnalepa,jszymanek}@future-processing.com

Abstract. Heterogeneity is a well-recognized feature of malignancy
associated with increased tumor aggression and treatment resistance.
Texture analysis (TA) of images of various modalities, including, among
others, CT, MRI or PET, can be applied to quantify the tumor heterogeneity and to extract useful information from images acquired in routine
clinical practice without additional radiation or expense of further procedures. In this paper, we elaborate on the filtration-based approach to
TA applied for extracting features from large sets of simulated images
reflecting various clinical circumstances. The areas under receiver operating characteristic curves were used to assess the diagnostic performance
of the derived biomarkers. We present and discuss their discriminative
abilities in identifying heterogeneity and classifying images with simulated lesions of various characteristics and localized density variations.

Keywords: texture analysis, image processing, image filtration, imaging marker.

1   Introduction

Texture analysis (TA) has attracted research interest not only in medical imaging
but also in a wide range of pattern recognition problems [1–4]. It is continuously
being developed as it proved to be a useful tool for assessing prognosis, diagnosing
patients with cancer, and differentiating between pathological and healthy tissue [5]. It was applied to identify heterogeneity of tumors across different imaging
modalities, including computed tomography (CT) [6], magnetic resonance imaging (MRI) [7], position emission tomography (PET) [8], and more [9]. TA can be
used to extract features (not perceptible by the naked eye) from images acquired

L.J. Chmielewski et al. (Eds.): ICCVG 2014, LNCS 8671, pp. 446–453, 2014.
© Springer International Publishing Switzerland 2014

in routine clinical practice to provide precision medical care. It does not require any additional acquisition or radiation procedures and is non-invasive.

The analysis of diagnostic images is usually based on evaluating image information such as size and shape. It strongly depends on the radiologist's knowledge, experience, and analytical skills. Therefore, extracting quantitative information from medical images is crucial for the in-depth analysis. It has been shown that the human visual system is unable to discriminate and interpret textural information resulting from local spatial variations in image brightness [10].

Most computer-aided diagnosis techniques follow a two stage scheme. Texture in an image is quantified at first, and various decision algorithms are applied to classify images based on the extracted features. The approaches to quantify texture in medical images include model based, frequency based, and structure or statistically based techniques [11]. In the first group, a mathematical model (e.g., fractal) reflecting prior information about the tissue is analyzed. Frequency and structure based algorithms are less commonly used since medical data are not periodic with individual pixel values reflecting intensity and variations. Thus, statistical approaches measuring spectral properties of data are given research interest. It is worth to note that the acceptance of some classification algorithms, e.g., artificial neural networks, is limited in the clinical arena due to the lack of a clear biological correlate for their outcome and difficulty in traceability [11].

In this paper, we discuss our TA algorithm to quantify heterogeneity in medical images. Large sets (with 800 images) of simulated lesions of various characteristics and localized density (i.e., pixel values) variations were used to assess the TA classification performance of images as either benign or malignant. Understanding the TA behavior for simulated data is crucial to tailor it for different modalities and cancer characteristics. We show the performance of the derived biomarkers in identifying heterogeneity and detecting image "defects" (objects) of a smaller density in the presence of defects of a larger density and vice versa.

This paper is organized as follows. Texture analysis is outlined in detail in Section 2. The discussion of the experimental results along with the description of generated data sets are given in Section 3. Section 4 concludes the paper.

2   Texture Analysis

The filtration-histogram approach to TA comprises image filtration performed to highlight image features of a specified size. This procedure is followed by histogram analysis for quantification of derived features.

2.1   Image Filtration

Each region of interest (ROI) within an image (usually annotated by a clinician during the review process) is filtered to highlight texture features at various spatial frequencies (scales). We used the Laplacian of Gaussian (LoG) filtration modulated to different scales. The 2D Gaussian distribution G is given as:

$$G(x,y) = \exp\left(-\frac{x^2 + y^2}{2\sigma^2}\right), \tag{1}$$

where σ denotes the standard deviation of this distribution, and x and y are the spatial coordinates. For generality, we consider the pixel size ps (varying between image modalities) and incorporate it into the *spatial scale factor (SSF)*:

$$SSF = ps \cdot \sigma\sqrt{2}. \tag{2}$$

This distribution blurs the image and removes features at scales much smaller than σ. It is smooth and localized in both the spatial and frequency domains, thus it is less likely to introduce changes to the input image and allows for highlighting image features at a particular scale.

After the Gaussian smoothening, we applied the Laplacian operator ($\triangledown^2$) to detect intensity changes, corresponding to the zero-crossings of the filter [12]. It is worth to note that Laplacian is the lowest-order isotropic (orientation-independent) differential operator. The LoG is given as:

$$\triangledown^2 G(x, y) = -\frac{1}{\pi\sigma^4}\left(1 - \frac{x^2 + y^2}{2\sigma^2}\right)\exp\left(-\left(\frac{x^2 + y^2}{2\sigma^2}\right)\right). \tag{3}$$

The filtration can be executed either in the spatial or frequency domain. In the former case, it would comprise convolving the filter with image which is quite computationally intensive. Also, this approach may suffer from the quantization errors, especially for small values of σ. Alternatively, the multiplication of the Fourier transforms of the filter mask and image in the frequency domain corresponds to the convolution in the spatial domain. Finally, the inverse Fourier transform of the filtered spectrum gives the resultant filtered image in the spatial domain. In this work, the images were filtered in the frequency domain.

2.2   Texture Quantification

The histogram of pixel values after image filtration was quantified and characterized by kurtosis (k), skewness (s) standard deviation (sd) and entropy (h):

$$k = \frac{n(n+1)}{(n-1)(n-2)(n-3)}\frac{\sum_{x,y}(v(x,y) - \bar{v})^4}{sd^4} - 3\frac{(n-1)^2}{(n-2)(n-3)}, \tag{4}$$

$$s = \frac{n}{(n-1)(n-2)}\frac{\sum_{x,y}(v(x,y) - \bar{v})^3}{sd^3}, \tag{5}$$

$$sd = \sqrt{\frac{1}{(n-1)}\sum_{x,y}(v(x,y) - \bar{v})^2}, \tag{6}$$

$$h = -\sum_i(p(v_i)\log_2 p(v_i)), \tag{7}$$

where $\bar{v}$ and n are the mean pixel value and total number of pixels within the ROI, and $p(v_i)$ is the probability mass function of the pixel value v_i. The meaning of various texture parameters derived from medical images along with their correlations with clinical data have been discussed in [13].

3   Experimental Results

In the experiments reported here, we varied the number of objects of a given density according to the ratio $\mathcal{T}_{\alpha\beta} = n_\alpha/n_\beta$, where n_α and n_β are the number of objects of the density d_α and d_β (relative to the background density). The radius (*size*) of circular defects was constant and equal to 3 pixels. The number of all objects within a generated ROI is given as $N_{\alpha\beta} = n_\alpha + n_\beta$. The statistical analysis of the experimental data was performed using TexRAD – a framework for image processing, visualization and statistical analysis of generated results[1].

3.1   Simulated Data Sets

Two simulated image sets were generated to assess the classification performance of our TA algorithm. Each set ($\mathcal{A}$ and $\mathcal{B}$) consists of 800 images with circular ROIs of radius 150. A ROI is filled in with random pixels following a Gaussian distribution ($d = 40$ and $sd = 20$) in step 1. Then, $N_{\alpha\beta}$ blobs are generated within the ROI according to n_α and n_β. Here, if an object has a density d then the values of pixels of this object (determined in step 1) are increased by d.

a) $N_{\alpha\beta} = 0$ b) $N_{\alpha\beta} = 40, n_\alpha = 40$ c) $N_{\alpha\beta} = 40, n_\beta = 40$ d) $N_{\alpha\beta} = 16, \mathcal{T}_{\alpha\beta} = 3$

e) $N_{\alpha\beta} = 12, \mathcal{T}_{\alpha\beta} = 1/3$ f) $N_{\alpha\beta} = 40, \mathcal{T}_{\alpha\beta} = 3$ g) $N_{\alpha\beta} = 20, \mathcal{T}_{\alpha\beta} = 1/3$ h) $N_{\alpha\beta} = 40, \mathcal{T}_{\alpha\beta} = 1/3$

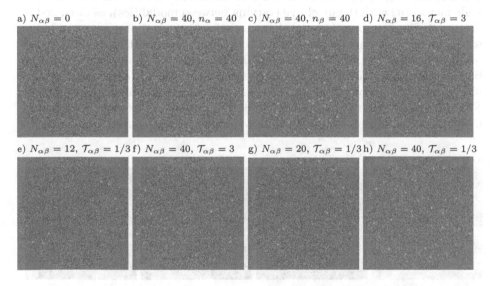

Fig. 1. Examples of simulated ROIs containing lesions with localized density variations

Examples of simulated images are given in Fig. 1. It is easy to note that the localized density variations are difficult to see by the naked eye, especially for relatively small d. Settings used to simulate the set $\mathcal{A}$ ($\mathcal{T}_{\alpha\beta} = 3$) are presented in Tab. 1. Each set ($\mathcal{A}$ and $\mathcal{B}$) is divided into 13 subsets containing images with different characteristics (see $\mathcal{A}_1$–$\mathcal{A}_{13}$). $\mathcal{I}^a$ denotes the number of images in each subset. The set $\mathcal{B}$ is generated analogously, however $\mathcal{T}_{\alpha\beta} = 1/3$. In both sets, the densities of objects were set to the following values: $d_\alpha = 15$ and $d_\beta = 30$.

---

[1] See http://www.texrad.com/ for more details.

Table 1. Settings used to simulate the set $\mathcal{A}$ ($\mathcal{T}_{\alpha\beta} = 3$) (the x/y notation allows for defining two subsets in one row – x is the value in the first subset, y – in the other)

Subset	n_α^a	n_β^a	$N_{\alpha\beta}^a$	$\mathcal{I}^a$
$\mathcal{A}_1$	0	0	0	200
$\mathcal{A}_{2/3}$	12/0	0/12	12	50/50
$\mathcal{A}_{4/5}$	16/0	0/16	16	50/50
$\mathcal{A}_{6/7}$	20/0	0/20	20	50/50
$\mathcal{A}_{8/9}$	40/0	0/40	40	50/50
$\mathcal{A}_{10}$	9	3	12	50
$\mathcal{A}_{11}$	12	4	16	50
$\mathcal{A}_{12}$	15	5	20	50
$\mathcal{A}_{13}$	30	10	40	50

3.2   Analysis and Discussion

TA comprised the LoG filtration of an input image followed by histogram analysis of resulting images. In the filtration stage we used eight SSF values (scales): 1.5, 2.0, 2.5, 3.0, 3.5, 4.0, 6.0 and 8.0. For real-life data sets SSF values relate the scale factors (σ) with the pixel size (varying between modalities), as discussed in Section 2. Since (in practice) the characteristics (e.g., size) of a potential lesion within an image are not known *a priori*, a range of scales must be used to extract textural features and to detect defects. In this study, we analyze the algorithm behavior for SSF's "close" to the size of simulated defects. An exemplary image filtered at various scales is given in Fig. 2. The defects are highlighted most for SSF correlated with their size (see $SSF = 3.0$). However, this scale is not known beforehand and images should be analyzed for a range of spatial frequencies.

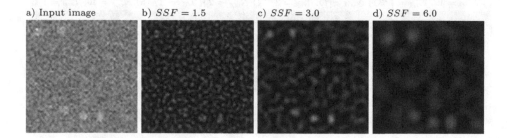

a) Input image   b) $SSF = 1.5$ c) $SSF = 3.0$ d) $SSF = 6.0$

Fig. 2. Parts of resulting filtered images (zoomed and cropped) for various SSF values

The filtration is followed by histogram analysis of resulting and original images (thus, we analyzed 7200 images here). Based on derived markers (outlined in Section 2.2), we classified images according to the heterogeneity variations. All investigated images (in both $\mathcal{A}$ and $\mathcal{B}$) are divided into four sets: without defects ($\mathcal{S}_1$), with d_α defects only ($\mathcal{S}_2$), with d_β defects only ($\mathcal{S}_4$), and these containing both d_α and d_β defects ($\mathcal{S}_3$). The sets are shown in Fig. 3 (for $\mathcal{A}$).

The performance of the markers was investigated for the following cases:

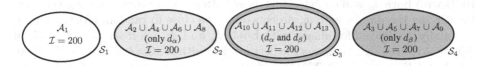

Fig. 3. Sets with defects of various densities (shown for $\mathcal{A}$)

1. Finding images with defects of a given density (d_α or d_β) in presence of defects of other density ($\mathcal{S}_3$ in $\mathcal{S}_2 \cup \mathcal{S}_3$ and $\mathcal{S}_3$ in $\mathcal{S}_3 \cup \mathcal{S}_4$),
2. Finding images with defects of a given density **only** (d_α or d_β) ($\mathcal{S}_2$ in $\mathcal{S}_1 \cup \mathcal{S}_2 \cup \mathcal{S}_3 \cup \mathcal{S}_4$ and $\mathcal{S}_4$ in $\mathcal{S}_1 \cup \mathcal{S}_2 \cup \mathcal{S}_3 \cup \mathcal{S}_4$),
3. Finding images with defects of **both** densities ($\mathcal{S}_3$ in $\mathcal{S}_1 \cup \mathcal{S}_2 \cup \mathcal{S}_3 \cup \mathcal{S}_4$).

The areas under receiver operating characteristic (ROC) curves (AUC) quantified the discriminative performance of individual markers (kurtosis, skewness, standard deviation and entropy). The results for $\mathcal{A}$ and $\mathcal{B}$ are given in Tab. 2.

Table 2. The best AUC and corresponding SSF values (AUC/SSF) obtained for $\mathcal{A}$ and $\mathcal{B}$ (the best indicated in boldface)

	Classification	k	s	sd	h
Set $\mathcal{A}$	$\mathcal{S}_3$ in $\mathcal{S}_2 \cup \mathcal{S}_3$	**0.98/4.0**	0.92/4.0	0.73/6.0	0.67/0.0
	$\mathcal{S}_3$ in $\mathcal{S}_3 \cup \mathcal{S}_4$	**0.37/1.5**	0.33/1.5	0.28/1.5	0.29/1.5
	$\mathcal{S}_2$ in $\mathcal{S}_1 \cup \mathcal{S}_2 \cup \mathcal{S}_3 \cup \mathcal{S}_4$	0.50/3.5	0.50/4.0	0.53/4.0	**0.56/4.0**
	$\mathcal{S}_4$ in $\mathcal{S}_1 \cup \mathcal{S}_2 \cup \mathcal{S}_3 \cup \mathcal{S}_4$	**0.99/3.0**	0.98/3.0	0.95/3.0	0.92/2.5
	$\mathcal{S}_3$ in $\mathcal{S}_1 \cup \mathcal{S}_2 \cup \mathcal{S}_3 \cup \mathcal{S}_4$	**0.67/3.0**	0.66/3.0	0.61/3.5	0.61/3.5
Set $\mathcal{B}$	$\mathcal{S}_3$ in $\mathcal{S}_2 \cup \mathcal{S}_3$	**0.99/2.5**	**0.99/3.5**	0.95/4.0	0.88/2.5
	$\mathcal{S}_3$ in $\mathcal{S}_3 \cup \mathcal{S}_4$	**0.48/1.5**	0.44/1.5	0.46/1.5	0.47/1.5
	$\mathcal{S}_2$ in $\mathcal{S}_1 \cup \mathcal{S}_2 \cup \mathcal{S}_3 \cup \mathcal{S}_4$	0.40/1.5	**0.42/1.5**	0.37/1.5	0.37/3.5
	$\mathcal{S}_4$ in $\mathcal{S}_1 \cup \mathcal{S}_2 \cup \mathcal{S}_3 \cup \mathcal{S}_4$	0.88/3.0	**0.89/3.0**	0.87/4.0	0.83/3.5
	$\mathcal{S}_3$ in $\mathcal{S}_1 \cup \mathcal{S}_2 \cup \mathcal{S}_3 \cup \mathcal{S}_4$	**0.80/3.0**	0.79/3.0	0.77/3.0	0.77/2.5

The best markers (with maximum AUC) to classify lesions with defects of various densities were skewness and kurtosis at a scale close to the defect size. Detecting images with objects of a higher density (d_β) in presence of d_α defects ($\mathcal{S}_3$ in $\mathcal{S}_2 \cup \mathcal{S}_3$) was accurate (AUC close to 1 for both kurtosis and skewness). It is worth noting that identifying the opposite case, i.e., defects of relatively small density in presence of a higher density objects ($\mathcal{S}_3$ in $\mathcal{S}_3 \cup \mathcal{S}_4$) is challenging, especially if the number of the latter ones is significant. AUC was less than 0.5 for each marker and it approached 0 for certain scales. The issue of obtaining AUC $\ll$ 0.5 and facing the opposite classification was discussed in detail in [14].

Similarly, identifying images with ROIs containing **only** defects of a given density appears more accurate if this density is larger (d_β). The resulting AUC values was close to 1 for $\mathcal{A}$ and to 0.9 for $\mathcal{B}$ (see $\mathcal{S}_4$ in $\mathcal{S}_1 \cup \mathcal{S}_2 \cup \mathcal{S}_3 \cup \mathcal{S}_4$). In the case of $\mathcal{A}$, $\mathcal{T}_{\alpha\beta} > 1$, thus $n_\alpha > n_\beta$. Therefore, the probability of misclassifying

ROIs with both d_α and d_β defects as those with d_β only drops, since n_α is larger. Identifying the images with d_α objects only was close to random (AUC ca. 0.5).

Finally, we looked for images with **both** d_α and d_β defects in $\mathcal{A}$ and $\mathcal{B}$ ($\mathcal{S}_3$ in $\mathcal{S}_1 \cup \mathcal{S}_2 \cup \mathcal{S}_3 \cup \mathcal{S}_4$). Kurtosis was the best marker with AUC= 0.67 and AUC=0.80, for $\mathcal{A}$ and $\mathcal{B}$, respectively. The classification performance obtained for skewness was very similar (AUC was ca. 0.01 smaller for both sets). The scatter plots (Fig. 4) present the relationships between the markers (for $\mathcal{A}$, $SSF = 3.0$), and show that they are correlated. The analysis of correlations between texture parameters can help determine which features (ideally non-correlated) should be combined into feature vectors to increase the level of extracted image information. These vectors can be classified using e.g., k-Nearest Neighbors algorithm.

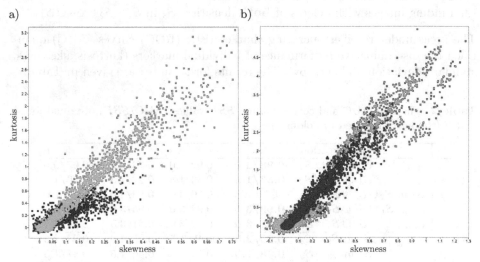

Fig. 4. Scatter plots of skewness vs. kurtosis (set $\mathcal{A}$, $SSF = 3.0$): a) $\mathcal{S}_3$ in $\mathcal{S}_2 \cup \mathcal{S}_3$, b) $\mathcal{S}_3$ in $\mathcal{S}_1 \cup \mathcal{S}_2 \cup \mathcal{S}_3 \cup \mathcal{S}_4$ (grey and black dots indicate two classes)

4   Conclusions and Future Work

In this paper, we discussed our TA algorithm comprising LoG filtration of images at a range of spatial frequencies followed by histogram analysis of filtered images. We investigated its classification capabilities using two sets containing simulated lesions with varying heterogeneity. The results show that classifying images with defects of a larger density (either in the presence of other density objects or not) is easier if the density is relatively high, and it depends on the ratio of defects of various characteristics. Our ongoing research includes combining the markers into feature vectors, and analyzing them using various classification algorithms. We aim at incorporating support vector machines to classify data [15].

References

1. Krichen, E., Allano, L., Garcia-Salicetti, S., Dorizzi, B.: Specific texture analysis for iris recognition. In: Kanade, T., Jain, A., Ratha, N.K. (eds.) AVBPA 2005. LNCS, vol. 3546, pp. 23–30. Springer, Heidelberg (2005)
2. Kawulok, M., Kawulok, J., Smolka, B.: Discriminative textural features for image and video colorization. IEICE Trans. on Inf. and Sys. 95-D(7), 1722–1730 (2012)
3. Kawulok, M., Smolka, B.: Texture-adaptive image colorization framework. EURASIP J. on Adv. in Signal Process. 2011(1), 1–15 (2011)
4. Kawulok, M., Kawulok, J., Nalepa, J.: Spatial-based skin detection using discriminative skin-presence features. Patt. Recogn. Letters 41, 3–13 (2014)
5. Parikh, J., Selmi, M., Charles-Edwards, G., Glendenning, J., Ganeshan, B., Verma, H., Mansi, J., Harries, M., Tutt, A., Goh, V.: Changes in primary breast cancer heterogeneity may augment midtreatment MR imaging assessment of response to neoadjuvant chemotherapy. Radiology (in press, 2014)
6. Ganeshan, B., Goh, V., Mandeville, H., Ng, Q., Hoskin, P., Miles, K.: Non-small cell lung cancer: histopathologic correlates for texture parameters at CT. Radiology 266(1), 326–336 (2013)
7. Zhang, J., Yu, C., Jiang, G., Liu, W., Tong, L.: 3D texture analysis on MRI images of Alzheimer's disease. Brain Imaging Behav. 6(1), 61–69 (2012)
8. Win, T., Miles, K., Janes, S., Ganeshan, B., Shastry, M., Endozo, R., Meagher, M., Shortman, R., Wan, S., Kayani, I., Ell, P., Groves, A.: Tumor heterogeneity and permeability as measured on the CT component of PET/CT predict survival in patients with non-small cell lung cancer. Clin. Cancer Res. 19(13), 3591–3599 (2013)
9. Castellano, G., Bonilha, L., Li, L., Cendes, F.: Texture analysis of medical images. Clin. Radiol. 59(12), 1061–1069 (2004)
10. Tourassi, G.D.: Journey towards computer-aided diagnosis: role of image texture analysis. Radiology 213, 317–320 (1999)
11. Ganeshan, B., Miles, K.A., Young, R.C., Chatwin, C.R.: Texture analysis in non-contrast enhanced CT: Impact of malignancy on texture in apparently disease-free areas of the liver. European J. of Radiol. 70(1), 101–110 (2009)
12. Marr, D.: Representing the image: zero-crossings and the raw primal sketch. In: Wilson, J., Monsour, P. (eds.) Vision, pp. 54–68 (1982)
13. Miles, K., Ganeshan, B., Hayball, M.: CT texture analysis using the filtration-histogram method: what do the measurements mean? Cancer Imag. 13(3), 400–406 (2013)
14. Perlich, C., Świrszcz, G.: On cross-validation and stacking: Building seemingly predictive models on random data. SIGKDD Explor. Newsl. 12(2), 11–15 (2011)
15. Kawulok, M., Nalepa, J.: Support vector machines training data selection using a genetic algorithm. In: Gimel'farb, G., Hancock, E., Imiya, A., Kuijper, A., Kudo, M., Omachi, S., Windeatt, T., Yamada, K. (eds.) SSPR&SPR 2012. LNCS, vol. 7626, pp. 557–565. Springer, Heidelberg (2012)

Enhancement of Despeckled Ultrasound Images by Forward-Backward Diffusion

Mariusz Nieniewski

Department of Mathematics and Informatics, University of Łódź
ul. Banacha 22, 90-238 Łódź, Poland
mnieniew@math.uni.lodz.pl

Abstract. The forward-backward diffusion (FBD) by itself does not remove speckles from the ultrasound (US) images. However, it can effectively improve results of methods intended for speckle removal. In this paper improvement of the results coming from the nonlinear coherent diffusion (NCD) is considered. The NCD-processed image still contains excessive amount of detail that cannot be attributed to the human tissues. The paper describes the details of the FBD approach and presents examples of the obtained results. Changes made to images by the FBD are quantitatively analyzed by considering statistical moments, textural measures, and image quality measures. It is shown that the FBD simplifies the image and improves visibility of the most important structures in the image.

1   Introduction

The US imaging is a common diagnostic tool used all over the world. However, the US images have some limitations due to the fact that they are covered with bright speckles. There exist many algorithms for speckle removal as described in the book [5] and review papers [2] and [6].

One of the best despeckling methods is the NCD [1]. However, the careful examination of effects of this method reveals that the quality of the filtered images might be further improved. There remain some traces of diagonal/antidiagional and possibly vertical/horizontal directions along which the calculations are performed. Furthermore, the tissue edges might be made more pronounced. The specific aim of the current paper is an improvement of the results of the NCD by the subsequent FBD [3]. Theoretically, one might increase the number of iteration steps of the NCD, and this would reduce the speckles. However, this number has to be limited even with the use of most up-to-date implementations because of computation time constraints. In fact the NCD uses a complicated implicit method of solving the diffusion equation [7]. On the contrary, the FBD uses an explicit method and hence can be made much faster. The choice of the FBD for US image enhancement is by no means obvious and has to be checked carefully. Originally in [3], the FBD is used for making the edges more steep while smoothing the approximately flat areas in the image. This is possible when the signal is relatively strong in comparison to noise, as is the case of natural scene images

L.J. Chmielewski et al. (Eds.): ICCVG 2014, LNCS 8671, pp. 454–461, 2014.
© Springer International Publishing Switzerland 2014

presented in [3]. When dealing with US images, the situation is more difficult since the remnants of the speckles exhibit gradients not so different from the gradients across the tissue contours. It follows from the analysis of the images that the FBD effectively smooths flat areas in US images while slightly improving high gradients. Changes introduced by the FBD are subtle and should be evaluated by comparing the image before and after enhancement. To the best of the author's knowledge the available means of image quality evaluation are not very helpful mainly because there is no single quantitative measure that would suit the case under consideration. In this paper changes made to images are evaluated via statistical moments, available textural measures, and image quality measures. Most of these measures confirm directly or indirectly the visual impression that the FBD improves visibility of the structure elements in the US image.

2   Nonlinear Coherent Diffusion

The NCD algorithm is quite complicated [1] and in the following only a short description is given in such a way that the parameters used in the computations are specified unequivocally. Initially the algorithm calculates vertical and horizontal components of the gradient of the input image. It then calculates the square of the vertical gradient, the square of the horizontal gradient, the product of vertical and horizontal gradients and subsequently filters the obtained three images by a convolution with a Gaussian filter. The obtained results are collected into a structure tensor. It was found that it is advantageous to normalize the eigenvectors of the structure tensor. The diffusion tensor needed for the diffusion equation, is then formulated using the eigenvalues and the eigenvectors of the structure tensor. In particular, the eigenvalues λ_1, λ_2 for the diffusion tensor are obtained by the nonlinear transformation of the eigenvalues of the structure tensor μ_1, μ_2 according to the equations

$$
\lambda_1 = \begin{cases} \alpha \left(1 - \frac{(\mu_1 - \mu_2)^2}{s^2}\right) & \text{if } (\mu_1 - \mu_2)^2 \le s^2 \\ 0 & \text{else} \end{cases} \tag{1}
$$
$$
\lambda_2 = \alpha
$$

where the parameters α and s have to be chosen. The resulting diffusion equation is quite lengthy [1], and it has both an explicit (diagonal) component and an implicit component. The numerical calculation of the implicit component involves solving a system of tridiagonal algebraic equations, which is the most time consuming operation in the NCD algorithm.

In our experiments the Gaussian filter used in the convolution has a mask of size 9×9 pixels with standard deviation $\sigma = 5$. The remaining, above mentioned parameters of the algorithm are $\alpha = 1$, $s = 800$, and the time increment is $\Delta t = 1$. Examples of image despeckling by the NCD is shown in Fig. 1(b) for a carotid artery, Fig. 3(b) for a vein, Fig. 3(e) for a breast. The size of images in Fig. 1 is 520×256 pixels, and the number of brightness levels is 256. The

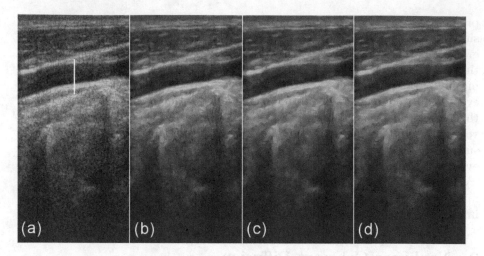

Fig. 1. Denoising an US image. a) Original image of a carotid artery. b) Result of three iterations of the NCD. c) Result of subsequent 12 iterations of the FBD. d) Result of 20 iterations of the FBD. The vertical line segment in (a) is a line along which brightness distribution is subsequently analyzed.

images were obtained by means of the SonixTouch ultrasound system, from its preprocessing output, hence the images are quite noisy. The results of despeckling after NCD as well as joint NCD, FBD iterations can be better appreciated by considering brightness distribution along some straight line segment in the image, such as shown in Fig. 2. Fig. 2 exemplifies the sharpening of the edges and the smoothing of flatter areas along the above mentioned line.

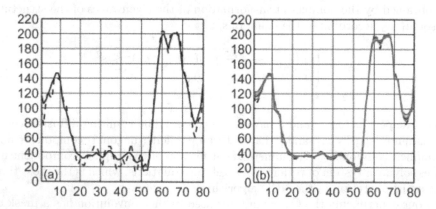

Fig. 2. Brightness along the vertical straight line segment shown in Fig. 1. a) For original image in Fig. 1(a) (dashed line) and NCD-despeckled image in Fig. 1(b) (continuous line). b) Brightness corresponding to Fig. 1 after 4, 8, 12, and 20 FBD iterations. The continuous curve from Fig. 2(a) for NCD-despeckled image is repeated now as a dashed line.

3   Forward-Backward Diffusion

The FBD in general follows developments in [8] with modification in calculations of the diffusion coefficient. The difference scheme for an iteration of the FBD is the following. The new brightness $I_{i,j}^{k+1}$ of the pixel with coordinates i, j, in iteration $k+1$ is calculated as a function of pixels in iteration k

$$I_{i,j}^{k+1} = I_{i,j}^{k} + \lambda[c_N \nabla_N I + c_S \nabla_S I + c_E \nabla_E I + c_W \nabla_W I]_{i,j}^{k} \qquad (2)$$

The delta increments in the above equation are defined in "geographical" N, S, E, W directions

$$\nabla_N I_{i,j} = I_{i-1,j} - I_{i,j} \qquad \nabla_S I_{i,j} = I_{i+1,j} - I_{i,j} \qquad (3)$$
$$\nabla_E I_{i,j} = I_{i,j+1} - I_{i,j} \qquad \nabla_W I_{i,j} = I_{i,j-1} - I_{i,j} \qquad (4)$$

The λ coefficient in Eq. (2) should lie in the range $[0, 0.25]$ for numerical stability [8]. The diffusion coefficients $c_N, \ldots, c_W$ are calculated at every iteration as a function of the magnitude of the brightness gradient $\|\nabla'.\|$ in the respective directions

$$c_{N_{i,j}}^{k} = c(\|\nabla'_N I_{i-1/2,j}^{k}\|) \qquad c_{S_{i,j}}^{k} = c(\|\nabla'_S I_{i+1/2,j}^{k}\|) \qquad (5)$$
$$c_{E_{i,j}}^{k} = c(\|\nabla'_E I_{i,j+1/2}^{k}\|) \qquad c_{W_{i,j}}^{k} = c(\|\nabla'_W I_{i,j-1/2}^{k}\|) \qquad (6)$$

The function $c(.)$ in the above equations is specific to the FBD, and in accordance with [3] it has two components, the first being responsible for the forward diffusion, and the second for the backward diffusion

$$c(s_1) = \frac{1}{1 + (s_1/k_f)^n} - \frac{\alpha_1}{1 + ((s_1 - k_b)/w)^{2m}} \qquad (7)$$

In Eq. (7), s_1 denotes the magnitude of the gradient component, and the parameters k_f, k_b, w, n, m, and α_1 define the shape of the $c(s_1)$ function. In our experiments the following values are assumed: $k_f = 10, k_b = 40, w = 20, n = 4, m = 1, \alpha_1 = 0.2$, and $\lambda = 0.1$. The gradients $\nabla'_N, \ldots, \nabla'_W$ in Eqs. (5) and (6) are replaced by respective delta increments in Eqs. (3) and (4). Experiments showed that using more refined gradient definitions with larger masks does not have a pronounced influence on the results. The parameters specified above were obtained experimentally and can be used for a relatively wide class of US images.

The results of FBD image denoising are illustrated by Figs. 1(c), (d) as well as 3(c) and (f). Fig. 1(d) depicts results of a larger number, that is 20 FBD iterations. This image indicates that bright parts of the image tend to form long stripes with clearly delineated edges. Subjective impression is that this might be an excessive modification of the image and that the FBD should be limited to a smaller number of iterations. Fig. 3 shows fragments of size 260×256 of the original images in order to improve the visibility of details.

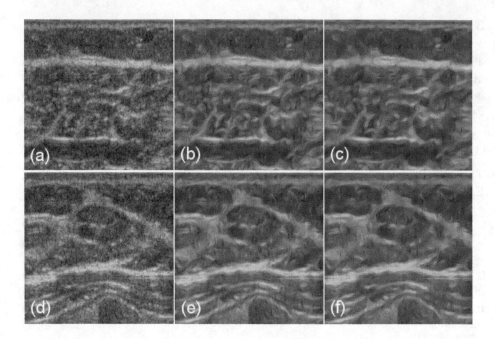

Fig. 3. Denoising an US image. Upper row: a) Original image of a vein. b) Result of three iterations of NCD. c) Result of subsequent 12 iterations of FBD. Lower row: d) Original image of a breast. e) Result of three iterations of NCD. f) Result of subsequent 12 iterations of FBD.

4   Analysis of the Influence of the FBD on Image Quality

Various methods of image quality evaluation are evolving all the time and a number of definitions are necessary. In order to cut things short we follow exactly the definitions given in [4]. In particular, we present results obtained with the functions *statmoments* and *statxture* taken from [4] as well as *graycomatrix* and *graycoprops* from the Image Processing Toolbox of Matlab. The first four central moments calculated for images from Figs. 1(a)–(c) are shown in the left hand part of Table 1. Normalizing the images by changing their gray levels from the range [0, 255] to [0, 1] gives the moments shown in the right hand part of Table 1. One can observe that the mean brightness, that is the first moment is practically the same for the original image and for despeckled images. The variance, that is the second moment, as well as higher moments are reduced by the NCD and to a smaller degree by the FBD. Table 2 specifies the mean, standard deviation, smoothness, third moment, uniformity, and entropy calculated by means of the *staxture*. Calculating the smoothness requires the variance from right hand side of Table 1. The third moment in Table 2 is obtained from the third moment in Table 1 by normalizing with the same factor as used for the variance [4]. Smoothness would be 0 for a constant image, and it is seen that it becomes smaller by performing the FBD. Uniformity would be maximum (1) for constant

Table 1. Centralized statistical moments for images in Figs. 1(a)–(c)

Moment's order	Unnormalized moments			Normalized moments		
	(a)	(b)	(c)	(a)	(b)	(c)
1st	58.003	57.982	57.978	0.2275	0.2274	0.2274
2nd	2220.2	2061.3	2034.3	0.0341	0.0317	0.0313
3rd	99800	94097	92084	0.00602	0.00567	0.00555
4th	$1.524 * 10^7$	$1.318 * 10^7$	$1.276 * 10^7$	0.00361	0.00312	0.00302

Table 2. Texture measures for images in Figs. 1(a)–(c)

Texture measure	(a)	(b)	(c)
Mean	58.00	57.98	57.98
Standard deviation	47.12	45.40	45.10
Smoothness	0.03302	0.03073	0.03034
3rd moment	1.5348	1.4471	1.4161
Uniformity	0.00812	0.01031	0.01065
Entropy	7.2268	7.0455	7.0139

Table 3. Texture properties for images in Figs. 1(a)–(c)

Property	Horizontal offset =1			Vertical offset =1		
	(a)	(b)	(c)	(a)	(b)	(c)
Contrast	200.42	18.60	14.05	176.37	41.66	41.88
Correlation	0.9549	0.9955	0.9965	0.9603	0.9899	0.9897
Energy	0.000200	0.001377	0.002697	0.000256	0.001709	0.002758
Homogeneity	0.17082	0.41833	0.54351	0.18942	0.41841	0.51723

image. Table 2 illustrates the increase of the uniformity as a result of the FBD. The entropy is slightly reduced by the FBD.

Table 3 summarizes the following texture properties: contrast, correlation, energy, and homogeneity, calculated for images in Figs. 1(a)–(c) based on the neighborhood gray level dependence matrix. The *graycomatrix* calculating the neighborhood gray level covariance matrix was used with the following options: number of gray levels in the image equals to 256, the symmetrical option of the offset is true. The horizontal offset of one pixel was used for the left hand part of Table 3 and vertical offset of one pixel for the right hand part. The symmetrical option means that the basic pixel and the offset pixel can be exchanged and both cases are included in the calculation of the neighborhood gray level dependence matrix. A larger group of 10 images representing a carotid artery, elbow, thyroid, abdomen, breast, ligament, muscle, and a vein were tested also, and the mean values for these images are given in Table 4. Inspection of this table, as well as of Table 3 reveals that as a result of the FBD the contrast has tendency to reduce, the correlation remains approximately the same, the energy increases, and the homogeneity increases.

Table 4. Mean texture properties for 10 US images

Property	Horizontal offset =1			Vertical offset =1		
	Original	3 NCD iterations	plus 12 FBD iterations	Original	3 NCD iterations	plus 12 FBD iterations
Contrast	227.38	30.94	25.26	189.74	41.91	41.11
Correlation	0.9221	0.9872	0.9892	0.9348	0.9831	0.9830
Energy	0.000190	0.000895	0.001649	0.000244	0.001051	0.001684
Homogeneity	0.16621	0.37264	0.48727	0.18056	0.37867	0.47378

Table 5. Image quality measures for images in Figs. 1(b) and (c)

	Median filter	Fig. 1(b)	Fig. 1(c)
MSE	162.331	92.365	124.927
RMSE	12.741	8.511	11.177
ERR3	15.416	11.434	13.272
ERR4	17.939	13.138	15.221
GAE	0	0	0
SNR	18.293	20.762	19.440
PSNR	26.027	28.476	27.164
Q	0.356	0.573	0.428
SSIN	0.389	0.598	0.461

Differences between the original and despeckled images were further evaluated by means of image quality evaluation measures, similarly to [5]. The exact definitions of these measures are given in [5]. The measures calculated are: MSE (mean square error), RMSE (root mean square error), ERR3 (norm of dissimilarity between the original and despeckled images calculated as Minkowski norm with the parameter equal to 3), ERR4 (Minkowski norm with the parameter equal to 4), GAE (geometric average error) SNR (signal-to-noise ratio), PSNR (peak signal-to-noise ratio), Q (universal image quality index), SSIN (structural similarity index). In Table 5 the measures for images in Figs. 1(b) and (c) are given in two right-most columns. For comparison the same measures were calculated for the image in Fig. 1(a) denoised by a median filter of size 7×7 pixels, similarly as in [5]. Inspection of Table 5 confirms that all the image quality measures are better for the NCD despeckled and FBD enhanced images than for the median filtered image. However, they do not reflect the fact that the tissues in the FBD enhanced images are more distinct than in the NCD denoised images. It seems that some more specialized measure of image quality might be desirable.

5   Conclusion

The use of several FBD iterations after NCD iterations smooths the image while maintaining or improving steep tissue edges. This improves the visibility of prominent edges in the US image. The FBD iterations give much less computational load in comparison with NCD iterations. The existing textural measures do not allow precise optimization of the number of FBD iterations. Experiments show, however, that several, up to 12 iterations give visually satisfactory results. It appears probable that the use of the FBD might be advantageous in the case of other despeckling methods, not only the NCD.

Acknowledgments The author would like to express his gratitude to Prof. Andrzej Nowicki, Institute of Fundamental Technological Research, Warsaw for providing the necessary images for this research.

References

1. Abd-Elmoniem, K.Z., Youssef, A.-B.M., Kadah, Y.M.: Real-time speckle reduction and coherence enhancement in ultrasound imaging via nonlinear anisotropic diffusion. IEEE Trans. Biomed. Eng. 49(9), 997–1014 (2002)
2. Contreras Ortiz, S.H., Chiu, T., Fox, M.D.: Ultrasound image enhancement: a review. Biomed. Sign. Proc. & Control. 7, 419–428 (2012)
3. Gilboa, G., Sochen, N., Zeevi, Y.Y.: Forward-and-backward diffusion processes for adaptive image enhancement and denoising. IEEE Trans. Image Process. 11(7), 689–703 (2002)
4. Gonzalez, R.C., Woods, R.E., Eddins, S.L.: Digital Image Processing Using MAT-LAB. Gatesmark Publishing (2009)
5. Loizou, C.P., Pattichis, C.S.: Despeckle Filtering Algorithms and Software for Ultrasound Imaging. Morgan & Claypool (2008)
6. Michailovich, O.V., Tannenbaum, A.: Despeckling of medical ultrasound images. IEEE Trans. Ultrason Ferroelect. Freq. Contr. 53(1), 64–78 (2006)
7. Nieniewski, M., Zajączkowski, P.: Real-time speckle reduction in ultrasound images by means of nonlinear coherent diffusion using GPU. In: ICCVG 2014. LNCS, vol. 8671, pp. 462–469. Springer, Heidelberg (2014)
8. Perona, P., Malik, J.: Scale-space and edge detection using anisotropic diffusion. IEEE Trans. Patt. Anal. Mach. Intell. 12(7), 629–639 (1990)

Real-Time Speckle Reduction
in Ultrasound Images by Means of Nonlinear
Coherent Diffusion Using GPU

Mariusz Nieniewski and Paweł Zajączkowski

Department of Mathematics and Informatics, University of Łódź
ul. Banacha 22, 90-238 Łódź, Poland
{mnieniew,zajaczkowski.pawel}@math.uni.lodz.pl

Abstract. The paper describes a novel GPU implementation of the nonlinear coherent diffusion (NCD) algorithm for speckle reduction in ultrasound (US) images. Although the NCD algorithm gives satisfactory results, its execution in the CPU is too slow for real-time applications typical for US images. The use of parallel computing in the GPU allowed us to reduce the processing time of a single iteration of the diffusion to 85.8 ms for an image of size $512 * 1024$ pixels.

1 Introduction

The speckle removal is a fundamental problem of ultrasound imagery and many algorithms exist that solve this problem [5]. The most refined methods are those based on the diffusion, such as the NCD [1]. By executing the computations in the GPU rather than CPU one can significantly reduce the processing time of medical images [2], [3]. The purpose of this paper is the development of a method for parallel execution of the NCD algorithm in real-time in the GPU.

2 Mathematical Preliminaries for the NCD Algorithm

A short description of the algorithm [1] is given here, with particular emphasis on the parameters needed for possible reimplementation of the numerical experiments. Initially the algorithm executes the preparatory steps: it calculates vertical and horizontal components of the gradient of the input image by means of the Sobel operator. It then calculates the square of the vertical gradient, square of the horizontal gradient, the product of vertical and horizontal gradients, and subsequently it convolves the obtained three images with a Gaussian filter. The three convolution results are collected in a structure tensor J

$$J = \begin{bmatrix} J_{11} & J_{12} \\ J_{12} & J_{22} \end{bmatrix} \equiv \begin{bmatrix} a & b \\ b & d \end{bmatrix} \tag{1}$$

with symbols a, b, d used in the following for brevity. Having the structure tensor defined, we can describe a single iteration of the NCD as follows.

L.J. Chmielewski et al. (Eds.): ICCVG 2014, LNCS 8671, pp. 462–469, 2014.

The eigenvalues of J are given by the equation

$$\mu_{1,2} = \frac{1}{2}[a + d \pm \sqrt{a^2 + 4b^2 - 2ad + d^2}] \tag{2}$$

We calculate the eigenvectors of the matrix J in Eq. (1) according to the equations

$$\begin{bmatrix} \{a - d + \sqrt{a^2 + 4b^2 - 2ad + d^2}\}/2 \\ b \end{bmatrix} \equiv \begin{bmatrix} w_a \\ w_b \end{bmatrix} \tag{3}$$

$$\begin{bmatrix} \{a - d - \sqrt{a^2 + 4b^2 - 2ad + d^2}\}/2 \\ b \end{bmatrix} \equiv \begin{bmatrix} w_d \\ w_b \end{bmatrix} \tag{4}$$

After normalization the eigenvectors can be written in the form $[v_a \; v_b]^T$, $[v_c \; v_d]^T$ with components $v_a, \ldots, v_d$ appropriately defined in terms of $w_a, \ldots, w_d$.

For the diffusion implementation, we now have to define the diffusion tensor. The diffusion tensor is obtained using the eigenvectors given above and calculating new eigenvalues λ_1, λ_2 in accordance with the conditions

$$\lambda_1 = \begin{cases} \alpha(1 - \frac{(\mu_1 - \mu_2)^2}{s^2}) & \text{if } (\mu_1 - \mu_2)^2 \leq s^2 \\ 0 & \text{otherwise} \end{cases} \tag{5}$$
$$\lambda_2 = \alpha$$

with parameters α and s defining the nonlinearity of the diffusion process [1]. The diffusion tensor is now calculated as a product of three matrices

$$D = \begin{bmatrix} D_{11} & D_{12} \\ D_{12} & D_{22} \end{bmatrix} = \begin{bmatrix} v_a & v_c \\ v_b & v_d \end{bmatrix} \begin{bmatrix} \lambda_1 & 0 \\ 0 & \lambda_2 \end{bmatrix} \begin{bmatrix} v_a & v_b \\ v_c & v_d \end{bmatrix} \equiv \begin{bmatrix} a_d & b_d \\ c_d & d_d \end{bmatrix} \tag{6}$$

with $a_d, \ldots, d_d$ representing terms obtained by carrying out the multiplications indicated in Eq. (6).

The difference scheme approximating the solution for the NCD is given jointly by the two following equations

$$J_{j,l}^{k+0.5} = I_{j,l}^k + \frac{\Delta t}{4}\{c_{d;j+1,l}^k(I_{j+1,l+1}^k - I_{j+1,l-1}^k) - c_{d;j-1,l}^k(I_{j-1,l+1}^k) - I_{j-1,l-1}^k)\}$$

$$+ \frac{\Delta t}{4}\{b_{d;j,l+1}^k(I_{j+1,l+1}^k - I_{j-1,l+1}^k) - b_{d;j,l-1}^k(I_{j+1,l-1}^k) - I_{j-1,l-1}^k)\} \tag{7}$$

$$I_{j,l}^{k+1} - \Delta t \left[\frac{d_{d;j,l}^k + d_{d;j,l+1}^k}{2}\left(I_{j,l+1}^{k+1} - I_{j,l}^{k+1}\right) + \frac{d_{d;j,l}^k + d_{d;j,l-1}^k}{2}\left(I_{j,l-1}^{k+1} - I_{j,l}^{k+1}\right) \right]$$

$$- \Delta t \left[\frac{a_{d;j,l}^k + a_{d;j+1,l}^k}{2}\left(I_{j+1,l}^{k+1} - I_{j,l}^{k+1}\right) + \frac{a_{d;j,l}^k + a_{d;j-1,l}^k}{2}\left(I_{j-1,l}^{k+1} - I_{j,l}^{k+1}\right) \right]$$

$$= J_{j,l}^{k+0.5} \tag{8}$$

The symbol $I_{j,l}^k$ in the above equations denotes the brightness in kth iteration of a pixel with coordinates j, l. The auxiliary variable (brightness) $J_{j,l}^{k+0.5}$ refers to explicit calculations along diagonal and cross-diagonal of the image matrix. Eq. (8) uses $J_{j,l}^{k+0.5}$ obtained from Eq. (7) and involves implicit calculations due to the unknown terms of type $I_{j,l}^{k+1}$ appearing more than one time in this equation. The Δt denotes the time step. Eq. (8) can be rewritten as Eq. (9) with appropriately defined coefficients $T_1, \ldots, T_6$

$$\{1 + \Delta t\, [T_1 + T_2]\}\, I_{j,l}^{k+1} - \Delta t\, \overbrace{\left[T_3 I_{j,l+1}^{k+1} + T_4 I_{j,l-1}^{k+1}\right]}^{\text{vertical}} - \Delta t\, \overbrace{\left[T_5 I_{j+1,l}^{k+1} + T_6 I_{j-1,l}^{k+1}\right]}^{\text{horizontal}}$$
$$= J_{j,l}^{k+0.5} \qquad (9)$$

Eq. (9) is subsequently decomposed into two equations describing the vertical and horizontal diffusion, respectively, both of which are solved via a tridiagonal system of algebraic equations

$$-\Delta T\, T_4 I_{j,l-1}^{k+1} + \{1 + \Delta T\, T_1\}\, I_{j,l}^{k+1} - \Delta T\, T_3 I_{j,l+1}^{k+1} = J_{j,l}^{k+0.5} \qquad (10)$$

$$-\Delta T\, T_6 I_{j-1,l}^{k+1} + \{1 + \Delta T\, T_2\}\, I_{j,l}^{k+1} - \Delta T\, T_5 I_{j+1,l}^{k+1} = J_{j,l}^{k+0.5} \qquad (11)$$

where $\Delta T = 2\Delta t$. Eqs. (10) and (11) are solved independently, and the final $I_{j,l}^{k+1}$ is obtained as the average of the results for the vertical and horizontal diffusion.

3   Implementation of the NCD Algorithm Using the GPU

The main principle of the presented algorithm is that the CPU program calls a number of GPU kernels that perform particular tasks corresponding to the computations specified above [4]. The sequence of kernels for one iteration of the diffusion is shown in Fig. 1. One exception is the CPU function cr, which solves systems of Eqs. (10) and (11) by calling several additional kernels. All of the kernels have block and grid dimensions, which are their dim3 parameters shown inside the symbol <<< . >>>. The other kernel parameters are specified after this symbol, within parentheses, where the output variables of each kernel are specified *in front of* the semicolon and the input variables are *after* the semicolon (see the list of symbols in the Appendix).

The kernels rowSobel and columnSobel execute filtering along the rows and columns. This means that the usual $3 * 3$ horizontal and vertical Sobel filters are both decomposed into two vectors for filtering sequentially along the rows and columns [6]. The kernel multiplyPixelbyPixel implements pixel-by-pixel multiplication as required for preparation of the structure tensor in Eq. (1). The kernels rowConv and columnConv similarly implement row and column convolution with a Gaussian mask [6]. It is worth noting that both the convolution and the Sobel filtering require processing the neighborhood of a pixel when calculating a new value for a given pixel. It means that in order to compute a portion of a new image one has to have access to a bigger portion of the input image including a so called apron surrounding the computed output data. As a result,

- rowSobel $<<<$ BGRC, TBRSC $>>$ (sTmp; Idble, filterVert, width, height)
- columnSobel $<<<$ BGCC, TBCC $>>>$ (Iv, Ivv; sTmp, filterHor, width, height)
- rowSobel $<<<$ BGRC, TBRSC $>>>$ (sTmp; Idble, filterHor, width, height)
- columnSobel $<<<$ BGCC, TBCC $>>>$ (Ih, Ihh; sTmp, filterVert, width, height)
- multiplyPixelbyPixel $<<<$ DG, DB $>>>$ (Ivh; Iv, Ih, width, height)
- rowConv $<<<$ BGRC, TBRC $>>>$ (gTmp; Ihh, width, height)
- columnConv $<<<$ BGCC, TBCC $>>>$ (J11; gTmp, width, height, filtRad, gauss)
- rowConv $<<<$ BGRC, TBRC $>>>$ (gTmp; Ihv, width, height, filtRad, gauss)
- columnConv $<<<$ BGCC, TBCC $>>>$ (J12; gTmp, width, height, filtRad, gauss)
- rowConv $<<<$ BGRC, TBRC $>>>$ (gTmp; Ivv, width, height, filtRad, gauss)
- columnConv $<<<$ BGCC, TBCC $>>>$ (J22; gTmp, width, height, filtRad, gauss)
- K1 $<<<$ DG, DB $>>>$ (D11, D12, D22; J11, J12, J22, alpha, s, delta_t, side, sigma, height, width)
- K2 $<<<$ DG, DB $>>>$ (J05; D12, alpha, s, delta_t, side, sigma, width, height)
- K3 $<<<$ DG, DB $>>>$ (T1 ..., T6; D11, D22, width, height)
- K4 $<<<$ DG, DB $>>>$ (diag_a, diag_b, diag_c; T1, T3, T4, width, height, delta_T)
- imagev $=$ cr(diag_a, diag_b, diag_c, J05, IS)
- K5 $<<<$ DG, DB $>>>$ (diag_a, diag_b, diag_c; T2, T5, T6, width, height, delta_T)
- transpose $<<<$ GT, TT $>>>$ (J05T; J05, width, height)
- tmp $=$ cr(diag_a, diag_b, diag_c, J05T, IS)
- transpose $<<<$ GT, TT $>>>$ (imageh; tmp, height, width)
- averaging $<<<$ DG, DB $>>>$ (outputImage; imagev, imageh, width, height)
- toInt $<<<$ DG, DB $>>>$ (imageInt; outputImage, height, width)

Fig. 1. List of kernels executed in the GPU during one iteration of the algorithm

when processing the image one has to differentiate between the tile and the block of image data [6]. Since Sobel filtering and Gaussian convolution are 2-D operations executed as a sequence of 1-D operations in vertical and horizontal directions, it follows that there are separate row and columns tiles and blocks of threads in the respective kernels. The assumed tile and block dimensions are specified in Fig. 2.

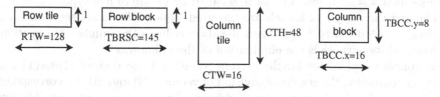

Fig. 2. Blocks and tiles used for Sobel filtering. In the case of the convolution TBRSC is replaced by TBRC.

The kernel K1 calculates the matrix elements $a_d, \ldots, d_d$ defined in Eq. (6). The kernel K2 calculates the matrix J_{05} according to Eq. (7). The kernel K3 calculates the coefficients $T_1, \ldots, T_6$ in Eqs. (10) – (11). These equations can be rewritten in a tridiagonal form

$$
\begin{bmatrix}
b_1 & c_1 & 0 & 0 & 0 & 0 & 0 & 0 \\
a_2 & b_2 & c_2 & 0 & 0 & 0 & 0 & 0 \\
\hdotsfor{8} \\
0 & 0 & 0 & 0 & 0 & a_{n-1} & b_{n-1} & c_{n-1} \\
0 & 0 & 0 & 0 & 0 & 0 & a_n & b_n
\end{bmatrix} X = Y \tag{12}
$$

where $X \equiv I^k$, $Y \equiv J^{k+0.5}$. The kernel K4 calculates the vectors of coefficients diag_a, diag_b and diag_c according to Eq. (12).

- crAlphaBeta $<<<$ dGSN, dBSN $>>>$ (alpha[i], beta[i]; a[i], b[i], c[i], Y[i], 2^i)
- crABC $<<<$ dGSN, dBSN $>>>$ (a_tmp, b_tmp, c_tmp, Y_tmp; a[i], b[i], c[i], Y[i], alpha[i], beta[i], 2^i)
- crCopy $<<<$ dGSN, dBSN $>>>$ (a[i−1], b[i−1], c[i−1], Y[i−1]; a_tmp, b_tmp, c_tmp, Y_tmp, 2^i)
- backsubstituteEven $<<<$ dGSN, dBSN $>>>$ (X[i]; X[i−1], a[i−1], b[i−1], c[i−1], Y[i−1], 2^i)
- backsubstituteOdd $<<<$ dGSN, dBSN $>>>$ (X[i]; X[i], a[i], b[i], c[i], Y[i], 2^i)

Fig. 3. Types of kernels executed in the GPU during one call of the function cr

The function cr uses the method of cyclic reduction (chapt. 7.2.2 in [7]) for finding the solution to Eq. (12) (cmp. Fig. 3). The assumption is made that the number of algebraic equations represented by Eq. (12) is 2^N, where N is a natural number. This equation set is solved be elimination of odd unknowns by substituting from odd equations into even equations. Iterating this operation N times we are left with a single equation with one unknown that is easy to solve. The remaining unknowns are then calculated by back substitution in subsequent iterations. The function cr calls a variable number of kernels depending on the image size IS (Appendix and Fig. 3). In the case of $1024 * 1024$ image all kernels are executed $N = 20$ times. The kernels called by cr are of five types.

The first three types of kernels are executed sequentially in an iteration starting from i = N down to i = 2. Each iteration reduces the number of equations by half and its purpose is the elimination of the unknowns:
- crAlphaBeta calculates for the current iteration i the vectors alpha[i] and beta[i] containing the results of division of vectors a[i] and c[i] by corresponding elements of b[i]. The parameter 2^i denotes the size of input vectors. The aim of this operation is the elimination of a division from subsequent operations [7].
- crABC calculates auxiliary vectors a_tmp, b_tmp, c_tmp, Y_tmp given vectors a[i], b[i], c[i], Y[i], and 2^i. In the first iteration of the cyclic reduction i = N and the vectors a[N] = diag_a, b[N] = diag_b, c[N] = diag_c, and Y[N] = J05 (or Y[N] = J05T in the second call of cr).
- cr3Copy copies even-position values from a_tmp, b_tmp, c_tmp, Y_tmp to a[i−1], b[i−1], c[i−1], Y[i−1].

The final iteration, for i = 1, calculates a single value of X[1] = Y[1]/b[1].

The last two types of kernels are executed sequentially for i = 1 up to N and implement back substitution:

- backsubstituteEven copies values from X[i−1] into even positions in X[i].
- backsubstituteOdd calculates missing values of X[i] in odd positions.

The final result of the cr function is a vertically (imagev) or horizontally (imageh) diffused image.

Returning now to Fig. 1, the kernel transpose calculates the transpose of a given matrix [8]. The kernel averaging calculates the mean value of the results of the vertical and horizontal diffusion, and the kernel toInt rounds the double precision result outputImage to the integer imageInt.

4   Experimental Results

Experimental results described below were obtained for the Gaussian filter with $9 * 9$ mask and standard deviation $\sigma = 15$ and other parameters of the algorithm as follows: $\alpha = 1, s = 120, \Delta t = 1$. An example of the results obtained is shown in Fig. 4. The GPU computation time as a function of the size of the image is given in Fig. 5. The individual times for all of the kernels are specified in Table 1.

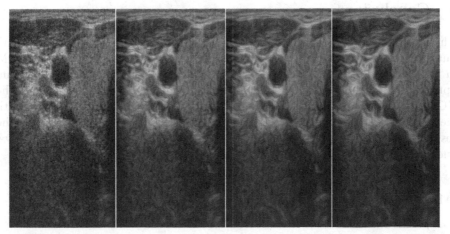

Fig. 4. Results of the filtering of a thyroid image. The original image is on the left. The subsequent images illustrate, respectively, the results of three, six, and nine iterations of the NCD.

Table 1. Individual kernel execution times for an image of $512 * 1024$ pixels

kernel/function	time	kernel/function	time
2 Sobel filters	2.1 ms each	function cr	28.5 ms
pixel-by-pixel multiplication	2.0 ms	K5	1.5 ms
3 Gaussian convolutions	2.5 ms each	transpose	0.2 ms
K1	7.2 ms	function cr	29.5 ms
K2 and K3 in parallel	2.4 ms	transpose	0.7 ms
K4	0.7 ms	average	0.5 ms

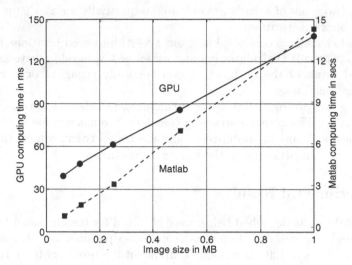

Fig. 5. GPU compute times as a function of image size

5   Conclusions

The obtained results confirm that there is a considerable reduction of the computation time, even with an average NVIDIA card of the type GeForce GT 650M in the Dell Inspiron 7720 computer, when compared with the Matlab program optimized for the sequential operation for the same computer. As a result the NCD algorithm has a potential for being used in US equipment. It is worth mentioning that testing the algorithm with 25 various images showed that the respective diffused images obtained with double precision arithmetic in CUDA and Matlab differed less than 1.54×10^{-9} in any pixel.

Appendix - List of Symbols

Input Parameters:
- `width`, `height` - width and height of the image,
- `alpha`, `s`, `delta_t`, `side`, `sigma` - diffusion parameters specified in section 2 above.
  Constants:
- BW $= 16$, BH $= 16$,
- RTW $= 128$ – row tile width (Fig. 2),
- CTW $= 16$ – column tile width, CTH $= 48$ - column title height (Fig. 2),
- FRA $= 16$ – FILTER_RADIUS_ALIGNED ([6]),
- TD $= 32$, BR $= 8$,
- `filterRow` $= [1, 0, -1]$ – row of the decomposed Sobel mask,
- `filterCol` $= [1, 2, 1]$ – column of the decomposed Sobel mask.

dim3 Variables:
- BGRC = ($\lceil$width, RTW$\rceil$, height) = ($\lceil$width, 128$\rceil$, height) = $(8, 1024)$ – width and height of a grid for row Sobel filter and row convolution,
- TBRSC = FRA + RTW + 1 = 16 + 128 + 1 = 145 – width of row block for Sobel filter,
- BGCC = ($\lceil$width, CTW$\rceil$, $\lceil$height, CTH$\rceil$) = ($\lceil$width, 16$\rceil$, $\lceil$height, 48$\rceil$) = $(64, 22)$ – width and height of a grid for column Sobel filter and column convolution,
- TBCC = (CTW, 8) = $(16, 8)$ – width and height of a block for column Sobel filter and column convolution,
- TBRC = FRA + RTW + filtRad = 16 + 128 + filtRad – width of a block for row convolution,
- DG = ($\lceil$width, BW$\rceil$, $\lceil$height, BH$\rceil$) = ($\lceil$width, 16$\rceil$, $\lceil$height, 16$\rceil$) - width and height of a grid for pixel-by-pixel multiplication,
- DB = (BW, BH) = $(16, 16)$ – width and height of a block for pixel-by-pixel multiplication,
- dGSN = $(1, \lceil 2^N, 1024 \rceil + 1)$ – width and height of grids used by kernels of the cr function, $N = 1, 2, \ldots, 20$,
- dBSN = $(1, \min\{2^N, 1024\})$ – width and height of blocks used by kernels of cr function, $N = 1, 2, \ldots, 20$,
- GT = ($\lceil$width, TD$\rceil$, $\lceil$height, TD$\rceil$) = ($\lceil$width, 32$\rceil$, $\lceil$height, 32$\rceil$) = $(32, 32)$ – width and height of a grid for matrix transposition,
- TT = (TD, BR) = $(32, 8)$ – width and height of a block for matrix transposition.

Other Variables:
- Idble – input image, **imageInt** – output image, IS = **width** $*$ **height** – image size,
- Ivv = Iv $*$ Iv, Ihh = Ih $*$ Ih, Ihv = Ih $*$ Iv,
- filtRad = $\lfloor$side/2$\rfloor$ – one half of a side of the Gaussian mask,
- gauss – row (or column) vector of a decomposed Gaussian mask.

Acknowledgments. The authors would like to express their gratitude to Prof. Andrzej Nowicki, Institute of Fundamental Technological Research, Warsaw for providing the necessary images for this research.

References

1. Abd-Elmoniem, K.Z., Youssef, A.-B.M., Kadah, Y.M.: Real-time speckle reduction and coherence enhancement in ultrasound imaging via nonlinear anisotropic diffusion. IEEE Transactions on Biomedical Engineering 49(9), 997–1014 (2002)
2. de Fontes, F.P.X., Barroso, G.A., Coupé, P., Hellier, P.: Real time ultrasound image denoising. Journal of Real-Time Image Processing 6, 15–22 (2011)
3. Eklund, A., Dufort, P., Forsberg, D., LaConte, S.M.: Medical image processing on the GPU – past, present and future. Medical Image Analysis 17, 1073–1094 (2013)
4. Kirk, D.B., Hwu, W.-M.W.: Programming Massively Parallel Processors. Elsevier (2010)
5. Loizou, C.P., Pattichis, C.S.: Despeckle Filtering Algorithms and Software for Ultrasound Imaging. Morgan & Claypool (2008)
6. Podlozhnyuk, V.: Image Convolution with CUDA. Nvidia (June 2007), http://docs.nvidia.com/cuda/samples/3_Imaging/convolutionSeparable/doc/convolutionSeparable.pdf
7. Rauber, T., Rünger, G.: Parallel Programming. Springer (2010)
8. Ruetsch, G., Micikevicius, P.: Optimizing Matrix Transpose in CUDA. Nvidia (January 2009), http://www.cs.colostate.edu/~cs675/MatrixTranspose.pdf

QWERTY- and *8pen*- Based Touchless Text Input with Hand Movement

Adam Nowosielski

West Pomeranian University of Technology in Szczecin
Faculty of Computer Science and Information Technology
Żolnierska 52, 71-210 Szczecin, Poland
anowosielski@wi.zut.edu.pl

Abstract. Natural user interface offer touchless and convenient medium for communication. Hands-free control of electronic devices is largely based on sophisticated methods of image processing and pattern recognition. While mouse alternative may be successfully achieved with the use of camera and body movements, the main problem is the text entry. New touchless interfaces are generally introduced for convenient manipulation in Graphical User Interface but casual text entry using the same medium of communication is still necessary. The problem of non-contact onscreen keyboard interface is addressed in the article. Two interfaces for touchless text input are proposed and compared. The first one uses standard onscreen QWERTY keyboard operated with hand movement in front of the camera. The second solution is the adaptation of a stroke-based text entry technique *8pen* [1] to touchless interface.

1 Introduction

Hands-free control of electronic devices by natural user interface is gaining more and more attention. New interfaces are mostly based on some kind of visual system and offer touchless and convenient medium for communication for the user. These solutions use sophisticated methods of image processing and pattern recognition.

Two most important tasks in human-computer interaction include text input and mouse control. It seems to be natural and convenient to interact with gestures with limited and adapted menus or to control character in the game. However, it becomes cumbersome with the text entry. In such cases the user is forced to use a physical device (i.e. keyboard) or use another solution such as a voice dictation. None of these is perfect since the user has to convert to different method of communication. The same medium of communication is expected to be used during the whole interaction. This is of particular importance in controlerless interface for large screens in public spaces or in homes. While hands-free mouse alternative may be successfully achieved with the use of camera and body movements, the main problem is the text entry. Casual short writing as one of the many elements of the touchless interface should be considered and addressed.

L.J. Chmielewski et al. (Eds.): ICCVG 2014, LNCS 8671, pp. 470–477, 2014.

The rest of the article is structured as follows. In Sect. 2 touchless techniques for input interfaces are considered. In Sect. 3 various techniques for text entry are presented. Section 4 describes two solutions proposed for touchless text input. Their evaluation and comparison are provided in Sect. 5. The article ends with a summary.

2   Touchless Techniques for Input Interfaces

There are several techniques for touchless interfaces and most popular of these include: computer vision approaches, eyetracking, speech recognition, brain computer interfaces.

Computer vision techniques offer new means for creating interfaces. The essential element of such systems is a camera which observes the user and his actions. There are solutions operating in visible or infrared light. Most systems track part of the body (hand, finger, head/face, mouth or eyes) or even the whole body. Some systems operate with the use of special marker. Special distinctive material or colour light source are used for easy foreground separation. Markers are usually placed on the selected part of the body.

Eyetracking offers sophisticated methods for capturing humans gaze direction. The most common eye trackers capture image of the pupil by a video camera sensitive to the infra-red spectrum. The eyes are exposed to direct invisible infra-red (IR) light and corresponding corneal reflections are measured enabling the estimation of observers gaze point [2]. The movement of the eyes is used: for activity analysis (usually off-line systems) or as control medium for human computer interaction (HCI) [3]. In the second case, eye movements replace traditional control devices: the mouse and the keyboard (e.g. Dasher [4] system to text entry for disabled).

Speech is another medium for input interfaces. Speech recognition technology has been a topic of research since the 1950s and is considered mature[5]. It is a significant medium in HCI having a great potential in dialogue systems, in device control (smartphones, operating systems) and used for dictation (eliminating the need to type). Voice to text solutions do not provide privacy and silence. However, there is an alternative in the form of silent speech. Silent speech interface operate in silence-required or high-background-noise environments [6]. It can be used as an aid for the speech-handicapped [6].

Brain-Computer Interfaces (BCI) constitute another group of solutions. BCI interfaces attract great attention with new proposals and prototypes being introduced. All solutions are based on the fact that any form of communication begins with the user's intent. Under normal conditions it activates certain brain areas and the nervous system transmits signals to the corresponding muscles. The BCI bypasses this process. Presence of specific patterns in a persons brain activity is analyzed. Measured brain activity associated with the users intent is converted into control signals for BCI applications [7].

3 Text Entry Methods

The first increased interest in text entry methods was connected with the office automation in 80's of. With the introduction of Graphical User Interfaces in 90's and with the spreading of mobile devices today it continues to be an important issue.

The most important feature of the keyboard is the layout. Modern keyboards are most often based on the QWERTY key arrangement designed in the 19th century. To make the text entry more efficient and ergonomic new alternatives are introduced. They tend to minimize finger path distance and make heavy use of the home row. The best-known alternative to QWERTY is the Dvorak keyboard. Another proposal is the Colemak. It bases on the QWERTY layout retaining position of many keys. All alternatives of full-sized keyboards share the same problem - difficulty of switching from well-known QWERTY layout and the need to learn new key arrangements.

With the increased interest in mobile devices new methods of text entry have been proposed. The key-based text entry is known from the first mobile phones where several letters are assigned to one physical key. Problems with ambiguity are obvious. Multi-tap and dictionary-based approaches are commonly used solutions. For finger-based and stylus-based text entry more techniques have been introduced. One of the first was shorthand handwriting recognition with simplified characters alphabet. *Unistroke* and *Graffiti* are recognized examples [8]. Another approach for entering text was *Quikwriting* [9]. To write a text the user moves from the centre to zones without lifting the stylus. Words are obtained with continuous gestures. In *SpeedScript* [10] there are two variants of keyboard layouts: smart and QWERTY. Both versions have special blue window (displayed as popup) for vowels and spaces. The need to reposition the pen is decreased since the window is displayed after selection of any letters. Special layouts designed for small mobile screens have also been introduced (e.g. *Opti*, *Fitaly*) but without spectacular commercial success. Users are reluctant to learn new key arrangement. Solutions that base on standard QWERTY layout (e.g. dictionary-based *Swype* [11]) gain most user interest.

4 Touchless Text Entry

Here, the problem of non-contact onscreen keyboard interface is addressed and two solution proposed. In each case the user operates with the hand movements. The first one processes a video stream from a webcam. User movements interpreted as gestures allow a key selection on the standard onscreen QWERTY keyboard. The second proposition is the adaptation of a stroke-based text entry technique *8pen* [1] to touchless interface. Proprietary *Kinect* sensor from Microsoft was used to track hand movements. Figure 1 presents a user interacting with the interface and enlarged layout of the interface itself (the *8pen* version). The details of both solutions are provided in the following sections.

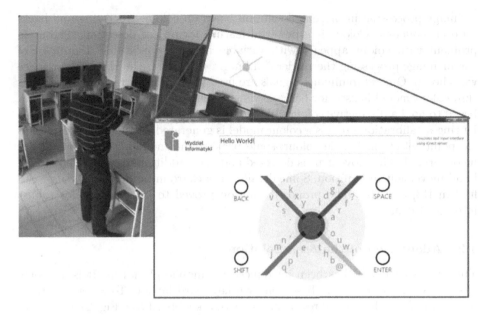

Fig. 1. Adaptation of the *8pen* solution for touchless screen

4.1 QWERTY Keyboard for Touchless Screens

The layout of the QWERTY keyboard is well-known and widely used. There is
no need for users to learn specific key arrangement. For this reason, the QW-
ERTY layout was used in the first solution. However, typing on this keyboard
requires a physical process of keystroke which is a problem in touchless interface.
The problem was solved with gesture interpreter. Each gesture consists of hand
movement in one of the four directions (left, right, top or down) and return to
the starting position (neutral position). Without the return new starting position is adopted. In this way, the user can freely move in front of the camera
without the need to stand still.

Selection of the appropriate letter is a two-step process and it consists of the
choice of the column and then a row on the QWERTY keyboard. The choice is
always made with the movement to the left or right side. Downward movement
is considered a confirmation while the upward movement is considered a can-
cellation. This procedure provides the text input using only moves in four basic
directions. After selecting the appropriate column (with left and right movements) the user approves the selection with downward motion. Then the user
selects the row (again with left and right movements) and confirms the choice
with the movement downward (or cancel the action with the upward gesture).
The row selection with left and right movement was indicated by some users at
first contact in interface learning stage as cumbersome. However, participants
agreed that accustomed it was no longer a problem.

Image processing in presented solution bases on colour processing and background modeling. Colour is a powerful feature for object detection. The main problem with colour appears with variable lighting conditions. Examples of colour image processing the reader can find in [12]. Here, the HSV colour space was chosen. Only chrominance signals are used (hue and saturation). By default skin-colour model is used for hand movement detection. However, the user is allowed to hold a distinctive colour object in hand which may be used as a marker. During a calibration process a colour model is generated automatically after single point selection. Beside colour, some background modeling mechanisms are incorporated. The movement is detected and used additionally in the process of hand movement recognition. Some details on background modeling the user can find in [13] and [14]. The proposed solution proved to be sufficient for robust interface testing.

4.2   Adaptation of the *8pen* Solution

The *8pen* solution [1] has been introduced for mobile platforms. It is a stroke-based text entry technique based on own keyboard layout. To enter a letter a user starts from the central region of the virtual keyboard (see Fig. 2) and moves in one of the four directions (top, down, left or right) thus selecting a sector with specially arranged letters. Which letter is selected depends on the further movement of the finger or pointer in the clockwise or anticlockwise direction. The number of sectors crossed in the turn indicates the successive letter on the boundary. Selection of the letters ends with the return to the center. Each letter is a loop and consecutive loops form a word which is entered with one continuous and fluid gesture [1]. The text entry method introduced in the *8pen* seems to be strange and surprising for new users.

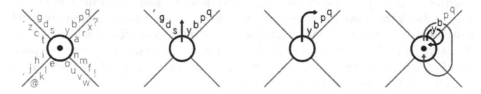

Fig. 2. Entering a letter on the *8pen* keyboard [1]

Text entry method introduced by the *8pen* is designed for touch screens. This raises an issue when the method is expected to be used on touchless screens. Special adjustment and modification need to be proposed. In touch screen a user can freely move the finger or pointer above the screen. The text entry begins with the touch on the center part of the keyboard. With the touchless interface hand movement of the user are recorded continuously. To distinguish the sequence of free hand movement from the sequence of text input the clench fist gesture has been introduced. When the user clenches fist text entry mode is activated.

5   Text Entry Methods Evaluation

It is difficult to compare studies on text entry performance since experimental data varies widely due to the use of different metrics and experimental designs [15]. Evaluations of text entry methods require the user to enter phrases of text while performance measures are gathered. The participant is usually instructed to write a text quickly and accurately [17]. The presented text and the transcribed text (produced by the user) are compared afterwards. There are three types of errors [16] [17]: substitutions, insertions, or deletions. The above errors can be seen as primitive operations required to convert the incorrectly entered text phrase to the correct one. The minimum number of these primitive operations for the given incorrect text is called the *Minimum String Distance (MSD)* [16]. What is more, a string can be transformed through more than one minimum set of transformations (alignments) [16] [17]. This uncertainty is adjusted by weighting the errors by the number of alignments in which they occurred [16]. Thus the error rate is calculated by dividing the error count by the average length of the alignments [16] [17]. Other error rate measures have also been introduced and the reader can find reference in [15].

There are three approaches of error correction in text entry experiments [15]: *none, recommended* and *forced* error correction. The *none* condition prohibits the participant to correct errors. In the *recommended* error correction, the participant is allowed to correct errors if he identifies them. With the *forced* condition participants are forced to correct each error. The effect of error correction conditions on the most common text entry performance metrics is presented in [15].

In our experiments we tested both propositions for touchless text input in forced error correction condition. There were 35 participants in the experiments, all of them computer science students, aged mostly 22-23 years. All participants were expert typist with fluent use of the QWERTY layout keyboard. Additionally, selection of participants was made among the candidates who do not have previous contact with the *8pen* keyboard.

All experiments were performed in front of the wall screen projector (see Fig. 1). Each participant was introduced at start to both interfaces with the task of typing a short text. After that, the participant proceeded to the proper experiment. Efforts were made to ensure a random selection of the first interface. As a result, approximately half of the participants began experiments with the QWERTY interface while the others with the *8pen*. All participants had the task to enter the same text in Polish (without diacritics) quickly and accurately (with the *forced* error correction condition). Forced correction of errors extends the process of text entry and ensures error-free resultant text. For these reasons, only the time of typing was measured. The results are provided in Fig. 3. The problem of errors was not addressed in this study.

The 35 participants took an average of 03:49 minutes for QWERTY and 02:06 minutes for *8pen* touchless text entry. The fastest text entry using QWERTY method was 02:33 minutes and it was slowest than the average for the *8pen* approach. The slowest text entry with the *8pen* (03:52) is almost equal of the average for the QWERTY approach (03:49). The QWERTY approach

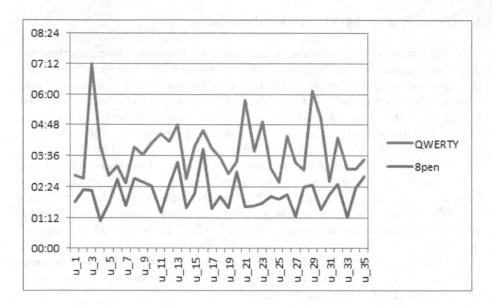

Fig. 3. Comparison of the *8pen* and QWERTY based interfaces

demonstrate higher values of standard deviation - 01:03 minutes to 00:38 in the *8pen*. It must be emphasized that for all participants the *8pen* approach was a novelty and they demonstrated faster writning skills.

6   Conclusions

The problem of non-contact onscreen keyboard interface has been addressed in the article and two solutions proposed. In both cases the user operates with the hand movements which are interpreted by each system. The first solution processes a video stream from a webcam and user movements interpreted as gestures allow a key selection on the standard QWERTY keyboard. The second proposition uses the *Kinect* sensor in visual system and the *8pen* [1] technique for text entry. In each case some adaptation for touchless text entry was required. Both solutions proved to work sable and efficiently.

Experiments conducted among 35 participants demonstrated some interesting results. All participants were expert typist with fluent use of the QWERTY layout keyboard. Additionally, they were selected from the candidates who did not have previous contact with the *8pen* keyboard. Despite these all participant demonstrated faster writing skills on the *8pen* keyboard. The process of entering a single character in the *8pen* solution consists of one continuous circular gesture. On the QWERTY approach usually a few gestures are required. The unfamiliarity of the *8pen* keyboard layout does not cause slower typing with gestures compared to QWERTY based solution.

References

1. 8pen (2014), http://www.the8pen.com/
2. Mantiuk, R., Kowalik, M., Nowosielski, A., Bazyluk, B.: Do-It-Yourself Eye Tracker: Low-Cost Pupil-Based Eye Tracker for Computer Graphics Applications. In: Schoeffmann, K., Merialdo, B., Hauptmann, A.G., Ngo, C.-W., Andreopoulos, Y., Breiteneder, C. (eds.) MMM 2012. LNCS, vol. 7131, pp. 115–125. Springer, Heidelberg (2012)
3. Jacob, R.J.K., Karn, K.S.: Eye tracking in human-computer interaction and usability research: Ready to deliver the promises. In: The Minds Eye: Cognitive and Applied Aspects of Eye Movement Research. Elsevier Science, Oxford (2003)
4. Dasher Project (2014), http://www.inference.phy.cam.ac.uk/dasher/
5. Rebman, C.M., Aiken, M.W., Cegielski, C.G.: Speech recognition in the human–computer interface. Information & Management 40(6), 509–519 (2003)
6. Denby, B., Schultz, T., Honda, K., Hueber, T., Gilbert, J.M., Brumberg, J.S.: Silent speech interfaces. Speech Communication 52(4), 270–287 (2010); Rebman, C.M., Aiken, M.W., Cegielski, C.G.: Speech recognition in the human-computer interface. Information & Management 40(6), 509–519 (2003)
7. Graimann, B., Allison, B.Z., Pfurtscheller, G.: Brain–Computer Interfaces: a gentle introduction. In: Graimann, B., Allison, B.Z., Pfurtscheller, G.(red.). (eds.) Brain Computer Interfaces Revolutionizing Human Computer Interaction. Springer Publishing, New York (2010)
8. Castellucci, S.J., MacKenzie, I.S.: Graffiti vs. Unistrokes: An empirical comparison. In: Proceedings of the ACM Conference on Human Factors in Computing Systems, CHI 2008, pp. 305–308 (2008)
9. Perlin, K.: Quikwriting: continuous stylus-based text entry. In: Proceedings of the ACM UIST 1998, pp. 215–216. ACM (1998)
10. SpeedScript (2014), http://www.speedscript.biz
11. Swype (2014), http://www.swype.com/
12. Bhattacharyya, S.: A Brief Survey of Color Image Preprocessing and Segmentation Techniques. Journal of Pattern Recognition Research 1(2011), 120–129 (2011)
13. Piccardi, M.: Background Subtraction Techniques: A Review. In: IEEE International Conference on Systems, Man and Cybernetics, vol. 4, pp. 3099–3104 (2005)
14. Bouwmans, T.: Recent Advanced Statistical Background Modeling for Foreground Detection: A Systematic Survey. Recent Patents on Computer Science 4(3), 147–176 (2011)
15. Arif, A.S., Stuerzlinger, W.: Analysis of text entry performance metrics. In: 2009 IEEE Toronto International Conference Science and Technology for Humanity (TIC-STH), pp. 100–105 (2009)
16. MacKenzie, I.S., Soukoreff, R.W.: A character-level error analysis technique for evaluating text entry methods. In: Proceedings of the Second Nordic Conference on Human-Computer Interaction, NordiCHI 2002, pp. 241–244 (2002)
17. Costagliola, G., Fuccella, V., DiCapua, M.: Interpretation of strokes in radial menus: The case of the KeyScratch text entry method. Journal of Visual Languages and Computing 24, 234–247 (2013)

Similarity Estimation of Textile Materials Based on Image Quality Assessment Methods

Krzysztof Okarma[1], Dariusz Frejlichowski[2], Piotr Czapiewski[2],
Paweł Forczmański[2], and Radosław Hofman[3]

[1] West Pomeranian University of Technology, Szczecin
Faculty of Electrical Engineering
26. Kwietnia 10, 71-126 Szczecin, Poland
okarma@zut.edu.pl
[2] West Pomeranian University of Technology, Szczecin
Faculty of Computer Science and Information Technology
Żołnierska 52, 71-210 Szczecin, Poland
{dfrejlichowski,pczapiewski,pforczmanski}@wi.zut.edu.pl
[3] FireFrog Media sp. z o.o.
Jeleniogórska 16, 60-179 Poznań, Poland
radekh@fire-frog.pl

Abstract. In this paper some experimental results obtained by the application of various image quality assessment methods for the estimation of similarity of textile materials are presented. Such approach is considered as a part of an artificial intelligence based system developed for the recognition of clothing styles based on multi-dimensional analysis of descriptors and features.

For the verification of the usefulness of image quality metrics for this purpose, mainly those based on the comparison of the local similarity of image fragments have been chosen. Nevertheless, since the most of them are applied only for grayscale images, various methods of color to grayscale conversion have been analyzed. Obtained results are promising and may be successfully applied in combination with some other algorithms used e.g. in CBIR systems. Since the analyzed metrics do not use any information related to shape of objects, further combination with shape and color descriptors may be used.

Keywords: textile recognition, image quality assessment, image analysis.

1   Introduction

Automatic estimation of clothing style similarity requires the analysis of various kinds of data. Recognition of the clothing style can be based not only on the image analysis methods but also utilize e.g. clustering of data expressed as experts knowledge. In order to obtain satisfactory results various approaches should be combined whereas a meaningful role is assigned to the analysis of image data. Nevertheless, the definition of a multi-dimensional similarity function based only

L.J. Chmielewski et al. (Eds.): ICCVG 2014, LNCS 8671, pp. 478–485, 2014.

on the image analysis may be insufficient for fully automatic clothing style esti-mation. However, similarity estimation of textile materials is possible and may be helpful as a relevant part of the whole system.

A fully automatic analysis of images representing persons wearing different clothes requires the application of several image analysis stages. The first ope-ration in such system is the detection of the person on the image plane. This task may be conducted using several approaches but it should be noticed that most of the methods based on the motion analysis and tracking which can be successfully applied e.g. for pedestrian detection in video surveillance systems may be useless for the analysis of static images. Many algorithms proposed by various researchers for people detection on images are dedicated to different applications e.g. related to solution of partially occluding silhouettes of moving persons, pedestrian detection for poor and changing lighting conditions, etc.

In the case of people detection on static images some other algorithms may be used, based on various descriptors e.g. the Histogram of Oriented Gradients (HOG) [3] or CENTRIST (CENsus TRansform hISTogram) [18].

After the extraction of the regions of images representing human bodies, the additional analysis of human pose would be necessary in order to locate the fragments representing different parts of clothing, conducting a specific kind of image segmentation. Such human pose estimation methods allow the divi-sion of the extracted human body representation into fragments corresponding typically, to head, torso, arms and legs. Combining the results with additional operations such as e.g. edge filtering allow the extraction of the shape informa-tion concerning the individual parts of outfit. For each of the image fragments representing such clothing parts, the similarity analysis with available reference textile patterns can be conducted leading to the extraction of the most similar textile materials for a specified fragment of the query image.

In this paper it is assumed that the above operations have been performed so the experiments are focused on the similarity estimation of the textile materials represented by extracted image fragments. For this purpose some popular simi-larity based image quality assessment methods have been applied. Since the most of state-of-the-art image quality metrics are typically dedicated for grayscale images and do not utilize the color information directly, the experiments have been conducted for different color spaces and popular color to grayscale conver-sion methods.

2   Texture Similarity Metrics

The analysis of textures is one of the typical problems in Content Based Image Retrieval (CBIR) systems since the similarity of images with different contents are typically compared i.a. considering the whole image as a texture or conduc-ting the segmentation before the comparison. Nevertheless, in most situations textures are represented by relatively high number of pixels so quite sophisti-cated methods can be successfully applied. Most of typical algorithms applied for texture recognition and classification purposes are quite demanding from the computational point of view so their applicability in the system comparing the clothing styles based on rather low resolution images captured from Internet social media seems to be limited.

Determining the image similarity, mostly for CBIR purposes, is typically applied using two major groups of methods. The first group is related to statistical analysis of some image features and probably the most popular approach is based on the co-occurrence matrices and classical Haralick features which can also be applied for color images [10]. Similar approach has also been considered for textile motifs [7], although resulting in computationally demanding algorithm. Some other methods are based on the correlation analysis for texture segmentation or Local Binary Patterns [8].

Another group of algorithms is based on the using spectral methods based on Fourier transform which are not directly related to texture features. Therefore such approach has been replaced by applications of wavelet decomposition [12] and Gabor filters with numerous modifications. Both approaches can also be combined leading to quite complex algorithms which are considered as not useful for assumed purposes.

An interesting idea, alternative both for spectral and statistical methods, is the use of structural methods, such as Structural Texture Similarity (STSIM) [14,21] or its modification denoted as STSIM2 [13].

Unfortunately, all the metrics discussed above are characterized by rather high computational complexity and require relatively high resolution texture information in order to assure good results. On the other hand, application of any of three kinds of texture descriptors defined in MPEG-7 standard also leads to unsatisfactory results.

Considering the idea of the STSIM, some common issues related to texture similarity and some of the image quality assessment methods can be noticed. One of them is the necessity of comparison of image structure, resulting in quite similar formulas used in the STSIM calculation and many previously defined image quality metrics. For this reason the application of chosen image quality assessment methods for simplified texture similarity estimation seems to be an interesting idea [9], especially considering possible combination with some other methods e.g. shape or color descriptors.

3   Image Quality Assessment Metrics Subjected to Experimental Verification

As the basic method chosen for the experimental verification in the project, the Structural Similarity (SSIM) metric proposed by Wang and Bovik [15] has been chosen. It is defined as the average of the local similarity indexes obtained for images x and y using the sliding window approach with the following formula, based on the local mean values, variances and the covariance:

$$SSIM = \frac{(2\bar{x}\bar{y} + C_1) \cdot (2\sigma_{xy} + C_2)}{(\sigma_x^2 + \sigma_y^2 + C_1) \cdot [(\bar{x})^2 + (\bar{y})^2 + C_2]}, \tag{1}$$

where the constants C_1 and C_2 are chosen typically as $C_1 = (0.01 \times 255)^2$ and $C_2 = (0.03 \times 255)^2$ in order to avoid any significant changes in the results, preventing only from the possible division by zero in flat and dark areas in the image.

Due to numerous modifications of the SSIM metric, the analysis of their image resolution requirements (for multi-scale extensions) and computational complexity has been performed as well as the necessity of some additional image analysis operations. Due to relatively high computational requirements and similar performance to standard SSIM metric, some of its modifications, such as Multi-Scale SSIM [17], Complex Wavelet SSIM (CW-SSIM) [11] or Information Weighting SSIM (IW-SSIM) [16], have been rejected from further experiments.

Considering the necessity of adjusting the edges for objects represented in compared images, metrics utilizing the division of images into regions representing edges, textures and smooth regions, such as Three-Component SSIM (3-SSIM) [5] or Four-Component SSIM (4-SSIM) [6] and similar extensions, have also been rejected.

As the result of the analysis of the state-of-the-art similarity based image quality metrics three additional proposals have been chosen: Gradient SSIM (GSSIM) with gradient images utilized for the structure and contrast comparison [2], variance-based metric denoted as Quality Index based on Local Variance (QILV) [1], Riesz based Feature Similarity (RFSIM) [20] and recently proposed Feature Similarity (FSIM) [19].

4   Description of Experiments and Verification Results

Since all the metrics, except the color version of Feature Similarity (referred to as FSIMc) are defined for grayscale images, they have been tested using different color to grayscale conversion methods. The 500 test images obtained from various Internet-based social media have been cropped to 32×32 pixels image fragments representing parts of clothing e.g. trousers or skirts. Then, the values of the SSIM metric have been calculated using six approaches: average of independently calculated metric's values for RGB channels, conversion to Y component according to ITU recommendation BT.601, using L component from CIELAB color space, average of independently calculated metric's values for CIELAB components, using value (V) from HSV color model and average of independently calculated metric's values for hue, saturation and value in HSV color space.

Considering the possibilities of using some more advanced color to grayscale conversion methods, their computational demands should be taken into account. An exemplary method which have been rejected for this reason is Color2Gray algorithm proposed in the paper [4].

In the second stage of experiments, the values of the modified SSIM index have been calculated obtained by changing the sliding window size from 11×11 to 8×8 pixels for the same six approaches to color analysis. Similar experiments have been also conducted for GSSIM, QILV and RFSIM metrics. For the FSIM metric, instead of the average of the values calculated for RGB channel, the values achieved using the original color implementation of the FSIMc metric have been calculated.

In order to limit the amount of presented data six representative textures have been chosen as query images corresponding to different textile materials: blue jeans (two different images), leather (3 images) or red pleated skirt. The original images and their cropped fragments are presented in Fig. 1.

Fig. 1. Example query images and their cropped fragments representing different textile materials

The chosen strategy of finding the most similar textile is similar to CBIR systems as several images with the highest values of the calculated similarity index have been chosen as the result and further verified with text descriptions of textile materials provided for each image. The results are visualized as images containing the cropped query image in the upper left corner and ordered 49 most similar textiles in view of each metric.

Since each found image is considered as positive or negative, the weighted accuracy can be determined for each image quality metric used in the experiments. Nevertheless, the most satisfactory results have been obtained using the HSV color model applied for the SSIM metric, especially for leather and jeans materials, as well as for QILV metric. For some of the test images satisfactory results can also be obtained using FSIM and GSSIM metrics, especially for the HSV color model (as the average of three metric's values).

Exemplary results obtained using some of the considered results have been presented in Figs. 2 - 5.

Fig. 2. Example results obtained for the SSIM metric using various approaches to color conversion - query image marked by a red rectangle and 9 closest matches in each row

Fig. 3. Example results obtained for the SSIM metric using various approaches to color conversion - query image marked by a red rectangle and 9 closest matches in each row

Fig. 4. Example results obtained for the QILV metric using various approaches to color conversion - query image marked by a red rectangle and 9 closest matches in each row

Fig. 5. Example results obtained for the FSIM metric using various approaches to color conversion - query image marked by a red rectangle and 9 closest matches in each row

5   Summary

Application of the image quality metrics for the extraction of similar textile materials on images leads to promising results. Nevertheless, obtained results are strongly dependent on the applied color model and color to grayscale conversion method. Since not all methods, both related to image quality assessment and color space conversions, can be considered as efficient enough in terms of computational demands, the obtained results are not perfect. Further increase of the recognition of similar clothes can be obtained by the combination of the presented methods together with some shape and color descriptors in order to analyze shape, color and structural information jointly.

Since the presented results have been obtained for low resolution images, often representing fragments of clothes of different physical size, the application of some additional image resizing algorithms based on the human pose estimation and detection of body parts would increase the recognition accuracy.

Acknowledgments. The project Construction of innovative recommendation based on users' styles system prototype: FireStyle (original title: Zbudowanie prototypu innowacyjnego systemu rekomendacji zgodnych ze stylami użytkowników: FireStyle) is the project co-founded by European Union (project number: UDA-POIG.01.04.00-30-196/12, value: 14.949.474,00 PLN, EU contribution: 7.879.581,50 PLN, realization period: 01.2013-10.2014). European funds – for the development of innovative economy (Fundusze Europejskie – dla rozwoju innowacyjnej gospodarki).

References

1. Aja-Fernandez, S., Estepar, R.S.J., Alberola-Lopez, C., Westiniu, C.F.: Image quality assessment based on local variance. In: Proc. 28th IEEE Int. Conf. Engineering in Medicine and Biology Society (EMBS), pp. 4815–4818 (2006)

2. Chen, G.H., Yang, C.L., Xie, S.L.: Gradient-based Structural Similarity for image quality assessment. In: Proc. IEEE Int. Conf. Image Processing (ICIP), pp. 2929–2932 (2006)
3. Dalal, N., Triggs, B.: Histograms of oriented gradients for human detection. In: IEEE Computer Society Conf. Computer Vision and Pattern Recognition (CVPR), vol. 1, pp. 886–893 (2005)
4. Gooch, A.A., Olsen, S.C., Tumblin, J., Gooch, B.B.: Color2gray: salience-preserving color removal. ACM Transactions on Graphics 24(3), 634–639 (2005)
5. Li, C., Bovik, A.: Three-component weighted structural similarity index. In: Proceedings of SPIE - Image Quality and System Performance VI, San Jose, California, vol. 72420, p. 72420Q (2009)
6. Li, C., Bovik, A.: Content-partitioned structural similarity index for image quality assessment. Signal Processing: Image Communication 25(7), 517–526 (2010)
7. Loke, K.S., Cheong, M.: Efficient textile recognition via decomposition of co-occurrence matrices. In: Proc. IEEE Int. Conf. Signal and Image Processing Applications (ICSIPA), pp. 257–261 (2009)
8. Ojala, T., Pietikäinen, M., Mäenpää, T.: Multiresolution gray-scale and rotation invariant texture classfication with local binary patterns. IEEE Trans. Pattern Anal. Machine Intell. 24(7), 971–987 (2002)
9. Okarma, K., Forczmański, P.: 2DLDA-based texture recognition in the aspect of objective image quality assessment. Annales UMCS - Informatica 8(1), 99–110 (2008)
10. Palm, C.: Color texture classification by integrative co-occurrence matrices. Pattern Recognition 37(5), 965–976 (2004)
11. Sampat, M., Wang, Z., Gupta, S., Bovik, A., Markey, M.: Complex wavelet structural similarity: A new image similarity index. IEEE Trans. Image Processing 18(11), 2385–2401 (2009)
12. Unser, M.: Texture classification and segmentation using wavelet frames. IEEE Trans. Image Processing 4(11), 1549–1560 (1995)
13. Žujović, J.: Perceptual Texture Similarity Metrics. PhD dissertation, Northwestern University, Evanston, Illinois (2011)
14. Žujović, J., Pappas, T.N., Neuhoff, D.L.: Structural similarity metrics for texture analysis and retrieval. In: Proc. 16 th IEEE Int. Conf. Image Processing ICIP, pp. 2225–2228 (2009)
15. Wang, Z., Bovik, A., Sheikh, H., Simoncelli, E.: Image quality assessment: From error measurement to Structural Similarity. IEEE Trans. Image Processing 13(4), 600–612 (2004)
16. Wang, Z., Li, Q.: Information content weighting for perceptual image quality assessment. IEEE Trans. Image Processing 20(5), 1185–1198 (2011)
17. Wang, Z., Simoncelli, E., Bovik, A.: Multi-Scale Structural Similarity for image quality assessment. In: Proc. 37th IEEE Asilomar Conf. Signals, Systems and Computers, Pacific Grove, California (2003)
18. Wu, J., Rehg, J.: CENTRIST: A visual descriptor for scene categorization. IEEE Trans. Pattern Anal. Machine Intell. 33(8), 1489–1501 (2011)
19. Zhang, L., Zhang, L., Mou, X., Zhang, D.: FSIM: A feature similarity index for image quality assessment. IEEE Trans. Image Processing 20(8), 2378–2386 (2011)
20. Zhang, L., Zhang, L., Mou, X.: RFSIM: A feature based image quality assessment metric using Riesz transforms. In: Proc. 17th IEEE Int. Conf. Image Processing (ICIP), pp. 321–324 (2010)
21. Zhao, X., Reyes, M.G., Pappas, T.N., Neuhoff, D.L.: Structural texture similarity metrics for retrieval applications. In: Proc. 15th IEEE Int. Conf. Image Processing (ICIP), pp. 1196–1199 (2008)

Lacunarity Based Estimator for the Analysis of Cell Nuclei from the Papanicolaou Smears

Dorota Oszutowska-Mazurek[1], Przemysław Mazurek[1], Kinga Sycz[2],
and Grażyna Waker-Wójciuk[2]

[1] West–Pomeranian University of Technology, Szczecin
Department of Signal Processing and Multimedia Engineering
26. Kwietnia 10 St., 71126 Szczecin, Poland
adorotta@op.pl, przemyslaw.mazurek@zut.edu.pl
[2] Independent Public Voivodeship United Hospital
Department of Pathomorphology
Arkońska 4 St., 71455 Szczecin, Poland
grazynka@blue.net.pl

Abstract. Computer aided medical diagnosis requires dedicated algorithms dependent on the content of acquired image. Cervical cytoscreening is cell nuclei and cytoplasm oriented. Lacunarity based estimator for cell nuclei texture analysis is proposed in the paper. The cell size in pre–classification is also applied as main criterion in discrimination. The application of lacunarity improves the separation between atypical and correct cells nuclei region with similar cells sizes. Five cases are tested related to the selection of proper color channel.

Keywords: Lacunarity, Image Analysis, Papanicolaou Smears, Cytology.

1 Introduction

Fractal geometry has a lot of applications [1], and biological objects image analysis is one of the active research areas. Cell nuclei are characterized by numerous parameters [2] and the fractal dimension (FD) is the coefficient that describes the complexity of the texture, even if the texture does not preserve self-similarity [3].

The estimation of parameters is essential for the supervised analysis of cells and for the automatic selection of the atypical cells. This pre–classification could be the important tool for improving of cell screening process. Identification of cervical intraepithelial lesions in a Papanicolaou screening test (Pap test) [4–6] is important, especially in women of reproduction age. Cytoscreening is a standard test for early detection of precancerous conditions, that could be effectively treated. The cell nuclei have different sizes [7]. The examples of cell nuclei are shown in Fig. 1.

1.1 Related Works

Many works are related to low magnifications ($100\times$ – objective $10\times$, and less then megapixel camera), so obtained results are insufficient due to lack of

L.J. Chmielewski et al. (Eds.): ICCVG 2014, LNCS 8671, pp. 486–493, 2014.

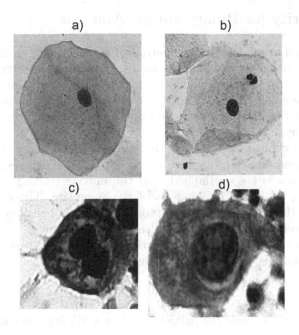

Fig. 1. Example images of cell nuclei (a,b – correct; c,d – atypical)

visibility of details and may provide to rejection of valuable estimation techniques. We use medium magnification (400× – objective 40×) and 5 megapixel camera so many details are visible and not omitted. Fractal dimension, that could be estimated using numerous techniques, is important factor in computer aided medical diagnosis [8–10]. Computer aided diagnosis needs dedicated image processing, including segmentation [11–14], also.

The Triangular Prism Method (TPM) [15], Tiled TPM [16], thresholded box–counting [17], variogram [18] as well as Area–Perimeter Method [19] are proposed for the fractal based analysis. The area of analysis (cell) is not square or rectangular, but irregular, and some techniques are not well fitted to such classes of objects.

1.2   Content and Contribution of the Paper

The proposed approach uses the lacunarity for binary images obtained using adaptive thresholding operation. The lacunarity shape is approximated using polynomial and one of the polynomial coefficient together with cell nucleus size are applied for the classification purposes. Lacunarity is introduced in Section 2, and the proposed estimation technique is considered in Section 3. The results for five cases of color channels are provided in Section 4. Discussion and final conclusions are provided in Section 5 and 6 respectively.

2   Lacunarity for Binary Image Analysis

Lacunarity could be applied for the analysis of 1D, 2D (images), 3D (volumetric objects). This analysis is based on the analysis grouping property of the object related to the object (ones) and holes (zeros) of the binary image. Grayscale image could be analyzed using directly or after a specific thresholding. In this paper adaptive thresholding is assumed and threshold criterion is the median value of the grayscale image.

The scale is defined as a side of the analysis box window applied to the image. Two approaches are applied for the analysis of images: the side–by–side window, that is not overlapped, and the moving (sliding) window where the overlapping is allowed by windows of the same size. The moving window is assumed in the paper, and this approach gives two behaviors: correlations between two overlapped windows and filtering of the result.

There are $r = R^2$ of pixels inside particular window ($R \times R$ resolution), so the following range is applied for the images:

$$s \in \langle 0, r \rangle. \tag{1}$$

The number of 1's inside the particular window W_i is computed:

$$s_i = \sum_i W_i, \tag{2}$$

where i is the index related to unique 2D position of the window.

The frequency of the occurrence of s–value for particular r is calculated successively using the following update formula:

$$n(s,r) \leftarrow n(s,r) + 1, \tag{3}$$

for the starting condition:

$$n(s,r) = 0. \tag{4}$$

The obtained frequency table n is transformed to the probability distribution (probability table) Q by the application of the following normalization:

$$Q(.,r) = \frac{n(.,r)}{\sum n(.,r)}. \tag{5}$$

This formula gives the proper distribution, so the following property is obtained:

$$\sum Q(.,r) = 1. \tag{6}$$

The calculation of lacunarity is based on the computation of two first moments for the distribution Q. The first moment is defined as:

$$Z_1(r) = \sum_i s_i Q(s_i, r), \tag{7}$$

and the second moment is defined as:

$$Z_2(r) = \sum_i s_i^2 Q(s_i, r).$$ (8)

The lacunarity $\Lambda(r)$ for the window $R \times R$ size is defined as:

$$\Lambda(r) = \frac{Z_2(r)}{[Z_1(r)]^2}.$$ (9)

The calculation is repeated for different window sizes and the maximal window size R_{max} is the half of the image side. This limitation is necessary, because the small number of cases (different positions of window) provides to low quality estimation. It is also connected with the phenomenon known as "fractal rabbits" [20], in which large scales may generate false result.

Obtained lacunarity is normalized $\Lambda_{norm}(r)$ and plot using double logarithmic plot (log10–log10). The normalization is necessary if the number of the 1's is different for multiple images, what is desired in typical applications:

$$\Lambda_{norm}(r) = \frac{\Lambda(r)}{\Lambda(1)}$$ (10)

The normalization is not necessary for fixed number of 1's for different images. A few synthetically generated images with different spatial properties are shown for example: randomly distributed, regularly distributed (b), clusters that are regularly distributed, and 2D fractal that is Cantor set with random component. Corresponding lacunarities are shown in Fig. 2 and the curves are specific for the appropriate spatial distribution classes.

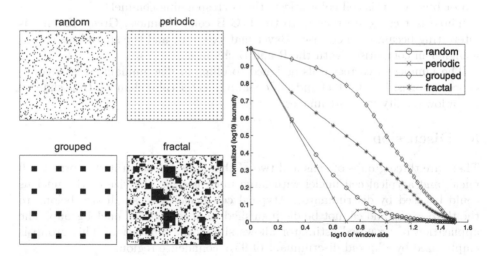

Fig. 2. Example images with different spatial properties and normalized lacunarity plots (log10–log10)

3   Proposed Estimator

The shape of the lacunarity is related to the specific classes of distributions so parametric approach is based on the approximation using polynomial. Third order polynomial is proposed:

$$\log_{10}(\Lambda(r)) = a_3 \left(\log_{10}(r)\right)^3 + a_2 \left(\log_{10}(r)\right)^2 + a_1 \left(\log_{10}(r)\right) + a_0, \qquad (11)$$

and the most important is the a_2 coefficient that is one of the important parameters for cells classification. The maximal window size is limited to the 10×10, because the variance of the cell nucleus sizes is large and the single technique of analysis is assumed for all cells. The small size is sufficient, because observed granularity is related to small scales.

The second parameter is the size of the cell nuclei, which is used during the analysis by cytoscreener.

4   Results

We use the database of separated cells nuclei classified as correct and atypical (there are many types of atypical cell nuclei types). There are 91 of correct and 59 of atypical cells nuclei from single pathomorphology laboratory in our database. Images have been acquired using AxioCamMRc5 color camera, that supports 2584×1936 resolution (5M pixels).

Five cases are tested (Fig. 3) related to the selection of proper channel. Images are color and converted to the grayscale, before adaptive thresholding. The first case is the grayscale image created from color channels using mean value. The channel switching case is based on properties of the images. Cells are stained in red or blue and this cell color selects the corresponding channel.

Three last cases are related to the R,G,B color channels. Green channel is interesting because camera used Bayer matrix sensor and the spatial resolution is higher in comparison with the R and B channels.

The number of correct cells assigned to ellipsoid discriminant of 95% confidence region is: $11, 13, 10, 11$ and 17 depending on the color channel. Blue channel has a low quality for most images.

5   Discussion

There are three groups of cells and two of them are well separated - correct cell nuclei and atypical cell nuclei with large nucleus size. The size of the nucleus could be used by discriminator. Atypical cell nuclei with small size belong to the third group and cannot be distinguished from correct cell nuclei group. The application of proposed estimator allows significant separation. This group is emphasized by ellipsoid discriminant of 95% confidence region.

The cells nuclei assigned to ellipsoid area should be carefully considered by cytoscreener as well as cells nuclei with large size. Computer aided cytoscreening using such pre–classification allows automatic detection of such cells. Even a single atypical cell nuclei is important for further histopathologic diagnosis.

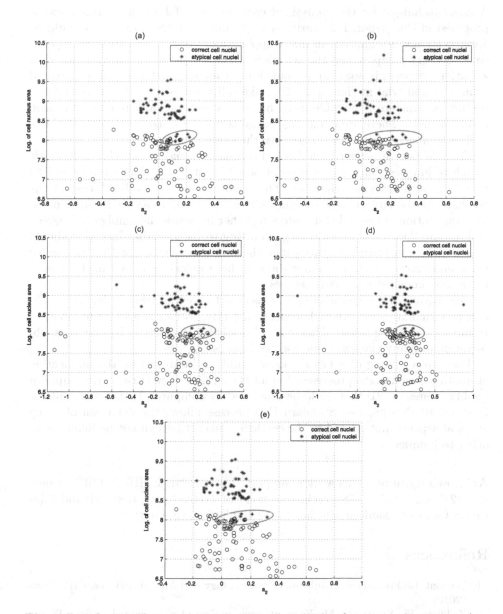

Fig. 3. Distribution of atypical and correct cell nuclei for the proposed estimator (a - grayscale image, b - channel switching, c - red channel, d - green channel, e - blue channel)

6 Conclusions

A novel technique for the analysis of color images of Pap smear cell nuclei is proposed in this paper. Lacunarity is very important technique, that could be applied for texture analysis in many applications. Images of biological objects, could be very complex and the selection of the important parameters for classification purposes is not simple. Some important parameters could be detected using test and trial method quite fast, like cell nucleus area. The estimation of texture parameters is possible using numerous methods and fractal dimension is one of them. There are numerous fractal techniques, like variogram, TPM as well as lacunarity, but they do not give the same values.

The selection of proper fractal based estimator could be based on automatic search techniques. Such exploration of possible estimators (solutions) could be based on optimization techniques. The problem is the possible fitting of the estimator to the particular set of images, so simple estimators are recommended. The application of multiple estimators together increases the number of Degree–of–Freedom (DoF) and provides to good fitting to the available data, that should be carefully considered. In this paper the minimal number of DoF is applied (two parameters only). The motivation of the application of cell nuclei area is the expert knowledge of cytoscreeners.

The texture of the cell nucleus is considered by cytoscreeners, but it is difficult to formulate such expert knowledge directly, so numerous texture analysis techniques could be tested. This expert knowledge is obtained by long time observation of many classes of microscopic images.

The cytoscreening of cervical cancer could be improved by the application of another preparation processes. Liquid Based Cytology (LBC) gives superior quality of images [21] that could be processed by computer, that is not available in standard Pap process. Standard Pap process allows the detection of many atypical aspects, not related to the cervical cancer, that can not be found using other techniques.

Acknowledgment. This work is supported by the UE EFRR ZPORR project Z/2.32/I/1.3.1/267/05 "Szczecin University of Technology – Research and Education Center of Modern Multimedia Technologies" (Poland).

References

1. Seuront, L.: Fractals and Multifractals in Ecology and Aquatic Science. CRC Press (2010)
2. Zieliński, K., Strzelecki, M.: Komputerowa analiza obrazu biomedycznego. Wstęp do morfometrii i patologii ilościowej. Wydawnictwo Naukowe PWN (2002)
3. Steven, I.: Linear Richardson plots from non-fractal data sets. Dutch Mathematical Geology 25 (6), 737–751 (1993)
4. Hoda, R., Hoda, S.: Fundamentals of Pap Test Cytology. Humana Press (2007)
5. Cibas, E., Ducatman, B.: Cytology. Diagnostic Principles and Clinical Correlates. Saunders Elsevier (2009)

6. Chosia, M., Domagała, W.: Cytologia szyjki macicy. Fundacja Pro Pharmacia Futura (2010)
7. IARC: Cytopathology of the urine cervix - digital atlas (2013)
8. Adam, R., Silva, R., Pereira, F., Leite, N., Lorand-Metze, I., Metze, K.: The fractal dimension of nuclear chromatin as a prognostic factor in acute precursor B lymphoblastic leukemia. Cellular Oncology 28, 55–59 (2006)
9. Metze, K.: Fractal dimension of chromatin and cancer prognosis. Epigenomics 2 (5), 601–604 (2010)
10. Ferro, D., Falconi, M., Adam, R., Ortega, M., Lima, C., de Souza, C., Lorand-Metze, I., Metze, K.: Fractal characteristics of May-Grünwald-Giemsa stained chromatin are independent prognostic factors for survival in multiple myeloma. PLoS ONE 6 (6), 1–8 (2011)
11. Hrebień, M., Korbicz, J., Obuchowicz, A.: Hough transform (1+1) search strategy and watershed algorithm in segmentation of cytological images. Advances in Soft Computing 45, 550–557 (2007)
12. Obuchowicz, A., Hrebień, M., Nieczkowski, T., Marciniak, A.: Computational intelligence techniques in image segmentation for cytopathology. Studies in Computational Intelligence 151, 169–199 (2008)
13. Frejlichowski, D.: Detection of erythrocyte cells in microscopy images. Electrical Review 88 (10b), 264–267 (2012)
14. Filipczuk, P., Wojtak, W., Obuchowicz, A.: Automatic nuclei detection on cytological images using the firefly optimization algorithm. In: Piętka, E., Kawa, J. (eds.) ITIB 2012. LNCS, vol. 7339, pp. 85–92. Springer, Heidelberg (2012)
15. Oszutowska-Mazurek, D., Mazurek, P., Sycz, K., Waker-Wójciuk, G.z.: Estimation of fractal dimension according to optical density of cell nuclei in papanicolaou smears. In: Piętka, E., Kawa, J. (eds.) ITIB 2012. LNCS, vol. 7339, pp. 456–463. Springer, Heidelberg (2012)
16. Oszutowska, D., Purczyński, J.: Estimation of the fractal dimension using tiled triangular prism method for biological non-rectangular objects. In: Electrical Review R.88 (10b), pp. 261–263 (2012)
17. Oszutowska–Mazurek, D., Mazurek, P., Sycz, K., Waker–Wójciuk, G.z.: Adaptive windowed threshold for box counting algorithm in cytoscreening applications. In: S. Choras, R. (ed.) Image Processing and Communications Challenges 5. Advances in Intelligent Systems and Computing, vol. 233, pp. 3–12. Springer, Heidelberg (2014)
18. Oszutowska–Mazurek, D., Mazurek, P., Sycz, K., Waker–Wójciuk, G.z.: Variogram Based Estimator of Fractal Dimension for the Analysis of Cell Nuclei from the Papanicolaou Smears. In: Choraś, R.S. (ed.) Image Processing and Communications Challenges 4. Advances in Intelligent Systems and Computing, vol. 184, pp. 47–54. Springer, Heidelberg (2013)
19. Mazurek, P., Oszutowska-Mazurek, D.: From Slit–Island Method to Ising Model – Analysis of Grayscale Images. Interational Journal of Applied Mathematics and Computer Science 24 (1), 49–63 (2014)
20. Kaye, B.: A Random Walk Through Fractal Dimensions. VCH (1994)
21. Bollmann, R.: Liquid-based cytology for risk-adapted cervical screening. Gynakol Geburtsmed Gynakol Endokrinol 4 (2), 164–180 (2008)

Detection of Vehicles in a Video Stream Using Spatial Frequency Domain Features

Wiesław Pamuła

Silesian University of Technology
Krasińskiego 8, 40-019 Katowice, Poland
wieslaw.pamula@polsl.pl

Abstract. The paper presents a method for detecting vehicles registered by a surveillance camera using their representation in spatial frequency domain. It mimics the operation of an optical processor with a ring-wedge detector (RWD). The values of the detector outputs constitute a time series of feature vectors. Chosen features, which are least sensitive to ambient light changes and strongly indicate the presence of vehicles are used as descriptors of the content of detection fields. When the values of the features surpass defined thresholds the field is regarded as occupied that is contains a vehicle. The choice of features is made by establishing statistical relations of the feature time series and corresponding reference vehicle presence data.

Keywords: vehicle detection, Fourier transform, ring-wedge detector.

1 Introduction

The term spatial frequency domain features is inextricably linked with optical processing. The idea of applying optical processing for object detection is investigated by researchers especially working in the field of target detection and tracking for military applications. Much work was done in the eighties, when the average processing power of computers was inadequate to calculate image transforms in real time [1], [2]. Diffraction patterns obtained by illuminating scene transparencies with laser light provide transform values with "the speed of light". Further processing is performed either by optical means or digitally after converting patterns to numerical data. Optical generation of combined test and template diffraction patterns or applying reference filters to test images gives direct indication of the presence of templates, i.e. objects in the scene. A hybrid approach utilizes auxiliary digital processing of transform values, which provides clues for objects presence.

The aim of the work is to develop an efficient algorithm for detecting vehicles on the approaches to traffic junctions. It may be an alternative solution to established vehicle videodetectors using background modelling. Adopted efficiency criteria include real time operation, highly parallelized computation exploiting logic resources instead of sequential processor based calculations. Implementation of FFT in logic circuits is well established and perfected since the introduction of specialized blocks such as MACs (multiply and accumulate unit) and

L.J. Chmielewski et al. (Eds.): ICCVG 2014, LNCS 8671, pp. 494–501, 2014.
© Springer International Publishing Switzerland 2014

DSP (digital signal processor) into the fabrics of field programmable gate arrays (FPGA). This potentially will enable the construction of video detector devices based on embedded circuits characterized by very high reliability of functioning.

The paper is organized as follows. Section 2 reviews works exposing the problems of utilising optical processing for object detection. Section 3 presents the main contribution of the paper that is the design of the vehicle detection algorithm. In the following sections the implementation results are discussed and concluded.

2   Related Works

Optical processing in pattern recognition takes advantage of generating diffraction patterns using coherent light passing though transparencies. Fig. 1. shows the basic setups of an optical processor. A coherent light source illuminates the spatial light modulator (SLM), which maps the input image. The modulated light is focused using L1 lens and a diffraction pattern of the depicted objects is formed on the focal plane (Fourier plane). The pattern is sampled using photo detectors or further optically processed using L2 lens to obtain data describing the objects on the input image. The aim of the processing is to recognize targets or classify the content of images. This is performed by filtering or finding correlograms.

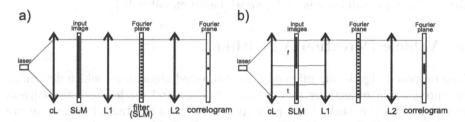

Fig. 1. Optical processor: a) Vander Lugt correlator, b) JCT - joint transform correlator

In the first case, fig. 1 a), the proper operation is determined by a precalculated matched filter, which is mapped by the SLM in the focal plane of L1 lens. Several methods of elaborating such filters were developed. Given a series of instances of a class, a Maximum Average Correlation Height (MACH) filter is designed to maximize a performance measure Average Correlation Height (ACH) while minimizing Average Similarity Measure (ASM) [3]. In practice, also other performance measures such as: Average Correlation Energy (ACE) and Output Noise Variance (ONV) are balanced to obtain an Optimum Trade-off (OT-MACH) filter to better suit different class characteristics. This procedure results in a two dimensional template that may express the general shape or appearance of a class of objects [4] [5].

The second setup fig. 1. b), may also be extended to a dual axis solution, works without the filter instead a compound diffraction pattern is formed using a pair of objects f, t depicted on the transparency [6]. One of the pair is the input image frame f and the other template t. If the frame contains examples of the template detection peaks appear on the correlogram after focusing with L2 lens.

This purely optical processing pipeline provides the results in the form of light patterns, which indicate target matches or object classes in the form of intensity peaks. These peaks are usually detected with photo detectors using simple thresholding techniques [7] [8].

Hybrid solutions of optical processors introduce digital processing at the focus plane of L1 lens. The diffraction pattern is sampled using a specialized photo detector and an A/D converter. George et al. introduced the ringwedge detector (RWD) having 32 annular rings and 32 radial sectors [9]. The outputs of the detector make up a feature vector, that represents the content of the image. Historically the main domains of applications are: recognition and classification of fingerprints, faces and tracking targets.

An important problem in using RWD is the optimization of the number and size of the detection areas. Ganotra et al. investigated the influence of the resolution of digital approximation of RWD on the error of face classification. Their work concludes that resolutions above the resolution of the SLM used do not contribute to better classification performance [13]. Niedziela and Cyran propose computer generation of RWD partitions for specific recognition tasks. The partitions are optimized in the course of selection of the feature space elements for feeding a probabilistic neural network based classifier [12].

3   Vehicle Detection Algorithm

The proposed algorithm, differently to established algorithms, which determine the presence of objects by subtracting a background model from the current frame, mimics the work of an optical processor from fig. 1a. All operations are carried out digitally in a pipeline as shown in fig 2. The image data is

Fig. 2. Vehicle detection algorithm

masked to extract detection fields. This is equivalent to applying a SLM. In the following stage the 2 dimensional FFT of the masked image $I(m, n)$ of the size $M \times N$ pixels is calculated:

$$F(p,q) = \sum_{m=0}^{M-1} [\sum_{n=0}^{N-1} I(m,n)e^{-j\frac{2\pi}{N}np}]e^{-j\frac{2\pi}{M}mq},$$
$$p = 0, 1, \ldots, N - 1, \quad q = 0, 1, \ldots, M - 1. \tag{1}$$

This frequency domain image is then centralized to obtain $F_c(p, q)$ so that the centre of the image corresponds to lower frequencies with the frequencies increasing away from the centre. This stage bears resemblance to the generation of the diffraction pattern using lens. The results are passed over to the RWD. The square modulus of FFT coefficients for each wedge and ring are accumulated. This is done for a ring R_j as follows:

$$R_j(r) = \sum_p \sum_q |F_c(p,q)|^2,$$
$$r \leq \sqrt{p^2 + q^2} < r + \Delta r \tag{2}$$

where: Δr is the width of the ring,
and for wedges W_i:

$$W_i(\varphi) = \sum_p \sum_q |F_c(p,q)|^2,$$
$$\varphi \leq \arctan(p/q) < \varphi + \Delta\varphi \tag{3}$$

where: $\Delta\varphi$ is the angular width of the wedge.

Square modulus is used as this represents the output of silicon sensor devices, which generate signals proportional to the power of the falling light. Such sensors are common in practical solutions of RWD circuits. R_j and W_i constitute the elements of the feature vector $f(R, W)$ generated by the RWD. In the last stage of the processing pipeline the state of the detection field is determined. This is done by comparing the values of particular feature elements with a predetermined threshold. Elements with higher than threshold values indicate the presence of objects, i.e. vehicles. The particular feature and detection threshold are defined in the course of finding statistical relations between the feature vector elements and reference detection data collected from registered video of road traffic.

Feature Selection for Vehicle Detection. The complex relations between features for describing the image content are usually captured using neural networks [12], [11]. This approach requires a careful selection of the network architecture and the associated training procedure.

The selection and training are sensitive to many factors which may impair the end result of describing the image content.

A different approach is presented in this work as the aim is less demanding than the description of content. The relation between the reference presence data and feature values was investigated and the following properties of the relations were established:

- time series of some wedge feature values resemble the graph of the states of the detection field,
- features with a high range of values over time indicate distinctly changes in the detection field,
- weak changes of feature values represent background illumination.

Fig. 3 gives examples of the time series of features collated with the graph of the presence data. There is no value legend as the graphs are appropriately scaled to enable a clear comparison.

$$R(f(i), p_v) = \frac{E[f(i) - \mu_f)(p_v - \mu_p)]}{\sigma_f \sigma_p} \tag{4}$$

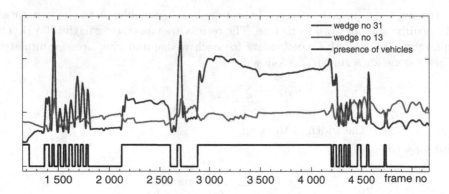

Fig. 3. Time series of RWD feature values compared with vehicle presence data

where: μ_f, μ_p are mean values, σ_f, σ_p are standard deviations of $f(i)$ - features, p_v - vehicle presence.

These initially determined properties are verified using statistical analysis. The goal is to find, which of the features most credibly indicate the presence of objects. The correlation coefficient $R(f(i), p_v)$ between the feature $f(i)$ and the detection field state p_v is used to evaluate the credibility (eq.4). It is assumed that there exists some linear dependency between these variables. Additionally feature values ranges are determined as a complementary measure of credibility.

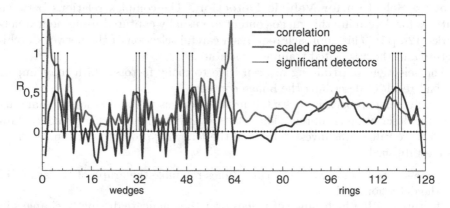

Fig. 4. RWD feature values

The graphs of correlation and ranges are overlaid in fig. 4. The superimposed peaks prove that the variables are consistent with each other and potentially indicate candidate features for vehicle detection. Features with highest correlation values are marked as significant detectors. Wedge features at the centre and on the edges of the wedge semicircle of the RWD are best suited for use in detection.

Ring features, apart from some placed near the centre of the RWD, are of little significance for detection.

Detection Threshold. The detection threshold is determined in parallel with the evaluation of the performance of candidate features for detection – significant detectors. Single features and pairs of features are tested. The threshold is determined by finding the value, which gives the lowest average error of mapping the presence of vehicles using the tested features. The search shows also, which of the features perform best and are least sensitive to the change of the threshold value.

4   Implementation Results

The native resolution of the video stream frames is 576×720 pixels. The frames are trimmed into square images $I(2^n, 2^n)$ of the size 512×512 in order to facilitate efficient FFT calculation. The image data is masked to extract detection fields, in the case of the tests there was one detection area marked on fig. 5 with a quadrangle. The size of the detection field is chosen to cover a whole average vehicle and some traffic lane background. Experiments with smaller fields proved less sensitive and prone to noise.

Fig. 5. Video frames of the test video stream

Consecutive images are transformed and the results are passed over to the RWD. The detector has the same size as the spectrum image which enables efficient calculation of features. It is a mask with marked detection areas, which is used to control the operation of summing up the values of the squared modulus of FFT coefficients. There are 64 rings and 64 wedges defined on the mask to enhance the capability of describing the image content and avoid ambiguous object clues. The RWD outputs feature vectors which are thresholded to determine whether the detection field is occupied. Successful detection of vehicles is done using single features or pairs of features out of the set of significant detectors as shown on fig. 4. The threshold value amounts to $1/3$ of the maximum of the feature values.

To illustrate the performance of the proposed detection algorithm the collected detection data was converted to road traffic flow rate values. The flow rates are compared to reference data extracted from the test films manually by human observers. In all over 50 hours of films were used for tests. The representative test stream consists of over 400 thousand frames of video. It is a compilation of film sequences from several days of road traffic observation. Fig. 5 shows examples of the stream frames: the left frame was registered on a rainy and cloudy day during low traffic, the centre frame depicts an average scene with two distinct vehicles, the right frame is highly disrupted by light reflections and additionally corrupted by oversaturated sensor pixels forming bright vertical lines. The test site is situated on a street with moderate traffic. Traffic peaks and stalls can be observed. Part of the traffic lane gets covered by moving shadows of nearby buildings.

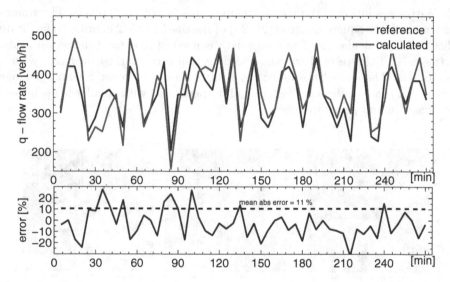

Fig. 6. Traffic flow rate graphs a) reference values, manually collected traffic data, b) derived from detection data based on spatial frequency features

Fig. 6 presents an example of a 4.5 hour test of the traffic flow measurements using the prepared test stream. The measured and reference flows are superimposed. The first part of the flow graphs (up to 120 min) presents the traffic flow with changing sunlight the rest traffic on a rainy day. About the 30 and 100 minute one can note substantial discrepancies, a detailed check reveals traffic stalls. One can conclude that the chosen feature represents fine details in the detection field and when vehicles tightly queue, one behind the other, the image of this lacks details, which leads to bad detection. The lower part of fig. 6. Shows the error of determining traffic flow in the test. The average value of absolute error amounts to 11%. Higher errors are in the first part of the test which was done in sunny conditions and with stalls of traffic.

5   Conclusions

The application of a RWD, usually used in optical processing, for the detection of vehicles proves to be successful. The core operation of the proposed algorithm is the calculation of the FFT, other operations include: accumulating of values and simple thresholding of the accumulated data. The characteristics of modules implemented in FPGA fabric, of the components performing these operations, cautiously permit to expect a complete device to operate in real time.

References

1. Ambs, P.: Advances in Optical Technologies: A 60-Year Adventure, Optical Computing, Vol. 2010, Article ID 372652, 1–15 (2010)
2. Cristobal, G., Schelkens, P., Thienpont, H.: Optical and Digital Image Processing: Fundamentals and Applications John Wiley and Sons, pp. 1–986 (2011)
3. Johnson, O.C., Edens, W., Lu, T., Chao, T.-H.: Optimization of OT-MACH filter generation for target recognition. In: Proc. SPIE, Optical Pattern Recognition XX, Pattern Recognition XX, vol. 7340 (2009)
4. Zhou, H., Chao, T.-H.: MACH filter synthesizing for detecting targets in cluttered environment for gray-scale optical correlator. In: SPIE, vol. 229, pp. 399–406 (1999)
5. Niedziela, T., Cyran, K.A.: Automatic recognition of the type of road vehicles with the use of optimised ring-wedge detector and neural network. Archives of Transport 18, 23–36 (2006)
6. Lee, T.C., Rebholz, J., Tamura, P.: Dual-axis joint-Fourier transform correlator. Optic Letters 4, 121–123 (1979)
7. Harasthy, T., Ovsenk, L., Turn, J.: Current summary of the practical using of optical correlators. Acta Electrotechnica et Informatica 12(4), 30–38 (2012)
8. Konnik, M.V., Starikov, S.N.: The use of a consumer grade photo camera in opticaldigital correlator for pattern recognition and input scene restoration. Optics Communications 282, 4210–4219 (2009)
9. George, N., Thommasson, J.D., Spindel, A.: Photodetector light pattern detector. US patent 3689772 (1972)
10. Fitz, A.P., Green, R.J.: Fingerprint classification using a hexagonal fast Fourier transform. Pattern Recognition 29, 1587–1597 (1996)
11. Trujillo, L., Pinto-Fernandez, S., Diaz-Ramirez, V.H.: Advances in Adaptive Composite Filters for Object Recognition. In: Kypraios, I. (ed.) Advances in Object Recognition Systems, InTech 2012, pp. 91–110 (2012)
12. Cyran, K.A., Niedziela, T.: Opto-electronic method of pattern recognition of motor vehicles in spatial frequency domain. Archives of Transport 21, 27–47 (2009)
13. Ganotra, D., Joseph, J., Singh, K.: Neural network based face recognition by using diffraction pattern sampling with a digital ring-wedge detector. Optics Communications 202, 61–68 (2002)

Accelerated Connected Component Labeling Using CUDA Framework

Fanny Nina Paravecino and David Kaeli

Northeastern University, Boston MA 02115, USA
fninaparavecino@coe.neu.edu, kaeli@ece.neu.edu

Abstract. Connected Component Labeling (CCL) is a well-known algorithm with many applications in image processing and computer vision. Given the growth in terms of inter-pixel relationships and the amount of information stored in a single pixel, the time to run CCL analysis on an image continues to increase rapidly. In this paper we present an accelerated version of CCL using NVIDIA's Compute Unified Device Architecture (CUDA) framework to address this growing overhead. Our parallelization approach decomposes CCL while respecting all global dependencies across the image. We compare our implementation against serial execution and parallelized implementations developed on OpenMP. We show that our parallelized CCL algorithm targeting NVIDIA's CUDA can significantly increase performance, while still ensuring labeling quality.

Keywords: connected component labeling, CUDA, HYPER-Q, dynamic parallelism.

1 Introduction

Image analysis plays an important role in many applications in biomedical, manufacturing and security applications. Connected Component Labeling has been used to identify blobs or regions in a graph. In many of these applications, the graph represents the contents of an image. Different approaches of Connected Component Labeling have been proposed [1,3,5].

Parallelization has been used effectively in image analysis implementations to accelerate a number of data-parallel tasks. Image analysis is typically easily parallelized, especially given the large amount of data that typically needs to processed using a common set of operations. Previous work has focused on parallelization of CCL [2,4], even though CCL involves some global synchronization. While speedups can be achieved, synchronization limits the amount of speedup that can be achieved.

However, recent advances in parallel architectures, such as NVIDIA's Kepler graphics processor [7], have improved support for the class of global synchronization operations present in CCL. The focus of our work here is to exploit this parallelism and global synchronization mechanism effectively. We present a new implementation of CCL which offers better performance compared against previous serial and parallel approaches [6].

L.J. Chmielewski et al. (Eds.): ICCVG 2014, LNCS 8671, pp. 502–509, 2014.

CCL has been using in a number of image analysis settings. Specifically, in the field of physical security, there are particular tasks such as luggage scanning at airports that require near real-time response with a very high rate of accuracy. Labeling is one of the first steps in the scanning pipeline; the accuracy of labeling will strongly affect the quality whole system. Unfortunately, labeling is a time-consuming operation. For this reason, we propose an efficient parallel CCL implementation which leverages the parallel architecture of NVIDIA's Kepler using the CUDA programming framework.

This paper is organized as follows. In the next section we review the state of the art in CCL algorithms, as well as consider previous work on parallel implementations. In Section 3, we review the Kepler GK110 architecture (equipped with compute capability 3.5), the target system used in our evaluation. In Section 4, we present the proposed algorithm and in Section 5 present results of running CCL on Kepler and compare against a serial implementation and a parallel OpenMP implementation. Finally, we conclude the paper in Section 6, and discuss directions for future work.

2 Connected Component Labeling

Connected Component Labeling utilizes hierarchical data structures and union-trees. CCL can be applied to graphs or images. When used on an image, typically CCL uses two scans of an image and performs an analysis of every pixel [4]. There has been previous work that attempts to perform a single scan of the image [3], but this form of CCL lacks inherent parallelism, making it difficult to tune execution efficiency.

When working with images, the CCL algorithm begins by labeling each pixel of an image I based on its neighbors. If a pixel belongs to the background, the label 0 is assigned to it. If the pixel is not part of the background, its label is determined by the labels of the neighboring pixels. In a sequential implementation of connectivity, we would consider the $North$ and $West$ pixels first in order to determine X's label. CCL constructs a tree in the first scan, by choosing a root label for the region. Then CCL performs a second scan, updating temporary labels based on their smallest neighboring labels.

There have been a number of attempts improve performance of CCL [1,2,3,4,5]. Stripe-based Connected Component Labeling [1] makes 3 passes over the image, performing: 1) *stripe extraction representation* during the first pass, 2) *stripe union* during the second scan, and 3) *label assignment* during the final step. The first scan can be run in parallel, processing multiple rows concurrently. However, the *stripe union* phase runs a *find root* task which explores all regions until a root label is found. This exploration is inherently sequential, and therefore very costly.

Klaiber et al. presented a memory-efficient parallel single pass CCL implementation targeting an FPGA [4] in 2012. Their improved the execution speed of Bayley et al.'s Single Pass CCL FPGA-based earlier implementation [3], reducing overhead due to memory allocation of labels while searching regions.

When processing large images, they tiled images into small slices and evaluated neighbors between slices. This approach reduced the memory requirements significantly.

A fast CCL implementation was presented in [5]. The regions are connected at region boundaries, which are identified during the second scan. This approach considers performing only a half scan, since in the previous step the image was divided into subregions and they used these subregions to merge components using boundary overlaps. The disadvantage of this approach is it inherently sacrifices accuracy. The approach uses semi-supervised learning, since the user needs to calibrate which regions she would like to segment.

2.1 GPU-Based CCL Implementations

Previous work has evaluated a GPU-based implementation [2] which builds off of a classical hierarchical structure, generates a root label for each component, locally merges them using block-based division of the image, and then performs a global merge to rejoin blocks. Since the *local merge* can be run in parallel, an *atomic* operation is used to control the many threads updating the same pixel label. Atomic operations impact performance due to thread waiting, and the multi-step merging process increases the number of memory accesses.

In [10] Mehta et al. presented a parallel implementation of a video surveillance algorithm run on a NVIDIA GPU using CUDA. Their CCL implementation divides input video frames into tiles and computes labels sequentially. To merge tiles, they choose the heaviest label from among the different tiles.

Riha et al. presented a promising GPU-based implementation of CCL using a single scan of an image [11]. Their approach creates an intermediate dynamic structure to store properties of groups of pixels on a per row basis. Their approach is very close to our own, though in their design, in order to merge and create the objects they need to run an extra step to update the connections between contiguous rows. The main problem with their approach is the sequential update of properties for every object in their dynamic structure.

3 NVIDIA's Compute Unified Device Architecture (CUDA)

With the advent of GPU computing, a number of computational barriers have been overcome, enabling researchers to push the limits of applications that were previously limited by performance. GPU computing architectures have been used across a wide range of applications [6]. NVIDIA's previous generation of GPUs, the Fermi family, has been used in a number of applications, promising peak single-precision floating performance of up to 1.5 TFLOPS. However, NVIDIA's Kepler GK110 GPU offers more than 3.5 TFLOPs of single-precision computing capability. The newest features provided on the Kepler enable programmers move a wider range of applications to the CUDA framework [8].

3.1   Kepler Advanced Features

Given the level of sophistication provided in the Kepler, we have focused our work on accelerating CCL while run on this particular architecture. Two new features, introduced on the Kepler GK110, are utilized in our approach:

1. Dynamic Parallelism: Kepler adds the capability to launch child kernels within a parent kernel. One typical pattern in sequential algorithms arc nested loops. Dynamic parallelism allows us to implement a nested loop with variable amounts of parallelism.
2. Hyper-Q: Kepler provides the ability to run multiples kernels assigned to different streams, concurrently. The Kepler GK110 supports up to 32 concurrent streams (as compared to 16 on the Fermi). Each stream is assigned to a different hardware queue.

Additional features included on the Kepler GK110 include texture memory, pinned memory, coalesced memory accesses, and new block/thread settings. Many of these features will be exploited in order to produce our optimized CCL implementation.

4   Accelerated Connected Component Labeling

The neighborhood operations present in CCL make it challenging to parallelize. We must modify the structure of the underlying algorithm if we want to exploit the massive thread-level parallelism present on the Kepler. Stripe-based CCL [1] modifies the first step of the algorithm by using row-level parallelization. We followed this approach in our design, but instead of only working on two rows at a time, we launched as many threads as rows in the image (I) during the first scan.

Formally, our Accelerated CCL (ACCL) uses two scanning phases, but our second phase simply updates a matrix that is half the size of the original image I. An intermediate stage reduces the size of labels associated with I.

4.1   Phase 0: Find Spans

We define a span as a group of pixels that have the same intensity in image I, and are located contiguously in the row. The structure of a span has two elements (y_{start}, y_{end}), which correspond to the column indices of the *starting* pixel and the *ending* pixel, respectively. $span_x$ defines a span in row x, and it is defined as follow:

$$span_x = \{(y_{start}, y_{end}) | I_{(x, y_{start})} = I_{(x, y_{start+1})} = \ldots = I_{(x, y_{end})}\} \quad (1)$$

An intermediate matrix stores spans on a per row basis. Once a span is found, a label is immediately assigned to the span in matrix L. Matrix L has half the number of columns of I, since labels are only associated with spans, not pixels. Processing I in this fashion, we reduce the number of updates performed during *Phase 1*.

A kernel *findSpans* is launched with as many threads as rows in the original image I. Each thread will process its corresponding row and fill the *Spans* matrix with indices. At the same time, the *Label* matrix L is assigned values found for each span. Figure 1 shows the behavior of this kernel.

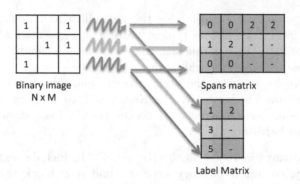

Fig. 1. The flow of the *findSpans* kernel

Our grid configuration attempts to maximize GPU occupancy. We launched 256 threads per block, where each image allocates 2 blocks. We can process up to 8 images per SMX before reaching full occupancy.

4.2   Phase 1: Merge Spans

In order to reduce the time taken for the *Union-Find* phase (which involves an exploration of previous regions to find the root), we record in matrix L the corresponding root label associated with each span.

Our second kernel *mergeSpans* joins two spans from contiguous rows, only if the indices of the spans overlap and both spans have the same intensity.

$$merge(span_x, spans_{x+1}) = \begin{cases} 1 & \text{merge if indexes } span_x \text{ and } span_{x+1} \text{ overlap} \\ 0 & \text{skip otherwise} \end{cases}$$

If the condition described above is satisfied, a *child* kernel is spawned with the one thread per label in L. These threads will update the respective labels of the newly added segment. Figure 2 shows the memory access pattern when the child kernel is launched. Spawming is enabled exploiting dynamic parallelism, which only became available in CUDA compute capability 3.5. The time to update multiple labels is the same as to update one single element of matrix L. We set up two grid configurations for this kernel. The parent kernel associates one block per image. The child kernel has 256 threads per block and 512 blocks.

Most of the memory accesses generated from threads of the same block perform read-only accesses of contiguous memory locations. This memory behavior is well-suited for the GPU *texture memory*. Texture memory is a read-only memory that is cached on-chip on the GPU. Utilizing texture memory can speed-up data transfer when threads of the same block access contiguous memory locations.

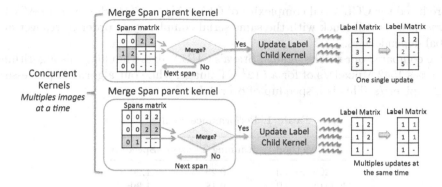

Fig. 2. The flow of the *mergeSpans* kernel

5   Performance Results and Analysis

Next, we present results of running real-world applications on an NVIDIA GK-110. Our experiments use DICOM images [9] of actual luggage scanned at airports. Each DICOM set contains more than 700 images (512x512) of the same luggage. All images were binarized and simplified (see Figure 3), even though ACCL works well with varying intensity values.

Our experiments were run on an Intel Core i7-3770K processor and with a NVIDIA GTX Titan GPU, compute capability 3.5 and CUDA 5.5. We used gcc compiler 3.7 and OpenMP 3.0.

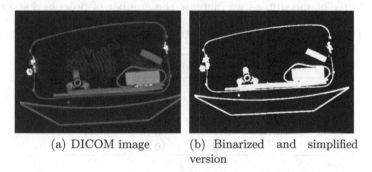

(a) DICOM image   (b) Binarized   and   simplified
version

Fig. 3. The input image used in this work

We provide results for optimized serial, OpenMP and CUDA implementations in Table 1, all achieving the same labeling accuracy. Computation was recorded for one image at a time. The OpenMP configuration that uses two threads and shared memory for matrix L obtains the best performance.

We can see that our proposed parallel ACCL algorithm achieves an average speedup of 5x over CCL serial. Our parallel implementation ACCL reduces the complexity of *Phase 0* from CCL Serial $O(N*M)$, where N and M are rows and columns of input matrix, to $O(N)$. Furthermore, for the relabeling in *Phase 1*, we reduced the CCL serial complexity of $O(N * M)$ to $O(1)$. However, in ACCL *mergeSpans* is still stuck with the same serial complexity in order to respect all global dependencies.

We compared our results against Stava's CUDA algorithm [6]. This algorithm processes 1542 Mpixels/s of for a 512^2 CT image, while our algorithm processes 5242 Mpixels/s. This is a speedup of over 3.3x.

Table 1. Performance results

Method	Running Time(s)	Speedup
CCL Serial	0.25	1.00x
CCL OpenMP	0.18	1.39x
ACCL	0.05	5.00x

In Table 2 the runtime our ACCL implementation using NVIDIA's Hyper-Q feature for processing multiple images concurrently is compared to the serial CCL runtime. Since we are using dynamic parallelism, there is a limitation in terms of the hardware, which restricts the number of child kernel threads that can be spawned. In the case where multiple images are processed concurrently, child kernel threads will not be able to be spawned, and labeling quality may suffer. In order to maintain labeling accuracy, we have added a sequential loop inside of the child kernel, and thus reduced the number of child kernel threads spawned. Adding the sequential loop reduces the speedup of our implementation (as is seen in Table 2 for Stream 1). Introducing the loop allows us to use the Hyper-Q feature effectively to process multiples images in parallel, and therefore achieve a degree of speedup as we increase the number of processed streams.

Table 2. Performance results comparing ACCL with Hyper-Q against CCL Serial

#Streams	CCL Serial(s)	ACCL(s)	Speedup
1	0.25	0.05	5.00x
2	1.08	0.10	10.80x
3	2.16	0.14	15.36x
4	4.18	0.19	21.44x
5	6.09	0.23	25.91x

We further investigated the cause of slowdown related to the loop added in the child kernel. Due to the nature of *mergeSpans* (parent kernel), a sequential analysis explores all spans. Thus, complexity of *mergeSpans* is $O(N * M)$. Since complexity of the child kernel is now increased from $O(1)$ to $O(M)$, the overall complexity of parent kernel becomes $O(N * M^2)$. Therefore, performance slowdown is reflected for stream 1.

The speed-up of any implementation that utilizes multiple streams greatly depends on the number of concurrent streams running, and partially depends on the image structure. As more streams run concurrently, we can continue to see benefits, though the speedup begins to tail off. The ideal performance for

Hyper-Q would be linear speedup (in the number of concurrent streams), but the work distributor inside the GPU starts distributing blocks as soon as the kernel is launched. If one kernel dominates the GPU, based on the intensity of the kernel (which is the case for our implementation for dynamic parallelism), then the second kernel will have to wait until first kernel is completed, at which point the second kernel can start execution. Thus, in this case we will only see a small amount of concurrent parallelism.

6 Conclusion

In this paper we presented Accelerated Connected Component Labeling (ACCL) using the CUDA framework. We experimented with new features of the NVIDIA Kepler GPU. Our proposed algorithm achieves improved performance versus prior serial and OpenMP parallel implementations. We also compared the serial CCL to processing multiples images concurrently using Hyper-Q running ACCL. The results showed that our algorithm could scale well as long as we increased the number of streams.

One interesting observation related to the parallelized algorithm we have presented here is that while dynamic parallelism improves performance for a small number of child kernels, it turns out to be a disadvantage when trying to use a larger number of child kernels. Hyper-Q, with dynamic parallelism, provides some benefits, but is not a perfect match for ACCL to scale performance.

References

1. Zhao, H.L., Fan, Y.B., Zhang, T.X., Sang, H.S.: Stripe-based connected components labelling. Electronics Letters 46(21), 1434–1436 (2010)
2. Oliveira, V., Lotufo, R.A.: A study on connected components labeling algorithms using GPUs. XXIII Sibgrapi, Graphics, Patterns and Images (2010)
3. Bailey, D., Johnston, C.: Singles Pass Connected Components Analysis. Image and Vision Computing (2007)
4. Klaiber, M., Rockstroh, L.Z., Wang, B.Y., Simon, S.: A memory-efficient parallel single pass architecture for connected component labeling of streamed images. Field-Programmable Technology (FPT), 159–165, 10–12 (2012)
5. Paralic, M.: Fast connected component labeling in binary images. In: 35th Telecommunications and Signal Processing (TSP), vol. 709, pp. 3–4 (2012)
6. Hwu, W.-M.: GPU Computing Gems Emerald Edition. M. Kaufmann (2011)
7. NVIDIA's Next Generation CUDA Compute Architecture Whitepaper: Kepler GK110. Nvidia (2013)
8. Foley, J.: Migrating your code from Tesla Fermi to Tesla K20X, with examples from QUDA Lattice QDC library. Microway, Inc. (2013)
9. National Electrical Manufacturers Association: Digital Imaging and Communications in Medicine (DICOM)., http://medical.nema.org/standard.html
10. Mehta, S., Misra, A., Singhal, A., Kumar, P., Mittal, A., Palaniappan, K.: Parallel implementation of video surveillance algorithms on GPU architectures using CUDA. In: 17th IEEE Int. Conf. Advanced Computing and Communications, ADCOM (2009)
11. Riha, L., Manohar, M.: GPU accelerated one-pass algorithm for computing minimal rectangles of connected components, pp. 479–484. IEEE Computer Society Press (2011)

Head Pose Estimation Relying
on Appearance-Based Nose Region Analysis[*]

Krzysztof Pawelczyk[1] and Michał Kawulok[2,1]

[1] Future Processing, Bojkowska 37A, 44-100 Gliwice, Poland
[2] Institute of Informatics, Silesian University of Technology
Akademicka 16, 44-100 Gliwice, Poland
kpawelczyk@future-processing.com, michal.kawulok@polsl.pl

Abstract. In this paper we explore the possibilities of recognizing head orientation based on the appearance of the nose. We demonstrate that the features extracted from that region possess high discriminating power with regards to the head orientation. Extensive experimental validation study, performed using the benchmark data, confirmed high effectiveness of the proposed approach compared with the baseline techniques that rely on the analysis of the entire facial region.

1 Introduction

Head pose estimation [15] consists in recognizing vertical and horizontal angles of a human head, given its coarse location in an input image. Recognition of the head pose is closely related to detecting the gaze direction [8], as people naturally turn their head towards an object they are looking at. However, there is a substantial difference in terms of the methods that are used to solve these problems. The gaze detection systems analyze the eye region, whilst the head estimation is based on global head features. The former require images of high resolution and quality, while the latter may operate well even with low-quality images, or when a person is far from the camera. There are numerous applications of head pose estimation, including human-computer interaction, surveillance and security, driver awareness monitoring, automatic video annotation, and more [7].

Recognition of the head pose is an active research topic which receives considerable attention from the computer vision community. The existing methods assume that the entire face area is visible in the image and they are highly sensitive to occlusions. First of all, the occlusions affect face and facial feature points detection, and they also modify the appearance-based features that are used by many methods. In the work reported here, we explore the possibilities of estimating the head pose exclusively based on the nose region, which we detect independently on the face detectors. Naturally, face detection may increase the accuracy of our nose detector, but its intrinsic effectiveness is not affected

---

[*] This work has been supported by the European Regional Development Fund under Operational Programme Innovative Economy 2007-2013, based on the Agreement No. UDA-POIG.01.04.00-24-138/11-01.

L.J. Chmielewski et al. (Eds.): ICCVG 2014, LNCS 8671, pp. 510–517, 2014.

when the face region is partially occluded, provided that the nose is visible. Our work was motivated by the need for counting people watching certain visual material (e.g., an advertisement), and measuring the time they are focused on it. The paper presents the results of our feasibility study which shows that head orientation can be estimated relying on the nose appearance with the accuracy comparable to the recognition from the entire facial region.

The paper is organized as follows. In Section 2, the existing methods are outlined. Later, in Section 3, our system is described in details, and the experimental validation is reported in Section 4. The paper is concluded in Section 5.

2   Related Work

Existing head pose estimation methods can be divided into the appearance-based ones, which operate using global facial features, and those that rely on the facial landmarks geometry. The majority of the existing solutions operate in 2D still images, but 3D imaging has also been exploited here. For example, in [4], random regression forests were used for classifying patches derived from depth images. There are also systems which benefit from tracking the heads in video sequences, which improves the estimation accuracy [3].

Facial appearance may be compared against a set of templates covering the full range of possible rotation angles, and the angle of the most similar template indicates the detected head orientation. In one of the first attempts, the similarity between a face and the template was defined in the image space [17], but since then a number of robust feature extraction techniques have been applied. The features can be extracted using dimensionality reduction techniques, such as principal components analysis [14], or by learning non-linear manifolds [1, 2]. It is worth noting that the subspace learning allows for interpolating the head pose between the most similar templates on the head orientation manifold, which increases the angle resolution over the discretized template grid. Among other feature extraction methods, Gabor wavelets and filter banks [12, 19] have also been used to extract the features useful for estimating a head pose. Instead of using a set of templates, multi-class classifiers such as support vector machines (SVMs) [18] or neural nets [21, 24], including linear auto-associative memories [6] were also applied to assign feature vectors to a certain orientation class. Recently, the biologically inspired features (BIFs) were combined with local binary patterns (LBP), and used as a head pose descriptor [13].

Another facial appearance-based approach consists in using multiple face detectors trained for different head poses [9, 25]. Such detectors are supposed to have low tolerance on head rotation, so a rotated head should be detected only by a single detector trained for a specific rotation angle. Thus, face detection is combined with head pose estimation, but the resolution is highly limited here due to the tolerance range of the detectors. Also, for real-time applications, a limited number of detectors can be run for a single image at the same time.

Detection of facial landmarks makes it possible to estimate the head pose as well [26]. However, in this case the efficacy strongly depends on the localization accuracy, as even small displacements of the feature points may lead to large errors in the estimated rotation angles. The most common methods for landmark detection rely on Gabor wavelets-based elastic graph matching or are based on active appearance models [22]. The orientation can be derived directly from the points' geometry, but also head pose manifolds may be trained here.

3   Nose Region-Based Head Pose Estimation

The proposed estimation of the head pose based on the nose region can be divided into several major steps presented in Fig. 1. In fact, two main tasks may be distinguished here, namely: (i) nose detection and localization, and (ii) head orientation estimation using features extracted from the nose area.

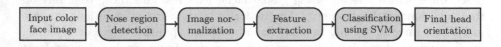

Fig. 1. Flowchart of the proposed method

For nose detection and localization we adopted the AdaBoost cascade of weak classifiers [23]. We relied on Haar-like wavelets (using original [23] and extended sets of masks) and local binary patterns (LBP) with different settings for extracting feature vectors. The cascade parameters were selected experimentally, which is presented in Section 4. Positive samples for training the cascades were collected based on the ground-truth data from the training set. The nose regions were normalized to the size of 34×51. The set of negative samples was created from randomly cropped images (excluding the nose) from the same training set. In order to increase the quantity of the learning samples, mirror images were added as well, and finally we used 3530 positive, and 17096 negative samples.

After detecting the nose region, the image is normalized to a fixed size of 17×26 and it is subject to feature extraction. We have observed that the most apparent differences between various head orientations are related to the alignment of the edges in the nose region. Hence, we have investigated the following feature extraction techniques: (i) histograms of oriented gradients (HOG), (ii) horizontal and vertical profiles of gradient magnitudes, (iii) gradient directions extracted using [10], as well as image filtered using (iv) Canny and (v) Sobel filters. Overall, we obtained the best results using the Sobel operator applied to a grayscale image, which is similar to the Stiefelhagen's method for facial images [21]. The grayscale image was obtained as the luminance component of the YCbCr color space, however other color spaces may be applied here, including those used in the image compression domain [20]. Afterwards, the image is represented as a long, 442-dimensional vector that is classified using SVMs.

Basically, SVMs is a supervised classifier for solving binary classification tasks, but it can be adapted for multi-class problems as well. In head pose estimation, there are $M = M_V \times M_H$ classes, were M_V and M_H indicate the vertical and horizontal resolution, respectively. Here, we used the one-against-all strategy, in which there are as many classifiers as classes, each of them trained to discriminate between the vectors from a particular class and those from the remaining classes. We have investigated three approaches here: (i) one classifier was trained per class, resulting in M classes (termed *grid scheme*), (ii) vertical and horizontal classes were treated separately, resulting in $M_V + M_H$ classes (termed *axis scheme*), and (iii) we classified a difference between two feature vectors, resulting in two classes (intra- or inter-class difference vectors).

In case of the multi-class classification, each vector is classified by every classifier, and assigned to that class, whose response is the strongest. In case of two-class classification, each vector is compared against a gallery of head poses, and the difference between that vector and each vector from the gallery is classified to find the best gallery template. We adopted here our evolutionary framework [11,16] for SVM training, but the obtained results were competitive only for large galleries, which required unacceptably long computation times. Hence, only the multi-class approaches were used for validation.

Fig. 2. Examples of input images with detected nose regions (top row), and magnified nose regions before and after applying the Sobel filter (bottom row)

4   Experimental Validation

We have validated our method using the Pointing'04 benchmark database [5]. It contains images of 15 individuals, whose head orientations are labeled using 13 horizontal and 10 vertical classes. Overall, there are 93 different head poses distinguished. We divided the set into two subsets, namely: a training set which contains images of 10 people, and a test set with the images of the remaining 5 individuals. Hence, the training and test sets contain images of different individuals. We implemented our algorithms in C++. The experiments were conducted using an Intel Core i7-3610QM 2.3 GHz computer with 16 GB RAM. An average recognition time was 9 ms for nose detection and 100 ms for orientation estimation. We compared the obtained results with two alternative works [6,21], in which the same database was used. These methods analyze the entire facial area and the head orientation is estimated using neural networks.

The ground-truth head orientation angles are quantized, hence for many images, they cannot be regarded as precise indicators of the real head orientation. In fact, quite often it is hard to determine whether a given image should be assigned to a certain class or to its neighbor. Therefore, when reporting the accuracy, we take into account two criteria, namely the *strict* (the estimated class must be identical with the ground-truth), and the *weak* one (the estimated class may be identical or adjacent to the ground-truth). Basically, the weak criterium consists in tolerating the estimation error of up to 15 degrees in horizontal and vertical directions. Actually, the same evaluation approach was presented in [6]. We report the estimation accuracy (i.e., the percentage of correctly classified samples) at two levels, namely: (i) the *exact orientation score* (EOS), i.e., both vertical and horizontal angle must be correct, and (ii) the *single axis accuracy* (SAA), i.e., the vertical and horizontal classes are assessed independently. Naturally, EOS is more restrictive than SAA. Also, we investigated both learning schemes (i.e., the grid and axis ones) outlined earlier in Section 3.

First of all, we trained the cascades for nose detection using discrete AdaBoost (we used the OpenCV implementation), and tuned the parameters: feature type, maximum number of stages (s_{max}), minimum hit rate (h_{min}), maximum false alarm rate (f_{max}), weight trim rate (r_{wt}), maximum depth (d_{max}), and maximum number of weak classifiers (n_{max}). Detection efficacy was verified based on the detection score (η) and false positive rate δ_{fp}. A detected nose region (**D**) is regarded as correctly detected, if it intersects with the ground-truth region (**G**), and the intersection coefficient $S_p > 0.85$. This coefficient is computed as $S_p = area(\mathbf{D} \cap \mathbf{G}) / \max(area(\mathbf{D}), area(\mathbf{G}))$. The selected results are presented in Table 1 (the settings from the top row were used).

Table 1. Nose detection scores obtained using different values of the parameters

Feature type ↓	s_{max}	h_{min}	f_{max}	r_{wt}	d_{max}	n_{max}	η	δ_{fp}
LBP	20	0.9	0.6	0.7	3	100	63.82%	23.71%
LBP	20	0.95	0.5	0.7	3	100	57.76%	15.13%
LBP	20	0.95	0.45	0.7	2	100	53.83%	13.00%
Haar (Extended masks)	20	0.95	0.5	0.7	3	100	70.25%	40.03%
Haar (Original masks)	20	0.95	0.5	0.7	2	100	49.67%	19.35%

In Table 2, we present EOSs, averaged over all the orientations, obtained using several feature extraction methods (see Section 3). We relied on the ground-truth nose locations, so as to avoid propagating the nose detection errors. The vectors were later classified by SVM learned using the grid scheme. We applied radial basis functions, and selected the kernel parameters using grid search with an exponential step. It can be clearly seen from the table that the best results (marked as bold) were obtained using the Sobel operator.

SAAs obtained for each horizontal and vertical angle using both ground-truth and detected nose locations are given in Table 3. In the latter case, we measured the accuracy only for true positives, hence for some angles the scores are higher than those achieved using ground-truth data. It can be seen, especially if the

Table 2. Average EOSs obtained using various feature extraction methods

Criterium ↓	Features →	HOG	Profiles	Directions	Canny	Sobel
Strict		5.33%	19.20%	17.53%	21.43%	**27.41%**
Weak			22.20%	58.80%	56.87%	58.90%	**73.46%**

Table 3. SAAs obtained based on ground-truth (GT) and detected (Det) nose locations, using grid (-g) and axis (-a) learning schemes

		Horizontal angle [degrees]												
		-90	-75	-60	-45	-30	-15	0	15	30	45	60	75	90
Strict	GT-a	0.74	0.28	0.41	0.52	0.50	0.56	0.81	0.56	0.53	0.54	0.43	0.24	0.75
	GT-g	0.74	0.30	0.39	0.53	0.61	0.59	0.88	0.58	0.62	0.52	0.41	0.29	0.74
	Det-g	0.50	0.30	0.35	0.50	0.68	0.59	0.79	0.55	0.65	0.64	0.42	0.27	0.79
Weak	GT-a	0.92	0.98	0.80	0.87	0.88	0.93	0.92	0.94	0.88	0.90	0.81	0.97	0.91
	GT-g	0.89	0.93	0.86	0.94	0.98	0.96	1.00	0.96	0.96	0.95	0.86	0.92	0.91
	Det-g	0.91	0.92	0.90	0.96	0.95	0.93	0.98	0.94	0.93	0.90	0.85	0.91	0.92

	Strict			Weak		
	GT -a	GT -g	Det -g	GT -a	GT -g	Det -g
Vertical angle [deg] 90	1.00	0.00	0.00	1.00	0.00	0.00
60	0.83	0.98	0.41	0.83	0.98	0.41
30	0.56	0.43	0.64	0.63	0.48	0.75
15	0.18	0.15	0.19	0.88	0.75	0.92
0	0.28	0.18	0.22	0.77	0.62	0.69
-15	0.29	0.27	0.40	0.83	0.79	0.85
-30	0.56	0.50	0.52	0.84	0.84	0.85
-60	0.64	0.74	0.42	0.64	0.74	0.42
-90	0.78	0.78	0.00	0.78	0.78	0.00

weak criterium is considered, that head orientation can be estimated very well in the horizontal plane relying on the nose region analysis. However, in case of the vertical angle, the accuracy is much worse. This is explainable, as the nose region appearance is more sensitive to the horizontal rotation. It can also be noticed that the grid scheme is superior to the axis-based one. In Fig. 3, EOSs are illustrated for each particular angle. Here, we used the grid scheme, and we demonstrate the results obtained for the ground-truth and detected nose locations under the weak criterium. The obtained values are rather low, mainly due to the errors in the vertical plane.

In Table 4, we compare our method with other existing approaches [6, 21]. Here, we demonstrate only SAAs, as EOSs were not given in those papers. In those works, it is assumed that the head location is known, hence for fair comparison, we also used the ground-truth data for the nose position. In case of the Gourier's method [6], the test set was determined in two different ways: (i) independently from the training set (as in our study), and (ii) including other images of the same individuals as in the training set. Following the latter approach, the results were definitely better, but they cannot be really compared with those obtained using other methods. In the table, they are given in (brackets). It may

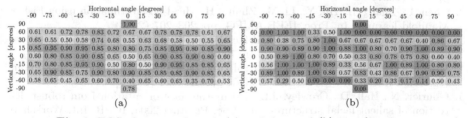

(a)   (b)

Fig. 3. EOSs for ground-truth (a) and detected (b) nose locations

Table 4. SAAs compared with other methods (bold values indicate the best score)

	Method ↓	Average angular error	Strict criterium	Weak criterium
Vertical	Proposed (grid)	12.36°± 15.80	47.91%	**77.80%**
	Proposed (axis)	14.70°± 18.90	45.60%	73.46%
	Gourier's [6] (grid)	16.80° (10.10°)	44.50% (61.70%)	–
	Gourier's [6] (axis)	15.90° (12.10°)	43.90% (53.80%)	–
	Stiefelhagen's [21]	**10.40°**	**66.30%**	–
Horizontal	Proposed (grid)	**8.18°± 11.52**	**56.99%**	**93.41%**
	Proposed (axis)	11.29°± 21.22	53.52%	90.22%
	Gourier's [6] (grid)	10.10° (8.50°)	50.00% (60.80%)	88.70% (90.10%)
	Gourier's [6] (axis)	10.30° (7.30°)	50.40% (61.30%)	88.10% (93.30%)
	Stiefelhagen's [21]	10.60°	52.00%	–

be seen that while for estimating the vertical angle, the Stiefelhagen's method is the most accurate, the horizontal angle is better estimated using our approach. Also, using our method, an average angular error is the lowest, and the accuracy is the highest, according to the weak and strict criterium.

5   Conclusions and Future Work

In this paper, we presented our study on estimating head pose exclusively based on nose region analysis. We have demonstrated that the nose location can be detected independently on the face detectors, and for estimating the horizontal rotation angle, our system is competitive with the methods that rely on analyzing the entire face area. Overall, our main contribution lies in proposing a new approach that may increase the performance of the state-of-the-art systems especially in cases when a face cannot be detected.

Our ongoing research is aimed at combining our system with face-based methods for head pose estimation. In particular, our goal is to improve the nose detector, given the outcome of face and skin detectors. Furthermore, we intend to apply dimensionality reduction methods and manifold learning techniques for better representation of the data that are classified using SVMs.

References

1. Balasubramanian, V.N., Ye, J., Panchanathan, S.: Biased manifold embedding: A framework for person-independent head pose estimation. In: Proc. IEEE CVPR, pp. 1–7 (2007)
2. Chen, L., Zhang, L., Hu, Y., Li, M., Zhang, H.: Head pose estimation using Fisher Manifold learning. In: Proc. IEEE AMFG, pp. 203–207 (2003)
3. Dornaika, F., Davoine, F.: Head and facial animation tracking using appearance-adaptive models and particle filters. In: Proc. IEEE CVPR, pp. 153–153 (2004)
4. Fanelli, G., Gall, J., Van Gool, L.: Real time head pose estimation with random regression forests. In: Proc. IEEE CVPR, pp. 617–624 (2011)
5. Gourier, N., Hall, D., Crowley, J.L.: Estimating face orientation from robust detection of salient facial structures. In: Proc. Pointing 2004, ICPR, Int. Workshop on Visual Observation of Deictic Gestures, pp. 1–9 (2004)

6. Gourier, N., Maisonnasse, J., Hall, D., Crowley, J.L.: Head pose estimation on low resolution images. In: Stiefelhagen, R., Garofolo, J.S. (eds.) CLEAR 2006. LNCS, vol. 4122, pp. 270–280. Springer, Heidelberg (2007)
7. Hachaj, T., Ogiela, M.R., Piekarczyk, M.: Real-time recognition of selected karate techniques using GDL approach. In: S. Choras, R. (ed.) Image Processing and Communications Challenges 5. Advances in Intelligent Systems and Computing, vol. 233, pp. 97–104. Springer, Heidelberg (2014)
8. Hansen, D.W., Ji, Q.: In the eye of the beholder: A survey of models for eyes and gaze. IEEE Trans. Pattern Anal. Mach. Intell. 32, 478–500 (2010)
9. Jones, M., Viola, P.: Fast multi-view face detection. Mitsubishi Electric Research Lab TR-20003-96 3 14 (2003)
10. Kawulok, M., Szymanek, J.: Precise multi-level face detector for advanced analysis of facial images. Image Process., IET 6(2), 95–103 (2012)
11. Kawulok, M., Nalepa, J.: Support vector machines training data selection using a genetic algorithm. In: Gimel'farb, G., Hancock, E., Imiya, A., Kuijper, A., Kudo, M., Omachi, S., Windeatt, T., Yamada, K. (eds.) SSPR&SPR 2012. LNCS, vol. 7626, pp. 557–565. Springer, Heidelberg (2012)
12. Krüger, V., Sommer, G.: Gabor wavelet networks for efficient head pose estimation. Image and Vision Comput 20(9), 665–672 (2002)
13. Ma, B., Chai, X., Wang, T.: A novel feature descriptor based on biologically inspired feature for head pose estimation. Neurocomputing 115, 1–10 (2013)
14. McKenna, S.J., Gong, S.: Real-time face pose estimation. Real-Time Imaging 4(5), 333–347 (1998)
15. Murphy-Chutorian, E., Trivedi, M.M.: Head pose estimation in computer vision: A survey. IEEE Trans. Pattern Anal. Mach. Intell. 31(4), 607–626 (2009)
16. Nalepa, J., Kawulok, M.: Adaptive genetic algorithm to select training data for support vector machines. In: EvoApplications 2014. EvoIASP. LNCS, Springer (in press 2014)
17. Niyogi, S., Freeman, W.T.: Example-based head tracking. In: Proc. IEEE FG, pp. 374–378 (1996)
18. Orozco, J., Gong, S., Xiang, T.: Head pose classification in crowded scenes. In: Proc. BMVC., vol. 1, p. 120 (2009)
19. Sherrah, J., Gong, S., Ong, E.J.: Understanding pose discrimination in similarity space. In: Proc. BMVC, pp. 1–10 (1999)
20. Starosolski, R.: New simple and efficient color space transformations for lossless image compression. J. of Vis. Commun. and Image Represent. 25(5), 1056–1063 (2014)
21. Stiefelhagen, R.: Estimating head pose with neural networks. In: Proc. Pointing 2004 ICPR Workshop (2004)
22. Storer, M., Urschler, M., Bischof, H.: 3D-MAM: 3D morphable appearance model for efficient fine head pose estimation from still images. In: Proc. IEEE ICCV Workshops, pp. 192–199 (2009)
23. Viola, P., Jones, M.: Rapid object detection using a boosted cascade of simple features. In: CVPR, vol. (1), pp. 511–518 (2001)
24. Voit, M., Nickel, K., Stiefelhagen, R.: Neural network-based head pose estimation and multi-view fusion. In: Stiefelhagen, R., Garofolo, J.S. (eds.) CLEAR 2006. LNCS, vol. 4122, pp. 291–298. Springer, Heidelberg (2007)
25. Zhang, Z., Hu, Y., Liu, M., Huang, T.: Head pose estimation in seminar room using multi view face detectors. In: Stiefelhagen, R., Garofolo, J.S. (eds.) CLEAR 2006. LNCS, vol. 4122, pp. 299–304. Springer, Heidelberg (2007)
26. Zhu, X., Ramanan, D.: Face detection, pose estimation, and landmark localization in the wild. In: Proc. IEEE CVPR, pp. 2879–2886 (2012)

Adaptive Non-local Means Filtering
for Speckle Noise Reduction

Krystian Radlak and Bogdan Smolka

Silesian University of Technology, Institute of Automatic Control
Akademicka 16, 44-100, Gliwice, Poland
{krystian.radlak,bogdan.smolka}@polsl.pl

Abstract. The aim of this study is to present the results of investigations concerning the evaluation of non-local means filter for multiplicative noise removal in ultrasonographic images. In this work a comparison
of different techniques based on the concept of the non-local means filtering and a novel application for a filter called trimmed non-local means
has been presented. The proposed modification is a generalization of the
non-local means algorithm, in which the pixels are ordered using rank-
ordered absolute differences statistic and only the most centrally located pixels in the filtering window are considered and used to calculate
the weights needed for the averaging operation. The experiments confirmed that the proposed algorithm achieves comparable results with the
existing state-of-the-art denoising schemes in suppressing multiplicative
noise in ultrasound images.

1   Introduction

Ultrasound imaging is widespread in diagnosing ailments or assessing the state
of the soft tissues in organs. The ultrasound imaging is non invasive, relatively
inexpensive and is performed in real time. However, the images are degraded by
speckle noise, which affects their quality reducing the contrast and concealing
the details. Consequently, a proper interpretation of the results and a correct
diagnosis can be difficult. Therefore, image denoising and enhancement is strongly needed and many approaches have been proposed. A survey on speckle noise
reduction methods can be found in [11,10].

Speckle noise is a kind of multiplicative distortion appearing due to signal
multiplication by a noise process and is quite difficult to remove [1]. This kind of
noise is common to laser, sonar and synthetic aperture radar (SAR) imagery and
depends on the structure of imaged tissue and various imaging parameters [8].
According to the literature, speckle noise can be approximated by the Gamma
distribution [16], the Rayleigh distribution [17] or the Fisher-Tippett distribution
[14]. A simplified speckle noise model can be defined as

$$u(x) = v(x) + v(x)^\gamma \cdot \eta(x)(0, \sigma^2), \qquad (1)$$

where $u(x)$ is the observed image, $v(x)$ is the original image and $\eta(x) \sim N(0, \sigma^2)$
is a zero-mean Gaussian noise. The factor γ depends on the kind of an ultrasound

L.J. Chmielewski et al. (Eds.): ICCVG 2014, LNCS 8671, pp. 518–525, 2014.
© Springer International Publishing Switzerland 2014

device and additional processing related to image formation. In [12] Loupas et al. have shown that the model described by Eq. (1) with $\gamma = 0.5$ fits better to data than the simple multiplicative model with $\gamma = 1$ or the Rayleigh model. This model has been employed in our work, since it has been used successfully in many studies [9,5,8].

The main aim of this research is to apply techniques based on the concept of Non-Local Means (NLM) to ultrasonographic images to suppress multiplicative noise. We also propose a novel method capable of denoising a speckle noise called Trimmed Non-Local Means (TNLM). The TNLM method is an extension of the NLM algorithm, in which the image pixels are restored by a weighted average of pixels, whose local neighborhood is similar to the local neighborhood of the pixel which is currently being processed.

This work is organized as follows. The next Section provides a short description of a basic version of NLM and introduced modification. In Section 3 we perform a comparison with existing state-of-the-art solutions and finally we conclude the paper.

2 Proposed Method

The Non-Local Means method was introduced by Buades et al. [3,2] and is considered as one of the best denoising technique for additive Gaussian noise. In our previous work [13], a novel scheme of weights calculation called Trimmed Non-Local Means for mixed Gaussian and impulsive noise reduction in color images has been proposed. In this work, we show that this method with optimally tuned parameters for grayscale images can be successfully used to suppress multiplicative noise. The experiments revealed that the proposed method significantly outperforms the standard NLM filter and yields results comparable with the stat-of-the-art denoising techniques.

Let x_i be the intensity value of the pixel at position i, where $i = 1, 2, \ldots N$ and N denotes the number of image pixels.

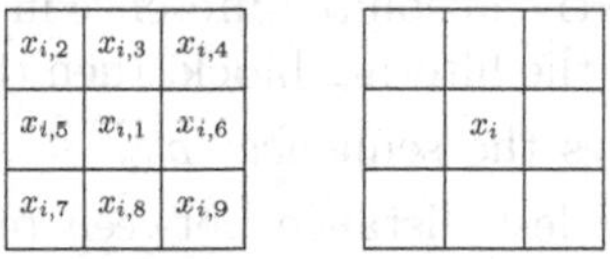

$x_{i,2}$	$x_{i,3}$	$x_{i,4}$
$x_{i,5}$	$x_{i,1}$	$x_{i,6}$
$x_{i,7}$	$x_{i,8}$	$x_{i,9}$

	x_i	

Fig. 1. Notation used for the pixels within the filtering window

Let us consider a set of pixels $W_i = (x_{i,1}, x_{i,2}, \ldots, x_{i,n})$ as a small square region (called a patch) centered at pixel x_i with the window size parameter n. The pixel x_i in image domain corresponds to $x_{i,1}$ in notation used for filtering (see Fig. 1). The dissimilarity measure $D(W_i, W_j)$ between the patches is defined as

$$D(W_i, W_j) = \frac{1}{n} \sum_{s=1}^{n} |x_{i,s} - x_{j,s}|^2. \tag{2}$$

Let us introduce a larger square image region $\mathcal{B}_i$ centered at pixel x_i, which will be called a filtering block with size parameter m. The restored value of pixel y_i is the weighted average of all pixels belonging to filtering block $\mathcal{B}_i$

$$y_i = \hat{x}_{i,1} = \frac{1}{\sum_{x_j \in \mathcal{B}_i} \omega_{ij}} \sum_{x_j \in \mathcal{B}_i} \omega_{ij} \cdot x_j. \tag{3}$$

The weight ω_{ij} assigned to the pixel at position i is calculated by comparing two patches $\mathcal{W}_i$ and $\mathcal{W}_j$, not just the pixel intensities. More formally, the weight ω_{ij} is defined as

$$\omega_{ij} = \exp\left(-\max\left(D(\mathcal{W}_i, \mathcal{W}_j) - 2\sigma^2, 0\right)/h^2\right), \tag{4}$$

where σ denotes the Gaussian noise standard deviation and h is a tuning parameters. This method is called *pixelwise implementation*.

In [4] Buades et al. introduced a simple modification of the basic NLM called *patchwise implementation*, where weights are calculated in the same manner, but instead of averaging a single pixel, all pixels within the patch are averaged. In this way, we obtain n different estimates of every pixel, while the values of pixels depend on the their position in the patch and their neighbors. In comparison to the basic version *patchwise implementation* is more computationally complex, but it improves the noise reduction process. Formally, it can be defined as

$$\hat{x}_{i,l} = \frac{1}{\sum_{x_j \in \mathcal{B}_i} \omega_{ij}} \sum_{x_j \in \mathcal{B}_i} \omega_{ij} \cdot x_{j,l}, \tag{5}$$

where $l = 1, 2, \ldots, n$. Finally, the output pixel y_i is the average of all of the estimates.

In the proposed approach, the pixels in the patch W_j are ordered using the Rank-Ordered Absolute Differences statistic (ROAD) introduced in [7] and the distance $D(W_i, W_j)$ is calculated for the first β pixels from W_j with the smallest ROAD values. In the previous version of TNLM a Generalized Vector Median Filter [15] for color pixel ordering was used. This subset of pixels will be used in the averaging step. A formal definition is presented below.

Let $\rho_{u,v} = |x_{j,u} - x_{j,v}|$ be the absolute difference in intensity of the pixels $x_{j,u}$ and $x_{j,v}$ belonging to W_j in the filtering block, then the set of ordered distances $\rho_{u,v}$ for $u, v = 1, \ldots, n$ gives the sequence: $\rho_{u,v}^{(1)} \leq \ldots \leq \rho_{u,v}^{(\alpha)} \leq \ldots \leq \rho_{u,v}^{(n)}$, where $\rho_{u,v}^{(\alpha)}$, is the α-th smallest distance between pixels $x_{j,u}, x_{j,v}$ and $\rho_{u,v}^{(1)} = |x_{j,u} - x_{j,u}| = 0$. Then, the ROAD statistic assigned to pixel $x_{j,u}$ is defined as

$$R_{j,u} = \sum_{l=1}^{\alpha} \rho_{u,v}^{(l)}. \tag{6}$$

The pixels are correspondingly ordered based on the ROAD measure

$$R_{j,(1)} \leq \ldots \leq R_{j,(\beta)} \leq \ldots R_{j,(n)} \Rightarrow x_{j,(1)} \leq \ldots \leq x_{j,(\beta)} \leq \ldots x_{j,(n)}. \tag{7}$$

Then, the set of the first β pixels $x_{j,(1)}, \ldots, x_{j,(\beta)}$ will be denoted as $\mathcal{W}_j^*$ and the corresponding pixels from $\mathcal{W}_i$ are taken to calculate the similarity between patches. The distance measure between W_i^* and W_j^* is defined as

$$\Delta(\mathcal{W}_i^*, \mathcal{W}_j^*) = \frac{1}{\beta} \sum_{l=1}^{\beta} |x_{i,[l]} - x_{j,[l]}|^2, \tag{8}$$

where $x_{i,[l]}$ denotes the corresponding pixel from the patch. The TNLM output for a pixel at position i is defined as

$$\hat{x}_{i,l} = \frac{1}{Z} \sum_{x_j \in \mathcal{B}_i} \delta(x_{j,l}) \cdot \omega_{ij}^* \cdot x_{j,l}, \tag{9}$$

where $l = 1, \ldots, n$ and Z is the normalizing constant

$$Z = \sum_{x_{j,l} \in \mathcal{B}_i} \delta(x_{j,l}) \cdot \omega_{ij}^*, \quad \delta(x_{j,l}) = \begin{cases} 1, & \text{if } x_{j,l} \in \mathcal{W}_j^* \\ 0, & \text{otherwise.} \end{cases} \tag{10}$$

To build the final denoised image, all estimates calculated at each pixel location i are averaged. The weights are defined as

$$\omega_{ij}^* = \exp\left(-\max\left(\Delta(\mathcal{W}_i^*, \mathcal{W}_j^*) - 2\sigma^2, 0\right)/h^2\right). \tag{11}$$

3 Experiments

The standard test images CAMERAMAN, GOLDHILL, BOAT and artificially generated PHANTOM were chosen to comparison, (see Fig. 2).

(a) CAMERAMAN   (b) GOLDHILL   (c) BOAT   (d) PHANTOM

Fig. 2. Test images

The evaluation of the proposed filter performance was made using a set of the filters based on the non-local means concept and state-of-the-art filtering designs capable of suppressing a speckle noise using source codes provided by authors. Following filters were used for comparison: Wiener Filter [10], Speckle Reducing Anisotropic Diffusion (SRAD) [20], Non-Local Means (NLM) [4], Optimized Bayesian Non-Local Means (OBNLM) [5], Probabilistic Non-Local Means (PNLM) [19], Probabilistic Patch-Based Weights (PPBW) [6]. The parameters of the filters were optimized according to suggestions provided in the respective papers. The control parameters α, β, σ and h for TNLM were selected experimentally to obtain optimal results in terms of the PSNR quality coefficient. The images were contaminated by the multiplicative noise described in Eq. (1) with mean $\mu = 0$ and $\sigma = 0.2, 0.4, 0.6$. The effectiveness is assessed in terms of Peak Signal to Noise Ratio (PSNR) and Structural SIMilarity index (SSIM) [18] and the restoration was also evaluated subjectively.

Fig. 3. Illustrative examples of the filtering efficiency of CAMERAMAN test image contaminated by multiplicative noise with $\sigma = 0.4$

The numerical results are summarized in Tab. 1. Analyzing PSNR metric we can be observed that for low level of speckle noise, the basic version of NLM gives almost the best results and OBNLM filter is superior for higher noise level. The proposed TNLM filter gives close results to the best filters in each category and outperforms other methods on PHANTOM image, in which the texture is simplified. Using the SSIM it is difficult to generalize the results.

The obtained results can be also assessed visually. Figure 3 exhibits the restoration quality achieved using the proposed design and other filters. As can be observed, any of the tested filters gives satisfactory results. Most filters suppressed speckle noise, but the small details like the hand in CAMERAMAN image

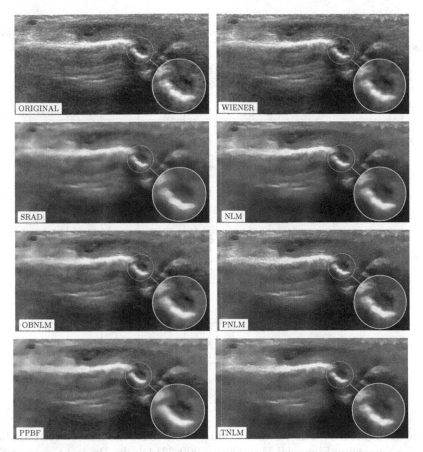

Fig. 4. Illustrative examples of the filtering efficiency evaluated on a real ultrasound image contaminated by multiplicative noise

were blurred. The exemplary restoration results of ultrasound images has been presented in Fig. 4. The results show that TNLM suppresses multiplicative noise and preserves the fine image details without introducing artifacts. The objective assessment of the real ultrasound can be evaluated for example, by segmentation efficiency, but currently it is out of scope in this work.

4 Conclusions

A comparison of algorithms based on the Non-Local Means concept and a novel filter for the suppression of multiplicative noise in ultrasound images has been presented. The tested techniques (especially the proposed TNLM filter) shows very good results in terms of image restoration quality measures and visual inspection, and confirm that filters based on Non-Local Means are capable of reducing the multiplicative noise. However, the tested filters are computationally demanding and the results strongly depend on used parameters. Therefore, there is still a need for development of an adaptive algorithm capable to yield optimal denoising results.

Table 1. Comparison of the quality metrics of noisy images restored by the non-local means filters and competitive techniques

Image		Noise σ	WF	SRAD	NLM	OBNLM	PNLM	PPBF	TNLM
CAMERAMAN		0.2	34.00	36.87	**37.35**	37.18	37.09	35.00	37.25
		0.4	28.01	28.78	29.38	**30.03**	28.13	28.70	29.52
		0.6	21.96	25.15	16.12	**25.95**	25.50	22.05	24.92
GOLDHILL		0.2	30.76	30.73	34.03	30.87	**34.20**	32.80	34.08
		0.4	27.09	27.26	27.35	**28.24**	27.18	27.11	27.48
	PSNR	0.6	22.24	23.69	16.49	**24.43**	22.75	18.56	24.37
BOAT		0.2	31.01	32.06	**35.40**	32.61	34.52	32.64	35.31
		0.4	26.69	26.96	27.68	**28.06**	27.34	26.91	27.47
		0.6	21.90	23.98	15.54	**24.13**	22.13	20.00	23.47
PHANTOM		0.2	37.36	42.52	43.07	38.64	42.21	37.01	**46.95**
		0.4	28.57	30.82	30.31	30.34	30.43	29.50	**32.49**
		0.6	21.19	24.14	20.15	23.76	23.00	21.15	**25.30**
CAMERAMAN		0.2	0.91	0.94	**0.95**	0.94	0.94	0.93	**0.95**
		0.4	0.71	0.80	0.73	**0.83**	0.64	0.79	0.77
		0.6	0.44	**0.75**	0.31	0.72	0.69	0.63	0.59
GOLDHILL		0.2	0.77	0.88	0.88	**0.90**	**0.90**	0.86	0.88
		0.4	0.64	0.67	0.65	**0.69**	0.64	**0.69**	0.66
	SSIM	0.6	0.43	0.54	0.20	**0.56**	0.42	0.35	0.53
BOAT		0.2	0.84	0.92	**0.93**	**0.93**	0.92	0.88	**0.93**
		0.4	0.67	0.72	0.69	0.69	0.67	**0.74**	0.72
		0.6	0.43	**0.65**	0.25	0.63	0.39	0.53	0.52
PHANTOM		0.2	0.98	0.99	0.99	**1.00**	0.98	0.95	0.99
		0.4	0.91	**0.96**	0.95	0.93	0.91	0.89	0.89
		0.6	0.67	**0.89**	0.56	0.79	0.80	0.68	0.76

Acknowledgments. The research leading to these results has received funding from the Norwegian Financial Mechanism 2009-2014 under Project Contract No. Pol-Nor/204256/16/2013. The research was performed using the infrastructure supported by POIG.02.03.01-24-099/13 grant: GCONiI - Upper-Silesian Center for Scientific Computation. Ultrasound images were created for MEDUSA project at Section for Rheumatology; Department for Neurology, Rheumatology and Physical Medicine, Central Hospital, Førde, Norway.

References

1. Achim, A., Bezerianos, A., Tsakalides, P.: Ultrasound image denoising via maximum a posteriori estimation of wavelet coefficients. In: Proc. of the 23rd Annual Intern. Conf. of the IEEE Engineering in Medicine and Biology Society, vol. 3, pp. 2553–2556 (2001)
2. Buades, A., Coll, B., Morel, J.: A review of image denoising algorithms, with a new one. Multiscale Modeling & Simulation 4(2), 490–530 (2005)
3. Buades, A., Coll, B., Morel, J.M.: A non-local algorithm for image denoising. In: IEEE Computer Society Conf. on Computer Vision and Pattern Recognition, vol. 2, pp. 60–65 (2005)
4. Buades, A., Coll, B., Morel, J.M.: Non-Local Means Denoising. Image Processing On Line 2011 (2011)

5. Coupe, P., Hellier, P., Kervrann, C., Barillot, C.: Nonlocal means-based speckle filtering for ultrasound images. IEEE Trans. on Image Proc. 18(10), 2221–2229 (2009)
6. Deledalle, C.A., Denis, L., Tupin, F.: Iterative weighted maximum likelihood denoising with probabilistic patch-based weights. IEEE Trans. on Image Proc. 18(12), 2661–2672 (2009)
7. Garnett, R., Huegerich, T., Chui, C., He, W.: A universal noise removal algorithm with an impulse detector. IEEE Trans. on Image Proc. 14(11), 1747–1754 (2005)
8. Hacini, M., Hachouf, F., Djemal, K.: A new speckle filtering method for ultrasound images based on a weighted multiplicative total variation. Signal Processing (2013)
9. Krissian, K., Kikinis, R., Westin, C.F., Vosburgh, K.: Speckle-constrained filtering of ultrasound images. In: IEEE Computer Society Conf. on Computer Vision and Pattern Recognition, vol. 2, pp. 547–552 (2005)
10. Loizou, C.P., Theofanous, C., Pantziaris, M., Kasparis, T.: Despeckle filtering software toolbox for ultrasound imaging of the common carotid artery. Computer Methods and Programs in Biomedicine 114(1), 109–124 (2014)
11. Loizou, C., Pattichis, C., Christodoulou, C., Istepanian, R.S.H., Pantziaris, M., Nicolaides, A.: Comparative evaluation of despeckle filtering in ultrasound imaging of the carotid artery. IEEE Trans. on Ultrasonics, Ferroelectrics and Frequency Control 52(10), 1653–1669 (2005)
12. Loupas, T., McDicken, W., Allan, P.: An adaptive weighted median filter for speckle suppression in medical ultrasonic images. IEEE Trans. on Circuits and Systems 36(1), 129–135 (1989)
13. Radlak, K., Smolka, B.: Trimmed non-local means technique for mixed noise removal in color images. In: IEEE International Symposium on Multimedia (ISM), pp. 405–406 (2013)
14. Slabaugh, G., Unal, G., Fang, T., Wels, M.: Ultrasound-specific segmentation via decorrelation and statistical region-based active contours. In: IEEE Comp. Soc. Conf. on Computer Vision and Pattern Recognition, vol. 1, pp. 45–53 (2006)
15. Smolka, B., Perczak, M.: Generalized vector median filter. In: 5th Inter. Symposium on Image and Signal Processing and Analysis, pp. 254–257 (2007)
16. Tao, Z., Tagare, H., Beaty, J.: Evaluation of four probability distribution models for speckle in clinical cardiac ultrasound images. IEEE Trans. on Medical Imaging 25(11), 1483–1491 (2006)
17. Wagner, R., Smith, S., Sandrik, J., Lopez, H.: Statistics of speckle in ultrasound b-scans. IEEE Trans. on Sonics and Ultrasonics 30(3), 156–163 (1983)
18. Wang, Z., Bovik, A., Sheikh, H., Simoncelli, E.: Image quality assessment: from error visibility to structural similarity. IEEE Trans. on Image Proc. 13(4), 600–612 (2004)
19. Wu, Y., Tracey, B., Natarajan, P., Noonan, J.: Probabilistic non-local means. IEEE Signal Processing Letters 20(8), 763–766 (2013)
20. Yu, Y., Acton, S.: Speckle reducing anisotropic diffusion. IEEE Trans. on Image Proc. 11(11), 1260–1270 (2002)

Semantic-Based Image Analysis with the Goal of Assisting Artistic Creation

Pilar Rosado[1], Ferran Reverter[2], Eva Figueras[1], and Miquel Planas[1]

[1] Fine Arts Faculty, University of Barcelona, Spain
pilarrosado@ub.edu
[2] Statistics Department, University of Barcelona, Spain

Abstract. We have approached the difficulties of automatic cataloguing of images on which the conception and design of sculptor M. Planas artistic production are based. In order to build up a visual vocabulary for basing image description on, we followed a procedure similar to the method Bag-of-Words (BOW). We have implemented a probabilistic latent semantic analysis (PLSA) that detects underlying topics in images. Whole image collection was clustered into different types that describe aesthetic preferences of the artist. The outcomes are promising, the described cataloguing method may provide new viewpoints for the artist in future works.

Keywords: Artificial vision, automated image cataloguing, Bag-of-Visual terms, probabilistic latent semantic analysis.

1 Introduction

Artists are image generators, since they constantly produce them in their creative process. Recently, an increasing community of researchers in computer vision, pattern recognition, image processing and art history have developed rigorous computer methods for addressing an increasing number of problems in the history of art [1]. In our case, the images used by the sculptor Miquel Planas [2] constitute an essential part of his creative process and he presents them as a large document collection on which subsequent work will be based, especially in the field of sculpture. The possibility was outlined that a study could be started to enable the creation of a system of image grouping and classification, not only with the aim of cataloguing them, but also in order to obtain new values, qualities and common characteristics of the compared images. In view of the fact that the piece of research of such characteristics was proposed within the field of fine arts, it was suggested that its results could be extrapolated to any kind of actions centred on creation, in which the comparison among images would be the main characteristic, with a view to create applications aimed at learning, knowledge acquisition and image research. This study extends previous work in assessing the performance of SIFT descriptors, BOW representation and spatial pyramid matching for automatic analysis of images that are the basis of the ideation and designing of art work [3].

L.J. Chmielewski et al. (Eds.): ICCVG 2014, LNCS 8671, pp. 526–533, 2014.

2   Methodology

Image representation In order to build up a visual vocabulary for basing image description on, we followed a procedure similar to the one used in automatic text analysis. The method is known as the "Bag-of-Words" (BOW) model because every document is represented as a distribution of frequencies of the words in the text, without considering the syntactic relationships among them. In the sphere of images we will refer to "Bag-of-Visual Terms" (BOV) representations. This approach consists in analysing images as a group of regions, describing only their appearance without taking into account their spatial structure. The BOV representation is built up based on the automatic extraction and quantization of local descriptors and it has proven to be one of the best techniques for solving different tasks in the field of computer vision. The BOV representation was first implemented [4] to develop an expert system specializing in image recognition. Figure 1 summarizes the process to be followed in order to obtain the BOV representation of the images of a collection [5,6]. This representation of an image does not contain information concerning the spatial relationships among visual words, in the same way that the BOW representation removes the information relating to word order in documents. To overcome the limitations of the BOV approach we have implemented a method using pyramid histograms that configure an increasingly fine grid sequence over the image and conducts a BOV type analysis in each of the grids, finally obtaining a weighted sum of the number of matches that occur in each resolution level of the pyramid [7].

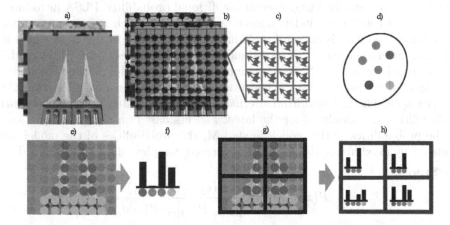

Fig. 1. BOW representation scheme. a) Collection of images b) A grid is defined over the images. c) Image descriptors are calculated. d) Descriptors are quantized in M clusters, which will define a visual vocabulary of M visual words. e) Once the vocabulary is available, the descriptors of each image are assigned to the nearest visual word. f) In order to obtain the BOV representation of a given image, the frequency of each visual word in the image is calculated. g),h) Sequence of grids on the image to draw histograms pyramid in order to take into account the spatial relationship between visual words.

Representation of Latent Aspects. The BOV representation is easy to construct. However, it has two drawbacks: polysemy - a single visual word may represent different scene contents - and synonymy - various visual words may characterize the same image content. As a partial solution to the previous drawbacks, we have found the probabilistic latent semantic analysis (PLSA), a methodology originated from text mining [8]. Extending PLSA to image analysis involves considering images as documents in a visual vocabulary established by means of a quantization process, as previously mentioned. The PLSA will detect categories of objects, formal patterns, within the images in such way that an image which contains different types of objects is modeled as a mixture of subjects. We have at our disposal an image collection $D = \{d_1, \ldots, d_N\}$ and a vocabulary of visual words $V = \{v_1, \ldots, v_M\}$. We can summarize the observations in a $N \times M$ table of frequencies $n(d_i, v_j)$, where $n(d_i, v_j)$ indicates how frequently the visual word v_j occurs in image d_i. The PLSA is a generative statistical model which associates a latent variable $z_l \in \{z_1, \ldots, z_K\}$ with each observation, an observation being understood as the occurrence of a visual word in a given image. These variables, normally known as aspects, are used to obtain a model of joint probability based on the images and visual words, defined as:

$$P(d_i, v_j) = P(d_i) \sum_{k=1}^{K} P(v_j|z_k) P(z_k|d_i)$$

where $P(d_i)$ represents the probability of d_i , $P(v_j|z_k)$ represents the conditional probability of a specific visual word conditioned on the latent aspect z_k , and $P(z_k|d_i)$ represents the image-specific conditional probability. PLSA introduces a concept of conditional independence, according to which it is assumed that the occurrence of a visual word v_j is independent of the image d_i in which it appears, given an aspect z_k. The estimation of probabilities of the PLSA model is performed by means of the maximum likelihood principle, using the image collection $D = \{d_1, \ldots, d_N\}$. The optimization is carried out using the EM algorithm [9]. The EM algorithm alternates two steps. In step E, the a posteriori probabilities are calculated for the latent aspects based on current estimations of the probabilities of the model; in step M, the probabilities of the model are updated by maximizing the so-called "expected complete data log-likelihood":

- **Step E**

$$P(z_k|d_i, v_j) = \frac{P(v_j|z_k) P(z_k|d_i)}{\sum_{l=1}^{K} P(v_j|z_l) P(z_l|d_i)}$$

- **Step M**

$$P(v_j|z_k) = \frac{\sum_{i=1}^{N} n(d_i, v_j) P(z_k|d_i, v_j)}{\sum_{m=1}^{M} \sum_{i=1}^{N} n(d_i, v_m) P(z_k|d_i, v_m)}$$

$$P(z_k|d_i) = \frac{\sum_{j=1}^{M} n(d_i, v_j) P(z_k|d_i, v_j)}{n(d_i)}, \quad n(d_i) = \sum_{j=1}^{M} n(d_i, v_j)$$

Steps E and M alternate repeatedly until a certain condition of termination is achieved. The iterative process is started by assigning random values to the set of probabilities $P(z_k|d_i)$ and $P(v_j|z_k)$. As a result of the previous process, a new representation is obtained for the images of the collection based on the aspect distribution,

$$(P(z_1|d_i), ..., P(z_K|d_i))$$

Actually, it is also possible to determine the aspect distribution for any image d that does not belong to the initial collection [10,11]. Using the previously described EM algorithm again will suffice, although in this case, in step M, only probabilities $P(z_k|d)$ will be updated, while probabilities $P(v_j|z_k)$, independent of the image and estimated from the collection in the learning stage, will remain fixed. Although the image representation based on aspects can be used as input for a scene classifier, we will focus on the use of said representation for image organization or ranking based on the distribution of underlying aspects. Given an aspect z, the images can be arranged according to the values of $P(z|d)$ thus, once the values of $P(z_k|d)$, $k = 1, ..., K$, for a given image d are estimated, we can arrange them in order and obtain an objective measure of the association between the image and every single aspect. As a result, we will associate the image with the aspect of higher probability. Based on this methodology, we have been able to analyse the image collection and determine underlying aspects by means of which the whole collection can be catalogued. The process has been carried out by means of scripts written in MATLAB, 2013a version (The MathWorks) (8.1.0.604). SIFT local descriptors [12] and the vocabulary of visual words have been implemented by means of functions available from the open code library VLFeat, 0.9.16 version [13]. The PLSA has been implemented by using functions developed by the authors themselves.

3   Results

The initial sample of our study is made up of 2,846 photographic images taken by the artist himself. It is a set of images, most of which were taken outside and from different angles and details (including fragments and special features which can be photographed as abstract and/or textured elements). The size of the images taken by the artist is between 480 x 480 pixels and 1400 x 1400 pixels, but the process rescales the images that exceed this size to 480 pixels. Taking into account the type of sample and the number of images, we have tested the system by setting the number of aspects to 10. For the outcome assessment of this set we will mainly take into consideration images categorized into a certain aspect with a probability equal to or exceeding 0.6. Computational evaluation is performed in greyscale. In light of these results, we perceive that the sample consists of two very distinct image types; a type of photographs which shows a single highly prominent aspect (we shall call them low entropy images), and another one which shows several simultaneously associated aspects (we shall call them high entropy images). To distinguish these two typologies, we have used

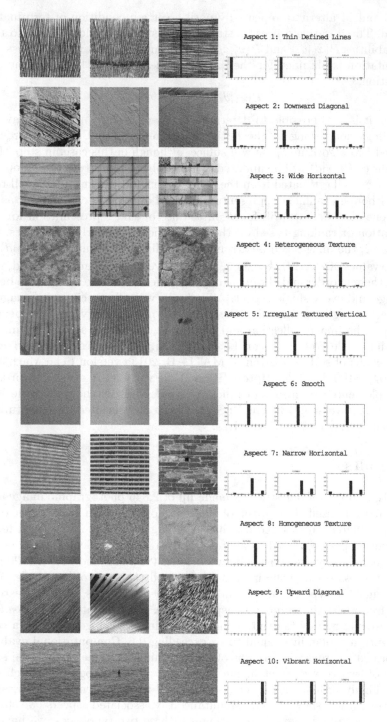

Fig. 2. Images and histogram of aspects obtained on the set of low entropy images

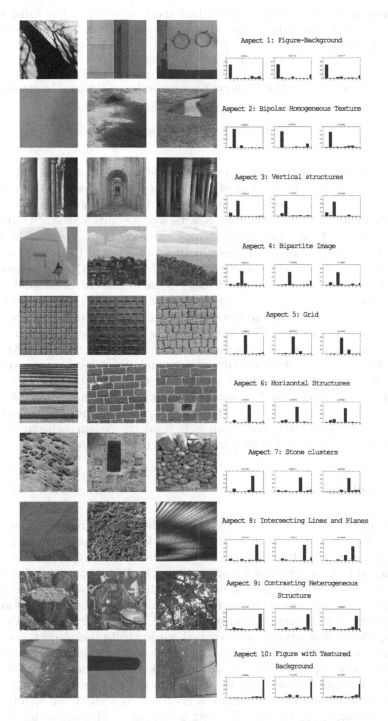

Fig. 3. Images and histogram of aspects obtained on the set of high entropy images

the Shannon entropy index [14]. The PLSA methodology provides a distribution of aspect probability in the images, that is, for a given image d, there is a vector of probabilities:

$$(P(z_1|d), P(z_2|d), ..., P(z_K|d))$$

hence, we can calculate the Shannon Entropy index of image d by means of

$$H(d) = -\sum_{i=1}^{K} P(z_i|d) \log P(z_i|d)$$

Thus, an image which is associated with a single aspect, that is, an image with a probability vector with all values of zero except for a one, will have a minimum entropy value equal to $H(d) = 0$; on the other hand, an image which is equally associated with all the aspects, that is, with a probability vector of $1/10$ in each component, will have a maximum entropy value equal to $H(d) = 2.3026$. The theoretical entropy ranges in respect of 10 aspects would be from 0 to 2.3026. Those noticed in our sample practically range from 0 to 2.17. The images which show high entropy are those which have been associated in an equiprobable manner with each and every aspect. It is decided to select the images with an entropic value of above 1.4 and restart the search for aspects in this new sample made up of 1,482 images. Thus, an attempt is being made to have the system establish new relationships between more visually complex images. Again the whole process of generating local descriptors and visual vocabulary is repeated, and thus an attempt is made to make the system be able to establish new relationships between visually complex images, resulting in new latent aspects different from the 10 first ones. The test is successful and different set of 10 aspects are generated on the new sample. In total, the system is able to categorize the total images analyzed in 20 groups, see Figures 2 and 3.

4 Conclusions

In view of the results obtained, we can conclude that, given a set of a large number of images, the system would enable a formal pre-selection by grouping them in a more objective manner. Artificial vision is not totally subject to or conditioned by human conceptual perception. The described cataloguing method may introduce new relationships, new sets which could provide the artist with new indications or viewpoints for future works. Thus, the results obtained in the different experiments previously described have enabled Miquel Planas to reapproach the photographic work carried out so far. In this respect, the artist's personal vocabulary will also be enriched by the new relationships obtained from the programmed classifications, as shown in the examples detailed in this study. The outcomes obtained will provide new ideas and nuances, which will directly benefit the final creative work. Thus, a creator's vocabulary can also be established, growing as the system is fed with new images. This will be highly useful in the creative, analytical, taxonomic and pedagogic process of the artwork.

References

1. Stork, D.G.: Computer image analysis of paintings and drawings: An introduction to the literature. In: Proc. of the Image Processing for Artist Identification Workshop. Van Gogh Museum (2008)
2. Planas, M.A.: Miquel Planas (2014), http://www.miquelplanas.eu
3. Reverter, F., Rosado, P., Figueras, E., Planas, M.A.: Artistic ideation based on computer vision methods. Journal of Theoretical and Applied Computer Science 6(2), 72–78 (2012)
4. Willamowski, J., Arregui, D., Csurka, G., Dance, C., Fan, L.: Categorizing nine visual classes using local appearance descriptors. In: Proceedings of LAVS Workshop, ICPR 2004, Cambridge (2004)
5. Lazebnik, S., Schmid, C., Ponce, J.: Beyond Bags of Features: Spatial Pyramid Matching for Recognizing Natural Scene Categories. In: IEEE Computer Society Conference on Computer Vision and Pattern Recognition, vol. 2, pp. 2169–2178 (2006), doi:ieeecomputersociety.org/10.1109/CVPR.2006.68
6. Fei-Fei, L., Perona, P.: A Bayesian hierarchical model for learning natural scene categories. In: Proc. CVPR (2005)
7. Grauman, K., Darrel, T.: The pyramid match kernel: Discriminative classification with sets of image features. In: Proceedings of IEEE International Conference on Computer Vision (ICCV), Beijing (2005)
8. Hofmann, T.: Unsupervised learning by probabilistic latent semantic analysis. Machine Learning 42, 177–196 (2001)
9. Dempster, A.P., Laird, N.M., Rubin, D.B.: Maximum likelihood from incomplete data via the EM algorithm. J. Royal Statist. Soc. B 39, 1–38 (1977)
10. Bosch, A., Zisserman, A., Muñoz, X.: Scene classification via pLSA. In: Leonardis, A., Bischof, H., Pinz, A. (eds.) ECCV 2006. LNCS, vol. 3954, pp. 517–530. Springer, Heidelberg (2006)
11. Quelhas, P., Monay, F., Odobez, J.M., Gatica-Perez, D., Tuytelaars, T., Van Gool, L.: Modeling scenes with local descriptors and latent aspects. In: Proceedings of the Tenth IEEE International Conference on Computer Vision (ICCV 2005), vol. 1, pp. 883–890 (2005), doi:10.1109/ICCV. 2005. 152
12. Lowe, D.G.: Distinctive Image Features from Scale Invariant Keypoints. Int. Journal of Computer Vision 60(2), 91–110 (2004)
13. Vedaldi, A., Fulkerson, B.: VLFeat - An open and portable library of computer vision algorithms (2008), http://www.vlfeat.org (retrieved)
14. Cover, T.M., Thomas, J.A.: Elements of Information Theory, 2nd edn. John Wiley & Sons, New Jersey (2006)

Mixing Graphics and Compute for Real-Time Multiview Human Body Tracking

Bogusław Rymut[2] and Bogdan Kwolek[1]

[1] AGH University of Science and Technology
30 Mickiewicza Av., 30-059 Krakow, Poland
bkw@agh.edu.pl
[2] Rzeszów University of Technology
Al. Powst. Warszawy 12, 35-959 Rzeszów, Poland
brymut@prz.edu.pl

Abstract. This paper presents an effective algorithm for 3D model-based human motion tracking using a GPU-accelerated particle swarm optimization. The tracking involves configuring the 3D human model in the pose described by each particle and then rasterizing it in each camera view. In order to accelerate the calculation of the fitness function, which is the most computationally demanding operation of the algorithm, the rendering of the 3D model has been realized using CUDA-OpenGL interoperability. Since CUDA and OpenGL both run on GPU and share data through common memory the CUDA-OpenGL interoperability is very fast. We demonstrate that thanks to GPU hardware rendering the time needed for calculation of the objective function is shorter. Owing to more precise rendering of the 3D model as well as better extraction of its edges the human motion tracing is more accurate.

1 Introduction

In the last decade, GPU computing has considerably evolved to deliver teraflops of floating-point compute power. Many real-time applications require a mix of compute and graphics capabilities, in addition to efficiently processing large amounts of data. Such applications include physically-based simulations, computer vision, augmented and virtual reality, motion capture and visualization, etc. In order to maximize performance, the applications must be designed to allow data to be passed efficiently between compute and graphics contexts. Owing to the CUDA-OpenGL interoperability we can avoid the back and forth data transfer between the host and device memories, and carry out all processing required for 3D rendering and display [10]. CUDA is a parallel computing platform and programming model, which interfaces CPU and of the graphics processing unit, whereas the OpenGL is well known programmer's interface to graphics hardware.

Model-based pose estimation algorithms aim at recovering human motion from one or more camera views and a 3D model representing the human body. An articulated human body can be perceived as a kinematic chain consisting

L.J. Chmielewski et al. (Eds.): ICCVG 2014, LNCS 8671, pp. 534–541, 2014.

of at least eleven parts corresponding to key parts of the human body. The human pose is typically represented by a vector of joint angles. Typically such a 3D human model consists of very simple geometric primitives like cylinders or truncated cones. The 3D articulated model is projected into each camera view. The majority of 3D motion tracking algorithms are based on minimizing an error function, which measures how well the 3D model projections fit the images. The model - image matching for pose estimation is usually formulated as an optimization of an error/likelihood function. The 3D model rasterization in the cameras' views is the most computationally demanding operation. As demonstrated in [5], a considerable speedup of the tracking can be achieved thanks to parallel computations on GPU, and particularly owing to GPU-based rendering of the 3D model.

Although the general purpose computing on GPU are becoming more popular because of its promise of massive parallel computation, achieving a good performance is still not a simple task. In order to achieve desired performance we have to keep all processors occupied and hide the memory latency. To attain such aim, CUDA supports running hundred or thousands of lightweight threads in parallel. The context switch is very fast because everything is stored in the registers and thus there is almost no data movement.

In general, the image processing and analysis algorithms are good candidates for GPU implementation, since the parallelization is naturally provided by per-pixel operations. Many research studies confirmed this by showing GPU acceleration of many image processing algorithms [1,3,8]. A recent study [7] reports a speedup of 30 times for low-level algorithms and up to 10 times for high-level functions, which contain more overhead and many steps that are not easy to parallelize.

Non intrusive human body tracking is a key issue in user-friendly human-computer communication. This is one of the most challenging problems in computer vision being at the same time one of the most computationally demanding tasks. Particle filters are typically employed to achieve articulated motion tracking. Several improvements of ordinary particle filter were done to achieve fast and reliable tracking of articulated motion [2] as well as to obtain the initialization of the tracking [11]. 3D motion tracking can be perceived as dynamic optimization problem. Recently, particle swarm optimization (PSO) [4] has been successfully applied to achieve human motion tracking [5]. The motion tracking is achieved by a sequence of static PSO-based optimizations, followed by re-diversification of the particles to cover the possible poses in the next time step. The calculation of the matching score is the most time consuming operation of the tracking algorithm. In turn, the rasterization of the 3D model in the cameras' views is the most computationally demanding operation in the evaluation of the fitness function. This motivated us to investigate the feasibility of mixing graphics and compute to speed-up the rasterization of the 3D model, i.e. by the use of CUDA-OpenGL interoperability.

2   Overview of CUDA-OpenGL Interoperability

A GPU is a dedicated processor that offloads 3D graphics rendering workload from the CPU. The synthesis of the image is traditionally implemented as a pipeline of specialized stages, which is called the graphics pipeline. The input to the graphics pipeline is a wireframe consisting of a set of primitives, which are defined by a group of one or more vertices. The basic graphics pipeline stages have evolved from fixed function graphics pipeline into powerful programmable co-processing units capable of performing general purpose computing. One such evolution was introduction of programmable processors consisting of:

- Vertex processor, which aim is to transform each input vertex to data required by the next graphics pipeline stages.
- Geometry processor, which processes a mesh at primitive level and produces vertices and attributes to define new primitives.
- Fragment processor, which determines the color of each fragment.

Such processors could be programmed with programs called shader programs. The three different shader types were merged into one unified shader model with a consistent instruction set across all three processor types. Thus, vertex, geometry, and pixel/fragment shaders became threads, running different programs on the programmable cores. These cores on NVidia platform are called CUDA Cores, and a streaming multiprocessor (SM) is composed of many CUDA cores.

In the CUDA programming model the GPU is treated as a coprocessor that executes data-parallel kernel functions. The kernel is typically executed in parallel through a set of parallel threads, which are grouped into parallel thread blocks and in each block the threads are scheduled for execution in groups containing 32 threads called warps. Each thread block consists of multiple concurrently running threads that can cooperate through shared memory and barrier synchronization. Blocks are mapped to streaming multiprocessors and each thread is mapped to a single core. The SM can issue and execute concurrently two warps.

The GPU consists of an array of SM multiprocessors, each of which is capable of supporting thousands co-resident concurrent threads. At each clock cycle, a multiprocessor executes the same instruction on a group of threads within a warp. Programming of SMs is based on SIMD paradigm, where the same instruction is utilized to process different data. In comparison to traditional multicore processors, GPGPUs have distinctly higher degrees of hardware multithreading (hundreds of hardware thread contexts vs. tens), memory architectures that deliver higher peak memory bandwidth (hundreds of gigabytes per second vs. tens), and smaller cache memories.

By using CUDA we can turn a GPU into a powerful image processor, by using OpenGL we can use the same GPU hardware to generate new images. Because CUDA and OpenGL both run on GPU and share data through common memory, the CUDA-OpenGL interoperability is very fast in practice.

3   GPU-Accelerated 3D Motion Tracking Using PSO

The motion tracking can by attained by dynamic optimization and incorporating the temporal continuity information into the ordinary PSO [5]. Consequently, it can be achieved by a sequence of static PSO-based optimizations, followed by re-diversification of the particles to cover the potential poses that can arise in the next frame. The re-diversification of the particles can be obtained on the basis of normal distribution concentrated around the best particle location found in the previous frame. The decomposition of the PSO on the available GPU resources has been discussed in [5]. In the following subsection we focus on the evaluation of the cost function since the time needed for the evaluation of the cost function is far larger in comparison time required by PSO-based optimization as well as time needed changing the configuration of the 3D articulated human model. Afterwards, we discuss how to accelerate the computation of the objective function using CUDA-OpenGL interoperability.

3.1   3D Human Body Model

The human body can be represented by a 3D articulated model formed by 11 rigid segments representing the key parts of the body. The 3D model specifies a kinematic chain, where the connections of body parts comprise a parent-child relationship, see Fig. 1. The pelvis is the root node in the kinematic chain and at the same time it is the parent of the upper legs, which are in turn the parents of the lower legs. In consequence, the position of a particular body limb is partially determined by the position of its parent body part and partially by its own pose parameters. In this way, the pose parameters of a body part are described with respect to the local coordinate frame determined by its parent. The 3D geometric model is utilized to simulate the human motion and to recover the persons's position, orientation and joint angles. To account for different body part sizes, limb lengths, and different ranges of motion we employ a set of pre-specified parameters, which express typical postures. For each degree of freedom there are constraints beyond which the movement is not allowed. The model is constructed from truncated square pyramids and is used to generate contours,

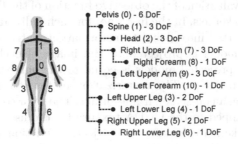

Fig. 1. 3D body model consisting of 11 segments (left), hierarchical structure (right)

which are then matched with the image contours. The configuration of the body is parameterized by the position and the orientation of the pelvis in the global coordinate system and the angles between the connected limbs. The rotation of the limb is done on the basis of the joint transformation matrix. The matrices are calculated on the basis of the joint rotation angles.

3.2   Cost Function

The most computationally demanding operation in 3D model-based human motion tracking is calculation of the objective function. In PSO-based approach each particle represents a hypothesis about possible person pose. In the evaluation of the particle's fitness score the projected model is matched with the current image observations. The fitness score depends on the amount of overlap between the extracted silhouette in the current image and the projected and rasterized 3D model in the hypothesized pose. The amount of overlap is calculated through checking the overlap degree from the silhouette to the rasterized model as well as from the rasterized model to the silhouette. The larger the overlap is, the larger is the fitness value. The objective function reflects also the normalized distance between the model's projected edges and the closest edges in the image. It is calculated on the basis of the edge distance map [9].

   The fitness score for i-th camera's view is calculated on the basis of following expression: $f^{(i)}(x) = 1 - ((f_1^{(i)}(x))^{w_1} \cdot (f_2^{(i)}(x))^{w_2})$, where w_1, w_2 denote weighting coefficients that were determined experimentally. The function $f_1^{(i)}(x)$ reflects the degree of overlap between the extracted body and the projected 3D model into 2D image corresponding to camera i. The function $f_2^{(i)}(x)$ reflects the edge distance map-based fitness in the image from the camera i. The objective function for all cameras is determined according to the following expression: $F(x) = \frac{1}{4} \sum_{i=1}^{4} f^{(i)}(x)$. The images acquired from the cameras are processed on CPU. The extracted foreground image and the distance map are then transferred onto the device [9]. Afterwards, they are mapped to the textures and then utilized by the PSO running on the GPU.

3.3   Computing the Cost Function on CUDA-OpenGL

In the phase of the evaluation of the objective function of the PSO running on the GPU we employ two kernels. In the first one, for each individual particle, the 3D model state is converted into global transformation matrix of the hierarchical body model. Each model is projected to the image of each camera, and the total number of the projected models is equal to the number of cameras times the number of the particles. The rasterization of the model is completed by OpenGL hardware on an off-screen frame-buffer. The color components of frame-buffer pixels are mapped to the CUDA texture for the use by the next CUDA kernel. The second kernel calculates the objective function for all particles. In our approach, in every thread block we calculate the fitness score $F(x)$ of single particle. Thus, the number of blocks is equal to the number of the particles, see

Fig. 2. The threads perform the summing of the fitness values of pixels belonging to the image region containing the rasterized model. Taking into account the available number of registers, in each block we run up to 512 threads and each thread is in charge of processing single or several columns of the image depending on the number of the running threads and the image width.

The partial results from each thread of the threaded block are stored in the shared memory and summed using parallel reduction. In each iteration we evaluate and store the sum of two consucitive shared memory cells and thus reduce the number of particpatitng threads by half. The loop is repeated down to complete thread reduction.

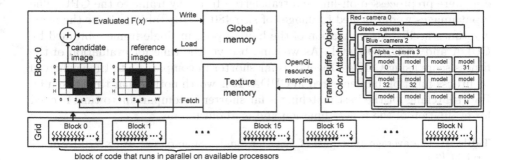

Fig. 2. Evaluation of the cost function using CUDA-OpenGL

The joint transformation matrices are stored in the Shader Storage Buffer Object (SSBO), whereas the indexes determining the order of painting of the triangles are stored in Index Buffer Object (IBO). The vertices are stored in the Vertex Buffer Object (VBO). The SSBO can be read and written by shaders programs written in GLSL language. The vertex attributes stored in VBO can be accessed by shaders programs. In addition to rendering of the model the programmable processors extract also the edges of the projected models. The OpenGL pipeline is executed twice for each camera, where in the first run the vertex shader projects the vertices from 3D to 2D plane using the Tsai camera model, and the fragment shader draws the visible triangles. In the second run the geometry shader extracts the edges of the projected models, which are then rendered in the frame-buffer. Thus, it stores the model edges in the frame-buffer. All models are rendered simultaneously for a given camera. The rendered images together with the extracted edges of a given camera are stored in one of RGBA components of Frame Buffer Object (FBO). The maximum size of the FBO on the utilized graphics card is 16384×16384 and this in turn allows us to put 32 images in one row of the FBO. The rendered image, which is stored in FBO is mapped to CUDA texture and is employed by a kernel responsible for calculating of the objective function. The SSBO, which is mapped to the linear memory, is used by the first kernel to store the model transformation matrixes, which in turn are used in OpenGL-based rendering.

4   Experimental Results

The experiments were conducted on a PC with Intel 3.46 GHz CPU, 8 GB RAM, and NVidia GeForce GTX 590 graphics card consisting of two CUDA devices. Each CUDA device has 16 multiprocessors and 32 cores per multiprocessor. The card is equipped with 3072 MB VRAM and 48 KB shared memory per multiprocessor. The OpenGL context was created by GLFW and GLEW libraries.

The performance of the algorithm has been evaluated on sequences with walking persons, which were used in our previous work [6]. In particular, in the discussed work above we demonstrated that the average speed-up of GPU over CPU is about 7.5. The images acquired from calibrated and synchronized cameras were preprocessed off-line and transferred frame by frame to the GPU. The input images were rescaled to images of size 480×270. Table 1 shows the average times needed for estimation of the human pose in single frame, obtained by CUDA and CUDA-OpenGL. As we can observe, the time for evaluation of the fitness score using CUDA-OpenGL is far shorter in comparison to time achieved by fitness function implemented in CUDA. It is worth noting that time taken by PSO searching for the best matching is far shorter in comparison to time needed for evaluation of the fitness function and is about 0.9 ms.

Table 1. The average time [ms] of PSO for single frame of size 480×270 (Seq. P1 straight [6])

# part.	10 it.		20 it.	
	CUDA	CUDA-OpenGL	CUDA	CUDA-OpenGL
64	69.5±3.6	49.4±1.7	135.2±6.9	92.9±3.7
128	67.5±3.5	56.7±2.1	147.6±6.9	119.9±4.9
192	86.6±3.2	70.2±3.0	173.2±7.0	137.6±6.1
256	90.3±3.8	82.6±4.0	179.9±7.0	163.7±8.0

Figure 3 depicts the accuracy of the 3D motion tracking for PSO with various number of particles and iterations, which was obtained on the sequence with a walking person [9]. As we can see, for PSO with the number of particles greater or equal to 128 and the number of iterations equal to 15 or 20 the average

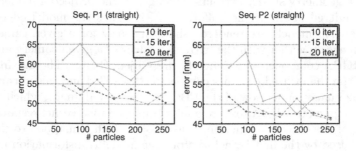

Fig. 3. Tracking errors [mm] versus particles number for CUDA-OpenGL PSO

error of 3D motion recovery is about 55 mm. The accuracy is slightly better in comparison to accuracy obtained in [9]. In particular, it is better for small number of particles. The results are better due to more precise rendering and different 3D model, since in [9] the model was built on truncated cones.

5   Conclusions

In this work we presented an algorithm for articulated human motion tracking. The tracking has been done in real-time using a parallel PSO that is executed on GPU. To accelerate the evaluation of the fitness function, which is the most computationally intensive operation of the tracking algorithm, the rendering of the 3D model has been realized using CUDA-OpenGL. We showed that thanks to rendering of the 3D model using GPU hardware the rendering time is shorter.

Acknowledgment. This work has been partially supported by the Polish Ministry of Science and Higher Education within a grant for young researchers (U-530/DS/M) and the National Science Center within the project N N516 483240.

References

1. Castano-Diez, D., Moser, D., Schoenegger, A., Pruggnaller, S., Frangakis, A.S.: Performance evaluation of image processing algorithms on the GPU. Journal of Structural Biology 164(1), 153–160 (2008)
2. Deutscher, J., Blake, A., Reid, I.: Articulated body motion capture by annealed particle filtering. In: IEEE Int. Conf. on Pattern Recognition, pp. 126–133 (2000)
3. Fung, J., Mann, S.: Using graphics devices in reverse: GPU-based image processing and computer vision. In: IEEE Int. Conf. on Multimedia and Expo., pp. 9–12 (2008)
4. Kennedy, J., Eberhart, R.: Particle swarm optimization. In: Proc. of IEEE Int. Conf. on Neural Networks, pp. 1942–1948. IEEE Press, Piscataway (1995)
5. Krzeszowski, T., Kwolek, B., Wojciechowski, K.: GPU-accelerated tracking of the motion of 3D articulated figure. In: Bolc, L., Tadeusiewicz, R., Chmielewski, L.J., Wojciechowski, K. (eds.) ICCVG 2010, Part I. LNCS, vol. 6374, pp. 155–162. Springer, Heidelberg (2010)
6. Kwolek, B., Krzeszowski, T., Gagalowicz, A., Wojciechowski, K., Josinski, H.: Real-time multi-view human motion tracking using particle swarm optimization with resampling. In: Perales, F.J., Fisher, R.B., Moeslund, T.B. (eds.) AMDO 2012. LNCS, vol. 7378, pp. 92–101. Springer, Heidelberg (2012)
7. Pulli, K., Baksheev, A., Kornyakov, K., Eruhimov, V.: Real-time computer vision with OpenCV. Comm. ACM 55(6), 61–69 (2012)
8. Rymut, B., Kwolek, B.: GPU-supported object tracking using adaptive appearance models and Particle Swarm Optimization. In: Bolc, L., Tadeusiewicz, R., Chmielewski, L.J., Wojciechowski, K. (eds.) ICCVG 2010, Part II. LNCS, vol. 6375, pp. 227–234. Springer, Heidelberg (2010)
9. Rymut, B., Kwolek, B., Krzeszowski, T.: GPU-accelerated human motion tracking using particle filter combined with PSO. In: Blanc-Talon, J., Kasinski, A., Philips, W., Popescu, D., Scheunders, P. (eds.) ACIVS 2013. LNCS, vol. 8192, pp. 426–437. Springer, Heidelberg (2013)
10. Stam, J.: What every CUDA programmer should know about OpenGL. In: GPU Technology Conference (2009)
11. Wu, C., Aghajan, H.: Real-time human pose estimation: A case study in algorithm design for smart camera networks. Proc. of the IEEE 96(10), 1715–1732 (2008)

Real-Time Laser Point Tracking

Artur Ryt, Dawid Sobel, Jan Kwiatkowski, Mariusz Domzal,
Karol Jedrasiak, and Aleksander Nawrat

Institute of Automatic Control, Silesian University of Technology
Akademicka 16, 44-100 Gliwice, Poland
{artur.ryt}@polsl.pl

Abstract. Laser Point Tracking is algorithm dedicated to rapidly moving lasergenerated blob. Even if common tracking problems like occlusion, intense background noises or illumination changes do not exist there we found it challenging to track that simple shape. Proposed method, by usage of few features: brightness, area and velocity, is able to overcome several problems, which occur there. Fast movement of laser makes its trail blurred and dark. We propose methodology to find optimal parameters for LPT. On the end of this paper there are test results comparison with novel trackers anddescription of real system, where our tracker found use.

Keywords: real-time tracking, blob tracking, shooting range.

1   Introduction

Modern tracking algorithms are focused on complicated objects, which can be described with complex methods [11]. Object tracking survey [1] lists 4 common visual features: color, edges, optical flow and texture. These features are used to build models, create templates and probability densities functions in order to find representation of object. Novel trackers can define and learn about the object not only by initialization but online as well [9]. However, tracking simple laser blob, which is seemingly immutable in real-time even in environment close to laboratorys one becomes difficult task.

The basic reason of problems is fast laser movement. Because of its small dimensions it can move by path of few diameters between two frames. What is more, rapid moves make blob blurred and darker. It means none of features listed above is preserved. Size of blob can get multiplied or divided by few times even every frame. Once area of the blob is too big information about relevant position of the laser is lost and cannot be calculated from just single frame. Our suggestion is to estimate new position using velocity vector.

Last, but not least, problem is realtime processing in high resolution. This is important task, because it can increase quality of the tracking. Ability to process frames with high frequency allows usage faster camera. Faster camera can have shorter exposure time, what leads less blurred blobs [7].

L.J. Chmielewski et al. (Eds.): ICCVG 2014, LNCS 8671, pp. 542–551, 2014.

Based on recent tracking review [2] we have chosen few trackers that can be able to handle problems connected with laser tracking. Fist of them, FragTrack [3] algorithm divides tracked object to set of fragmented images, where each fragment is represented and identified by histogram.

Second algorithm, called VTD [4], is based on 2 steps: first is defining object's observation and movement model. Usage of this data can make tracker robust to simultaneous changes of movement and shape. In second step tracking is divided to group of elements, where each one traces single, different type of object change. In order to combine results of elements together it uses Interactive Markov Chain Monte Carlo (IMCMC) method.

Locally Orderless Tracking (LOT) [5] method is based on the combination of the image space and object appearance which allows tracking of targets that are deformed. Method adapts its operation to form of the object that is being tracked. If the object is a solid body, then the value of the arrangement coefficient is close to zero and can be used in methods based on spatial alignment such as pattern matching. Otherwise, when the shape of the object is changing, LOT method cannot take advantage of spatial fit and works by matching the histogram.

2 Laser Tracking

The algorithm describes feature based tracker. In order to determine whenever found blob is laser point or noise we use two features: color and area of the blob. Both of them must match predefined, parametrized thresholds.

Tracking processing for every frame works in two different modes: regional or global search of blob.

In regional mode search is performed only in boundaries around previous laser position. In case of fast blob' movement it starts to estimate position of the laser using the blob's velocity and contour.

If regional search fails or position of the laser in previous frame is unknown the global search is made. It scans whole frame for blob, which can be possibly the lasers one. Algorithms returns new position of the laser as centroid of the blob or flag that the laser does not exist if none blob has been found.

Schema 1 represents flowchart of single frame processing. It contains 17 blocks, which are separated in two possible modes.

Block 1: Initialization memory allocation, loading of configuration parameters and previous laser position.

Decision block 2: One of two modes is selected. It goes for regional scanning if last position of laser is known (block 3) or for global search of blob otherwise (block 11).

2.1 Mode A: Region Search

Blocks 3: Perform regional scan for first unused pixel in region which contains in defined color interval. In order to achieve faster performance the loop step is parametrized.

Block 4: Create blob by using flood fill algorithm with same loop step. Mark all pixels in the blob as used.

Decision block 5: Test does the blob's size meets the minimal requirements. If it is passed, continue processing in block 7. Otherwise return to the search for blob by going to block 6.

Decision block 6: If whole region has been scanned, the global search is required, therefore algorithm switches to second mode, which starts on block 11. Otherwise it continues region scan loop on block 3.

Decision block 7: Estimation of laser point is not always triggered, because it is not always required and sometimes can decrease the quality of tracking [10]. We perform it only when the blobs area is bigger than defined threshold. If that is true, algorithm continues to block 8, otherwise it goes to block 10.

Block 8: Calculate velocity vector as subtraction of two positions: centroid of the blob and the laser previous position.

Block 9: Estimate and set new laser position as cross point of blob's edge and calculated velocity vector. Search for this frame is finished, continue to end block 17.

Block 10. Set new laser position as centroid of the blob. Search for this frame is finished, continue to end block 17.

2.2   Mode B: Global Search

Block 11: Perform loop on whole frame with parametrized step and push every pixel with proper shade of grey on list. Continue to block 12.

Block 12: Select median pixel in the list. If frame does not contain too much of noise pixels and lasers blob exist on image it should select one of the blob's pixels.

Block 13: Filter noise data by removal from the list every pixel which is too far from median pixel. Radius of filtering is parametrized.

Decision block 14: If median pixel is one of laser blob's pixels the filtering in block 13 will return just blob with few noise pixels. Otherwise list will be filtered around random noise pixel, so it will get almost empty, containing only a little number of noise pixels. In the first case, when size of the list is bigger than given threshold we can continue processing of the blob in block 17. Otherwise laser was not found and algorithm continues to block 15.

Block 15: Laser was not found. Search for this frame is finished, continue to end block 17.

Block 16: Set new laser position as centroid of the blob. Search for this frame is finished, continue to end block 17.

End block 17: Return new position of the laser or set flag of its absence.

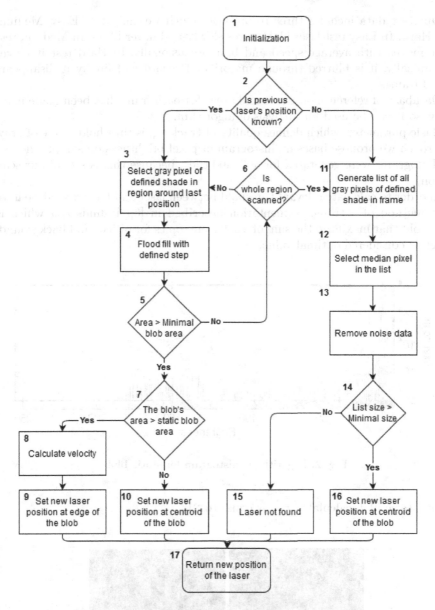

Fig. 1. Processing flowchart

3   Test-Based Parameters Selection

There are several parameters used to control performance speed and quality of tracking. All of them should be selected empirically because it can vary depending on configuration of used system e.g. camera frame rate and resolution, laser power, background noise intensity.

Our test data includes three recordings, which we named as Easy, Medium and Hard. In Easy test laser blob moves slowly and never blurs. In Medium test laser moves with average speed and blurs occasionally. In Hard test it moves dynamically, it is blurred through majority of record and finally it disappears for 13 frames.

Database of reference positions and areas for each frame has been made manually, so it can be used for analysis of algorithm.

Basic parameter, which defines quality of tracking, is threshold shade of gray. Approach we propose bases on histogram of pixel brightness on sample tiles.

Histograms were generated for 400x400 tiles, because this is size of our scan region.

In order to calculate relevant threshold between laser and background we have used method of entropic segmentation described in [6]. It finds t_{opt} which is threshold that maximize the sum of Tsallis entropies for object and background, which is considered optimal value.

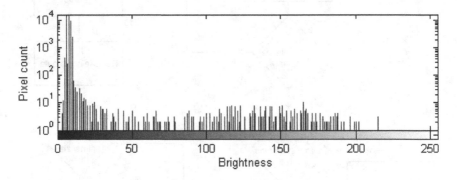

Fig. 2. Logarithmic histogram for static blob

For static blob calculated t_{opt} is equal to 21.

Fig. 3. Comparison of static blob (left image) and its threshold bitmask (right image)

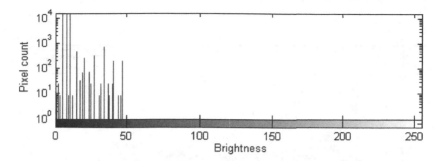

Fig. 4. Logarithmic histogram for blurred blob

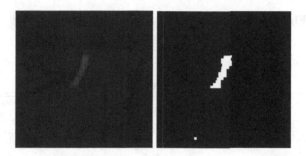

Fig. 5. Comparison of blurred blob (left image) and its threshold bitmask (right image)

For blurred blob calculated t_{opt} is equal to 12.

We have decided to use bigger threshold $t_{opt} = 21$, because its more safe solution, more proof to enviromental background changes [8].

Three other parameters can be selected by analysis of blobs velocity and area in listed tests. These are: dimension of scan region, minimal area of blob, trigger area for position estimation.

In order to track laser efficiently it cannot leave scan region even during fast movement. The biggest recorded velocity in this test set is 129. It means region should be square with half of side length equal to 129. We have added safety reserve in case of faster moves and set this variable 400.

Minimal area of the blob can be calculated as minimal non-zero area of *Easy* test, which contains only static blobs. In our test it was equal 357.

For triggering position estimation we have used double of minimal area of the blob.

In order to achieve speed boost we can increase step variables of search loops and flood fill. It not only decreases number of iterations required, but also decreases noise influence. It happens because there is chance of stepping over noise blobs, which dimensions are smaller than step size. These parameters should be calibrated online to get desired frames per second processing ratio.

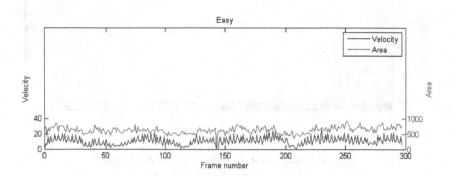

Fig. 6. Relation between area and velocity in test *Easy*

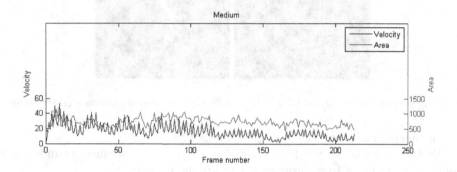

Fig. 7. Relation between area and velocity in test *Medium*

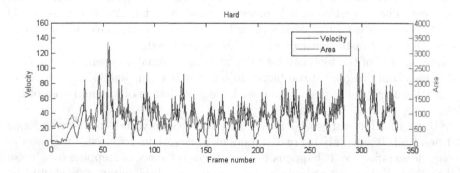

Fig. 8. Relation between area and velocity in test *Hard*

4   Test Results

We have tested proposed Laser Point Tracker (LPT) on three test records described earlier. We have compared results with three other trackers: LOT, FragTrack and VTD. Tests were run on default parameters on implementations published by their authors. Quality factor q was calculated as follows:

$$q = \begin{cases} 2\frac{A \cap B}{A+B} & \text{if } A > 0, B > 0 \\ 0 & \text{if } A = 0, B > 0 \\ 1 & \text{if } A = 0, B = 0 \end{cases} \tag{1}$$

where A is blob area in reference data, B is blob area returned by tracker. It represents how identical are these areas. Values vary from 0 to 1. Area value is equal to 0, when no blob was found on frame.

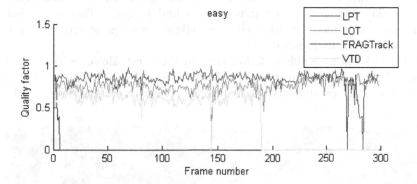

Fig. 9. Quality factor for different tracker over time for *Easy* test

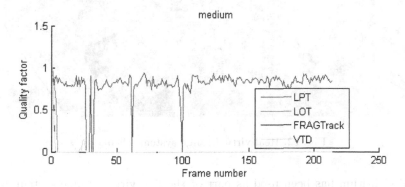

Fig. 10. Quality factor for different tracker over time for *Medium* test

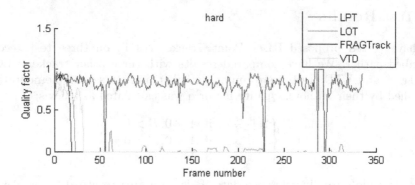

Fig. 11. Quality factor for different tracker over time for *Hard* test

Proposed algorithm LPT is able to track laser point almost constantly. Even if it loses laser for few frames it is able to find it again. This is the biggest advantage that it has over other trackers. High speed and strong blur in Hard test were successfully handled.

LOT and VTD were able to follow laser in Easy test. However, once the blob stated to blur in Medium test both of them have got stuck. Unfortunately static laser blob was not complicated enough to get properly recognized by FragTrack.

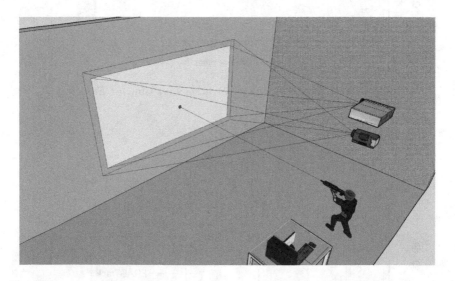

Fig. 12. Real virtual range system schema

LPT algorithm has been used as part of the real virtual range system. This system includes gun-shaped, wireless marker with IR laser attached, projector, high resolution, fast camera (1600x1200, 60FPS) with IR filter and central computer unit. Usage of IR wavelength allows filtering out majority of background noise. Game scene is shown on screen by projector, player can point at desired target with marker. Camera's stream is constantly processed, so position of the laser is known. Player can interact with game by built-in marker's buttons.

Acknowledgement. This work has been supported by Applied Research Programme of the National Centre for Research and Development as a project ID 178438 path A - Costume for acquisition of human movement based on IMU sensors with collection, visualization and data analysis software.

References

1. Yilmaz, A., Javed, O., Shah, M.: Object Tracking: A Survey. ACM Computing Surveys (CSUR) 38(4) (2006)
2. Yang, H., Shao, L., Zheng, F., Wang, L., Song, Z.: Recent advances and trends in visual tracking: A review. Neurocomputing 74(18), 3823–3831 (2011)
3. Adam, A., Rivlin, E., Shimshoni, I.: Robust Fragments-based Tracking using the Integral Histogram. In: 2006 IEEE Computer Society Conference on Computer Vision and Pattern Recognition, pp. 798–805 (2006)
4. Kwon, J., Lee, K.M.: Visual tracking decomposition. In: 2010 IEEE Conference on Computer Vision and Pattern Recognition (CVPR), pp. 1269–1276 (2010)
5. Oron, S., Bar-Hillel, A., Levi, D., Avidan, S.: Locally Orderless Tracking. In: 2012 IEEE Conference on Computer Vision and Pattern Recognition (CVPR), pp. 1940–1947 (2012)
6. Portes de Albuquerquea, M., Esquef, I.A., Gesualdi Mello, A.R., Portes de Albuquerque, M.: Image thresholding using Tsallis entropy. Pattern Recognition Lett. 25, 1059–1065 (2004)
7. Jędrasiak, K., Nawrat, A., Daniec, K., Koteras, R., Mikulski, M., Grzejszczak, T.: A Prototype Device for Concealed Weapon Detection Using IR and CMOS Cameras Fast Image Fusion. In: Bolc, L., Tadeusiewicz, R., Chmielewski, L.J., Wojciechowski, K. (eds.) ICCVG 2012. LNCS, vol. 7594, pp. 423–432. Springer, Heidelberg (2012)
8. Świtoński, A., Josiński, H., Jędrasiak, K., Polański, A., Wojciechowski, K.: Classification of Poses and Movement Phases. In: Bolc, L., Tadeusiewicz, R., Chmielewski, L.J., Wojciechowski, K. (eds.) ICCVG 2010, Part I. LNCS, vol. 6374, pp. 193–200. Springer, Heidelberg (2010)
9. Jędrasiak, K., Nawrat, A.: Image Recognition Technique for Unmanned Aerial Vehicles. In: Bolc, L., Kulikowski, J.L., Wojciechowski, K. (eds.) ICCVG 2008. LNCS, vol. 5337, pp. 391–399. Springer, Heidelberg (2009)
10. Iwaneczko, P., Jędrasiak, K., Daniec, K., Nawrat, A.: A Prototype of Unmanned Aerial Vehicle for Image Acquisition. In: Bolc, L., Tadeusiewicz, R., Chmielewski, L.J., Wojciechowski, K. (eds.) ICCVG 2012. LNCS, vol. 7594, pp. 87–94. Springer, Heidelberg (2012)
11. Nawrat, A., Jedrasiak, K.: SETh system spatio-temporal object tracking using combined color and motion features. In: 9th WSEAS International Conference on Robotics, Control and Manufacturing Technology, Hangzhou, China (2009)

An Easy to Use Mobile Augmented Reality Platform for Assisted Living Using Pico-projectors

Rafael F.V. Saracchini and Carlos C. Ortega

Technical Institute of Castilla y León, Burgos, Spain
{rafael.saracchini,calberto}@itcl.es www.itcl.es

Abstract. We present in this paper an easy to use Computer Vision based platform for real-time 3D mapping, and augmented reality in indoors environments and its innovative application in Assisted Living. The information is displayed to the user by projecting it into the environment by a wearable device with embedded pico-projector. The system does not need markers or complicated set-ups, using low cost off-the-shelf equipment. It is also robust to small changes of the environment, and can make use of surrounding objects to provide more stable camera tracking. Pilot tests in health care centres and residences demonstrated the efficacy of the initial prototype.

1 Introduction

Assisted Living systems aims to improve life quality of people with mental or physical disabilities. This support can be provided either in form of advice, warning of hazards, aid in interaction with relatives or improved supervision of caregivers, with desired minimal intrusion in his/her living habits. However, the adoption of such systems is difficult since they require constant interaction from users, which are unfamiliar with technology and expensive/complex infrastructure.

It was shown by Mist et al.[11] that realistic visual cues can be added into the user's surroundings by using *Augmented Reality* (AR) and a wearable set of camera and pico-projector, being a promising approach to interact with the user. State-of-art AR and *Simultaneous Localisation and Mapping* (SLAM) methods do not need introduction of markers or complicated calibration procedures, recognising locations and tracking the user movement with low cost equipment. Moreover, they are better suited for this task than most commercial real-time localisation systems [15] since the 3D orientation of the wearable device is necessary for AR.

Our contribution consists in the design of an innovative approach for an mobile augmented reality system and its potential application in assisted living. It also uses infrastructure already available in most of residences and healthcare centres. In our platform, we recover the environment map through a robust RGBD SLAM algorithm and generate a suitable input to a monocular visual

L.J. Chmielewski et al. (Eds.): ICCVG 2014, LNCS 8671, pp. 552–561, 2014.

tracker. Instead providing information to the user through a screen, or mounted heads-up display, we project a seamlessly merged overlay into the environment by a wearable portable device, with minimal user interaction. See figure 1.

Fig. 1. Our concept of Assisted Living system with on-site augmented reality by use of a wearable device

2   Related Work

Visual SLAM approaches aims to provide on-line 3D mapping of indoors environments to use in Augmented Reality, location and tracking applications. Those approaches can be either sparse, or patch-based approaches such as presented by Karlsson et al. [7], Klein et al. [1,8] or dense approaches, introduced by the seminal work of Newcombe et al. [13] and Engel et al. [2]. They retrieve a set of 3D map of reference patches or points, enough for visual tracking, but difficult to an operator to interact and determine interest regions with accuracy. Retrieval of a high-quality 3D map requires the application of dense stereo reconstruction [4,3], which not always provide an accurate result.

RGBD SLAM algorithms makes use of depth maps coupled with a RGB image retrieved by range sensors as additional information, offering a more robust solution. High quality models of small places and objects in metric scale were obtained by the innovative work of Newcombe et al. in the Kinect Fusion algorithm [12] by using *Truncated Signal Distance Function* (TSDF) clouds. This work was later extended to allow larger reconstructions by Henry et al. [6], and Whelan et al. [16]. This approach was used in high quality AR applications as presented in the original Kinect Fusion´s paper and by Meilland et al. [9]. Their output, in general, is a 3D mesh or dense point cloud, allowing much easier manipulation and determination of regions of interest. Despite their advantages over visual methods, most RGBD cameras lacks portability and requires a sizeable power supply, being unsuitable to be adapted to a portable device.

3   System Design

Our goal is to provide an autonomous Augmented Reality system that is able to display context-dependent information (in form of sound or projected information in walls or furniture) by a wearable device. This device acts as input/output source only, when resource-intensive tasks such as tracking, mapping and management of context-dependent data are done by a stationary computer, communicating through a standard wireless network. We opted to this design since most system-on-chip boards haven't enough processing power, and to keep the mobile device costs and battery usage low. We will refer to the portable device as *Device with Camera and a Pico-projector for Augmented Reality* (DCPAR) and the computer as *AR PC*.

3.1   DCPAR

The DCPAR is a portable device which contains a embedded web-cam, a commercial pico-projector and wireless module controlled by a battery-powered Raspberry Pi board. The device sends images from the camera, and exhibits an response overlay image from the AR PC, reproducing sounds when requested. The projector's relative "point of view" towards the device camera is known and calibrated *a priori*, so it can be used directly by an AR module. It also has straps to allow the user wear the device. See figure 2.

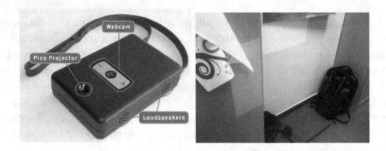

Fig. 2. DCPAR prototype (left) and an example of augmented reality: the 3D "painting" of a cabinet and the wall with distinct colours

3.2   AR PC

The *AR PC* is a standard PC responsible by the augmented reality module, context processing, network communications as well to perform tracking and mapping processing. It requires a GLSL/CUDA enabled graphics card for fast compute feature matching and RGBD odometry and roughly 2-4 GB of RAM. A RGBD camera such as Kinect or Asus Xtion Pro is needed for 3D mapping.

4   Implementation

Our software is divided in two different applications, the *RGBD SLAM* application, which captures the 3D map from the desired environment, and the *Visual Tracker*, which does determine the DCPAR's orientation and position in the previously mapped environment by the first application. Its main purpose is to provide the camera pose to an AR module, which can determine the user context and send an overlay image to the DCPAR's projector.

4.1   Map Representation

We represent an environment with a *global map* and an associated *inverted file*. They are used by in two important procedures for our system: the *visual consistency check* and *similarity search*.

The global map is an undirected graph $G = (V, E)$ with a set of vertices V and edges E. A vertex V_i stores the key-frame data, its camera pose and a *parent key-frame* denoted P_i, which is the oldest key-frame in the map which is possible determine its relative position. The key-frame data is composed by a RGB image I_i, its registered depth map D_i and SIFT features F_i. An edge $E_{ij} \in G$ stores the relative transform between the key-frames V_i and V_j and a set of matched features Fo_{ij} between I_i and I_j. This representation of the scene geometry allows perform loop closure operations with low computational costs.

The inverted file is a data structure used for image classification and fast search. It contains a list of indexing *visual words*, where an entry stores a list of every vertex where the visual word is present and its number of occurrences. In our implementation, visual words corresponds to the leaves of a indexing n-ary vocabulary tree [14], computed from a large image database. An image histogram is computed by mapping each feature $f_k \in F_i$ into a tree leaf by recursively navigating through the tree using the L_2 norm to choose the best branch. Image comparison can be done by a TF-IDF search [14] using the histogram of visual words of a query image, returning candidate vertices ordered by their IDF score.

Visual Consistency Check - The *visual consistency check* tries to evaluate a possible the relative camera pose M_c from a given set of features F_c with known position D_c. In this step we compute the frame SIFT descriptors F and perform a robust distance-ratio matching with F_c. The camera's relative pose is then computed by minimising the re-projection error between the matched features from F and the depths D_c using an iterative Levenberg-Marquardt optimisation with RANSAC. Features with re-projection error smaller than 3.0 are considered inliers and the check fails if their number is smaller than a parameter k.

Similarity Search - The *similarity search* test returns the most similar vertex V_{best} from the map and a set of reference features F_{best}, which can be used for camera calibration or detect a revisited local. Given a query image, we compute its histogram of visual words and determine a set S of the N candidates with lowest score from the TF-IDF search in the inverted file. Instead merely choosing the candidate with smallest L_1 distance [14], we cluster the candidates by their connectivity in the global map G into clusters C, where its score is the sum of matched visual words of each vertex $V_i \in C_j$. The best cluster C_{best} is then the cluster with highest score and the vertex V_{best} is defined as the cluster member with highest number of matched words. F_{best} is composed by each feature f_k such that $\{f_k \in F_{best} \Leftrightarrow f_k \in F_i | f_k \notin Fo_{ij} | V_i, V_j \in C_{best}\}$, that is, all non-overlapping features from members of the cluster C_{best}.

4.2   RGBD SLAM

We designed a RGBD SLAM algorithm which takes advantage of TSDF dense tracking with the robustness offered by pose-graph approaches. See figure 3.

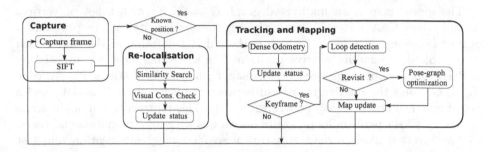

Fig. 3. RGBD SLAM work-flow

Hybrid Mapping - along the global map, our RGBD SLAM approach uses a *local map*. It is a TSDF cloud adapted to larger environments by the use of sliding a voxel cube as proposed by Whelan et al. [16]. This structure is used solely for local tracking since it suffers from drifting effects at large scale mapping and due the very high computational cost to perform a loop-closure operation.

Capture - For each new frame, we always compute its SIFT features and a tracking or re-localisation step is performed depending if the camera pose is known. The system is initialized by adding the first frame into the map with default pose, and itself as parent key-frame.

Tracking and Mapping - in this step, we perform dense odometry by computing a coarse motion estimate M_c by visual consistency check with the previous frame, matching tracked points detected by FAST. We then refine M_c by the GPU-based ICP between the frame's point cloud and surface predicted by ray-casting the local map TSDF as described by Newcombe [12]. If the camera relative displacement from the previous mapped vertex V_j is higher than a threshold,we add it in the map as key-frame, creating a new vertex V_i and edge E_{ij}. Its parent vertex is determined by a visual consistency check between it and the parent frame P_j, setting $P_i = P_j$ if successful, otherwise, we set $P_i = j$.

Loop Closure - For each new vertex V_i we perform a similarity search and choose the candidate V_j with highest number of votes where the conditions $P_i \neq P_j$ and $E_{ij} \notin G$ are satisfied. The first condition do not allow to close loops between recently mapped frames which the consistency is already ensured by the local map. The second avoids the detection of an already existing edge as loop, instead two revisited regions still not connected in the map.

If the aforementioned condition holds for V_j and a visual consistency check between V_i and V_j is successful, a loop is detected. The closure operation is performed by adding a new edge E_{ij} to the global map and minimizing the error between the edges with the TORO algorithm [5]. Since the local map will be inconsistent with the global map, a new one is generated by the vertices adjacent to the current camera pose.

Re-localisation - In the event of a tracking loss, we perform a similarity search of the current frame followed by a visual consistency check between the best vertex V_{best} and features F_{best}. If the test is successful we refine the estimated relative transform by ICP and calibrate the camera accordingly. We also add the recovered frame as a new vertex V_j and the edge $E_{j,best}$ into the map, setting its parent vertex $P_j = V_{best}$. In this case, we do not perform loop detection.

4.3   Visual Tracker

The Visual Tracker is designed to compute the DCPAR's orientation and position autonomously using the pose-graph map G. Its work-flow is shown in the figure 4.

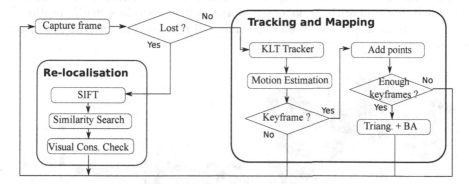

Fig. 4. Visual Tracker work-flow

Due the potential changes in the environment movement, some original features in the map used to calibrate the camera may be lost. This and the constant user movement reduces the tracking stability. To cope with this problem we perform a temporary mapping step, adding new reference points whenever is possible.

Initialisation / Re-localisation - In the event of a system initialisation or tracking loss, the Visual Tracker estimates the camera pose by computing its SIFT features and then performing a recovery step (similarity search followed by a visual consistency check) and switches to tracking mode in case of success.

Tracking and mapping - Once the camera pose is determined, we re-project the known 3D points tracked into the image plane of the previous calibrated frame and compute their displacement by the Lucas-Kanade tracker. The motion estimation is then done by minimising the re-projection error by iterative Levenberg-Marquardt using the previous camera pose as initial guess.

To perform a local mapping, we start to store key-frames by using the same criteria as in section 4.2 after the initial calibration. For the first added keyframe we also add new candidate points with unknown position detected by

FAST. When tracker have enough key-frames (in order of 3 to 5), we triangulate the unknown points and refine the camera pose by a local bundle adjustment step [17], minimising the re-projection error of all tracked points. In order to avoid degenerated triangulation, we use only key-frames that have enough rotation and translation(a minimum baseline of 10 degrees of rotation and 10 cm of translation). If the camera calibration turns out to be inconsistent or the number of tracked points is smaller than k, we discard all the key-frames stored and switch back to the re-localisation stage.

5   Tests

We have tested our framework successfully in several environments such as residences and health-care centres (from $60m^2$ to $215m^2$). Our reconstructions were on par with the PCL library implementation of KinectFusion, however we noticed that both algorithms do not perform well in corridors, with rotational errors of 5 to 20 degrees between two connected regions. The outputs produced by the system are shown in figure 5.

Fig. 5. Recovered 3D map(left and middle) and system in use (right)

Execution times: Although the execution times are slower than the original KinectFusion, we achieved an acceptable speed of $5-10$ frames per second during the capture, allowing the on-site retrieval of the map, which can be readily used by the Visual Tracker. The Visual tracker, in its turn, is able to run at very high speeds, with slower frame-rate only when in localisation mode, providing fluid tracking at ≈ 110 frames per second. The timings for a standard AR PC (Intel processor I5-3470 3.2 Ghz, with 4 GB of RAM, Nvidia GTX 650 GPU, 64-bit Debian Linux) are shown in table 1.

Initialisation/Re-localisation: We tested our recovery step using labelled frame sequences comparing a frame label with the label of the estimated location from the similarity search. We classified places accordingly the following categories: Rooms with high and low amount of distinguishable features, and zones with ambiguous appearance (corridors, almost blank walls). We used a vocabulary tree contained $W = 10^6$ words (6 levels, 10 leaves), and calibrated the camera with at least $k = 12$ inliers. The graph-based allows infer the user location even when not able to calibrate the camera. Regions with few details, however, are very problematic, requiring the user to look at some region with some recognizable feature like a painting or furniture. See table 2. The average camera pose error is around $\approx 0.5 - 7$ cm, which is acceptable for most of the advises to be displayed, but it tends be much larger ($\approx 40 - 60$ cm) when the camera is calibrated using far away planar regions.

Tracking Accuracy: To verify the accuracy of our visual tracker, we compared its computed trajectory with a ground truth calculated by a robust algorithm, the AFFTrack [10]. We also compared the trajectory error with a simple frame-to-frame tracking using the Lucas-Kanade tracker without the local mapping step. For these tests we used two scenes with circular trajectory: one easy to track scene (planar markers in a non-coplanar disposition), and a complex 3D object with occluding features. The tracking results were superior than simple tracking, and acceptable to close-range Augmented Reality. As limitation, the tracker is not robust to incremental drifting and occlusions. See figure 6.

Table 1. RGBD SLAM/Visual tracker timings for a standard AR PC

RGBD SLAM		Visual Tracker	
Step	time	Step	time
SIFT computation	40.5ms	Initialisation/Recovery	53.2ms
Tracking	102.2ms	Tracking	6ms
Similarity search	5.2ms	Similarity search	2.5ms
Loop closure	355.7ms	Triang. + B.A.	32ms
Avg. time	187.6ms	Avg. time	8ms

Table 2. Recognition rates of the re-localisation algorithm for N vertex candidates

	Recognition rate				Recovery rate			
Region type	$N = 1$	$N = 5$	$N = 7$	$N = 15$	$N = 1$	$N = 5$	$N = 7$	$N = 15$
High detailed	62.6%	72.0%	73.2%	75.5%	53.8%	59.0%	59.3%	61.5%
Few details	29.7%	39.9%	40.4%	42.8%	10.6%	14.6%	15.2%	16.2%
Ambiguous	16.0%	12.6%	27.6%	27.7%	4.5%	7.0%	7.5%	7.5%

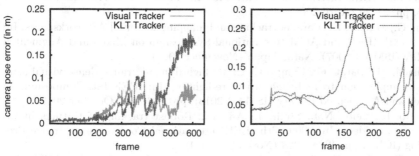

Fig. 6. Trajectory error for a simple (left) and a complex scene (right)

6   Conclusions and Acknowledgements

Our initial tests showed that the system is robust enough to be used in daily usage and makes use of infrastructure already existent in most of residences and health-care centres, being able to be used in monitoring and assisted living tools. We plan to incorporate a real-time implementation of the AFFTrack [10] algorithm for calibration and tracking, and initial tests showed improved accuracy and stability. Future iterations also aim to make use of accelerometers present in most mobile platforms, and be compatible with emerging wearable technology such as Google Glass. This work is part of the Natural Communication Device for Assisted Living project (NACODEAL - www.nacodeal.eu), funded by the Ambient Assisted Living Joint Programme, grant ref. AAL-2010-3-116.

References

1. Castle, R.O., Murray, D.W.: Object recognition and localization while tracking and mapping. In: 8th IEEE International Symposium on Mixed and Augmented Reality, ISMAR 2009, pp. 179–180 (October 2009)
2. Engel, J., Sturm, J., Cremers, D.: Semi-dense visual odometry for a monocular camera. In: IEEE International Conference on Computer Vision (ICCV 2013), pp. 1449–1456 (December 2013)
3. Furukawa, Y., Ponce, J.: Accurate, dense, and robust multiview stereopsis. IEEE Trans. on Pattern Analysis and Machine Intelligence 32(8), 1362–1376 (2010)
4. Goesele, M., Snavely, N., Curless, B., Hoppe, H., Seitz, S.M.: Multi-view stereo for community photo collections. In: IEEE 11th International Conference on Computer Vision, ICCV 2007, pp. 1–8 (October 2007)
5. Grisetti, Stachniss, Grzonka, Burgard: A tree parameterization for efficiently computing maximum likelihood maps using gradient descent. In: Proc. of Robotics: Science and Systems (2007)
6. Henry, P., Krainin, M., Herbst, E., Ren, X., Fox, D.: Rgb-d mapping: Using kinect-style depth cameras for dense 3d modeling of indoor environments. Int. Journal of Robotics Research 31(5), 647–663 (2012)
7. Karlsson, N., di Bernardo, E., Ostrowski, J., Goncalves, L., Pirjanian, P., Munich, M.E.: The vSLAM algorithm for robust localization and mapping. In: Proceedings of the 2005 IEEE International Conference on Robotics and Automation, ICRA 2005, pp. 24–29 (April 2005)
8. Klein, G., Murray, D.: Parallel tracking and mapping for small AR workspaces. In: Proc. Sixth IEEE and ACM International Symposium on Mixed and Augmented Reality (ISMAR 2007), Nara, Japan (November 2007)
9. Meilland, M., Barat, C., Comport, A.: 3D high dynamic range dense visual slam and its application to real-time object re-lighting. In: IEEE Int. Symposium on Mixed and Augmented Reality (ISMAR 2013), pp. 143–152 (October 2013)
10. Minetto, R., Leite, N.J., Stolfi, J.: Afftrack: Robust tracking of features in variable-zoom videos. In: 2009 16th IEEE International Conference on Image Processing (ICIP), pp. 4285–4288 (November 2009)
11. Mistry, P., Maes, P.: Sixthsense: A wearable gestural interface. In: ACM SIGGRAPH, pp. 11:1–11:1. ACM, New York (2009)

12. Newcombe, Izadi, Hillige, Molyneaux, Kim, Davison, Kohi, Shotton, Hodges, Fitzgibbon: Kinectfusion: Real-time dense surface mapping and tracking. In: IEEE Int. Symp. on Mixed and Augmented Reality (ISMAR), pp. 127–136 (October 2011)
13. Newcombe, Lovegrove, Davison: Dtam: Dense tracking and mapping in real-time. In: IEEE Int. Conf. on Computer Vision (ICCV), pp. 2320–2327 (2011)
14. Nister, D., Stewenius, H.: Scalable recognition with a vocabulary tree. In: IEEE Computer Society Conference on Computer Vision and Pattern Recognition, vol. 2, pp. 2161–2168 (2006)
15. Engineering System Technologies, Ekahau Vision, Sonitor Technologies, and Ubisense (2014)
16. Whelan, Kaess, Fallon, Johannsson, Leonard, McDonald: Kintinuous: Spatially extended kinectfusion. Technical Report MIT-CSAIL-TR-2012-020
17. Wu, Agarwal, Curless, Seitz: Multicore bundle adjustment. In: IEEE Conf. on Computer Vision and Pattern Recognition (CVPR), pp. 3057–3064 (2011)

Multi-robot, EKF-Based Visual SLAM System

Adam Schmidt

Poznań University of Technology, Poznań, Poland
Institute of Control and Information Engineering
Adam.Schmidt@put.poznan.pl

Abstract. This paper presents the multi-robot visual SLAM system based on the Extended Kalman Filter. The widely known MonoSLAM system was modified to allow cooperation of several heterogeneous mobile robots. Moreover, the mechanism for mutual observations of the mobile robots was developed. The proposed system was evaluated using the video sequences gathered using two mobile robots. The incorporation of the relative pose measurements resulted in the reduction of the RMS of the trajectories' reconstruction error by over 20%.

Keywords: SLAM, multi-robot, robot navigation.

1 Introduction

The ability to operate in an unknown environment is one of the basic requirements for autonomous operation of mobile robots. Over the years a significant effort has been put into development of the simultaneous localization and mapping (SLAM) algorithms with much of the attention focusing on the vision-based solution. Several widely recognized visual SLAM systems have been developed including the MonoSLAM [3], the FastSLAM [9], the PTAM [6], the FrameSLAM[7] or the systems based on the g2o framework [8]. Though those systems significantly differ in the approach to the SLAM problem they are all similar in the fact, that they are designed specifically for a single camera or mobile robot scenario.

Recently an increasing attention is given to the development of the multi-robot visual SLAM systems allowing the cooperative exploration of the environment. Ballesta et al. proposed a system for merging maps that are independently obtained using the FastSLAM algorithm [1] whereas Gil et al. extended the FastSLAM to cope with the multi-robot scenario directly [5]. In their work Forster et al. [4] presented a cooperative SLAM system for UAVs. They noted that the multi-robot SLAM is computationally demanding and proposed specialized data structures to cope with this problem. The same issue was noticed by Riazuelo et al. who proposed a distributed, cloud-based framework [10].

This paper presents an attempt to adapt the widely known and recognized MonoSLAM [3] system to the multi-robot scenarios. Moreover, a mechanism for mutual observations of the mobile robots using markers attached to the robots is proposed. This extension facilitates the initialization of the system and increases

L.J. Chmielewski et al. (Eds.): ICCVG 2014, LNCS 8671, pp. 562–569, 2014.

the trajectory reconstruction precision. Section 2 presents the proposed multi-robot SLAM system. The algorithms for detection and pose calculation of the markers attached to the robots are described in Section 3. The experimental evaluation of the proposed system is given in Section 4 and Section 5 concludes the paper.

2 Multi-robot Visual SLAM System

2.1 Environment Model

The probabilistic map approach of the MonoSLAM system [3] was adopted to model the environment. It is assumed that the environment consists of an arbitrary number of heterogeneous mobile robots carrying a given number of cameras and markers and of point features represented using the inverse depth parametrization [2].

$$x = [\, x_r^1 \, \dots \, x_r^{nR} \, x_c^1 \, \dots \, x_c^{nC} \, x_m^1 \, \dots \, x_m^{nM} \, x_f^1 \, \dots \, x_f^{nF} \,]^T \tag{1}$$

where nR, nC, nM and nF stand for the number of robots, cameras, markers and point features respectively. The Extended Kalman Filter (EKF) is used to update the state estimates and the uncertainty of those estimates is modeled as a single, multi-variate Gaussian represented by the covariance matrix P. The 'agile' model of the robot's movement [3] was used.

2.2 Initialization

During the system initialization the global coordinates system is instantiated at the coordinates of the first robot. No prior knowledge regarding the relative pose of the robots is assumed, thus the other robots are added to the SLAM system after being involved in a robot observation for the first time. Two possible variants of such initialization are possible. Either the uninitialized robot is observing a previously initialized one or is being observed by such.

In the first scenario the position vector r_{new} and the orientation quaternion q_{new} of the robot being initialized are calculated as:

$$r_{new} = R(q_{init}) \left(R(q_m) R(q_h)^T \left(-R(q_c)^T r_c - r_h \right) + r_m \right) + r_{init} \tag{2}$$

$$q_{new} = q_{init} \times q_m \times q_h^* \times q_c^* \tag{3}$$

in the latter they are given by:

$$r_{new} = R(q_{init}) \left(R(q_c) \left(-R(q_h) R(q_m)^T r_m + r_h \right) + r_c \right) + r_{init} \tag{4}$$

$$q_{new} = q_{init} \times q_c \times q_h \times q_m \tag{5}$$

where q_{init} and r_{init}, q_c and r_c, q_m and r_m stand for the orientation quaternion and position vector of the already initialized robot, the camera and the marker respectively. The measurement of the marker's pose w.r.t. the observing camera's coordinates is denoted as q_h and r_h, $R(q)$ is the rotation matrix equivalent to the quaternion q, q^* is the conjugate quaternion and $\times$ stands for the Hamilton product.

2.3   Prediction

Similarly to the MonoSLAM system [3] it is assumed that the robots are the only dynamic elements of the environment. During the prediction stage, the state of the robots is modified according to the 'agile model' while the state of all the other elements remains unchanged. As the proposed system allows cooperation of arbitrary number of robots it is assumed that the robots move independently.

2.4   Measurements and Update

The state vector's estimate is updated using the standard EKF procedure according to two types of measurements (Figure 1 - left):

$$h = \begin{bmatrix} h_f^1 \dots h_f^{nF} \; h_{rel}^1 \dots h_{rel}^{nRel} \end{bmatrix}^T \tag{6}$$

The first kind (h_f^i) is the observations of the point features' projections onto the current camera frames similarly to the method of the original MonoSLAM [3]. The second kind is the measurements of the relative pose of the mobile robots obtained by observations of the markers attached to the robots. The predicted relative pose of two robots is calculated as:

$$h_{rel} = \begin{bmatrix} h_r \\ h_q \end{bmatrix} = \begin{bmatrix} R(q_c)^T \left(R(q_{act})^T \left((R(q_{pas})r_m + r_{pas}) - r_{act} \right) - r_c \right) \\ q_c^* \times q_{act}^* \times q_{pas} \times q_m \end{bmatrix} \tag{7}$$

where r_{act} and q_{act}, r_{pas} and q_{pas} stand for the position and orientation of the active robot (carrying the camera) and the passive robot (carrying the marker) respectively.

Fig. 1. The effects of a robot passing through the field of view of other's robot camera: left - point features and robot marker observations, right - occlusion

3   Robot Markers

Each of the markers used in the proposed system consists of a black frame on a white background separating the marker from the texture of its neighborhood. Four circles are regularly distributed within the frame. The center of the black circle identifies the origin of the marker coordinate system, the second and the fourth circle define the x and y axes correspondingly. The three non-black circles can be either red, green or blue allowing for easy identification of 27 instances of the marker.

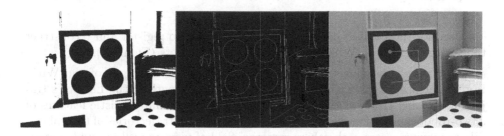

Fig. 2. The marker detection: left - thresholded image, center - detected contours, right - detected marker

The markers are detected by thresholding the image with some predefined threshold value. As the markers consist of four circles on a white background surrounded by a black frame this facilitates further processing. Afterwards the hierarchy of contours is constructed using the algorithm by Suzuki[14]. The groups of four contours lying on the same level of the hierarchy (i.e. within the same object) are analyzed further. If all the shapes are circular, their relative positions are correct, only one circle is black and all the others are either green, blue or red the group is considered to be a marker (Figure 2).

The pose of the marker w.r.t. the observed camera is calculated in two steps. First, the homography between the marker plane and the image plane is calculated. The rotation and position extracted from the homography matrix serve as a starting point for the second stage. The Levenberg-Marquardt algorithm is used to find the orientation quaternion and position vector minimizing the reprojection error between the observed centers of circles and their calculated position.

4   Experiments

4.1   Data

The evaluation of the proposed system required recording video sequences from two mobile robots equipped with cameras and markers. The robot motion registration system described by Schmidt et al. [12] and procedure similar to the

Fig. 3. The robots used in the experiment: LabBOT - left, WiFiBot - right

one used for the PUT RGBD dataset [11] were used to register and reconstruct the trajectories of the WiFiBot and the LabBOT robots (Figure 3).

A sequence consisting of 700 steps was recorded. The length of the WiFi-Bot's reference trajectory equaled $8.67[m]$ while the length of the LabBot's trajectory equaled $11.97[m]$. The registered data involved characteristic features of a two-robot exploration scenario involving intersecting trajectories of two robots, robots moving across each others cameras' field of view as well as sudden stops and changes of the movement's direction.

4.2 Results

The absolute trajectory error (ATE) metric presented by Sturm et al. [13] was used to evaluate the presented system. The estimated sequences of the robots' positions $r_j(i)$ where i is the number of the frame and j is the number of the robot were compared with the known, reference positions $r_j^{GT}(i)$. The reconstructed trajectories were expressed in the coordinate system coinciding with the initial coordinates of the first robot. To allow the comparison and to remove the ambiguity of the scale the rotation R, translation t and scale s aligning the obtained trajectories with the reference trajectories in terms of least-squares were determined. Once the trajectories were aligned the ATE of the j-th robot at iteration i was be calculated as:

$$\text{ATE}_j(i) = ||r_j^{GT}(i) - (sRr_j(i) + t)|| \tag{8}$$

The quality of the reconstructed trajectories was measured using the RMS of the errors:

$$\text{RMSE} = \sqrt{\frac{1}{n}\sum_{j=1}^{2}\sum_{i=1}^{n}\left(\text{ATE}_j(i)\right)^2} \tag{9}$$

The two variants of the system were evaluated. In the first one the markers observations were used solely for the purpose of initialization. In the second one, the mutual observations of the robots relative pose were incorporated into the measurements vector.

Table 1. The RMS and maximum ATE error

Mutual observations	RMSE [m]	max. ATE [m]
no	0.220	0.447
yes	0.173	0.425

Table 1 contains the numerical values of the maximal ATE and RMSE. Although the maximal ATE was similar in both cases, using the additional robot observations resulted in the reduction of the RMSE by over 20%. The obtained trajectories are presented in Figure 4.

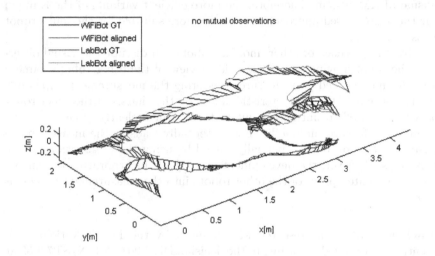

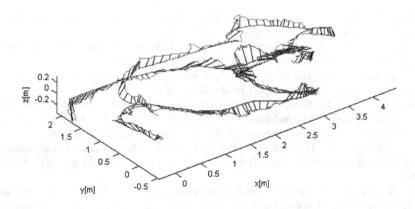

Fig. 4. The trajectories obtained during the two-robots experiments

5   Conclusions

This paper presented an successful attempt to track the trajectories of two mobile robots using the EKF-based visual SLAM system. Moreover, the mechanism for mutual observations of robots was proposed and incorporation of such measurements improved the quality of the reconstructed trajectories.

However, two main limitations of the EKF-based multi-robot system were observed. Firstly, the length of the state and the measurement vectors is approximately doubled. The quadratic complexity of the Kalman filter results in a significant increase of the processing time hindering the real-time operation of such visual SLAM system. Therefore, the more efficient variants of the Kalman filter or the graph-based approach may prove more suitable for the multi-robot scenarios.

Secondly, the presence of other, moving robots can disrupt the visual observations. The robot moving across the field of view of the other robot's camera can occlude the observed point features rendering the measurement impossible (Figure 1). Moreover, the characteristic points on the chassis of the other robot can be wrongly used to initialize point features, which clearly violates the assumption of the features immobility and potentially leads to the measurements inconsistency. This problem is partially solved by using the observations of the robot markers. However, the development of methods incorporating the knowledge of the estimated poses of the other robots into the measurement process is necessary.

Acknowledgment. This research was financed by the Polish National Science Centre grant funded according to the decision DEC-2011/01/N/ST7/05940, which is gratefully acknowledged.

References

1. Ballesta, M., Gil, A., Reinoso, O., Juliá, M., Jiménez, L.M.: Multi-robot map alignment in visual SLAM. WTOS 9(2), 213–222 (2010)
2. Civera, J., Davison, A.J., Montiel, J.: Inverse depth parametrization for monocular SLAM. IEEE Transactions on Robotics 24(5), 932–945 (2008)
3. Davison, A.J., Reid, I.D., Molton, N.D., Stasse, O.: Monoslam: Real-time single camera slam. IEEE J PAMI 29(6), 1052–1067 (2007)
4. Forster, C., Lynen, S., Kneip, L., Scaramuzza, D.: Collaborative monocular SLAM with multiple micro aerial vehicles. In: 2013 IEEE/RSJ International Conference on Intelligent Robots and Systems (IROS), pp. 3962–3970. IEEE (2013)
5. Gil, A., Reinoso, Ó., Ballesta, M., Juliá, M.: Multi-robot visual SLAM using a Rao-Blackwellized particle filter. Robotics and Autonomous Systems 58(1), 68–80 (2010)
6. Klein, G., Murray, D.: Parallel tracking and mapping for small AR workspaces. In: 6th IEEE and ACM International Symposium on Mixed and Augmented Reality, ISMAR 2007, pp. 225–234. IEEE (2007)
7. Konolige, K., Agrawal, M.: Frameslam: From bundle adjustment to real-time visual mapping. IEEE Transactions on Robotics 24(5), 1066–1077 (2008)

8. Kummerle, R., Grisetti, G., Strasdat, H., Konolige, K., Burgard, W.: g2o: A general framework for graph optimization. In: 2011 IEEE International Conference on Robotics and Automation (ICRA), pp. 3607–3613. IEEE (2011)
9. Montemerlo, M., Thrun, S., Koller, D., Wegbreit, B., et al.: FastSLAM: A factored solution to the simultaneous localization and mapping problem. In: AAAI 2002 Proceedings (2002)
10. Riazuelo, L., Civera, J., Montiel, J.: C2TAM: A cloud framework for cooperative tracking and mapping. Robotics and Autonomous Systems 62(4), 401–413 (2013)
11. Schmidt, A., Fularz, M., Kraft, M., Kasiński, A., Nowicki, M.: An indoor RGB-D dataset for the evaluation of robot navigation algorithms. In: Blanc-Talon, J., Kasinski, A., Philips, W., Popescu, D., Scheunders, P. (eds.) ACIVS 2013. LNCS, vol. 8192, pp. 321–329. Springer, Heidelberg (2013)
12. Schmidt, A., Kraft, M., Fularz, M., Domagała, Z.: The registration system for the evaluation of indoor visual slam and odometry algorithms. Journal of Automation, Mobile Robotics & Intelligent Systems 7(2), 46–51 (2013)
13. Sturm, J., Magnenat, S., Engelhard, N., Pomerleau, F., Colas, F., Burgard, W., Cremers, D., Siegwart, R.: Towards a benchmark for RGB-D slam evaluation. In: Proc. of the RGB-D Workshop on Advanced Reasoning with Depth Cameras at Robotics: Science and Systems Conf. (RSS), Los Angeles, USA (June 2011)
14. Suzuki, S.: Topological structural analysis of digitized binary images by border following. Computer Vision, Graphics, and Image Processing 30(1), 32–46 (1985)

The EKF-Based Visual SLAM System with Relative Map Orientation Measurements

Adam Schmidt

Poznań University of Technology, Poznań, Poland
Institute of Control and Information Engineering
Adam.Schmidt@put.poznan.pl

Abstract. This paper presents the extension of the feature-based, visual SLAM with additional measurements of the relative orientation between the current and past poses of the camera. The well known inverse depth representation of the point features was replaced with the combination of local maps and simplified features to allow orientation measurements via the estimation of the essential matrix. The proposed modification was evaluated using the openly available PUT RGB-D database. The incorporation of additional measurements resulted in reduction of the RMS of the trajectory reconstruction error by 17%.

Keywords: visual SLAM, feature-based SLAM, keyframe-based SLAM.

1 Introduction

The simultaneous localization and mapping (SLAM) is an important area of the autonomous robots' navigation. Due to the availability of cheap cameras, relative simplicity of their mathematical models and rich information content of images a significant attention is paid to the vision-based SLAM systems. Several approaches to the problem have been developed over the years and two main paradigms have emerged.

In the first one the environment is modeled as a set of distinct features (e.g. characteristic points) as in the widely recognized MonoSLAM [2] and Fast-SLAM [10] systems. The state of each feature is independently modeled which results in larger dimensionality of the problem. However, individual measurements are based on relatively simple observations of particular features. Usually, the filtration methods such as the Extended Kalman Filter(EKF) [2] or the Particle Filter [10] are used to track the state of the system.

The second approach models the environment using a number of past camera positions (so called key-frames) and relations between them. Examples of such systems include the PTAM [6], the FrameSLAM [7] and the g2o framework [9]. The state vector of those systems includes only the current pose of the robot and the poses of the key-frames which significantly reduces its size. However, the measurements require calculation of relative poses between the current pose of the robot and its past poses, which can be computationally demanding. The

L.J. Chmielewski et al. (Eds.): ICCVG 2014, LNCS 8671, pp. 570–577, 2014.
© Springer International Publishing Switzerland 2014

systems using key-frame representation are generally based on the global optimization methods.

The two paradigms of the visual SLAM have been extensively compared by Strasdat et al. who have shown the advantages and limitations of both approaches [14]. Recently, Schmidt et al. have presented a visual SLAM system that, while being feature-based, incorporates the measurements of the mobile robot's orientation change similarly to the key-frame systems [12] [13].

This paper presents an attempt to extend the feature-based visual SLAM system with additional measurements of relative orientation between the current and the past poses of the cameras. Section 2 presents a brief outline of the visual SLAM system and Section 3 describes the introduced models of local maps and simplified features. The performed experiments are presented in Section 4 and Section 5 concludes the paper.

2   Visual SLAM

2.1   Environment Model

The environment is modeled using the probabilistic map approach similar to the one used in the MonoSLAM system [2]. It was assumed that it consists of a mobile robot, cameras attached to the robot, local maps and point features:

$$x = [\, x_r \; x_c^1 \ldots x_c^{nC} \; x_m^1 \ldots x_m^{nM} \; x_f^1 \ldots x_f^{nF} \,]^T \tag{1}$$

where nC, nM and nF stand for the number of robot cameras, local maps and point features correspondingly. The uncertainty of the state estimate is modeled as a single, multi-variate Gaussian represented by the covariance matrix P. The estimates are updated according to the visual measurements within the EKF.

2.2   Prediction

At each iteration of the EKF the new state of the mobile robot is predicted according to the 'agile model' adopted from the MonoSLAM [2]. The agile model is based on the assumption that the robot is affected by random accelerations resulting in its smooth movement. The robot's environment is assumed to be static, thus the state estimates of all the other elements remain unchanged.

2.3   Measurements and Update

The state estimate is updated according to two types of measurements. The first are the observations of the point features' projections onto the current image observed by one of the robot's cameras. The predicted positions of the features' projections are calculated similarly to the MonoSLAM system using the inverse depth parametrization [1]. The second are the measurements of the relative rotation between the local maps' coordinate systems and the current pose of the robot's camera. The mechanism for the relative rotation measurements is described in section 3.3. Thus, the measurements vector is defined as:

$$h = \begin{bmatrix} h_f^1 \dots h_f^N \ h_m^1 \dots h_m^M \end{bmatrix}^T \qquad (2)$$

where N and M stand for the number of point features observations and relative orientation measurements respectively. The update of the state vector's estimate is executed according to the standard EKF procedure.

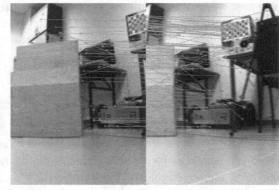

Fig. 1. The two types of measurements: left - sparse observations of point features, right - dense matching used for relative rotation estimation

2.4 Maintenance

After each iteration of the EKF the maintenance stage commences. The features that have not been observed for a number of iterations and those which have been wrongly matched are removed from the system in order to keep the length of the state vector within predefined limits. Similarly, the maps with too few features are also discarded. Afterwards, if the number of visible features is too low, new local maps and features are initialized as described in Section 3.3.

3   Local Maps and Features

3.1 Model

The inverse depth parametrization [1] is one of the most popular representations of the point features in SLAM. Each feature is represented with the Cartesian coordinates of the point from which it has been initialized (x_0, y_0, z_0), azimuth and elevation angles (ϕ and θ) expressed in the global coordinates which define a line passing through both the feature's 3D position and the point of initialization (POI) and the inverse of the distance between the POI and the feature (ρ):

$$x_{id} = \begin{bmatrix} x_0 \ y_0 \ z_0 \ \phi \ \theta \ \rho \end{bmatrix}^T \qquad (3)$$

The main advantage of such representation is the fact that the initial uncertainty of the feature's depth affects only a single variable. However, if mutliple features are added from a single camera position it becomes redundant. Moreover, expressing the angles and elevation in the global coordinates may introduce significant linearization errors for some spatial configurations.

Those problems can be alleviated by decomposing the the feature representation into two parts. The first, called a local map, represents the pose of the camera during the features' initialization and consists of the Cartesian position and quaternion describing the orientation:

$$x_m = \begin{bmatrix} r_m \ q_m \end{bmatrix}^T \tag{4}$$

Once the pose of the camera is preserved the initialized features can be represented w.r.t. the map's coordinates. Moreover, the POI for all the features lies in the map's coordinates' origin and thus can be omitted. The state vector of the simplified inverse depth feature contains only the azimuth and elevation angles as well as the inverse of the depth:

$$x_{sid} = \begin{bmatrix} \phi \ \theta \ \rho \end{bmatrix}^T \tag{5}$$

3.2   Initialization

The current pose of the camera within the global coordinates required to initialize a local map is calculated as:

$$r_m = r_r + R(q_r)r_c \tag{6}$$

$$q_m = q_r \times q_c \tag{7}$$

where $R(q)$ is the rotation matrix equivalent to the quaternion q and $\times$ stands for the Hamilton quaternion product.

Once the pose of the camera is known the state vectors of the features being initialized are calculated. As the azimuth and elevation angles are defined w.r.t. local coordinates the state of the i-th feature depends only on the observed image coordinates of the feature and the arbitrary selected initial estimate of the inverse depth (ρ_0):

$$\begin{bmatrix} h_x^i \ h_y^i \ h_z^i \end{bmatrix}^T = p^{-1} \left(\begin{bmatrix} u^i \ v^i \end{bmatrix}^T \right) \tag{8}$$

$$\phi^i = \arctan \left(\frac{h_y^i}{\sqrt{(h_x^i)^2 + (h_z^i)^2}} \right) \tag{9}$$

$$\theta^i = \arctan \left(\frac{h_x^i}{h_z^i} \right) \tag{10}$$

$$\rho^i = \rho_0 \tag{11}$$

where u^i and v^i are the image coordinates of the i-th feature's projection, p^{-1} is the inverse of the camera's projection function and h_x^i, h_y^i, h_z^i define the vector passing through both the camera focal point and the feature.

3.3   Relative Orientation Measurement

The local maps can play another important role besides serving as a reference frame for the features. At the moment of initialization the map coordinate system coincides with the coordinate system of a camera. As the camera moves its current pose changes but the map stores its past pose. The relation between the past pose of the camera and the current pose can be described by the means of the essential matrix [5]:

$$E = [t]_\times R \tag{12}$$

where t and R are the translation vector and rotation matrix transforming the current pose into the past pose of the camera, $[t]_\times$ stands for the matrix representation of the cross product with t.

The essential matrix describes the relation between projections of $3D$ points onto the current camera image and the image captured during the map initialization:

$$p^c E p^m = 0 \tag{13}$$

$$p^c = \begin{bmatrix} u^c & v^c & 1 \end{bmatrix}^T \tag{14}$$

$$p^m = \begin{bmatrix} u^m & v^m & 1 \end{bmatrix}^T \tag{15}$$

where p^c and p^m are the normalized image coordinates of the projections of point P on the current and the past camera image correspondingly. The essential matrix can be estimated by using the positions of the corresponding point features on the images captured from both poses of the camera using the 8-point [5] algorithm. In order to allow for such measurements the image captured by the camera during the map initialization is stored and associated with the map.

In order to use such observation the measurement function has to be defined. The quaternion describing the rotation between an onboard camera ($x_c = \begin{bmatrix} r_c & q_c \end{bmatrix}$) attached to a robot ($x_r = \begin{bmatrix} r_r & q_r & \ldots \end{bmatrix}$) and a map ($x_c = \begin{bmatrix} r_m & q_m \end{bmatrix}$) can be calculated as:

$$h_o(x) = q_c^* \times (q_r)^* \times q_m \tag{16}$$

where q^* is the conjugate of the quaternion q.

The actual measurement starts with detecting, describing and matching feature points on the current camera image and the stored map image by using the selected interest point detector and descriptor. Afterwards, the normalized image coordinates of the matched points are calculated by using the chosen camera model. The essential matrix is estimated using the 8-point [5] algorithm. As some of the features may be matched incorrectly a robust estimation based on the random sample consensus (RANSAC) framework [3] is used. The RANSAC allows for finding the estimate of the essential matrix supported by the biggest set of matches (so called inliers) with an assumed probability. The ratio between the number of inliers and the overall number of matches can be considered a measure of the estimation confidence and only measurements with this ratio bigger than the assumed threshold are considered successful.

4   Experiments

The proposed system was tested using the data available in the PUT RGB-D database [11]. A video sequence consisting of 800 images was selected. The length of the robot's trajectory equaled $9.28[m]$. This particular sequence was selected as it contains the elements characteristic for the indoor exploration scenario such as alternating turns, forward and backwards movement, loop closing, varying lighting conditions and slight motion blur. In order to reduce the correlation between the observations of the point features and the orientation measurements the ORB algorithm was used to detect and match the point features while the SIFT algorithm was used for the essential matrix and relative rotation estimation.

Table 1. The RMS and maximum ATE for the canonical system and the system using relative orientation measurements

Orientation measurements	RMSE [m]	max. ATE [m]
no	0.099	0.190
yes	0.082	0.137

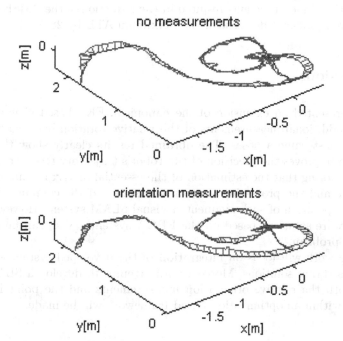

Fig. 2. The trajectories obtained for the canonical system and the system using relative orientation measurements: blue - gt trajectory, green - aligned trajectory

The results were evaluated using the absolute trajectory error (ATE) metric presented by Sturm et al. [15]. The SLAM system outputs a sequence of the estimated robot's positions $r(i)$ where i is the number of the frame. The known, reference positions of the robot are denoted as $r_{GT}(i)$. In order to allow the comparison and to remove the scale ambiguity inherent to the monocular algorithms the rotation R, translation t and scale s aligning the obtained trajectory with the reference trajectory in terms of least-squares were determined. Once both trajectories were aligned the ATE at iteration i can be calculated as:

$$\text{ATE}(i) = \|r_{GT}(i) - (sRr(i) + t)\| \tag{17}$$

In order to assess the quality of the reconstructed trajectories the RMS of the errors was calculated:

$$\text{RMSE} = \sqrt{\frac{1}{n}\sum_{i=1}^{n}(\text{ATE}(i))^2} \tag{18}$$

Figure 2 presents the trajectories obtained with the canonical system and with the system using the additional relative orientation measurements. It is clearly visible that the additional measurements smoothed the estimated trajectory and improved the tracking accuracy. The numerical results contained in Table 1 show that the additional measurements resulted in the reduction of the RMSE by 17% and even more significant decrease of the maximum ATE by 28%.

5   Conclusions

This paper presented an extension of the canonical, EKF-based visual SLAM system with additional measurements of the relative rotation between the current and the past camera poses. The obtained results clearly show that such augmentation improves the precision of the robot's trajectory reconstruction.

It is worth noting that the estimation of the essential matrix is computationally expensive and the processing time on the standard PC computer hinders the real-time operation of such augmented visual SLAM system. However, specialized hardware solutions based on the FPGA systems [8] [4] can be used to alleviate this problem.

The future work will focus on integration of the developed system with the specialized hardware solutions. Moreover, an attempt to develop a SLAM system using both the relative orientation measurements and the point features observations within an optimization-based framework will be made.

Acknowledgment. This research was financed by the Polish National Science Centre grant funded according to the decision DEC-2011/01/N/ST7/05940, which is gratefully acknowledged.

References

1. Civera, J., Davison, A.J., Montiel, J.: Inverse depth parametrization for monocular SLAM. IEEE Transactions on Robotics 24(5), 932–945 (2008)
2. Davison, A.J., Reid, I.D., Molton, N.D., Stasse, O.: Monoslam: Real-time single camera slam. IEEE J. PAMI 29(6), 1052–1067 (2007)
3. Fischler, M.A., Bolles, R.C.: Random sample consensus: A paradigm for model fitting with applications to image analysis and automated cartography. Communications of the ACM 24(6), 381–395 (1981)
4. Fularz, M., Kraft, M., Schmidt, A., Kasiński, A.: Fpga implementation of the robust essential matrix estimation with RANSAC and the 8-point and the 5-point method. In: Keller, R., Kramer, D., Weiss, J.-P. (eds.) Facing the Multicore - Challenge II. LNCS, vol. 7174, pp. 60–71. Springer, Heidelberg (2012)
5. Hartley, R., Zisserman, A.: Multiple view geometry in computer vision, 2nd edn. Cambridge Univ. Press (2000)
6. Klein, G., Murray, D.: Parallel tracking and mapping for small AR workspaces. In: 6th IEEE and ACM International Symposium on Mixed and Augmented Reality, ISMAR 2007, pp. 225–234. IEEE (2007)
7. Konolige, K., Agrawal, M.: Frameslam: From bundle adjustment to real-time visual mapping. IEEE Transactions on Robotics 24(5), 1066–1077 (2008)
8. Kraft, M., Fularz, M., Kasiński, A.: System on chip coprocessors for high speed image feature detection and matching. In: Blanc-Talon, J., Kleihorst, R., Philips, W., Popescu, D., Scheunders, P. (eds.) ACIVS 2011. LNCS, vol. 6915, pp. 599–610. Springer, Heidelberg (2011)
9. Kummerle, R., Grisetti, G., Strasdat, H., Konolige, K., Burgard, W.: g 2 o: A general framework for graph optimization. In: 2011 IEEE International Conference on Robotics and Automation (ICRA), pp. 3607–3613. IEEE (2011)
10. Montemerlo, M., Thrun, S., Koller, D., Wegbreit, B., et al.: FastSLAM: A factored solution to the simultaneous localization and mapping problem. In: AAAI 2002 Proceedings (2002)
11. Schmidt, A., Fularz, M., Kraft, M., Kasiński, A., Nowicki, M.: An indoor RGB-D dataset for the evaluation of robot navigation algorithms. In: Blanc-Talon, J., Kasinski, A., Philips, W., Popescu, D., Scheunders, P. (eds.) ACIVS 2013. LNCS, vol. 8192, pp. 321–329. Springer, Heidelberg (2013)
12. Schmidt, A., Kraft, M., Fularz, M., Domagała, Z.: On augmenting the visual SLAM with direct orientation measurement using the 5-point algorithm. Journal of Automation, Mobile Robotics & Intelligent Systems 7(1), 5–10 (2013)
13. Schmidt, A., Kraft, M., Fularz, M., Domagała, Z.: Visual simultaneous localization and mapping with direct orientation change measurements. In: Gruca, A., Czachórski, T., Kozielski, S. (eds.) Man-Machine Interactions 3. AISC, vol. 242, pp. 127–134. Springer, Heidelberg (2014)
14. Strasdat, H., Montiel, J.M., Davison, A.J.: Visual slam: Why filter? Image and Vision Computing 30(2), 65–77 (2012)
15. Sturm, J., Magnenat, S., Engelhard, N., Pomerleau, F., Colas, F., Burgard, W., Cremers, D., Siegwart, R.: Towards a benchmark for RGB-D slam evaluation. In: Proc. of the RGB-D Workshop on Advanced Reasoning with Depth Cameras at Robotics: Science and Systems Conf (RSS), Los Angeles, USA (June 2011)

Geometrical Models of Old Curvilinear Paintings

Marek Skłodowski[1], Piotr Pawłowski[1], and Katarzyna Górecka[2]

[1] Institute of Fundamental Technological Research Polish Academy of Sciences,
Pawińskiego 5b, 02-106 Warsaw, Poland
msklod@ippt.gov.pl, ppawl@ippt.pan.pl
[2] Academy of Fine Arts in Warsaw, Faculty of Conservation and Restoration of Art
Wybrzeże Kościuszkowskie 37, 00-379 Warsaw, Poland
katarzyna_gorecka@wp.pl

Abstract. The presented research is based on the on-site geometrical measurements analysis related to conservation works of the canvas "Adoration of the Magi" carried out in the Saint Aubain cathedral in Namur (Belgium). The paper presents considerations related to geometrical modeling of the painting shape based on 3D point cloud measurements and experimental and theoretical analysis of fundamentals of stretching of large curvilinear canvas. The considerations can be extended to multi-surface curvilinear canvas paintings.

1 Introduction

Curvilinear paintings on large canvases became a decorative element of churches and palaces interiors several centuries ago. One of the earliest religious curvilinear painting is "Apostles discovering the empty tomb of Mary" by Camillo Procaccini [1] from 1594, placed in Basilica di Santa Maria Maggiore in Bergamo (Italy). Convex curvilinear paintings can be found on pillars for example in St. Jacob's church in Antwerp (Belgium) or in Frauenkirche in Nuremberg (Germany). This kind of paintings can also be found in palaces e.g. a giant vault decoration at the Hall of Mirrors in the Palace of Versailles composed of the canvas cycle executed by Charles Le Brun [2]. It was the Baroque period when the large size plafond canvas were painted with an aim to provide an illusion of open-space architecture with view of the sky. Curvilinear shape of canvases' surface intensified the illusion. The next step in development of curvilinear canvas paintings are panoramas (semi-circular of 1792, by Robert Barker [3], and full circle paintings developed in XIX century). These large size paintings require special stretching of the substrate to avoid disturbance of the assumed visual impression and possible destruction of a paint layer. Currently many of the curvilinear canvases require comprehensive maintenance including conservation and redevelopment of stretching systems.

The presented research is based on the on-site geometrical measurements analysis related to conservation works of the canvas "Adoration of the Magi" carried out in the Saint-Aubain cathedral in Namur (Belgium). The painting is one of a group of four large-size canvas paintings, presenting the scenes of the Christ's

L.J. Chmielewski et al. (Eds.): ICCVG 2014, LNCS 8671, pp. 578–585, 2014.

childhood by Mauritius Heinrich Loder. It has an unusual form adapted to the shape of the apse walls [4] and has dimensions of 3,70 m in height and 4,50 m in width. The painting is bowed in the horizontal plane and the sagitta of the arc of its stretcher frame is 37 cm.

The paper presents considerations related to geometrical modeling of the painting shape based on 3D point cloud measurements and experimental and theoretical analysis of fundamentals of stretching of large curvilinear canvas. It shows that a curvilinear canvas has to be a ruled surface and that rational shaping of stretchers based on visual measurements and mathematical modeling can be successfully suggested.

2   On-site Measurements

One of the requirements for conservation activity planning was canvas shape measurement of "Adoration of the Magi" painting prior to its taking off the cathedral wall. The painting had to be placed on a correctly shaped conservation table to avoid undesirable straining of the canvas. The shape of the table had to follow average curvature of the actual deformed state of the painting (Fig. 1).

Fig. 1. Photogrammetry session of deformation measurements of "Adoration of the Magi" by Mauritius Heinrich Loder

Direct curvature and shape measurements were not possible for practical reasons because of the painting dimensions and its placement nearly 10 m above the church floor level. Therefore it was decided that remote optical shape measurements and geometry processing methods should be used to get the precise curvature, dimensions and actual deformed shape knowledge necessary for proper design and manufacturing of convex and concave conservation tables.

Fig. 2. Laser scanner position in Cathedral's presbytery

Two methods of painting shape remote measurements were chosen. First one was laser scanning with aid of 3D Surphaser 25HSX [5] and the other one close range photogrammetry with software reconstruction of camera orientation [6]. Figure 2 presents Surphaser scanner in cathedral presbytery during measurements. Full painting surface was scanned from a single position and there was no need of merging partial point clouds.

Opposite to laser scanning data merging from various images is the inherent feature of close range photogrammetry. A quality and accuracy of the painting surface reconstruction depends on many factors among which proper positioning of the camera with relation to the object is a crucial one. It is seen from Fig. 3

Fig. 3. SmartPoints and restored cameras positions after processing of photogrammetry data in PhotoModeler Scanner [6]

that camera positions were far from optimal for the painting geometry measurement. This was a consequence of the limited space available inside the cathedral and the painting hanging high above the floor level as shown in Fig. 1.

SmartPoints shown in Fig. 3 did not cover the whole painting surface due to lack of visible texture in the dark oil paitning layer. Despite of that an adequate reconstruction of painting stretcher shape was possible on the basis of the photogrammetry data. Accuracy of various remote optical measurement methods with application to large canvas paintings is discussed in the report [7].

3   Geometry Modeling

Based on 3D laser scan data, the actual deformed shape of the painting was modeled. Gauss curvature representing so called "surface roughness" was calculated to emphasize folds and warps existing in the painting prior to its conservation. The roughness surface is illustrated in Fig. 4 [8]. Then modeling of the stretcher shape was done for two purposes - a design of the convex and concave conservation tables [4] and a design of a stretching system for the renovated painting.

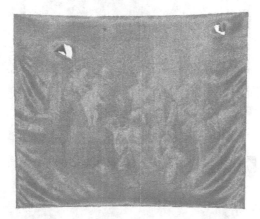

Fig. 4. Canvas deformations modeled on the basis of laser 3D scanning data

Solving the problem of looking for the original curvilinear canvas shape which the most probably existed centuries ago and which cannot be directly computed from 3D measurements of deformed surface is not a trivial one. Calculating a least mean square error surfaces which "the best" approximate the measurement results is not a correct approach in the case of curvilinear canvases.

Convex shape of the paint layer surface required a special stretching which differed from the standard ones used for plane canvases. Preliminary theoretical considerations showed that any out-of-plane tensions should result in folding of the canvas. In our case when the canvas has a non-planar but convex shape the out-of-plane component of the tensile force disappears in one situation only. This happens when tensile force is tangent to the surface.

The convex canvas was modeled in a laboratory by a simple "string model" to confirm the above considerations. The strings were parallel and all were stretched in the same vertical direction. String model deformations due to tensions introduced additionally in directions inclined to the strings (Fig. 5) confirmed the above expectations.

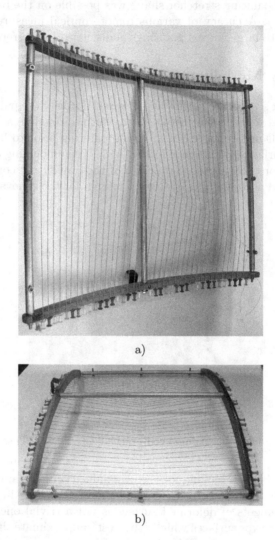

a)

b)

Fig. 5. Canvas string model deformed by diagonal (a) and lateral (b) stretching

It became obvious that a canvas can be properly stretched when forces at its boundaries act along straight lines tangent to the canvas surface. This is possible only if the canvas is a ruled surface and the forces directions coincide with the surface rulings.

A ruled surface S is generated by continuous motion of a straight line (ruling) along a base curve (directrix). This means that for each point of S one can draw at least one straight line on the surface. Ruled surfaces can be described by a parameterization [12]:

$$S(u, v) = a(u) + vr(u) \qquad (1)$$

where $a(u)$ is the directrix, and $r(u)$ is a unit vector providing direction of the ruling. Alternative representation is in the form [11]:

$$S(u, v) = (1 - v)a(u) + vb(u) \qquad (2)$$

where S is a point on the surface, $a(u)$ and $b(u)$ are two directrix curves, and u, v are parametrization variables. Straight lines connecting points on directrix curves in this case define the ruled surface.

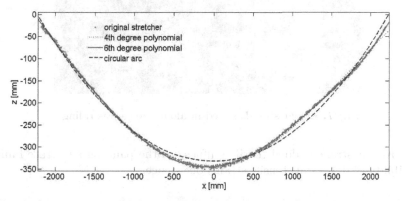

Fig. 6. Approximation of the strecher's shape based on laser 3D scanning data

One of possible approaches for finding initial shape of the analysed painting's surface is to approximate two boundary lines and use them as directrix curves for the searched ruled surface (cf. eq.2). Figure 6 depicts different approximations of the data obtained by 3D laser sacnning. Original shape of the stretcher's frame is compared with circular arc segment approximation and two approximations by polynomials of degree four and six, respectively. In all three cases obtained discrepances are acceptable, however polynomial-based approximation provides more accurate results. This fact can be related to the nature of solutions resulting

Table 1. Root mean square errors for the stretcher's frame approximations

Approximation type	RMS error [mm]
4th degree polynomial	4.34
6th degree polynomial	2.76
cricular arc	10.30

from the Euler-Bernoulli beam theory. Table 1 presents root mean square errors for the approximations of the stretcher's frame.

In the case of "Adoration of the Magi" predominant stretching of the canvas in the vertical direction was chosen. To avoid over-tensioning of the painting in that direction the knowledge gained during geometry analysis step was used and Kevlar strands (Fig.7) were sewed-in along the ruling directions.

Fig. 7. Kevlar strands sewed-in along the canvas rulings

The Kevlar strands added tensile stiffness to the painting substrate limiting a possibility of dangerous tensile strains occurence.

4   Conclusions

Analysis showed that correct initial canvas shape without out-of-surface deformations can be secured under two conditions:

- canvas must have a form of a ruled surface, and
- external tractions applied to the canvas need to be co-linear with surface rulings.

Remote optical 3D measurements are a useful tool in analysis of old large canvases shape and deformations and combined with reverse enginnering calculations based on additional geometrical assumptions may help us to discover the adequate ruled surface shape of the curvilinear painting prior to beginning of its conservation. Hence additional strengthening of a painting substrate can be rationally designed.

Taking the above into account one may suggest a new form of canvas paintings consisting of properly combined together (attached along common rulings) various ruled surfaces forming a multidimensional canvas.

Acknowledgements. Technical assistance of Mr. Jan Całka in manufacturing of the string model is thankfully acknowledged. The research was partly supported by National Science Centre under Grant "Innovative measurement of deformations in large - size canvas paintings by remote optical methods and its application in documenting, designing and evaluation of technical conservation solutions" No.165419.

References

1. Neilson, N.W.: Camillo Procaccini: paintings and drawings, New York (1979)
2. La galerie des Glaces, Charles Lebrun, maître d'oeuvre. Édition de la Réunion des Musées Nationaux, Paris (2007)
3. Comment, B.: The Painted Panorama, New York (1999)
4. Górecka, K., Skłodowski, M., Pawłowski, P., Szpor, J.: New Materials and Methods Used in the Conservation of the XVIIIth Century Curvilinear Canvas Painting "Adoration of The Magi" from the Saint Aubain Cathedral Church in Namur (Belgium). In: 6th European Symposium on Religious Art Restoration & Conservation ESRAC 2014, Florence (2014)
5. Surphaser: 3D Surphaser 25HSX. Basis Software Inc., USA, Internet: http://www.surphaser.com/surphaser.html
6. EOS Systems Inc.: PhotoMedeler Scanner, Internet: http://www.photomodeler.com/products/scanner/default.html
7. Skłodowski, M., Pawłowski, P.: Sprawozdanie z badań obrazu Pokłon Trzech Króli M. H. Lodera, z katedry St. Aubin de Namur w Belgii- Etap I i Etap II. Projekt NCN Preludium 2, Nr UMO-2011/N/HS2/01936 unpublished report (2012) (in Polish)
8. Górecka, K., Skłodowski, M., Pawłowski, P., Szpor, J., Arendarski, H.: XVIII Century Wooden Stretchers Structure Designed for Large Canvas and an Example of the Assessment Method. Advanced Materials Research 778, 113–118 (2013), doi:10.4028/www.scientific.net/AMR.778.113
9. Skłodowski, M., Pawłowski, G.K., Wójcicki, P.: Stretching of Curvilinear Religious Canvas. In: 6th European Symposium on Religious Art Restoration & Conservation, ESRAC 2014, Florence (2014)
10. Fischer, G.: Mathematische Modelle, Kommentarband. Friedr. Vieweg & Sohn Verlagsgesellschaft GmbH, Braunschweig (1986), http://download.springer.com/static/pdf/322/bok%253A978-3-322-85045-4.pdf?
11. Pottmann, H., Wallner, J.: Computational Line Geometry. Springer, Heidelberg (2001)
12. Wolfram MathWorld, Internet: http://mathworld.wolfram.com/RuledSurface.html (accessed March 04, 2014)

Novel Lightweight Quaternion Filter for Determining Orientation Based on Indications of Gyroscope, Magnetometer and Accelerometer

Janusz Słupik[1], Agnieszka Szczęsna[2], and Andrzej Polański[3]

[1] The Silesian University of Technology, Institute of Mathematics
ul. Kaszubska 23, Gliwice, Poland
Janusz.Slupik@polsl.pl
[2] The Silesian University of Technology, Institute of Informatics
ul. Akademicka 16, Gliwice, Poland
Agnieszka.Szczesna@polsl.pl
[3] Polish-Japanese Institute of Information Technology
Aleja Legionów 2, 41-902 Bytom, Poland
apolanski@pjwstk.edu.pl

Abstract. The costume for acquisition of motion is example on MO-CAP system based on IMU sensors using fusion of their measurements (like inertial, gyroscopic and magnetic measurements) for estimating motion parameters. In this paper a new simple and efficient fusion algorithm Lightweight Quaternion Filter is developed and implemented for estimation orientation in three dimensions. The result of estimations are compared to implemented Extended Quaternion Kalman Filter algorithm.

1 Introduction

The need for broadly defined measure of human motion and estimation of motion parameters occurs in many research disciplines from orthopedics through sport, art to entertainment [1], [2], [3]. The research described in this article are necessary for the construction of sensor-based IMU (*Inertial Measurement Unit*) type system for out-door acquisition and motion analysis. Miniature IMU sensors contain a triad of orthogonally mounted linear accelerometers, a triad of orthogonally mounted angular rate sensors, and a triad of orthogonally mounted magnetometers.

The angle of rotation necessary to determine the orientation is determined by integrating the output signal from the gyroscope, so the accuracy of determining the angle to the greatest extent depends on the sensor stability of zero. Zero drift (for example due to changes in temperature) results in a short time of the large error values in determined angle. The integration accumulates the noise over time and turns noise into the drift, which yields unacceptable results. Besides the gyroscope, in IMU the accelerometers measure the sum of linear acceleration and gravitation acceleration. The magnetometers measure the direction of the local magnetic field. For a stationary sensor in an environment free of magnetic

L.J. Chmielewski et al. (Eds.): ICCVG 2014, LNCS 8671, pp. 586–593, 2014.

anomalies, it is simple to determine the orientation by measuring Earth's gravitational and magnetic fields along all three axes of the orthogonally mounted sensors. The combination of the two resulting vectors can provide complete roll, pitch and yaw (RPY) angles information. In more dynamic applications, high frequency angular rate information can be combined in a complementary manner with accelerometer and magnetometer data through the use of a sensor fusion algorithms like complementary or Kalman filters [4], [5], [6], [7].

In this paper we are focusing only on filters based on quaternion representation of body orientation. Quaternions are used to represent orientation to improve computational efficiency and avoid singularities. In addition, the use of quaternions eliminates the need for computing trigonometric functions. That filters are based on the well-known correlation between the angular velocity ω and the quaternion derivative (1).

$$\dot{q} = \frac{1}{2} q \otimes \omega \tag{1}$$

In this paper we are focusing on the problem of the fusion of inertial (acceleration vector y^A), gyroscopic (angular velocity vector y^G) and magnetic (magnetic field vector y^M) measurements for estimation of orientation of the IMU sensors. We have developed new simple and efficiency filter based on quaternions algebra as **Lightweight Quaternion Filter** (LQF). The main goal of this filter design was the use of the minimum number of matrices and calculations on them. This makes the algorithm very efficient and easy to implement online with low memory resources. For comparison we have implemented other approaches known in the literature: **Extended Quaternion Kalman Filter** ($EQKF$). We performed a series of tests using the Xsens sensor raw data and the simulation data.

Section 2 describes our new orientation estimation algorithm - Lightweight Quaternion Filter. Section 3 presents Extended Quaternion Kalman Filter algorithm implemented for tests. Next section concerns experiments and results based on Xsens sensor. The last section is a summary.

2   Lightweight Quaternion Filter

The **Lightweight Quaternion Filter** (LQF) allows estimating the orientation of a body segment, which is represented with quaternions.

The orientation is estimated in two independent blocks (Fig. 1). The first one uses angular velocity and the orientation previously calculated. The process of integration gives a new orientation of the q^G, unfortunately dependent on drift problem. Orientation calculation based on correlation between the angular velocity and the quaternion derivative (1). Thus, we obtain equation:

$$q_{k+1}^G = \exp\left(\frac{T}{2} y_{k+1}^G\right) q_k, \quad k = 0, 1, \ldots \tag{2}$$

where q_0 is an orientation estimated by second block in the first frame and T is the length of the sampling period.

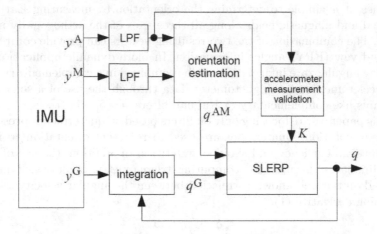

Fig. 1. The Lightweight Quaternion Filter structure

The second block uses measurements from the accelerometer and magnetometer to determine the orientation q^{AM}. The measurement of the accelerometer and magnetometer are subjected to pre-filtered using a low pass filter (LPF). That filters are firewall for sensors self-noise, thus improving the orientation estimation result in that block. The quaternion q^{AM} describes rotation between two orthogonal vector systems. These systems are obtained by the Gram-Schmidt process of vector systems: y^A, y^M, $y^A \times y^M$ and g, h, $g \times h$ respectively (where g is the earth gravity vector, h is the earth magnetic field vector).

The estimation of orientation of the second block is dependent on the occurrence of an external sensor acceleration. If such acceleration occurs, the block incorrectly calculate orientation. Therefore, it is used acceleration measurement validation function, which produces an parameter K. This parameter specifies the proportions in which the orientations of the two blocks affect the final orientation q. For this purpose we use spherical linear interpolation (SLERP):

$$q = q^G \left((q^G)^{-1} q^{AM} \right)^K \tag{3}$$

If $K = 0$, this means that external acceleration was too large, so $q = q^G$. If $K = 1$, then $q = q^{AM}$.

The acceleration measurement validation function f is defined by the rule:

$$f : y^A \mapsto K$$

$$f(y^A) = \begin{cases} 0 & d_y > 9 \cdot \sigma \\ -\frac{d_y}{9 \cdot \sigma} + 1 & d_y \leqslant 9 \cdot \sigma \end{cases} \tag{4}$$

where $d_y = \left| |y^{AM}| - |g| \right|$ and σ is the standard deviation of the accelerometer. Also the delay of non-zero value of the parameter K is used. If $K_i \neq 0$ (K_i is a value of K at i-th frame) and there exists a $j \in \{i - \epsilon, \ldots, i - 1\}$, that $K_j = 0$, then K_i is set also to zero.

3 Extended Quaternion Kalman Filter (EQKF)

In [6], the filter continuously corrects drift based on the assumption that human segments acceleration is bounded, and averages to zero over any extended period of time. It adopts a two-layer filter architecture (Fig. 2), in which first block pre-processes accelerometer and magnetometer data and find a corresponding orientation quaternion. In that block algorithms to solve the Wahba problem can be used. In [6] the Quest algorithm was used. In similar solutions the Gauss-Newton iteration method was used [8] and FQA (Factored Quaternion Algorithm) [9]. This preprocessing step reduces the dimension of the state vector and makes the measurement equations linear.

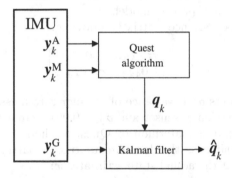

Fig. 2. The Extended Quaternion Kalman Filter block diagram

The QUEST algorithm is a popular algorithm for a single-frame estimation of an attitude quaternion [10]. The algorithm was created to solve Wahba's problem that involved determination of the attitude of a rigid body in reference to a fixed coordinate system based on a set of measurement or observation vectors using a closed form solution. The minimum number of measurement vectors required to compute orientation is two.

The state vector x is 7-D, with the first three components being the angular rate y^G, and the last four components being the quaternion q (5).

$$x_k = \begin{bmatrix} y_k^G \\ q_k \end{bmatrix} \tag{5}$$

Based on a process model representing motion dynamics the state equation $\dot{x} = f(x)$ is given by:

$$\dot{x}_k = \begin{bmatrix} \frac{1}{\tau}(-y_k^G + w_k) \\ \frac{1}{2} q_k \otimes y_k^G \end{bmatrix} \tag{6}$$

where q is the orientation quaternion, y^G is the angular velocity, w is a white noise, and τ is the time constant.

The measurement equations (7) are linear:

$$z_k = x_k + v_k \tag{7}$$

where v_k is the white noise measurement.

It should be noted that equitation (6) is non-linear differential equations. The Extended Kalman filter linearizes a non-linear process model about the estimated trajectory of the filter.

The system covariance matrix is following:

$$Q = \begin{bmatrix} \frac{D}{2\tau}(1 - e^{-\frac{2\Delta t}{\tau}}) \cdot I_{3\times3} & 0_{3\times4} \\ 0_{4\times3} & 0_{4\times4} \end{bmatrix} \tag{8}$$

where D is the variance of continuous white noise with zero mean. In experiments $D = 50$ was taken from publication where the variance and time constant was estimated in simulation of process model.

The measurement covariance matrix is following:

$$R = \begin{bmatrix} \sigma_1^2 \cdot I_{3\times3} & 0_{3\times4} \\ 0_{4\times3} & \sigma_2^2 \cdot I_{4\times4} \end{bmatrix} \tag{9}$$

where diagonal elements σ_1^2 is variance of angular rate measurements and were taken from documentation of sensor and $\sigma_2^2 = 0.001$ were experimentally determined based on computed quaternion by Quest method.

State transition matrix is the Jacobian matrix of partial derivatives of the state equation $f(x)$ at the actual state estimates $\hat{x}$:

$$\Phi_k = \begin{bmatrix} e^{-\frac{\Delta t}{\tau}} \cdot I_{3\times3} & 0_{3\times4} \\ \frac{\Delta t}{2} \cdot A_{4\times3} & I_{4\times4} + \frac{\Delta t}{2} \cdot B_{4\times4} \end{bmatrix} \tag{10}$$

where

$$A_{4\times3} = \begin{bmatrix} -\hat{x}_5 & -\hat{x}_6 & -\hat{x}_7 \\ \hat{x}_4 & -\hat{x}_7 & \hat{x}_6 \\ \hat{x}_7 & \hat{x}_4 & -\hat{x}_5 \\ -\hat{x}_6 & \hat{x}_5 & \hat{x}_4 \end{bmatrix}, \quad B_{4\times4} = \begin{bmatrix} 0 & -\hat{x}_1 & -\hat{x}_2 & -\hat{x}_3 \\ \hat{x}_1 & 0 & \hat{x}_3 & -\hat{x}_2 \\ \hat{x}_2 & -\hat{x}_3 & 0 & \hat{x}_1 \\ \hat{x}_3 & \hat{x}_2 & -\hat{x}_1 & 0 \end{bmatrix}. \tag{11}$$

4   Experiments

Experiments were carried out using a wand (T-stick) made of plastic to which the Xsens sensor (type MTi-G-28 A53 G35) were attached. We have performed a wand rotations around different axes. The raw signals of accelerometer, magnetometer and gyroscope are input of implemented filters. The roll, pitch and yaw angles estimated by sensor are treated as a reference. Also experiments with simulation data were performed. All data were sampled with a sampling rate

100 Hz. Cut-off frequency digital low-pass filters were set at 5Hz. Parameter ϵ in the acceleration measurement validation function was set to 4. The standard deviation of the accelerometer was taken from documentation of sensor ($\sigma = 0.160$) and for simulation experiments was experimentally determined ($\sigma = 0.0088$).

In Fig. 3 the plot of roll angle estimation is presented. As a reference data we use the estimation taken from Xsens sensor. Estimation errors are presented in Fig. 4.

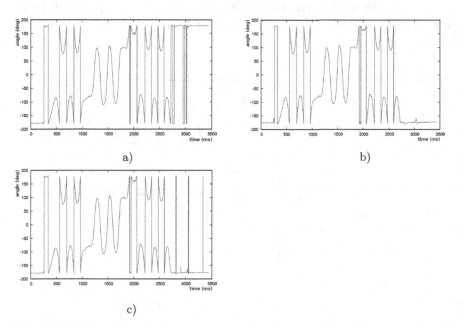

Fig. 3. Experiments with Xsens sensor, roll angle estimation a) estimated by Xsens sensor, b) estimated by EQKF c) estimated by LQF

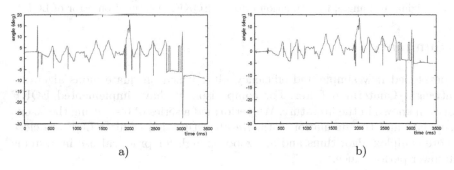

Fig. 4. Roll angle estimation errors: a) EQKF, b) LQF

The results of the estimation of filter LQF are close to the estimation obtained by algorithm implemented in the Xsens sensor and similar to the more complex solutions like EQKF. Numerous experiments revealed, that the filter LQF achieves better results than the filter EQKF by leveling influence of external acceleration. For example, this can be observed in Fig. 5.

In short periods of time, the filter LQF determines the orientation based solely on integrating of gyroscope measurements, when external accelerations occurs. In such periods, orientation estimation is distorted by the drift errors. Adaptive character of the filter LQF provides, that such errors do not grow with time. Results analysis confirms that thesis. For example, in Fig. 5 error is bounded with time.

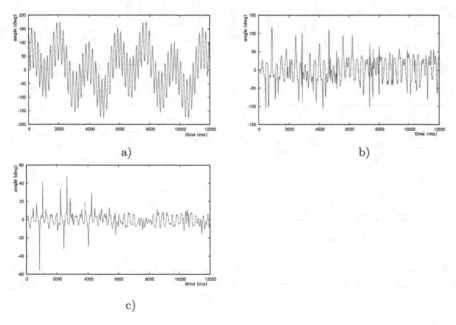

Fig. 5. Experiments with simulation data with extern acceleration, roll angle estimation a) original roll angle, b) estimation error of EQKF, c) estimation error of LQF

5   Summary

We developed new simple and efficiency filter based on quaternions algebra - Lightweight Quaternion Filter. For comparison we have implemented EQKF algorithm known in the literature. We performed a series of tests using the Xsens sensor data and the simulation data. Result estimation of filter LQF are close to more complex algorithms and are good enough for practical use in systems with lower performance.

Acknowledgment. This work was supported by projects PBS I ID 178438 path A from the Polish National Centre for Research and Development.

This work was partly performed using the infrastructure supported by POIG.02.03.01-24-099/13 grant: GCONiI - Upper-Silesian Center for Scientific Computation.

References

1. Szczęsna, A., Słupik, J., Janiak, M.: The Smooth Quaternion Lifting Scheme Transform for Multi-resolution Motion Analysis. In: Bolc, L., Tadeusiewicz, R., Chmielewski, L.J., Wojciechowski, K. (eds.) ICCVG 2012. LNCS, vol. 7594, pp. 657–668. Springer, Heidelberg (2012)
2. Świtoński, A., Polański, A., Wojciechowski, K.: Human identification based on gait paths. In: Blanc-Talon, J., Kleihorst, R., Philips, W., Popescu, D., Scheunders, P. (eds.) ACIVS 2011. LNCS, vol. 6915, pp. 531–542. Springer, Heidelberg (2011)
3. Beth, T., Boesnach, I., Haimerl, M., Moldenhauer, J., Bos, K., Wank, V.: Characteristics in Human Motion - From Acquisition to Analysis. In: IEEE International Conference on Humanoid Robots (2003)
4. Sabatini, A.M.: Kalman-Filter-Based Orientation Determination Using Inertial/Magnetic Sensors: Observability Analysis and Performance Evaluation. Sensors (2011)
5. Mahony, R., Hamel, T., Pflimlin, J.M.: Nonlinear Complementary Filters on the Special Orthogonal Group, Automatic Control. IEEE Transactions on Automatic Control 53(5), 1203–1218 (2008)
6. Yun, X., Bachmann, E.R.: Design, Implementation, and Experimental Results of a Quaternion-Based Kalman Filter for Human Body Motion Tracking. IEEE Transactions on Robotics 22(6), 1216–1227 (2006)
7. Sabatini, A.M.: Quaternion-Based Extended Kalman Filter for Determining Orientation by Inertial and Magnetic Sensing. IEEE Tran. Biomedical Eng. 53(7), 1346–1356 (2006)
8. Yun, X., Lizarraga, M., Bachmann, E.R., McGhee, R.B.: An Improved Quaternion-Based Kalman Filter for Real-Time Tracking of Rigid Body Orientation. In: Proceedings of the 2003 IEEE/RSJ International Conference on Intelligent Robots and Systems, pp. 1074–1079 (2003)
9. Yun, X., Aparicio, C., Bachmann, E.R., McGhee, R.B.: Implementation and Experimental Results of a Quaternion-Based Kalman Filter for Human Body Motion Tracking. IEEE Transactions on Robotics 22(6), 317–322 (2006)
10. Shuster, M.D., Oh, S.D.: Three-Axis Attitude Determination from Vector Observations. Journal of Guidance and Control 4(1), 70–77 (1981)

Range of Motion Measurements Using Motion Capture Data and Augmented Reality Visualisation

Dawid Sobel[1], Jan Kwiatkowski[1], Artur Ryt[1], Mariusz Domzal[1],
Karol Jedrasiak[1], Lukasz Janik[2], and Aleksander Nawrat[1]

[1] Institute of Automatic Control, Silesian University of Technology
Akademicka 16, 44-100 Gliwice, Poland
{dawid.sobel}@polsl.pl
[2] Institute of Computer Science, Silesian University of Technology
Akademicka 16, 44-100 Gliwice, Poland
{lukasz.janik}@polsl.pl

Abstract. Range of motion measurements are used by physicians, physical therapists and veterinarians. There is a need for a solution that would increase the accuracy and repeatability of the measurements obtained. Commonly used methods are based on tests using a classical goniometer are often inaccurate and depend on the individual interpretation of result by the therapist. The use of motion capture data to RoM measurements results in an accuracy of order of tens of micrometers, which is mainly due to the precision of the Motion Capture system. During the test, patient is not constrained by any device and has a total freedom of movement. It allows to carry out a medical examination not only during flexion and extension of the one limb but more limbs during dynamic movement such as walking. Clear visualization based on elements of the augmented reality in a simple manner presents measured angles, drawn on the image directly on the limbs of the patient.

Keywords: range of motion, camera calibration, augmented reality, motion capture.

1 Introduction

Modern medicine is able to deal with many diseases once thought to be incurable. The development of medical knowledge, familiarity with the human body as well as new technologies, enables implementation of complicated operations, while the medical equipment is becoming more and more precise and reliable. Specialised tools support the work of a doctor, sometimes even replacing him during operations in which the precision unattainable by a human is required.

One of the basic tests in physiotherapy is examination of the range of motion of a person, who as a result of an accident or due to some other cause cannot be physically fit [1]. The range of motion is measured with aid of a tool called goniometer, which is placed at a patient's joint, and then with its two movable

L.J. Chmielewski et al. (Eds.): ICCVG 2014, LNCS 8671, pp. 594–601, 2014.

arms, the angle formed by the flexion or extension of the limb is determined. Unfortunately, the measurements carried out with this method are sensitive to the human factor, i.e. they depend on how the tool is placed at the body and with what accuracy the value of the angle is read. The measurements done by different people can also differ and are dependent on individual interpretation. Furthermore, the examination itself requires restriction of the patient's movements and, at the same time, the therapist uses both hands to conduct the measurement. In conjunction with the above, there is a need for such a method of measurement, which is insensitive to the reading error and to the interpretation of the measurements results. The new method should also simplify the measurement as well as give the patient greater freedom of movement. It would also be great if such measurements could be taken in motion, in normal conditions during walking, running, jumping, or other exercises. It would be even better if there was a possibility of measuring a few or all the angles simultaneously.

2 Review of Medical Solutions

The main tool used for the measurements of the range of motion is a goniometer mentioned in the introduction. It is a tool consisting of two arms connected together. The arms are placed alongside parts of body between which the angle is to be meas-ured and then, the angle at which they are positioned is read (Fig. 1.a). An advantage of such solution is the simplicity of the measurement, while a disadvantage is that the measurement largely depends on the validity of the reading from the scale and exactness of placing of the goniometer at the body. Theoretically, Gajdosik and Lusin [1] show that by obeying strictly specified procedures a repeatable and reliable measurement can be made but it is still dependent on individual interpretation.

Another solution is an electronic goniometer allowing a measurement of the range of motion with the use of two sensors connected with a spring (Fig 1.b). The device enables a measurement in one or two planes, it is comfortable, especially on uneven surfaces of body and does not require constant holding by the doctor as it is attached directly to the patient. The result of the measurement is precise and can be simply read in a digital form. Manufacturer of an exemplary device, *Biometrics LTD UK* gives the accuracy of the measurement to be +/-2° in range +/-90° [3].

A laser goniometer HALO (Fig 1.c) has also been introduced in the market. It stands out due to the ease and speed of the measurement, because it only needs to be placed over the limb whose range is to be measured, then a button is pressed to determine the point of reference. The device needs to be held in the same position during the movement. At the end of the movement, the result can be read from a digital display and its accuracy is +/- 1° [4]. The manufacturer states that such a solution makes the obtained results independent of the individual measuring technique for each therapist, because independently of a person, every measurement is done identically, unlike in a classic goniometer. An additional advantage is recording of the results in the memory of the device.

The only disadvantage that can be observed is that the result is dependent on how the Halo device is held during the measurement above or directly on the limb. Because it can never be held over it in exactly the same position, the obtained results can vary insignificantly.

3   Proposed Solution

The new method of measurement of the range of movement and also processing of the results is based on the use of the data reading from Motion Capture. Motion Capture is a system of few or over a dozen of cameras calibrated to one system of coordinates and directed onto a common space. If in this space an object designated with aid of markers is found, the system is able to determine the position of every visible marker in a 3D space. The principle of operation is based on the application of diodes emitting infrared light, which reflects from the reflective markers and is later registered by the cameras. Afterwards, in the process of triangulation based on 2D images from the cameras, the position of the markers in space is determined. These markers are located on the tested limbs and joints on the patient's body (Fig. 2). Connecting these points into straight lines, selected angles in the patients body are computed.

In order to create a clear visualisation of the test results of the range of motion, elements of augmented reality were used. Selected points connected with lines and angles between them were imposed onto the image obtained from the camera registering the test. In this way, after the test, a therapist can monitor the angles changing during the examination. In order to make the obtained image overlap with the lines drawn, it is necessary to calibrate the camera.

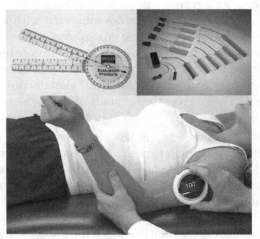

(a) - upper left, (b) upper right [3], (c) bottom [4]

Fig. 1. Classic goniometer (a), electronic goniometer (b), laser goniometer

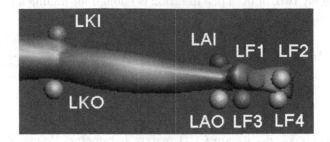

Fig. 2. Markers on the left leg

Calibration of the camera is to find intrinsic and extrinsic camera parameters. Intrinsic parameters are related to the optical and electronic properties of a camera, i.e.: focal length, radial and tangential distortion coefficients, and real coordinates of centre of the camera image. Extrinsic parameters describe transformation, rotation and translation of the system related to the observed 3D scene to the camera system. Based on this transformation, we are able to find for the points positioned in space, corresponding points on the image registered by the camera (Fig. 3). Calibration is usually done by directing the camera onto an object of a known shape and pattern or an object of known 3D coordinates its characteristic points. In case of the presented solution, the object used for the calibration was data for a few basic exercises, from Motion Capture system. It is worth noting, that if the position of the camera registering the image does not change, it is enough to run the calibration procedure once.

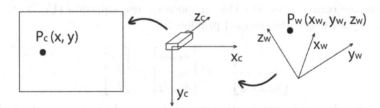

Fig. 3. Transformation of 3D coordinates into 2D image coordinates

Calibration method applied was developed by Tsai [5]. Special calibration techniques using a noncoplanar ser of point, which was used was described in detail in another publication [6]. After splitting the calibration procedure into two subprob-lems, we improve the speed of the calculation as well as the precision. The first step of the calibration algorithm is the implementation of linear methods to find approximated intrinsic and extrinsic parameter values of the camera followed by their use in the second step as the initial values in the non-linear optimisation process of the equations below (Eq. 1, Eq. 2). Thus, in the second step, only two, or even one iteration is enough for finding a solution with a good precision.

$$s_x^{-1}d_x'X + s_x^{-1}d_x'Xk_1r^2 = f\frac{r_1x_w + r_2y_w + r_2z_w + T_x}{r_7x_w + r_2y_w + r_9z_w + T_z}, \tag{1}$$

$$d_y'Y + d_y'Yk_1r^2 = f\frac{r_4x_w + r_5y_w + r_6z_w + T_y}{r_7x_w + r_2y_w + r_9z_w + T_z}, \tag{2}$$

where parameter s_x, d_x, d_y are CCD matrix parameter. Points X and Y are the coordinates of an image pixel horizontally and vertically respectively, and x_w, y_w, z_w are the corresponding coordinates in the 3D scene. Radial distortion coefficient k_1 and focal length f, represent the intrinsic parameters of the camera, while the rotation matrix elements $r_1...r_9$ and translation vector elements T_x, T_y, T_z represent the extrinsic parameters.

Nonlinear optimisation was carried out using a ready-made implementation of the Levenberg-Marquardt method from the Levenberg-Marquardt.NET library [7], which is a combination of the gradient descent method and the Gauss-Newton method [8].

After the calibration, we obtain a full camera model with intrinsic and extrinsic parameters. Knowing the camera model, we can utilise it for drawing a virtual object, i.e. in this case lines and the angles between them in the space. The problem of merg-ing the real image with the virtual one is a matter of the augmented reality mentioned before. In order to add a virtual object to the image, it is necessary to create its 3D model. To add straight line on the image why it was necessary to find in the 3D space the equation of a straight line based on the points through which it was supposed to go. The next step was discretisation of the line into a series of points and transfor-mation of each point into the image coordinates. For this purpose we use equation (Eq. 3) based on the camera parameters determined previously.

$$\begin{bmatrix} x_{camera} \\ y_{camera} \\ z_{camera} \end{bmatrix} = R\begin{bmatrix} x_{word} \\ y_{word} \\ z_{word} \end{bmatrix} + \begin{bmatrix} T_x \\ T_y \\ T_z \end{bmatrix} \tag{3}$$

The obtained coordinates are the coordinated in the camera system. This is why we need to recalculate them into the image coordinates in two steps. We use equations (Eq.4) to transfer from the camera system to the image system with the origin of the system in its centre.

$$x = f\left(\frac{x_{camera}}{y_{camera}}\right), \qquad y = f\left(\frac{x_{camera}}{y_{camera}}\right), \tag{4}$$

Next, in the second step we "distort" the position (x, y) of our point in order to adjust it to the naturally distorted image (Eq. 5). The equations presented below are invented by Silesian University of Technology researchers [9] and their application produces the best results:

$$x_d = x(1 - \gamma) + C_x, \qquad\qquad y_d = y(1 - \gamma) + C_y, \qquad\qquad (5)$$

where γ id described by the below equations (Eq.6, Eq. 7).

$$\gamma = \lambda \frac{x^2 + y^2}{x_c y_c}, \qquad\qquad (6)$$

$$x = x_r - x_c, \qquad\qquad y = y_r - y_c. \qquad\qquad (7)$$

Hence, knowing the position of the points from the 3D space on the image we can perfectly draw the selected lines overlapping with the patient's real movements in the subsequent frames (Fig. 4).

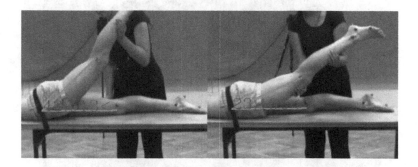

Fig. 4. Visualization of the angle in each frame

The angle presented in the form of digits and the lines are located on the image using ready-made functions of OpenCV library [10]. To calculate the equation of the line, the set of equations (Eq. 8) was used. The subsequent points of the line arise from the multiplication of the line directional coefficients with the increasing coefficient s [9]. The equations of the line and the angles between them are calculated and drawn for every subsequent frame of the film.

$$\begin{cases} x = x_0 + ms \\ y = y_0 + ns \\ z = z_0 + ls \end{cases} \qquad\qquad (8)$$

where:

m, n, l – the directional coefficients of the straight line,

s – a number different from zero,

$(x0, y0, z0)$ – starting point of the line,

(x, y, z) – currently calculated point

The application software that supports calibration and drawing angles has also a function of adding reference static points and lines, which allows measuring the flexion or extension with respect to, e.g. a vertical line, or another line, placed arbitrarily in space.

4   Summary

As a final result, the measurement of the range of motion with accuracy of order
of tens of micrometers was obtained, which is mainly due to the precision of
the Motion Capture system. If the position of camera does not change, it is
enough to run a single calibration. The obtained measurement is independent
on the individual measurement technique of every therapist and his subjective
interpretation of the results, as it was the case for a classic goniometer.

Fig. 5. Augmented Reality visualization of measurements

The measurement is convenient because after placing markers on the patient,
he has practically total freedom of movement and it is not necessary to hold
the device or a measuring tool by a doctor, who can at the same time pay
more attention to the patient. Such a solution allows simultaneous measurement
of lager number of joints than just one and because the neighbouring joints
are dependent on each other, it influences the way in which the body moves.
Additionally, the patient can easily do exercises or actions such as normal walking
through a room, a squat or even a jump. A clear visualisation on a computer
screen, possible to be created also in real time, enables a detailed analysis of
motion and angles in the joints that change during exercising (Fig. 5).

Another quality of the solution is automatic registration of the measurements
in a data base in the form of 3D coordinates of the markers position as well as
films registered by the cameras. In this way, every patient has his own catalogue
with med-ical history visualised in the form of films with exercises, which allows
a quick judgement of the rehabilitation progress. It is worth to mention that
develop technique for image calibration could be applied in various applications
e.g. UAV gimbal's cameras calibration [13-15].

Acknowledgement.. Lukasz Janik is scholarship holder of the "Doktoris scholarship program for innovative Silesia" co-financed by the EU under the European Social Fund.

References

1. Gajdosik, R.L., Bohannon, R.W.: Clinical measurement of range of motion review of goniometry emphasizing reliability and validity. Physical Therapy 67(12), 1867–1872 (1987)
2. Rothstein, J.M., Miller, P.J., Rottger, R.F.: Goniometry Reliability in a Clinical Setting: Elbow and Knee Measurments. Physical Therapy 63(10), 1611–1615 (1983)
3. Biometrics Ltd: Goniometr and torsiometer operating manual, access via Internet: http://www.biometricsltd.com (access: April 2014)
4. HALO Proffesional Digital Goniometers, access via Internet, http://www.halo-goniometer.com (access: April 2014)
5. Tsai, R.Y.: A Versatile Camera Calibration Technique for High-Accuracy 3D Machine Vision Metrology Using Off-the-Shelf TV Cameras and Lenses. IEE Journal of Robotics and Automation 3(4), 323–344 (1987)
6. Sobel, D., Jedrasiak, K., Daniec, K., Wrona, J., Nawrat, A.: Camera Calibration for Tracked Vehicles Augmented Reality Applications. In: Innovative Control Systems for Tracked Vehicle Platforms, pp. 147–162 (2014)
7. Kniaz, K.: LMA, access via Internet, http://kniaz.net/software/LMA.aspx (acces: Febuary 2014)
8. Gavin, H.P.: The Levenberg-Marquardt metod for nonlinear east squares curiefitting problems, Department of Civil and Environmental Engineering. Duke University (2013)
9. Babiarz, A., Bieda, R., Jaskot, K.: Vision System for Group of Mobile Robots. In: Nawrat, A., Kuś, Z. (eds.) Vision Based Systems for UAV Applications. SCI, vol. 481, pp. 139–156. Springer, Heidelberg (2013)
10. Official OpenCv website, acces via Internet: http://opencv.org/ (acces: March 2014)
11. Grzejszczak, T., Mikulski, M., Szkodny, T., Jędrasiak, K.: Gesture Based Robot Control. In: Bolc, L., Tadeusiewicz, R., Chmielewski, L.J., Wojciechowski, K. (eds.) ICCVG 2012. LNCS, vol. 7594, pp. 407–413. Springer, Heidelberg (2012)
12. Świtoński, A., Josiński, H., Jędrasiak, K., Polański, A., Wojciechowski, K.: Classification of Poses and Movement Phases. In: Bolc, L., Tadeusiewicz, R., Chmielewski, L.J., Wojciechowski, K. (eds.) ICCVG 2010, Part I. LNCS, vol. 6374, pp. 193–200. Springer, Heidelberg (2010)
13. Iwaneczko, P., Jędrasiak, K., Daniec, K., Nawrat, A.: A Prototype of Unmanned Aerial Vehicle for Image Acquisition. In: Bolc, L., Tadeusiewicz, R., Chmielewski, L.J., Wojciechowski, K. (eds.) ICCVG 2012. LNCS, vol. 7594, pp. 87–94. Springer, Heidelberg (2012)
14. Nawrat, A., Jedrasiak, K.: SETh system spatio-temporal object tracking using combined color and motion features. In: 9th WSEAS International Conference on Robotics, Control and Manufacturing Technology, Hangzhou, China (2009)
15. Jędrasiak, K., Nawrat, A., Daniec, K., Koteras, R., Mikulski, M., Grzejszczak, T.: A Prototype Device for Concealed Weapon Detection Using IR and CMOS Cameras Fast Image Fusion. In: Bolc, L., Tadeusiewicz, R., Chmielewski, L.J., Wojciechowski, K. (eds.) ICCVG 2012. LNCS, vol. 7594, pp. 423–432. Springer, Heidelberg (2012)

Analysis of Frame Partitioning in HEVC

Jakub Stankowski, Tomasz Grajek, Damian Karwowski,
Krzysztof Klimaszewski, Olgierd Stankiewicz,
Krzysztof Wegner, and Marek Domański

Chair of Multimedia Telecommunications and Microelectronics
Poznań University of Technology, ul. Polanka 3, 60-965 Poznań, Poland
{jstankowski,tgrajek,dkarwow,kklima,ostank,kwegner}@multimedia.edu.pl

Abstract. The paper presents analysis of frame partitioning in the next generation video coding standard HEVC. Complex study on frequency of the particular coding unit, prediction unit and transform unit sizes selection made by the encoder compliant with HEVC technology is included. General conclusions based on extensive experiments for HD video sequences are presented. Such knowledge may be the first step to the development of more efficient mode selection algorithms.

1 Introduction

In the last years the growing importance of multimedia systems transmitting high quality videos is observed. In this context, studies on efficient representation of high resolution images are crucial. Such works have been conducted in last years, and as a result the new High Efficiency Video Coding (HEVC) technology has been developed. The technology has been standardized as ISO/IEC 23008-2 (MPEG-H part 2) and ITU-T H.265 in 2013 [1].

HEVC allows for encoding of high resolution video at half of bitrate of previous technology namely AVC (MPEG-4 Part 10 and H.264)[2]. Higher coding efficiency came at a price of higher encoder complexity.

General idea of the HEVC technology is very similar to the older generation solutions (e.g. MPEG-2, H.263, AVS, VC-1, AVC) [3] and exploits intra- and inter-frame correlation by using prediction coding of image blocks together with block-based transform coding of residual data. But the HEVC allows for greater flexibility in terms of image partitioning and prediction mode selection leading to a stronger compression of high resolution video [4]. Classical macroblock structure has been replaced by more flexible coding tree block structure (CTB). Each CTB allows to quad tree block partitioning from size of 64x64 pixels downto 8x8 pixels. Each block in a partitioning tree is called a coding unit (CU) and can be encoded in intra-frame or inter-frame mode. Within the CU, prediction is performed in prediction units (PU) of various size (both square and rectangular shapes of PU are available). Each CU can also be further recursively divided into transform units (TU) of various sizes from 32x32 downto 4x4 in which transform-based coding of residual data is performed. Size of PU and TU can not exceed the size of CU.

L.J. Chmielewski et al. (Eds.): ICCVG 2014, LNCS 8671, pp. 602–609, 2014.

CTB partitioning with PU and TU partitioning leads to almost 3000 combinations in case of intra-frames and more than 4500 combinations in case of inter-frames to be analysed by encoder for a single CTB. In other words, great number of combinations is available in the encoder and all of them should be checked in order to choose the optimal one. However, huge computational complexity is the main drawback of such approach. Therefore, not all of combinations are evaluated in practice during encoding. Various methods of speeding up encoder decision have been developed so far, for example [5–8]. Basically all of them are based on observation that some partitioning schemes are very rarely used by the encoder, so they can be omitted resulting in negligible coding efficiency loss.

Nevertheless there are no complex studies of frequency of the particular partitioning selection made by the encoder. Such a knowledge can be further used to develop even more efficient encoder mode selection algorithms. Thorough analysis of image partitioning makes the topic of the paper.

2 Research Problem and Goal of the Work

In this paper we have evaluated frequency of particular CU, PU and TU sizes selection made by the encoder. In particular we are interested in the knowledge of image area covered/encoded with particular CU, PU and TU sizes. The goal is to make detailed analysis for individual frames types used in the HEVC encoder.

3 Methodology of the Research

In extensive experiments, seven HD 1920x1080 test video sequences (Fig. 1): *Bluesky, Pedestrianarea, Riverbed, Rushhour, Station2, Sunflower* and *Tractor*, recommended by ISO/IEC MPEG and ITU-T VCEG working groups have been encoded by the HEVC encoder. In particular HM 10.0 reference software [9] working under Common Test Condition (CTC) [10] was used. CTC defines a set of conditions and encoder configurations designed as a common ground for evaluation of HEVC related technology. In experiments "Random Access" scenario has been used to make the research for high efficiency mode (Fig. 2). Each sequence was encoded multiple times, each time with different quantization parameter (QP) value from a range $10 \div 48$ resulting in a wide range of bitrates. It must be emphasized that, the "Random Access" scenario assumes different values of QP for individual types of frames in the hierarchical coding structure.

4 Experimental Results

Coding Unit Analysis. QP value affects the statistics of CU sizes in frames. Experimental results averaged over all sequences and all frames allow to draw the following general conclusions:

- In the case of small QPs, the large CU (i.e. 64x64) is rarely used (below 5%). In such a case the most commonly used sizes of CU are 32x32 and 16x16 (about 75%).

Fig. 1. Test video sequences used in experiments in order from top-left: *Bluesky, Pedestrianarea, Riverbed, Rushhour, Station2, Sunflower* and *Tractor*

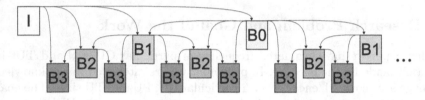

Fig. 2. Hierarchical structure of frame prediction used in experiments (according to CTC). Only part of inter-prediction sources is marked

- With the increase of QP the amount of big CUs also increases (up to 90%). In particular, for really high QPs 16x16 CUs and smaller ones are rarely used by encoder (below 10%).

Going into details there is a large convergence of the results obtained for $B0$, $B1$, $B2$, and $B3$ frames, but these results are significantly different from those obtained for I frames. In particular, significantly higher percentage contribution of 8x8 CUs is observed in I frames in the case of small QPs. Why is this happening? In the HEVC encoder the size of CU determines the size of PUs in which image prediction is realized. Selected size of CU is the upper limit for the size of PUs and TUs. In the case of complex image textures, CU is divided into smaller blocks in order to increase encoding efficiency. Thus, the increased use of smaller CUs for small QP values, where details of textures are preserved (for intra- and inter-frames). In addition, the prediction of complex image parts is more demanding in the case of intra-frames, hence more frequent (than in inter-frames) selection of small CUs. Detailed data for these experiments are shown in Fig. 3 for a wide range of QP values. The most likely explanation for this is the following. By strong data quantization (high QP values) the vast majority of transform coefficients take zero value. Therefore, it is more reasonable to carry out encoding in smaller CUs in order to preserve from sending large amount of control data. In this case, large CUs are more often applied.

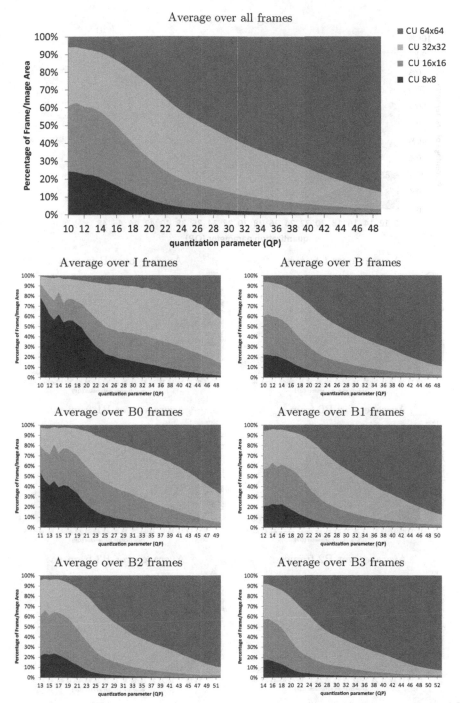

Fig. 3. Percentage of frame/image area covered by different sizes of CU. The QP values for individual types of frames in the hierarchical coding structure are adjusted according to "Random Access" scenario.

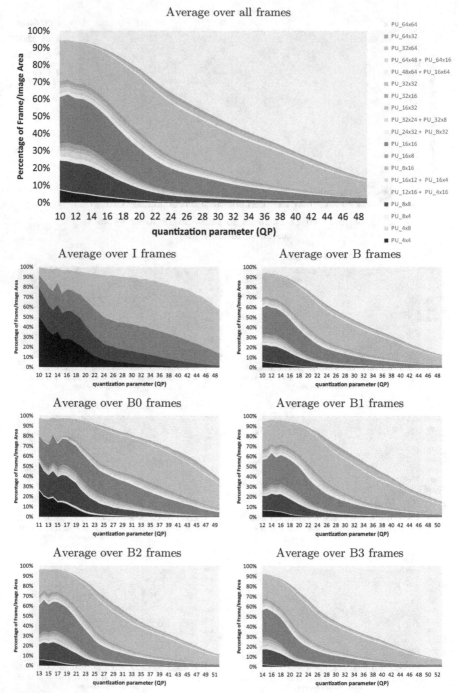

Fig. 4. Percentage of frame/image area covered by different sizes of PU. The QP values for individual types of frames in the hierarchical coding structure are adjusted according to "Random Access" scenario.

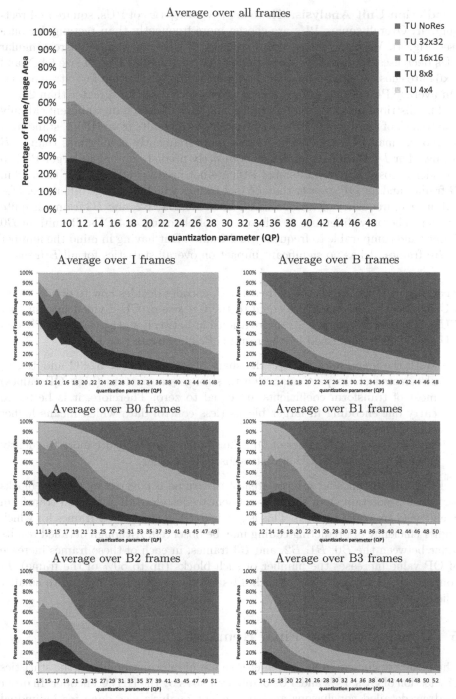

Fig. 5. Percentage of frame/image area covered by different sizes of TU. The QP values for individual types of frames in the hierarchical coding structure are adjusted according to "Random Access" scenario.

Prediction Unit Analysis. There are two categories of PUs: square and rectangular. Overall square PUs are chosen more frequently than rectangular ones (see Fig. 4). With increasing QP, frequency of choosing small and rectangular PUs decreases. Interesting observation is that rectangular PUs of size 64xN and Nx64 are chosen more frequently for average values of QP than for extreme ones. On average PUs of size 4x4 are hardly ever selected for QP greater than 24.

The distribution of PUs for I frames and B frames is quite different. Mainly due to lack of rectangular PUs in I frames (which results from HEVC standard). Moreover small PUs are chosen 5 times more frequently in I frames than in B frames. For I frames it is harder to accurately predict content in larger PUs so encoder chooses smaller units. 4x4 PUs are not used for QPs greater than 18 in B frames and for QP greater than 36 in I frames which is a huge difference. Distribution of frequency of various sizes PUs in $B0$, $B1$, $B2$, and $B3$ frames is quite similar. The only difference is a frequency of choosing 4x4 PUs. Results in $B0$ frames and comparable to frequency in I frames. But having in mind the number of $B0$ frames, it has no significant impact on overall statistics for all B frames.

Transform Unit Analysis. For each CU, encoder decides how to divide it into TU blocks (i.e. TU block size equal to the CU size or CU divided into smaller TUs). Therefore there is a strong relationship between statistics of the TU and CU size. This is confirmed by the results of experiments (see Fig. 5):

- With the increase of the QP the share of large TUs (i.e 32x32 and 16x16) also increases. In particular, due to strong quantization (high QP values) most of transform coefficients are equal to zero. Therefore, it is better to carry out encoding in larger blocks (less control data which means higher coding efficiency).
- In the case of small values of QP, the smaller sized TUs are more frequently used. It is related to CU statistics discussed earlier.

In the HEVC encoder a large area of the frame is covered by the TU blocks for which prediction error signal is not sent to decoder (all quantized transform coefficients are equal to zero). This is particularly evident for B frames for which higher efficiency of predicting coding may be observed. Although detailed results differ between the $B0$, $B1$, $B2$, and $B3$ frames, in each of these frames increase of QP value increases the number of such blocks (up to 50% of the frame). In contrary, for I frames share of such TUs is very low (below 5% due to smaller efficiency of intra prediction).

5   Conclusions and Final Remarks

The results documented in the paper give useful information about the statistics of selection of CUs, PUs and TUs of different sizes by the HEVC encoder. In order to draw detailed conclusions an independent analysis was done for individual frame types (I, $B0$, $B1$, $B2$, and $B3$). Additionally all the results were averaged and presented in the paper to highlight the general remarks. Huge collection of experimental results enables analysis of frame partitioning for a wide range of bitrates (QP values from 10 to 48). Achieved results allow to formulate two general conclusions:

1) The higher QP the major area of the frame is covered by larger CUs, PUs and TUs (up to 80%, 83% and 87% respectively).

2) There is a significant difference between results obtained for I and B frames. For the same QP value for I frames smaller sizes of CUs, PUs and TUs than for B frames are used.

The results are the basis for further study leading to the development of fast mode decisions in the HEVC encoder. The knowledge on statistics of frame partitioning acquired in the paper gives direct information which combinations of CU, PU and TU can be omitted in order to speed up the encoder mode selection process. Appropriate remarks have been presented in experimental section.

Acknowledgement. Project was supported by The National Centre for Research and Development, Poland. Grant no. LIDER/023/541/L-4/12/NCBR/2013.

References

1. ISO/IEC 23008-2 (MPEG-H Part 2) / ITU-T Rec. H.265: High Efficiency Video Coding, HEVC (2013)
2. Ohm, J.-R., Sullivan, G.J., Schwarz, H., Tan, T.-K., Wiegand, T.: Comparison of the Coding Efficiency of Video Coding Standards Including High Efficiency Video Coding (HEVC). IEEE Transactions on Circuits and Systems for Video Technology 22(12), 1669–1684 (2012)
3. Shi, Y.Q., Sun, H.: Image and Video Compression for Multimedia Engineering: Fundamentals, Algorithms, and Standards, 2nd edn. CRC Press, New York (2008) ISBN 978-0-8493-7364-0
4. Sullivan, G.J., Ohm, J.-R., Han, W.-J., Wiegand, T.: Overview of the High Efficiency Video Coding (HEVC) Standard. IEEE Transactions on Circuits and Systems for Video Technology 22(12), 1649–1668 (2012)
5. Zhao, L., Zhang, L., Ma, S., Zhao, D.: Fast mode decision algorithm for intra prediction in HEVC. In: IEEE Visual Communications and Image Processing (VCIP), Tainan, Taiwan, pp. 1–4 (2011)
6. Palomino, D., Cavichioli, E., Susin, A., Agostini, L., Shafique, M., Henkel, J.: Fast HEVC Intra Mode Decision Algorithm Based on New Evaluation Order in the Coding Tree Block. In: Picture Coding Symposium PCS, San Jose, USA, pp. 209–212 (2013)
7. Xiong, J., Li, H., Wu, Q., Meng, F.: A Fast HEVC Inter CU Selection Method Based on Pyramid Motion Divergence. IEEE Transactions on Multimedia 16(2), 559–564 (2014)
8. Yoo, H.M., Suh, J.W.: Fast coding unit decision algorithm based on inter and intra prediction unit termination for HEVC. In: 2013 IEEE International Conference on Consumer Electronics (ICCE), Las Vegas, USA, pp. 300–301 (2013)
9. HEVC test model reference software, https://hevc.hhi.fraunhofer.de/svn/
10. Bossen, F.: Common test conditions and software reference configurations. Joint Collaborative Team on Video Coding (JCT-VC) of ITU-T SG16 WP3 and ISO/IEC JTC1/SC29/WG11, doc. JCTVC-J1100, Stockholm, Sweden (2012)

Comparison of Appearance-Based and Geometry-Based Bubble Detectors

Nataliya Strokina[1], Roman Juránek[2], Tuomas Eerola[3], Lasse Lensu[3],
Pavel Zemčik[2], and Heikki Kälviäinen[3]

[1] Tampere University of Technology, Department of Signal Processing
P.O. Box 527, FI-33101 Tampere, Finland
nataliya.strokina@tut.fi
[2] Brno University of Technology, Department of Computer Graphics and Multimedia
Brno, Czech Republic
{ijuranek, zemcik}@fit.vutbr.cz
[3] Lappeenranta University of Technology
Machine Vision and Pattern Recognition Laboratory
P.O. Box 20, FI-53851 Lappeenranta, Finland
{teerola, ltl, kalviai}@lut.fi

Abstract. Bubble detection is a complicated tasks since varying lighting conditions changes considerably the appearance of bubbles in liquid. The two common techniques to detect circular objects such as bubbles, the geometry-based and appearance-based approaches, have their advantages and weaknesses. The geometry-based methods often fail to detect small blob-like bubbles that do not match the used geometrical model, and appearance-based approaches are vulnerable to appearance changes caused by, e.g., illumination. In this paper, we compare a geometry-based concentric circular arrangements (CCA) and appearance-based sliding window methods as well as their combinations in terms of bubble detection, gas volume computation, and size distribution estimation. The best bubble detection performance was achieved with the sliding window method whereas the most precise volume estimate was produced by the CCA method. The combination of the two approaches gave only a minor advantage compared to the base methods.

1 Introduction

The paper focuses on the problem of detecting bubbles, or more generally, transparent roughly spherical objects with multiple interfaces. The total gas volume and gas volume distribution in pulp suspensions, estimated here from the size and number of detected bubbles, are the important factors in the decision to terminate the bleaching stage of pulp processing [2]. Due to the varying lighting conditions, the appearance of bubbles varies from a pair of ring-like, bright ridge edges to blurred dark edges with contrast reversal and multiple interreflections. Experiments show that oriented filter responses caused by such objects form a set of concentric arcs with a common center point as shown in Fig. 1.

L.J. Chmielewski et al. (Eds.): ICCVG 2014, LNCS 8671, pp. 610–617, 2014.
© Springer International Publishing Switzerland 2014

The problem of bubble detection appears in a number of applications, for example, dispersion of oil drops in water [3], segmentation of spherical particles in transmitted light image stacks [9], and air bubble detection in dense dispersion [14]. Bubbles or drops manifest themselves as roughly circular objects, which motivates to solve the problem as the detection of circles. There are two common approaches that are used to detect circular objects: geometry-based and appearance-based approaches. In the geometry-based approach, a circular model parameterized by its center and radius is fitted to the image edge map. These methods typically utilize a voting technique, such as the Hough Transform (HT) [4] or its modifications [7]. The HT-like approaches suffer from a large number of false positives and are sensitive to noise. Moreover, they do not take into account the appearance of the bubbles as an object with multiple light interreflections. The appearance-based approach works with grayscale images, or in some cases, with edge-maps. The approach is typically based on the sliding window where a template of the object of interest is created and the grayscale image is convolved with the template. In order to find the objects, the maxima of the filtering responses are searched. Template matching techniques are difficult to apply for the bubble detection since the bubbles may appear differently (bright ring-like edge or dark moon-like shape as shown in Fig. 1) depending on the bubble location in the image and lighting.

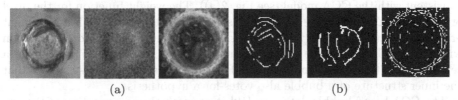

(a)   (b)

Fig. 1. Examples of images of bubbles: (a) bubbles; (b) local maxima (in spatial and orientation domains) of oriented ridge filters

In [10], the bubble detection problem was formulated as a search for Concentric Circular Arrangements (CCAs) and was solved in a hypothesize-optimize-verify framework. The CCA detection method demonstrated a satisfactory performance in the task of gas volume computation outperforming the standard Circular Hough Transform [11]. However, the estimation of gas volume distribution with respect to bubble sizes remained challenging. Small blob like bubbles were not detected in most cases because there is no ridge edge expected by the model. Although the small bubbles do not have a big impact on the volume value, they affect the volume distribution histogram.

In this work, we tackle the problem of detecting also small bubbles by applying the appearance-based approach for bubble detection using WaldBoost [13]. Moreover, the two methods are combined in two ways. In the first case (Combination 1), the bubble hypotheses are generated by the CCA method and postprocessing is done by verification of the results by the sliding window approach. In the second case (Combination 2), the bubbles are detected by the sliding window approach and verified by the CCA method.

The main contributions of the paper are (i) a novel sliding window based bubble detection method, (ii) comparison of the sliding window based approach and the previously developed CCA method, and (iii) analysis of the method combination results, when one of the methods is used as a post-processing of the other. The methods are evaluated on a dataset comprising pulp suspension images and bubble annotations produced by pulpmaking experts. The data reflect real industrial problems, giving us a challenging and meaningful test set.

2   CCA for Bubble Detection

Concentric Circular Arrangement $H = (\mathcal{A}, c, r, \theta)$ is a set of concentric circular arcs $\mathcal{A}$ with a center c located within an annulus of radius r and width 2θ (see Fig. 2(a)) [10]. An arc is a connected component $A = (P, r_a)$ parameterized by a pixel list P and a radius r_a. The score of a CCA is comprised by the contribution of separate pixels located within the CCA area. The contribution of a pixel $p \in A$ with an orientation α_p to the support of a CCA hypothesis with a center c is computed as

$$f_p = g(\Delta\alpha) \cdot q(r_a) \tag{1}$$

where $\Delta\alpha = \left| \alpha_p - \arctan\left(\frac{|x_c - x_p|}{|y_c - y_p|} \right) \right|$ describes if the orientation of the pixel is consistent with the CCA model (see Fig. 2(a)). The weight function for the pixel orientation $g(\Delta\alpha) = 1/(1 + \Delta\alpha)$ puts less weight to the edges with inconsistent orientation. The function $q(r_a)$ weights the pixel input depending on its location within the CCA area. The weight function $q(r)$ for the edge distance from a center used in this work is presented in Fig. 2(b). Its shape reflects the fact that the inner structure of a bubble also votes for a hypothesis.

The CCA-based bubble detection [10] starts with the computation of the oriented edge map by filtering image with second derivative zero-mean oriented Gaussian filters in eight directions followed by non-maximum suppression [1]. After that, the CCA hypotheses are generated by sampling from the edge map using procedure similar to RANSAC [5]. A CCA hypothesis is generated from the arc if it satisfies the following requirements: (i) it receives sufficient support from the pixels located within the CCA area and (ii) the support comes from a

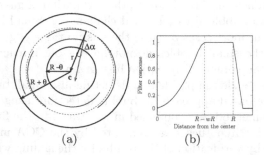

(a)   (b)

Fig. 2. CCA: (a) The model; (b) The weight function for the edge distance from the center

sufficient number of directions. The center location and the radius of the hypothesis are optimized by maximizing the support with the Neadler-Mead Simplex method [8]. Finally, the non-maximum suppression is performed on the CCA parameters to prevent multiple hypotheses for a single bubble.

3   Sliding Window Approach for Bubble Detection

For appearance-based detection, we use WaldBoost detector [13], which process the input image in sliding window manner. WaldBoost builds on AdaBoost [12] and uses *Sequential Probability Ratio Test* (SPRT) to reject samples whose probability of negative classification reaches a certain level, based on measurements provided by weak hypotheses. This mechanism allows the classifier function to be terminated just after the evaluation of several weak hypotheses. The classifier is represented by a sequence of weak hypotheses $h^{(t)}$ and decision thresholds $\theta^{(t)}$ where $t = (1, \ldots, T)$. The response of the classifier on a sample $\mathbf{x}$ for a step t is obtained by accumulating the responses of weak hypotheses from 1 to t:

$$H^{(t)}(\mathbf{x}) = \sum_{k=1}^{t} h^{(k)}(\mathbf{x}). \qquad (2)$$

After every step, the sample can be rejected as background in the case that the sum falls below the threshold, or otherwise the next step is evaluated:

$$S^{(t)}(\mathbf{x}) = \begin{cases} 0 & H^{(t)}(\mathbf{x}) < \theta^{(t)} \\ S^{(t+1)}(\mathbf{x}) & \text{otherwise} \end{cases} \qquad (3)$$

If the evaluation passes the last weak hypothesis, the final decision is positive if the final response is greater than some user defined threshold. During the detection, every suitable sub-window of the input image is analyzed with the classifier. Final detections are obtained by simple clustering of the detected sub-windows

A significant advantage of this detection method is that it is easy to implement on various platforms. It has been demonstrated that a GPU implementation can process HD video in real-time [6], and FPGA implementation can run at over 100 fps on 640×480 image [15].

4   Experiments

4.1   Data

The data consisted of 24 fully annotated microscopic pulp suspension images with a resolution of 1600×1200 pixels. In total, 1141 image regions of interest were marked as bubbles by an expert. The ground truth volume was computed from the marked bubbles. The volume of a bubble with radius R was calculated as $V = \frac{4}{3}\pi R^3$, assuming that the bubbles have an approximately spherical shape. The mean relative error of volume estimation for M images was computed as

$V_{err} = \frac{1}{M}\sum_{i=1}^{M}(\frac{|V_{est_i}-V_{gt_i}|}{V_{gt_i}})$, where V_{gt_i} is the ground truth volume and V_{est_i} is the estimated volume. The annotations contained a large number of blurry and noisy bubbles and, on the other hand, not all bubbles were marked. Thus, the detectors are expected to produce higher number of false detections (detecting unmarked bubbles), with slightly lower detection rate as some marked bubbles are hard to detect.

The detectors were evaluated by checking the overlap with ground truth:

$$O(A, B) = \frac{\text{area(intersect}(A, B))}{\max(\text{area}(A), \text{area}(B))}, \tag{4}$$

where A is the detection and B is the ground truth. Detections with an overlap higher than 0.5 were accepted as true positives. Detector evaluation is reported in terms of precision, recall, and F-measure representing the harmonic mean of precision and recall. Better detectors are those with higher F values.

4.2 Method Training

The data was divided into a training set containing eight randomly selected images (397 bubbles) and a test set containing the rest of the images, 16 images (744 bubbles). CCA parameters were selected by minimizing the volume estimation error in the training set. The experiment was repeated 4 times, and the following parameter values were selected: the number of CCA sectors $N = 10$, the number of sectors where the support of the hypothesis is not zero $K_s = 4$, the maximum radius of bubbles $R_{max} = 1.52$ mm, the filter response threshold $T_{filt} = 0.93$, the width of the annulus $\theta = 0.5R$, the minimum length of an arc from which a hypothesis is generated $L_{min} = 15$, the parameter of the cost-function $W = 0.6R$.

WaldBoost was trained using a set of bubble samples (see Fig. 1(a)) obtained from the labeled training images. The set was expanded by random rotations of every bubble image. The background set was extracted from areas not containing bubbles (parts of bubbles, like edges, were included). All samples were re-scaled to common size and used as the training set. Eight different WaldBoost detectors were trained with four size configurations (20, 24, 28, and 32 pixel samples) and two feature configurations. The first feature configuration contained all LBP features without any restriction, the second configuration contained only features with block sizes up to 2×2 pixels per block. This restriction is important for possible implementation in programmable hardware [15]. All detectors consisted of 1000 weak hypotheses. The best detector was the one with 24 pixel window ($F = 0.67$, and $F = 0.62$ with restricted feature setting).

4.3 Combination of the Approaches

To see whether the approaches could benefit from each other, the detection results obtained by the CCA and WaldBoost detectors were combined. One of the methods was used as the base method for hypothesis generation and the other for verifying the results. The verification was done by checking overlaps between the detection results using (4). Hypotheses of the base method that have a high overlap with a verification detection were accepted as the final detection. The experiments were performed by using CCA as the base method and WaldBoost as verification method (Combination 1) and vice versa (Combination 2). In Combination 1 the filter response threshold T_{filt} was set deliberately lower in order to produce more detection that are subsequently verified by the WaldBoost. The CCA with a lower filter response threshold is referred to as CCA(extra).

4.4   Results

Fig. 3 shows Precision-Recall and ROC curves of the WaldBoost and CCA detectors on the test set. The detection results on few example images are shown in Fig. 7. From the detection results, statistics of the bubble size and gas volume were evaluated and compared to the ground truth data. The bubble size distribution is shown in Fig. 4. WaldBoost and Combination 2 detectors were closer to the ground truth compared to the other detectors. Gas volume estimation is

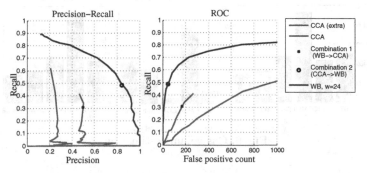

Fig. 3. Precision-Recall and ROC curves of two CCA detectors and best WaldBoost detector

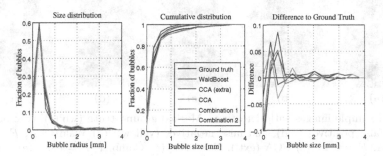

Fig. 4. Bubble size distribution

summarized in Fig. 5. WaldBoost and Combination 2 were again better in estimating the volume distribution. However, as Fig. 6 shows, CCA is better in predicting the total gas volume. Combination 2 underestimates the volume.

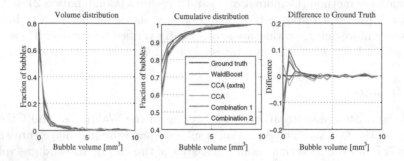

Fig. 5. Bubble volume distribution

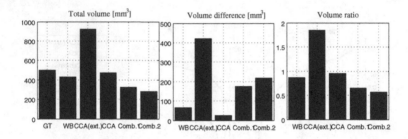

Fig. 6. Gas volume estimation

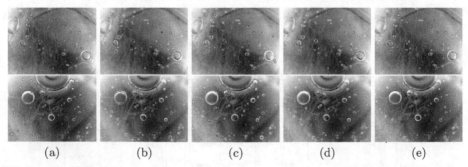

(a)   (b)   (c)   (d)   (e)

Fig. 7. Example images with detections. Marked ground truth (white), true positives (blue), false positives (red), and false negatives (yellow): (a) WaldBoost, $F = 0.67$; (b) CCA, $F = 0.43$; (c) CCA (ext.), $F = 0.31$; (d) Comb. 1, $F = 0.49$; (e) Comb. 2, $F = 0.61$.

5 Conclusion

We compared the performance of an appearance-based (WaldBoost) and geometry-based (CCA) approaches for bubble detection applied to the industrial problem of gas volume estimation in the pulp suspension. WaldBoost performed well in bubble detection with an acceptable volume estimation accuracy. Moreover, it can be efficiently implemented on PC and programmable hardware allowing a real-time performance in industrial applications. The results showed that the CCA method is slightly worse at bubble detection but it can very precisely estimate the gas volume. Combinations of the two approaches did not show significant benefit over the base methods. The question of the ground truth coverage and validity should be addressed in the future.

Acknowledgments. The research was supported by PulpVision EU TEKES 70010/10, 70040/11, IT4I, MSMT, CZ.1.05/1.1.00/02.0070, V3C, TACR, TE01010415 projects, and by expertise of Dr. J Käyhkö and H. Mutikainen from MAMK FiberLaboratory.

References

1. Canny, J.: A computational approach to edge detection. PAMI 8(6), 679–698 (1986)
2. Dence, C.W., Reeve, D.W.: Pulp Bleaching, Principles and Practice. TAPPI (1996)
3. Dominguez, R.A., Corkidi, G.: Automated recognition of oil drops in images of multiphase dispersions via gradient direction pattern. In: CISP, vol. 3, pp. 1209–1213 (2011)
4. Duda, R., Hart, P.: Using the hough transform to detect lines and curves in pictures. Comm ACM, pp. 11–15 (1972)
5. Fischler, M.A., Bolles, R.C.: Random sample consensus: A paradigm for model fitt. with appl. to image anal. and autom. cartogr. Comm ACM 24(6), 381–395 (1981)
6. Herout, A., Jošth, R., Juránek, R., Havel, J., Hradiš, M., Zemčík, P.: Real-time object detection on cuda. JRIP (2011)
7. Leavers, V.: Which Hough Transform? GMIP: IU 58(2), 250–264 (1993)
8. Press, W., Flannery, B., Teukolsky, S., Vetterling, W.: Numerical Recipes in C: The Art of Scientific Computing. Cambridge University Press (1992)
9. Ronneberger, O., Wang, Q., Burkhardt, H.: Fast and robust segm. of sph.l particles in vol. data sets from brightfield microsc. In: Proc. ISBI, pp. 372–375 (2008)
10. Strokina, N., Matas, J., Eerola, T., Lensu, L., Kälviäinen, H.: Detection of bubbles as concentric circular arrangements. In: ICPR, pp. 2655–2659 (2012)
11. Strokina, N.: Machine vision methods for process measurements in pulping. Ph.D. thesis, LUT (2013)
12. Viola, P., Jones, M.J.: Robust real-time face detection. IJCV (2004)
13. Šochman, J., Matas, J.: Waldboost - learning for time constrained sequential detection. In: CVPR (2005)
14. Zabulis, X., Papara, M., Chatziargyriou, A., Karapantsios, T.D.: Detection of densely dispersed spherical bubbles in dig. images based on a templ. matching technique. appl. to wet foams. Colloids and Surfaces A: PEA 309, 96–106 (2007)
15. Zemčík, P., Juránek, R., Musil, M., Musil, P., Hradiš, M.: High performance architecture for object detection in streamed videos. In: Proc ICFPLA (2013)

Analysis of the Hand's Small Vessels Based on MR Angiography and Level-Set Approach

Michał Strzelecki, Tomasz Woźniak, Marek Olszycki,
Konrad Szymczyk, and Ludomir Stefańczyk

Institute of Electronics, Lodz University of Technology
Wólczańska 211/215, 90-924, Łódź, Poland
Department of Diagnostic Imaging, Medical University of Lodz
Kopcińskiego 22, 90-154 Łódź, Poland
michal.strzelecki@p.lodz.pl, ludomir.stefanczyk@umed.lodz.pl

Abstract. The article describes a method for segmentation and analysis of small blood hand vessels in 3D magnetic resonance contrast angiography data obtained with collaboration of Department of Diagnostic Imaging, Medical University of Lodz. The main algorithm used for vasculature extraction implements a 3D version of level-set method based on Chan-Vese mathematical model. The image analysis was performed for two different contrast agents. Preliminary segmentation results were presented and discussed, along with further research plans.

1 Introduction

Visualization of small blood vessels in hands is a big challenge in diagnostic imaging. The first difficulty is the small diameter of the vessels, their omnicourse and a multitude of anatomical variants. The second is an overlap in the image of veins and arteries that is obvious in the peripheral area. The reference method in the evaluation of the vessels is X-ray angiography, which guarantees the highest spatial resolution images and the ability to assess the dynamic flow. Angiography, however, is a costly and invasive approach since it requires arterial catheterization, utilizing ionizing radiation and intra-arterial iodinated contrast agent. Thus, the attempts to replace it with non-invasive methods such as Doppler ultrasonography or, finally, nuclear magnetic resonance.

The recent development of new MRI blood pool agents offers a new approach for monitoring the vessel in magnetic resonance angiography (MRA). They produce a higher signal and have a longer half-life, in comparison to standard agents, so a specific region of interest can be evaluated with a longer time of acquisition at a higher spatial resolution [1–3]. Thus MRA is preferable for diagnosing upper extremity vascular disorders and characterization of complex arteriovenous anatomy such as in vascular malformations and for evaluation of dialysis fistulas and grafts [4]. Also, a wide variety of diseases like atherosclerosis or embolism, which are the most common in affecting the upper extremity can be diagnosed by MRA techniques.

L.J. Chmielewski et al. (Eds.): ICCVG 2014, LNCS 8671, pp. 618–625, 2014.
© Springer International Publishing Switzerland 2014

There are not many references related to the quantitative analysis of vessels in extremities images. In [5] the vascular abnormalities in the upper extremities echo images were described by an image-based flow model to detect major bleeding. Maximum intensity projection maps were applied in [1–4] to identify and qualitatively assess vessel abnormalities. Thus there is need to develop an approach for quantitative MR images assessment [6] aimed at applications in MR angiography. The aim of this study was to evaluate MRA images of the small vessels of the hands fingers, obtained for a blood pool contrast agent (Vasovist) and a standard one (Gadovist). For analysis, the own software was developed. It implements level-set approach for vessel segmentation, a widely used technique for analysis of brain vasculature [7, 8]. The software not only visualizes the hand vascularity but also estimates the blood vessel volume in each finger along with the volume of remaining tissues.

2   Materials and Methods

This research was performed on fourteen volunteers, with obtained a consent to participate in this study. Six people were injected with a contrast agent Gadovist, while the rest of them with contrast agent Vasovist. For image acquisition, the 3D MR T2 sequence was applied (Siemens Avanto 1.5T).

For Gadovist study four images were acquired for each patient: without contrast, just after contrast injection, then 6 and 12 minutes after injection. The same imaging was performed for Vasovist contrast agent, except additional image was taken 3 min. after contrast injection. Moreover, left patients hands were cooled, while right were preserved in the room temperature. For cooled hands, the cold water immersion tests were carried out (in 5°C water for 1 min). Sample MR images (maximum intensity projections, MIP) obtained for both contrast agents are shown in Fig. 1 and Fig. 2. The acquired 36 images were stored using 16 bits DICOM format, although only 12 bits are allocated. Image resolution was 704x704 pixels with 96 slices recorded. The voxel size was 0,424 x 0,424 x 0,4 mm.

The method used for blood vessels segmentation in fingers region is level-set approach based on Chan-Vese mathematical model [9, 10]. This technique is versatile and widely used also for analysis of other biomedical images [11].

In order to perform blood vessels segmentation, pre-processing of the images was required. All MR images used in this study have slightly different brightness and contrast. Firstly, it is essential to adjust these values to obtain a comparable range of gray level that corresponds to vessels in each image. ImageJ [12] software was used to adjust these parameters - the brightness and contrast were normalized to the same values.

Some of the data included with the MR images are useless and interfere in the process of segmentation of blood vessels. This regards to image background noise and finger bones regions. The analysis of normalized imaged demonstrated that bones and background have pixel intensity in the approximate range [0...500], while the vessel brightness is larger than 700. Histogram of sample image is

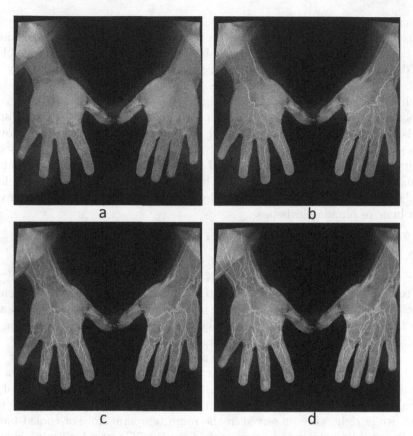

Fig. 1. MIPs of images acquired for Vasovist study: image without contrast agent (a), just after contrast injection (b), 6 min. (c) and 12 min. later (d)

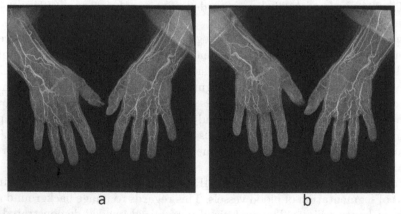

Fig. 2. Fig. 2. MIPs of images acquired for Gadovist study (left hand cooled) after contrast injection (a) and 6 min. later (b)

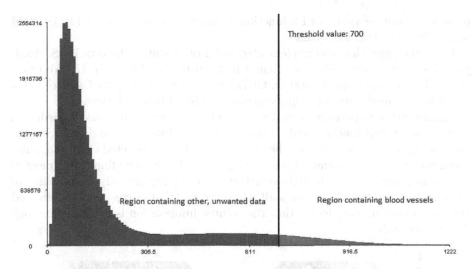

Fig. 3. Histogram from examplary MR sequence with marked threshold value

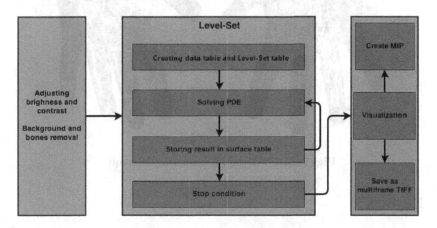

Fig. 4. Segmentation method block diagram

shown in Fig. 3. Thus, to remove unwanted data simple thresholding (threshold equal to 700) was applied. After that the remaining image content represents blood vessels and soft palm and finger tissues only.

The main idea in level-set active contour model is to iteratively evolve a curve that is controlled by some parameters estimated from the image. The motion of the curve is obtained by solving the curve evolution partial differential equations (PDE) [9], adapted to three-dimensional data space. Finally, the curve ends its evolution by fitting to objects boundaries within the given image.

Fig. 4 presents block diagram of the algorithm used for blood vessels segmentation. After image preprocessing image data is passed to level-set (LS) module. Next, the level-set table that corresponds to LS function is filled with initial values; in this case sphere equations were used. After solving PDEs, LS table preserves resulting values of LS function. Segmented image is stored in DICOM or multiframe TIFF file formats.

First, the algorithm was implemented in C♯ on 64-bits Windows 7 OS. Analysis of sample image took more than 3 hours using Intel Core i7-4700MQ processor. In the final implementation CUDA technology for nVidia GeForce GTX 760M was applied reducing segmentation time to 10 min. (18 times).

Segmentation is performed on the whole image, except regions discarded in preprocessing step (background, bones). However, since medical doctors are interested on finger veins volume, the analysis results are collected excluding palm fragments. One needs manually select every finger by drawing lines in segmented images as shown in Fig. 5. It is sufficient to select fingers only in one slice of the image. The algorithm counts all white voxels (that correspond to detected vessels) in each marked ROIs, thus the volume information is available for each finger separately.

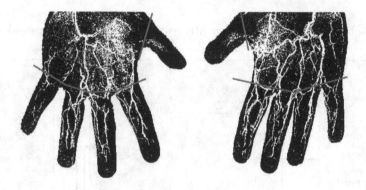

Fig. 5. MIP of sample segmentation result

3   Results

Obtained vessel volumes for both contrast agents are presented in Figs. 6 and 7. These results were estimated as an average values for left or right hand including all volunteers in given study. Plots are made for time points indicating initial image acquisition (without contrast), the moment of contrast injection and after 6 and 12 minutes (for Gadovist, additional images were taken 3 min. after contrast injection). As described in Section 2, for Gadovist study left hand were cooled after contrast injection while right remained in the room temperature. In the initially acquired images blood vessels were not detected. This is explained by the fact that T2 image sequence is unable to visualize blood flow. Vasculature visualization is possible after contrast injection since contrast agent increases T2 time significantly, increasing image contrast between vessels and adjacent tissues.

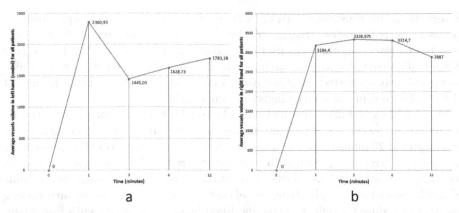

Fig. 6. Average vessels volume (Vasovist study) in left cooled hand (a) and in right hand (room temperature) (b)

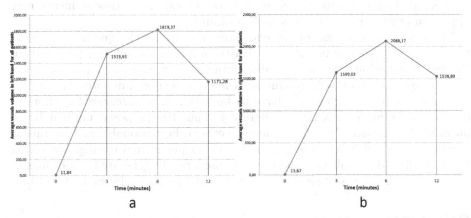

Fig. 7. Average vessels volume (Gadovist study) in left hand (a) and in right hand (b)

4   Discussion and Conlusion

With good quality data provided by the MR angiography, it was possible to build an algorithm that allows quantitative analysis of fingers blood vessels in acquired images. This is a great advantage in comparison with the previous only subjective qualitative assessment, typical for routine analysis of standard MRI. An analysis of the data obtained enables detection of vascular anatomy differences between patients hands, and even between each finger. So far, such differences were perceptible subjective and dependent on the observer, including his experience, knowledge of anatomy, as well as the time spent on assessment tests. The applied algorithm helped demonstrate the influence of vanishing contrast agent in each successive measurement time to the image quality. Especially it is important for Gadovist study where statistically significant differences in the contrast evolution for successive time instants in cooled down hands were observed. These observations are consistent with data from other diagnostic techniques used to assess these pathologies - thermography and ultrasound-Doppler. Also, it was possible to reveal another feature of vascular reactivity in response to the cool down test - vascular spasm in the hands of the control (not cooled down), which was previously suggested by other studies (ultrasound, thermography), but not clearly observed in our study diagnostic angio-MR.

Segmentation results are sometimes blurred by motion artifacts resulted by unconscious movements of patients hands and arms during long lasting acquisition (approx. 20 minutes). Also, due to limited scanner resolution thin vessels are not always correctly represented in the images (reduced part of vessel is visible, its continuity is lost). This affects segmentation accuracy and estimated volume of hand vasculature. Emphasizing vessel contrast when compared to surrounding tissues can reduce this effect. Thus, modified level-set approach with implementation of vesselnes-dependent weight [13] will be applied. To further improve detection of blood vessels, image data acquired in different time instants will be merged. This way some vessels fragments missing in one time sequence may appear in other one, enhancing vessel continuity.

The obvious application of presented segmentation technique is to evaluate the course and patency in patients with trauma and those being prepared for the treatment of arteriovenous malformations. Techniques for reimplantation and transplantation of limbs require accurate diagnosis and monitoring of grafts perfusion, quite often the tests have to be repeated at intervals too short to be able to perform an X-ray angiography. Thus the proposed method based on much less invasive MR angiography seems to be reasonable and promising approach, however it still requires further development and testing. For future tests, medical data will be supported by numerically generated vessel images obtained by the means of recently developed MR angiography simulator [14].

References

1. Corot, C., Violas, X., Robert, P., Gagneur, G., Port, M.: Comparison of different types of blood pool agents (P792, MS325, USPIO) in a rabbit MR angiography-like protocol. Invest. Radiol. 38(6), 311–319 (2003)
2. Gutzeit, A., et al.: Clinical experience in timed arterial compression contrast-enhanced magnetic resonance angiography of the hand. CA Radiologist Journal 61, 206–216 (2010)
3. Kassamali, R.H., Hoey, E., Ganeshan, A., Littlehales, T.: A comparative analysis of noncontrast flow-spoiled versus contrast-enhanced magnetic resonance angiography for evaluation of peripheral arterial disease. Diagnostic and Interventional Radiology 19(2), 119–125 (2013)
4. Nikolaou, K., Kramer, H., Grosse, C., Clevert, D., Dietrich, O., Hartmann, M.: High-spatial-resolution multistation MR angiography with parallel imaging and blood pool contrast agent: initial experience. Radiology 241(3), 861–872 (2006)
5. Wang, A.S., Bech, F., Lee, J., Taylor, C.A., Liang, D.H.: Developing an arterial bleed detection algorithm for diagnostic ultrasound. In: Proc. of IEEE International Ultrasonics Symposium, IUS 2008, Beijing, China, November 2-5, pp. 1627–1630 (2008)

6. Strzelecki, M., Szczypinski, P., Materka, A., Klepaczko, A.: A software tool for automatic classification and segmentation of 2D/3D medical images. Nuclear Instruments & Methods in Physics Research A 702, 137–140 (2013)
7. Lesage, D., Angelini, E., Bloch, I., Funka-Lea, G.: A review of 3D vessel lumen segmentation techniques: Models, features and extraction schemes. Medical Image Analysis 13, 819–845 (2009)
8. Strzelecki, M., Szczypinski, P., Materka, A., Kocinski, M., Sankowski, A.: Levelset segmentation of noisy 3D images of numerically simulated blood vessels and vascular trees. In: Proceedings of 6th International Symposium on Image and Signal Processing and Analysis, Salzburg, Austria, September 16-18, pp. 742–747 (2009)
9. Chan, T.F., Vese, L.A.: Active Contours Without Edges. IEEE Transaction on Image Processing 10(2), 266–277 (2001)
10. Getreuer, P.: Chan-Vese Segmentation. Image Processing on Line 2, 214–224 (2012)
11. Suri, J.S., Liu, K., Singh, S., Laxminarayan, S.N., Zeng, X., Reden, L.: Shape Recovery Algorithms Using Level Sets in 2-D/3-D Medical Imagery: A State-of-the-Art Review. IEEE Transactions on Information Technology in Biomedicine 6(1), 8–28 (2002)
12. ImageJ official website, http://imagej.nih.gov/ij/ (visited April 10, 2014)
13. Forkert, N.D., Schmidt-Richberg, A., Fiehler, J., Illies, T., Möller, D., Säring, D., Handels, H., Ehrhardt, J.: 3D cerebrovascular segmentation combining fuzzy vessel enhancement and level-sets with anisotropic energy weights. Magnetic Resonance Imaging 31, 262–271 (2013)
14. Klepaczko, A., Szczypinski, P., Dwojakowski, G., Strzelecki, M., Materka, A.: Computer Simulation of Magnetic Resonance Angiography Imaging. Model Description and Validation 9(4) (April 2014), doi:10.1371/journal.pone.0093689

Identifying a Joint in Medical Ultrasound Images Using Trained Classifiers

Kamil Wereszczyński[1], Jakub Segen[1], Marek Kulbacki[1], Paweł Mielnik[2],
Marcin Fojcik[3], and Konrad Wojciechowski[1]

[1] Polish-Japanese Institute of Information Technology
Koszykowa 86, 02-008 Warsaw, Poland
[2] Revmatologisk Avdeling, Førde sentralsjukehus
Svanehaugvegen 2, 6812 Førde, Norway
[3] Sogn og Fjordane University College
Vievegen 2, 6812 Førde, Norway
mk@pjwstk.edu.pl

Abstract. A novel learning approach for detecting the joint in ultrasound images is proposed as a first step of an automated method of assessment of synovitis activity. The training and test data sets consist of images with labeled pixels of the joint region. Feature descriptors based on a pixel's neighborhood, are selected among SURF, SIFT, FAST, ORB, BRISK, FREAK descriptors, and their mixtures, to define the feature vectors for a trainable pixel classifier. Multiple pixel classifiers, including k-nearest neighbor, support vector machine, and decision tree classifier, are constructed by supervised learning. The AUC measure computed from ROC curves is used as the performance criterion for evaluation. The measure is used to compare and select the best mixture of image descriptors, forming a feature vector for the classifier, the best classifier and the best chain of image preprocessing operations. The final joint detector is a result of clustering the pixels classified as "joint". The results of experiments using the proposed method on a set of ultrasound images are presented, demonstrating the method's applicability and usefulness.

Keywords: medical ultrasound images, machine learning, classifier, image feature descriptor, synovitis.

1 Introduction

Medical examiners use ultrasound images to assess the degree of synovitis, the inflammation of the synovial membrane of a joint frequently associated with arthritis [8,9]. Automating the assessment of synovitis activity would reduce the range of discrepancies in human evaluation, and may help in clinical trials and patient screening. The work described in this paper is a part of the project MEDUSA, which aims at automated assessments of synovitis activity through analysis of ultrasound images of fingers. Medical literature [10] suggests, that measurements of image features relative to the location of the joint, provides useful information towards the project's objective. Performing such measurements

L.J. Chmielewski et al. (Eds.): ICCVG 2014, LNCS 8671, pp. 626–635, 2014.

necessitates localization of the joint in an ultrasound image. The approach to the joint localization, that is being pursued, consist of two steps. The first step, and the focus of this paper, uses a detector trained to identify the joint based on analysis of the neighborhoods of pixels, and similar detectors for other parts of finger's image, such as bones. The results of this step may have errors, such as detecting a joint where there is none. The second step attempts to reduce such errors, and improve the joint localization by mapping the results of detectors to a structural model, in the spirit of recognition-by-components theory [11].

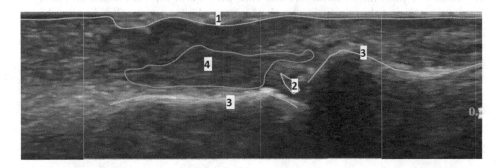

Fig. 1. Human fingers USG image with example biological structures marked: 1-skin, 2-joint, 3-bones, and 4-inflamation area

This paper presents a novel approach to identification of a joint that uses supervised learning to construct a pixel classifier from the provided set of training examples with labeled joint pixels. Fig. 1 presents an example of an ultrasound image that shows a finger joint, annotated by drawn outlines of the joint, bones, skin and a region of synovitis. Multiple image feature descriptors and their mixtures are evaluated as the basis for the classifier's feature vector, including SURF [1,2], FAST [3], ORB [4], BRISK [5], FREAK [6], and three classification methods: Nearest neighbor classifier, Support Vector Machines or SVM [12], and Decision trees [13]. The evaluation of performance is based on the AUC (Area Under the Curve) [7] measure, computed from ROC curves. This measure guides the choice of the classifier, feature descriptor, and the preprocessing filters. Pixels predicted by the classifier as being in class "in joint", are clustered into a small group of locations, which are the possible joint locations. The final joint location will be found by the above mentioned second step method, which will be described in another paper. The learning method are extensively used in recent research work for image feature identification, however in most cases such as [14] they are applied to learn a library of non-specific features useful for object classification, while the proposed here method learns specifically to detect the pixels of a joint. The following section describes preprocessing of the images, labeling and screening of pixels and formation of feature vectors for classification, Section 3 describes the classifiers and their learning, Section 4 describes the performance evaluation measure and Section 5 presents the results of experiments on ultrasound finger images and demonstrates the usefulness of the proposed approach.

2 Image Preprocessing and Feature Extraction

Before applying the learning and classification methods, data must be obtained from the images, in an appropriate format for these methods. An image is first processed by a sequence of image preprocessing operations, with the purpose of enhancing the image characteristics that are useful for classification. Each of these operations takes an image as the input and returns another image. After preprocessing, the pixels of the resulting image are screened, and for each pixel that passes, a descriptor is computed from this pixel's neighborhood, which gives the vector of features for the learning and classification. In the training and testing phases, such pixel is also given a label. The purpose of the screening is the reduction of the number of pixels subject to the expensive descriptor computation.

2.1 Image Preprocessing

The image preprocessing step consists of a conversion of a color image to a gray scale image, followed by the application of filters, such as a smoothing filter (for example a Gaussian blur), histogram equalization, or a denoising filter. As an example, this step can consists of the following operations: gray scale → Gaussian blur → histogram equalization → denoising.

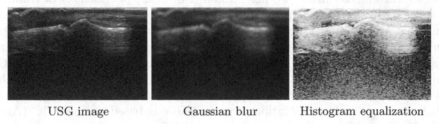

USG image   Gaussian blur   Histogram equalization

Fig. 2. Image processing operations applied to a USG image

The smoothing filter has a positive effect on the results of nearly all classifiers. A description of the combined influence of the preprocessing operations on the results of tests with classifiers, and their best combinations is given in Section 5.

2.2 Labeling Pixels

For the purpose of learning, the pixels in the joint region are labeled as positive examples or in joint, and remaining pixels are negative examples or outside joint. The example labels are computed from the information provided by a human expert, who marks the joint center C and points belonging to a joint region

$J = p_1, p_2, ..., p_n$ from which ball $B(C, \varepsilon\sigma_{||c-p_i||})^1$ is computed. The symbol ε is scale coefficient and it is a parameter of feature labeling process. For one-class classifiers, such as the nearest neighbor classifier, all in joint labeled pixels are the examples of the learned class. For two class classifiers, such as the two-class Support Vector Machine (SVM) [12], the pixels labeled in joint and outside joint are the examples of the two classes. As described further, experiments show that for the SVM classifier, dividing the class outside joint into multiple classes improves the classification. The outside joint is divided into 3 classes: near - 1, far - 2, and remaining - 3, defined by near coefficient (ε_n), and far coefficient (ε_f). The in joint class is labeled 0. All four classes are defined as follows:

$$label(p \in I) = \begin{cases} 3 \Leftrightarrow d(p,c) \in [0, \varepsilon] \\ 2 \Leftrightarrow d(p,c) \in [\varepsilon, \varepsilon_n] \\ 1 \Leftrightarrow d(p,c) \in [\varepsilon_n, \varepsilon_f] \\ 0 \Leftrightarrow d(p,c) \in [\varepsilon_f, \infty] \end{cases} \qquad (1)$$

where d is a distance in image space, c is the joint center and ε is a scale coefficient defining the radius of the joint region (see Fig. 3)

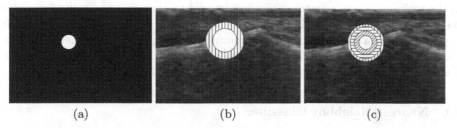

(a)   (b)   (c)

Fig. 3. Screening and labeling. Example of screening pixel in training perspective (a). Pixel assignment into one in joint class (solid fill) and one (b) or three (c) out joint classes (pattern fill).

2.3   Screening Pixels

Computing a descriptor on a pixel's neighborhood is a costly operation. Without some preselection or screening, it would have to be applied to about 400K pixels per image. A simple sub-sampling on a grid with 7-pixel spacing is used as the screening method. In the training phase, the set of preselected pixels is extended by adding the pixels labeled in joint, near and far (see Fig. 3). We also have attempted to screen pixels using a feature detector such as including SURF [1,2], FAST [3], ORB [4], BRISK [5], FREAK [6]. However, none of these detectors was found adequate, under the requirement that at least one pixel in the in joint region is selected. Setting the detector's sensitivity high enough to satisfy this requirement resulted in half or more image pixels passing the screening, while much higher reduction results from the sub-sampling based screener.

---

[1] σ is a standard deviation.

2.4   Feature Extraction

Features are attributes which, taken as a set, distinguish one object from another. Joint detection problem come to pixel qualification; that's why features is information concerned with pixels. The simplest but not sufficient attribute of pixel is its color or gray level. The objects that are subject to classification are individual pixels. For each pixel, a vector of features is formed as a function of a pixel's neighborhood. Local image descriptors such as SURF [1] are used as the basis of features for pixel classification. The feature vector is constructed as a mixture of multiple descriptors. Let $D_1, D_2, , D_n$ be n different descriptors of the same pixel, in a vector form. The mixture feature vector F is formed as a concatenation of weighted descriptors $F = [w_1 D_1{}^T, w_2 D_2{}^T, \ldots, w_n D_n{}^T]^T$, where w_i is a weight of D_i descriptor; n is called mixture length. The results shown in this paper were obtained using a mixture of the SURF [1].

3   Learning Pixel Classifiers

A classifier, in the context of this presentation, is a function that is applied to a neighborhood of an image pixel, which outputs or predicts the label of this pixel. In the training phase, a learning method is used to construct a specific form of a classifier, using images with labeled pixels as input data. The presented approach to pixel classification allows one to use many different classification methods. The classifiers used in the experiments which are shown in Results section are the Nearest Neighbor classifier and the Support Vector Machine [12].

3.1   Nearest Neighbor Classifier

Let I be an image, $p, q \in I$ - a pixel, J joint area, $c \in J$ joint center, $delta_p$-descriptor of pixel p, λ affiliation threshold, d square Euclidean metric in descriptor space. In learning phase so called Ground truth set (GT) is created composed of clustered descriptors of pixels belonging to the in joint class collected from all training images. In the classification phase, a label is assigned to a pixel according to:

$$label(p \in I) = \begin{cases} 0 \Leftrightarrow min_{g \in GT}\{d(\delta_p, \delta_g)\} < \lambda_n \\ 1 \Leftrightarrow min_{g \in GT}\{d(\delta_p, \delta_g)\} \geq \lambda_n. \end{cases} \tag{2}$$

λ_n is a normalized affiliation threshold, 0 means the in joint class and 1 the outside joint. Normalization is applied for each image separately assigning weights proportionally in range $[0,1] \in \mathbb{R}$ with the sum of weights equal to 1 (scaled to $[0, 1020] \in \mathbb{N}$ for visualization). For labeling k nearest neighbors search algorithm is used cite15 with $k = 1$. For each pixel nearest point in Ground Truth using knn-search is founded. If distance to this point is smaller than threshold given pixel is labeled as in joint else as outside joint. This value is used as a variable control parameter in ROC analysis. An example of such a procedure is shown in Fig. 4. For each pixel descriptor distance from the Ground Truth is shown using colors ($distance = 0$ is marked with black color the biggest with red color). On the left picture only distances are shown. On the right picture a yellow spot shows pixels that have distances closer to Ground Truth then τ.

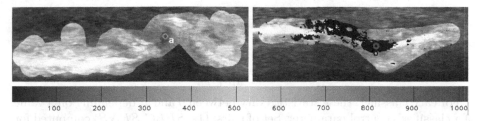

Fig. 4. Distances of pixel descriptors to joint center pixel descriptor (a) with classified in joint area by nearest neighbor classifier marked with black spot (b); height map of descriptor normalized distances legend showed on picture below

3.2 Support Vector Machine

The publicly available version of SVM [12] version was used in this work. The SVM library includes classification, regression and one-class classification functionalities using idea of support vectors. The multi-classification was used, with penalty C multiplier for outliers. Optimization considerations are described in [12]. Radial basis kernel function that was used for evaluation is: $K(x_i, x_j) = e^{-\gamma ||x_i - x_j||^2}, \gamma > 0$. Using auto train method from used library $\gamma = 0.85$ was fixed as most proper. For ROC analysis purpose C was changed in range $[0.5, 25]$. Best results was for C close to 15.

3.3 Decision Trees

Decision Trees was introduced by Breiman in [13]. In the current study, the implementation from the library OpenCV was used. Tree was used with surrogate splits, 10-fold built-in cross-validation, pruned branches was physically removed from tree. The so called 1 SE rule was used, which leads to making the tree more compact and more resistant to training data noise.

4 Evaluation Methods

In a test phase, each of the classifiers is applied to the image pixels, after screening, to predict the pixel's label. The classified pixel obtains one of four qualifiers, based on the prediction correctness: *true positive, false positive, true negative* and *false negative*. True positive is the case when both the predicted and assigned label are in joint, false positive when the predicted label is in joint and the assigned outside joint, true negative when both the predicted and assigned label are outside joint, and false negative when the predicted label is outside joint and assigned in joint. The numbers of pixels in all test images that obtained a specific qualifier are denoted by *tp, fp, tn* and *fn,* for *true positive, false positive, true negative* and *false negative* pixels, respectively. From these four numbers we compute two statistics: 1-specificity (1-SPEC) also called false positive rate (fpr), and sensitivity (SENS) otherwise called true positive rate (tpr).

$$1 - SPEC = \frac{fp}{fp + tn} \qquad (3)$$

$$SENS = \frac{tp}{tp + fn}. \qquad (4)$$

For each classifier, these statistics vary between 0 and 1, depending on a value of a classifier's control parameter. Set of pairs, $(1 - SPEC, SENS)$ computed for a range of values of the control parameter forms a curve, called ROC curve [7], which is used to judge the performance of a classifier. Three evaluation measures computed from this curve are described below: *area under the curve* (AUC).

5   Results

For initial comparison of different joint detection methods measures described above was applied to results of some experiments. Each experiment was made implementing one scenario of preparation, feature collection and training. Number of tests was proceeded and some of them are presented in this section. Several scenarios with best results are specified in table below.

Table 1. Scenarios of several joint detection methods with AUC value. GS - gray scale, HE - histogram equalization, GB - Gaussian blur.

marking	preparation	Feature collection	training method	AUC
SVM1	GS , HE, GB	SURF mixture	SVM	0,966
SVM2	GS	SURF mixture	SVM	0,981
SVM3	GS , HE, GB	SURF	SVM	0,961
SVM4	GS	SURF	SVM	0,975
NN1	GS , HE, GB	SURF mixture	Nearest Neighbor	0,911
NN2	GS	SURF mixture	Nearest Neighbor	0,928
NN3	GS , HE, GB	SURF	Nearest Neighbor	0,912
NN4	GS	SURF	Nearest Neighbor	0,925
DT1	GS , HE, GB	SURF mixture	Decision Tree	0,710
DT2	GS	SURF mixture	Decision Tree	0,749
DT3	GS , HE, GB	SURF	Decision Tree	0,889
DT4	GS	SURF	Decision Tree	0,877

Parameters of applied methods was selected basing on many experiments and are the same in all above scenarios. In detail, parameters are: Gaussian blur: $\sigma = 7$, window size=37; SURF: octaves count: 8, octaves layers: 2, window size: 200, orientation was computed, SURF mixture: first element descritpor has the same parameters as SURF, second one: octaves count: 6, octaves layers: 2,

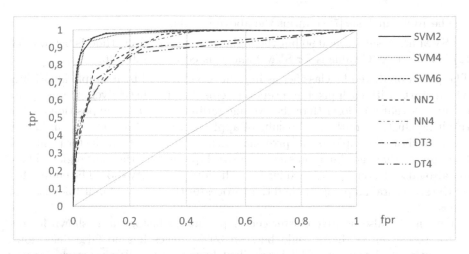

Fig. 5. ROC curves for some algorithms which scenarios are shown in Table 1

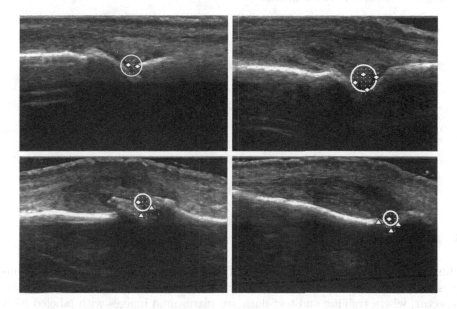

Fig. 6. Example results of pixel classification (light dots: in joint class, white circle: joint area, diamonds: positive detected cluster centers, triangles: false detected clusters centers)

window size: 80, orientation was computed; Nearest Neighbor: τ was parameter changing during creating ROC curve; SVM: C was parameter changing during creating ROC curve, class peantely weight: [15, 0.1, 0.1, 0.1] (see section Support Vector Machine) and for details about using 4 classes, Radial Basis Function was used as kernel with $\gamma = 0.85$. As could be seen on Fig. 5 ROC curves for all SVM are closer to point (0, 1), than curves for NN algorithms. It means, that this algorithm is more proper for joint detection problem.

The ROC analysis [7] confirms the above insights:

(1) SVM has results over 0,96 but the highest value for NN method is below 0,93.
(2) The best AUC value is for SVM2 and it is equal to 0,98146.

The pixels predicted by classifier as in joint are clustered by a simple algorithm, which starts with each pixel in a separate cluster, and successively merges pairs of clusters that are closer than the average radius of a joint. The positions of the resulting clusters are the final results of applying the joint detector to an image.

Fig. 6 shows examples of the pixel classification and the final cluster positions. One can see that each image has a cluster overlapping with the joint region. There are also false clusters, positioned far from the joint, but they should be eliminated by the structural mapping method that processes the output of multiple detector types.

On Fig. 7. false positive cluster center per image histogram is shown for detector based on SVM. As could be seen 30% images has no false detections, consecutive 30% only one. This is excellent base for the following works leading to finger structural model building.

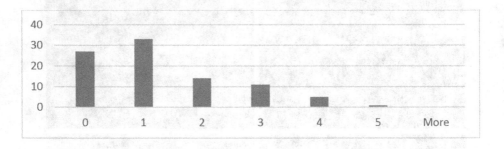

Fig. 7. Histogram of false positive cluster center per image

6   Conclusions

The presented novel approach to identifying a joint in medical ultrasound images uses supervised learning to construct a pixel classifier that acts as the joint detector, where training and test data are ultrasound images with labeled joint region pixels. The feature vectors used by the classifier are built from image feature descriptors such as SIFT, SURF or FAST. The ROC Area Under the Curve (AUC) is used as a measure of the classifier's performance. This measure helps to select the best classifier, mixture of descriptors used as the feature vector and the combination of preprocessing filters. The pixels classified as in joint are clustered, which results in a small number of potential joint locations. In the example results from ultrasound images of a joint, the correct joint location is always found, along with one or more incorrect locations, which are expected to be filtered out by a structural mapping method, which is a subject of an ongoing work.

Acknowledgement. The research leading to these results has received funding from the Polish-Norwegian Research Programme operated by the National Centre for Research and Development under the Norwegian Financial Mechanism 2009-2014 in the frame of Project Contract No. Pol-Nor/204256/16/2013.

References

1. Bay, H., Tuytelaars, T., Van Gool, L.: SURF: Speeded Up Robust Features. In: Leonardis, A., Bischof, H., Pinz, A. (eds.) ECCV 2006, Part I. LNCS, vol. 3951, pp. 404–417. Springer, Heidelberg (2006)
2. Lowe, D.G.: Distinctive Image Features from Scale-Invariant Keypoints. International Journal of Computer Vision 60, 91–110 (2004)
3. Rosten, E., Drummond, T.: Machine Learning for High-Speed Corner Detection. In: Leonardis, A., Bischof, H., Pinz, A. (eds.) ECCV 2006, Part I. LNCS, vol. 3951, pp. 430–443. Springer, Heidelberg (2006)
4. Rublee, E., Rabaud, V., Kurt Konolige, K., Bradski, G.R.: ORB: An efficient alternative to SIFT or SURF. In: ICCV, Barcelona, Spain, pp. 2564–2571 (2011)
5. Leutenegger, S., Chli, M., Siegwart, R.: BRISK: Binary Robust Invariant Scalable Keypoints. In: ICCV, pp. 2548–2555 (2011)
6. Alahi, A., Ortiz, R., Vandergheyns, P.: FREAK: Fast Retina Keypoint. EPFL Lausanne, Switzerland (2012)
7. Till, D.J., Hand, R.J.: A Simple Generalisation of the Area Under the ROC Curve for Multiple Class Classification Problems. Machine Learning 45, 171–186 (2012)
8. Østergaard, M., Szkudlarek, M.: Ultrasonography: a valid method for assessing rheumatoid arthritis? Arthritis Rheum. 52(3), 681–686 (2005)
9. Zuffereya, P., Tamborrinib, G., Gabayc, C., Krebsd, A., Kyburze, D., Michele, B., Moserf, U., Villigerg, P.M., Soa, A., Ziswilerh, H.R.: Recommendations for the use of ultrasound in rheumatoid arthritis: literature review and SONAR score experience. Swiss Medical Weekly 143, w13861 (2013)
10. Vlad, V., Berghea, F., Libianu, S., Balanescu, A., Bojinca, A., Constantinescu, A., Abobului, M., Predeteanu, D., Ionescu, R.: Ultrasound in rheumatoid arthritis - volar versus dorsal synovitis evaluation and scoring. BMC Musculoskeletal Disorders, 12–124 (2011)
11. Biederman, I.: Recognition-by-components: a theory of human image understanding. Psychol. Rev. 94(2) (April 1987)
12. Chang, C.-C., Lin, C.-J.: A Library for Support Vector Machines. National Taiwan University, Taipei (2013)
13. Breiman, L., Friedman, J.H., Olshen, R.A., Stone, C.J.: Classification and regression trees. Chapman & Hall/CRC, Wadsworth (1984)
14. Becker, C., Rigamonti, R., Lepetit, V., Fua, P.: Kernel-Boost: Supervised Learning of Image Features For Classification. Technical Report. Lausanne: School of Computer and Communication Sciences, Swiss Federal Institute of Technology, Lausanne (February 2014)
15. Muja, M., Lowe, D.G.: Fast Approximate Nearest Neighbors with Automatic Algorithm Configuration. In: International Conference on Computer Vision Theory and Applications (VISAPP), Lisbon, Portugal (2009)

Robust Eye Gaze Estimation

Joanna Wiśniewska[1], Mahdi Rezaei[2], and Reinhard Klette[2]

[1] Warsaw University of Technology
Plac Politechniki 1, 00-661 Warsaw, Poland
J.Wisniewska@stud.elka.pw.edu.pl
[2] The University of Auckland, Department of Computer Science
Private Bag 92019, Auckland 1142, New Zealand
{m.rezaei,r.klette}@auckland.ac.nz

Abstract. Eye gaze detection under challenging lighting conditions is a non-trivial task. Pixel intensity and the shades around the eye region may change depending on the time of day, location, or due to artificial lighting. This paper introduces a lighting-adaptive solution for robust eye gaze detection. First, we propose a binarization and cropping technique to limit our region of interest. Then we develop a gradient-based method for eye-pupil detection; and finally, we introduce an adaptive eye-corner detection technique that altogether lead to robust eye gaze estimation. Experimental results show the outperformance of the proposed method compared with related techniques.

1 Introduction and Related Work

Eye gaze estimation is an active research topic in computer vision. The development of such systems depends on the quality of the target camera, for example a high-resolution one which focuses only on the eye region, or a simple low-resolution webcam. The first option supports very accurate results for the detection of eye features. Due to cost limitations or varying head poses it may not be applicable. Images captured by a webcam typically contain the whole face and some background, and may require noise removal or image enhancement. A webcam is a widely used device due to its low cost.

High-resolution and infrared cameras were used, for example, in [9,21], with a focus on high resolution images of the eye-region which simplifies eye-features detection. Both papers use infrared lighting to ease eye-region detection. The Starburst algorithm is often used for detecting the pupil, see [9,11,13,14]. The algorithm applies simple thresholding, fits an ellipse to the pupil, and then refines the ellipse by consideration of a pupil's "edge points". When testing along the basic idea of this algorithm, we noticed that it cannot be applied to noisy and low-resolution images.

Some other researchers use a Hough circle transform for detecting the position of a pupil [17]. When dealing with low resolution images, the first issue is the localization of the eye center. Different methods are proposed to achieve this goal. Typically, methods are based on the usage of an edge detector. Then, a

L.J. Chmielewski et al. (Eds.): ICCVG 2014, LNCS 8671, pp. 636–644, 2014.
© Springer International Publishing Switzerland 2014

Hough circle transform is suggested to detect the iris or pupil [5,7]. Published research typically uses test images recorded under ideal lighting conditions where the eye region is not dark, e.g., due to the shadows. The curvature of isophotes (i.e. points of equal intensity) is used in [19] to design a voting scheme for the localization of the pupil. Next, they extend the method by using SIFT features for each pupil candidate and match such features with examples from a database before obtaining a final decision. The approach in [12] is based on an ensemble of randomized regression trees.

An extension to Logarithmic Type Image Processing (LTIP) is presented in [4]. The parametric extensions of LTIP models were used to built a reliable auto-focus mechanism for cameras working under extreme light conditions. According to facts presented by the authors, LTIP resembles properties of the human visual system. It could be used to enhance images acquired under extreme lighting.

This paper provides an eye gaze detection method for using a low resolution camera, especially also for challenging lighting conditions. Recorded images are assumed to contain an entire face region. The proposed algorithm consists of four major steps. At first, we apply a face-detection algorithm using Haar-features. Then we detect the eye region followed by a processing step to find the eye-pupil. Inspired by the work in [18] we implement pupil localization by analyzing gradients in the eye region. The method defines a function which takes a maximum at a location where many of the gradients intersect. This location is expected to correspond to the position of the pupil. Finally, in order to estimate eye-gaze, we detect the eye corner. Eye-corner detection in [23] proposes a method based on spatial filtering and the application of corner-shape masks. More recent work, e.g. [3,22], uses Harris corner detection with additional improvements such as active shape models (ASM). The authors of [6] also follow [23] and use additionally weighted variance-projection functions for determining approximately the corner area. In this research we use FAST features [16] with added adaptive thresholds for eye-corner detection.

We evaluate our eye-gaze detection algorithm based on experimental results performed on the BioID database [2] and video sequences recorded from different subjects under various lighting conditions.

2 Proposed Method

The method is structured into five steps: face and eyes detection, adaptive binarization, pupil detection, eye corner detection and gaze estimation.

2.1 Face and Eyes Detection

A fundamental requirement for any eye-tracking system is accurate face and eye socket detection. This can be achieved by Haar-like object detectors which were proposed in [20] and improved in [10]. Under non-ideal lighting conditions it is possible that one half of the face is darker than the other half. By applying face partitioning into two halves, and by changing the detector parameters for each half, we obtained better results under non-ideal lighting conditions than when using a standard detection approach. This idea was inspired by [15].

To improve accuracy, a hard-coded method was also used to estimate locations where eye sockets are expected to be. Even if a Haar-like face detector temporarily fails, non-rotated eye regions can be expected to be almost at their previous locations. As a result, it is possible to estimate their positions depending on the face width and height. Our experiments show that the eye-region width can be assumed to be around 33% of the face's width, and the eye-region height is around 25% of the face's height. The position of the left eye begins at about 13% from the left border of the face, and at about 27% from the top of the face.

2.2   Adaptive Binarization

We apply four hierarchical steps to limit the eye-socket region where we search for the pupil: binarization, edge (or contour) detection, determining the longest contour, and image cropping.

We tested various thresholding techniques [8], e.g. a basic *inverted* thresholding based on the minimum pixel value T of the eye region:

$$D(x,y) = \begin{cases} 0 & \text{if } S(x,y) > T \\ 255 & \text{otherwise} \end{cases} \tag{1}$$

This proved to be too unstable and worked only reasonable under very ideal lighting conditions. Otsu's adaptive thresholding had the same problems; results were also not adaptive to lighting conditions.

Due to the failures of the above mentioned thresholding methods, we decided to use *p-tile thresholding* as described in [1]. An adaptation to the light conditions according to pixel intensities was added to the basic technique. The first step of this method is the creation of a grey-level histogram of the image. The choice of threshold value T depends then on the chosen percentage parameter *p-value*. This parameter is a percentage value by which the size of the vector is multiplied. By taking the total value of the multiplication result, the position in a vector is obtained. The value hidden under this position is the query threshold value T. Using the calculated T, we applied basic thresholding as described in Equ. (1). In order to find an appropriate p-value, we calculate *mean* and *mode* M of pixel intensities. By combining these two parameters we identify a parameter I_p which determines the appropriate p-value. We describe I_p as follows:

$$I_p(\alpha) = \alpha * M_P + \frac{1-\alpha}{n} \cdot \sum_{i=1}^{n} P(x_i, y_i) \tag{2}$$

where P is the considered input window having n pixels. Following [15], this process (i.e. calculation of p-value and binarization) is performed independently for both eye regions. An adjustable parameter α is used to manipulate the influence of mean and mode values. Experimentally we identified $\alpha = 0.6$ as the mode intensity which led to better evaluations of the brightness of the pixels.

The next step is to perform a dilation in the binarized image and to find the smaller eye region by cropping the window for the largest region. Results of these steps are illustrated in Fig. 1.

Fig. 1. Steps for extracting smaller eye regions. *Left to right:* Input image, *p-tile thresholding*, dilation result, and the final cropped eye region.

2.3 Pupil Detection

We use the gradient method [18] for pupil detection due to its efficiency. Applying the method on the BioID database [2] we obtained very reasonable results. The method may fail in cases when the image is too blurry or the eyelashes are very long and dark. Among all the tested methods the method led to a smaller number of false positives. Figure 2 illustrates samples of positive and negative results on the BioID database [2].

Fig. 2. Examples of pupil detection on BioID images. Both images on the left supported correct detections, and the other two led to incorrect detections.

In a video sequence, errors can be reduced by applying some averaging over the last few frames. At the start of the program, we spend a few seconds to calibrate the gradient method. During calibration, the recorded subject is expected to look straight into the camera. After 20 frames, the averaging process starts for subsequent pupil detection.

2.4 Eye Corner Detection

Pupil detection is followed by localizing eye corners. For corner detection we use FAST features [16] with added adaptive thresholds. Parameters for the FAST algorithm are adjusted depending on pixel intensities, by following the same idea of using mean and mode values of the eye region as already discussed for the binarization process. The eye region is divided into two parts according to the location of the pupil, and two independent feature detection algorithms are applied on both halves.

Some of the detected FAST features could be false positives (e.g. at eyelashes, borders of glasses, or iris). To reject such FPs we assume that eye corners are maximally 50% of eye width and 30% of eye height away from the pupil. All features which satisfy this constraint are stored in a vector and averaging defines the final feature position. For more accurate results, we find the features that are most extreme to the left or right within the defined border.

In a video sequence, the errors can be reduced using temporally averaged positions of eye corners. We describe our algorithm by the following equations. First, we define the mean feature position $A(x, y)$ in one iteration as follows:

$$A(x,y) = \sum_{i=1}^{n} f(x_i, y_i) \quad \text{if} \quad P_y - b_y + c \leq f_{y_i} \leq P_y + b_y \tag{3}$$

where f is the set of detected features, P_y is a pupil location, b_y is an off-set for y-values, and c is an adjusting parameter. In our experiments we consider c as equals to 20% of the height of the eye region. The new corner position can be described as follows:

$$C(x,y) = \begin{cases} \frac{E(x,y)+A(x,y)}{2} & \text{if } (P_y - b_y + c \leq E_y \leq P_y + b_y) \wedge \\ & \quad (P_x \pm b_x \leq E_x \leq P_x \pm b_x + d) \\ E(x,y) & \text{if } A_x < P_x - 0.3 \cdot b_x \\ A(x,y) & \text{otherwise} \end{cases} \tag{4}$$

where $E(x, y)$ is the most extreme (towards left or right) feature, b_y is again a y-offset and b_x is an offset for x values, $P(x, y)$ is the pupil location, and d is an adjusting parameter, which is experimentally set to an optimum value of 24% of the width of the eye region for the inner corner, and to 15% for the outer corner. The sign in front of b_x depends upon whether we calculate a new position for the inner or outer corner.

Finally we need to check whether our new corner candidates are not too far away from the averaged corner position of the last few frames, described as

$$A_f(x,y) = \frac{1}{20} \sum_{i=1}^{20} C'(x_i, y_i). \tag{5}$$

after having already the first 20 frames (before this time the average corner position is not yet calculated for avoiding false results). The final corner position is as follows:

$$C'(x,y) = \begin{cases} C(x,y) & \text{if } (A_{f_x} - 10 < C_x < A_{f_x} + 10) \wedge (A_{f_y} - 10 < C_y < A_{f_y} + 10) \\ A_f(x,y) & \text{otherwise} \end{cases}$$

2.5   Gaze Estimation

We consider the distance between the pupil and the eye corners for estimating the horizontal direction. We also use the distance between the center of an eye region and the pupil for estimating the vertical direction.

First, we define a line segment which connects both eye corners. Then we calculate the distance from the pupil to the line as follows:

$$d = \frac{(P_x - S_x) \cdot (D_y - S_y) - (P_y - S_y) \cdot (D_x - S_x)}{\sqrt{(D_x - S_x)^2 + (D_y - S_y)^2}} \qquad (6)$$

where $P(x, y)$ is the pupil location, $S(x, y)$ is the one corner position, and $D(x, y)$ is the other one. We also calculate the distances between x-values of the pupil and both corners. Then we check the values of these three distances.

The information from both eyes is used in order to avoid estimation errors. For example, for our camera parameters, if the distance from the pupil to the line is less than -2 pixels, we assumed that the person is looking downward; if it is less than 3.5 and more than -1.8 we assume that the person is looking straight forward; if it is more than 3.5 we consider that the person is looking upward.

To determine whether a person is looking to the right or to the left, first, we check whether the distance between pupil and the outer left corner is less than 18 pixels. At the same time we check whether the distance between pupil and inner right corner is less than 20. To reduce errors, we also check whether the distance from the inner left corner and the outer right corner is more than 28. If 'yes' then we assume that the person is looking to the right. Similar conditions are checked for looking to the left. If none of the conditions are fulfilled then we assume that the person is looking straight forward.

3   Experimental Results

First, we performed face and eye-socket detection on the BioID database [2]. A combination of Haar-feature based eye detection and a hard-coded method for detecting eye sockets provided good results; only 0.15% of correctly detected faces had incorrectly detected eyes. Adaptive binarization also provided very good results: above 99.5% of images had a smaller eye region cropped correctly.

As a next experiment, we tested our method on six different subjects under different lighting conditions, including varying colors, from natural light condition to different artificial lights, obtained from various light sources. All the video sequences had a resolution of 640×48 pixels. Test subjects were at various age and of different gender. We also used two different webcams, one external and the other one integrated in a laptop. We used the first 20 frames for system calibration and for estimating potential pupil and eye-corner positions, in order to calculate mean positions for these eye features. Then the subjects were asked to look several times in four basically different directions (up, down, left, and right), and in four additional directions (e.g. upper left and right, bottom left and right). All results are recorded, frames are analyzed, and error rates are calculated. The evaluation of results has its limits; for example, with a naked eye, it is not feasible to determine the exact direction of the subject's eye gaze in dark, noisy, and low-resolution images. In order to evaluate the results it was assumed that a false detection of eye corners or of the pupil causes incorrect eye-gaze estimation. This might not be exactly true always. In some cases, pupil or eye corners are detected incorrectly but the detections are not too far away from the correct position, and it is still possible to have a correct final result for gaze estimation. Figure 3 presents results of eye-feature detection obtained for six different subjects, where the circles are symbolizing pupil and corner positions and a line between the corners.

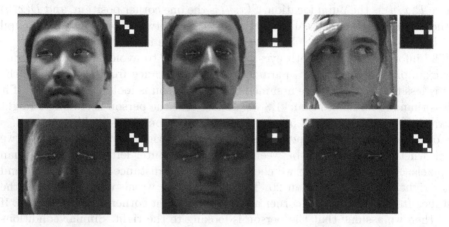

Fig. 3. Samples of eye-gaze detection under various lighting conditions

Table 1 presents the final results obtained from 13 performed tests. The first ten were performed using an external webcam with higher image quality, and the last three are obtained using an integrated webcam in a laptop with poorer image quality. Also, the last three tests were performed for very dark faces and challenging lighting conditions (in shadows), as also illustrated in Fig. 3. The table confirms that the less noisy images support better results.

Table 1. Percentages of correct eye-feature detections, separately for both eyes

Number of test	1	2	3	4	5	6	7	8	9	10	11	12	13
Left eye [True positive (%)]	100	100	99	96	98	98	97	95	100	94	98	87	78
Right eye [True positive (%)]	98	100	99	100	93	96	100	95	100	77	64	57	59

We realized that the most common reason of failures are dark spots near the eye regions (e.g. a very thick and dark frame of eyeglasses). Another problem appears if there are multiple dark and bright areas in the same eye; then the algorithm misses the eye-corner position and replaces it with a false-positive. We believe that this kind of problem could be avoided by adding an eye tracking solution into the algorithm. This could improve the stability of the gaze detection. When the eyes are closed then a (non-existing) false pupil might be detected as well; however, in most cases the eye corners are detected correctly. Our adaptive binarization and cropping algorithm worked efficiently in all the tested cases.

4   Conclusions

The detection of face features under non-ideal lighting conditions and in low-resolution images is a challenging issue. We had to face various complications for detecting points of interest accurately. The proposed and implemented adaptive algorithm ensures less vulnerability due to changes in lighting conditions. The paper outlined a robust solution for eye-gaze detection and suggests in particular a method for minimizing the region of interest. By using light-adapting *p-tile thresholding*, the method provides robustness and efficiency over a comprehensive range of experimental tests. For future work, the algorithm might be more stable by adding a tracking module and eye state detection. This can further reduce errors generated when the eyes are closed.

References

1. Al-amri, S.S., Kalyankar, N.V.: Image segmentation by using threshold techniques. arXiv preprint arXiv:1005, 4020 (2010)
2. BioID database (2014), http://www.bioid.com/index.php?q=downloads/software/bioid-face-database.html
3. Bengoechea, J.J., Cerrolaza, J.J., Villanueva, A., Cabeza, R.: Evaluation of accurate eye corner detection methods for gaze estimation. Int. Worksh. Pervasive Eye Tracking Mobile Eye-Based Interaction (2013)
4. Florea, C., Florea, L.: Parametric logarithmic type image processing for contrast based auto-focus in extreme lighting conditions. Int. J. Applied Mathematics Computer Science 23, 637–648 (2013)
5. Fu, B., Yang, R.: Display control based on eye gaze estimation. IEEE Int. Conf. Image Signal Processing 1, 399–403 (2011)
6. Haiying, X., Guoping, Y.: A novel method for eye corner detection based on weighted variance projection function. In: IEEE Int. Conf. Image Signal Processing, pp. 1–4 (2009)
7. Khilari, R.: Iris tracking and blink detection for human-computer interaction using a low resolution webcam. In: Indian Conf. Computer Vision Graphics Image Processing, pp. 456–463. ACM (2010)
8. Klette, R.: Concise Computer Vision. Springer, London (2014)
9. Li, D., Winfield, D., Parkhurst, D.J.: Starburst: A hybrid algorithm for video-based eye tracking combining feature-based and model-based approaches. In: CVPR Workshops, vol. 3, pp. 79–86 (2005)
10. Lienhart, R., Maydt, J.: An extended set of Haar-like features for rapid object detection. In: IEEE Conf. ICIP 2002, vol. 1, pp. 900–903 (2002)
11. Lupu, R.G., Ungureanu, F., Siriteanu, V.: Eye tracking mouse for human computer interaction. In: E-Health and Bioengineering Conference (EHB), pp. 1–4. IEEE (2013)
12. Markuš, N., Frljak, M., Pandžič, I.S., Ahlberg, J., Forchheimer, R.: Eye pupil localization with an ensemble of randomized trees. Pattern Rec. 47, 578–587 (2014)
13. McMurrough, C.D., Metsis, V., Kosmopoulos, D., Maglogiannis, I., Makedon, F.: A dataset for point of gaze detection using head poses and eye images. J. Multimodal User Interfaces 7, 207–215 (2013)

14. Nagel, J.A., Kutschker, C., Beck, C., Gengenbach, U., Guth, H., Bretthauer, G.: Comparison of different algorithms for robust detection of pupils in real-time eye-tracking experiments. Biomed Tech 58, 1 (2013)
15. Rezaei, M., Klette, R.: Adaptive Haar-like classifier for eye status detection under non-ideal lighting conditions. In: Int. Conf. Image Vision Computing New Zealand, pp. 521–526. ACM (2012)
16. Rosten, E., Porter, R., Drummond, T.: Faster and better: a machine learning approach to corner detection. IEEE Trans. PAMI 32, 105–119 (2010)
17. Schwarz, L., Gamba, H.R., Pacheco, F.C., Ramos, R.B., Sovierzoski, M.A.: Pupil and iris detection in dynamic pupillometry using the OpenCV library. In: IEEE Int. Conf. Image Signal Processing, pp. 211–215 (2012)
18. Timm, F., Barth, E.: Accurate eye centre localisation by means of gradients. In: Int. Conf. Computer Vision Theory Applications, vol. 1, pp. 125–130 (2011)
19. Valenti, R., Gevers, T.: Accurate eye center location through invariant isocentric patterns. IEEE Trans. PAMI 34, 1785–1798 (2012)
20. Viola, P., Jones, M.J.: Rapid object detection using a boosted cascade of simple features. In: IEEE Conf. CVPR (2001)
21. Zhang, W., Zhang, T.-N., Chang, S.-J.: Eye gaze estimation from the elliptical features of one iris. Optical Engineering 50(4), 47003–47003 (2011)
22. Zhou, R., He, Q., Wu, J., Hu, C., Meng, Q.H.: Inner and outer eye corners detection for facial features extraction based on ctgf algorithm. Applied Mechanics Materials 58, 1966–1971 (2011)
23. Zhu, J., Yang, L.: Subpixel eye gaze tracking. In: IEEE Int. Conf. Automatic Face Gesture Recognition, pp. 124–129 (2002)

Exponentially Smoothed Interactive Gaze Tracking Method

Adam Wojciechowski[1] and Krzysztof Fornalczyk[1,2]

[1] Institute of Information Technology, Technical University of Łódź, Poland
[2] Binar::Apps, Łódź, Poland
adam.wojciechowski@p.lodz.pl, krz.fornalczyk@gmail.com

Abstract. Gaze tracking is an aspect of human-computer interaction still growing in popularity. Tracking human eye fixation points can help control user interfaces and eventually may help in the interface evaluation or optimization. Unfortunately professional eye-trackers are very expensive and thus hardly available for researchers and small companies. The paper presents very effective, exponentially smoothed, low cost, appearance based, improved gaze tracking method. The method achieves very high absolute precision (1 deg) at 20 fps, exploiting a simple HD web camera with reasonable environment restrictions. The paper describes results of experimental tests, both static on absolute gaze point estimation, and dynamic on gaze controlled path following.

1 Introduction

Due to computer vision methods development and digital cameras increasing performance, non-intrusive, appearance based gaze tracking methods have been still growing in popularity [1] [2]. Using computer vision and geometrical properties of the eyes, gaze direction can be estimated without the need of any kind of physical contact with the user. Among them there are professional image-based eye trackers which prices may exceed 10000 Euro (i.e.: Tobii eye-tracker).

Whereas authors claim that, non-professional equipment without dedicated light sources can work sufficiently. Simple video cameras for about 20 Euro supported by appropriately elaborated gaze tracking method, can become a powerful interactive eye-tracking system. Though Hansen [17] review has shown that appearance based methods, considering environment illuminated with natural light are confined to a precision of about 5 deg, authors have elaborated a method of considerably higher precision (1 deg).

Presented paper describes an improved, interactive method for effective tracking eye movements. Method did not enforce any sophisticated lighting condition, and exploited simple HD web camera. Newly proposed geometric eyes features vectors can be very effectively calculated for low resolution eyes images and after simple calibration have provided gaze point estimation high accuracy. Additional exponential prediction smoothen collected samples resulting in a very stable and reliable solution. Very promising tests on implemented method, were also provided.

L.J. Chmielewski et al. (Eds.): ICCVG 2014, LNCS 8671, pp. 645–652, 2014.

2   Related Work

Interactive eye-gaze tracking systems provide solutions mainly for selective and gaze-contingent human computer interaction [1][3][6][7][8][9][10][11][12]. Though interactive gaze tracking systems have relatively lower precision then diagnostic one, such systems assure fully functional, robust, real-time response and system reaction [1]. There were several attempts, where interactive solutions stability and precision improvement was considerably enhanced by system intrusiveness. Due to special devices in direct contact with skin or enforcing users to wear uncomfortable glasses or helmets [13] [14] [15], systems have reduced, eyes and tracking device related, coordinating systems correlation costs.

In selective interactive systems, eyes actively control the system by means of gaze direction. Possible use of eye trackers typically employ gaze as a pointing modality, i.e. in similar manner to a mouse pointer. It can enable a user interface to be sensitive to the attention of a user. Sibert and Jacob [18] showed that eye tracking interfaces are both usable and superior to mouse driven interfaces for some metrics. Possible applications involve selection of interface items as well as selection of objects or areas of virtual environment. Jacob [3] demonstrated an intelligent gaze-based informational display. The *What You Look At Is What You Get* idea lets to scroll the window to show information on visually selected items. Starker and Bolt [4] presented gaze-controlled navigation in a three dimensional environment. Tanriverdi and Jacob [5] elaborated an eye-based interactive system with gaze acting as a selective mechanism in VR. Another prototypical application of interactive eye tracking was, handicapped users dedicated, screen displayed keyboard typing [6][7], screen gaze controlled drawing [8] or blink controlled web browsing [10]. Santalla et al. [9] adaptively cropped photographs basing on averaged region of interest.

Within quoted applications, powered by non-intrusive, single camera, interactive, gaze tracking methods, the approach tending to evaluate geometric characteristics of eye components (pupil, iris, sclera, limbus) interrelations and analyze them in order to estimate gaze direction were mainly researched [2][17][19][20][21][22].

Betke [20], Liu [21] and Kao [22] suggested tracking characteristic features of the eye regions throughout all subsequent camera frames. Ones recorded, fragment of eye ball was located in subsequent frames basing on the best correlation coefficients [20], mean-shift algorithm [21] or pattern voting scheme [22]. Authors reported that direct mapping of eye center onto mouse cursor position, had resulted in a miserable precision. Magee [23] has evaluated gaze direction basing on adjustment of eyes images. Subtraction of left and right eyes images (one of the eye images was mirrored) let evaluate gaze direction. Nevertheless methods tests have limited its functionality to moving cursor horizontally, to the left or to the right respectively.

Yamazoe [24] and Ishikawa [25] have proposed eye model based gaze estimation exploiting iris centre, eye ball centre and eye corners interrelations. However, the obtained precision was only about 5 deg. horizontally and 7 deg. vertically.

Yet method presented in the paper, neither imposes severe lighting conditions nor requires long training. Assuming that user, being interested in some point of the screen, is enforced to freeze his head for at least several frames, the head and eyes were tracked on frames by direct highly optimized Haar-like classifier and upgraded between similar frames. Thus method does not use any sophisticated features tracking algorithm. Similarly to Yamazoe and Magee, gaze estimation was based on eyes images features, but features retrieval was performed only in image space. Introductory concept of the method was presented in [2]. Its developed and improved version, is presented further in the paper. Due to improvements its precision had increased more then twice.

3   Smoothed Gaze Tracking Method

The main goal of the method was to determine the point on which the user's eyes are focused (gaze point) and proceed analysis to determine whether the user is looking at certain place, or the gaze point is moving. This task can be divided into five general steps:

1. Finding user's face in the image.
2. Finding (on the face) eyes.
3. Determining whether the eyes are opened.
4. If eyes are opened, finding where the user looks (gaze point).

In order to find user's face on the image, the cascade of Haar-like features classifiers (describing face) was used [26]. The weak point of this approach was the ordinary operation's speed, but to some extent it has been compensated by simple optimizations. The first optimization was that only one, the first found and the biggest region satisfying Haar-like classifier was chosen as the valid face region. Additionally new iteration of the face localization was initiated if the region pixels brightness has overall changed more than 2%. Otherwise previous face region was set as valid for at maximum 3 iterations. The latest performance boosting improvement was to conduct the face finding step on a scaled down image.

The next step was to find the user's eyes within the face region. For this purpose the cascade of Haar-like features classifiers (describing eyes pair) was used [26] [27]. Additional boosting assumption was that stripe containing eyes should be localized within upper part of the face region.

The next step was to determine whether users eyes were opened. For this purpose part of image containing both eyes, was retrieved form original size image and divided into two parts right and left eye respectively. All of further operations were performed on both parts separately as the brightness of each eye may differ. Then a histogram equalization operation was performed. The next operation was inversed binary threshold - thanks to that the darkest parts (pupil and upper eyelid) of image became white and the rest black. The values of thresholds were set by user. To delete possible noise which may appear in result, operations of erosion and double dilatation were used. Then, in both images separately (left and right eye), all contours were being sought and the largest was selected from them - these were contours of the pupils and/or the upper eyelids. Further processing should crop all contours that do not belong to eye pupil and eliminate them from the further considered contours. Sometimes contour was divided into two or more parts. To avoid omission of smaller parts we added to the biggest one all contours lying within its image height range.

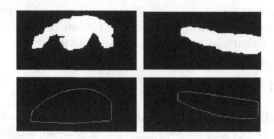

Fig. 1. Eye contours and theirs convex hulls for opened (left) and closed (right) eye

Analyzing the groups of contours and their curved outlines of opened and closed (fig. 1) eyes, it was easy to notice a dependency closed eyes contours had similar area as their convex outlines, while contours of opened eyes were significantly different in size from their convex outlines. A condition to distinguish two cases was formulated - if a convex perimeter constitutes more than 85% (usually more than 90%) of the contour's perimeter the eyes were closed, if less eyes were opened (normally 60%-80%).

The last step was to determine the gaze point. This was done in several steps:

- calculating the geometric center (SG) and center of mass (SM) for each of the contours (fig. 2);
- calculating the vector v connecting the above points (eq. 1) within image coordinate system;

$$v =< v_x; v_y >=< SM_x - SG_x; SM_y - SG_y > \tag{1}$$

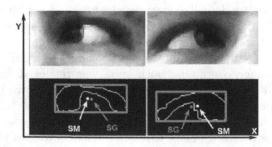

Fig. 2. Eye contours, theirs bounding rectangles, centers of mass (white points - SM) and geometric centers (grey points - SG)

- dividing the v_x coordinate by the width and v_y coordinate by the height of the bounding rectangle of the contour (fig. 2);

As it was shown in the figure 2 - relation between the center of mass (SM) and the geometric center (SG) of the contour was different depending in which direction the eyes were oriented. Analysis of the vector v allowed, to determine gaze point, upon previous system calibration.

Calibration was simply to retrieve a specific number of samples for each of the corners of the screen. Then, for each characteristic point, the arithmetic mean of all corresponding samples was calculated. In this way, we got 4 points A,B,C,D representing the screen corners (fig. 3). In theory, the extreme points (A,B,C,D) should create the rectangle, but due to various reasons, the points usually form a quadrangle (fig. 3a), which should be normalized so that the subsequent vertices were located at (0, 0), (1, 0), (1, 1), (0, 1) (fig. 3b). Calibration coefficients were used for further gaze point calculation.

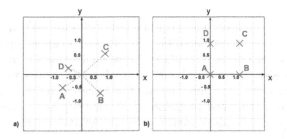

Fig. 3. Set of points A,B,C,D representing averaged screen corners. a) averaged screen corners values before normalization; b) averaged corners values after normalization

After calibration, the screen corners related gaze point tracking was proceeded. For smoothing gaze points trajectory new prediction method was implemented. On contrary to previous one where a certain number of samples was averaged the second exploiting exponential smoothing prediction (ESP) [28] was added. For collected samples, smoothened position of the gaze point was calculated and normalized with calibration coefficients. If one of the resulting points coordinates exceeded [0,1] range it has meant that the user was not looking at the screen.

4   Tests

Efficiency of the method was tested on a group of 10 students without glasses (21 to 23 years old). All the tests were performed using Creative Live! Cam Sync HD 720p web camera (1280x720 pixels at 30 fps) and laptop with screen resolution 1366x768 pixels and corresponding physical dimension 34.5x19.5 centimeters. In result 1 centimeter corresponded to about 40 pixels.

The first group of tests goal was to measure the static position of the gaze point fixation in relation to the mouse cursor position, the eyes were concentrated on. The testers were placed about 75cm away from the monitor and the camera was positioned on the laptop keyboard, midway between the screen and the user. Tests were carried out under unified lighting conditions. For each test 25 measurements were made. Achieved averaged results are presented in table 1.

Table 1. The average results of exponentially smoothed method accuracy tests for 50 and 100 calibration samples

Calibration samples no.	α coefficient	Avg. x error [pix]	Avg. y error [pix]	Total distance error [pix]
50	0.5	69	58	99
50	0.1	62	48	88
50	0.05	37	69	86
100	0.5	46	16	51
100	0.1	54	40	75
100	0.05	50	45	70

As one may notice, after longer calibration (100 samples) the working mode x coordinates errors have oscillated between 46 and 54 pixels (median 50 pixels) and y coordinates errors have oscillated between 16 and 45 (median 40 pixels) with absolute position error of about 70 pixels. The results were much better then in previous tests [2] where the most advantageous distance errors have reached 163 pixels. Obtained precision of about 40 pixels horizontally and 50 pixels vertically corresponds to metric precision of about 1 cm horizontally and 1.25 cm vertically.

Second group of tests goal was to verify functional aspects of the eye-tracking method, while dynamic gaze pointing. Users were asked to guide, gaze controlled cursor, along provided path (fig. 4), from the darkest segment to the lightest one. The cursor was controlled by web camera supported with authors gaze tracking method. The segment was accepted as visited if the cursor spent inside at least 0.5 second. During experiments, the followed path had two, so far the most challenging [2] thicknesses: 50 and 100 pixels.

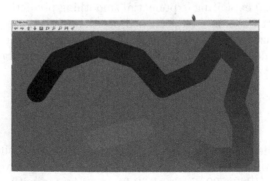

Fig. 4. Trajectory followed by cursor controlled with gaze tracking method

Total time of cursor passage was measured and percentage of time spent inside the path in comparison with total time was collected. For each test 10 measurements were made. Achieved averaged results were collected in a table 2. Speed of whole system during test was about 20 frames per second.

Table 2. The average results of path controlling test

	50 pixels width			100 pixels width		
ESP coefficient α	0.5	0.1	0.05	0.5	0.1	0.05
Camera total time [s]	36	42.88	44.56	28.45	29.25	36.63
Camera time inside the path [%]	52.4	55.15	53	76.82	77.25	81.13

Results presented in table 2 revealed that applied improvements mainly increased cursor controllability to 55% (previously 40%) for 50 pixels path. Very successful rate of about 80% for eye-gaze cursor control over wider path (100 px) also seems to be promising. Moreover tested functionality was assured without perceptible cursor reaction lag and provided noticeable movement fluency.

5   Conclusions

Provided paper has described simple and very effective eye-gaze tracking method. The analysis of the results has shown that method metric resolution was about 1.0 cm horizontally and 1.25 cm vertically what corresponds to angular resolution of about 1 degree, considering user-screen distance (75 cm).

The gaze tracking system performance was about 20 fps what suited for most of interactive application requirements. System performance has decreased to about 18 fps on user rapid head movements due to time demanding process of searching for face and eyes. In this context using some techniques of optical flow analysis, or two correlated cameras, one capturing the face and second searching for eyes within the face, instead of current solution, may beacome a further, frame rate increasing, improvement.

Method was tested not only statically, on its absolute precision, but also on its dynamic functionality. Achieved results let exploit the elaborated solution as a fully professional input device for human computer interaction selective tasks.

References

1. Duchowski, A.: Eye Tracking Methodology: Theory and Practice. Springer (2007)
2. Wojciechowski, A.: Wspomaganie interakcji czlowiek-komputer w środowiskach wirtualnych. Exit (2013)
3. Jacob, R.J.: What You Look Is What You Get: Eye Movement-Based Interaction Techniques. In: HF in CS: Conf. Proc. ACM CHI, pp. 11–18 (2000)
4. Starker, I., Bolt, R.A.: A Gaze-Responsive Self-Disclosing Display. Human Factors in Comp. Syst. In: ACM CHI Conf. Proc., pp. 3–9 (1990)
5. Tanriverdi, V., Jacob, R.J.K.: Interacting with eye movements in Virtual Environments. In: Human Factors in CS, ACM CHI Conf. Proc., pp. 265–272 (2000)
6. Kotze, P., et al.: Accessible computer interaction for people with disabilities: The case of quadriplegics. In: 6th Int. Conf. on Ent. Inf. Sys. (2004)

7. Majaranta, P., Raiha, K.: Twenty years of eye typing: Systems and Design Issues. In: Proc. of ETRA, pp. 15–22 (2002)
8. Hornof, A.J., Cavender, A.: EyeDraw: Enabling Children with Severe Motor Impairments to draw with their eyes. In: ACM Proc. of SIGCHI Conf. on HF in CS, pp. 161–170 (2005)
9. Santella, A., et al.: Gaze-Based Interaction for Semi-Automatic Photo Cropping. In: Proc. of the ACM SIGCHI Conf. on Human Factors in Comp. Syst., pp. 781–790 (2006)
10. Królak, A., Strumillo, P.: Eye-blink detection system for human-computer interaction. Univers. Access Inf. Soc. 10, 1–11 (2011)
11. Wiak, S., Napieralski, P.: Visualization method of magnetic fields with dynamic particle systems. El. Rev. 88(7B), 56–59 (2012)
12. Glonek, G., Pietruszka, M.: Natural User Interfaces (NUI): Review. JACS 20(2), 27–46 (2012)
13. Lin, C.S., et al.: Design of a computer game using an eye-tracking device for eye's activity rehabilitation. Optics and Lasers in Engineering 42(1), 91–108 (2004)
14. Schneider, N., et al.: An open-source low-cost eye-tracking system for portable real-time and offline tracking. In: Proc. of the Conf. on Novel Gaze-Contr. App., pp. 1–4 (2011)
15. Ishiguro, Y., et al.: Aided eyes: eye activity sensing for daily life. In: Proc. of the 1st Augmented Human Int. Conf., ACM, vol. 25 (2010)
16. McMurrough, C.D., et al.: An eye tracking dataset for point of gaze detection. In: Proc. of ETRA, pp. 305–308 (2012)
17. Hansen, D.W., Ji, Q.: In the eye of the beholder: A survey of models for eyes and gaze. IEEE Trans. on Pattern Anal. and Mach. Int. 32(3), 478–500 (2010)
18. Sibert, L.E., Jacob, R.J.: Evaluation of eye gaze interaction. In: Proc. of the ACM SIGCHI Conf. on HF in CS, pp. 281–288 (2000)
19. Kim, K.N., Ramakrishna, R.S.: Vision-Based Eye-Gaze Tracking for Human Computer Interface. In: Proc. of IEEE Int. Conf. on Sys. Man and Cyber., pp. 324–329 (1999)
20. Betke, M., Gips, J., Fleming, P.: The camera mouse: visual tracking of body features to provide computer access for people with severe disabilities. IEEE Neural Syst. and Rehab. Eng. 10(1), 1–10 (2002)
21. Liu, T., Pang, C.: Eye-gaze Tracking Research Based on Image Processing. In: IEEE Congr. on Im. and Sign. Proc., pp. 176–180 (2008)
22. Kao, C.W., et al.: Eye Gaze Tracking Based on Pattern Voting Scheme for Mobile Device. In: Proc. of the IEEE Int. Conf. on IMCCC, pp. 337–340 (2011)
23. Magee, J.J., et al.: Eyekeys: A real-time vision interface based on gaze detection from a low-grade video camera. In: IEEE CVPR, pp. 159–159 (2004)
24. Yamazoe, H., et al.: Remote Gaze Estimation with a Single Camera Based on Facial-Feature Tracking without Special Calibration Actions. In: Proc. of ETRA, pp. 140–145 (2008)
25. Ishikawa, T., et al.: Passive Driver Gaze Tracking with Active Appearance Models. In: Proc. 11th World Cong. Int. Transp. Syst. (2004)
26. Lienhart, R., Maydt, J.: An Extended Set of Haar-like Features for Rapid Object Detection. In: IEEE ICIP 2002, vol. 1, pp. 900–903 (2002)
27. Viola, P.A., Jones, M.J.: Rapid object detection using a boosted cascade of simple features. In: IEEE CS Conf. on CVPR, vol. 518, pp. 511–518 (2001)
28. LaViola Jr., J.J.: An Experiment Comparing Double Exponential Smoothing and Kalman Filter-Based Predictive Tracking Algorithms. VR 3, 283–284 (2003)

Quantitative and Qualitative Evaluation of Selected Lung MR Image Registration Techniques

Artur Wujcicki and Andrzej Materka

Institute of Electronics, Łódź University of Technology
Wólczańska 211/215, 90-924 Łódź, Poland
arturwujcicki@gmail.com

Abstract. In medical applications, non-rigid image registration is often a first step for further actions, including more sophisticated image processing and pre-operative planning. In this study, we compared the performance of two non-rigid image registration algorithms. The first one, implemented in ANTs open source project, and second, a variational registration algorithm were used for registering MR lung images, that were processed afterwards to create functional lung images. To conduct a quantitative assessment of registered lung images, we used well known metrics (including Dice and Jaccard coefficients). The results were compared for thirteen MR lung image sequences recorded for five volunteers. Using this assessment, and visual evaluation of functional lung images that were derived from the registered ones, we found that variational image registration outperforms the ANTs registration algorithm, selected recently as highest ranking algorithm for human brain MRI registration. We found also, that variational registration algorithm is sensitive to regularization parameters, which means that variational registration algorithm may outperform ANTs algorithm only when optimal regularization parameters are chosen.

Keywords: image registration, ANTs, Fourier Decomposition MRI.

1 Introduction

Image registration is the process of finding a transform that maps homologous points from one image into another image [1]. In medical applications, image registration is a step that is performed before major image processing [2,3], as well as for pre-operative planning or treatment verification [4,5]. In case of the lungs, image registration is done to align their shape which is subject to deformation due to breathing.

Recently, a non-invasive method - Fourier Decomposition MRI (FD MRI), was developed for determining lung perfusion and ventilation [3,6]. FD MRI method processes a time sequence of registered MR lung images. Registration is needed to align the shape of the lung within the sequence. Due to breathing and

L.J. Chmielewski et al. (Eds.): ICCVG 2014, LNCS 8671, pp. 653–660, 2014.

pulsatile blood flow, image intensity inside the registered lung areas varies from image to image in the MR images sequence, which is the mechanism the FD MRI method relies on. Information about blood flow is mapped into the perfusion image, and information about gas exchange is mapped into the ventilation image. Separation of perfusion and ventilation information is done by filtering signals constructed as time series of pixel intensities taken from the sequence (for each (x, y) location inside the considered lung 2D cross-section, one signal is constructed). The pixel intensities that construct the signal should correspond to the same lung tissue along the sequence. If not, artifacts occur in ventilation and perfusion images caused by registration errors. Registration error artifacts are visible in perfusion images as artificial venous shadows. In the case of ventilation images, lung image texture may be corrupted. Hence, the registration algorithm used for FD MRI method is essential to obtain satisfactory results.

In the FD MRI method, a variational image registration algorithm [7] was used to compensate for lung motion [3]. On the other hand, there exists ANTs (Advanced Normalization Tools) - an open source project, dedicated for medical images registration and segmentation [8]. ANTs provides SyN (Symmetric Normalization transformation) registration algorithm, proven as one of the highest ranking algorithm for human brain MRI registration [9].

In this work, we compared the performance of ANTs' SyN, and variational registration algorithms. After images registration, we used them as an input for FD MRI method. Evaluation was performed using quantitative measures proposed in [9]. Those measures were calculated using labeled images, prepared with Atropos image segmentation tool, which is one of the ANTs modules. As the FD MRI method is sensitive to registration errors, visual assessment was also performed to provide guidance on the choice of the registration algorithm for FD MRI.

2 Materials and Methods

Image Acquisition

Written informed consent was obtained from five healthy volunteers (23-28 years) in this study, which was approved by the institutional review board of the Medical Faculty Mannheim at Heidelberg University. The lung images were obtained on a 1.5T MR system (Magnetom Avanto, Siemens Healthcare, Erlangen, Germany) using a balanced steady-state free-precession sequence with the following parameters: TE/TR = 0.9/1.8 ms, voxel sizes (3.5 mm x 3.5 mm x 10 mm) and (3.5 mm x 3.5 mm x 15 mm), flip angle = 75 degrees, bandwidth = 1302 Hz/px, and parallel imaging reduction factor = 3.

Lung images were formed into 13 separable sequences. Seven sequences consist of 256x256 sized images, while remaining consist of 128x128 images. The sequences consist of 192 or 90 lung images, respectively, acquired at sample rate of 3,33Hz.

Reference Image Selection

Comparison of the registration algorithms requires the reference image (the one for which other images from the sequence will be registered) to be the same for both examined algorithms for a given image sequence. An image, in which lung diaphragm was located approximately in the middle position between the full inhalation and full exhalation phases, was selected as the reference image. Such approach was expected to provide high registration quality due to small residual lung image deformations in the registration process.

Selection of the lung image with diaphragm in the middle position is based on calculating mean difference between the lung image that is expected to be the reference image, and all other lung images from the sequence. When diaphragm is in the middle position in the reference image, the images difference is positive for images showing full inhalation phase, and negative for images showing full exhalation phase, respectively. Thus the mean difference between the lung image with diaphragm in the middle position and all other images is close to zero.

Lung Image Registration with ANTs

Registration was performed between the reference image, and other images from the time-sequence. It was found that SyN diffeomorphic registration scheme with cross correlation as a similarity measure gives best results that can be achieved using ANTs. Cross correlation measure was selected to use window with radius of two. Scale-space approach (with three scales) was used to improve image registration. According to ANTs documentation, Gaussian smoothing of the velocity field with variance of three was used for default regularization.

Lung Image Registration with Variational Registration Framework

The second considered image registration algorithm is an implementation of a method introduced in [7]. This algorithm uses calculus of variations to align two images together, which is done by minimization of statistical dissimilarity measure. In the case of MR lung images, that are obviously in the same modality across the entire sequence, local cross correlation similarity measure was used. This approach was applied initially in [3]. The algorithm iteratively computes a deformation field $\mathbf{h}(\mathbf{x})$ between reference image I_1 and target image I_2, given by partial differential equation (1) [7].

$$\frac{\partial \mathbf{h}}{\partial t}(t, \mathbf{x}) = -L_{CC}^l(I_1(\mathbf{x}), I_2(\mathbf{x} + \mathbf{h}(\mathbf{x})))\nabla I_2(\mathbf{x} + \mathbf{h}(\mathbf{x})) + \alpha\Delta\mathbf{h}(\mathbf{x})$$
$$\mathbf{h}(0, \mathbf{x}) = \mathbf{0} \tag{1}$$

In (1), L_{CC}^l is cross correlation based local similarity measure between I_1 and I_2 [7], and α is the coefficient that controls regularization, initialized with a value of 0.1.

The algorithm uses scale-space approach to improve registration results. In the case of lung images, four scales were used. Cross correlation was computed using a square 9x9 window for the coarsest scale, and 7x7 window for the finest scale. After each iteration, deformation field was smoothed using Gaussian filter with mask size of 7x7 for the coarsest scale, and 3x3 for the finest scale.

Regularization parameter α, cross correlation window size and Gaussian filter mask size were selected experimentally to achieve minimum mean absolute error (MAE) calculated between the reference image and the registered image, for all images in the sequence. In addition, visual evaluation of perfusion and ventilation images was performed to make sure the regularization parameters have correct values.

As in the ANTs case, the registration was performed between the reference image and other images from the sequence.

Lung Image Segmentation and Labeling

The metrics [9] need labeled images, which was obtained using images segmentation. Atropos tool from ANTs package was used to create segmented lung images. Image segmentation was performed to produce segmented images with 8 labels.

FD MRI method creates lung ventilation and perfusion images. It is expected to create proper images in image area containing at least lungs. Other parts of the image are not really important. The segmentation was performed only in a rectangular region containing lungs. This rectangular region defines a mask used to a segmentation. One mask was used for each images sequence. The masks for all the processed image sequences were created manually and then converted to a format accepted by Atropos using XMedCon tool (open source toolkit for medical image conversion).

Due to changes of image intensity within a registered lung images sequence (caused by breathing and blood flow), which is a feature of the FD MRI method, the shape of a region identified by a label in segmented image may differ slightly within a sequence of segmented lung images. To reduce this effect, and make the shapes of regions in segmented images more coherent, a prior information was used to perform image segmentation [10]. This information was created with Atropos tool from the reference image, and was applied to other images in the sequence. However, to drive segmentation with information mainly from lung image, not from a prior, a weight that balances contribution to prior information was set to 0.05. It means, according to Atropos documentation, that segmentation is performed using information from input image with a weight of 0.95. Weight of prior information greater than 0.05 caused the segmentation results were too much correlated with the image used to creating the prior information.

An example of labeled lung image is shown in Fig. 1. Atropos tool creates labeled images according to input image intensity, i.e. the darkest part of image is attributed with label 1, and brighter image areas are labeled in ascending order. As lungs are visible as dark objects in MRI, the lung parenchyma has a label with number 1. This label covers most area in segmented lung image. The veins which are visible as bright objects in MR images, after segmentation have labels numbered with relatively big value.

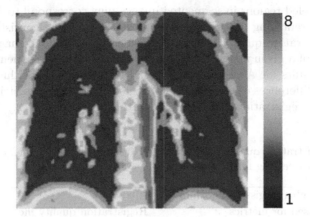

Fig. 1. Example of MR lung image segmented with Atropos tool, visualized with color map. Segmented image was created with 8 labels, numbered from 1 to 8, respectively.

Registration Quality Metrics

In this project we used registration quality metrics proposed in [9]. These metrics operate on labeled images, and are computed between 2 images, for regions assigned with the same label value. We used a Target Overlap, Dice (DC) and Jaccard (JC) coefficients, False Negative (FN) and False Positive (FP) errors and Volume Similarity (VS) metrics. Due to different notation[1] used in [9], we called the Target Overlap as Reference Overlap (RO). As opposed to definition of VS metric proposed in [9], we computed absolute value of that metric.

For perfect registration, the reference overlap, Dice and Jaccard coefficients should have a value of 1, and false negative error, false positive error, volume similarity should have a value of 0.

3   Results

Registration quality metrics were computed as a mean value for labels stored in segmented images, from a given lung image sequence. Mean value of a metric was computed for components that were determined between reference lung image from a sequence, and all other images from that sequence. Furthermore, we computed metrics for a label with value of 1, which cover regions of lung parenchyma without lung veins, since those labels cover the lung shape and are well defined across all lung sequences.

Labels with value greater than one describe well image characteristics within a lung image sequence. On the other hand, brightness of veins relative to brightness of lung parenchyma may differ in different lung image sequences. This may

---

[1] We denoted the target image as the image that is warped to be aligned with the reference image. In [9], the reference image is called a target image, and the target image is called a source image.

cause that labeled regions in segmented images may correspond to different lung tissues in different lung image sequences. Hence, to allow a consistent interpretation of registration quality metrics between registered lung image sequences, a mean value of a given metric for all labels, for given image sequence, was computed. The results for ANTs and variational registration algorithms are shown in Table 1[2]. Differences of mean values of registration quality metrics computed for variational registration and ANTs SyN are shown in Table 2.

Table 1. Registration quality metrics for ANTs and variational registration (VR) algorithm, for three lung image sequences

Seq. number, registr. algorithm, labels used for metrics	Registration quality metrics					
	RO	DC	JC	FN	FP	VS
#1, ANTs, all labels	0.892	0.880	0.790	0.108	0.131	0.046
#1, VR, all labels	0.905	0.893	0.811	0.095	0.116	0.042
#1, ANTs, label 1	0.935	0.959	0.922	0.065	0.015	0.052
#1, VR, label 1	0.943	0.965	0.932	0.057	0.012	0.047
#2, ANTs, all labels	0.869	0.851	0.744	0.131	0.163	0.051
#2, VR, all labels	0.931	0.917	0.847	0.069	0.095	0.040
#2, ANTs, label 1	0.918	0.933	0.874	0.082	0.052	0.033
#2, VR, label 1	0.951	0.960	0.924	0.049	0.030	0.021
#3, ANTs, all labels	0.893	0.877	0.786	0.107	0.135	0.060
#3, VR, all labels	0.907	0.893	0.810	0.093	0.119	0.055
#3, ANTs, label 1	0.935	0.965	0.932	0.065	0.004	0.063
#3, VR, label 1	0.943	0.969	0.941	0.057	0.002	0.056

Table 2. Difference of mean values of quality metrics for variational registration (VR) and ANTs SyN, computed for thirteen lung image sequences

Labels used for metrics	Difference of mean values of quality metrics [%]					
	$\Delta(RO)$	$\Delta(DC)$	$\Delta(JC)$	$\Delta(FN)$	$\Delta(FP)$	$\Delta(VS)$
(VR-ANTs), all labels	2.30	2.42	3.58	-2.30	-2.47	-0.77
(VR-ANTs), label 1	1.47	1.12	2.04	-1.48	-0.78	-0.74

Registered lung image sequences were used as input for FD MRI algorithm to create lung ventilation and perfusion images. Example of ventilation and perfusion images, obtained using ANTs and variational algorithm, are shown in Fig. 2 and Fig. 3.

---

[2] Table 1 shows results for three lung sequences. Results for remaining ten sequences are similar.

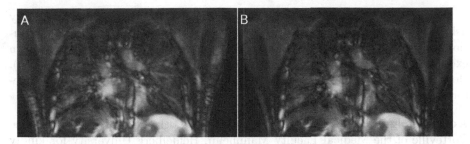

Fig. 2. Example of ventilation lung images, created using lung image sequence registered with ANTs (A), and variational registration algorithm (B)

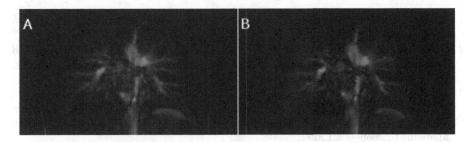

Fig. 3. Example of perfusion lung images, created using lung image sequence registered with ANTs (A), and variational registration algorithm (B)

4   Discussion and Conclusion

For all lung sequences considered, variational registration algorithm with local cross correlation similarity outperforms ANTs SyN algorithm. However, variational registration algorithms seems to be more sensitive to regularization parameters like Gaussian filter size for smoothing the deformation field, as well as cross correlation window size. Hence, ANTs SyN parameters are less dependent on input data to be registered.

The registered lung sequences were used as input for FD MRI algorithm to create lung ventilation and perfusion images. Ventilation images created with ANTs' registered data tend to be more noisy, as well as texture of the lungs is more grained, compared to results obtained with variational registration algorithm. This is clearly visible in Fig. 2A in lungs region, as well as on edges of the subject's body (at the height of the diaphragm). Perfusion images created using sequence of images registered with ANTs and variational algorithm are similar. Visibility of details of lung veins in perfusion images is also similar, Fig. 3.

Table 2 shows difference of mean values of registration quality metrics. Because all registration quality metrics used in this paper are in range [0;1], the magnitude of the difference between them is equivalent to improvement of registration quality of variational algorithm over the ANTs SyN algorithm.

To sum up, FD MRI method provides better lung ventilation images quality using input data registered with variational registration algorithm, while perfusion images quality is similar. The registration quality of variational algorithm exceeds 2-3% the ANTs SyN algorithm (depending on used quality metric). However, for the variational registration algorithm the regularization parameters have to be optimized to achieve good results.

Acknowledgments. The Authors thank Prof. Lothar Schad and Dominique Corteville of the Medical Faculty Mannheim, Heidelberg University for kindly providing lung image sequences.

References

1. Zitová, B., Flusser, J.: Image registration methods: a survey. Image and Vision Computing 21, 977–1000 (2003)
2. Rueckert, D., Sonoda, L., Hayes, C., Hill, D., Leach, M., Hawkes, D.: Nonrigid Registration Using Free-Form Deformations: Application to Breast MR Images. IEEE Transactions on Medical Imaging 18, 712–721 (1999)
3. Bauman, G., Puderbach, M., Deimling, M., Jellus, V., Chefd'hotel, C., Dinkel, J., et al.: Non-Contrast-Enhanced Perfusion and Ventilation Assessment of the Human Lung by Means of Fourier Decomposition in Proton MRI. Magnetic Resonance in Medicine 62, 656–664 (2009)
4. Risholm, P., Golby, A., Wells, W.: Multi-Modal Image Registration for Pre-Operative planning and Image Guided Neurosurgical Procedures, Neurosurg. Clin. N Am. 22(2), 197–206 (2011)
5. Maintz, J., Viergever, M.: A survey of medical image registration. Medical Image Analysis 2, 1–36 (1998)
6. Lederlin, M., Bauman, G., Eichinger, M., Dinkel, J., Brault, M., Biederer, J., et al.: Functional MRI using Fourier decomposition of lung signal: Reproducibility of ventilation- and perfusion-weighted imaging in healthy volunteers. European Journal of Radiology 82, 1015–1022 (2013)
7. Hermosillo, G., Chefdhotel, C., Faugeras, O.: Variational Methods for Multimodal Image Matching. International Journal of Computer Vision 50, 329–343 (2002)
8. Avants, B., Tustison, N., Song, G., Cook, P., Klein, A., Gee, J.: A Reproducible Evaluation of ANTs Similarity Metric Performance in Brain Image Registration. Neuroimage 54, 2033–2044 (2011)
9. Klein, A., Andersson, J., Ardekani, B., Ashburner, J., Avants, B.: Evaluation of 14 nonlinear deformation algorithms applied to human brain MRI registration. NeuroImage 46, 786–802 (2009)
10. Avants, B., Tustison, N., Song, G.: Advanced Normalization Tools (ANTS) Release 1.5 (2013),
    ftp://ftp3.ie.freebsd.org/pub/sourceforge/a/project/ad/advants/
    (accessed 19 April 2013)

Image-Based 3D Semantic Modeling
of Building Facade*

Jun Yang[1] and Zhongke Shi[2]

[1] School of Mechanics, Civil Engineering and Architecture
Northwestern Polytechnical University
Xi'an 710072, China
junyang@nwpu.edu.cn
[2] School of Automation, Northwestern Polytechnical University
Xi'an 710072, China
zkeshi@nwpu.edu.cn

Abstract. 3D building modeling has many potential uses in the fields of construction, city planning and public security. An image-based 3D semantic modeling method of building facade is proposed in this paper. Dense point clouds are generated from inputting images by structure from motion and cluster based multi-view-stereo algorithms. Planar components are extracted from generated point clouds by random sample consensus and further recognized as structural components based on prior knowledge. Windows are detected through a multi-layer complementary strategy with binary image processing techniques. Experimental results from two building facades verify the proposed method.

1 Introduction

Various society fields demand three-dimensional (3D) building models. In the Architecture, Engineering and Construction (AEC) industry, semantically rich 3D building models are increasingly used throughout a building's life cycle, from design, through construction, and into facility management phase [1]. These models are generally known as building information models (BIMs). Recently, automatic generation of as-built BIMs is a hot issue being studied extensively, which is used not only for as-built documentation [2], but also for construction progress monitoring [3][4]. In urban planning domain, it is helpful to adopt 3D building models since analyzing in 3D world is much more efficient than on 2D maps. For public security, accurate 3D building models are indispensable to make strategies during emergency situations. Other fields, such as automobile navigation and virtual tourism also benefit from realistic 3D building models [5].

Automatic 3D building modeling are based on remote sensing technologies, such as laser scanning [1][5][8][9], photogrammetry [3][14] or the combination

---

* This work was supported by National Natural Science Foundation of China (No.51208425) and Research Foundation of Northwestern Polytechnical University (No.JCY20130127).

L.J. Chmielewski et al. (Eds.): ICCVG 2014, LNCS 8671, pp. 661–671, 2014.

of these two [6][7]. Laser scanners have been widely applied for its precise generation of dense 3D point clouds. Tang et al [8] outlined a scheme from laser scanning generated point clouds to as-built BIM, composed of three core operations: geometric modeling, object recognition and object relationship modeling. Xiong et al [1] focused on the creation of semantically rich 3D models of building interior. The proposed algorithm extracted planar patches from input point cloud, learned to label patches as walls, ceilings or floors and performed an analysis on surface openings, such as windows and doorways. Special reasoning were used to deal with occlusions and holes. Pu and Vosselman [5] presented a knowledge based approach for reconstruction of building facade models using terrestrial laser scanning data. Segmented plane surfaces were classified into various semantic features based on generic knowledge and a polyhedron facade model containing both detailed geometry and sematic meaning were generated. Martinez et al [9] proposed a novel facade contour detection method by converting point cloud data into a profile distribution function and looking for distribution peaks and valleys.

With its prevalence, laser scanner has limitations in reality due to expensive and fragile equipments, lack of portability, need of skilled operators [12] and a long preparation time for setting up. In addition, laser scanners only provide Cartesian coordinate information of the scanned scene. These featureless data without semantic information is especially challenging for high level 3D modeling [3]. On the contrary, photogrammetry offers a lower cost, lower skill, portable solution with abundant features such as color and texture. Different to laser scanning, a computation flow involving camera calibration based on multiple view geometry and cross view feature points matching are required to obtain 3D point clouds in photogrammetry. Compared to the millimeter accuracy of laser scanner, photogrammetry can only achieve centimeter level [2]. References [12][13] evaluated the accuracy of image-based 3D modeling and verified the serviceability of photogrammetry in 3D modeling.

Unlike the extensive studies of 3D modeling by laser scanning, there are not so many progresses on photogrammetry side. Golparvar-Fard et al [3] solved the photographer's locations, orientations and a sparse 3D geometric representation of the as-built site using daily progress photographs and superimposed the reconstructed scene over as-planned 4D models for progress estimation. Even generating a sparse 3D point cloud, the study was not about 3D modeling but geo-registration of daily photographs. Son and Kim [4] proposed an efficient, automated 3D structural component recognition and modeling method using color and 3D data acquired from a stereo vision system. However the structural component under consideration is just a simple steel structure specifically designed for experiments. Kim et al [14] designed a framework consisting of 3D photogrammetric data acquisition, refinement and concrete detection for progress measurement of buildings under construction. The study accomplished dense reconstruction of 3D point cloud using a commercial system. However 3D building modeling was not involved.

How photogrammetry performs in realistic 3D building model is still unknown. In this paper, we mean to demonstrate that a monocular handheld camera is capable of densely reconstructing and modeling building facade. Instead of only generating sparse point cloud, we propose to move to a dense reconstruction level, which can supply more features for further analysis. As for the 3D semantic modeling, we present a knowledge based semantic reasoning strategy, together with a novel window detection method.

The remaining of the paper is organized as follows: Section 2 explains the dense reconstruction workflow. Section 3 elaborates on the 3D semantic modeling procedure. Starting from plane segmentation, semantic structural components are recognized based on prior-knowledge, followed by a novel window detection procedure. Experimental results and conclusions are given in section 4 and 5 accordingly.

2   Dense 3D Point Clouds Generation

Most previous studies on image-based building reconstruction only generated sparse 3D point cloud, which is far more than enough for higher level semantic modeling. The paper proposes to move beyond sparse point cloud to dense reconstruction. The inputs are the images of building facade captured by un-calibrated handheld cameras from multiple points of view. And the outputs are dense reconstructed 3D point clouds.

The first step of reconstruction is feature points detection and matching. Robust feature detector which can result in reasonable dense feature points and are not sensitive to point-of-view, illumination change, scale change, etc, need to be used. The most frequently used detector is scale-invariant feature transform (SIFT)[15] for its invariance to scale and rotation and robustness to small affine or projective deformations and illumination changes. Once detected, feature points are matched by measuring the distance between their SIFT descriptors, which describe the intensity gradient over an image window centered at a feature point. Since false matches always exist and will have negative influence on the following reconstruction, a RANSAC (RANdom SAmple Consensus) procedure is evoked to remove false matches.

Starting from the initial successful feature matching between two images, the camera extrinsic and intrinsic parameters for each image and the 3D coordinates of each feature point are solved incrementally by repeatedly adding matched images,triangulating feature matches and bundle-adjusting the structure and motion.

The preceding Structure From Motion (SFM) procedure outputs a sparse 3D point cloud by computing the 3D position associated to each match. A Cluster based Multi-View-Stereo (CMVS) algorithm [22] is followed for dense point cloud generation. It decomposes the set of input images into clusters that have small overlap. Once clustered, a multi-view-stereo algorithm is applied to reconstruct dense 3D points. The resulting reconstructions are merged into a single dense point-based model.

3   3D Semantic Modeling

The geometry of a reconstruction 3D model can be described with boundary representation (B-Rep), constructive solid geometry (CSG) and spatial enumeration. Spatial enumeration decomposes the 3D space into a set of identical cells. CSG represents the target as a combination of certain fixed primitives using Boolean operators. B-Rep describe the 3D world by connected surface elements. Considering the nature of building facades, B-Rep is the most suitable method. B-Rep models are usually composed of two parts: topology and geometry (surfaces, curves and points). We model the building facade as several connected surfaces under certain topology. Three semantic components: wall, window and protrusion are considered in our model. The 3D reconstruction from images is first segmented into several planes. Then these planes are further recognized as semantic components based on prior knowledge.

3.1   Segmentation

Common buildings are usually polyhedrons consisted of multiple planes. Though other shape primitives, such as spheres or cylinders, may also exist in modern buildings, they are out of the paper's scope currently. The first step of 3D modeling is to segment planes from 3D reconstruction result. Three widely used segmentation methods are RANdom SAmple Consensus (RANSAC), Hough Transform and region growing. Hough transform is a voting scheme that extracts a parameterized shape primitive from a discretized parameter space. A primitive with a large number of parameters results in a high-dimensional discretized parameter domain, which causes memory issues. So the main application area of Hough transform remains in 2D. Region growing in 3D space usually takes normals at different points as features and starts growing at an initial seed region. So the selection of seed region has a strong impact on the segmentation result, especially for noisy data [11]. RANSAC is a robust estimator of parametric model even for data containing a high degree of noise and outliers, which serves our purpose best.

The principle of RANSAC is to search the best plane fitting the 3D data. It selects randomly three points and calculates the parameters of the corresponding plane. Then it detects all points in the original data belonging to the calculated plane, according to a given threshold. Afterwards, it repeats these procedures N times. In each iteration, it compares the obtained result with the last saved one. If the new result is better, then it replaces the saved result by the new one [19].

The basic RANSAC algorithm assumes that only one model can be fit to the data. In order to detect all the planar components in the 3D reconstruction result, an iterative strategy is applied. First, RANSAC is applied on the data returning the plane with the most inliers (referred as dominant plane). Then all inliers for this plane are removed the data. RANSAC is performed on the residue to find the next largest plane. The process terminates when no plane with a sufficient number of points can be found.

3.2   Semantic Components Recognition

Segmentation finds out planar components of building facades. The semantic roles of these components are to be recognized based on prior knowledge. A common building facade is usually composed of walls, windows and protrusions. Wall is the largest plane perpendicular to the ground. (Notice that ground plane is assumed as a user defined information in our proposed scheme. Naturally, we set up the coordinates system following the right hand rule, with plane XY being the ground plane and the dominant plane in point clouds parallel to plane YZ.) Windows are usually small rectangle planes embedded in the wall surface. Other structures, such as balconies or friezes, are a little outside the wall, are all sorted as protrusions.

It can be seen from the above description that the semantic components of the building facade can be recognized based on their geometric features. These features are listed as below:

Area: The area of a plane is a dominant feature in the semantic reasoning. Wall plane usually has the biggest area. A threshold can be set up to filter out too tiny planes for noise depression.

Position: The location of the plane, its orientation and its connection relationship with other components are also important for recognition. We use the centroid of the plane's convex hull for its location, the plane normal for its orientation and the intersection line of two planes as judgement of connection relationship.

Shape: As aforementioned, windows are usually in the shape of rectangle.

Due to light reflection, point cloud in the glass window area is usually much sparser compared to other parts. So the point cloud density is also a significant feature for semantic reasoning, especially for window detection, which will be illustrated later.

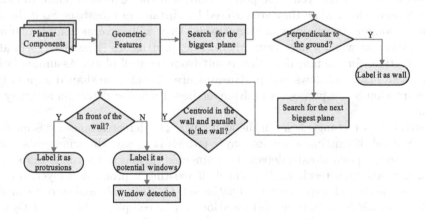

Fig. 1. Flowchart of semantic component recognition

In general, the semantic component recognition procedure is concluded in Fig. 1 . We follow a coarse to fine, bottom to up searching strategy, starting from the dominant wall plane and finally going to the windows and protrusions.

3.3   Window Detection

As a distinguishable component in building facade, window detection has been discussed several times in the literature. Most studies, no matter laser scanning-based or image-based, have used the low point cloud density in window area as a dominant feature. The rectangle shape, with two horizontal edges and two vertical edges, is often regarded as another accompanying feature for window detection.

Xiong et al [1] regarded windows as rectangular-shaped openings in laser scanned point cloud and used a support vector machine (SVM) classifier to detect partially occluded windows. Pu and Vosselman [5] extracted boundary points around holes in point cloud, grouped them and fitted a minimum bounding rectangle as detected window. Martinez et al [9] used the 3D point cloud density to distinguish points into multiple layers which corresponded to wall, windows, etc. Radopoulou et al [20] tested a depth-encoded Hough voting for window detection. Bohm et al [7] detected windows based on edge in laser scanning point cloud and integrated images for detail recovery, such as window crossbars. Bauer et al [21] applied a sweep based method to scan the density change in point cloud line by line and searched for windows. Machine learning based methods [1][20] require a labor-intensive training stage. Boundary or edge based methods [5][7] are sensitive to noise. Sweep based method [21] is inefficient.

Based on the previous semantic reasoning procedure, we have the following basic observations. Windows (intrusions) and protrusions both result in holes in the point clouds of the wall plane. On the other hand, though the glass itself does not appear as feature rich area in images due to reflection and hence corresponds to very sparse even none point cloud, windows may still relate to dense enough point cloud when they are covered by curtains or crossbars. So if the 3D points belonging to windows are detectable, they will serve as complementary information for window detection. Meanwhile, protrusions (if existing) will also be corrections for the hole detection result from the wall plane. Assuming holes in the wall plane, windows and protrusions are all rectangle shaped area in the 3D point clouds, we propose a multi-layer based window detection strategy as follows.

First, detect rectangle holes in the wall layer. The detected holes set is marked as Φ. Second, if existing a window layer (which is to say, the windows are detectable in the point cloud), detect the connected regions in rectangle shape and mark the detection result as Ω_1. Third, if existing a protrusion layer, do the same as the second step and ends up the set Ω_2. Both Ω_1 and Φ confirm the existence of windows and their information can be complementary. And Ω_2 will be the correction since it indicates not all the holes in wall layer are introduced by windows. So the final window detection result is:

$$Windows = \Phi \cup \Omega_1 - \Omega_2$$

For both hole detection in the wall layer or connected region detection in other layers, we propose an uniform method taking advantages of binary image processing. First, the point clouds are converted into a binary image through the following procedures. All the y, z coordinates of the 3D points are amplified by a certain factor, centralized by subtracting mean values of y, z accordingly, shifted by adding minimum values, and finally rounded up. Consequently, the converted y, z coordinates correspond to pixels with value 1 in the binary image. And the rest area is marked by value 0. A binary image is generated by now. Preprocessing steps include morphological open operation for small connected components removal and holes filling up. Then all objects in the binary image are traced with two properties measured. One is the *area*, which is the actual number of pixels in the object region; the other is the *extent*, which is defined by the ratio of pixels in the region to pixels in the total bounding box. If $area >= T_1$ and $extent >= T_2$, then the region is marked as a candidate window. T_1 is given by users according to experiences. A too small area can not be a window. In our experiment, it is around 100 pixels. T_2 is a key threshold to indicate the shape of the region. Technically, when $extent = 1$, the region is an exact rectangle. Considering the imperfection of the realistic situation, we usually set T_2 loosely, e.g. around 0.8. Notice all the above mentioned procedure is targeted at locating connect white regions in binary image. So for operation in the wall layer which has windows as holes (black area), its binary image needs to be inverted beforehand.

4   Experimental Results

Two groups of experiments have been set up for validation of the proposed scheme. Targets to be reconstructed are the teaching building and the office building on campus. The device used to capture images is a Canon IXUS 950 IS digital camera, which is a portable low-end product. The selection of the device is because in reality site inspectors usually prefer portable devices. The proposed system lays no restriction on the quality of images and means to take daily log photos as input. The only requirement is that the camera parameters, such as focal length, image resolution and zoom have to remain fixed during capturing. And at least a 50% overlap between continues images must be assured for stable feature matching. Notice that in the experiment we only focus on the reconstruction of a single building facade. A more complete reconstruction of the entire building will be explored in the future work.

4.1   The Teaching Building

The teaching building has embedded windows without any protrusions. As shown in Fig.2(a), 37 images are captured in resolution 3648 x 2736. The generated dense point clouds are shown in Fig.2(b). The plane segmentation results in two planes, which are further analyzed by their geometry features and recognized as wall layer and window layer. As in Fig.3, the magenta color represents the wall layer and the cyan color represents the window layer. Windows are detected on each layer separately as shown in Fig.3(a),3(b). After the combination procedure, windows are finally unified as in Fig.3(c). We can see that most windows are correctly located. A few windows on the point clouds edge are not stably detected because of the low point density there.

(a) Snapshots of the teaching building.

(b) Dense point clouds of the teaching building.

Fig. 2. The snapshots and point clouds of the teaching building

(a) Windows detected in the wall layer.

(b) Windows detected in the window layer.

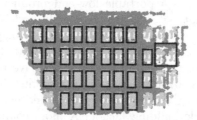

(c) Final windows after combination of results from all layers.

Wall Layer   Window Layer

(d) legend

Fig. 3. The structural components recognition and window detection result

(a) Snapshots of the office building.

(b) Dense point clouds of the office building.

Fig. 4. The snapshots and point clouds of the office building

4.2 The Office Building

The office building is a regular four stories building. It has embedded windows and protrusions serving as air conditioners holders. As shown in Fig.4(a), we took 45 images in resolution 2048 x 1536. The generated dense point clouds are shown in Fig.4(b). Applying plane segmentation on the dense point clouds, results in three planes. These planes are further recognized as wall layer, window layer and protrusion layer. As in Fig.5, the magenta color represents the wall layer,

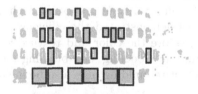

(a) Windows detected in the wall layer.

(b) Windows detected in the window layer.

(c) Windows detected in the protrusion layer.

(d) Final windows after combination of results from all layers.

■ Wall Layer   □ Window Layer   ■ Protrusion Layer

(e) legend

Fig. 5. Structural components recognition and window detection results for the office building

the cyan color represents the window layer and the green color represents the protrusion layer. After segmentation, we detect windows on each layer separately as shown in Fig.5(a),5(b),5(c). It can be seen that the detection result is not very satisfying in a single layer. But after the combination procedure as shown in Fig.5(d), nearly all the windows are correctly located and those protrusion areas are successfully removed.

From the above experimental results, we can see that the proposed scheme works successfully for various scenarios. It can generates a 3D sematic model by segmenting the 3D point clouds and recognizing structural components correctly. The proposed multi-layer based window detection method can stably locate windows and reject the potential ambiguous protrusions. The undetected windows are mainly from low density area of the point cloud.

5   Conclusions

This paper proposed an image-based 3D semantic modeling scheme of building facade. 3D point clouds were generated from handheld camera captured images using SFM and CMVS. For semantic modeling, planar components were extracted from generated point cloud by Random Sample Consensus. Knowledge-based strategy was applied for semantic structural components recognition. The building facade was modelled as the combination of wall, windows and protrusions. Windows are detected through a multi-layer complementary strategy with binary image processing techniques. Experiment on two real building facades demonstrated the efficiency of the proposed scheme. Future work seeks to explore the color and texture features of 3D points clouds for higher level semantic modeling, e.g. building material recognition. A complete modeling of the entire building may also be included.

References

1. Xiong, X., Adan, A., Akinci, B., Huber, D.: Automatic creation of semantically rich 3D building models from laser scanner data. Automation in Construction 31, 325–337 (2013)
2. Klein, L., Li, N., Becerik-Gerber, B.: Imaged-based verification of as-built documentation of operational buildings. Automation in Construction 21, 161–171 (2012)
3. Goldparvar-Fard, M., Peña-Mora, F., Savarese, S.: D4AR-a 4-dimensional augmented reality model for automating construction progress monitoring data collection, processing and communication. Journal of Information Technology in Construction 14, 129–153 (2009)
4. Son, H., Kim, C.: 3D structural component recognition and modeling method using color and 3D data for construction progress monitoring. Automation in Construction 19, 844–854 (2010)
5. Pu, S., Vosselman, G.: Knowledge based reconstruction of building models from terrestrial laser scanning data. ISPRS Journal of Photogrammetry and Remote Sensing 64, 575–584 (2009)

6. Brilakis, I., Lourakis, M., Sacks, R., Savarese, S., Christodoulou, S., Teizer, J., Makhmalbaf, A.: Toward automated generation of parametric BIMs based on hybrid video and laser scanning data. Advanced Engineering Informatics 24, 456–465 (2010)
7. Bohm, J., Becker, S., Haala, N.: Model refinement by integrated processing of laser scanning and photogrammetry. In: Proceedings of 2nd International Workshop on 3D Virtual Reconstruction and Visualization of Complex Architectures (3D-Arch) (2007)
8. Tang, P., Huber, D., Akinci, B., Lipman, R., Lytle, A.: Automatic reconstruction of as-built building information models from laser-scanned point clouds: A review of related techniques. Automation in construction 19, 829–843 (2010)
9. Martinez, J., Soria-Medina, A., Arias, P., Buffara-Antunes, A.F.: Automatic processing of Terrestrial Laser Scanning data of building facades. Automation in Construction 22, 298–305 (2012)
10. Gonzalvez, P.R., Aguilera, D.G., Lahoz, J.G.: From point cloud to surface: Modeling structures in laser scanner point clouds. In: ISPRS Workshop on Laser Scanning, pp. 338–344 (2007)
11. Schnabel, R., Wessel, R., Wahl, R., Klein, R.: Shape recognition in 3d point-clouds. In: Proc. Conf. in Central Europe on Computer Graphics, Visualization and Computer Vision, vol. 2 (2008)
12. Bhatla, A., Choe, S.Y., Fierro, O., Leite, F.: Evaluation of accuracy of as-built 3D modeling from photos taken by handheld digital cameras. Automation in construction 28, 116–127 (2012)
13. Golparvar-Fard, M., Bohn, J., Teizer, J., Savarese, S., Pena-Mora, F.: Evaluation of image-based modeling and laser scanning accuracy for emerging automated performance monitoring techniques. Automation in Construction 20, 1143–1155 (2011)
14. Kim, C., Son, H., Kim, C.: The effective acquisition and processing of 3D photogrammetric data from digital photogrammetry for construction progress measurement. In: ASCE International Workshop on Computing in Civil Engineering, pp. 178–185 (2011)
15. Lowe, D.G.: Distinctive image features from scale-invariant keypoints. International Journal of Computer Vision 60, 91–110 (2004)
16. Wu, C.: Towards Linear-time Incremental Structure from Motion
17. Labatut, P., Pons, J.-P., Keriven, R.: Efficient multi-view reconstruction of large-scale scenes using interest points, delaunay triangulation and graph cuts. In: IEEE 11th International Conference on Computer Vision, pp. 1–8 (2007)
18. Jancosek, M., Pajdla, T.: Multi-view reconstruction preserving weakly-supported surfaces. In: IEEE Conference on Computer Vision and Pattern Recognition, pp. 3121–3128 (2011)
19. Yang, M.Y., Förstner, W.: Plane detection in point cloud data. In: Proceedings of the 2nd Int. Conf. on machine control guidance, vol. 1, pp. 95–104 (2010)
20. Radopoulou, S.C., Sun, M., Dai, F., Brilakis, I., Savarese, S.: Testing of Depth-Encoded Hough Voting for Infrastructure Object Detection. In: ASCE International Workshop on Computing in Civil Engineering, pp. 309–316 (2012)
21. Bauer, J., Karner, K., Schindler, K., Klaus, A., Zach, C.: Segmentation of building models from dense 3D point-clouds. In: Proc. 27th Workshop of the Austrian Association for Pattern Recognition, pp. 253–258 (2003)
22. Furukawa, Y., Curless, B., Seitz, S.M., Szeliski, R.: Towards internet-scale multiview stereo. In: 2010 IEEE Conference on Computer Vision and Pattern Recognition, pp. 1434–1441 (2010)

3D Pose Refinement Using Rendering and Texture-Based Matching

Xenophon Zabulis[1], Manolis I.A. Lourakis[1], and Stefanos S. Stefanou[2]

[1] Institute of Computer Science, FORTH
Nikolaou Plastira 100, GR - 70013, Heraklion, Greece
[2] Institute of Molecular Biology and Biotechnology, FORTH
Nikolaou Plastira 100, GR - 70013, Heraklion, Greece
{zabulis,lourakis}@ics.forth.gr, stefanou@imbb.forth.gr

Abstract. This paper presents a method for accurately determining the pose of Lambertian rigid objects present in an image. An initial pose estimate computed with the aid of local point features is ameliorated by considering all visible object texture. This is achieved by combining a textured mesh model of the object with a graphics renderer to synthesize an image of the object as would be captured by the camera at a particular pose. A rendered image is compared against the acquired one with the aid of a visual dissimilarity score involving cross-correlation. Population-based stochastic optimization is used to efficiently search the pose space and minimize the dissimilarity between rendered images corresponding to candidate poses and the acquired image. The method is demonstrated with the aid of real and synthetic images.

1 Introduction

Object pose estimation refers to determining the six degrees of freedom defining the position and orientation of a rigid object relative to a camera. Typically, a 3D model is used to provide pose estimation with geometric knowledge about the object of interest. Such model-based approaches are usually preferred due to their increased robustness and fail-safety [10].

This work is concerned with the refinement of an initial pose estimate in order to improve its accuracy. This initial estimate is determined by extracting natural features from an image, matching them to an object model constructed offline and, finally, using the 3D coordinates of matched model points to estimate the 3D pose of the object relative to the camera. Refinement of the initial estimate is based on matching all observed object pixels against synthetic images of a textured triangle mesh model of the object. Derivative-free particle swarm optimization is used to explore the pose space with a population of candidate poses, without resorting to exhaustive search. Each candidate pose is evaluated by generating a synthetic image which predicts the appearance of the model at that pose and then measuring the photoconsistency between the synthetic image and the acquired one. The proposed approach employs a fully projective imaging formulation, improves the accuracy of feature-based pose estimates and

L.J. Chmielewski et al. (Eds.): ICCVG 2014, LNCS 8671, pp. 672–679, 2014.

can serve as the basis for drift-free tracking. Furthermore, it does not require any image preprocessing (e.g. no edges or silhouette need to be extracted) and employs all available texture information.

2   Related Work

Using features to estimate pose originated with [13]. Subsequent developments in covariant detectors and descriptors for image patches enabled the construction of compact object representations. For example, geometric models are combined with feature matching in [22] to track rigid objects in 3D. In [19], the appearance of object surface patches is captured using affine invariant local descriptors and their spatial relationships using multi-view geometric constraints. In [8], a system is described based on SIFT features for recognizing learnt models in new images and solving for their pose. By relying on randomized trees to learn both appearance and geometry during a training phase, [15] circumvents the need to construct a prior 3D model. Similar to our feature-based pose estimation is the work in [18], that describes a system based on natural features.

Often, pose estimation with sparse features suffers from inaccuracies due to the limited number of correspondences. This boils down to the substantial differences in viewpoints among the images used to build the model and those used to estimate its pose. Feature-based pose estimates can be refined with the aim of increasing their accuracy, relying on information provided by pixels inside the object's projection in the form of optical flow, matched templates or edges. Relevant existing approaches are briefly reviewed next; a more detailed review can be found in [10]. In [2], the object contour is combined with optical flow. However, it is assumed that the initial pose is known accurately whereas tracking failures cannot be recovered from. In [3], dense optical flow is complemented with tracked SIFT features. Wide-baseline stereo tracking is performed in [6] by augmenting the object contour with local descriptors of interest points. The idea of analysis by synthesis is also used in our approach, however we do not need to extract point features or contours from the rendered images. Reference [7] extends [6] to track articulated objects in the presence of self-occlusions, multiple moving objects and clutter using a combination of patch-based and region-based matching. The PWP3D algorithm in [17] adopts a probabilistic framework for simultaneous segmentation and pose tracking. PDFs are used to model image regions in [20], without needing to explicitly estimate contours in images. Among the reviewed methods, only [6,7] use rendering-based synthesis.

3   Proposed Method

3.1   Model Acquisition

The object model is comprised of two view-independent parts, namely a textured 3D mesh and a set of sparse 3D points upon its surface. To obtain a complete mesh, several images depicting the object from multiple unknown viewpoints are provided to a multiview, dense stereo reconstruction system [23]. The model is represented by a textured mesh of triangles, let M, which is comprised by an ordered set of 3D points V and an ordered set T of triplets of indices on V that determine the triangles of the mesh. A composite image I collecting pixels from the images used in the reconstruction, is used to texture the 3D model. An ordered set C of 2D points provides the texture coordinates in I for each point from V.

Features from the surface of the object are also recovered. The images used to obtain the mesh are employed in a feature-based, structure-from-motion pipeline to recover a 3D point cloud [21]. These 3D points may not exactly occur on the surface of the mesh due to inaccuracies between the two reconstructions. The 3D coordinates of the reconstructed points are associated with a SIFT feature descriptor [14]. A descriptor may be available from each image where a particular 3D point is imaged. We select the descriptor from the image in which the imaged surface is close enough and most frontal to the camera, guided by the surface normal as availed from the closest triangle in M. The true scale of the model is estimated as explained in [11].

3.2   Pose Initialization

The monocular pose estimation approach employed for initializing pose is outlined next and described in more detail in [12]. First, SIFT keypoints are extracted from the image region occupied by the object and matched against those of its model to establish putative 2D-3D point correspondences. A P3P solver embedded into a RANSAC [5] framework estimates a preliminary pose estimate along with a classification of correspondences into inliers and outliers. The pose computed by RANSAC is next refined to take into account all inlying correspondences by minimizing a non-linear cost function amounting to their total reprojection error. Denoting by $\mathbf{K}$ the 3×3 intrinsic calibration matrix and corresponding 2D-3D points by $\mathbf{m}_i$ and $\mathbf{M}_i$, the cumulative image reprojection error is minimized with

$$\min_{\mathbf{r},\mathbf{t}} \sum_{i=1}^{n} d(\mathbf{K} \cdot [\mathbf{R}(\mathbf{r}) \,|\, \mathbf{t}] \cdot \mathbf{M}_i, \, \mathbf{m}_i)^2, \tag{1}$$

where $\mathbf{t}$ and $\mathbf{R}(\mathbf{r})$ are respectively the sought translation and rotation matrix parameterized using the Rodrigues rotation vector $\mathbf{r}$, $\mathbf{K} \cdot [\mathbf{R}(\mathbf{r}) \,|\, \mathbf{t}] \cdot \mathbf{M}_i$ is the predicted projection on the image of the homogeneous point $\mathbf{M}_i$ and $d(\mathbf{x}, \mathbf{y})$ denotes the reprojection error, i.e. the distance between points $\mathbf{x}$ and $\mathbf{y}$.

3.3   Rendering Pose Hypotheses

During evaluation of candidate poses, the model is rendered accordingly in synthetic images. The simulated virtual camera shares the same intrinsic and extrinsic parameters with the actual one, as were obtained via grid-based calibration.

Fig. 1. Rendering pose hypotheses. Original image from an experiment (left) and a synthetic image generated for the evaluation of a pose hypothesis (right).

It is assumed that the 3D model M is already transformed by the initial pose estimate (see Sec. 3.2), which is to be refined. Let $\mathbf{R}_i$, $\mathbf{t}_i$ be the i-th candidate pose for which the synthetic image S_i is rendered. M is transformed according to $\mathbf{R}_i$, $\mathbf{t}_i$ and S_i is rendered as follows. Transformation $\mathbf{R}_i$, is an "in place" rotation. In other words, denoting by $\mathbf{c}$ the centroid of the points in V, the model is first translated by $-\mathbf{c}$, then rotated by $\mathbf{R}_i$, and finally translated back in place by $\mathbf{c}$. Translation $\mathbf{t}_i$ is applied and the resulting model is rendered. Thus, model point $\mathbf{x}$ is transformed as $\mathbf{R}_i \cdot (\mathbf{x} - \mathbf{c}) + \mathbf{c} + \mathbf{t}_i$. Taking also into account the transform, let $\mathbf{R}_0$, $\mathbf{t}_0$, availed from pose initialization (cf. Sec. 3.2), the overall transformation is $\mathbf{R}_i \cdot \mathbf{R}_0 \cdot \mathbf{x} + \mathbf{R}_i \cdot (\mathbf{t}_0 - \mathbf{c}) + \mathbf{c} + \mathbf{t}_i$.

Rendering of the synthetic image is carried out on the GPU and is implemented through OpenGL calls. The process employs Z-buffering to respect visibility and thereby project the 3D model realistically to the image plane.

3.4 Evaluating Pose Hypotheses

The accuracy of a candidate pose is evaluated with respect to its similarity to the acquired image. Normalized Cross Correlation (NCC) is used as a metric to quantify this similarity. Similarity is assessed pixel-wise and in the intensity domain. No segmentation procedure is involved in this process; thus for inaccurate poses, the rendered object is compared against pixels of the background.

The rendering process depicts the object against a neutral background and provides a mask indicating the foreground pixels. NCC is computed only for these pixels. Each foreground pixel is corresponded with the pixel of the acquired image at the same coordinates. The two pixel sets are collected with their elements being in a 1-1 correspondence. This is illustrated in Fig. 1: pixels rendered in the right image are being compared to the corresponding ones in the left. The NCC score is obtained from these pixel sets and is in $[-1, 1]$, with -1 and 1 amounting to no similarity and maximum similarity, respectively.

3.5   Pose Refinement

Pose is refined by searching the space around the initial estimate obtained in Sec. 3.2. Searching this space exhaustively incurs high computational costs, therefore a numerical optimization approach is adopted. The objective function is the similarity between the rendered and the imaged objects. The domain of optimization is restricted to a 6D neighborhood around the initial pose estimate. The objective function $\mathcal{O}$ is defined as the opposite of the NCC score.

The objective function $\mathcal{O}$ exhibits local minima [17]. Thus, local optimization methods (e.g. gradient descent, Gauss-Newton or Levenberg-Marquardt) assuming a smooth, continuous and unimodal objective function are expected to run into difficulties if applied to optimizing $\mathcal{O}$ far from the global minimum.

In our work, the minimization of the objective function $\mathcal{O}$ is based on Particle Swarm Optimization (PSO) [4], which is known to be an effective and efficient computational method for solving other vision optimization problems (e.g. [16,9,24]). Canonical PSO, the simplest of PSO variants, has several attractive properties. Most importantly, it does not require knowledge of the derivatives of the objective function, depends on very few parameters, and requires a relatively low number of objective function evaluations until convergence [1]. In our formulation, the rotation component of candidate poses is parameterized in terms of yaw, pitch, and roll angles, respectively. Translation is parameterized by its Euclidean coordinates.

4   Experiments

The accuracy benefits obtained using the proposed method are evaluated in this section. For brevity, FEATPOSE will refer to the feature-based pose estimation of Sec. 3.2 and TEXTPOSE to the proposed method. In all experiments, PSO employed 64 particles evolved through 64 generations. Search ranges were $\pm 20\,mm$ for the translational parameters and $\pm 20\,°$ for the rotational ones. These bounds could be tightened for faster PSO performance.

An experiment with synthetic images was conducted first, utilizing our renderer to accurately avail ground truth. A model of a densely textured rectangular cuboid of size $45 \times 45 \times 90\,mm^3$ was rendered in 59 images (1280×960 pixels, $22.2° \times 16.7°$ FOV) circumnavigating the object in a full circle perpendicular to its major symmetry axis and pointing at the object (see Fig. 2). The experiment was performed in three conditions, for circle radii of 500, 1000, and $1500\,mm$. Using the ground truth data, we were able to calculate the error in the estimates. More specifically, denoting by $\mathbf{R}$, $\mathbf{t}$ the true object pose and by $\widehat{\mathbf{R}}$, $\widehat{\mathbf{t}}$ a pose estimate, the translational error is computed as $|\mathbf{t} - \widehat{\mathbf{t}}|$, whereas the rotational error is $\arccos((\mathrm{trace}(\mathbf{R}^{-1}\widehat{\mathbf{R}}) - 1)/2)$ and corresponds to the amount of rotation about a unit vector that transfers $\mathbf{R}$ to $\widehat{\mathbf{R}}$. Table 1 summarizes the mean and standard deviation of the errors. TEXTPOSE improves the estimates of FEATPOSE, whereas all errors increase with the distance of the object from the camera, as expected.

Fig. 2. Three of the synthetic images rendering the test object at $500\,mm$

Table 1. Mean and standard deviation for the translational ($\mathbf{t}$, mm) and rotational ($\mathbf{R}$, °) pose errors for methods FEATPOSE and TEXTPOSE

Radius	$\mathbf{t}_{\text{FEATPOSE}}$	$\mathbf{R}_{\text{FEATPOSE}}$	$\mathbf{t}_{\text{TEXTPOSE}}$	$\mathbf{R}_{\text{TEXTPOSE}}$
500mm	6.948 (3.839)	0.260 (0.121)	4.931 (1.915)	0.167 (0.064)
1000mm	12.211 (8.218)	0.492 (0.256)	5.389 (9.067)	0.167 (0.270)
1500mm	13.654 (7.508)	0.532 (0.269)	6.237 (3.049)	0.165 (0.101)

The FEATPOSE and TEXTPOSE methods are compared next with the aid of real images of an object with sparser texture relative to the previous one. The object and the experimental setup are shown in Fig. 3. To obtain ground truth for object poses, a checkerboard was used to guide object laying, facilitating its placement on checkers and alignment with them. The object was placed upon every white checker of the 9×10 checkerboard. The checkerboard was at a distance of $\approx 0.75\,m$ from the camera (960×1280 pixels, $16° \times 21°$ FOV) and each checker was $19 \times 19\,mm^2$. As we lacked any information on the orientation of the intrinsic reference frame of the object, we only measured the translational error. The mean error in these 45 trials was $13.25\,mm$ ($2.19\,mm$ std) for FEATPOSE and $8.3\,mm$ ($4.65\,mm$ std) for TEXTPOSE.

We also compared the methods with the aid of a more elaborate object, shown in Fig. 4. Due to its complex shape, ground truth regarding its pose was difficult to obtain. The initial pose provided by FEATPOSE was quite accurate owing

Fig. 3. Left to right: original image, FEATPOSE, and TEXTPOSE results. The original image is converted to grayscale and shown on the blue and green channels of an RGB color image. The red channel of each color image shows the estimate. The misalignment caused by an inaccurate FEATPOSE estimate is visible in the right vertical edge of the object in the middle image, whereas it has been corrected in the right image.

Fig. 4. Left to right: original image, FEATPOSE, and TEXTPOSE results with magnified detail near the eye, shown in the bottom-right. Results are encoded as in Fig. 3.

to the very dense texture of the object, leaving little room for improvement. Nevertheless, the proposed method still managed to improve the pose estimate.

The execution time of the TEXTPOSE method is determined by the following factors. The number of pixels by which the model is rendered in the generated images increases linearly the complexity of the method. The complexity of the PSO algorithm is linear to the number of particles P and generations G considered. Finally, the number of triangles in the model also linearly increases computational complexity. Indicatively, when the method was executed for images of 960×1280 and a model of $5 \cdot 10^4$ triangles, execution time was $10\,sec$ on an Intel Core i7 CPU 950 @ 3.07GHz and a GeForce GTX 580 GPU.

The experiments confirm that the proposed method provides accurate refinements to the feature-based initial pose estimate. The method is most effective when the texture of the object of interest is weak (i.e. as in Fig. 3), as in such cases the inaccuracy of the feature-based initialization is prone to be larger. Nevertheless, improvements are observed even for objects with dense texture.

5   Conclusions

This paper has presented an approach for rigid object pose estimation that was shown experimentally to be highly accurate and versatile. The approach combines feature and texture-based matching for pose estimation and is applicable to any kind of rigid free-form objects. Future work will address the extension of the method to multiple views and its application to the problem of continuous tracking of moving objects. Another direction concerns the tuning of PSO implementation and parameters in order to minimize execution time.

Acknowledgements. This work has received funding from the EC FP7 programme under grant no. 270138 DARWIN.

References

1. Angeline, P.: Evolutionary Optimization Versus Particle Swarm Optimization: Philosophy and Performance Differences. In: Porto, V.W., Waagen, D. (eds.) EP 1998. LNCS, vol. 1447, pp. 601–610. Springer, Heidelberg (1998)
2. Brox, T., Rosenhahn, B., Cremers, D., Seidel, H.-P.: High accuracy optical flow serves 3-D pose tracking: Exploiting contour and flow based constraints. In: Leonardis, A., Bischof, H., Pinz, A. (eds.) ECCV 2006. LNCS, vol. 3952, pp. 98–111. Springer, Heidelberg (2006)

3. Brox, T., Rosenhahn, B., Gall, J., Cremers, D.: Combined Region and Motion-Based 3D Tracking of Rigid and Articulated Objects. PAMI 32(3), 402–415 (2010)
4. Eberhart, R., Shi, Y., Kennedy, J.: Swarm Intelligence. Morgan Kaufmann (2001)
5. Fischler, M., Bolles, R.: Random Sample Consensus: A Paradigm for Model Fitting with Applications to Image Analysis and Automated Cartography. CACM 24, 381–395 (1981)
6. Gall, J., Rosenhahn, B., Seidel, H.P.: Robust Pose Estimation with 3D Textured Models. In: Chang, L.-W., Lie, W.-N. (eds.) PSIVT 2006. LNCS, vol. 4319, pp. 84–95. Springer, Heidelberg (2006)
7. Gall, J., Rosenhahn, B., Seidel, H.P.: Drift-Free Tracking of Rigid and Articulated Objects. In: Proc. of CVPR 2008, pp. 1–8 (2008)
8. Gordon, I., Lowe, D.G.: What and Where: 3D Object Recognition with Accurate Pose. In: Ponce, J., Hebert, M., Schmid, C., Zisserman, A. (eds.) Toward Category-Level Object Recognition. LNCS, vol. 4170, pp. 67–82. Springer, Heidelberg (2006)
9. Iveković, S., Trucco, E., Petillot, Y.: Human Body Pose Estimation with Particle Swarm Optimisation. Evolutionary Computation 16(4), 509–528 (2008)
10. Lepetit, V., Fua, P.: Monocular Model-Based 3D Tracking of Rigid Objects. Found. Trends. Comput. Graph. Vis. 1(1), 1–89 (2005)
11. Lourakis, M., Zabulis, X.: Accurate Scale Factor Estimation in 3D Reconstruction. In: Wilson, R., Hancock, E., Bors, A., Smith, W. (eds.) CAIP 2013, Part I. LNCS, vol. 8047, pp. 498–506. Springer, Heidelberg (2013)
12. Lourakis, M., Zabulis, X.: Model-Based Pose Estimation for Rigid Objects. In: Chen, M., Leibe, B., Neumann, B. (eds.) ICVS 2013. LNCS, vol. 7963, pp. 83–92. Springer, Heidelberg (2013)
13. Lowe, D.: Three-Dimensional Object Recognition from Single Two-Dimensional Images. Artificial Intelligence 31(3), 355–395 (1987)
14. Lowe, D.: Distinctive Image Features from Scale-Invariant Keypoints. Int. J. Comput. Vis. 60(2), 91–110 (2004)
15. Özuysal, M., Lepetit, V., Fleuret, F., Fua, P.: Feature Harvesting for Tracking-by-Detection. In: Leonardis, A., Bischof, H., Pinz, A. (eds.) ECCV 2006. LNCS, vol. 3953, pp. 592–605. Springer, Heidelberg (2006)
16. Padeleris, P., Zabulis, X., Argyros, A.: Head Pose Estimation on Depth Data Based on Particle Swarm Optimization. In: CVPR Workshops, pp. 42–49 (2012)
17. Prisacariu, V., Reid, I.: PWP3D: Real-Time Segmentation and Tracking of 3D Objects. Int. J. Comput. Vis., 1–20 (2012)
18. Romea, A., Berenson, D., Srinivasa, S., Ferguson, D.: Object recognition and full pose registration from a single image for robotic manipulation. In: ICRA (2009)
19. Rothganger, F., Lazebnik, S., Schmid, C., Ponce, J.: 3D Object Modeling and Recognition Using Local Affine-Invariant Image Descriptors and Multi-View Spatial Constraints. Int. J. Comput. Vis. 66(3), 231–259 (2006)
20. Schmaltz, C., Rosenhahn, B., Brox, T., Weickert, J.: Region-Based Pose Tracking with Occlusions Using 3D Models. Mach. Vision Appl. 23(3), 557–577 (2012)
21. Snavely, N., Seitz, S., Szeliski, R.: Photo Tourism: Exploring Photo Collections in 3D. ACM Trans. Graph. 25(3), 835–846 (2006)
22. Vacchetti, L., Lepetit, V., Fua, P.: Stable Real-Time 3D Tracking Using Online and Offline Information. PAMI 26(10), 1385–1391 (2004)
23. Vergauwen, M., Gool, L.V.: Web-based 3D Reconstruction Service. Mach. Vision Appl. 17(6), 411–426 (2006)
24. Zhang, X., Hu, W., Maybank, S., Li, X., Zhu, M.: Sequential Particle Swarm Optimization for Visual Tracking. In: CVPR, pp. 1–8 (2008)

Protected Pooling Method of Sparse Coding in Visual Classification*

Zhichen Zhao, Huimin Ma, and Xiaozhi Chen

Department of Electrical Engineering, Tsinghua University, 100084, China
zhaozc10@tsinghua.mail.edu.cn, mhmpub@tsinghua.edu.cn

Abstract. Sparse Coding, a popular feature coding method, has shown superior performance in visual recognition tasks. Different pooling methods, such as average pooling and max pooling, are commonly employed after feature coding. However, it has not been explained clearly what characteristic accounts for the success of pooling method. In this paper, a new pooling method, namely protected pooling, is proposed. Our method produces features putting more emphasis on weak codes. What's more, we prove that all other pooling methods follow the same rules. Experiments on Scene 15, Caltech-101 and Flowers 17 demonstrate our improvements.

1 Introduction

Feature coding, which transforms local features into a more seperatable feature space, is a common step in visual recognition tasks. The original feature coding is VQ coding (Vector Quantization Coding[8], also called Hard Coding). Later, yang[1] has introduced a helpful solution called SC (Sparse Coding). The latter has been proved to be more powerful and employed to achieve excellent performance on various datasets. Thus, we choose SC to demonstrate our proposed pooling method.

Pooling operation can capture spatial structures to a certain extent and reduce dimensionality of features. The pooling features are commonly fed into a classifier (e.g. SVM) to learn data patterns. The code produced by average pooling is the concatenation of sums of feature responses within the same grid. Max pooling keeps only the strongest response within each grid. Boureau etc. have explained the difference between these two methods[2]. Besides, more pooling methods, such as MaxExp, Gamma and AxMin[3] have been proposed and proved to be useful.

In this paper, we are hammering at finding out the critical reason that affects results of pooling method. Also, we compared different pooling methods on datasets, inspected the property of them. At last, we raised a new pooling method to improve the accuracy, and carried out some verified experiments to prove our improvement.

---

* This work was supported by National Science Foundation of China(No.61171113).

L.J. Chmielewski et al. (Eds.): ICCVG 2014, LNCS 8671, pp. 680–687, 2014.

2   Recent Works

2.1   Primary Pooling Methods

For present a image, we need to compute a single feature vector to classify. Let
$\mathbf{U}$ (a matrix) be the result after the coding. We compute the image feature by
using pooling function

$$\mathbf{z} = \mathcal{F}(\mathbf{U}) \tag{1}$$

where $\mathcal{F}$ is defined on each column of $\mathbf{U}$. Different pooling functions construct
different image statistics. In VQ coding, we always use the *averaging* pooling

$$\mathbf{z} = \frac{1}{M} \sum_{m=1}^{M} \mathbf{u}_m \tag{2}$$

which is also known as *histogram*. People names it according to its most obvious
feature: counting numbers of descriptors belong to some "word", just like a
histogram using on codebook. Of course this function can be used in SC, but in
SC there is a more efficient pooling called *max* pooling

$$\mathbf{z}_j = \max\{|\mathbf{u}_{1j}|, ...|\mathbf{u}_{Mj}|\} \tag{3}$$

where $\mathbf{z}_j$ is the j-th element of $\mathbf{z}$, $\mathbf{u}_{ij}$ is the (i, j) entry of $\mathbf{U}$. Max pooling
is thought to be supported by biophysical evidence in visual cortex. In most
applications, max pooling has been found to be superior than many other pooling
methods including average pooling.

2.2   Recent Pooling Methods

Likelihood based pooling methods have recently shed new light on the role of
the pooling step in Bag-of-Words. Under the hypothesis of Bernoulli distribution,
the mean of max pooling could be expressed as $1 - (1 - \alpha)^M$[2], Estimating α as
the average of mid-level feature activations. Inspired by this, a pooling method
named *MaxExp* is proposed, defined by

$$\mathbf{z} = 1 - (1 - \frac{1}{M} \sum_{m=1}^{M} \mathbf{u}_m)^{\widehat{M}}, \widehat{M} = |M| \tag{4}$$

M is the number of elements. To using this method we should confirm that
$0 \leq \mathbf{u}_m \leq 1$ or the result will be totally wrong because there may appear
negative elements in $\mathbf{z}$. This constraint is always satisfied in SC coding.

Another method, called *Gamma*, was introduced from a phenomenon that a
given visual word appears in an image more often than is statistically expected[4].
Gamma acts on average pooling to improve the similarity of image signatures
belonging to each class of objects and it is defined by:

$$\mathbf{z} = (\frac{1}{M} \sum_{m=1}^{M} \mathbf{u}_m)^{\gamma} \tag{5}$$

The correction factor $0 < \gamma < 1$ is usually chosen by cross-validation. It is closely related to MaxExp. It is not difficult for us to find that these two methods both promote the function curve beyond $y = x$ (fig. 1). This property will be discussed later and our following method takes this more completely.

Knoiusz[3] introduced a close approximation of MaxExp that has a parameter β accounting for the interdependence of descriptors. The method, named Approximate Pooling *(AxMin)*, is defined by:

$$\mathbf{z} = \min[1, \beta(\frac{1}{M} \sum_{m=1}^{M} \mathbf{u}_m)] \tag{6}$$

AxMin pooling implies that the confidence in the visual word can increase until it reaches the saturation threshold (full confidence). Once reached, any strong variations have no effect. This means elements have different status according to their value, and big enough elements needs less details than small ones.

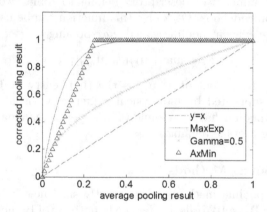

Fig. 1. A figure of these three method: MaxExp, Gamma and AxMin. They are all functions using average pooling result as independent variable and promote data bigger than $y = x$, the reason will be explained in section 3.2.

All these three methods are effective in application. For AxMin, Knoiusz made improvement by taking only the top n largest elements to calculate average each column while ignoring others. It is obvious that max pooling is its special case where n=1, so it equals to taking self-adaption between 1 and M. In section 3, we will discuss what influences performance among these methods and design a new method to obtain better pooling features.

3   Methods

Through the discuss above, we found that all the three methods, MaxExp, Gamma and AxMin, boost average pooling codes in certain ways (Fig 1). This enlightens us to find out the critical factor that affects pooling method and it is exactly our stand point. In this section, we will give discussion on characteristics of pooling and feature coding, then find out the factor behind different methods. First, we will begin from average and max pooling.

3.1   Behind Average and Max Pooling

During researching on the average pooling and max pooling. An interesting phenomenon drew our attention: the data of $\mathbf{z}$ after max pooling always has smaller variance and its minimum except zero is bigger than that of average pooling. The fact reminded us that a very small data nearby zero will be baneful. we found that data in average pooling has a bigger gap, which makes tiny numbers approach zero after normalization. Too tiny elements are easy to be ignored and message will be lost. The advantage of max pooling is the protection of tiny data and figuring out if there exists the word in codebook correctly. Notice that max pooling indeed reduces the variance but variance is not the critical factor. More insights will be seen through experiments in section 4.

Max pooling reaches a better result. It could be seen as a improvement of average pooling, though there is no functional relationship between average and max pooling. It also gives an important thinking that if we could boost these tiny elements without changing the order in data, we could probably obtain a more accurate result.

3.2   Theory with Pooling Methods

With the help of analysis above, a new way comes to be reasonable: Let average pooling result be our input, we could find a function to modify it as

$$\mathbf{y} = \mathcal{F}(\frac{1}{M} \sum_{m=1}^{M} \mathbf{u}_m) \tag{7}$$

Where $\mathbf{y}$ is a change over $\mathbf{z}$, average could give basic messages we need, so usage of the function will modify data as we expect. Of course we need to hold most properties obtained by average pooling such as order and existence of messages. To modify correctly, this function should have properties below

- $\mathcal{F}(0) = 0$ and $\mathcal{F}(1) = 1$.
  Means no extra messages or change of the boundary.
- $\forall x_1 \leq x_2, \mathcal{F}(x_1) \leq \mathcal{F}(x_2)$.
  A monotone increasing function will not change the order of data, so does the status behind them.
- $\mathcal{F}''(x) \leq 0, \forall x \in [0, 1]$.
  A concave function is required for boosting weak codes.

In fact, there are already methods satisfying the conditions above. We could easily check out that MaxExp, Gamma and AxMin are all up to these rules. This truth also confirms our theory. Notice even though a concave function could be helpful, the degree should be controlled, otherwise it will bring bad consequence finally. As the goal of designing above rules is to protect the weak codes which may contain discriminative information, we define all these methods "Protected Pooling Methods".

3.3   Improve the Method Thoroughly

Among MaxExp, Gamma and AxMin, AxMin@n[3] performs best in many occasions. It finds where the data should be protected and where the details of order are not important. However, using two straight lines is two simple to make full use of the above properties and the roughness around intersection point also brings errors. Further more, parameter β is difficult to control in SC because data in $\mathbf{U}$ are too small. According to those points, we improve AxMin@n in 3 views:

- use a concave function to replace straight line, it is supposed to protect weak codes and it is more smooth around intersection point.
- use sum operation instead of average to be input. Data in SC are small while M is big(nearly 2000). Division on average result may lose precision. In fact, AxMin@n is a ideal model for its using on n largest numbers, we will also use this improvement.
- change parameter β to be horizontal, the place we choose where to cut off should be decided by the value of funtion rather than slope. What's more, a horizontal parameter is easier to tune.

Above all, we choose $\log_2(x + 1)$ to be the concave function. Using all the improvement, the final pooling method we use is

$$\mathbf{z} = \min[\log_2(\sum_{m=1}^{N} \mathbf{u'}_m + 1), \beta] \tag{8}$$

Where $\mathbf{u'}$ has been sorted from large to small, β is the parameter controlling position to cut and N is the number of top largest elements we used. we call this function as *protected-AxMin@n(p-AxMin@n)*. And this, is our **Protected Pooling method**.

As so far, the whole method has been introduced. To check the accuracy of our improvements, in the next section, we will carry out experiments to confirm our theory and compare pooling methods in different datasets.

4   Experiments

Firstly we analyze the influence of different factors such as the completeness of information and the degree of boosting weak codes. We design an experiment using Scene 15[11] dataset. A codebook with 1K words is trained and SVM is used as classifier throughout all experiments. Table 1 is our results.

Table 1. Classification rate compared on Scene 15

Pooling Method	classification rate
bool	75.35± 0.64
average	76.30± 0.87
sum	78.96± 0.53
ex-variance	77.66± 0.47
re-variance	77.21± 0.56

The method "bool" refers to a method that operate on average result. Set all non-zero elements in z to be 1. Notice that it floats all the details in z but could get a near accuracy with average pooling. This verified our theory that the completeness of messages is the most important point. Ex-variance expands the variance, re-variance reduces the variance, this two results implies variance is not the critical factor. Moreover, we could find sum pooling performs better than average pooling just because of its protection on precision. A division operation may be usual but in SC we should be careful.

4.1 Results on Scene 15

We tried our algorithm on the Scene 15 dataset. This dataset contains totally 4485 images about 15 categories, including living room, kitchen and so on. we took 100 images per class for training and the left for testing (the same as yang[1]). Comparison results are shown in Table 2. It could be seen easily that with or without @n, protected(p-) methods always perform better than previous methods.

Table 2. Classification rate compared on Scene 15

Pooling Method	classification rate
max[1]	80.28± 0.93
max	81.30± 0.49
Gamma	80.62± 0.99
AxMin	82.13± 0.92
p-AxMin	82.59± 0.81
AxMin@n	82.42± 0.77
p-AxMin@n	**82.79± 0.85**

4.2 Results on Caltech101

The Caltech-101 dataset[9] contains 101 classes, we follow yang's condition to experiment. We take 30 images per class to train and the size of codebook is 1K.

Notice that AxMin@n has a lower accuracy compared with max pooling. Max pooling could be regarded as a method to protect weak codes from average pooling though there is no explicit mapping function. MaxExp, Gamma and

Table 3. Classification rate compared on Caltech101

Pooling Method	classification rate
max[1]	73.20± 0.54
max	**72.32± 0.61**
AxMin@n	71.60± 0.97
p-AxMin@n	72.28± 0.56

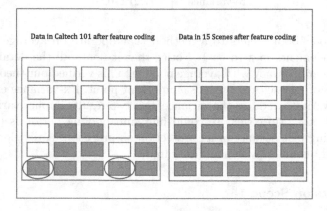

Fig. 2. Data in two datasets after feature coding. White elements are zero ones, black elements are nonzero ones. Max pooling is especially effectively to "isolated point".

AxMin do the same thing. Using these methods can insure better accuracy than average pooling, but AxMin@n not always obtain better accuracy than max pooling because they both protect weak codes just in different ways.

Further on, we will find out the cause of different display on Caltech101 and Scene 15. The data **u** (has been sorted from small to large) is showed in Figure 2. of two different datasets. Data in red circle shows there are many "isolated point". Using AxMin@n, we can not protected them to the maximum extent. However it is easy for max pooling. This phenomenon also agrees our theory.

4.3   Results on Flowers 17

The dataset Flowers 17[12] consists of 17 classes of flowers with 80 images of each. Characteristic has changed from a problem to another, but it doesn't affect the comparison with different pooling methods. The size of codebook in Flower 17 is also 1K and results are showed in Table 4

Notice that flowers have their own characteristics. because of the low baseline, our method could get more gain from other methods. With results on 3 different datasets our theory proves to be correct, and our method is efficient. So we can draw the conclusion that the protection of weak codes is the critical factor in pooling.

Table 4. classification rate compared on Flowers 17

Pooling Method	classification rate
max	67.29± 0.87
AxMin@n	67.78± 1.10
p-AxMin@n	**68.76± 0.71**

5   Conclusion

We have analyzed several popular pooling methods and proposed a hypothesis that protecting weak codes is the critical factors for pooling operation. The design of a proper pooling strategy is supposed to follow three rules: maintaining the completeness of information, preserving magnitude order and boosting weak codes. Experiments have demonstrated improvements over previous pooling methods. The proposed pooling rules are independent of feature coding stage, so combining both feature coding and pooling to design a unified coding-pooling strategy is supposed to be promising, which is our future work.

References

1. Yang, J., Yu, K., Gong, Y.: Linear Spatial Pyramid Matching Using Sparse Coding for Image Classification. In: CVPR (2009)
2. Boureau, Y., Ponce, J., LeCun, Y.: A Theoretical Analysis of Feature Pooling in Visual Recognition. In: ICML (2010)
3. Koniusz, P., Yan, F., Mikolajczyk, K.: Comparison of Mid-Level Feature Coding Approaches And Pooling Strategies in Visual Concept Detection. CVIU 117(5), 479–492 (2013)
4. Jegou, H., Douze, M., Schmid, C.: On the Burstiness of Visual Elements. In: CVPR (2009)
5. Yu, K., Zhang, T., Gong, Y.: Nonlinear Learning using Local Coordinate Coding. In: NIPS (2009)
6. Zhou, X., Yu, K., Zhang, T., Huang, T.S.: Image Classification Using Super-Vector Coding of Local Image Descriptors. In: Daniilidis, K., Maragos, P., Paragios, N. (eds.) ECCV 2010, Part V. LNCS, vol. 6315, pp. 141–154. Springer, Heidelberg (2010)
7. Wang, J., Yang, J., Yu, K., Lv, F., Huang, T.S., Gong, Y.: Locality-constrained Linear Coding for Image Classification. In: CVPR (2010)
8. Chatfield, K., Lempitsky, V., Vedaldi, A., Zisserman, A.: The devil is in the details: an evaluation of recent feature encoding methods. In: BMVC (2011)
9. Fei-Fei, L., Fergus, R., Perona, P.: Learning generative visual models from few training examples: an incremental bayesian approach tested on 101 object categories. In: GMBV (2004), http://www.vision.caltech.edu/Image_Datasets/Caltech101/
10. Chang, C.C., Lin, C.J.: LIBSVM-a library for support vector machines
11. Lazebnik, S., Schmid, C., Ponce, J.: Beyond Bags of Features: Spatial Pyramid Matching for Recognizing Natural Scene Categories. In: Lazebnik, S., Schmid, C., Ponce, J. (eds.) CVPR (2006), http://www-cvr.ai.uiuc.edu/ponce_grp/data/
12. Nilsback, M.-E., Zisserman, A.: A Visual Vocabulary for Flower Classification. In: CVPR (2006), http://www.robots.ox.ac.uk/~vgg/data/flowers/17/

Author Index